PENGUIN BOOKS
LIFE RARELY TELLS

Jack Lindsay comes from one of the most distinguished and prolific Australian literary and artistic families. His father was Norman Lindsay, the artist and writer, and together they helped build a movement that pushed Australia towards a universal approach to art, while rejecting national enthusiasms.

Born in Melbourne in 1900, Lindsay has lived in England since 1926 and is an author and critic of remarkable energy and output. His works include poetry, novels, biography and translations and run into dozens of volumes. This is the first time that his three volumes of autobiography have been published in a single book. Jack Lindsay's distinguished contribution to Australian literature was recognized in 1981 when he was awarded membership of the Order of Australia.

JACK LINDSAY

LIFE RARELY TELLS

An autobiography in three volumes

· LIFE RARELY TELLS
· THE ROARING TWENTIES
· FANFROLICO AND AFTER

PENGUIN BOOKS

Penguin Books Australia Ltd,
487 Maroondah Highway, P.O. Box 257
Ringwood, Victoria, 3134, Australia
Penguin Books Ltd,
Harmondsworth, Middlesex, England
Penguin Books,
625 Madison Avenue, New York, N.Y. 10022, U.S.A.
Penguin Books Canada Ltd,
2801 John Street, Markham, Ontario, Canada
Penguin Books (N.Z.) Ltd,
182-190 Wairau Road, Auckland 10, New Zealand

First published in three volumes by The Bodley Head as *Life Rarely Tells*, *The Roaring Twenties*, and
Fanfrolico and After
Published as a trilogy in Australia by Penguin Books, 1982
Copyright © Jack Lindsay, 1958, 1960, 1962, and 1982
Introduction to this edition © Michael Wilding, 1982
Select bibliography this edition © John Arnold, 1982
Typeset in Baskerville by The Dova Type Shop, Melbourne
Made and printed in Australia at
The Dominion Press, Blackburn, Victoria

CIP

Lindsay, Jack, 1900-.
Life rarely tells.

First published as separate v.: London: Bodley Head,
1958-1962.
Bibliography.
Includes index.
Contents: Life rarely tells – The roaring twenties –
Franfrolico and after.
ISBN 0 14 005913 X.

1. Lindsay, Jack, 1900- – Biography. 2. Authors,
Australian – Biography. I. Title. II. Title: The
roaring twenties. II. Title: Franfrolico and after.

A828'.209

CONTENTS

INTRODUCTION

JACK LINDSAY's autobiographical trilogy is one of the classics of Australian writing, an unforgettable memoir of an Edwardian colonial childhood in pre-World War I Sydney and Brisbane, of the hectic world of Sydney's bohemia in the 'roaring twenties', and of an Australian cultural invasion of literary London in the late twenties and thirties.

Australian literary life from the 1890s to World War I is well documented; this is the archetypal period of the 'legend'. Norman Lindsay's *A Curate in Bohemia* (1913) recorded the nineties. And Marcus Clarke had fondly recalled Melbourne's literary bohemia of the 1860s and 1870s. The twenties have been comparatively unexplored: the sagas of Bloomsbury, Paris, and Greenwich village have become better known than Australia's own bohemian tradition. Jack Lindsay establishes the significance, the feeling and above all the complexity of those years. The great figures of the nineties are still present, brooding presences of rejection, ruin, decline and isolation. Christopher Brennan, dismissed from the university, his daughter Anna, S. A. Rosa; Randolph Bedford, Henry Lawson, A. G. Stephens, Fred Broomfield, Hugh McCrae – figures from Norman Lindsay's *Bohemians of the Bulletin* (1965). These were the ghosts of the great radical nationalist achievement of Australian writing. By the twenties the radicalism had been undermined, defeated in the maritime and shearers' strikes, the failure of New Australia, the destruction of the I.W.W. Insofar as it survived, it had retreated strategically into the attempt to work within the system of the parliamentary Labor Party, itself split and out of power as a result of the conscription issue. Nationalism looked tired and compromised, particularly after the slaughter of World War I. The horrors of the war break through the Edwardian adolescence of the first volume – the shell-shocked soldier who comes to tea. Norman Lindsay withdrew from the social realm, into a realm of pure art, absolute value. It was a reactive formation in fear and distaste of the mass slaughter, compounded with the fear of mass revolutionary action unleashed by war, as in 1917. The Nietzschean, neo-Platonic vitalism that Norman Lindsay expounded in *Creative Effort* (1920) found a ready social acceptance. Jack became its prophet in the literary world.

Jack, Philip, and Ray were the three sons of Norman Lindsay (1879–1969) by his first marriage to Katie Parkinson. Jack was born in Melbourne in 1900, when Norman was twenty-one. The family moved to Sydney, and Jack recalls the years at Lavender Bay up to the end of the marriage in 1909, and Katie's taking the three boys to Brisbane. Norman married Rose Soady, who had modelled many of his paintings and, by the time Jack returned to Sydney in 1920, was living 75 kilometres from Sydney, near Springwood in the Blue Mountains, amid satyrs and nymphs and spectacular bush walks. Now a National Trust property, left to the nation by Norman Lindsay and open to the public, the house and grounds provide a permanent exhibition of his paintings, etchings, shipmodels, sculptures, drawings, books, manuscripts, and memorabilia. Norman's own memoirs are in *My Mask* (1970), Rose's in *Model Wife* (1967) and the eldest of their two daughters', Jane's, in *Portrait of Pa: Norman Lindsay at Springwood* (1973). Jack's arrival in Sydney was both an entry into the life of literature, and a rediscovery of the father; and not only the father but also the artist brothers: the eldest, Percy, always ready to have a drink; Lionel, who had no contact with Norman because of a quarrel over spiritualism. Lionel's memoirs *Comedy of Life* (1967) and those of the youngest brother Daryl, *The Leafy Tree: My Family* (1965) and of Daryl's wife Joan, *Time Without Clocks* (1962) offer further documentation of this remarkably talented and extensive family. Joan Lindsay, who wrote *Picnic at Hanging Rock* (1967) married into the family, as did Will Dyson, cartoonist on the *Bulletin* and on the London *Daily Herald*, who married Norman's younger sister Ruby, herself an artist. John Hetherington's *Norman Lindsay: The Embattled Olympian* (1973) is the authorized biography.

Together with Kenneth Slessor and Frank Johnson, Jack established a little magazine, *Vision*, which lasted four issues, expounding and expressing the new movement. In reaction to the laconic economy of Lawson, in reaction to realist recording of an unappealing social reality, they sought a richer, glittering literary texture. Why shouldn't Australian poetry have the jewels? It was an attempt to enrich, to create a self-conscious 'culture'. It was in opposition to mercantile norms, but it was determined by the same socio-economic system: it was producing identifiable commodities, labelled 'art'. Its polar opposition to the philistine material norms of the society was a flight away from social perception, from considering art in any social way: its élitism and idealist denial of the social bases of culture were precisely the aesthetic that suited the preservation of the élite social structure. And its aesthetic was firmly anti-modernist; it saw modernism – Pound, Joyce, Eliot, Lawrence – as the expression of decadence. Australia, preserved from the wars of Europe and the materialist vulgarity of the United States would be the clear space for a renaissance of classical vitality and innocence and purity in culture. The rich, punning, echoing language – we can find that in Joyce among the accepted pantheon of modernists, we can find the archaisms in Pound, the vortex of language in Wyndham Lewis, the return to the seventeenth-century lyric and Elizabethan drama in Eliot. But the mix Lindsay and *Vision* were offering was different. 'It was the difficult task set themselves by some Australian writers after the war to re-interpret colonial experience' wrote Stephen Murray-Smith in Geoffrey Dutton's *Literature of Australia* (1964); Evan Jones wrote, in the same volume, 'at no other time have Australians had the confidence, so buoyantly expressed . . . that they were the übermenschen of the cultural world . . . the Western cultural heritage had fled a sickened Europe and a vulgar America'.

The feel of the period is conveyed by Lindsay's drawing on some stories he wrote at the time, and a novel he wrote about the period ten years later; the texture of the period is caught in the packed language. In the end Lindsay won through to a functional clarity which is the overall manner of the trilogy, a manner shaped by the needs of the work, the development of the thought, the imparting of the necessary information. The new manner can encompass the manner of the old; the old could never have encompassed the manner of the new. Similarly, he incorporates letters and comments from Lionel Lindsay, Ray Lindsay, R. D. Fitzgerald; these different voices, different perspectives, allow a modernist collage of a multiplicity of accounts.

Vision was the first of the 'little magazines' in Australia. John Tregenza begins from it in *Australian Little Magazines, 1923–54* (1964). Slessor in later years tended to distance himself from close involvement with the *Vision* world. 'I wasn't part of it. I was a very amused and detached observer. I can't say I belonged to that Bohemian world . . . but I was able to observe some extraordinary characters – I think a lot more outrageous, more colourful, more humorous than their equivalent, the "beats" today.' (*Southerly* XXVI 1966). Jack, Norman and Slessor all offered differing assessments of *Vision*'s role and nature in an exchange in the Sydney quarterly *Southerly* 1952–53. They are collected in *Critical Essays on Kenneth Slessor*, ed. A. K. Thompson (1968). Some of Slessor's memoirs of the period are in his *Bread and Wine* (1970); and in his life of Slessor, *A Man of Sydney* (1977), Douglas Stewart discusses the *Vision* period. R. D. Fitzgerald's recollections are in *Of Places and Poetry* (1975). And Philip Lindsay, Jack's younger brother, was the first of the autobiographers with *I'd Live the Same Life Over* (1941).

In allying a literary impulse to Norman Lindsay's visual aesthetic, *Vision*'s vitalist assertion was a focal point in Australian literary and cultural development. As Vincent Buckley wrote in *Essays in Poetry, Mainly Australian* (1957):

It is an important strain in our modern poetry; it dominates in a direct way the first books of both Slessor and Fitzgerald. In a more indirect way, it has heavily influenced the poetry of Douglas Stewart and Kenneth Mackenzie, the poetry and prose of Eve Langley, even the work of Judith Wright and Brian Vrepont.

Slessor's list of those influenced by Norman Lindsay's 'doctrine of poetic values' also included Hugh McCrae, Rupert Atkinson, Leon Gellert, Jack Lindsay, Ronald McCuaig, Francis

Webb, Louis Stone, Leslie Miller, Godfrey Blunden, and Brian Penton. Christina Stead offers an external view in *For Love Alone* (1945). The magazine Teresa lends to Jonathan is surely *Vision*:

written and illustrated by the young artistic set in Sydney, run by the Brimley family, dominated by the Brimley family, in which, with imitations of Marlowe and Shakespeare, Donne and free verse, it was chiefly a question of free love and naked women; on each page were drawings of voluptuous, fat-faced, naked women, running away from a crowd of satyrs, carried off by centaurs or tempted by evil-eyed fauns . . .

As well as *Vision*, Slessor and Jack edited a manifesto anthology, *Poetry in Australia, 1923*, whose contributors included Brennan, Shaw Neilson, McCrae, Slessor, Fitzgerald, Jack Lindsay, Gellert, Hugh McKay, Dorothea Mackellar (known to generations as the author of 'I love a sunburnt country') and with a foreword by Norman.

This is the world Jack recalls, these the publications, these the artists: Adolf Beutler, Elioth Gruner, Guy Lynch and his brother Joe Lynch (whose death is the subject of Slessor's 'Five Bells'), David McKee Wright, Zora Cross, Les Robinson, George Finey, Unk White, Francis Croslé, Bertram Stevens, Hugh McKay. Jack's wife, Janet Beaton, was grand-daughter of William Bede Dalley, made Australia's first Privy Councillor for despatching the Soudan contingent when he was premier of New South Wales in 1885. His sons, Will and John, were part of Norman's world. John Dalley wrote three novels, *No Armour* (1928), *Max Flambard* (1929), and *Only the Morning* (1930). And the café's – Mockbells' chain of coffee shops, the Greek club in Park Street, Amendolas in Wilmot Street near the Liverpool Street Central Courts. Frank Johnson introduced Jack to J. T. Kirtley, who was interested in limited editions and fine press books and had just bought a Chandler and Price Bench-platen press for £20. The first book printed was Jack's first book of poems, *Fauns and Ladies* (1923). In 1925 the press was named Fanfrolico, published Jack's translation of *Lysistrata*, and launched on the Lindsayan–Nietzschean vitalist path. In 1926 Kirtley and Jack invaded London. 'All that vindicates the human spirit, all that frankly, heroically, or delightedly, faces the problems of life, all that allies fantasy with realism and defines the subtle and complex colour of earth and man; all such works have their place in (the Fanfrolico) aesthetic.' (Quoted, Richard Fotheringham, 'Expatriate Publishing: Jack Lindsay and the Fanfrolico Press,' *Meanjin*, XXXI, March 1972). Jack's narrative and analysis of these years is, apart from its sheer enjoyability, basic to any account of the period – and cultural historians have all offered their versions of *Vision* – Judith Wright in *Preoccupations in Australian Poetry* (1965), Robert Hughes in *The Art of Australia* (1970), Geoffrey Serle in *From Deserts the Prophets Come* (1973), John Docker in *Australian Cultural Elites* (1974), Humphrey McQueen in *The Black Swan of Trespass* (1979).

When Kirtley returned to Australia, Jack was joined by P. R. Stephensen, who had edited the Queensland university magazine, *Galmahra*, in which one of Jack's poems had been found obscene by the university authorities. After Stephensen left, Jack was joined on Fanfrolico by Brian Penton, who wrote the novels *Landtakers* (1934) and *Inheritors* (1936) and by Philip Lindsay, his younger brother, on the verge of his career as novelist and screenwriter. Phil's baby daughter, glimpsed briefly, grew up in England and established herself as a novelist in the 1960s, Cressida Lindsay. Fanfrolico published some forty titles and has a treasured role among fine press collectors. The titles are described in Harry F. Chaplin's *The Fanfrolico Press* (1976) and in Will Ransom, *Private Presses and Their Books* (1929) supplemented by William Ridler, *British Modern Press Books* (1971). Titles included Hugh McCrae's *Satyrs and Sunlight* (Douglas Stewart speculated that this edition was 'the only way to read him'), Slessor's *Earth Visitors*, Norman Lindsay's *Hyperboroea* and *Madam Life's Lovers*, Stephensen's version of Nietzsche's *Antichrist*, and Jack's *Dionysos, or Nietzsche contra Nietzsche*, his poems and verse plays and his translations that became a staple of the press, like Petronius's *Satyricon* and Catullus. They published an edition of Beddoes's poetry edited by Edmund Gosse, librarian of the House of Commons, and author of that classic Victorian memoir *Father and Son*; and of Cyril Tourneur's plays edited by Allardyce Nicholl, later professor of English at the University of Birmingham and founder of the Shakespeare Institute. It was this 'sumptuous critical edition' that T. S. Eliot reviewed for his famous revaluation of Tourneur in *Selected Essays* (1932).

In England the darker side of bohemia revealed itself further. Murger's *Scenes de la vie bohème* and Puccini's opera have their tragic note. Whether caught up and tossed around by the force of the creative fire or sacrificed on the altar of male sexuality, bohemia left its succession of victims. Jack's mother had been a warning from the world of artists in the first volume; Anna Brennan in volume two; Elza de Locre in volume three. Jack's scrupulous and agonizing account of his relationship with Elza, of the exploration and understanding of sexual roles, social conditioning, and the attempt to rethink possibilities is an important document. A novel is based on them, Edith Young's *Lisa* (1930). Another bohemian figure encountered was musician and writer Philip Heseltine, also known as Peter Warlock, drawn in Lawrence's *Women in Love* as Halliday and in Huxley's *Antic Hay* as Coleman. D. H. Lawrence, Huxley, Augustus John, Nina Hamnett, Edgell Rickword, Harold Monro, Norman Douglas, Basil Bunting, Robert Graves, Tom Driberg, and the expatriates Anna Wickham and Constant Lambert are among the figures glimpsed in fine evocation of the period. And on the edges, hashish, cocaine, ether, Aleister Crowley, espionage, sex-magic, the occult, death.

Lindsay and Stephensen collaborated on a magazine, *The London Aphrodite*, named in response to J. C. Squire's *London Mercury*, carrying Australian writing and art work into England: Jack, Philip, Norman, Stephensen, Penton, McCrae, Slessor, together with Australian expatriates W. J. Turner, Bertram Higgins and Rupert Atkinson, and British contributors Liam O'Flaherty, Rhys Davies, Philip Owens, T. F. Powys. Jack declared in the first issue:

We stand for a point of view which equally outrages the modernist and the reactionary. It is certain that J. C. Squire and T. S. Eliot, Wyndham Lewis and Dean Inge, Humbert Wolfe and Robert Graves, e.e. cummings and Alfred Noyes, Maritain and James Douglas, Roger Fry and William Orpen would, if compelled by physical force to read our magazine, heartily (or at least irritatedly) dislike it.

The English were not wholly impressed. Huxley described Stephensen as Cuthbert Arkwright and Lindsay as Willy Weaver in *Point Counter Point* (1928):

[Arkwright] made his living, and in the process convinced himself that he was serving the arts, by printing limited and expensive editions of the more scabrous specimens of the native and foreign literatures. Blond, beef-red, with green and bulging eyes, his large face shining, he approached vociferating greetings. Willie Weaver jauntily followed, a little man perpetually smiling, spectacles astride his long nose, bubbling with good humour and an inexhaustible verbiage.

Stephensen later wrote his own account of the Fanfrolico years in *Kookaburras and Satyrs* (1954). A letter of D. H. Lawrence's dated 14 December 1929 confirms Lindsay's account that the Lawrence paintings were originally offered to Fanfrolico.

Dear Mr Lindsay

Orioli wrote me from Florence that the Fanfrolico Press might do a portfolio of reproductions of my pictures, that hang now in Dorothy Warren's gallery. I think the idea is fun, if you'd really care to do it. I would write a little introductory essay on painting, modern painting if you wished.

Would you let me know if you actually think of going on with the thing? I've heard of Fanfrolico from Rhys Davies – hope you're having a good time with it.

Yours sincerely
D. H. Lawrence

John Arnold, *Australian Literary Studies*, IX, October 1979

Stephensen ran Mandrake Press for a while, wrote *The Legend of Aleister Crowley* and returned to Sydney to start Endeavour Press with the support of Norman Lindsay and the backing of the *Bulletin*. He left after a year and established his own imprint, and in 1935 *The Australian Mercury*, which survived only one issue. Frank Johnson's own imprint published all Slessor's major poetry. Hal Porter recalls in *The Paper Chase* (1966) sending his stories to Norman Lindsay 'a young man's sort of deity in 1932' and 'P. R. Stephensen, to whom Lindsay has passed on some of my poems . . . dashes off letters on the startling orange writing-paper of *The Australian Mercury*, a one-number-only publication, telling me that my work is "ideally suited to a *real* literary magazine". And have I £200 to finance such a magazine?' It can look like a succession of disasters, comedies, absurdities. Yet it was through these short-lived Australian presses and magazines that Australian writers emerged and remained in print. It was through the energies of Johnson, Kirtley, Stephensen and the Lindsays that works of Slessor, Penton, Miles Franklin, Eleanor Dark, McCrae, Henry Handel Richardson, Xavier Herbert, Norman, Philip and Jack Lindsay, and many others were published. According to Norman Lindsay it was Brian Penton who at this time 'seduced me into publishing a novel' by taking off the manuscript of *Redheap* to England, where it was published in 1930 – and a further ten very popular, very successful works of fiction followed into print.

In 1936 Stephensen joined with W. J. Miles in *The Publicist*, 'the paper loyal to Australia first'. Stephensen's involvement in the Australia First Movement, a right-wing, nationalist organization, led to his being interned in 1942 for three and a half years. Kirtley, a *Publicist* contributor, was interned for two years. Bruce Muirden describes the episode in *The Puzzled Patriots* (1968). Nietzsche, vitalism, and nationalism had led towards fascism. Stephensen and Kirtley were not rare in their sympathies: T. S. Eliot, Charles Maurras, Ezra Pound, Wyndham Lewis, Montherlant, Henry Williamson, Yeats, Céline, Roy Campbell, Pirandello, d'Annunzio were all at some stage sympathetic to aspects of fascism, but they were rare in paying the price of internment.

Meanwhile in England Jack withdrew from the literary life and profound period of self-analysis, fasting, to come to understand his relationship with Elza, and to understand his relationship with Norman Lindsay and Norman's socio-cultural beliefs. 'At the crucial point, reached round the New Year of 1936, the new balance triumphantly asserted itself as a definitely organized system, and I found it was Marxism.'

One of the first works to issue from this new orientation was *John Bunyan* (1937); its pioneering strength has been attested by the historian Christopher Hill, though it is best known to generations of literary students from the attack on it by F. R. Leavis collected in *The Common Pursuit* (1952):

Bunyan, according to Mr Lindsay, 'wanted to get outside the cramping, distorting social discord of his day into the fuller life of fellowship.' Though Mr Lindsay talks of 'fuller life' he proffers emptiness; like most marxist writers who undertake to explain art and culture, he produces the effect of having emptied life of content and everything of meaning. It is impossible in any case to believe that the classless society produced by the process that the marxist's history has determined on could have a cultural content comparable with that represented by *The Pilgrims Progress*.

We are into the political polarizations of the late thirties, the foundations of the cold-war anti-communism of the fifties; and what Leavis found it impossible to believe, Jack Lindsay always has continued to believe. And his vision of human fulfilment and human possibility, his sense of the dialectic of change, his understanding of historical process and the creative spirit have shaped the great achievement of the works that now ensued.

Published in one volume for the first time, the trilogy gains in impact: we see the full sweep of movement, the romantic poet leaving Brisbane first for Sydney, then for London, going through processes of understanding, regaining and then breaking free from the father, coming under enchantments, coming to self-knowledge. Here are the archetypal, the mythic, materials: the portrait of the artist as a young man, dog, the scenes from bohemian life, the figures of tragic ruin. But though it is a story of struggle, of confusion, of emergence, of change, it is not a story of lost illusions. It is the story of coming through. The narrative ends at the end of the thirties, at the beginning of the first of the new periods of Lindsay's maturity, at that point at which E. Morris Miller characterized him in *Australian Literature: From its Beginnings to 1935* (1940): 'Probably the most versatile of the younger generation of Australian authors.'

MICHAEL WILDING
Sydney, 1981

LIFE RARELY TELLS

CONTENTS

1 · A GLIMPSE OF BRISBANE

AN OVERGROWN country town, terminus for the thirsty drovers. Cattle converging on it for hundreds of thousands of square miles, down from the sparse spinifex ridges and the gullies of grey stones, across the drab speargrass plains or through the twisted ti-tree scrub. My home town, if I have any. A sprawling mass of galvanized-iron and slated roofs dully glinting as I looked down from the crest of One Tree Hill, with the broad river winding silver among them. Houses perched on tall tarred poles with tin plates turned upside down on the top to keep out the white ants.

> *The pretty girls of Brisbane*
> *were hanging out their duds.*
> *I wished to have a chat with them,*
> *so steered straight for the tubs.*
> *Some dirty urchins saw me,*
> *and soon they raised my dander,*
> *crying, 'Mother, quick, take in the clothes,*
> *here comes an Overlander!'*

Echoes of the songs clung about the dusty streets. But the drovers' road now sheered off round the town to the meat works on the river banks. What I saw was a vast herd of red cattle pike-horned and bony, wearily staring with a sullen daze from behind the fences of wire and gum-sapling. Standing dejected with bloodshot eyes and a sort of hellish patience amid the fine brown dirt and the few meagre scraped trees.

I never put any faith in those gaunt fences with their bits of limp rusting wire. Every time I trailed along the hard rutted lane between the cattle hordes, leading my two brothers, I felt that only an incomprehensible chance lay between us and a trampled death. But my mother with her small bright parasol was unafraid.

Not another human being in sight. Only the hard red-brown earth pounded by the sun, the miles of cattle, and the fiery crystal of the heavens. Not a bird song in the heavy droning silence, the breaking wave of a taut drum-crescendo that never broke. The cattle seemed to have grown there, come up straight out of the bare bushless earth inside the huge pens; and I walked with circumspect fear, with a polite aloofness, scared of doing or saying the one tabooed thing which would break the uncertain armistice and bring the cattle charging over us.

We made this passage often on Saturdays, visiting my uncle who managed a big meat works by the river. A man with clear-cut apopleptic features, whose bookshelves held works only on the meat trade and on Napoleon, and who himself still had a tinct of strange courtesies learned in the Argentine and overlaying his brusqueness like the remnants of a courtly fancy dress (hired cheaply at a theatrical shop). His large bungalow stood above the rambling works of discoloured white, the involved water towers, the tall chimney where bones and offal were burned for manure, hashmagandy, the corridors down which on weekdays the cattle went lurching to the hammer-blow, the refrigerating chambers where we wandered in an endless forest of chilly hanging corpses.

While we drank tea or meandered by the revetted river-banks, watching for the fish that came to the pipes still bloodclotted, I put aside all thought of the cattle ordeal. But when we passed along the rutted track between the bloodshot eyes, I knew that I had been remembering it all the while, dreading it all the week, yet accepting it as a sort of necessary danger, a test which, when met and overcome, quickened my life.

Then after the quiet stroll between the miles of cattle came a differently difficult moment. We encountered a smaller works, silent during the weekend stoppage, and had to hasten through the slaughter-yards, over the swabbed cement and through the drowsy flies, the thick sticky stink of blood. The stink hung in a clammy cobweb from the shadowy rafters and wisped up from the muddy purplish puddles in the gutters. I used to hold my breath till we came out the other end into the shrill sunlight. Blood smells, I thought, as a penny tastes when you've been holding it in your sweaty palm.

After that it was exhilarating to wait at the box of a station which had no platform, its name-board almost hidden under gum leaves. We hunted round for flags of bracken or boughs of the scanty gum trees with their flat-curved leaves and slight blossom, which we waved to stop the train. We were sure that without the signals the driver would never notice our small group and we should have to spend the night in the wilds inhabited by hordes of cattle ghosts. There was a breathless moment of uncertainty before the engine slackened. Then came the dash of stumbling triumph along the metalled lines, the struggle with the lofty door-handle, the scratched knees of the scramble into the cigarette butts of the carriage floor. My mother closed her parasol with a faint sigh and held her throat as she stared dreamily out at the flickering telegraph posts.

But even if I carried my fern plume all the way home, it was no use to wave away the stinging flies, the bloodshot alien eyes, from the dusk of memory. On the edge of sleep I heard again the snorting bellow of a single steer and saw the lean heaving sides, and expected a thousand throats to answer in implacable anger. Nothing happened. The steer's eyes glazed and it listened mournfully to the echo of its cry. The others gave no sign. The patiently accusing eyes regarded me, and that was all. Under the mosquito net on the boarding-house balcony a hot deep sleep took me into its broad lap.

But though the cattle had gone out of town, other companions of the Overlander lingered only a few yards from my bed. Brisbane, with a couple of hundred thousand inhabitants, had trams but no sewerage system, and many tokens of its pioneer days. Our boarding-house of the moment was in George Street, next door to the Queensland Club, that lair of grimly rich squatters with discreet venetian blinds and grey dignity. Now and then I intruded with a bold panic on its trim reserve, slithering over the back wall to retrieve a lost ball among the dusty genteel shrubs. Round the corner, by the frangipani trees with their bold loose flowers, was one of the three entrances to the

Botanical Gardens, where my mother used to annoy me by blandly ignoring all notices, picking any flower that pleased her, and striking up conversations with gardeners. Now I can recall only her encouraging smile. She had a knack of making friends with anyone on sight and could never pass an empty house without trying to get inside and see what was there. She would look round, planning what use to make of the rooms if the house (as now suddenly seemed likely) were hers, and I'd keep an eye open for the arrival of a policeman – though the only time one did ask us what we were doing, he ended by telling her all about his family troubles. (Always I see her in a parasol nimbus, a glistening underwater fluorescence of shadow, listening.)

Within a hundred yards of club and boarding-house stood the Queensland Parliament House with a giant jacaranda in front, a cathedral mass of light bright blue blossoms filling half the summer sky and carpeting the ground in azure for the unworthy feet of M.P.s. Premier Ryan, also a resident at our boarding-house, patted my head, asked me questions that I disdained to answer, and Irishly made my mother smile in her plump peach-coloured remoteness. Yet at the other end of our block, near the second entrance to the gardens, stood a couple of nondescript shops with varnish or blankets over their windows and a Chinese laundry breathing out a hot starchy smell and displaying a fly-blown shirt beside a ginger jar. Amid these shops rose a tall archway with a large double gate spiked across the top. A small door was inset in the gate; and when I loitered home at evening from the playing ground in the gardens I noticed that women came out of this door, bringing stools or chairs, to sit on the pavement under a fitfully coughing gas jet.

I paused to look, to wonder without conjecture. There was no note of family feeling in the ways of the group, in their looks or their postures. They sat in a row and said nothing to one another. They all seemed young to me, but that may have been because they were all lavishly painted white and pink, and some had their hair falling lank or ringleted on their bared shoulders. They wore dressing-gowns, flowered or striped, and when they crossed or uncrossed their legs, as they often did, the gowns fell open and revealed bare legs or big careless breasts, with a flash of frill or ribbon. I stared and wandered on.

But the strangeness of the women grew stronger every time I saw them. I felt a difference between these loungers of the first gas flares of dusk and the other people. I looked forward to walking home round their side of the block. They had something about them that reminded me of circus or pantomime, those rare treats, with their gaudiness and paint, their scanty clothes, their odd bird-bright eyes, their silence broken occasionally by hoarse whispers as if preluding an unpredictable show which never happened.

Sitting in their row, relaxed but uncomfortable, they smoked cigarettes or fastened a rosetted garter. At times, as I approached a man was speaking with one of them, and he and she went in, ducking down, through the small door. I tried to time my steps so as to come up just at the moment when I'd get a peep through, into the world from which the women emerged; but I never managed it. Once, when I lingered, a woman with a fuzz of yellow hair called something with a strident laugh and I ran off in panic.

Years later, when we had left the neighbourhood, I realized that the women were relics of the old roaring days. The chap from way back with a cheque to blue liked to have his woman-wares set out conveniently for leisurely consideration. There had been several such houses round the area, mixed up with the engineering works which clanged and belched by day, and the swimming baths that floated on the river mud by the ferry punt. One night P.R.S., riding by at a late hour, was hailed by one of the tarts at a galvanized-iron gate: 'Come on in, bike and all!'

And once, taking a short cut near the shopping centre of the Valley, I stumbled on a day-street of such unashamed bitchery. I was in a hurry and my pace gave offence to a blowsy wench lounging broad-bosomed in a doorway among the strings of a bead curtain. She shouted an insult or a proposal, and when I hurried faster, she shouted yet more loudly. Scarlet-mouthed trollops in frowsy lace petticoats or slack dressing-gowns came out yawning and puffy-eyed to watch the fun. I suppose they thought I was trying to bilk one of the sisterhood. Anyway they joined in the noise, and I ran, dodging into safety, into the normal traffic of the Valley, past a girl who opened her kimono to hedge me in, showing swollen breasts with the silky opalescent sheen of a Rubensesque *Kermes*.

A second multitude of encircling eyes, Brisbane-born, hovered on the edge of my sleep. Eyes wilder and larger than those of lethargic cattle; more dangerous in their ambush of the unknown. Eyes with a malicious glassy glare, bright as water, flowing in filleted hair-thickets.

Hordes of resentful tired-out cattle waiting to be smashed on the head in the narrow slaughter-way that allowed no turning-back; and flaunted womanflesh spread coldly on slabs for sale. These were the two images that floated up out of the drover-past, out of the incomprehensible present. The walls of the solid day crumbled before their piercing power, which left an unanswered question like an acid eating silently through the acknowledged surface of things.

But before I tackle what happened in Brisbane, let me briefly glance at the Sydney years that preceded it.

2 · EARLY YEARS IN SYDNEY

Out of the multitudinous shifting of images, momentary unexplained events and faces caught in an evanescent shaft of light, which make up my earliest childhood in Melbourne, I come to the clearing vistas of Sydney, my brother Ray born in my third year and all the worries over feeding him and, as a central vignette framed in cockle-shells, my mother pushing a perambulator down the broad steps of a garden. I cannot see her face hidden in the straw-hat that a blue ribbon ties under her chin; it is dissolved in lemon-yellow shadows.

When I first felt myself the member of a group, detached from the broad lap of the family, we were living in a house built over the spot where the train from Milson's Point plunged into a tunnel on its way to North Sydney suburbs. Between our house and the landing stage of the ferry at Lavender Bay was a stretch of beach with some weatherboard shacks of fishermen (soon to be pulled down). There, playing under the afternoon-eyes of my mother, I had come to know half a dozen lads, fishermen's sons, who knocked down my sandcastles and kicked my cap seawards, charged on broomhandle-horses, jumped over me like the wind, disappeared into damp crannies under their derelict homes. Barefooted lads, about my own age or a little older, with stubborn untidy hair and torn breeches, scrambling with scarred toes among the driftwood and smelling of tar, putty, and crushed ants. My mother, when not taken up with watching that Ray didn't swallow too much sand, made friends with the whooping pack and reconciled them to me. She asked them up to our house for tea, and they ate loudly and hungrily, leaving sand and seaweed on the floor. After tumbling me about and falling on me, they communicated something of their own seashore smell to my hair and clothes, and took me in as one of themselves.

We played on the beach, skimming stones across the waves and racing the mongrel-dogs. We put jellyfish down one another's backs. We stood between the rails at the tunnel entrance as the trains came roaring up, stood there defiantly, shouting, as long as we dared. We went on rambling walks, planned with piratic strategies, over the hills of sparse grass and lantana bushes that lay inland.

We sang as we went, because we had a common purpose which could be uttered only in song. We were together and defiant. We chafed all the while against one another, taking a dare or giving it, wrestling, tossing a penny, running, climbing trees. 'I saw it first. I got higher than you did. I touched it first.' I felt myself distinct because I was part of them; I was part of them because I detached myself in the ceaseless dares and claims.

We sang in a tramping yell, about moonlight and somebody's daughter washing her feet in soda water, and Hell O Hell O Helen most divine. Also, without any intention of championing the policy of White Australia:

> *Rule Britannia, Britannia rule the waves,*
> *No more Chinamen in New South Wales –*

though we liked Chinamen and merely felt that the words were somehow a defiance of authority. Also:

> *Forward Christian Soldiers*
> *to the Battle of Waterloo.*
> *The wind blew off my trow-ow-sers*
> *and I didn't know what to do.*

For the moment it seems that I too could sing. Indeed the echoes from the dry gritty hills must have somehow drifted under the arch of our front gate. For my mother taught me the words of *We Sailed by the Lowlands Low*, and once I was cajoled into singing the ballad in the drawing-room, to ladies in a rustling circle, all dressed in lilies and lavender, white kid gloves and clouds of lace. Ladies who exclaimed at the clever and well-behaved little boy, and whose voices had the tinkle of frail silver teaspoons on bone china, in a light of milk. But my mother was far too absorbed in her children to entertain much, and the ladies soon receded into the bright domes of their fringed parasols, patting a dear little boy on the cheek and climbing into carriages curved like the sepals of their own flowering selves. There remained only the clash of my mother's many thin silver bracelets, the froufrou of her petticoats with their eyelets of broderie anglaise into which I wanted to thread pieces of string.

And the voices on the hills. The singing was indistinguishable from the movement of arms and legs, and loudest when all sound was torn from the mouth by the wind of our speed as we ran down the stony slopes. Grey grass and lantana bushes with hard green unripe berries in clusters; stones and grey grass and a tin-shack mouldering red and old barbed wire with a few dirty tufts of wool. Endlessly shelving sunlight, a silent explosion of light, and birds squawking on the telegraph poles. Nothing but hills of harsh gold, spiky with grey grass.

Afterwards, the crunch of stolen apples in a hollow of snug heat, among the tumbling sandboys who laughed and used lots of words that I hadn't heard before – words which I knew by some masonic understanding must not be repeated in adult company. The body as a secret source of delight, one's own inestimable possession, and an awareness of the forbidden.

My fifth birthday was nearing. We discussed it in a big back room of the house where we played with various objects found in its lumber, a genuine blunted cutlass and a phonograph with cylinder records that emitted Negro songs across the hiccups of cracks. Perhaps because the whole gang had gathered in a room that was mine, I saw them all together, saw them as *my friends, myself, us.* We drank water out of discarded beer bottles. 'I've drunk beer,' said the eldest boy, Harry, wrinkling his snubnose and reeling about. 'I drank a whole bottle.'

That evening my mother, coaxing me to bed, remarked, 'You can do whatever you like on your birthday.'

And I replied, feeling very sly and somewhat frightened, doubling up in the armchair, 'Oh no, I can't.'

We moved to a house not far away, a house with terraces reaching right down to the harbour. It lay on a slope, so steep that only the top of its three storeys came up to street level and there were hundreds of stone steps down from the front gate. My mother's throat was swathed and she spoke huskily. Then my other brother, Philip, was born in 1906. And one day my tousle-haired dog strayed down after my father to the city-ferry and was never seen again. We wept every night for weeks.

One day my mother took out the little shining round box in which my father had been collecting sixpences and broke it open with an axe in the coal shed under the stone steps. We laughed and cheered. I remember angry voices through venetian blinds. I listened and then ran down the path winding on the terraces, fell and sprained my thumb.

Down by the water was a large boating-shed and a closed space for bathing. A small wooden jetty led out into the water and at low tide several yards of slimy rock were uncovered. One day the tide had turned and was coming in, but I went on paddling among the rocks in one foot, two feet, of water. Ray was chasing himself round on the grass and our mother sat on the jetty with the baby on her opened lap, dreaming in the shade of one of her large straw-hats with a huge pink rose on one side, her eyes gently hidden. Suddenly I had a sick conviction of danger, of a world heeling over and engulfing me, of monstrous tentacles reaching out all around. A fear so intense that the body seemed contracting inside itself to a point of nothingness.

The next moment I was safe on dry land, hugged wet to my mother's bosom and weeping. A small octopus had come out from under one of the rocks and decided to investigate me. When I had recovered enough to feel angry, I collected all the stones near at hand and threw them down in the region of the underwater where the octopus had been lurking. But I could not so easily reply to monsters laired under the waters of sleep.

When I closed my eyes, I saw the waters in a slow whirlpool, a white rose of fury, coming and going in complicated graceful motion round the central maw. But sometimes my will conquered, and I saw them as a smooth moonwaste on which I walked. All I had to do, I argued, was to move each foot before it had time to sink. The logic was impeccable, and so I found nothing impossible in walking the moonwaters on the edge of sleep; but I never tried to put the method to the test on the umplumbed octopus-lairing waters of day.

We had two girl cousins, who emerged living in an old shady house among twisted fig trees on cracked terraces. And soon we ourselves moved from our terraced house to one not far off, higher up, where the street in front dropped quickly away and left a considerable man-made cliff at the end of the garden. We discussed if a cat, pushed off, would have to use up one of its nine lives before it picked itself up at the bottom. For my birthday my father bought a fine lot of fireworks, which wrecked the rose-garden; and early next morning most of the plaster fell from the ceiling of the large drawing-room. The party had been a huge success, proved by the fact that our shouts and songs had brought down the roof of the world. Shouting, Ray and I pried among the debris for sections of moulded designs, flowers and flying cupids. Most of all we wanted to find one of the fat cupids that had circled the chandelier with an odd confusion of limbs – I had often lain on the floor trying to allocate the legs to the right bodies despite the wisps of drapery or cloud that got in the way at the essential points of juncture. But we were shooed from the room where we were trampling the plaster into the carpets.

We had met the two girls of our own age from next door and soon had many communicating holes between the sheds at the side of our house and the outbuildings that lay against them. Polly's place owned extensive grounds with many trees and bush lairs, and beyond it was empty ground with really vast lantana thickets in which we could establish tunnels and shelters on a satisfying scale. We worked out a system of hidden connections. From the roof of our sheds we climbed over the slates to a precarious window in the outbuildings, or we slid into the coach-room, clambered up manger-racks into a skylight, whence we fell on an old mattress in a next door lumber-room, or we crawled behind a rose bush, removed a paling, swung out on a bough, and dropped some ten feet, then crept among rhododendra till a final dash brought us to a side door in the stables. Or, if we wanted a long way round, we wormed among tree-roots and small bushes all along the front fence of Polly's place, then near the gate, shielded by big trees, crossed the drive and crouched behind the reeds with tall silky plumes. There we slipped through a broken piece of fence and made for the H.Q., where the lantana tunnel ended against a slight hillock, and we had dug something of a cave. In this inadequate cave we kept a couple of biscuit tins and the toy revolvers fed with caps for banging noises; also an exercise book in which I drew a plan of the tunnels and wrote out a list of our valuables. We had picked up rumours of a Japanese invasion: probably the adults had been talking about one of the periodic arrests of a Jap spy. And so we wanted to be ready for the coming irruption. But buns or slices of bread, the food most easily obtainable, had a way of going hard as bricks or crumbly as sand: and any more delectable articles were likely to be eaten up before we'd had them an hour. Still, we had a compass that wouldn't work, a rusty gardening knife, five medicine bottles and a beer bottle full of water, an old pillow and a tin opener. One rejoicing day we got away with a tin of sardines from the pantry. In the H.Q. we sat huddled, watched ants, or scraped out a little more cave with broken glass and a skewer.

The alternative lair was the shed-stables agglomeration, which had more variety but lacked the security of the cave. We could, however, get into the top part of Polly's stables and then pull up the ladder after us, which gave us almost as good a feeling of being alone in the world. There was the added attraction that we were right up against the adult world and must talk in hushed tones, having been forbidden to play in the stables on account of their dirt. Once the ladder was pulled up – which needed care if we weren't to knock it through the tiled roof – we were stranded conspirators. If the worst came, we could slide down the rope that still hung out of a wall hatch; and meanwhile we could throw small objects into the servants' room opposite.

The stables, the sheds, the coach loft, tumble together in my memory, alike filled with dust, rust, ironmongery and sacks, ancient chaff and stiffened bits of leather harness, broken glass and tins with a little paint left under a thick crust, motiveless wrestlings and obscure military operations. Vast stand those ribs of monstrous metal, shadows that rattled at a breath, winding caverns of the hush, and old buckets where mice had nested. Ridiculous crockery of giants. In the late afternoon the choked stillness was that of a den cluttered with brazen bones by some untidy ogre, and the hot smell of rust was like dried blood. Old bedsteads and carpet rolls long sealed with the silvery cobweb of romance; spraying plumes of dust from wire mattresses that jingled like spinets prodigiously out of tune; underworld lights that straggled through brown paper and dirty glass, cupolas of rich gloom. Lead pipes that might be telescopes, if you took care not to pour dust in your eye when you held them up to the window; or blowpipes, like the eagerly sought reeds that always broke. Stinking garden of wrought-iron flowers and chipped jugs, old photos stained from the wet ring of a cup, spoutless teapots that came in handy as urinals, and tin baths that served as reverberating boats on a voyage to the country we shall never reach.

There were enemies in this secretive Eden with its involved communication lines invisible to the adult eye. Bob, the brother of the two girls, was about fourteen, too old to share in our games, too young to shade off into the ignored worlds of grown-ups. Both Polly, blonde and dumpy, and Sara, small and dark-flashing, were his tongue-tied handmaids; but as he was away at school, it was only at weekends that their obsequious attitudes spoiled our games.

Two male cousins, aged about ten, were however open and violent foes. When they paid one of their rare visits, we were harried and tormented. They were brigands, with their hands red against all the world, and they showed a fiendish ingenuity. Pretending to be friends, they lured us to the end of the garden where they had a hosepipe ready, or they tied us to trees and cut our hair with garden-shears on pretence of scalping us. Once when they had roped us on the bough of a tree, they lighted a fire underneath. They put us in the wash-house copper and tried to boil us. Once, when the family was out, they shut us up in a pitch dark cupboard and left us till someone came home. They gave us sweets full of cayenne pepper and cakes in which the cream turned out to be toothpaste. They even sent us a matchbox full of dead flies through the post.

They had winning ways and the adults never took their

pranks seriously. We ourselves, deceived again and again, were always convinced of their good intentions when they smiled and swore that they'd turned over a new leaf. (I met one of them later and he had become a shy young man madly addicted to motor bikes.)

They had no special dislike of Ray and myself. They tormented the girls, too, though in less furious ways. They put frogs down their backs and treacle in their hair, in Polly's straw-coloured and careless locks and Sara's neat-fringed black helmet. Once, when Mrs C. had some ladies to tea, they took all Polly's clothes off and sent her running tearful into the house.

Phil, an outrageously screaming baby, had a nurse-girl Betty, with whom I used often to go down towards the ferry, where the land was still rocky and untamed. Of her I remember only the lifted upper lip (her mouth was never closed), the bitten fingernails, and the birthmark on the left knee. And the day is always a day of gold, the wool of light caught in dazzling tatters on the trees as though the sky-sheep had been pushing through. Over on the right, people are going down to, or coming up from, the ferry, walking fast because the asphalt is hot under the soles of their shoes. The heat flows down the steps in vaporous eddies of glass, mixed up with the parasol blossoms and the twinkling hands. Ladies float langorously along in Edwardian fullness and old gentlemen take out handkerchiefs to pick the burs of heat from their beards. But the birds, bathing in the song-trickles that they toss in the air, are enjoying themselves, and so am I, tearing up patches of grass. Where we lie is shady, against the shaggy coat of rock peeling with a minute grey-green skin of age. We see everyone and nobody sees us.

Betty is restless. The rocking-horses of the harbour waters make their unadvancing charge against the land. Small sailing boats glisten and lean round a curve of slow wind. Blue-bloused Betty with her bitten nails has taken off her shoes and stockings, she pulls me over and kisses me; and I am too astounded to resist. The kiss is not like those of family ritual, being large and loose and wet, altogether ridiculous and unfair and unacceptable.

Shortly before we left the pleasant one-storeyed old colonial house, the cook left us. Minnie was a stolid solid woman with a brick-red face. One day when I was in the kitchen she made herself a cup of tea and added a greedy dose of what she thought was sugar. But it was salt. She declared that the mistake was God's punishment and waste-not-want-not. So she drank the whole cup off and then ran wheezing and coughing to the sink. 'Let that be a lesson to you,' she moaned.

She was short-sighted, but hated to admit it; and when she made one of her mistakes over the ingredients of a dish, she produced any far-fetched excuse rather than confess the truth. She carried on long monologues with the Lord when she thought she was alone; and she used to take her false teeth out and mislay them. Then her mumbles grew so bad that one could not tell if she were addressing God or the Devil. But she was kind hearted and told me stories about the wrongs of Ireland and the habits of the fairy folk, so that I got a confused picture of policemen shooting down the fairies for making moonshine whiskey in a bog, with the moral 'God will have mercy on Ireland yet.' She and my mother were at odds about the window. My mother opened it as soon as she came into the kitchen, and sent Minnie grumbling and coughing piteously over the stove, then, the moment she went out, Minnie rushed and closed the window, no matter how hot the day was.

She was engaged to a small sunburnt fellow with a long pointed nose, who must have been a fisherman. At least once a week he brought her a present of fish. Finally he produced two big fish with strange rainbow-coloured skins, which my mother refused to have cooked for dinner. Minnie took the refusal as a mortal insult, a wicked waste and a charge that she and her man were conspiring to poison the family. So she went, implacable.

3 · LEARNING TO READ

WE MOVED to a newly built bungalow, just across the road from the terraced house with the octopus, on the higher slope. It had been bought by the *Bulletin*, on which my father worked as chief cartoonist, and was intended to be our settled home. The deeds were settled on my mother.

I was sent to a kindergarten school in a new sailor-suit. I had already somehow managed to acquire the rudiments of reading. My aunt Mary had given me *Treasure Island*, and while I was in bed recovering from chickenpox, my father Norman roughed out drawings of the characters. I learned to read out of sheer determination to interpret the drawings. Our new cook, amiable Harriet, who was in love with a big bronzed carter, helped me. The carter used to sit in the kitchen on visits, drinking tea out of the biggest cup and saying nothing; but one day to my surprise I heard Harriet remark to my mother that he had declared I was a brainy one and I'd make my way, mark his word. After that I had a high opinion of him.

At the same time I gained my first sense of style in art. For Norman decided to collect all the joke drawings he had done in the *Bulletin*, perhaps with the idea of making some extra money out of a book of them. He offered me sixpence for every one I cut out of the tall pack of *Bulletins* in the cupboard. I cut hundreds out and never needed to look at the signatures. But after the first payment I failed to get any more sixpences; and it was a result of this let down that I said loudly one breakfast when Ray was complaining at not having been brought a promised present, 'Don't you know daddy never keeps his promises?' (Behind this precocious sense of parental frailty I feel sure there must have been conversations between my mother and Harriet overheard, in which my father's short-

comings were canvassed. I distrust my powers of generalizing
character so succinctly at this early age.)

But for non-Australian eyes I had perhaps better here
intrude a few words about Norman, who already by 1905-6 was
a national figure. Born in 1879 at Creswick, a mining township
near Ballarat, Victoria, he was one of a large family with a doctor as father. In his early years he had little but the family Bible
and Knight's *London* as art-exemplars, which provided an historical apparatus for the drawings he began making to Dumas
and Shakespeare. Almost all the children had some art faculty;
and Norman at the age of fifteen followed his elder brother
Lionel in the flight to Melbourne. For some years he lived precariously on drawings for crime sheets and boxing papers; then
in 1900 he married and soon after by a sequence of chances
found himself a cartoonist on the *Bulletin*, then the radical
centre of all that was vigorous in Australian art and writing.
He was hardly a member of its staff, he told me, when the
premises were attacked and partly wrecked by drunken sol-
diery for the weekly's anti-Boer War policy. In Melbourne he
had avidly read and studied, deeply affected by the pre-
Raphaelites (mainly through Sandys), Rubens, the Greeks,
Dürer, Leonardo, and learning much from such more or less
contemporary black-and-white artists as Keene, Menzel, Doré,
Vierge, May. In literature he fastened in particular on Shakespeare, Rabelais, the Greek poets, Catullus, Boccaccio, Villon,
Dickens, Petronius, and for a while, through Lionel's influence,
the French dissidents from Baudelaire to Flaubert.

Partly through his position on the *Bulletin*, partly through
the fact that his exhibitions roused the press and the churches
to a frantic demand for his suppression, he soon became known
to the whole Australian public, whether they were interested
in art or not. He had found in Nietzsche the idiom of his revolt
against the society around him; and both in such direct polemics as *Pollice Verso, The Scoffers*, or *The Crucified Venus*, or in
his bacchanals and the like, in which he sought to express an
uncompromising affirmation of the fertilities and laughters of
life, he appeared anathema. By the age of twenty-five he had
gained such a mastery of his medium that he was producing
works like *Pollice Verso* and *Dionysus*, in which virtuosity of

draughtsmanship was matched with tonal richness, and rhythmic certainty of composition. For the time being he was combatively at home in the Australian world. While fiercely rejecting all its respectable conventions, he was gaily secure in his sense of a great imaginative journey, merging without strain Athens and Pompeii and Woolloomooloo. He was absorbed in mastering the grand tradition of art, but felt this process one with the struggle against all that was inert and life-denying in his society. He was emotionally in harmony with the down-to-earth independence, the damn-all integrity, the frank acceptances, of the pioneering world which was fading out – though he had apparently severed all points of contact by lifting these elements to a new level. He could for the moment draw effectively thus on the Australian spirit, pre-1900 vintage, unbothered by the fact that much of the values that supported him derived from the pioneers who were also largely responsible for the things he hated. For the pioneer as he settles down into a good citizen breeds aggressively a petty bourgeois philistinism, and the spirit of dogged indepen-dence becomes a blinkered sense of property – unless its pos-sessors realize what is happening and get together accordingly. (The stage at which Norman's original impetus could not but be staggered and checked came in 1914–18; and he then had to face a new set of choices.)

He has always had an all-round craft skill of the Renaissance kind, working in pen-and-ink, wash drawings, etchings, engravings, wood cuts, water colours, oil paintings, and turn-ing at various moments of his career to anything from wood carving to minutely correct ship models or life-size concrete statues. He knew every rope on a full-rigged sailing ship, its name and function, and was friendly with sailors and boxers – for long he had a retired bruiser as his studio retainer. In the Sydney days of which I am writing occurred the Burns–Johnson match; I can recall the excitement it roused, the hectic emotion that the white supremacy depended on Burns win-ning. Norman was in the thick of it, particularly liking John-son; he was now a pal of MacIntosh the promoter, who later introduced, among other things, dirt-track racing and milk bars into England. And he must have been living lavishly; for besides his cartoons he was drawing many hundreds of joke blocks for the *Bulletin* and producing advertisements, postcards, book illustrations – not to mention writing tales, though it was later that he began steadily turning out novels as well as philosophical diatribes. His economic sense is embalmed in the family tale that after his *Bulletin* début he was informed by the bank that he was overdrawn, and answered in bewilderment that he still had some cheques in the cheque-book. Another time, seeing a starved-looking man peer into a food shop, he pressed a sovereign into his hand, and the man muttered, 'Are you God?' He did so many joke drawings for the *Bulletin* that they remarked on it, and he retorted that he'd never do another one; not long after there was a fire in the office and the store of drawings-in-hand was burnt, but he refused to take back his refusal.

At the kindergarten, run by two old maids, the pupils were mostly girls. To reach the suburban slate-tiled house with its front garden of mangy mignonette, I had to take more than half an hour's walk and soon found the passage perilous. There were dire feuds between the boys of the Preparatory Grammar School and the less well-off who went to the public school (that is, the state school in Australianese). These often led to street brawls and I was continually near to getting caught in some clash or other. For one thing I had no idea which side I was on. So far there had been little in my daily life to develop a class sense. Our friends had always been simply those who lived close at hand, the fisher-lads or Polly and Sara; and I had not yet taken to reading the threepenny school magazines, *Gem* and *Magnet*, which carefully inculcated a thorough snobbishness.

Then, after I had ventured through the ambushed streets with Ray's hand in mine, I had the grievously long day of the kindergarten to endure, ill at ease among the many skinny pigtailed girls and soon convinced that the teachers didn't like me. No doubt I was already striving to show off my knowledge, such as it was. Several times I had to don the tall pointed dunce's cap and stand in the corner by the glistening globe, trying to pass the time by reading the titles of the books on the shelf out of the edge of my eye. Already I collected stamps and matchbox labels, and had a peculiar smattering of history deviously acquired.

The lunch-hour, spent in the asphalted backyard, was my worst trial. The girls, mostly older than I, despised me. They ignored me or suddenly penned me in a corner by the draggled bed of geraniums and wallflowers, which it was a crime to tread on. There they chanted insulting slogans which they punctuated by lifting their skirts and flapping them at me, showing serge bloomers and bony knees. But there was also one of them named Helen, whose golden curls were so bright that I cannot recall her face, who sometimes walked home with me.

I used all my wiles to divert my mother from what seemed the unnecessary and foolish project of school. The simplest plan was to hide my boots. But soon most of the hiding places became known. So, when my boots had been ignominiously fished out for the tenth time from behind the piano or the top of the wardrobe, I fell back on pathos. I lingered on the steps while my mother told me to hurry or I'd be late. 'This might be the very day I'm going to be run over. Think how sorry you'd be for sending me.' She could seldom bear up long against this argument. Under her big floppy hat she weakened, 'Very well, just this once. But remember you *must* go tomorrow.' Then, feeling secure and absolved in her firm resolve about the next day, she was quite happy in having surrendered for the moment. At heart she didn't believe in schools any more than I did. So Ray had a holiday too, and if the day was hot, I'd have to watch that he didn't eat any of the melting asphalt in the yard, picking at the places where a clothes-prop had dug in. We splashed one another in the bath and spent the rest of the morning running naked round the yard.

'You're weak with them, Mrs Lindsay,' Harriet would remark with a shake of her coppery head.

'Still, it does them good to be out in the sun,' my mother consoled herself. 'Better than being shut up in school.'

Dudley, a slightly older boy, who lived across the road from our previous house, had continued to be a friend. For one thing we could now signal from our backyard to the attic-window in his house; and he was a keen boy scout. I occasionally slept in his garden in a tent; and we went together to the new kind of show that had opened – magic lantern slides, sometimes illustrating a popular song (which the audience sang) and brief films of horseplay or a train rushing alarmingly straight at us. I too became a boy scout and learned to tie knots; and Dudley, who had a box-camera, let me watch him develop films. One day we went to take a photo of the docks visible on the other side of the headland; we climbed a high rocky point and wormed our way along a narrow track, with a clear fall of some fifty feet, into a cave, from which we looked out over the harbour.

Prize day came at the school. Even Ray got something, but I was left out. Infuriated, I hurried home and wept to my grandmother, a small fattish Victorian lady in black glistening clothes with jet decorations, and she comforted me with a shilling and an assurance that I was cleverer than everyone else.

At the moving pictures we tried to join in the ballads, and Dudley always knew the words afterwards. At the big drapers on the other side of the harbour there were Christmas shows of Punch and Judy, which enraptured us. Here in Punch was somebody with whom one could feel wholly in sympathy as he banged and battered his way through all the authorities of the world. His reckless rage and his demoniac chuckle, his defeat of police and hangman, death and devil, stirred me beyond laughter.

And we ourselves played the game of Ned Kelly, which I had first learned with the fisher-lads. Ned Kelly the outstanding outlaw-hero of Australian folklore:

> Then come, my hearties, we'll roam the mountains high.
> Together we will plunder, together we will die.
> We'll wander over mountains and we'll gallop over plains,
> for we scorn to live in slavery bound down with iron chains.

Many are the ballad-heroes of the bushranging days, the dare-devils who, when alluvial petered out and small selector came up against big squatter, decided to help themselves to ill-gotten gold.

> Farewell to Burke, O'Meally, Young Gilbert and Ben Hall,
> likewise to Daniel Morgan, who fell by rifle-ball.

But the Kellys left the deepest mark, with Ned the unforgettable hero making his last stand in improvised armour. His memory is kept green every time an Australian boy puts a bucket or a chamber-pot on his head and defies the minions of the law.

I had assumed the bucket, with an old rubbish tin top for shield. But I was captured at last and the enemy tied me with a belt, pinioning my arms. In a last defiance, as we wrestled on the upper-terrace where my mother had given up trying to grow flowers. I swelled out my muscles and to my astonishment the leathern belt broke. No doubt it was rotten with age, but such a possibility did not intrude on my heroic sensation of power. I had burst my fetters with one shrug of my outlaw limbs and I was free.

Shortly after, in a hurricane, a great piece of sheet iron was torn from the Lavender Bay Baths and flung on to our roof; it crashed through over my bed. But that night I had had toothache and my mother had taken me into her bed, her providential bed. (When she managed to coax one of my teeth out with a length of thread, she ceremonially inserted it into a mouse-hole.)

Early in our stay in this house, I had been given an illustrated book of the story of Bluebeard and his murdered wives. There was one drawing in it that I could not bear. My revulsion was so deep that I cannot remember in the least what it was like; and I hated having to look at the book or listen to the story. But for some reason I could not mention my hate and fear. Nor could I destroy the book; all I could do was to hide it. And every time it was found again and presented to me as if I ought to be delighted, I took it and tried to invent a better hiding-place.

One day, after I had gone to school, I was seated on the stone steps leading up to our house from the street, with the Bay and its dolphin waters bounding below. I was reading a penny-dreadful about a mystery gang under a master crook. One of the characters had found out something or other, and then, instead of rushing to give up his evidence, he thinks: Why should I tell? Why shouldn't I keep it all to myself? Why should

I tell? And the author commented: 'The mystery had him too in its grips.' No explanation.

The words somehow came home to me with a sense of strange spiritual power. I sat on the steps trembling. The words had been spoken to me. Why should I tell? The mystery had me too in its grips. I made no effort to find an explanation, to think out what the author had meant or what the words now meant to me. I felt the exaltation of an accepted mystery, the power of spiritual loneliness. After some fifty years I can revive the moment, entire, to the least shrug of ecstasy in my scalp, feel again the gritty heat in the stone, see the small bit of fern growing from a crack in the crumbling wall-face, hear the apocalyptic voice separating me out into silence.

My father had taken to horse riding, drawn into John D's smart set and the attempt to form a proper hunting tallyho group. He was afraid of horses – how I knew this, I cannot tell – but I enjoyed going with him to the stables and watching him ride off. Finally, to his relief, the horse ran into a cart shaft while a groom was looking after it, and had to be shot.

Norman had his studios in town, across the harbour, and was less and less at home. He had fallen in love and my mother cannot long have been ignorant; for Will Dyson told her all about it. (Bill we called him.) W.D. had a deep fondness for her; I have read the letter he wrote to her about this time before going off to England, in which he warmly pressed her to call on him for any help whatever that she needed. He made a water-colour sketch of her in a blue suit, which she long kept. I think it had little of her except her way of turning her face aside, keeping herself gently enclosed in the lair of herself, in the shadow of her hair.*

*I was looking for the words in my mind that would define the far-off image of Will Dyson in those days when I found Hugh McCrae's description: 'Now and then Will Dyson came in: young and good-looking, with eyes full of brightness, and flushed cheeks, while he said something not to be missed, smilingly, out of the corner of his mouth. Tightly fitting clothes emphasized the sinuous lines of his body; and, instead of a collar, he wore a black silk

A family legend told that she went to dine once with Bill, and Norman bribed the waiter to be allowed to hide under the table. I feel that this tale must be symbolic rather than factual; but jealousy can be an odd gadfly. Another such legend recounted how Bill came one evening to chat; as usual Norman wasn't at home; a storm blew up and Bill was pressed to stay for the night. My mother vacated her own bed for him and slept with me. A day or so later when Norman was at home, I remarked to him at the dining-table, 'Bill Dyson slept in mummy's bed.' He rushed out of the house. I do not remember the episode, but tell it as I have heard it told.

What I do remember is the New Year's Eve when we had been given permission to stay up, with Dudley, and see the New Year in. 'After all, it only comes once a year,' my mother said apologetically to Harriet. (Harriet was now married to her carter, but had come back to us after a few months' absence, complaining that once men got a woman they showed what brutes they were.)

About eleven o'clock Norman came home. Noticing us with our tins and a number of bangers brought by Dudley, under the castor-oil tree, he asked why we weren't in bed. My mother answered that of course we were staying up to see the New Year in; everybody was staying up; Dudley was staying up; she wasn't going to see her children deprived of the pleasures which all the others had.

He went inside. In due time the noises began and we took our cue. We let off the bangers, we blew our whistles, we yelled, we beat on tins. All round us a medley of noises were going on, boat whistles blowing and fireworks cracking, a tumult mixed with the hot gold light beating up over the city and licking out the cold stars. Light wriggled and jiggled in the waters. Ray tried to climb the castor tree, a tree which looks as if designed by a small child and which quite lacks stamina. One half of the tree split off and Ray fell on the nasturtiums. He yelled, we all yelled, our mother made small laughing noises,

---

scarf wound many times round his throat . . . full of mockery, humour, and discontent.' He married one of Norman's sisters, Ruby, who had much talent as a black-and-white artist. In these days a fiery socialist, he played an important part in the early *Daily Herald*.

even Harriet came out and yelled. We beat on our tin cans with all the licence of a world gone mad.

Norman reappeared and suggested that the confounded children might stop their hellish noise and go to the bed where they should have been long ago.

'Nonsense, they've got a right to enjoy themselves once a year. Everybody else is making a noise. Go on, boys.'

We beat our tins with enhanced glee. Against such a noise no human retort was possible. Without his hat Norman went off down the steps, retreating to the city and his studio. We beat on. My mother sat veiled benignantly under a big cashmere shawl.

We had beaten a corybantic funeral march for the marriage. Norman went off in 1909 to England, where he stayed a couple of years; my mother removed to Brisbane, where her strong-minded sister Mary was living. They never met again – except for a brief moment when Norman had returned from London and was thought to be dying of pleurisy. My mother and I came down from Brisbane to visit him in hospital – staying at an odd hotel in a city arcade, where I was laid up with an ankle poisoned by a mosquito bite. But for the moment the drama of departure gathered round the wicked-eyed white cockatoo that had been my mother's main pet. He used to roam about the house with the gait of a drunken seaman, perhaps accentuated by a liking for beer in a spoon, now and then giving coarse chuckles and showing his blunt tongue. Harriet had agreed to keep him, but as the hour of our going neared, my mother went on saying, 'Poor cocky, you're going to be left behind . . . So, the day before we departed, he got in first and flew away.

Harriet wept and said she'd have another shot at married life. Her carter promised to desert the two-up school for ever-more and make a home for her. Mother cried too and said that she and Harriet must constantly exchange postcards; and she gave the girl a consoling portmanteau of clothes.

We travelled by sea and the voyage was perfectly calm and bright. I, who a few years before had been unmoved by a terrific storm on a visit to Hobart, was seasick all the while. By the time we berthed in the river at Brisbane, I had vomited up the last drop of bile in my racked system.

4 · SCHOOL AT LAST

THE BRIEF kindergarten period held all I was to know of school till I was about twelve. When we first came to Brisbane, my mother arranged for me to go to the big public school in the middle of the town. I went for a few days, but was unhappy. I knew no one. Plunged into the alien turmoil, the bleak churchlike buildings, I wept in the lofty lavatory and after two days told my mother that I couldn't bear it. She was the sort of person who could never be really trained to think that people should do things they disliked, least of all her own sons. In her heart she never understood or liked the world, and couldn't see why everyone shouldn't be happy, perpetually setting out on a new holiday. She ran away from home to marry Norman because, brought for a meal one evening by her brother Ray, he lingered in the kitchen – afraid to go into a room where he might betray the imperfectly patched backside of his trousers. (They had a hasty courtship in the Fitzroy Gardens, chaperoned by her big dog Carlo, and I was begotten there amid the bright scents of flowers.) In all my young years I cannot remember one slap or harsh word.

I don't know why the inspectors failed in their duty, but they did. Perhaps our assiduity in moving threw them off the trail. No sooner was my mother in a boarding-house than she yearned for a house of her own. Maybe we never had enough money to get into a nice enough boarding-house or to find a nice enough house of our own; but I think the restlessness went deeper. She had come to Brisbane to be near her tower-of-strength sister; but a dim yet pervasive resistance made her refuse to do the things of which Mary approved. She needed the impressive shadow, but pulled in her own direction, away from Mary's idea of a correct and respectable existence. She knew what she didn't want, but not what she did. Unable to find a world that satisfied her being happy and ceaselessly inventing new holidays, she wavered between one dissatisfaction and the next. She was sure that she'd be in heaven if she could have her own garden or if she didn't have to keep on cooking sausage and mashed potatoes (which with porridge and suet pudding seem to have constituted her whole food system); but when she had a garden, she soon lost interest in tending it and couldn't understand why flowers lacked the intelligence to grow in masses of their own accord; and as soon as she was once more eating boarding-house fare, she dreamed of all the things she would cook in her own kitchen – anything but sausage and mash, porridge and suet pudding. Then the moment she did get the coveted kitchen, she reverted to sausage and mash, etcetera. After all, what else was there to cook? Oh, to be back in a boarding-house without domestic chores and with all sorts of people to talk to.

No longer having roots in a neighbourhood, we lacked friends. There were only the slight acquaintances of boy or girl passing through the boarding-house. We played cricket together in the narrow lane or went looking for brazil nuts in the gardens, and then the others were gone. The nearest thing to friends were the B's who lived by the house into which Aunt Mary had moved, out Hamilton way, a house of one-storey like most Brisbane houses but built over a steep gully with a stream running beneath. The poles on which the place was set reached enormous lengths, though two sides rested on the ground. When wind came up under the house, one felt it shake and strain. Below a fine garden had been constructed with roses and rhododendrons and great ferns – stag ferns hanging from the poles like strange trophies – amid the unceasing brabble of spring water.

In the house itself Mary had a wonderful mess, a magpie heap of objects, some valuable, some sheer junk. Tiger-skins and bear-skins and Indian draperies with millions of glass-eyelets sewn into the woollen embroiderings, Mahratta swords and armour, folk-things from the village and brummagem models, Malay krises and swords made up of Chinese coins with square holes in their middle, huge and horrible irons that had been used in the Tasmanian convict jails, Australian Aboriginal shields with symbolic patterns, frescoes of fowls and dogs that Norman had painted once while staying with her in Melbourne, Wedgwood plates and ebony elephants, old lace and knuckledusters. Here, using her typewriter, I learned to type, and here my uncle Raymond died of consumption.

My mother's father had been a postmaster in India and she herself was born in Allahabad. In the 1890s he had been smitted by the desire to farm in Tasmania and had bought an orchard there. Sending his family ahead, he died before he could join them. His wife had been gently nurtured into a total incapacity to do anything except fuss pleasantly about a household. Faced with a difficult financial situation and no domestic lord to give her orders, she collapsed. Her eldest daughter Mary took charge, moved the family over to Victoria, and pulled strings till she obtained the only job then open to a distressed gentlewoman in Australia apart from governessing: the office of postmistress. The family lived for some time at Lorne on the Victorian coast, then moved to Melbourne, where she married John Elkington, son of a professor at the University, and proceeded to work out the destinies of her brother and sisters.* As a destiny moulder she was a considerable failure, but she never gave up trying. My mother, Catherine, married Norman, then a penniless artist; the other sister Lottie married against Mary's advice, not at all wisely; the brother Raymond took up journalism and showed more devotion to literature

---

*In reading H. H. Richardson's *The Fortunes of Richard Mahoney* I felt again and again my own family background. Here too the genteel turn to the post office appears; and the whole early life of Mahoney in Victoria's gold areas is close to Norman's family basis – though N's father as a doctor was very different from Mahoney, being a man of great cheerful overbearing gusto. The legend goes that he could not resist the appeals of girls in trouble, had to leave the mining town, worked as a ship's doctor and died nobly in helping during a mining disaster. Almost all his children were highly talented in art – besides Norman, Lionel, Percy, Daryl and Ruby had their own style. The Lindsays came of a Jacobite family that emigrated to Northern Ireland after 1745. (On the Parkinson side I believe the roots were West Country, though with a strain of French emigrés from the 1790s.)

than to career building. Only with John she had some success, but even there to her cost. An irascible, highly skilled and capable man, he clearly had no talent as a G.P. and was directed into public health; but though for many years Mary pushed him steadily up the ladder of promotion, he as steadily nursed a rebellion against her passion for propriety and social status. More and more he realized that what he had wanted out of life was to be the captain of some leaky South-Sea steamer or even a feckless boozer on a Pacific beach, not an official with a regular timetable.

But for the moment she seemed to have the universe well under control. Jack was in charge of public health in Queensland; her two sisters, confessing their marriage errors, had flocked to her side, abandoning their husbands; and she had nephews and nieces to dominate. Her brother Raymond too had come to Queensland; but that was a matter of grief, for he was dying.

Across the road from the house straddling the gully lived the B.'s. Fifi was about my age and the boy was about Ray's. We climbed the trees for loquats and tumbled down the higher reaches of the steep gully and hid in silky grass or among old creaking harness in the stable. Once a number of trees and bushes were cut in the large front region below the house, and the boughs and sprays were piled all together, so that we could tunnel a way into the middle of the mountain of greenery and entangled wood. I recall the wind glistening over the flowering tops of grass as Fifi and I lay curled like hares in their forme, the light curling in her soft hair, the warm silence; thinking what a pity it was that we could not hide like that for ever, and suddenly feeling the bright nested moment as a single thing, a rich interweaving, which was outside me, tantalizingly lost by the act of recognition.

But the B.'s house caught fire one windy night and the family moved away. Not long after I received a printed invitation to a party they were giving, but I refused to go – partly out of the shyness that was coming over me, partly out of a sense of our poverty which would mean something wrong about my clothes. My mother tried to make me go, but I couldn't tell her why I refused. I didn't know why.

In our unstable situation, without school or friends, I was turning more and more to reading. A clear inner world, opposed to the outer world, was forming. In Sydney an invitation to a party would have been something to be accepted without question; the excitement of the occasion might produce diarrhoea and even shattering dreams (as did visits to the zoo or a pantomime), but there would have been no problem, no matter of divided choice.

I read voraciously, coming at last across various adventure tales and historical novels to Dumas's *Three Musketeers*, which for years I was to reread. And every now and then I slipped into strange territory. Among my mother's books I found such things as Ritson's collection of Robin Hood ballads and a Baldwin Spencer work on the Arunta – things that had no doubt been Norman's, though she had her own definite taste in reading: among her favourites I remember Gissing and George Moore. One day, shopping with her in an omnibus store, she rewarded me by a visit to the book department where I bought a volume of Shakespeare's plays, a green-bound book, the type of which is still sharp in my mind. I read *Titus Andronicus* and thought it not bad at all, though somewhat puzzling.

The person to whom I came nearest to saying something about the things which interested me was my grandmother, who lived with her masterful daughter Mary, pleased to be permitted to do nothing with a certain mild grace. Dressed in her black moire, she told us tales of her experiences as a girl in the Indian Mutiny – a long night ride seemed the worst she had suffered – and she sang us Jacobite ballads. She was convinced about the reality of Indian magics and particularly frightened us with an account of how an offended fakir, seeking a hair of his enemy but given instead a bristle from a tiger skin by an accomplice servant, charmed the skin flopping out of the house one midnight into a great bonfire.

At moments a chance to play came about and then I let myself go in absorbed miming. This happened mostly when I joined with my younger brothers in a concerted game of make-believe, with costumes laboriously made up out of our mother's oddments. I found that I possessed a moveable scalp and could wiggle my ears; and my gift of facial contortion and mimicry earned me for a while the nickname of Max Linder. (Max was our favourite comedian on the films; and of films themselves we were becoming more aware, going now and then to the converted hall near the Bridge where at times a funny man with a small moustache named Charlie flickered on the screen.)

The days drifted on. I listened to the German band blaring in the street, but never had a lemon at the right moment to test the theory that one could stop them all in mid-blow by prominently sucking. One day my mother hustled me into the synagogue in the side street to see a marriage. The moment when the glass was broken is preserved in my mind in Rembrandtesque chiaroscuro, in mysteriously gold penumbras. I saw that life could hold colours outside the daily spectrum of Brisbane, strange smells like that given out by burning joss sticks in Chinese laundries or the chi-chi jars that the Chinese vegetable-man with his slab of fine silk hidden under the cabbages had presented every Sydney Christmas. (Always amiably grinning, handing out the silk, 'Just touchee, no buyee, just touchee, mum, see how good,' rejoicing in the delicate texture with a bland repudiation of all commercial aims, then padding off with his two rushwoven baskets dangling from the pole across his shoulders, padding with a gentle undulating rhythm.)

At last our uncle Jack put his foot down and took me to a preparatory school where he knew the headmaster. I experienced the extreme shame of sitting in the infants' class. Filled with a bitter sense of unrecognized superiority, I worked furiously to raise my school status and moved by a series of jumps from class to class. In about a year I had attained the lower sixth. I, an expert malingerer and truant in Sydney, never missed a day and was never late – a record that I kept up later through my four years at the Grammar School. After the first incredulous shock, my mother said that she had always known I was like that, a student, like her brother Raymond.

Raymond died. For the first time I was near death. He came from some sanatorium to be near his mother. I knew that he was ill, tubercular, and I hated the moments when we had to

go in and speak to him in the room that Mary gave him in
her gully-house. I tried to hold my breath, as I did when passing a hospital. The news of his death was phoned to our
boarding-house; and when the three of us were told, Ray and
Phil looked blank and went on with their game. But I took the
news decorously and shed a few tears. I felt nothing and was
proud that I knew how to make the correct response to an adult
phenomenon like death. And then, a couple of days later, as
I was going down the stairs and almost tripped on the torn carpet, I suddenly realized what had happened. He was dead. I
was terrified, sorry, anguished. Not so much for an uncle whom
I scarcely knew, but because I had at last discovered the existence of death. The cold wind had come close, under the skin;
a clammy darkness pressed its bony hand into the nape of my
neck. I ran down the dim corridor out into the backyard, fur-
tively looking round and in no way proud of myself.

For a while we moved out towards the Hamilton
Racecourse, to be near Mary. Ever since Norman's period in
England and our departure to Brisbane, the marriage break
had been definite. But now something happened that made it
all explicit. Our mother was extremely miserable and gave all
Norman's pictures and drawings to Mary. From this moment
she went steadily down into a distractedness that ended in a
settled melancholia. Of the brief stay in the house I recall little
except noisy racehorse crowds, wanderings on the riverbanks,
fields and fields of pineapples, and a tussle naked in bath with
Ray which cut open my upper lip and scarred me for life. And
lying stealthily awake all one Christmas night watching my
mother creep in and out with the presents that went in stockings or were heaped by the beds.

A little later I won the first prize in a competition set by the
Society for Prevention of Cruely to Dumb Animals. The theme
was pets (of which I had none). My aunt pushed me into the
thing and provided me with books and hints on the care of
dogs, canaries and horses. To my surprise I won. But the prize
turned out a well-bound copy of *Black Beauty*, a book about a
horse, which I despised and of which my grandmother had
given me a copy some time before.

At school I played cricket or football on Saturday afternoons at the boarders' house some way inland out of Brisbane. There were so many on each side that a player who had no wish to shine could lose himself in the mob of forwards or linger at the end of a long line of batsmen to that he only went in in time to gain the unimpeachable score of nought not out. Fielding, I chose long stop far behind the wicket keeper. Some afternoons we swam in the river; but my sharpest memory is the colour and taste of the lemons we pulled from the trees at half-time in a match. At the boarding-house I had fixed up a private gymnasium out of old bedsteads from a store-room and the back gate. An iron post laid across the open gates gave me an excellent bar on which to swing and hook my knee.

On account of my rapid movement from class to class, I had no time to become friendly with the boys among whom I briefly sat. But now and then I let go my miming powers. Once, in a group that had gone to a park at lunch time under a master, I acted the part of Mrs Pankhurst. The subject of suffragettes must have come up, though I remember nothing of it. Egged on by laughter, I threw myself into the role, making Mrs Pankhurst into a female Max Linder and Charlie Chaplin. Then after my excitement had died down during the march back to school, I was mysteriously summoned to the headmaster's study and a lot of incomprehensible questions asked. What they were, I cannot recall; and in retrospect it seems hard to imagine what on earth they could have been. But clearly I was being suspected of ambitions to act a feminine part.

Dismissed inconsequentially at last, I was left with a sense of shame and nausea. A sort of doubt as to my own identity, a fear that by pretending to be someone else I might become permanently warped into the mask. Was I myself or Mrs Pankhurst? Jack L. or a clown with indelible paint on my face? And deeper still was the conviction of something contaminating, an effluence from the dirty-minded headmaster that had become stuck on my hands. What had I felt in my mime? What had been the sense of power and delight as if I were insulting the world and riding above it on the wind of applauding laughter? Now the world had taken its revenge and treated me as something doubtfully mad or ugly or dangerous.

I never again let go my miming faculty.

5 · GRAMMAR SCHOOL

FROM THE lower sixth I won a three-years' scholarship to the Grammar School over the heads of the middle and upper sixth. My first year at the new school was 1914; and now at last I began to feel that there had been both rhyme and reason in my reading. I had found *The Golden Treasury* among my mother's books and I chanced to buy Smith's *Classical Dictionary* from a cheap stall. Suddenly it struck me that it was possible to write poetry as well as read it. Reading up Diana in the *Dictionary* and tapping out the beats with my finger, I composed a poem in iambic lines, with only a few metrical casualties.

O thou who hauntest still the forest-deeps
and blow'st thy horn across the rocky steeps. . .

Further, in the midst of one of the Shakespeare lessons, I discovered that I could improvise blank verse – lines no more subtle than 'And now the clock is ticking near the hour', but none the less remarkable in my thought. I tried talking in rhymed couplets, and sometimes did it.

The play, *Julius Caesar*, on which we were working, at once became a new thing. What had appeared a meaningless jargon devised for some undisclosed purpose of school torture, was seen at a glance as a stirring vehicle of superior expression. And this abrupt revelation of verse as a sort of lordly speech, at once private and bombastic, hidden from the world and yet shouting at it, was bound up with the first extrusions of puberty. The secure retreat into schoolwork, achieved at the preparatory school, was broken down, but I fought to maintain it. I wanted to keep on inhabiting the territory in which I seemed capable of mastery, capable of extorting the world's admiration. Once I moved outside those boundaries, I was liable to be filled with a daimon and driven madly to assume strange masks, after which I would find myself hauled up before a grave authority insinuating that I was mad, doomed, criminal. Yet the school-work itself had now led me to poetry, in which daimons thrived. It seemed all the more necessary to go warily, to play with the masks without being caught out.

It was hard to shut the world away, but I was determined to do it. I watched my mother closely. She seemed to have changed. There were more and more things about her that irritated me, the way she ate and the way she talked to people. Each of her new friends seemed worse than the others. One, Mrs Brown-Brown, smelt of something that I now know as gin, and she was cosmeticked so superbly that even I couldn't help seeing it. Every now and then she had attacks which spread her out on the sofa and made her snore; these she attributed always to eating lobster. I wondered why she went on eating such a disturbing food, which I had never tasted. Also she kept on promising me presents which never materialized – a wrist watch, a bicycle, a fountain pen.

There was further a patched-up French aviator, who spoke a cynical English and pinched my ear; and a portly red-faced Australian stockbroker, who wore spats clumsily and patted me on the head. I couldn't make out why we had such friends all of a sudden; I resented and disliked them all. Finally the day came when she herself lay dozing on the sofa, feeling ill because of too much lobster.

In our family, truncated of its father, I was the eldest male. Now I half realized that fact, in a revulsion of anger and confused distaste. I knew that my mother was unhappy and didn't know what to do with herself; but I shrank from the knowledge, which imposed on me a responsibility far beyond my powers and comprehension. My refuge was poetry.

Only the *Classical Dictionary* had greater charms. I spent hours working out complex genealogical trees for all the Greek deities and heroes. Zeus with his many amours and families was a nuisance; I could never fit him on to a single sheet. In the classroom I had an eccentric reputation for being able to solve any classical reference. At first it was hard to say if I looked on poems as an extension of the classical dictionary or the dictionary as the key to poems. I read avidly any book on Greek myths, from Kingsley's *Heroes* to *The Muses Pageant* in Everyman Library. The world of Greek myth became more real than anything in the newspapers; I had the sense of having come home, of hearing afresh the stories I had heard long ago but half forgotten. The events around me were broken-down or weakened forms of the clear episodes enshrined in the myths; they could be understood only by a reference back; in themselves they were chaotic, fragmentary, looking to the Hesperides for their fulfilled meanings.

But if the actual world could be explained only as a derelict form of what stood complete in the myth, the poem, there was also, it seemed to me, a sharp opposition between myth and actuality. The latter existed expressly by means of a rejection of the world of poetry, the Hesperidean truth. It was no mere neutral space where poems came or went, indirectly generated; it was essentially hostile. As partisan of poetry, I began to feel that I must hate and resist the world around me, which seemed either dead or virulently stupid.

I found my slogan on the title page of Everyman Poets – Shelley's voice crying that poets are the trumpets which sing to battle . . . the unacknowledged legislators of the world. I got hold of his *Defence of Poetry* and read it, reread it, recited its sentences through the darkness of my meditations under the mosquito net on the verandah. I was not alone; I had allies. Shelley had lived; there must be others echoing his words at this dark moment. Someday I would meet them. The light turned on in a room further down the street might be shining on a girl who murmured as she combed her hair: *O wild west wind* . . .

I grew conceited in my reading. When the brown-tweeded master commenting on the *Epitaph on the Countess of Pembroke*, took a look at the notes at the back of his book and told the class, 'That is by Ben Jonson,' I interjected, 'No, it isn't, it's by William Browne of Tavistock.' The class laughed and I was ordered outside. After, the master called me in. 'Look here, Lindsay, probably you're right, blast you, but don't contradict me in front of the class, do you hear?'

Another day, looking at my name inside my *Latin Grammar*,

I scribbled in pencil under it: *What did the Wind Say?* The rhyme struck me as uncannily brilliant and sang on in my head for weeks. *J. Lindsay, what did the Wind Say?* Me, it said. I was the word of the wind and the wind was the voice of me. I was one with the elemental force, the spirit blowing at its will, the spirit mysteriously still. I was the force uttering myself. I felt endless overtones of strange inspiration, which seemed dated from all eternity, yet a mere freak of spontaneous will. I blow over the faces of the waters – and then?

In August that first year came the war. The headmaster, on receiving the news, went round class by class. We happened to be in the gymnasium. On his entry we left the parallel bars and the rings, and assembled along the wall under the ladder. He spoke politely about king, old country, and empire, staring all the while at us with his coldly suspicious protruding eyes. We gave a cheer and went on turning over on the bars.

6 · POPULARITY

I⊤ ᴡᴀꜱ the last class of the afternoon and the boys were restless. Sunlight poured thickly through the tall windows across the broad outer passage of the upper floor in the new building; and there came the rattle and screech of a train from the bottom of the valley. Beyond the line lay the football field on which many of the boys' thoughts were set. Mr Ervine the master sat glumly on the dais, tilting his chair forwards as he leant over the table, clasping his thin long hands. His black hair was lank, black, dead-black; his lean sallow face was a mask locked with anger and distrust.

The boys felt the emotion behind that mask face and responded to it with a desire to provoke. Ervine had tried hard at first to win them over and had succeeded to some extent when taking English, for he had a knack of telling little fables and stories. But he lost his temper easily, lost it in a way that the boys could not understand; he was especially irritable during mathematics. The class didn't mind old Hoskins who now and then foamed at them with fury; they understood him with his straggling grey moustaches and his ideas on class-behaviour. But one day Ervine was as charming and unexpected as a vaudeville-turn, then he became a nervy tyrant trying to crush out the slackness and familiarity which he had himself created.

Under the trees along the path outside the sparrows were twittering, still busily searching for the many crumbs scattered by the day boys at lunch time. The master heard and his face stiffened. 'What are you doing there, Leach?' he snapped, rapping the table with his bony knuckles.

'Nothing, sir,' said Leach, a snub-nosed boy with curly hair.

'Hold up your hands.'

Leach held his hands up and something fell to the floor. Ervine swooped down between the desks and picked up a paper dart.

'What do you mean by wasting your time on these idiocies? Half an hour's detention.'

Then he rushed back to the dais and hurled the dart into the big waste-paper basket. Trembling, he glared round and spoke with a helpless snarl, 'Are you human children or the lineal offspring of cabbages?'

The boys stared with dull obstinacy as he raged on. They hated these mouthings of his, which they couldn't follow. In his outbursts he seemed to speak deliberately in as obscure and far-fetched a style of insult as possible; and resentment drew the whole class into rigid opposition, into an appearance of stupidity. Only I was of a double mind, confused and worried.

Leach was encouraged by the deepening mood of revolt; he began muttering to the boy at his side, his plump face heavy and dull with a sulky anger. 'I'm not going to detention, I'm going down to practice. He's a beast.'

'You're talking, Leach,' said Ervine, swinging round and indicating Leach with the pointer.

Leach rose sullenly. 'I wasn't talking. But I've got to go to football practice.'

'You've got to stay in detention, do you hear? I'll take you across myself, as the book's been round.' Leach mumbled. 'Speak up, boy.' He nodded at the algebraic equations on the board. 'What was I saying about that?' Leach went on mumbling.

The class was tensely united in a fierce antagonism. The boys glanced covertly at one another, their lips curling in unspoken insulting nicknames.

'Tell the fool, Lindsay,' said Ervine in a softer voice.

I rose. I could feel the anger of the class all round me, hedging me in, forbidding me to give a correct answer. But even stronger than my fear of the other boys was my wish to exhibit my cleverness, and if I had known what to say I'd have said it. 'I don't know,' I stammered.

Ervine included me in his embittered frown that swept the classroom. 'Wool-gathering, you too.'

I sat down, hoping that the class would think I hadn't answered out of bravado. Leach set to work on another paper dart. Ervine, staring at his algebra book, had resumed his seat and seemed to have forgotten us all. We waited. The spell of master rule had snapped. Under that spell, though the class was drawn together in submission, each boy was aware only of his relation to the master; but when it went, he saw himself as a free unit, aware primarily of the other boys, his accomplices and supporters. The master was merely the common object of derision.

The class knew that in the last few weeks other classes had proved unruly; it was rumoured that Ervine had been reprimanded by the headmaster. A sense of power was being gleefully born. The class felt that they held the master's destiny in their hands. A restless buzz, hard to locate, sprang up. Ervine heard it and glanced around without lifting his head. For a moment he stayed with bowed head, then he rose and resumed his sarcastic remarks, his voice taking a sharp shrill edge.

'Stand out from your desk, Leach.'

Leach stood out with a clatter, knocking his books over and kicking the iron frame. His pen rolled down the polished maplewood of the desk-top and rattled on to his seat. But his hands were empty; he had pushed the dart into the lap of Willis, his desk mate. Willis was a timid boy with strongly magnifying spectacles; but there was a wild look aswim in his goggling eyes as he took advantage of Ervine's turning to the blackboard to hand the dart to the boy behind. This boy wrote on it *Ervine the Stinker* and handed it on again; other insults were added as the dart progressed round the class.

There had been no concerted plan; but as the dart moved along with its incriminating inscriptions, it became a sign and a weapon of warfare. Anyone caught with it would be sure of extreme punishment, and so it became invested with increasing importance, stimulating the class's resistance and zest of daring. At last it came to me and I read the words on it, then hid it on my lap.

Ever since I had failed to answer the question, I had been growing more excited, sure that the boys were admiring an act of defiance and that Ervine resented it. The gathering revolt of the class had a heady effect. Gone was the sensitive and charming English master, who only yesterday, in reading Shelley's *Lines Written in the Euganean Hills* had given me a chance to explain who Amphitrite was: 'You, Lindsay, our gossip of Olympus . . .' A tyrannical dummy, a mere creation of the class's rebellious dislike, was standing on the dais; and against this dummy I felt an intensifying antagonism. This tyrant I'd gladly have seen guillotined, yet Ervine the kindly and fine-mannered enthusiast I revered. For the moment the two aspects of the master were cut far apart; yet, somewhere behind the clamorous pulse of execration, I knew that the distinction was false, that Ervine was suffering, that he was a sick man with nerves tormented beyond endurance. But I fought to drown this knowledge, which isolated me from the other boys and merged me with the enemy that they wanted to destroy. I was safe only while I felt and acted like the others.

Here at last I was being given a chance to stand out as a leader, to gain popularity, to enter into the collective life of the boys. An intoxicating recklessness made my heart throb painfully and I found it hard to breathe. On my lap, resting between my legs, lay the dart; waiting till the master had turned once more to the sliding wall-blackboard, I dipped the point in the inkwell and flung the missile. Ervine looked round and the dart struck him on the cheek splashing his face with ink. Startled, he stepped back and hit his head against the blackboard. This recoil of panic was the last thing needed to release the class. They burst into a roar of defiant laughter, stamping on the floor and banging their books. I sat dumb with fear and regret, yet exultant. Ervine did not seem to hear anything. Dazed, he bent and picked up the dart, then stood reading the pencilled gibes. His full scarlet lips twitched in his swarthy pallid face, his black hair hanging streakily over his eyes.

Ervine looked at me. Perhaps he suspected, perhaps he wanted to see if his one chosen pupil had joined the persecutors. I felt the glint of his dark suffering eyes as an intolerable accusation. I stopped banging and the blood ebbed from my strangled heart. Then a new fear came. In a moment the noise would bring the headmaster along and a strict inquiry would be made for the dart-thrower.

Ervine lifted his hand and his lips moved. There was no anger on his face, no appeal, only a kind of suffering exaltation and despair. The boys banged on, unable to stop now even if they had wished. Yet they too were beginning to be afraid, wanting to find some way of ending the tumult before the headmaster arrived.

Then we saw Ervine walk out of the room, staggering a little, his long hair falling forward over his face. The uproar promptly slackened and we heard the dismissal bell. Snatching at the chance, we poured out, talking tumultuously and joining the boys from the other classes, crushed on the connecting bridge that led from the new school to the higher ground of the old.

Slapped on the back, I shoved my way out, wanting to savour the delights of being a hailed hero, unable to shut out the image of Ervine's exalted despairing face. Then the groups broke up and thinned away, seeing the headmaster in his flapping gown stride across the quadrangle.

I went over to the water tanks under the shadow of the sham Gothic of the hall and drank from one of the chained metal cups. I wanted to see if Ervine was in the masters' commonroom. The door swung open and the athletic Mr Sprinkler emerged. I saw several masters inside, but no Ervine. Then Leach ran up. 'He walked straight out of the grounds, round the back of School House, without his hat or anything.

I sped off round the hall, across the space trodden grassless by countless schoolboy shoes. There was no one on the path that led to the exit behind the house. On one side lay the wooden building of the Bacteriological Institute, and below stretched the valley in which lay Roma Street station. There was no one in the street.

I was panting and heard my difficult breathing turn to sobs. I checked myself and drifted back round the front of the hall to the tennis courts, skirting the shed of a temporary classroom (thrown up to meet the sudden increase in scholars through the new state scholarships). I went across the first court to the school shop under the spreading Moreton Bay fig, with its dark metallic lustres. I trod on some of the round ruddy fruit, which squashed flat, like coins; then I passed through the gate in the wall of wire-netting that kept out tennis balls. I was frightened. There was nothing to trust. And I too was not to be trusted. I had been forced to recognize that the cruelty and hatred, which ravaged the world, was laired deeply and strongly in my own heart.

I fingered the threepence in my pocket and pushed into a group of boys discussing the rebellion.

'Somebody threw a dart in his eye.'

'Yes, I did it. It was me.'

There was no conviction in my voice; only a pleading desire for belief and praise. The boys, who belonged to a higher class, looked curiously at me. 'It was Leach,' said one of them.

'It wasn't,' I protested. 'It was me.'

'All right, keep your hair on.'

Somehow my intrusion had killed the subject. I felt only a bitter hostility to the others, who refused to believe me or felt something queer about me. I pushed past and went to the counter fixed on a cottage verandah rail, embowered in trailing roses. The fat wife of the caretaker, dressed in blue with a white apron, was in smiling charge. I looked unhappily at the boxes and jars of sweets, the ranged bottles of lemonade, gingerbeer, sarsaparilla.

'Give me . . .' To my dismay I found that I was on the verge of tears. 'Give me . . .' I wanted to die. I pointed to a chocolate bar and laid the threepence down; then I took the chocolate and bolted off down the side of the hill. Tears were burning on my cheeks and the Girls Grammar School on the hill opposite wavered and blurred like an ark on the dazzling waters. I clutched the chocolate, but couldn't bring myself to eat any of it. How could I ever get the courage to return to the locker-room and collect my satchel and cap? I wept, grateful for the long grassy slope devoid of people. Far off, on the other side of the railway line, boys were moving about the football field.

'I didn't mean to do it,' I muttered, without any idea who it was that I wanted to deceive.

7 · MOVES AND BAPTISMS

ON THE WHOLE I got on better at school with the rough-tough lads, the boys with state scholarships; and one, rough as bags, took me under his wing. Only once did I have bother with a bully, but at last I turned on him and challenged him to fight me that afternoon in the gym. Luckily he was a coward, even more scared than I was, and he took care to be afflicted with detention, so that the whole thing fizzled out. I was now in the senior cadets and did not dislike the drill as a variation from lessons inside doors, especially the route marches. When we went shooting on a long-distance range, I turned out a very good shot and was later picked for the school team in some competition. But then we had to shoot on a miniature range, and though I was a crackshot at a thousand yards I found it hard to hit the target at thirty.

Once by some accident I was detailed off as a bugler and spent two drill-afternoons doing nothing before it was discovered that I had no sense of pitch and could not blow a note. We lounged about in the most unfrequented part of the grounds, near the no-man's-land between the Boys and the Girls Grammar School. Girl boarders playing tennis waved to us; and one of the buglers, a boarder, described how he met a grammar girl nightly in the hollow. In proof he produced a manuscript she had given him, which purported to be letters written by a girl on her honeymoon to her best friend. Though extremely curious, I could not bring myself to read the lurid text at all carefully.

Only a few days before I had reached a clear understanding of what it was all about. I was walking home through the park with three others, including the rough-as-bags lad; and one of them made a remark I didn't understand. I answered in a way that betrayed my lack of understanding, and there was a roar of laughter from the others. At once I saw it all, plain as a pikestaff. A thousand known facts fell into obvious connection. I had known it all along. I seemed to have been putting up for years an elaborate pretence that I didn't know. But why? why had I had to pretend to myself? what had I been afraid of?

For the moment however, as my mind reeled under the shock of realization, what I was mainly concerned about was to save my face. I wildly gagged and joked to cover up my *faux pas*, to make it seem I had been acting the innocent; but I took nobody in.

My aunt had moved, up the inland line, across the river from Indooroopilly. She in her own way was as restless as my mother. This time she and Jack decided to build for themselves; and because she was impatient and distrustful, she decided to be on the spot while the building went on. She camped in the grounds in a large double tent kept from the days when J. had travelled round in India as a district health commissioner. A shed housed my grandmother; another shed served for kitchen. The tent, set up on wooden flooring, impressed us boys and we hoped a storm would blow up, to test the moorings. With its tiger-skins and oriental embroideries it had an exotic effect; and I read Shelley's *Revolt of Asia* and Byron's *Giaour* inside it on sunny Saturday afternoons, curled on a couch with gilded cushions and a sleek panther skin, an image of Shiva level with my eyes.

Uncle J., still health commissioner, did carpentry as a hobby. One day as he was hastening the building operations by putting up the front gate, a car drove by and some women asked him the way. Touching his cap, he told them, and they said. 'Thank you, my man.' He was delighted. As he again was when he sent off the parson puzzled with the statement that he was a Scotch Mohammedan. Under his irritable eye I learned the elements of carpentry, lathe-work and bits of joinery, and helped to turn out chairs. As the grounds ran down to the river, we made a rowing boat.

This was in the latter part of 1914. My grandmother was the one who worried about the war, repeating, 'It must be over by Christmas. The Germans can't hold out.' She said that all the while till 1918. For us boys the war was long only a matter of coloured flags stuck on wall maps, a reason at last for geography.

Uncle J.'s offices were in a building by the bridge, on the third or fourth floor, more like an aquarium than a government department. He was tackling the problem of getting rid of the mosquito curse by destroying the larvae, and one idea was to find the right sort of fish, gifted with the appetite to eat up the larvae fast enough. There were rooms full of tall tanks with peculiar fishes floating around and pervading the whole situation. Faintly glowing shadows from goldfish wavered on the cheeks of girl clerks, and fine rococo designs of coral and seaweed were tangled with the faces reflected in the glass of bookcases. Fish with long chiffony fins seemed drifting in the black-and-white sky, as in an etching by Meryon.

We went on to the high balconies on festival days when there was a procession along the main streets, particularly on May day, Eight hour day. As far back at 1865 Queensland had had its Eight-hour-day celebrations, with the stonemasons in the van of the fight for limiting work hours. The old name was still used, though already the fight was for a forty-four-hour week, not a forty-eight-hour one. The procession was a national event, watched even by such rabid anti-trade unionists as Mary. We had little idea what it was all about, but enjoyed the show.

The procession wandered with cheers and vast banners down the crowded street. The bands brassily pompommed. More banners of red velvet with gold designs, upheld on crosspieces like football goals, with many steadying ropes. Wagons, and more and more men, steadily marching, more and more. 'It's simply a provocation,' said Mary, pursing up her heavy lips.

My aunt was coming more into my life as my mother retreated behind a dim pane of unconcern. A large dark handsome tigerish woman, with an enormous vitality and appetite for life, she had surrendered personal ambition at the price of being allowed to organize the careers of all connected males. Jack, her husband, she had so far steered along fairly successfully after recognizing that he was too short-tempered for a general practitioner; but she had never been quite reconciled to the fact that in public health he could not hope to make anything like the money possible from a general practice. So she tried to drive him to the top of his branch. Having pushed him to the position of public health commissioner for Queensland, he dug in his heels and began to revolt, showing more interest in his fishing holidays than in seeking any further advancement. Inordinately ambitious, Mary yet had little time for entertaining people or visiting; she was too deeply preoccupied with the family circle for that. Though not mean, she wanted money as a tangible form of the powers that she felt frustrated in herself, the fame and the prestige that none of her men-folk coveted.

More and more J. was yearning for the sea; and Mary was beginning to feel that perhaps I would be the one through whom she was to gratify her itch for success.

About this time I discovered religion. I do not mean that I was converted to a creed; I mean that I noticed the existence of religion, of churches and clergymen. At the prep school I had been taught Biblical history, which I liked and did well in; but now for the first time a personal query was heard. The only prayer that my mother had taught me was, Gentle Jesus meek and mild look upon a little child, something something something me and pity me my simplicity, God bless daddy and mummy and whoever else happened to be in the house. But that had been many years before.

Something troubled me. I told my mother that I wanted to go to church. She was rather disturbed by such an odd request, but could find nothing to urge against it. After thinking it over, she began to approve. She liked to think I was serious, unlike other boys who thought only of games and girls.

She decided against a parish church, where she felt that the clergyman or someone might ask her why she hadn't come before. So we went to the Cathedral, twice. On the first occasion I was so taken up with fear of doing the wrong thing, standing up when everyone else sat down, and so on, and with inability to find the place in the hymn book, that I had no attention to spare for anything else. On the second occasion I fainted – for the first, and so far the only time in my life. Why,

I did not know. Perhaps it was dislike of the organ, a wuffing bumbling ragged-edged pompous instrument that I still detest. Perhaps I felt God roaring at me in the organ thunder beating about the clouds of stone. Anyway I fainted. Both my mother and myself felt that this was not the right thing to do, and neither of us ever referred to the incident or to church-going again.

However, my brief concern with churches may have been the starting-off in my mother's mind of a train of thoughts which led not long after to a collective christening. Her sister Lottie, having left her husband, had carried on the family tradition by becoming a postmistress. At the time she was working at Indooroopilly, on the other side of the river below Graceville; and she and my mother decided to have all their children baptized in one fell swoop. We three boys stoutly objected till we extracted a promise that there would be no strangers present. Lottie further soothed us with the assurance that the clergyman was very old, so old that he probably wouldn't notice we weren't the usual babies held over the font.

Everything went well. We were alone in the small church and the clergyman was very benevolently old. As the eldest of the five children I felt especially foolish and promised to get myself confirmed. Afterwards we all five ran off and asserted ourselves by walking over the railway bridge with its narrow plankway, pretending that we were walking on tightropes, and dropping apple cores between the girders.

At last Mary's new house was built. It consisted of one huge room, surrounded by a verandah which was cut up into various small rooms (bedrooms, study, kitchen, bathroom) or left open for lounging in. The whole, of course, was perched on poles with lattice-work between. A shed surrounded by roses, some way from the house, was given to me for weekends; and J. and I built a concrete jetty for the flat-bottomed boat which we had caulked and seamed. J. showed me how to set concrete under water in holes we had drilled in the rocks.

Before long my mother moved out of town along the same line, a mile or so away from Mary's place. Immediately she hated living so far out, with no shops reachable without a train, and nobody she knew but Mary and her mother. The husky stockbroker called a few times with a car load of champagne, but that was all. She was beginning to give up the ghost. How can I adequately characterize her, since she was already fading out by the time I was able to look people in the face and see them as part of the confused thing, life, flowing in and on and around us? I am tempted to say that she was too gently detached, too subtly but guilelessly amused, for anything but a role in a pastoral poem, a charade of the Hesperides; but there was certainly much more to her, and less, than that. She was obstinate without will-power, she knew what she didn't like much more than what she did. In the years before the break, she had long had no link with Norman except the children; and yet she had clutched them away from him by her amiable indulgence, and had ended by excluding him from the warmth of her bosom. That was her side of the blame. And his? He had resented an early marriage (thrust on him by my insistence on being born); he had been haunted by all the day dreams of a weak Balzacian hero; he had not wanted to make that surrender in love which alone can bring out the rich qualities of a girl like Kate Parkinson. That is how it now seems to me. Both my parents lacked all capacity for organizing things, themselves or other people. My mother liked hats that hid her eyes, hair fashions that hid her ears. (She had refused to let Bill Dyson draw her ears.) Soft fluent muslin dresses suited her, and soft blues. She would have made a devoted wife for a poor man if his heart had been good; she could have carried on, happily or unhappily married; in some green manor-world of prosperous charities and hospitalities. What she wasn't fitted for was the lonely bringing-up of three boys on a very restricted income.

Going home in the train to Graceville, I sometimes found myself alone in a carriage full of girls from the Grammar School. Singly they were most lady-like; in a bunch, hoydens in a Restoration comedy who asked nothing better than a shy schoolboy at their teasing mercy.

The enticement and the terror of things seemed equally balanced. Everything that happened was what I wanted to happen, but its advent gave me gooseflesh of shrinking. I had the sensation that my face melted away and that my eyes became as eerily blind as the slits in a pumpkin lighted from within by a candle in a graveyard's midnight. I sat stricken; but out of my loins leaped another self, a reckless ghost whose face was beautiful and who danced. This ghost got in my way; I expected the others to see him and forget all about me, to caress him and acclaim his grace and strength. I wanted to dive out of sight and exist only as the doll into which the puppeteer's hand has gone with masterful ease of gesticulation and simplified devices of meaning. I had the conviction that I had only to put out my hand to break into that sphere, to bring the ghost back with a delicious penetration of union, to become myself the perfect puppet and the beautiful dancer.

But no force in heaven or earth could make me put out my hand; and in that realization I felt an exultation of loneliness and power. Without the endless ache for involvement, where would lie the virtue of renunciation? So I buried my head in the sheltering book, the secret bush of poetry, the echoing sea-cave of pure seclusion; and acquired a persistent bloom of pimples.

It was growing harder to avoid the fact that we were a family without a father, that I owned two younger brothers who shared none of my thoughts and a mother who considered that any train she walked into became the train going to her station. (We were more than once carried on to Ipswich, the next main-line station of the line, before I assumed the responsibility of reading notice-boards and asking porters.)

The last play operation I shared with my brothers took place at Graceville. We decided to build a trench and bring the war into our own backyard. Not at all clear as to what constituted a trench, we achieved a big square pit. The spades had little effect on the hard yellowish clay. As we had no pickaxe, the only way was to attack the earth with an axe and then shovel the broken-up pieces out. When we were about five feet down, Jeff (a friend of Phil's) hit me across the left hand with the axe and almost broke three fingers. However, that only made me more determined. With bandaged hand I continued digging after the others had tired of the game. I dug on and delved more than six feet into the hard clay before I gave up. By that time the swinging of the axe and the throwing-up of the debris was very difficult, but I resented having to stop.

One day I was poking about in the store room under Mary's house and found several drawings and paintings by Norman that my mother had handed over in her misery. One of them I had never seen before. It was called *The Rejected* and showed a Christ figure stumbling with downcast head amid a desert scene of sand and stones. Something of both *The Scapegoat* and *The Light of the World* by Holman Hunt had been fused in an image simultaneously scornful and sympathetic. The artist rejected the prophet together with the populace, and yet was one with him. I looked a long time at this pen-drawing and then found myself with quivering lip, my eyes blurring. I hastily pushed the sheet away behind the other works and ran out into the sunlight, where my grandmother's pet raven hopped from under the stairs and pecked furiously at my bare feet, triumphantly croaking.

8 · FLOWING RIVER

AMID FLYBUZZ and heat-murmur of the afternoon I lay on the cool linoleum of the big central room, side by side with the lion-skin carpet in which the stuffed head had glassy eyes. I was wearing only a thin pair of cotton shorts. Through the window in the alcove came a faint rich golden light, passing through the filter of masses of nasturtium flowers. There was a dead flickering silence, as if only insects lived. Norman's painting of tall disdainful girls, yellow-haired in heavy green bushes glimmered across the room out of the woodframe which he had himself carved with satyr-heads. Everyone was out except the Aboriginal girl whom Mary had obtained from a mission to do the housework. I heard her bare heel thud slightly in the passage as she swept. I read on and all things were clear, all things, suddenly, quietly, inevitably.

Like a single buffet of joy I realized the unity of the poetic image and my entire rejection of the world. For the first time I climbed right inside a music, to the sure throb of the sustaining heart; I held a poem simple and complete as a flower on my palm, and knew the timeless moment, the rhythm seen as a clear structure held together by its own inner tensions. And in the words 'Beauty is Truth, Truth Beauty', this experience was given its articulate seal, its open statement, which in turn became a demand, an inescapable demand for full allegiance. I knew my allegiance like an oath of love; in the poem I possessed an alien body which was also my own.

The process of possession was a complex one; no simple narcissistic discovery of my own face, between the lilies, in the pool of poetry, the pool of my senses penetrated by a single beam of light. True, the spirit world was darkly and powerfully one with the new life seething in my loins and only by renunciation

had I come to this secret tryst among the parted maidenhair
ferns at the crystal bubbling source. It was my own body rising
up from the waters reddened with the murder, the primal castration; but it was also the body of Venus curved from her own
genital shell. The continual movement of detachment from the
world had inverted itself into this discovery of a perfected sensuous essence, a nacreous bubble of light precariously united
with my leaping heart. I reject, to accept; I turn away, to find;
I am blinded, to see; I give up all, to possess all; I die, to
live.

With an Irish terrier named Kelly for companion I used to row
up the river in our dinghy. The region was still sparsely
inhabited. Across the river were a few small farms and up past
the reach where my uncle had built his house the country was
wild. I landed in the more entangled parts, on slopes of fir trees,
where I climbed by clinging to bushes and tree roots, into a
thick resinous silence, or among clumps of lantana – that ver-
bena introduced as an ornamental shrub from tropical America and now classified in Australia as a noxious plant; carried
by birds that eat its berries when they have changed from hard
green beads to soft black. I stripped and walked round regardless of scratches. I lay in wiry grass to watch a ground lark
piping its pretty song aloft and then descending with a circling
dive to its eggs of spotted grey-white, to its cup-nest of grass
on a tufted spot. I watched the ants at their haulages along the
red canyons streaked by the rain beside a rotted tree bole. I
read Shelley and Theocritos to my terrier, who yawned.

We splashed round a small rocky islet in the fierce current
and lay wetly naked on the burning altar of the stone, under
a contorted fir. Stretched in sacrificial calm, stunned by the
hammers of the sun, while the song rose high and higher, and
I reached up and caught the fir-bough and wrenched it off and
held it up to the sun, bleeding. In joy, in a gust of entire joy.
In the hard light, the sculptural Australian light, under cloud-
swags of brittle lilac-silver the voice was Shelley. Under the
hanging lichened boughs, in the Australian dusk with its heavy
liquid incrustation of stars, the voice was Keats. In the coil of
the grass I opened eyes on a silken-rustling silence, on the

golden shadow of dwarf apples and the glistening reflections of the gum bark, and the voice was Herrick.

When I was almost drowned in the welter of the islet, when I scrambled breathless and bloody up the teeth of the stone, it was good; it was an initiation.

Kelly bayed the sun and moon. I ran across the waters. I hung from the rag of rock. I twitted the eagle-hawk face to ugly face. I went to sleep on the hand of the stone which opened and shut around me.

'Take care of yourself, be a good boy,' said my mother. She couldn't bear the country any longer. We moved back to town, to an unpleasant small house not far from the Grammar School, right on the tramline down to the main streets. I was deadly ashamed of this house. When school was over, I walked in the park or went devious ways to escape letting my school-fellows know where I lived. Sometimes, with a familiar face behind me, I would walk on a couple of blocks and then come round in a zigzag route through back streets. Once I lost my way.

One night my uncle C., the meat-works manager, turned up tipsy with a suitcase full of live crabs which he let loose in the meagre living-room. They scuttled over the floor, making horrid dry scraping noises with their claws, and Ray and I refused to come down from the sofa. He told us that we were cowards and he was sorry to see any of his blood relations disgracing themselves before some harmless crabs. We hoped that the crabs would nip him, but they didn't; they seemed to respect him.

Another time he came also tipsy, and breathed all over me, holding my arm and insisting that I tell him what writers I really liked. 'Don't say Shakespeare and Macaulay, and all that crap. Say what you really think. Don't be a hypocrite. I can stand anything but hypocrites. Come on, tell me,' Finally uncle J., rung by my mother, arrived to take him away.

I read *The Faery Queen* right through on the narrow front verandah while the trams rattled by outside the curtains of split bamboo cane. Grim-faced women passed with shopping baskets, drunks hugged bottles of beer, once some boys got a kite wrecked on the overhead tram cable. I tried vainly to grow

some flowers in a box in the backyard. The Catholics next door
had a house full of red prints of the Sacred Heart and gawdy
plaster casts; the daughter who slept on the side of the verandah wore red woollen stockings home knitted; we sometimes
stared at one another, but never smiled; her father had meek
moustaches and once in a boozy fit threw his boot out of the
window, landing it in my mother's room. I was reading canto
xi of book V: 'It often falls in course of common life. That right
long time is overborne of wrong . . .'

However I had my weekends at Mary's place, when I could
row into the turbulent river and make a small fire of resinous
twigs on a flat stone. I slept in my garden hut, cut off by the
streams of jasmine-scented darkness, reading by lamplight
wreathed with white moths. I read Beddoes or Poe late at night
amid the banging fists of a Gothic storm, or recited *Tom o' Bedlam* by moonlight which threw the shadow of a rose across my
eyes. I read Racine in the lucid eternal early morning, with
hoarse ribald kookaburra laughs for punctuation, waiting for
the Aboriginal girl Lucy to bring my cup of tea.

She rubbed red geranium petals on her cheeks for rouge,
though she denied it to my aunt, and was always cheerful,
sleekly graceful under her short chintz frock. I wanted to talk
to her but didn't know what to say. I was frightened that she
would misunderstand and the watchful Mary would accuse me
of trying to make love to her. I wanted Lucy to know that I
looked on her with the utmost respect – and at the same time
I did want to make love to her. She'd come rushing in barefoot,
holding the tea unspilled without looking at it, curling up her
big toe. 'Your tea, Mast' Jack,' she'd smile with gleaming teeth,
beautiful and friendly.

'Oh, thanks, Lucy, nice day, isn't it?'

She'd laugh and toss her head and stand for a moment
scratching her left calf with the strong toes of her right foot,
balanced on the tight-rope of my admiration. She'd laugh and
look as if she was thinking of something else, and say, 'Yes,
Mast' Jack' – though she considered all days nice, bright or
glowering.

So I said, 'You can take the sugar. I never use sugar.'

She insisted on bringing the sugar every morning. Now, with

another smile, she went off swinging lightly inside the unnecessary chintz dress, and I drank my tea and read Darley's
Nepenthe.

There had been an Abo boy, as handsome as Lucy, but he
didn't like being pushed to work. He answered back and Mary
returned him to the mission. But Lucy stayed on near two
years, till she was got with child by a returned soldier. Nothing
could stop her rubbing the geraniums on her cheeks and laughing. Nothing could stop her tying up the alarm clock with
string.

'But, Lucy,' my aunt would argue with a deadly patience
in her voice, 'who else could tie the clock up? who else could
get into your room to do it? who else would want to tie it up?'

Lucy stared at her with her big wet-dark eyes and said
gravely, 'I don't know, mam. Who was it?' as if she was tolerantly putting up with a silly conundrum; and no force or logic
could bring her to an admission. She went to Sunday school
and retailed what she learned, generally in a system worked
out by herself to make sense of a lot of strange information.
Thus, she refused to revise the notion that Joan of Arc was
Noah's daughter.

Now I heard her chattering at the foot of the steps to the
diabolic raven with its passion for pecking at bare legs and feet.
'Go away, William. You got no business here. Go away, William, or I tell on you.'

The river was my solace. On still nights I went down to the
banks and climbed a tree with a big bough thrust out over the
waters. I lay on the bough and watched the rapid clear-dark
stream. Suddenly a dimple of milky light broke it or a fish
leaped on the edge of vision. Maybe a lantern twinkled on the
further bank. The river was still broad here; and with its rapid
current I had not yet managed to swim right across. I broke
off a fragment of bough and dropped it down, watching it
abruptly whirled out of sight. I heard the deep flowing of the
river like the underlayer of silence.

I endowed the scene with all the decor of European lyricism,
untouched by the fact that our spring, coming in September,
was very unlike the spring of the songs I read, the round dance

of the English May, the carole on the heavenly meads of Fra
Angelico's pictures. Later I was to hear the theory that Australia could not produce a satisfactory poetry because its spring
did not burst forth in lush blossoming, with a quick world of
green mantling over wintry bareness; but such an idea would
have been gibberish to me. On the one hand, there were indeed
many changing manifestos of colour; the jacaranda riding the
heavens with largesse of blue, blue, and yet more blue; the
frangipani lolling its big tongues of scarlet over the fences; the
wax plant with its willow leaves putting out pink stars and
hairy filaments, soon to explode its valves with a crack on hot
days and scatter its finely rattling seeds on the palm of a leaf;
even the universal gum tree drooping with a faint fuzz of
flowers. Not that I ever saw these changes as a broad onset of
spring. But I added in my mind what was lacking. My own
ardour was the spring of the world, sending up flower
fountains. A lawn, watered into emerald-green with a scatter
of daisies, was enough to stand for Chaucer in a medieval
illumination; or the flight of the great hulking clouds of silver
across the topless towers of morning gave me all of Shelley I
expected to see in the tarnished mirror of earth.

Snow indeed was lacking. Once, when I was about seven, we
had gone on a visit to Hobart where J. was then health commissioner for Tasmania. We stayed in the old barracks, sleeping in a room that must have once bedded a hundred soldiers,
and playing on the ancient cannons. On a mountain peak overlooking the town we beheld snow; and we set out to ascend the
slopes and see the snow at close quarters. But we stopped at
tea-gardens near a brewery, where a cold clear stream brabbled
and rippled over glassy rocks, and the snow seemed scarcely
nearer. We waded in the numbing waters and ran about on
the grass.

9 · EXPEDITIONS

I WENT on several camping holidays with my uncle. Once we went to Currumbin on the south coast with the professor of physics from the university. The men had pistols as well as rifles; but when I shot with a pistol at a bottle on a stump, I hit another bottle about ten yards off. They thought I had aimed at this second bottle, so I accepted their praises and kept to the rifles.

J. was a crack shot. When we wanted a quick meal, he used to shoot fish. He waited till one came up to snap or nibble at something on the surface of the water; then the moment its snout made a dint he shot. Thus in a few moments he had supplied our lunch. I hurried out in the boat and picked up the fish floating with white bellies uppermost. We rolled them in a ball of mud, threw them into the camp fire, and left them to bake in the embers. I drew them out with a stick, let them cool a bit, cracked the mud off, and slit the belly open. The innards would be waiting in a neat ball to be dropped out.

Here among the swamps and the endless scrub, or on the long beach with a lonely cabbage palm and an odd rock hump that looked like the invention of a late Flemish Gothic painter for the abode of St Jerome, I savoured Australian space, its hard brightness, its depthless lucidity: the height of the sky which did not however flatten a man upon a belittled earth, but which opened new dimensions in the curve of hill, the fall of water, the aspiring spirit.

Wake at midnight to hear for a moment the dull thudding call of the mopoke, solemn as some dead hero's handclap, in a distant fern-valley of the night. And watch the stars, so quick-silver clear, scattered at that very heartbeat like water drops wrung from the hair of Aphrodite, giving the heavens a definite amplitude and compact infinity.

At dawn the sky went on sliding back veil after veil till the eye was lost. Lying on a veined rock, I watched the slow undulations of the water weeds as a great mottled cod came through a thing of subtly mobile bronze with red patinas, and darted with preying mouth into the rock shadow, shot with chilly long translucencies. And so the call came to breakfast across a drift of tiny yellow butterflies.

The cow, bloated dead in the bog, stuck out its legs like the pipes of a monstrous bagpipe. The droning heat was tasselled with reed plumes.

We went shooting nearer Brisbane too, in the swamp opposite the meatworks of my other uncle. To find the place, we did not take the train, but trammed to Hamilton Reach and ferried across, then walked down the bank till we sighted the tall chimney of the works, the conglomeration of buildings, the villas of the management on the hill crest, the chutes, the stands of coiling pipes that carried water to the refrigerating rooms. On the jetty sat the old caretaker whose boat we were going to borrow, a little blackened man with a lonely front tooth and an overpowering stink of hashmagandy. With him sat his dog, a prick-eared kelpie of a glistening slaty-blue colour with a white patch on his chest. As the others got things ready, he fixed me with his wild kindly eye.

'Aye, some say the black-and-tan's a more brainy breed. Mebbe it goes for the general run of dogs, but Sam's one of a sort, he's Sam, eh, Sam, aren't you?' His voice rose in a rusty shout and Sam lay down with his head between his paws, his eyes turned up to watch his master. 'He frets a bit, Sam does, having no sheep to muster. Mebbe I does myself, but I've got a peck of rheumatic in my bones, I've got to stay put.' Sam gave a long snorting sigh and shut his eyes. 'Many's the time I've made him little boots o' basil to save his poor feet from the thorns of the bindi-eye out on the plains, and now he just sits and looks at me while I fish. Just as if he wonders what's come over me and made me stupid. It gets me shouting sometimes, but what's the use of that, blame me cats? I get as jumpy as a bag of old fleas, sitting here with an ache in my bones.

I wouldn't care if the whole bloody show went up in smoke, would I, Sam?'

J. called me down into the boat and the caretaker went on talking after us. 'What the stinking hell do you want to go shooting off flying foxes for? Better stay and fish, you silly sods. Fishing's good round here, what with all the blood going into the water. Under the pipe there, that's the place . . .'

On the other side, we stepped cautiously ashore. Grey mangrove trees stretched all along the bank as far as we could see, serried lines of close desperate trees, melancholy as emblems in an old edition of Quarles, funereally standing in a sort of abject and obstinate penury, abjuring any part in the gay waters of the spring or the bright skirts of the girls in the launch that sent frills of frothy foam lapping up against the mudfringe and the stones of the breakwater. Their leaves had a varnished coat for protection against the sun's rays. Tide was low and criss-cross cracks in the mud showed where the water had run out. Crabs scuttled among the breather-roots that stuck up out of the other roots branching and digging into the mud.

Slithering in smooth slime, I grabbed at a trunk, then, walking gingerly, followed into the mudflat. J. scratched at one of the trees. 'Rotten soft? not a bit of it. The tissues interlock. It's used for mallets, stonemasons' mallets, and bullock-yokes . . .' So one could be tough as well as soft amid corruption.

The trees had shot up high and higher in the pocked mud away from the banks, grey and sparse against the blue. For a while I couldn't see any foxes of the sky. Then I made out a dark bundle hanging from one of the topmost branches. J. fired and the crack thudded dully away across the grey-black mud. The bundle gave a jump, but still hung there unmoving. J. shot again and again the fox shook with the impact of the bullet. But it still hung there.

I fired and the same thing happened.

Then J. fired again, at the fox's feet. The thing came down with a crash through the small boughs and splashed in the mud. I went towards the lump of reddish-yellow grey fur blood-mud-dabbled. 'Don't touch it,' shouted J., 'or it'll take you weeks to get the smell off . . . You saw what I did? Shot the claws off?'

We went on tramping through the heavy mud that sucked at our feet, into the soggy mangrove silence. The heat stank. Every now and then J. killed a fox, an orchard thief. I had now slipped and sat a couple of times in the mud. I had mud in my hair, black sticky mud. My toes wriggled over roots and small crabs and rotting wood. The rest of the world had disappeared. There were only the stretches of mud and a foul smell; nothing to kill except uneatable carrion.

We stayed too on Bribie Island in the north of Moreton Bay, near the southern end of the Great Barrier Reef, a flat treeless length of sand swept by wind and sun. Here my main job was to catch bait. First I had to find some of the meaty ugarie shells, smooth wedge-shaped bivalves purple in the wash of the tide or dug from the sand where the surf had buried them. Then, after prizing them open, I laid out the halves on the ocean beach. Before long an unwary sandworm poked its red-brown head out of the sand and emerged for a bite of ugarie.

A skilful worm catcher knew the exact moment when to drive down and catch the worm between two fingers. The act of catching had to be simultaneously a lift upwards, a smart wrench out. Otherwise the worm went rigid and got its grip in the sand. If you were slow, you missed the thing altogether – which was quite easy, as it could withdraw at lightning speed. If you were quick enough to get hold of the head between your fingers, but failed in the lift, you were likely to whip off only a few miserable inches and you lost the worm unless you were ready to spend half an hour digging. If you were properly trained, you pulled the whole damn thing out in one long sweeping gesture.

After a while I grew fairly good at catching the worm before it shrank back into the sand, but rarely did I get the full surprising length. Mostly I got anything between two inches and a foot.

I wandered into the beaten bushes and ti-trees that looked as if they had been reared by one of the more fantastic Japanese artists, and was lost. But on a very long and very narrow island even I could not stay lost for more than half an hour. I wrote couplets on the flat brown sand with a fir-bough, then with a broken oar washed up by the waves. O blood of light, pour from the wounded sun, here Philoctetes cursed, the cheated one.

I created out of a song and a statue of sand an island nymph, Bribia, who hid from me among the battered bushes, but left her footprints on a track between two rocks. I found two blue stones that were her eyes, a slit shell draped with delicate weed for her maidenhood, slivers of red coral for her breasts. I embedded these in a statue of sand which the wind had gnawed. I found a bottle without a message in it and sent it again adrift with a few words addressed to Apollo, telling him that I was learning Greek from a master as round as a hairy gooseberry and red as the inside of a Moreton Bay fig. I lay in the rough windy boughs of ti-trees and the disk of a crystal world spun under me. O Bribia come forth in archaic nakedness, with two plaits of golden hair, and take my respectful hand, you nereid born from a rib of the old Giant Sand. Balanced upon the spinning wind, come lithely forth, one leg from the south, one leg from the north. Come with a flash of foam, bright as milk, and make my hand your home. Come with a billow-leap and ride upon my sleep, sunburnt goddess.

I found her footprints again and tracked them for a hundred yards, then lost them.

The cymbal clashes of light on the heaving waters, the hoarse rumbling like a host of maenad-tambours, the shrill conches of the wind blowing through the beards of dried seaweed caught up in the trees – I turned and saw the sea, the Pacific Ocean, and cried *Thalassa!* with the voice of ten thousand.

I found the slender footprints again and tracked them home. Bribia turned out to be the slatternly girl who did the cooking in the sole ram-shackle building of the island, a group of long huts in various stages of mange. Her hair was mousey-fair, but matted, a pleasant thicket from which her pert eyes twinkled. She wore a brown dress rotted at the armpits and her scratched feet were bare.

I asked her if she liked bathing; and she said she didn't like it much, but it wasn't so bad in the Christmas holidays when there were lots of daily visitors.

I asked her what she did if she disliked bathing, and she said she didn't do anything much, there wasn't anything to do, but it was good in the Christmas holidays with the boats coming in.

She yawned with shapeless mouth and our conversation flagged. I didn't ask her to come bathing with me. Instead I went a mile down the oceanic side and ran naked in the buffets of the wind and skimmed a stone along the waters. The foam flashed and stung my eyes and mouth. Mother of men, the sea was mine, a wet sheet and a flowing sea. I dug myself in the warm sands a cradle-and-grave, a womb-and-tomb exultant in resurrection.

What does the wind say? J. Lindsay.

That night my uncle and the professor gave me a large draught of rum, which tasted like boiled ants with a dash of gingerbeer. I said it was fine and felt like the old bold mate of Henry Morgan. J. sang sea-chanties: *Rolling home* and *Boney was Warrior* and *Rio* and the others in his rumbling bass. And told fabulous stories of his adventures in the South Seas and on the Barrier Reef, escapes from giant clams that had caught his foot, discoveries of pearls in a Jap's tobacco pouch. 'You didn't know Joe Hicks, did you, Tom? He had a glass eye. He knew how to keep the kanakas working when he wasn't there. He'd take out his eye and put it on a leaf . . .'

That night in response a storm came up and crashed all over the island, flinging a thousand miles of Pacific breakers at a spit of sand. I stood at the door of my hut, under the clashing shields of thunder, whipped by the tassels of rain, and perhaps the rum made it nobler than it was. But it was noble all the same, with devil-packs of clouds careering close overhead, trailing ropes of vapour that mixed with the mist of foam. The spindrift was blown right across to the nook of the huts, spindrift and rain gusts mingled. Only in a storm could I now sing.

And in the morning I tramped over the stricken island that glittered in the lick of a breeze, and wrote more couplets in the eternal sands. And moulded afresh a statue to undefiled Bribia.

I went camping also with boys from the school and often

tramped with them from One Tree Hill among the ridges and gullies around. I learned how easy it was to get lost in the criss-crossing gullies where one vista seemed much like another. From a bush-wise friend of these wanderings I acquired various maxims. If you haven't got a compass (and I never had), keep your eye on the sun and watch your relation to its movement. Work towards a watershed. Better still, go down a creek: you'll come sooner or later to a larger creek and some sort of house – in the wilds, a shepherd's hut or a small farm or at least a paddock fence. At first glance it may well seem hard to tell whether you're going up or down a gully; but if you look at the way the bushes grow along it, you could make out the flow of the stream in torrent-time.

Climbing along the scattered bones of a dry course, we found a pool left in some deep bowl of rock and had a dip, then lay about trying to smoke dry pieces of lawyer-vine in which the small perforations allowed at least something of a free passage for the smoke. Or we slid down a slope, catching at the roots or the saplings when the pace threatened to get out of control, and ending in a green nook from which we watched a brown-green water snake slide in a sinuous zigzag across the stream. Or listened to a flight of chattering lories among the tree tops.

Alone and naked on a flat stone like the opened palm of the sun lifting me out of time and space, I still felt a compelling union with the earth. As though moving through successive rings of tightening light, and yet at the same time flowing out-wards to clash against the horizon. Aware with crystalline intensity of a leaf shape, the shadow of an ant, the pleats of a water plant, and yet lost in the undulating fields of gold, the earth spinning below like a small shadowy globe. The universe broke into countless pieces of bright glass and I rose steadily from the dark centre, a frail eternal fountain, going up against the ghostly debris, falling. And at last, coming back from the four corners of the rounded distance, I heard my heart beating deep in the earth and waited with a patience beyond all thought till it had crept back into my breast.

10 · VISION OF PLATO

ALONE, with water, fire and air, I was happy. The prinking flow of the water was not distinct from the rhythmical structure of the song; the leap of the wind and all the moods of the sky. The beautiful drowned woman smiled up at me from the river depths and became the sly nymph; every flowering shadow was a tryst with Keats and with Amaryllis.

My solitude was a marriage with the earth. One night, formally so. Mary had had a couple of trees cut down and the fall of a tree was always a belly blow, a pang of humiliation, a crash of loss. A great heap of boughs and leaves was piled one end of the garden. The moon came up at midnight and made me restless with a flickering breeze. Mice of shadowy light stole under the door. A leaf-finger tapped. I went on to the moonpyre of greenery and lay there naked. Dozing a moment, I woke on a fear, clinging to the boughs. The raft of the earth shook on the dark waters, the moon was veiled, something fluttered across the sky, and the cradle of greenery rocked me, comforted me. My sister the tree had also been severed from the earth and we were one in the buoyant bed of darkness. Far away, inside my head, a bird wailed. And then, as the wind slid the cloud away, the fountain of light burst up out of the earth, out of a hole in my side.

Mostly the spell held. But there were moments when it slipped and I was lost in the mockery of chaos. Sometimes I couldn't stop saying the same word over and over till it ceased to have meaning and became a strange clot of alien life, a cut-off thing, lodged hostilely in my head and refusing to go. The word of magical meaning became the clot of madness, the blind ticking death of meaning. Words were then locusts in the crops, stripping the earth of green and familiar life. And this treachery of the word was the very loss of self. The alien and hostile world swelled up inside and burst like an abscess and left a raw void; and an obliquity of angles entangled the world. Reach out and the object moved aside, ever so little, but enough to make you miss it. The gap between your straddling feet grew wider. You felt the turn of the mad earth in every pause. Whatever you did was broken apart, a separate mechanism in which you were inexplicably and agonizedly caught. Time, the mad clot beating; death, a dusty spiral in the dank repellent smell; sleep, the pit of the body in which lurked terrible snakes. Fear of involuntary emission, of V.D. (obscurely learnt about from warnings in public lavatories and the tantalizing pedantries of encyclopaedias), of blindness and strange privies, of people talking and talking on the other side of the wall, beyond the window pane, of absolute cruelties seen in the street, a kicked dog or a fallen horse between two trams, a man glimpsed through a window savagely beating a small girl with a belt. Lying in bed, you felt on the edge of sleep your body puffing up, grown huge and doughy, floating away out of control; nothing of you left but a peculiar hot taste in the mouth or your heart rattling and swinging at the end of a piece of string tied to the iron bar of the bed.

Mary however knew that I wrote verse and wanted me to do something about it: have it read, published, utilized. I resisted her with a stubborn silence, but she had helped to break the spell, the single-minded independence of my movement. I couldn't help thinking for the first time how my verses would seem to someone else; and once I thought like that, I couldn't rest calmly on my delight in the sun-game, the prismatic modulations among the cubes and arcs of nature.

I needed Plato for my defence and I found him through Shelley, in the Everyman translations, and then (as I learned more Greek) in the original.

Till now the separation of poetry and world, of sensuous essence (or spirit) and everyday experience, had been a matter of simple and direct oppositions – even if it had its moments of anger and despair. The world was interested in things that seemed to me futile: money-making and sausage machines and fashions and shop windows. The world was concerned with penning large numbers of people in unclean prison systems called towns. And I was absorbed in what I thought the real things, colour harmonies and symmetries of rhyme, the relation of a Shakespearean sonnet to the balances of a bough in the wind. The only person who could enter into my sphere was another preoccupied with the same problems – and though the advent of such another was theoretically possible, it seemed so remote a chance that I never thought about it. My mind to me a kingdom is; in a cell I still own the universe of my body.

But now an argument had begun in the cell, in the universe; and I couldn't halt it. For, unforeseeably, I was arguing with myself. My aunt's frowned-off intrusion had merely opened the door to the stranger, myself. Experience had to find an intellectual idiom.

The exultations had previously faded out in a sick dizziness, a bacchic wrenching at the roots of my hair, a sense of milky lightnings in the blood, a straining of the entire body upwards as if by becoming cruelly aware of the limiting structure of bone I could achieve a liberating discipline of wings. But now my thoughts had to pass beyond this annihilating moment, into some schoolroom of Apollo, where they would be required to explain and justify themselves. They could no longer rely on the blank and blind opposition of the world; they had to find ways of speaking which would at a pinch enable them to smile with a safe guile.

Now it was not a matter of my spirit-self against the lumpish world, with a neutral mask between. The mask was also myself, also the world. I was myself double, inside and outside, and two voices claimed the mouth of the mask. Mask and face could change places and roles with indefinite address and prolixity. The flame spiral of song, consuming the world and escaping into ethereal acrobatics, was no longer the only possible graph of the free spirit. The social extension of the inturned and organic experience was discovered to be possible, necessary – an unexplored aspect of the single reality. Yet my total rejection of the world's values made that extension conceivable only as an imaginative act peopling solitude.

The war too was beginning to change its face and play its part in the new perturbations. No longer it kept its tidy and

distant place on the wall map. I had long given up taking
Mary's weekly edition of *The Times*, to cut out the little black
silhouettes of naval losses. Wounded men were returning.
Some of the boys at school had lost brothers. One or two of
Norman's cartoons in the *Bulletin* had had a forceful protest
against a vicious circle of madness and brutality. If the world
were murderous as well as pointless, could poetry stand in a
vague sort of neutral opposition? The question was dimly formulated, yet was present.

Besides, my success at school, coupled with my mother's
slackening grip, made me emerge further as family head. My
aunt's insistence on worldly fame seemed aimed at riveting me
in the home responsibility which I could neither evade nor
accept.

I had carried my enthusiasm for water into my schooldays
and found at last a sport I could welcome. I showed myself a
reasonably good bow in a four or an eight on the river, and
practised at least a couple of afternoons a week – along the
reach over which the main bridge was built. We had now
moved to a boarding-house on the banks, not far from the
rowing club which the school used.

Thus, rowing, which had been my main instrument for getting away into the wilds, had become a means of participating
in an organized sport.

I became acutely aware of my dreams and tried to remember
them in the hurry of morning. There were caves and oceanic
islands in which obscure trysts were held; but the main dream,
which I grew to desire strongly, was one of abstract forms in
motion. A simultaneous progression in and out, an outward
pressure bellying and building big lines of force and an inward
pressure of converging curves. A ceaseless struggle went on
between the two pulls; and in my dream I grew more and more
excited as to the result. If the outward pull triumphed, everything would fly into scattered pieces; if the inward, then everything would contract into nothingness. What I sought was the
difficult and precarious moment of perfect balance when the
hidden centre which conditioned the whole struggle would
manifest itself with decisive power and all would interlock on
a pure harmony, a subtle equilibrium of apparently disparate

elements, a symmetry of mated opposites which were held apart on the edge of joy or disaster. A voice said to me: Here is the secret of the universe, the clue to the maze. Then, at the very pulse of solution, the toppling into action, the adjustment into a yet finer equipoise, the rich geometry was wiped out and I awoke.

As yet I knew nothing of abstract art, but my dreams seemed to define that art as a preparation of fear and desire for the movement into a new unity of self – or as a breakdown from a previous level, coagulating the vital entanglements of a situation into a dead draft, a thingified death.

I still had not heard, as far as I knew, any classical music; but I had built up a complicated idea of what such music was, even what the music composed by the famous names was like. Once a lad in my class, who fancied himself a pianist, said that his favourite musician was Chopin. I argued at length that Wagner was much superior, though I had not heard a note of the music of either musician.

All the more reason then to strive to grasp Plato's logic, to find the points where my own inner argument coincided with the voices arguing like learned birds among the Athenian pillars or the green walks of the Ilyssos.

Plato turned the passionate moment of realization (the creation of a living image) into a dialogue where the diverse aspects of the self were cunningly given the faces of diverse persons; and so his method provided me with a scheme of dramatization which alone could serve as a bridge from my crystalline of music to the disorderly sphere of people. I had no words from my word-obsessed life to exchange with the inhabitants of that latter sphere: but I could in seclusion transpose the valueless words of actual discourse into a discussion which to some extent broke down the division between the passionate moment and the analytic instrument, between poetry and prose. Plato showed how to use the deadly instrument against itself, against the world and its contaminated or dead judgements.

Poetry had been the achievement of furious wings of ascent in a storm of my own magical unloosing; but the platonic system implied a group of people speaking and listening. I replaced the burning goddess-mask and the gyre of elemental transfiguration by the give-and-take of equal voices all my own. I sought to dramatize the lyrical moment as the refutation of the enemy.

Shelley had crystallized my previous position: in the lines about the poet watching all day the yellow bees in the ivy-bloom and the lake-reflected light, seeking not mortal blisses and creating forms more real than living man. The trumpets singing to battle do not feel what they inspire. The poet is one with the elemental energies; self is still the enfolding whole, with self-awareness submerged in the activity of union. Is every faintest flitter of movement, every sweetness hived, every dimple of water. The outgoing current of union absorbs all forces and things, and leaves nothing to jerk back into a separate consciousness. The creation of form occurs through an entire identification of the inner world with the network of light and scent, the hiving elementals. An orgasm in a dream leaves a smiling baby in the hands of waking. A miracle: something that never happens is yet at the root of all creative activity. Shelley's *Witch of Atlas* the textbook.

When I had first read Wyatt's line 'like bended moon that leans her lusty side', I had known only an incandescence and a curving, a length of naked legs (round as the surfaces of a late Titian nude) under the strange light and a wind of steady rhythm: a tumble of naughty schoolgirls in the shell-hush of night, Aphrodite curdling from the fluted waves; and, the flash gone, only the trembling of my hands. Now I felt the light burst less purely, less stormily; but I held the moon afterwards on my anxious palm, a faintly quivering figurine of stone, and said: Here is the image of the moon, more real than the coin of light spun nightly in the trivial sky. I said: What does one do with a captured moon?

People and my own thoughts had thrust between my senses and the poetic image. Though the dialogue was only that of green tongues of solitude, there stirred implicit in the formulations a belief that life, despite all the evidence, could be gracious and graceful. The earth could be the song, people the singing. Perhaps had once been, therefore could be again, a society of equal voices. For the first time, uneasily, I began to feel lonely. Till now I had been simply alone.

Plato on memory and on inspiration. In *Ion* I recognized the transcription of my own daimonic experience. Here was more than the brotherly testimony of the poets in their ravishing images, which took me into their queenly lap (like Betty). Here was more than the oracular moment of Keats or Wordsworth when the doorway of the majestic loins was neatly decorated with a lightning scroll, a nicely turned motto of eternity, a note from God in a Christmas cracker. Here was a logically extended defence, the full map of the detailed country previously viewed only by blinding flashlight through a fissure in the skull.

In the *Meno* I verified all my doubts about schools. When the slaveboy saw, in the pure and mad moment of knowledge, the side of the larger square identify itself with the diagonal of the square half its area, I rose and ran from the room. To sit still at such a moment, unless one had the power of chanting a paean, would be irreverent. The one thing needful to be proved had been proved.

For this picture of a boy's mind wrestling over a problem of forms was the exact picture of my own mind in the testing moment of realization. I grasped what had happened that time in the park when the mocking laughter of my friends broke down my fear and forced me to know what I knew. Here was the plain clue to the pang of Aphrodite's rhythmic birth and the uncurling of a poem's petals. Now I was sure that I wasn't going mad; I was safe under the skirt of lapsing water, I knew what the others knew but feared to know.

From that moment I was pledged to detest all veils, to look on all veils as lies, to identify poetry and nakedness and truth. My life had once before become Keats' Ode; now the Ode moved outwards and became experience. Beauty is Truth, Truth is Beauty. Here at the secret rose-heart, where all is nakedness. The rose glows under the social tissues, under shame and shelter, and I worship it in every girl as the sinewy point where time and eternity meet.

I walked along the banks of the river, I wanted to plunge

in, clothes and all, and swim straight to the bottom, out of the world to a level of pure rest. The pellucid cloudless afternoon sky, clear as a single drop of welling dew, curved in its depthless depth over my thought; and my thought went beyond it. Drank the drop of dew and was still thirsty. That leap of the slaveboy's mind was a leap over the moon, over the chattering years, into my hands, my wholeness. How could I ever utter my gratitude?

I sat on the bank while the water sucked at a riddled rock and a dog tried frantically to gain the courage to jump in. A girl with a skin of transparent wax went by, holding her hat in her hand. Body and dress flowed in a single elemental rhythm, as in a figure drawn by Blake in a dream. I wanted to touch her. I felt that then we should both go up in a single flame. Heart of my heart, our heaven is here, is won. I have immortal longings, and this girl is part of them, closer than breathing, and she will never know.

But I had to go back past the hordes of rude wenches pouring out of the bottle factory as the whistle blew. They laughed and joined hands and pushed me into the road; they sang and babbled and laughed; they called out invitations and would have been as scared as I if I had taken them at their word. I blushed and hurried on. How could they ever know how wonderful I thought them all?

For me the myths were the most immediate parts of Plato's work, explaining the here-and-now, not the past or the future. The two winged steeds that draw the charioteer in the great procession of gods moving to their eternal ends in the place above the heavens. The moulting of the wings and the fall into the coiling horror of the winds, the sudden darkness and turmoil of gnats. How could I fail to read here the stations of my stoical golgotha, the detailed physiology of adolescence? the skeleton rattling in my nightly bed, the swelling of the snakesting in old Adam, the tunnel of separations?

For we have seen that in life and in death it is best to choose thus. And it was now midnight, there was a clap of thunder and an earthquake; and in a moment the souls were carried up to their birth, this way and that, like shooting stars. I remember nothing but the Form of Beauty.

The gravel, the broken bits, the oddments and offal of corrupted thought and desire, the innumerable splinters of the mirror of the titans. The night of confusion and the unjust arithmetics of money; the world as it is. Falling through a sieve, the mind. And memory, the organizing structure, which is art and wholeness.

And at last the vision is revealed to him of a single science which is the science of beauty everywhere. Nothing can be remembered but the Form of Beauty.

I felt no need to talk to other people of the things in my mind since I talked nightly with the drinkers of the *Symposion*. Plato had become a city in my dreams. I saw how Aphrodite rose from the gyres of Betty's navel into the moon-niche; the burning image consumed the lovely bodies which rose again in the purer light of the Form. And the Form was the quick of myself, the axis of the sun turning in the sockets of flesh. I, O Dionysos.

There was no division between myself and every leap of growth, every curl of the song.

Yet I, who had simply been alone, was now lonely. I knew loneliness because I projected the image of its antithesis, the jewel-pageant in the eye of the sun, the rapt and merry gods, the talkers round Aristophanes.

It happened as I was walking out of the dull and dusty Public Library on the bank near the Bridge, on a day of windy sunlight and little whitegold flame-tendrils in the grasses. In front, the small Treasury Gardens held a tall girl in a short blue frock going down the steps towards the iridescent spray and the silver sky. Beyond her was the stationer's shop where I once found on sale some early hack-humorous postcards drawn by Norman, all about Mr Damn, Mrs Damn and the Whole Damn Family.

What I saw was caught out of the corner of my eye, just past the edge of distraction, without surprise. A naked brown-legged ephebos with a brief gold cloak streaming from his shoulders and buckled across his throat. His body was close and lithe against me for a moment of delighted inattention and then was nonchalantly gone, into Athenai, down the Propylaia. I had not seen his face. I thought: I need not be alone.

I felt as gay as a flock of finches. For the moment I was satisfied with the warmth of symbols and the simple contrasts of irony. I followed the tall girl through the gardens and along George Street, past the Government Printing Works with the devil in his niche, enjoying the spectacle of her graceful ease because I was still quite sure that we walked along different streets.

11 · REVULSIONS

For a while I lingered in the imagic world of Keats, in his letters and their praise of negative sensibility. But though in *Endymion* the quest for the image (and the girl) through the elemental spirals and the oceanic whorls might solace, in *Hyperion* I felt driven out into the open of conflict, into the Apollonian birthpang. 'Those for whom the miseries of the world are misery and will not let them rest' fell across my thoughts like an icy bar. Why had Keats died so young? The fear of dying touched me; and now it was desperately important that I should leave something immortal on my doorstep. But the milky shadow of a goddess on my virginal bed was barren.

I recalled my uncle Raymond, pressed my hands against my ribs and wondered why the next breath of wind did not flatten the feeble thing of water and corruption that was I. I feared as a noon-siren the girl who danced in the windy tree; I feared the hole in the earth, the navel of the waters. I remembered the cow swollen in the Currumbin bog, red and foul, and the delicate skeleton of a bird found on a kingly cushion of moss. The blood of the abbatoirs and the hosts of carcasses streaked white and pink in the ice-chambers of the meat works. The flying fox with its claws shot off. The day at Hobart when we played at the back of the barracks (where our bedroom was like a colonnaded vista inside a mirror) and Ray upset a bottle of acid on himself, so that suddenly all his clothes started disappearing.

A lovely girl came one Saturday to tea at Mary's house. She seemed to have materialized that moment from a world of apple-blossom light. She moved in the halo of her own beauty, with long grave eyes. I hardly dared to look at her; she sat on the edge of my eyes, a young Kore throned on acanthus-leaves of syenite with a pomegranate, yet soft as the Welsh heroine made from the flowers of the oak and the flowers of the broom and the flowers of meadowsweet. Olwen with the slender eye-brows and the pure heart, out of whose every footprint sprang four white trefoils and whose fingers were like wood-anemones in the spray of the meadow-fountain.

Then, about a fortnight later, my aunt said casually to some-one, 'Yes, that poor girl, she died of blood poisoning last night – a mosquito bite ...' I went down to the river and the skein of reflected lights dancing on the smooth-skinned water was now more lively than the senses of the daughter of the moon.

My flesh crept with worms as I recalled the words some-where cited in Poe: 'And will you now please discard your mask?' 'I am not wearing a mask.'

I reread the later poems of Donne and all the sixteenth cen-tury dirges I knew. *Timor mortis conturbat me.* Brightness falls from the air. I sought to undergo the ritual of repentance and redemption without a preliminary conviction of sin, feeling only that no other ritual adequately dramatized the fear of death. Oh, to vex me, contraries meet in one. Crashaw's Teresa bloomed in the blonde amorous flames of her martyrdom, but I could not find in that big sweat-nimbused bosom the home I sought.

I was nearing the aesthetic of the Troubadours, the paradox of loss as the sole key to stable possession, of distance as the sole perspective of sure vision. Once the girl had been merged with the tree-dance and the luxurious clouds, the cyclopean spring and the festival of the daisies, so warmly present, so teasingly round the corner of a scent, that the ethic of renunciation had no meaning. All things are here, here in the gyration of blossoming light, even the spin of the pirouetting dryad on the axis of green water. The jagged-tail bower bird swallowing the fruit of the bitterbark spoke the same language as the girl out of Goya hiding behind her fan under the flirt of black leaves.

But now, in the sense of loneliness which had become the fear of death, I was forced to see that the girl wasn't really there with the shawl of leaves and the fillets of the wind, coming down the roadway of the larch. The bubbles sidling up from the grass roots at the river edge were not the breathing naiads. The moongirl did not stroll down the wake of my boat in the night waters.

It seemed then that I must choose between the peopled street and the moonwake. But at once that appeared as a choice between the making of money and the creation of art. There could be no hesitation. I chose the silence of the urn and the tomb of the goddess, the book and the river of night. As I came through the desert, thus it was. The world that I now wanted was wholly of stone and harsh light, sterile. The cell of water, the sackcloth of the harsh sun.

One aspect of my stoicism was a determination not to fall ill. Ilness seemed to me an illegitimate form of suffering. I wanted my pangs, my loss, to go deeper than any submission to disease. A disease appeared as the imposition of the pang from without – or from the blind necessities of the body, which was the same thing. A blasphemy against the pure will. To keep my suffering uncorrupted and tragic I decided to refuse any illness. About the age of six I had had measles and chicken-pox; but that must be the end of an undignified surrender. And so, apart from the sneezes of brief colds, I was not ill. If I remained true to my own deepest needs of struggle, I success-fully told myself, I should not need to invoke the vulgar alter-nations of health and un-health by which others dramatized weakly their desires and fears, their hopes and frustrations.

Mary thought it would be patriotic to have some wounded soldiers to tea. She asked a friend, who worked in the hospital on the Point, to send along a few convalescents. Two turned up. One was a squat fellow who sat on the rim of his chair and had a deep red ridge across his brow; he kept screwing up his eyes and seemed taken aback when addressed. The other was lanky and confidently loud-voiced, with tunic wide open at neck, and he sprawled in his chair. He began talking the moment he entered, and talked most of the time when not drinking tea. 'Got a fire or something inside,' he remarked. 'Can't quench it. Everlasting fire. Wouldn't mind another cup, mum.'

I was there to hand biscuits and cakes round. My aunt tried

to put in a firm and tactful word to show how much she appreciated the soldiers going overseas to fight the Huns and save Australia from the horrors afflicting Europe. Lanky didn't give her much of a chance to talk. She had made some of her excellent very thin sandwiches, and when she wasn't looking I was eating up the tomato ones. The new servant girl, a rather slummocky person who kept her baby in the kitchen, had done her hair more carefully than usual; and after the way the soldiers looked at her, my aunt went out herself to get some more hot water.

After the fourth cup, Lanky became even faster in his talk, tripping over his words. Squat still sat on chair-rim, frowning to himself and occasionally throwing a sharp blinking look at Lanky. 'How I longed for a cup of tea,' the latter was saying. 'One bloody thing I couldn't get used to going without. How many is that I've had?'

'Four,' said Squat, speaking for the first time.

'I was never much good at counting,' said Lanky, with an odd titter.

I wanted to slip away and as next best I managed to get behind the lavish vase of zinnias. 'Four five six it's all one to me, I always counted them Jackos wrong. Four five six.' He tittered again while Squat scowled into his teacup. 'Funny how the shrapnel always got them. Wasn't any use counting right, was it, mum? Take them prisoners down to the beach, corporal! Okay, sarge. So off we go down the bridle track. Just round the corner there comes a bad drop. Just out of sight too, mighty convenient, eh? Off we march, mum. Round the corner of the hill.' He tittered more loudly, then coughed and spluttered. Mary offered him a slice of cake, but he waved her away. 'So when we report on the beach, not a bloody prisoner left. Not the smell of one. Ten killed by shrapnel and the other two shot trying to escape. Four five six. That's the way it was. Very good, sir. Salute, right about bloody-turn, and off again. What's the use of counting? And nobody offered us a cup of tea for doing it. I wouldn't mind if I did have another.' Again he tittered. 'All the buggers dead. One two three. Bloody funny wasn't it. Oh Christ, wasn't it? Why the hell don't you laugh?' He began sobbing.

'You better shut up,' said Squat unemotionally. He rose smartly, 'I'll take him back, mum. It's nothing. He gets like this.'

My aunt did not ever discuss with me the soldier's Gallipoli experiences. And no more soldiers were asked to tea.

She decided to give up her Graceville house after J. had a physical breakdown. Moving right into town, she closed my one sure weekend passage into the wilds. On a Saturday afternoon I rowed the dinghy the many miles down to Kangaroo Point and tied up to a jetty amid a couple of old steamers and heaps of rusting boilers. Crossing a paddock, I climbed the back fence to the new house, a charming old colonial bungalow with a grass tennis court, a clump of mango trees and bananas at the side. I was offered the court (to lure me into keeping it in condition) and a small room by the kitchen, where I kept my books.

We ourselves were still in the boarding-house near the rowing club. The proprietress, an efficient hard-faced woman with a scar over one eye, had taken up with a discharged soldier who had been wounded in the left arm. He sat drooping on the piano stool, picking out tunes with one hand or playing with the ginger cat. He was proud of being able to roll cigarettes with his one free hand. Once, as I sat on the verandah, waiting for the factory girls to go noisily by, he stood over me, 'What the devil do you keep on finding to read?' He scowled, 'Your mother says you write things? I'll tell you my life some day and let's see if you could write that up. Nobody'd believe it. I could make a pot of money if I had the patience to write it all out. But I can't read for ten minutes on end, let alone write. Anyone who can stick it must be a bit potty.'

Then the girls came pouring out of the galvanized-iron gates and saved me from his suggestions.

A week later he tried to burn the house down. He filled the room next to us, on the first floor, with petrol, and set match to it. The police found the wardrobe full of petrol tins. It happened late one night and I never discovered how the plan was frustrated or why the man didn't go to jail. As far as I could make out from the comments I heard, he and the proprietress had hoped to cheat an insurance company; and with the evidence of the petrol tins there could hardly have been any question of an accident. Still, he wasn't arrested. He merely gave up shaving more than once a week and didn't try to hide his drinking habits. What I objected to was the dirty trick of attempting to start the conflagration in the room next to ours. Probably that was the only convenient empty room. But it was next to ours all the same and our mother had been quite friendly with Mrs M. the proprietress. If the petrol had properly blazed up, we'd have all no doubt been burned alive.

Most of the other boarders promptly and rudely moved out, but we stayed on. My mother said we were moving, but we didn't. The wounded man was looking more like a criminal with arson on his mind every day, though he did nothing worse than grumble and drink. Then a few new boarders appeared and we had pleasant musical evenings dominated by a girl Gladys, aged about eighteen, who treated me with condescending hauteur, ordered me about, and held a cigarette with her little finger in genteel detachment.

I had become interested in medieval and early renascence art. The official Art Gallery was a room on the top of one of the government offices in George Street, full for the most part of amateurish local work. But the Public Library had a number of art books, and I studied them, in particular looking for anything connected with Francis of Assisi. Also I copied out in the medieval texts as many miracle plays as I could find.

One afternoon I was out rowing in an eight, near the south side, at the upper turn of the bridge-reach. Out of the near house came running a young woman, unclad, with her hair down. She stood for a second on the slight rise in the scantily grassed yard which sloped to the water, as if the slap of light had dazed her. She didn't seem to see us, stockily built, black-haired. Then she fell over before the impact of a man with pulled-down cap who had run after her from the back door. He pushed her down the slope, and they both slid out of view as we rowed on, a disused wood yard intervening. The master who was coxing sternly bade us keep up our speed.

When we reached the punt and carried the boat in, I had a shower and went off, not wanting to discuss with the others the miraculous episode. I knew and accepted that behind the normally blank wall lay the hidden faces, places, graces, traces, embraces of poetry. But now I had seen with a shock, still felt in my navel, that behind the world which my aunt described as the only true and possible world there lay all sorts of strange, forbidden and disordering things.

Death was one of the dark winds that broke up the world of trim pretences. A naked woman was an equal force of jolting confusion and defiance, ruffling all the given surfaces.

It broke up the rational systems and yet could not be made to serve as the basis for a new system. I could not relate death or the naked woman to anything in my daily life, my habitual environment. And yet what was any system worth when it could not include death and nakedness?

I went up to my verandah corner and tried to read Herrick. But the image of the white body, repellent and yet striking sweetly on every string of the senses, put all lyrics out of tune. I had the feeling that there was something in my pockets I ought to hide from the police, some evidence of crime needing to be washed away. But it was myself I wanted to hide, in the pocket of the image. I wanted to become one with the rhythmical drive of the long lean boat through the yielding waters.

We moved along to another boarding-house on the river bank, a three-storeyed old colonial wooden building with wide creaking verandahs under the shadow of fig trees. I had a small room of my own, made by enclosing a length of the verandah outside my mother's room. There was just enough width between table and wall to squeeze in.

Another boarder was a handsome drowsy woman come from Bundaberg to say goodbye to her enlisted husband. For his pocket-book overseas he took some dozen photos of her in bridal undress and she must have handed them over to my mother in a confiding pride. For, opening one of the drawers for a tie, I came on the neat little heap and recognized with an incredulous perturbation the woman who sat a few feet away from me in the dining-room and to whom I often passed the salt. She was this – lovely, terrifying, sweeter-than-honeycomb, and also (strangely) banal, familiar, faintly ugly, disproportionate, heavy, pathetic. This, all the while; this, while I passed her the salt; this, met in the street; this.

What was revealed was not only the awful fact of this broad implacable offering presence, which, with its emphases in unexpected places, made all statues seem impertinent and puritanic rationalizations. Rather, it was the thought, the brazen and yet impenetrable thought behind the half-open mouth and the eyes so gaily afraid. What was she thinking of as she arranged herself with graceless pride on the sacrificial block, plumply foreshortened and baroquely distorted, a sleepy monument of relaxed but unsatisfied appetites? Patiently opened to the camera's clinical and fantastic eye, she was like a neurotic on the psychiatric couch who wildly invents baseless episodes of rape in order to satiate the boring scrutiny of the questioner and regain a normal posture in the streets of anonymity. As with the case of the girl surprised on the south bank, there seemed no relation between this unlicensed exposure and the partial denudings of a bathing beach. The ungainly form, disturbing in a quite different way, seemed dragged by its own wilful weight from a broken point of centralizing rhythm; and its very unseemliness, its floundering uncoordinations, gave it a rude and shaggy force that I felt at this moment to own an attraction beyond all the smooth adjustments or simplified constructions of a work of art.

I shuffled the photos back and fled before the creak of my mother's coming; and next day there was nothing in the drawer but my ties and handkerchiefs.

Shortly after, the woman returned to Bundaberg. She went back into her own tunnel of light and shadow, turning over and over like a soundless acrobat, to reappear faceless in my dreams. A crouching sphinx whose inexorable question was her lack of questions. Leaving me the unsolved problem of the social enforcement of shame and the private need to throw all shame off, the gap between the accepted pretences of the world and the seething realities behind the drawn blinds, the closed faces.

12 · READING AND WRITING

My reading for years had been almost entirely of poetry. The only critic I respected was Hazlitt. Without guidance, by putting out my hands to shelves, I made up my list of worthy poets. The first to stand heaven high were Shakespeare, Keats, Shelley, Marlowe, Coleridge. But by 1917 I had read most of the poets with any place in English literature up to the end of the nineteenth century. All the Mermaid dramatists, the complete works of Jonson, Beaumont and Fletcher, Dryden, Spenser, Chaucer, even of men like Gower or Phineas Fletcher, Barnaby Barnes or Taylor the Water-poet. Charlotte Smith or Bloomfield, Orion Horne or Festus Bayley.

Prose I scorned. Only in verse did I feel the air-treading, the sea-cleaving, the fire-dancing, the irreconcilable rejection of the world. I found the one bookshop with a good second-hand section and saved every penny to build up my library of poets. That one could seriously use money for any other purpose never crossed my mind, and I should certainly have starved rather than turn my expenditure from books to food. I got a shilling or so from my mother, and half-a-crown a week from my grandmother; and then the coins jingled complainingly in my pocket till I reached the shop and nosed among the odd piles in the dim corners. I was always liable to find some prize within my means, Gifford's edition of Ben Jonson or the folio of Temple's works, *Rejected Addresses* of Goldsmith's edition of Parnell. Such a find kept me happy for days. The Muses Library gave me Donne, Vaughan, Browne of Tavistock, Drummond and other seventeenth century poets. By following up their trails I came on writers like Traherne or the Countess of Winchelsea.

I went on trying to write sonnets on Marlowe or long narra-

tives in Spenserian stanzas, love poems in choriambics, odes on
the nature of man. It was all entirely derivative in theme and
form. Then, after coming to Plato, I tried dialogues. Reading
the Greek, my mind was full of new ideas tangentially struck
off; but when I took up the pen, I tamely repeated. After a
while I tried dialogues between poets, creating the conversation and company I wanted. Arguments between Coleridge
and Wordsworth, with material taken from the preface to
Lyrical Ballads or Biographia Literaria led on to Scenes at the
Mermaid, with Jonson and Shakespeare, Greene and Peele,
debating, or to Pastoral Parties where Theocritos put his
friends in their places amid cyclamen and tame grasshoppers.
An attempt at a Death of Marlowe was my first intrusion into
drama proper.

My aunt had decided to speed up my school career. I had
taken the scholarship at the prep school long ahead of normal,
so why shouldn't I enter for the university scholarship in my
fourth instead of my fifth year at the Grammar? I had come
top of the candidates for a continuation scholarship at the end
of 1916, and she insisted that I could easily cram two years'
work into one.

The idea appealed to my vanity, but was scaring. No one
had done it before as far as I could find out. What a fool I'd
look if I failed and had to go back to school. But while I tempor-
ized, she went behind my back and fixed things with the headmaster. He agreed to find one of the masters to coach me in
mathematics for an extra fee. I had no choice; and though I
did my best to hide the project, it leaked out and many sarcastic comments were made.

The master giving me the extra lessons on conic sections and
the like (I did no extra work on history, Latin, Greek and the
other subjects) happened to be the son of the old clergyman,
a naturalized German, at the seaside resort to which Lottie had
moved as postmistress: Redcliffe, on Moreton Bay.

We started going there for the long summer holidays over
Christmas. Lottie, patient and hardworking, put us up at the
post office, a rambling weatherboard building with grapevines
all over the back. We slept on camp beds in a back room and
spent the day swimming, wandering on the endless beach or

in the bush at the rear. In the evening we read by lamplight, slapping at mosquitoes, or went to the open-air cinema where scratchy films jumped and blurred on the whitewashed screen. Sometimes the films snapped at the most exciting bits and roused the audience to feet stamping. Sometimes a dog fight broke out under the chairs or a bench collapsed under skylarking youngsters. One dog strongly objected to cowboy films and raced up and down after the chases on horseback. The pianist thumped out set pieces everlastingly repeated, tried to catch a quickening beat, or made a mere racket when a climax was reached on the screen, anxiously turning his head to watch.

An ungainly seaside resort, with low reddish cliffs and stretches of sand where one could leap from fallen boulder to boulder, a long spindly pier, a few nondescript boarding-houses and residence, a creek that lost itself in sand under the bridge, and dank undressing sheds on the main beach. No dance halls, no smartness, no fabricated excitements of any kind. Clearly some of the visitors were better off than others; but there was not much evidence of social differentiation. Unless you swam *all* the time and rolled about drunk, you could merge with the others. We strolled down to watch the daily boat disgorge its trippers or sat under the thick grapevine shadowing the back of the post office. Ray fell from a tree and broke his arm. It was most alarming to see the bone suddenly pointing in the wrong direction; but after he had carried it about in splints, it set as if nothing had happened.

On our first visit I started on Browning, going straight through from *Pauline*. And after a strenuous day with my brothers and our cousins Nancy and Molly, I lay creaking in the brown canvas bed, with the solitary candle of the last awake, and never solved the difficult problem of lying comfortably, with bare arms tucked from the mosquitoes, and yet turning the pages of the book. Sometimes I read and reread the same page before giving in and blowing out the candle with a furious puff.

For a while now I developed improvization. I could never manage it in a room. I needed the open air, a broad sweep of land or sea, solitude. Most helpful of all were the golden expanses of sea-sand with the wind careering over the great breakers. Then as I strode barefooted along it was easy to compose in stanzaic forms such as those of Swinburne's *Dolores* or in Skeltonesque doggerel with a repeated rhyme. The diction was dithyrambic, poor stuff for cold scrutiny on a sheet of paper, but owning its scaldic intoxications when shouted at the wave flattening and frilling up the sand or clucking in the perforated rocks.

Once I was chanting into the sea wind and waving my arms, and round a rock came two girls. I didn't see them at once, with the wind in my eye, in the lull between a wave and a wave. One of them giggled as I passed, the small one with a blue ribbon tied across dark maenad curls and a broad small catface. I felt foolish and dashed, pleased and exalted; but they had spoiled my bardic solitude. Always after they hovered on the edge of my expectation, an unreturning audience.

At times I chanted poems that I knew by heart such as Wordsworth's *Ode on Imitations of Immortality*, Keats' *Nightingale*, large chunks from the first book of *Paradise Lost*, Antony's speech from *Julius Caesar*, Tamburlaine's address to Zenocrate. Always while I strode. I kept mostly to the beach, which was sometimes littered with jelly fish, especially the stinging portuguese men-of-war with their livid blue prong. Even a few yards back from the sand would bring a fury of mosquitoes; and if I rested there a moment, it would be to see how many I could kill at a single blow on my forearm or leg. The big scots-greys were thickly about. Chanting or lost in a choric silence, I walked all round to Sandgate and back, or the length of Bribie.

At Redcliffe the bathing was safe. There was a big sand reef some way out, over which, with its thumping surf, the sharks found it hard to come. This lack of sharks, unusual on the Pacific coast, made bathing a blither matter.

It was at Redcliffe that I heard the results of the examination. I had come third in Queensland. That meant three years of reading and writing clear ahead, all problems of money earning temporarily banished; for the first dozen won university scholarships. Later I found that the two who beat me had been at the examinations the year before, but had come up again so as to enter the university with high scholarship places.

I had now gone into long pants. This consummation had

been a little delayed even by Australian standards; I had still been only sixteen when I sat for the examination. My mother wept when she saw me in adult trousers. She kept several large photos of me as a naked baby; and a curly lock of my hair which was a soft gold. She had wept too as that was cut off when I was about four: a fact hard to credit in view of my dark-brown lank hair of later years. Every step of mine on the road of growing up was a blow, pushing her outside life; it seemed I could develop only at her expense. Now she often did little except sit at a window or on a balcony, smoking and looking out under eyelids slightly dropped. But after the shock of my long trousers she bought a dog, a semi-mongrel fox terrier, who sat beside her, on the sill or at the foot of her chair, also looking out. The dog's occasionally pricked ears, his growls, showed a more direct interest in the passers than did her steady aloofness.

I had an incessant wrestle with my sense of pity. Trying not to think of her for whom I could do nothing. There was always a fear that she might do some incalculable thing, ridiculous or pathetic, through mere failure to reckon with convention or through trying to palliate her ineffably dull routine with the mild dissipation of a bottle of beer or stout. Her resistances having been thrown away, she needed little drink to be stupefied. But what could a son do? There seemed room only for a useless pity. No changes or movements did more than break down briefly and imperfectly her growing accidie.

My aunt was the dominant family figure then in my life – that is, actively dominant: my mother, having moved out of all complicity and participation, remained a shadowy omnipresent form, mistily magnified, from which my thoughts were carefully averted. To my aunt with her busybody schemes I could turn an aggressive face. Her ideas and attitudes became of great importance to me; she provided me with the valuable shape of a spiritual foe, whom in many ways I personally like but who in all ultimates was doggedly set against my needs. By stubborn and largely silent struggle against her plans I did much to clarify my own line of movement.

She wanted me to be a scholar, a correct and famous scholar. She approved of my career so far, to the extent that it seemed likely to lift me to an honourable and profitable place in society, her society. Literary activity was smiled on as long as it helped that lifting. My counter-idea was that if I was any good as a poet I could never reach the position she coveted for me. On the contrary my progress must be a deepening fight against all that constituted honour and profit in her eyes.

I did not for long see the matter as simply as all that; but I fought every inch of the way on the various aspects of the career plan that came up. Gradually she represented for me all that sought by guile, corruption or force to destroy art. I blamed her for Keats's consumption, Chatterton's suicide, Collins's small sad madness, Tennyson's Victorian smugness. She it was who had prevented Byron from living with his half-sister; who had denied Keats her pretty libidinous breasts; as Sara Walker she had closed her smooth knees to hectic Hazlitt. I even found her in poetry itself, the mother whose paddling palm drove Hamlet mad, the slut Cressid who cracked the crystal youth of Troilus, the Dark Lady who shadowed Shakespeare's sonnets with the musk-night of her hair. She was the masked force luring men into the slough of money-filths and cheating them of her O sweet body.

When I found that she looked through my papers during my absence from the house, I wrote things meant to annoy or upset her. I made explicit statements which I would never have been able to formulate under her dark smouldering eyes. I started a series of sonnets (imitating Rossetti's *House of Life*) to alarm her prudish side. Looking back, I see more than a devious defiance of her in those notebooks: I was also trying to persuade her, to win her over, to compel her to my will, binding her to me by the satisfaction that I knew she would find in thus coming close to my apparently hidden self (which was also my really hidden self, more than I knew).

13 · THE WAR

BUT OUR contest was coming out into the open on an angrier issue, the war. Though I had long given up interest in war-maps and rarely looked at newspapers, I had been confusedly roused by the second referendum about conscription. Queensland was a state which stoutly rejected the proposal. I heard anecdotes bandied by Mary and Jack. The Labor government, they said, was kept in power only because the dead voted every election – that is, dead persons were kept on the lists and officials dropped their papers in the box. Scandals about corn and mines were always on the point of bursting, so J. said. He was also very anti-Irish on the conscription issue, and most of all anti-Archbishop Mannix, the rallying point of Irish opposition to the empire. He told gleefully of an old Irishwoman who had been brought into hospital with inflammation of the bowels; she had taken off her wooden lavatory seat and used its oval to frame a photo of the Archbishop. (The only child-hood memory I had of working-class action related to some Sydney strike when our supplies of gas were cut off and we built a big bonfire in the asphalted backyard to do the cooking. We turned the hose on ourselves and danced naked round the fire. Altogether a strike had seemed a pleasant occasion.)

But it was the reading of a handful of Sassoon's poems that brought to a head my contempt for Mary's war attitude. And my bitterness was in no way lessened by finding that for all her fire-eating she had no intention of letting me become one of the slaughtered. If the war went on long enough, she had decided to use her influence to gain me a job in the censor's department. She had selected this job as respectably a part of the war machine, something that could probably be combined with my academic work and was quite safe. My capacity for languages convinced her that she would have no difficulty in fitting me into the censorship system. (At the time, in my quest for lyrics, I was browsing over several European languages, including Old Icelandic.)

Her plan, far from earning the gratitude she thought it merited, was for me the final proof of her insincerity and corruption. I was putting an impossibly heavy burden of guilt on her shoulders; but she stood in my thoughts and feelings as the world's express envoy, and it was necessary for me to see her as the prostitute who sold everything, every value and expression, and who most of all wanted to sell me.

My revulsion was all the stronger after her efforts to talk to me frankly. 'Sex is a wonderful thing. Wait till you meet some nice girl you can love, and then marry her. I'm the last person to deny what a wonderful thing it can be; but that's the very reason why I say all this. So do be patient and don't wreck your life. You know how far you can go if only you're sensible . . .'

What did she take me for? I who so far hadn't even asked a girl out to afternoon tea, lacking the cash even if I had the nerve – I was being talked at as a prowling lecher. The bait of marriage, the bawd's offer of a nice clean body buyable by marriage and a good secure salary, outraged me into a sullen silence. I decided I would never marry.

One day I was in a fairly crowded tram, and a half-drunk soldier, annoyed in some way by the conductor, stood up and grabbed one of the leather straps. Swinging about, he denounced everyone around him. Scroungers and dirty lickspittles, thinking only of saving their filthy skins, grubbing away in the safety of their own little backyards, swine . . . At first he accused them for not being in the army, not taking the rap; then he changed his line of attack and denounced the war itself. A bloody mess, useful only to profiteers. Anyone who enlisted was a fool, and anyone who voted for conscription was a murderer. 'I've had my whack and it's enough. They couldn't prod me back with bayonets. I wash my hands of the whole bloody lot of you.' Then he became grossly personal, picking on a well-dressed man nearby and taunting him as a bloodsucker.

The conductor wandered round him, trying to shut him up.

'Come on, Billjim, we know all that.'

The soldier knocked him aside and jumped off the tram between two stops, sprawling in a gutter.

I had been afraid all the while that he'd turn on me; otherwise I had been fiercely on his side. And I returned to Sassoon's poems, feeling in them now a challenge that I could not ignore. I knew them all by heart. They leaped up cheerily and savagely into my mind at moments when my thoughts were furthest from the war, in the midst of a psychology lecture or as I looked at a girl coming up the gravel path. 'Goodmorning goodmorning the general said . . . But he did for them both with his plan of attack.' Whenever I heard a piano thumping, I recalled the lines about the tanks lurching into a music-hall to the tune of the war-time songs, the kind that my aunt liked – lurching in and shooting the audience down, ending the garish lie 'that mocks the riddled corpses round Bapaume'. The war, so long elbowed aside by my adventure into poetry, now crowded all around me, invading my senses with a ceaseless gun-rattle and scream. It had begun almost to a day with my puberty; now it seemed that my movement into manhood had been accompanied at every moment by the vile thing, a deepening murder threat.

The problem of murder, of blood-guilt, the curse of Cain, began to obsess me. Before, even in my periods of wildest renunciation, I had not been aware of guilt. I had wanted to separate myself from a polluted world, but the separation had cleansed me. Guilt lay on the other side of the page of poetry, the stream of silver-scaled water. But now I no longer felt that one could withdraw so easily. When one had swum the stream, one found that there were shrouded ways round the back of it, infiltrations of the enemy into the promised land.

On a midnight, while the stars flattened their noses on my pane and the ghosts of murderers inhabited the mouse gnawing in my wall, I wrote in my notebook:

Dry leaves of shadow falling falling. Every flicker of light is a death twitch and sends the shadows falling all over again.

It is happening here this very moment and always. Between my hands, a last judgement. Who cares? Even death is defiled and there is no way out. The evil of the world is its triviality.

Siegfried Sassoon. *Intimations of Mortality.*

> *In a world scarce understood*
> *crying out for the forbidden*
> *fruits of evil and of good,*
> *to taste and know the thing that's hidden,*
> *thanks five thousand miles I send*
> *to where the murder roars all day,*
> *roars all night, and call you friend,*
> *who tore the cruel mask away.*

I felt an urgent need of some renunciatory act; some way of life absolutely opposed to a world of personally owned things. Sell all and give it to the poor. But I had nothing to sell. I had only a contrite heart to offer on a nameless altar. It seemed necessary to reject all human relationships except those of self-less love and unweeping pity. Above all I knew that one must guard against the self-assertions which under one pretence or another, morality or law, love or art, made a thing, a means, an instrument of another human being. There was no good will. I read Epicurus and Marcus Aurelius. I aspired to a form of living that seemed to purge the spirit of all the pulls of the law of gravity, all the pressures drawing one into a nexus of relations where one had continually to commit a 'lesser evil.' I ate as little as possible; I walked long unnecessary distances; I enjoyed the fall of the shower water over my lean ribs. I stood at the river-edge taking long measured breaths and my body seemed a slight amenable thing which I could throw away without a second thought at the signal, the call to bear witness.

14 · DANCER

THE UNIVERSITY was situated on the curve of land at the end of the bridge-reach, past Parliament House and the Technical College. Its main building, where the arts sections were located, was the old Government House, a handsome two-storey structure. The professor of Latin and Greek, Michie, a large shy Scot, I liked very much; and though in class he always seemed daunted by the presence of girl undergraduates, in private chat he was able to let out his warm-hearted interest and to be very helpful. I was ostensibly in the full stream of things: attending all events, debating society or dance, and rowing in a four. I even at times attended the choral society, though, as I had now lost all sense of pitch, I only pretended to sing. As for debating, I, who prided myself on living in the world of ideas, had no ideas at all on the discussed subjects and I was astounded at the glibness of some of the speakers. How on earth did they think up such things, arguments for and against disarmament or the freedom of the press? My utmost effort of thought could not get beyond the statement: Anyone not a lunatic wants total disarmament. Anyone not a worm wants the press free, really free. As for dancing I, who found in the very word *dance* an incredibly magical power of evocation, couldn't dance a single orthodox step.

Still, I enjoyed the dances. Mostly I stood out on the verandah towards the river and watched the couples through the glass doors (or watched the stars through the trees). Nobody was likely to bother about me there and I could yield myself up to my rapturous melancholy. In resisting the pull of the music I gave my loneliness a positive value. I felt that the life of a Desert Father must have been a magnificent life as long as the topsy-turvy Venuses and the Birdwomen with pouted breasts and the upended Sphinxwomen and the wittily obscene snakes and all the rest of the crafty tumblers kept on tempting. To resist temptation was easy and delightful; to have no temptations offering their various mouths was the deadly thing.

Still, now and then I joined in. I even went later for a few weeks to dance classes – when I came to give talks to the W.E.A. and some of my students asked me to attend. But I never managed to master the steps unless I thought hard about them all the time, and if one thought hard one couldn't dance pleasantly with another person. I consoled myself by saying that my sense of inner rhythm was too strong and complex, breaking up my weak attempts to move in submissive time. If I could dance a ballroom dance, I would cease to be a poet; I would become a musician – and my dances would be Dionysian.

Those early ragtime tunes burst brilliantly on the world of the second decade of the century, which was still clinging to Edwardian notions despite the assaults of the war. Childish little explosions in the dark of a great fear. The tawdry homesickness, the rhythms at once jejeune and novel, were exactly what I thought the world was: something galvanically twitching and smeared with saccharine of tears. The music gave me strength to resist its own blandishments. In its pretty brittle chords and thin concussions I saw the faces of the girls transfigured by the cheap cosmetics of the quack music. Their hearts of mass-produced metal turned and turning to the magnet of a kiss. Their bodies of suburban flowers caught on the unbuttoning moment of spring. In the new light of the music they all seemed blinded, looking for me through the impassive shirts or over the shoulders of their partners; but I was hidden behind the screen, hypnotizing them with my distant devotion. Only I saw past the socially adjusted face into the face of the kiss, I who would never kiss them. Only I knew the lift and lilt of the sweet syncopation in their limbs, after which the music limped, I who would never touch them. Now and then I turned and stared into the outer dark of the stars, which were precisely cut like many faceted diamonds, and saw the vanishing blur of a light frock in the bushes edging the football field; and the

music from the room was counterpointed with a faint pizzi-
cato, a moaning semitone, from the shelving night.

Until now I had never thought of the night-time except as
a period convenient for reading poetry or for wandering among
the trees of a river. True, there had been the few visits to the
cinema, but little else. (Among the last films I saw at this time
were *The Birth of a Nation* and *Intolerance*, films which profoundly affected me and had a considerable influence on the
way in which later I approached the historical novel – as I recognized when I saw them once again in the 1940s. But, finding
that my brothers had become real film fans, writing to stars
for photographs and talking about them at meals, I announced
that I should never set foot in a cinema again; and I kept my
word till I left Brisbane. My high moral tone however had no
effect at all on my brothers.)

The night events of the university had shown that one could
do other things after dusk than read, write and brood. I wanted
to enter a pub, but felt awkward without a companion. However, after much hesitation, I bought a ticket for the theatre
in Albert Street – I forget its name. The more imposing theatres
I avoided through a deep suspicion of anything gilded and an
economy forced on me by my lack of money. So I sensibly
missed the touring companies, the third-rate imported companies giving fifth-rate imported plays or musical comedies,
Instead, in Albert Street, I patronized local stock companies
putting out local melodrama.

The plays were close in blood to the Victorian English type,
crowded with top-hatted villains and blooming village-
innocents, blueblooded murderers and noble sons of labour.
But they were generally remoulded to Australian circumstance. The heroic miner or prospector, the bluff stockman, the
Chinese servant saying 'Velly-well' and finally unveiling the
plot of his clubman employer, were all important characters.
Once, when an irate father was raising his hand and shouting
at his wayward but good-at-heart son 'Never darken my doorstep again,' his celluloid cuff shot off and landed in the front
rows of the stalls.

Now it was no longer sufficient to read and to work over the given space of imagery and technique. A while back I had rewritten one of the Mabinogion tales in Spenserian stanzas, but never thought of comparing the result with Spenser or with other imitations of Spenser by Thomson, Keats and so on. Nor did I think of the result as 'my work'. The poem had been one aspect of my discovery of the region signposted Spenser *Faerie Queen*. A daydreaming aspect related to the activity of reading Spenser, but not detached into any consideration of good or bad, into competitive criticisms. I no more thought of getting it published than of getting the *Faerie Queen* published.

But the dialogue of Plato and the diatribe of Sassoon, the revolt against Mary and the war, had brought about a cleavage between my own writings and the broad continent of poetry. My experience assumed its own urgent value and significance, and because it was now sharply my own I felt the beginning of a need to communicate it to others. At once it was a foolish and trite deed to turn the Mabinogion into ambling stanzas or to write Wordsworthian lines on the discovery of the daisy. The medieval Welsh tale in the rewriting was no better than prettified dummies in the shopwindows; the daisy had not been discovered at all. I no longer had a title to contempt of the world.

Certain themes emerged as significant: morning noon and evening as the changes of my spirit; stars as my defiance nailed on the sky; sea and island, my senses beating in on myself and flowing out into the universal sun; light through bars and a flower opening; a valley with the spark of water in its cleft. And suddenly, imposed on all the images of nature, the thick and murderous street where the distorting lie and the naked truth walked side by side, where the beast strode in pinstriped trousers and the human lay in the gutter, where an invisible acid of cruelty and greed was corroding the faces.

A vast inchoate emotion tore at unrealized fetters which (in the throes of composition) became identified with the exigencies of metre and the weight of words – though the metric impulsions and the need to grasp the components of the word were at the core of my very desire to write.

'Star of the Morning fledged and shod with Fire': thus begins the interminable sonnet of Marlowe. The words are as dead as a doornail, without a simmer of fire or a quiver of wing tissues. I let my mind drift and scribble. *Star bar car mar far tar cigar starfledged windsedged blind-edged . . . the blind-edged wind is sedged with furry fire . . . starshod trod God on the thin floor of space.* Such lines pleased me, but I could never work them into my theme. *Star of the Morning scarred with scorn afar. The flirt of scorning squirted with the star out of the telescope of hairy light, my tattered betty on the fork of matter O spread your breasted mercy on the night.* All very well but nothing to do with Marlowe. The stars have scarred my face with penny blotches. I pulled the sounds down over my head with a sense of obscure revenge. *Gush lush fire mire lasht with shoddy lust.* The words irritate me and I tear the paper into little bits which I shove into a mouse-hole. The words are stale and flat or they break into wicked little fragments that know too much about me. Falling back into my navel of meditation, the fountain splashing level with the earth-hole, the misty glitter gone. Not a statue, however small and cock-eyed, left in my palm, but the damp sweat. Metronome invocations of wind-blown Venus.

Start again. *Starfledged with Morning, shod with rebel song.* Two *withs*: won't do. *Shod with the morning, fledged with daring song.* Ditto. Let the song dare, but how? *Out of the cloven dawn-cloud milk the fire.* That was better, but didn't seem Marlowe. Turn from Swinburne to the actual dawn over the housetops. *The insidious spread of light with glaucous fans.* That wasn't too bad, I must make a note of it for a different poem. The cloud-clash and the wings of jagged gold. *Out of the morning came the son of fire..* I saw Zenocrate on One Tree Hill, a fragile mask of gold with slitted eyes, and Marlowe god-shod with the morning skies . . . No, I wanted something different, but what? The bulls and bells of Babylon are babbling in bogs of blue and baffling-bellied betties. Crumple the paper and burn it slowly at the candle that runs with translucent gouts of lovely stinging grease.

Try again. *O mighty son of clapping morning-stars.* Leafglints of rustling glass and scalding tears. *Fledged with the rebel fires of Lucifer.* Loose a fur. Take out the star-pins from a velvet betty and let the scarlight drip. The sweating pores of night the mother poor. Blue hands in star-muffs of loose puffy lasses. You

fell from heaven, dislodging half the stars, in Southwark stews
you rose again and laughed. *The morning stars clapped hands and
you were born, scorn horn thorn morn shorn torn.*

Now it was midnight and I gave up. But next morning the
struggle began again. I got a flying start. Noon –

> *O perfect hour of outstretcht wings grown absolute,*
> *heraldic tree of truth, here in my heart take root. . .*

but then the words wandered again. I couldn't get rid of the
stars of last night. Crusted with stars the watery hull of night.
The pearl-encrusted skirt of Night the whore. Star-holes
phosphoric rotting with a glow. Star-bubbles rising in the well
of dark. Star-orris from the scented venus-toilet. Light-bells in
quivering towers of brittle glass. Daggering flick-holes flocking
thick and ugly. Aspen-quivering eternity, quickspit quackspots
tightly nightly aphrobaffledite. Out of the navel of the Rose,
Venus jumped without her clothes.

> *The gods are all abroad tonight*
> *in starry frills of muslin light.*

I had moved on to quite a different poem. Then that too got
stuck and suddenly Marlowe burst through the remnants of his
bloody sonnet.

> *I saw a King go reeling down the air*
> *through jagged space.*

But he went on falling falling. I could not bring him to earth.
All the same I was encouraged. The junk of stars, piled
together, would in time add up to a kiss-weight; the slithering
left and right would in time achieve the wing-symmetry of a
successful rhythm.

My aunt had inherited a pianola – I think after the death
of her father-in-law in Melbourne. To her annoyance I took
charge of the library list of available records and hungrily
marked off all those by Beethoven, Mozart, Wagner: my three
favourite musicians, of whose work I hadn't heard a note.
Among the first obtained were the *Appassionata* and the *Liebestod*. I heard them through a confused tumult of reactions like
a familiar voice emerging now and then from a storm of foreign

tongues. Then I set to work to control my impressions.
I did it by means of the pianola record itself. As I treadled,
the record unwound before my eyes, with the sounds trans-
posed into a shifting series of geometrical patterns. My strong
visual sense came to the rescue of my auditory chaos. First I
got a rough idea of what the main patterns were, picked out
the recurrent themes (shapes), saw how one related to another,
how they were spaced or linked. I then tried to find the unifying system, the structural connections within a single focus.
Whereas a gramophone would have set me insoluble problems,
the pianola gave me music in the mode most rapidly assimi-
lable. I was soon able to get a grasp of sonata form, of fugal
movement, of variation; within a few months I had organized
my impressions well enough to follow the development of form,
the emotional significance.

With Beethoven a new dimension opened in my life, in the
universe. All my imaginings up to this point were revealed as
trivial things. In the tremendous echoes all that I had learned
of poetry took on fresh sonorities. Here was the complete
Dionysia. The space of Plato was filled with such gay and furious colourations that it seemed to have been a faint grey and
spectral gold before these trumpets broke down all doors and
the violins filled the interstices between the stars with an endless coil and glint. With a single step this music could cross the
world; with one gasp, one pause, it could end the world; in the
void thus created it could summon life back and from a lonely
throb release the full unstaunchable flow as deep as history and
as broad as nature.

My aunt insisted that I couldn't possibly understand and
enjoy such music when I had no ear and no training. I once
again took refuge in a mute obstinacy.

Besides the melodramas I went to a large variety show on
the right hand side over the Bridge. Here I saw my first bits
of opera. Once a valiant attempt was made to give a potted
version of *Carmen*. There was a permanent group of artists for
the season, who often played the most varied roles. I liked the
sketches which had the air of being made up as they went along
– as indeed they doubtless were. But most of all I liked the
dancer.

A young girl well built with a rounded clearly modelled face and eyes of blue enamelled flower flame. She came on the stage as the answer to my Dionysian prayer. (I was always seated rather far back as I could afford only the cheapest seats.) Perhaps she really was a talented young dancer with some of the poetic feeling I attributed to her. Perhaps at this stage any comely young girl who could dance with a modicum of grace would have seemed one of the everdancing dryads whisked straight from an oakgrove on Ida. But however that may be, I felt in her the verification of my awe for the word *dance*. I hadn't been wrong in thinking that a dancer could revive all the buried years, all the snows of yesteryear and the girls of crumbled kisses, the giant red flowers of Babylon and the hyakinth of the Arkadian copse, Aphrodite the fountain of swaying milk and Artemis with long slender legs and ribs faintly showing under the scarcely risen breasts. Here was the point where poetry at last met earth in full union and the body was free.

I wrote many poems for her. The one I liked best described the music as her lover and her dance as the flight from the embrace which at last claims her.

> She steps into the limelight: the gold round
> of the stage-moon stares blankly. Wickedgay
> her dark eyes gleam and a soft silken sound
> spreads from the violins about her way.
>
> A flower become a flame is she:
> her eyes burn wide with ecstasy.
> The music like a nimble lover
> chases and races, leaping after,
> made her lost beauty to recover,
> casting bright chains of tangled laughter
> about her feet and many a snare
> of curving joy all round her there.
>
> She, thought already won, desires
> to bend through mazes till she tires,
> liking the exquisite quick fear
> of clutching fingers come so near.

At last the music turns and presses,
catches her up in its embrace,
folds every limb with bold caresses
and lifts to joy her haloed face.

The violins sink smoothly, strokingly,
like tremulous tendrils that in darkness go
seeking. Abandoned to her lover, she,
closed by invisible hands, leans backward slow.

When I had half a dozen poems that didn't seem too bad, I wrote her a long letter of admiration and enclosed them, without giving my address. I knew where she lived; for I had waited round the theatre to watch her emerge after the show, and had followed her back to the boarding-house where she stayed. In the street she always had her mother with her. I was glad of this obstacle that saved me from having to admit that I lacked the courage to approach her.

Slight as the verses to her were, they gave me at last a point of rest in actuality where I could begin to reassemble such powers as I owned.

About a year later I heard from a half-French lad M. that she had been very excited and thrilled at my letter and poems; and in 1924-25 I met her in Sydney. By that time she was doing turns at picture shows, a sort of between films variety extra. She was partnering a tall handsome fellow on the edge of running to seed. I went behind the scenes with J.R. who was playing the piano for the cinema. I told her that I'd enjoyed her dance (a feeble bit of phoney Egyptianism, postures with flat hands, meant to go with *The Ten Commandments*). She smiled uncomfortably, aware of the insincerity, and neither of us had anything more to say to one another. Certainly by that time her dancing was without distinction, and she herself had a washed out look. J.R. told me that he had mentioned I was the Brisbane poet, but neither of us referred to it.

15 · AN OATH

BLAKE NOW became real for me, suddenly moving to the centre of my being. Through him the elegant geometries of the platonic paradox, the threefold movement of the self and of nature, were filled out with richer stuffs of light and shadow, with all the passionate angers and protests that had been breeding in me. I found that a poet might harmonize his attack on the existing world with an enjoyment of man and nature, his acceptance of all-that-lives with a demand for total change. Thus the integrity of the ascetic rage could be preserved through the participations of action.

Blake brought immediacy of emotion and rarefied symbol together in a new texture of fusion; and the first effect was to strengthen my antagonism to the world. Pity, born of anger, became the organizing force; and yet by its place within an aesthetically realized universe, an accepted universe, it brought its own solvents. I saw the world as it is; therefore, saw it as symbol. Saw it in the unity of process, with past-present-future as one, saw what-might-be moulding what-is, what-is determined by what-was, in an involved revolving sphere that was simultaneously history, evolution, myself, life-and-death, and the eternal here-and-now.

The Platonic algebra of trifid change became the passionate transformation by the conflict of opposites. The *eidos*, the creative form in its pure ether, became the clear-edged definite image of multitudinous life. The abstraction, indistinguishable from all repressive positions, all deathly efforts to arrest the rich flow of man and nature, was the spectre whom I had always fought. Vagueness, indeterminate form, sentimentality and its lies, fear and its lies, all lies, were of the same coinage, the other

side of the abstraction. From the struggle of spectre and emanation emerged the self purged of all egoism and confusion.
Poetic activity was a ceaseless fight against empire, against
war, against all the cruelties and fears known as law and order,
against the satanic mills of exploitation, against the money
forces that deadened men into things. Jerusalem was the secure
position of this activity, vitalizing the self and redeeming the
earth. It necessitated by its very nature a true relation between
man and his fellows – that is, a relation from which all lies and
veils have been removed; and a common objective, a common
humanity, discovered. Out of an unending crucifixion, the
whole man proceeded, the poet, the lover, the revolutionary.

Not that the system came to me in a flash, with all its difficulties removed and its labels annotated. I began on the edition
of Yeats and Ellis, reacting at once to the indignant pity and
the libertarian demands, but confused by mystical interpretations. Gradually however, working from the lyrics and the
aphorisms, I got rid of much of the blurring lumber and saw
at least to some extent what was the detritus of the great poetic
upheavals, and what the upheavals themselves were.

Let me glance back at the distance traversed since I wrote the
Hymn to Diana. The poetic image, come up out of the bodily
and spiritual changes of puberty, had cut me off from the
world. The union with nature had isolated me from society.
Certain forces of fear and separation, operating domestically
for several years, had thus thrown me off my balance: in com-
pensation opening triumphal gates in stone and maidenhair
tunnels of valley light. The social relations were unexplored,
ignored.

Then the Platonic dialogue cut me in turn from the simple
passage rite and its *ekstasis* by making the experience a subject
of discourse, a matter of analysis. Thus I maintained my position under the pressure of increasing intellectualization, of
domestic and social disturbances which I did not want to
realize as part of the emotional situation. The conflict was
rationalized in the new high terms. An immaculate asphodel
sun sent its beams over my belittled earth, but I had found the

eidos as a principle of the unity of process, an explanation of the heart of self-sufficient life beating in the poetic image once it had been detached into the completed work of art.

But the effort to evade the conflict all around and inside me soon reached a point of intolerable tension. There was a break, a leap. Blake brought into a single focus the platonic heaven and the wild earth of poetry. The conflict which the ideas, the experience, of mechanism and pollution had introduced into poetry was thus finding its first large objectification, its first attempted resolution.

Experience was no longer the breathless hush of an immediate union; no longer the dimensionless rapture, the apotheosis inside a jewel. Its transcendencies were not beyond nature; they were thrusts of necessary creation. Their structure was not the graph of a glancing blow struck at an impenetrable sphere; within it there strained a wrestling and a mating, a dying and a birth, a rhythm by which both earth and spirit were shaped, released, realized. The image was not the goddess doll in the adoring hand; it was the organic pattern of the fountaining body. And the body was at every point inside both society and nature.

The mask melted into the face, into a multiplicity of faces. Every face passing in the street, seen through the dark pane of a moment: in the beams of the blossom, beautiful and pitiful. I was a part of it all, it was all a part of me, every restless hand, quick in the net of the leaves or hanging dead in the shop windows, every whisper in the enormous bed of the night. All men were cut into half; and to build the wholeness of the image the poet must fight that deadly force in men and in himself which clove life in half, in fragments. A fragment was a thing. Man must be alive; man must not be fragmentary.

I had regained nature, but now nature was not enough. Not enough the desert of inspired birds and the waters of rebirth. Communion had been won, but not communication. Athens was only an after-image of the rock in the rolling waters reflected in Shelley's mirror, the slanted shadows of the white afternoon. Athens had to become Brisbane in order to be Jerusalem.

One way in which I interpreted these positions was to make an irreconcilable opposition of poetry and money. Poetry stood for freedom, for all that sought to build the wholeness of man, the regained unity with nature and the brotherhood opposed to a society of repression and fragmentation. Money stood for enslavement, for all that sought to cut men into halves and to estrange them from nature, from themselves and their fellows. Money was the obvious and vile emblem of the forces turning men into things, the free and organic changes and chances of life into the compulsions of the market.

Though my application of these ideas has varied, I have never since that moment receded from the position I had reached. But my application then was one of severe simplicity.

Only in love, poetry and revolt was there freedom. The outer world in all aspects not directly related to this freedom was identified with mechanism. The idea of a remorseless machine represented the world which denied or ignored love, poetry, revolt. Mechanism of any kind and money were seen as different aspects of the same enslavement. All habitual acceptances, associations and directions were implicated in it.

There was however a point where the opposed forces met and could no longer maintain an irreconcilable hostility. The body, which revealed the principle of mechanism, going on unconsciously with its decomposition and rebuilding, its complex blind necessary life; and which was also the source of all organic energy and ecstasy. The principles of freedom and necessity were indeed most hopelessly and happily entangled in the intensest moments of bodily life, in sex. Beauty in the genitals, said Blake. But here too was a blind mechanism, with the deepest pressures of fear and pollution. The cave of rotten death and the new man rising up in acclamation of all that lives as holy. The embraced girl, releasing the lover from the hell of separateness, became otherness at the moment of penetrating union, an instrument of pleasure and not the absorbed and absorbing universe.

I have mentioned my decision that I must not fall ill, since illness reduced the bodily life to deranged mechanism, left the spiritual life at its mercy. And sexual emotion, gathering the onanistic fears of castration and the Dionysiac releases of union with all life, seemed to concentrate endlessly the conflict of death and life, mechanism and organism.*

Because of the deep-locked conflict, sketched above, in the sexual life, poetry enclosed both the forbidden and the hidden, the defiant and the naked. It expressed by its very nature the anxiety and the ecstasy which people in their everyday lives spent their whole time in ignoring, denying, attacking.

One afternoon of mealy summer light I took the oath. It arose out of a meeting with a chap whom I had known at the prep school. I met him at my aunt's place, where he had come with his mother. He was going to take up a position at Dalgety's, the big wool firm, where his father had some interest. My aunt was spreading herself about my brilliant scholastic career; perhaps to keep his end up and stress his own importance, he suggested that I should go into the firm with him. His father, he assured me, would find me a starting job which would soon be made a quite good one. The only way to make a decent income was to enter one of the big businesses with the right backing. He flattered me by assuming that we both belonged to the ruling class – or that I might so belong by accepting the right patronage. To get in well with the wool interest was to be among the Australian elect.

For the first time I was directly confronted with the issue of a job. True, my aunt often talked of my academic future, as she talked that afternoon; but such talk did not evoke any defi-

---

*What all these ideas and formulations omitted was the existence and nature of productive activity, where again both the pressures of repression, estrangement and enslavement, and those of creative energy and free development, met in their clearest form. It will be seen that I subsumed this activity inside that of sex and so lacked a sense of the full relations that would have prevented my isolation of the sexual life. I brought estrangement into the very core of my image and idea of organic wholeness. But it was to be long before I understood this failure; indeed the story of that understanding lies outside the compass of this book. Therefore, I hope that what I say here in this note will be kept in mind, so that I need not repeat it at every new turn of the quest I describe.

nite picture or pose me with the decision of accepting a role in the existing system of things. It merely suggested an indefinite study of Latin and Greek. Any further problems that it might raise could be tackled when they arose. But the urgings of this lad, whose name I have forgotten, but not his clear false voice, drove me from my covert. A vague gesture of disdain and disquiet would not suffice. The lad's flattering and urbane words, whether or not seriously meant, remained with me for days, like the chuckles of a devil skulking round an anchorite's cell with a delicious sulphurous smell of pomp and lust.

I suppose the anchorite was merely irritated by the devil's smugness and angrily ashamed at the high opinion that devilesses had of their anatomy. Certainly the lure of Dalgety gold did not tempt me in the least; it merely annoyed me with the need to put into formal terms the decision long past taken irrevocably in the silent depths. But it did also provide a certain relief – as when the forcing of an enemy into the open makes him expose the extreme weakness of his resources.

Crossing in the Kangaroo Point ferry, I looked across the dim sliding waters and saw the big building of successful sin. I won't ever compromise with the world of money, I told myself. I won't ever have anything to do with the buying and selling of commodities, not even if I die for it. I'll be a poet, and if that doesn't keep me somehow alive, to hell with the earth.

I searched in my pockets for the old envelope which was my usual composing sheet – as if I meant to dispatch my poems to some other world or to some address in antiquity. And I wrote some lines which though slight have remained imprinted on my memory.

> They have taken the beautiful woman and cropped off her young bright hair.
> They have broken the thews of Apollo with a dark and bitter snare.
> Their word is the fear in the darkness, they move with a smell of decay, and all that on earth is most lovely turns loathliest under their sway.
> And this is the world they have builded, the world where alone I roam with a statue only friended, with only a song for home.
> And this is the world I am bidden to accept and build more

> *secure, or starve. But an oath I have taken, and come what*
> *may come, I'll endure.*

The first line states the revulsion I was undergoing from Christianity and St Francis: it refers to the saint's cropping of Clare's locks. This revulsion appears also in the metrical reminiscence of Swinburne: Thou has conquered, O pale Galilean . . . My attitude to religion kept wavering as I regarded it as the accomplice of the money ethic or its enemy.

I carried the envelope, with the poems blurring dirtily, in my pocket for a long time: in my aunt's presence or in the streets of shops, feeling like the hero in a folk tale who carries a talisman through witch haunts and devil thickets.

16 · WANDERINGS
AND DISCOVERIES

THE SHARP emergence of the guilt sense drove me back to Shakespeare and started me off on the Russian novelists – my first serious attempt (apart from enjoying Dickens) to read prose. I read every Russian novel I could lay hands on, from Gogol and Pushkin to Bunin and Sologub, except Tolstoy who repelled me with his mixed naturalism of method, his hard variously disguised egoism which I vaguely felt was based in a terror of death. Dostoevsky it was who hit me in the red of my heart; and through him and Blake I began to understand Shakespeare for the first time. For years I had been steadily reading the latter, getting from him what I was getting at each stage from other poets. Craggy exultation or sweep of movement, mythological compendium or gay company of folk alive to the tingling fingertips or mysterious space of hooded figures. Now at last I began to penetrate simply the poetic meaning, the revelation of the human condition.

Still, it was Dostoevsky who came home with the direct impact out of the very streets of my anger and hope, explaining my own evil. The problem of the war in itself gave way to the problem of what underlay the war. I began to understand more deeply my oath, to see why I shrank from the unions and compacts which others so easily accepted. My poetic conscience had made me shudder away from all compromises, all bargaining; my aesthetic of nakedness had made it impossible to accept a morality of veils, evasions, lies (the whole of contemporary ethics and politics which had come into my view); where I smelt shame, I smelt bad art; and the correlative of bad art was a tyrannous society. Now I saw how all the things I detested were gathered in the forces that produced the split man, the half man who was the normal citizen of my world. Dostoevsky depicted the everyday actuality of the state of being which Blake had anatomized and defined in myth, aphorism, and lyrical denunciation.

I found myself in Raskolnikov, my other self, my anti-self. If one accepted a world where the dominant values were egoism and the preying of man on man, then the only way to be in harmony with the world was to commit murder – the simple reality behind the abstract commercial terms and the assertion of will against will. In Raskolnikov the impulse to the truth drives on to the act; having committed the act, he finds that he has joined himself with all that he most hates and fears and that the only solution is a rejection as total and uncompromising as his effort of union had been.

The Idiot gave me back my fool-self transfigured; *The Brothers Karamazov* set out the drama of the sons united against the tyrannous father, yet torn by the division inescapable in a world where such a father image determines revolt and renunciation, hate and love, rejection and acceptance.

I do not mean that the readings of these novels brought me level at a leap with the things I feared; that they educed a clear working-out of all that I had sought to keep sealed up in a dream. What happened was that the pattern of their revelation impacted on the lines of my interlocked conflict, partly hidden, partly stirring in my thoughts. The submerged conflict heaved and began breaking loose, emerging into consciousness. Years would have to pass before the full effects were apparent; but the deep liberating blow had been given.

And the intolerable strain inside Shakespeare's work began revealing itself in all its universality and its particular immediacy: the tragic and comedic pattern that reached from Dionysiac initiation ritual to unguessed at levels of development in the human future, but also the face of the clown and shrewd businessman, the tallowdip light and the restless hand of composition, the suffering pride, and the bitter integrity, the steadfast eye and the unfaltering gaiety. Though it was long here too before I dared to face more than a brief moment of that titanic struggle in its overwhelming truth.

My aunt decided to build at the side of her present place. As a preparation, she cut her house into half and let one half. I disliked the plan, which dismembered a charming house (old for Brisbane) and robbed me of the tennis court. The new house was to be built on what had been a garden with trees, and I hated this crushing of a new concrete structure into the space, destroying the whole dignity of the setting. I had a feeling that Mary had developed the unsettling scheme as an emotional retort to Jack, who had rebelled strongly enough to leave his position in public health and to take up direction of quarantine – a job that gave him much movement on water and involved a yearly trip to Darwin.

J. sometimes drove his wife frantic at the dinner-table by unloading on to the guests various tall stories which he had read or heard. He made himself the chief character and went on undeterred by acidulous comments, kicks under the table, or the ringing of the bell for the next course. Not that Mary entertained much. Generous in many ways, she was parsimonious with people outside the family; and she was delighted with a notice I painted for her, directing visitors to the back half of the house where she now lived. This notice had some addition in Greek asking the guests to come without their stomachs.

I had used the tennis court but little, though with one or two attempts at parties at my aunt's goadings. One result was that I was asked out myself and became a member of a group known as Starry's (from M. Starr the main vivacious character in it, a blonde with a pointed chin). But I still couldn't dance. I did my best to attach myself to G., an excellent clowner, who played the Shakespearean fool in the dramatic society's productions. At the commemoration festivities I sat jolted on one of the wagons through the town, among the fancy-dressers, or collected money from the pavement crowd. There were tableaux devised by G. making fun of local politics and the university dignitaries; and that night he led us in an assault on the picture show near the Bridge. Perhaps we all of us merely decided to get in at the same time. Anyway the police turned up in force and tried to drive us away so that there was shoving and shouting and frays for some hours. At last the police tried to arrest everyone; they drew batons and charged. I was near the bank at the corner of George Street when a policeman made for me. For some reason (I can hardly think it was presence of mind) I took out my handkerchief and started calmly blowing my nose. The disconcerted policeman swerved off with his baton after someone dancing in a cap of streamers across the road. I promptly went off in the other direction, discarding the various remnants of my clown disguises, and deviously reached home. After that I decided it was both costly and unrewarding to spend all one's spare cash on crême de menthe, and I took to beer.

I was completing my training as a cadet at a depot since I could no longer belong to the school corps. One afternoon as the roll-call was being called, the sergeant came to *Christ, J.* – presumably the son of some German immigrant. There was no reply; then someone shouted, 'Not present!' and the whole company burst into yells of laughter. A truly Australian episode, expressing the almost total lack of religious resonances in the social scene, an aspect of the diminution of feudal elements in the economy.

But I had at last acquired a friend A.B.G., come from Melbourne University, to censor letters in Russian. He had to leave at the end of the year to continue his work in philosophy and Mary had planned my taking-over of his job. She introduced him and I felt no objections to learning Russian from him, though I had no intention of doing any censoring. For one thing, while trying to master printed Russian, I gave up the ghost at once before the angular scrawl of the written language; and so I should not have been able to censor any letters even if I had not rejected the job with every fibre of my being. (Brisbane at this time was thick with emigrant Russians come via Vladivostok.)

A. was the first person at all near my own age with really wide reading whom I had met. Not that he shared my poetic fanaticism. But we could at least find some elements of a common idiom and got on well together. He was patient in helping me to read Pushkin and Lermontov. His mind was clear dry decisive, opposed to my intuitive discursiveness: which enabled us to argue amiably, but not to meet closely. I was not surprised when some half a dozen years later I saw that he had published a book on Descartes.

With him I went to several public meetings. Later I realized that we attended to see if sedition was talked; but at the time I did not question or probe the reasons for our attendances. Now for the first time I heard discussions on socialism, but I was so little prepared for such a theme that much of what was said went in one ear and out the other. Still, I can recall being intellectually stirred by a sharp discussion on the social basis of value, the socially necessary time embodied in objects, and the non-typical nature, say, of sponges washed up on a shore, undived for.

My brother and our cousins now and then still combined to compose and stage plays. Once, with A., I agreed to act as manager: I think it was the last large-scale attempt at these home theatricals. The actors sketched out the play beforehand and then extemporized before the audience. Ray, with huge walrus moustaches, enacted the thundering villain while Molly in her best frock was the prim village maiden. Phil was the rollicking bumpkin with George Robey eyebrows and Nancy the good heart who put all to rights. The four of them had continually to put on different hats and appear in new roles. The drunken rustic, combing his hair, assumed a buttonhole and swaggered on as the hero; the village maiden, rubbing two big spots of rouge on her cheeks, became a wicked lady. Alex sang some Russian songs, inaudibly aided by myself, in a high-pitched voice as a comic turn.

The results of the first year's examination came out. I was marked A except in logic and psychology, where I failed. Proud in knowledge of books like *Biographia Literaria*, Boyle's *Sceptical Chemist*, Bergson's *Time and Free Will* – of philosophers like Plato and Spinoza – I had taken no notice of the lectures, which seemed dull and unimportant. As a result I couldn't answer a single question. The types of syllogism I had forgotten, and I felt sure I must be reading the wrong paper when under psychology I found: 'Describe the organ of Corti.' I thought it was a musical instrument. There seemed no logic in the logic paper, no psychology in the psychology, though I took advantage of some allusion in one of the papers (can it have been the logic?) to write an account of the very latest treatment for tapeworm, having recently heard that theme discussed by my uncle and an American working under the Rockefeller Institute. (The other theme elaborated by the American, that of pumpkin pie, I could not work in.) So, during the vacation, I had to swot at syllogisms and physiology, and scraped through in a second exam.

The war had ended. Fireworks on the water. We of the Starry group lay on a high lawn overlooking the turn of the river that led on to the Botanical Gardens. Starry had nicknamed me Plato by some odd insight, and as Plato I found a minor fool-place in the gaddings of the group. G. was there too, the great fool, the reckless japer with rasping voice and coarse granitic Jewish face. He and I had decided to enlist after Christmas if there was still a war. Since I was now flatly hostile to the war, it may seem illogical that I had decided to enlist. But I had no intention of fighting; I was merely carrying out, as I have ever since carried out, the policy of taking the most difficult way out, the line of most resistance. I was going into the army because no other way seemed to enable me to face the ghosts of the murdered and to protest against my aunt's behaviour: the patriotic front and the private wangling. That some organized effort could be made to stop the war was still far from my thoughts. I felt only the emotional need for expiation and self-sacrifice.

But the war had ended and G. was kissing a girl nearby. I had no one to hold. It was enough, however, to be accepted into a group that were merry, scornful, with their own code of honour and laughter. Enough to lie among the musing girls on the high lawn, looking down on the sprays of fire, the exploding stars, the blazons of gold and the whining rockets. Down in the waters another celebration was going on, a blurred tangle of fiery reflections. The river still flowed, mixing its patches of dully oily silver with the sharp gold; everything flowed. Under the waters the dead were holding their ironic celebrations; and I felt myself suspended in a cradle of extreme contradictions, loyal to the dead, the murdered young men my brothers, and loyal to the living, the quiet girls in their bright blouses that smouldered through the dusk of flowers, and G.

the mocking fool who held nothing sacred. The bells rang on into my sleep.

Several of the Starry group, including some of my fellows in the classics course, were going to a camp held in Victoria by the Students Christian Association. On being assured that several weren't members of the S.C.A. and that one didn't need to profess any creed, I decided to join them. The camp would give me a chance to look at the coast near Lorne and get at least as near as Geelong to the Ballarat area from which Norman had come. Also, it would enable me to spend a week with Alex and his family, whose summer holidays were being spent on the coast not far from the camp.

There were about a dozen in the party, with a couple of thousand miles to cover. We arrived three days later at the camp, crushed, dusty, bonesore, still chattering. It had been bitterly cold during the night of our departure when the train began to climb; and we all piled on top of one another, exquisitely uncomfortable and ignoring the shouts every now and then of some small farmer or railway gang along the track, 'Newspaper!' Besides, we had long past thrown out all our papers to the news-hungry backblockers. Gulping large cups of black railway-tea at Wallangarra as we changed trains and rushed for forgotten parcels. Stared on the broad cornlands of the Darling Downs; crossed the Namoi in its upper stretches and steamed into Tamworth; turned to the coast at Werris Creek and came across the ranges to Newcastle with its blackened works, and at last reached Sydney, where we scrambled round a few moments and went on again, eating ever staler sandwiches, intimate and irritable, dozing and hot-eyed. I wrote a parody of a sonnet by Brooke: 'Opposite me two lovers sweat and paw,' which was passed round with much acclaim among all but the lovers – though they finally read it themselves on the notice-board of the camp, where some admirer pinned it. And then, as we were rushing to make the connection at Melbourne I picked up a ten-shilling note on the platform, a good omen of something or other.

The camp was pleasant, amid bush and fir trees on the coast. We slept in tents and ate communally, and the only event I attended apart from concerts was a discussion group led by a mild clergyman who chatted with me about Virgil. I wrote more verses of circumstance and flytings, which were passed round or stuck on the notice-board. Verse, if kept at a level of low intensity, had a social value, a ceremonial virtue, in a communal group. The common interest was factitious and temporary. What, it struck me, if the bond went deeper? Would poetry in its deeper aspects then find a place?

The pair on whom I had written my first successful jeu d'esprit consisted of a tall handsome athletic Christian (the only one of our group who had gone to the camp for other than holidaying reasons) and a small dainty stepping girl with a hint of perishable gold. The girl was kind-hearted and so did not discourage my attentions as the more imperious lovelies did. Once I walked from the university to the station with her, carrying her suitcase; and the wretched thing burst open in the middle of the main street, amid clanging trams. I dived about, rescuing underclothes and combs and such things. Once too, I even had enough money to ask her to afternoon tea at the cafe in the Gardens – the first time I ever asked anyone to such an expensive event. It cost me 2s.1d., and I grudged the money that could have bought a couple of books. I had a scholarship grant of £26 a year, out of which came my clothes.

I spent a week with the B.Gs. One of the younger brothers had an effective gift of fantasy: I recall tales of eccentric angels and tigers on a visit, that came out at breakfast. The mother was a sensible sensitive person holding everything together with a myriad strings of warm understanding; I have since heard that she perished in a house fire. Once we all went for a long walk, during which my bladder almost burst but I was too shy to ask for a halt and withdraw behind one of the meagre trees. Particularly as a girl, also a guest, had glued herself to my side with an earnest conversation that went on for hours, about the terrible dangers of Bolshevism breaking out in Germany. Russia, left to its incompetent self, would certainly collapse; but if the Germans too rose for socialism, there would be a real danger to civilization. The subject interested me, though I had no clear ideas on it beyond a strong sympathy for the Russians as for anyone whom the newspapers and my aunt attacked. Also, I knew vaguely that the Russians had declared for peace as well as socialism when they broke away. From the meetings that I had attended with A. I had taken away at least a sense of seething ideas and indignations among the working class – though the very idea *working class* was strange to me; it seemed an abstraction, which I was ashamed to use, and at the same time an unknown dimension, into which I was afraid to cross. My idea of *workers* (as distinct from that of individuals who did work of various kinds) was mainly derived from my aunt, the only person I knew who used the term; for her workers were lazy, grasping creatures who formed associations called trade unions to tyrannize over their betters and keep themselves in a regimented state of doing as little as possible for as much as possible. As the objects of her enmity they filled me with a lot of fellow feeling, but they still remained vaguely outside my direct experience. Now, however, I began to feel that they had a real and urgent existence and meaning, which made them my allies in an adventure still nebulous and incredible, yet fiercely necessary.

I wanted to grapple with the girl's arguments; but my physical obsession made it impossible to do more than grunt a few assents or dissents. Still, as I knew so little of the subject, perhaps those grunts were as valuable an intellectual contribution as my full powers of speech would have made. The important thing was the girl had evoked for the first time in my head the image of revolution, had convinced me that we lived in a revolutionary epoch, had communicated her fears to me as exciting possibilities.

Arriving on my own in Melbourne, I wandered round and wondered where to put up. Finally I went into a hostel of the Salvation Army for men only – because it was near the station, because it was the only building that seemed to be asking me in, because after the Christian camp the Salvation Army seemed my natural home. I was given a poky room and left with the new enormous problem of finding what to do with myself in a strange city.

What I did was to spend hours in the bookshops, preferably the second-hand ones, with periods along the riverside or in the

Fitzroy Gardens. My purchases included some thirty volumes of eighteenth-century drama, fortunately small in size. (My uncle had donated a few pounds; I had saved a little out of my scholarship allowance; my grandmother had dug into her jetfringed purse. Never had I had so much money in my pocket. At night I put it under my pillow, and one morning I forgot all about it, then rushed back after breakfast to find that the bed was already made and the maid had put the money carefully on the wash stand.)

For the first time in my life I felt boredom. In Brisbane, however much at loose ends, I had all sorts of routines of action or reading to drift through. Now I felt a sheer blankness, a chilly isolation from the world about me. In the day it was unpleasant, but tolerable; the nights were infernal. Yet I stayed on, feeling that something would happen, somebody stop and speak, some spot somehow glow with the burning bush of revelation in this my natal city.

I walked the streets, looked in shop windows, leaned against a lamp-post. And watched people. The idea of a cinema or pub did not enter my mind. I watched and waited. For the first time I savoured the deadly glamour of the modern city, the deliberate place of estrangement, the populous desert of loneliness. The changing maze of lights caught in a hole of horse urine opalescent with spilt petrol, the slouch of involving shadows, the slits of alien intent eyes, the scuffle of flat shapes behind the pink curtain, the poster harlots winking at the taxis, the accordion wheeze from a hidden attic, the swinging faces momently seen in a brutish glow beyond the pub door, the bird bright chatter of passing girls (jingling like keys to the door of the unknown), the incessant hurrying of gnatlike purposes in a darkness like some huge wound. Or the dank gloom empty except for rat-scattered garbage in a side-street, a furtive cat stalking the starved moon on a brickwall with jagged glass, a face suddenly haloed by a cigarette puff. The Baudelairean city of self-alienation. The puffy face of a whore like something dead stung back into life by the insatiable snake of sin, the withered hand of a beggar stretched from the coffining shadows, the morgues of the shop windows in which imbecile dummies wooed the wan-eyed living into the money-snares.

Something infinitely horrible, edged with a callous hypnotic fascination: a skein of incalculable possibilities, unravelled by mean malices and abruptly ending in nothing, like a penny that rolled down a sewer grating.

So this was the world. Seen in its obvious truth once the blinkers of habit and customary protection were removed. The world that poetry must reveal and redeem.

Then, more scared than spelled, I tore myself away. My baggage was weighted with books, with more books tied on by uncertain bits of string. I was glad at lodging so near the station. After one more visit to the rambling book arcade where I knew from my uncle that Norman had found his great loves twenty years before – Rabelais and Theocritos, Villon and Petronius – I set out for Sydney. I intended to stay there at least a week. Though I never read newspapers, I gathered from overheard conversations that there was an epidemic, Spanish influenza, sweeping the world, and that it had reached Australia. I decided not to bother; but on reaching Sydney I tried a couple of hotels, found them full, and learned that there was the probability of state borders soon being closed. After a cheap meal of buns in the Domain and a rapid glance at the endless Victorian anecdotes painted in the Art Gallery, I suddenly lost heart and yearned for Brisbane. I went to the station and took the next train. It was the last train over the Queensland border before quarantine restrictions came into action.

My uncle J. had just come back from his yearly trip to Darwin. Part of the way back he had taken over medical control of a ship where half the crew were down with the new plague. They had just managed to make Brisbane. He could do that sort of thing angrily, efficiently, modestly. It was only when his daydreams were provoked that he bragged.

My own reaction to the general panic was to ignore it. Here, I told myself, is my first test. If I feel or show the least concern, I'll never be able to look Keats or Shelley in the eye again. Everyone went round wearing muslin masks impregnated against infection. I refused to wear one and took up the job of canvassing advertisements for the university magazine which I was to edit for the coming year and which was sinking under financial difficulties.

The influenza killed my grandmother – by stirring up
malarial germs which had survived in her system from an early
illness. My aunt had too much sense to involve any of us in
the funeral. Mrs Parkinson's end was rather a disappearance
than a death. One more of the ties still holding my mother to
life had been broken. I regretted, without strong feeling, the
loss of someone who had a fine store of proverbs and folk songs,
but who had surrendered all responsibility for the world since
her husband's death.

In my canvasses I acquired a new friend. At an optician's
shop near the G.P.O. I saw on the wall what seemed at a glance
one of Norman's pen-and-inks. A second look showed it a
painstaking copy. I mentioned it to the optician, who had a
foreign accent, and he said it was his son's work. The son was
called in and I was asked to visit the family.

The optician was a Frenchman by birth, with a passion for
romantic music. Through him I heard the music of Berlioz and
Meyerbeer. Sometimes he played a whole opera through on the
piano, growing more and more excited, singing bits of all the
parts, hopping about on the stool, and finally, turning a page
of the score so furiously as to hurl the book across the room.
The hurling always occurred when he played the part about
the massacre in *Les Huguenots*.

His son Maurice was a talented lad, capable of everything
except originality. He could draw and play and write in the
style of anyone he admired, and only a close scrutiny showed
up the hesitations of the copying hand. I enjoyed his household. Here at last were people who in their own way were preoccupied with art matters. During a weekend spent at their
seaside bungalow (with a puncture on the way) they gave me
my first glass of wine. I drank two large tumblers and then
under benevolent eyes went out to vomit under the peppercorn
trees.

The separation between my parents now issued in a divorce.
I went down with my mother to Sydney to look after her while
she gave some evidence and saw a solicitor about the alimony.
She hated the whole thing and sank into dire depression. I too
was unhappy in a dull sort of way. However, I met Bertram

Stevens, grey-faced owl-eyed and kindly, an untalented critic of some importance in Australian letters; he had published a damnably dull anthology of Australian verse, which had been taken seriously; he and Sydney Ure Smith, at Norman's suggestion, were founding *Art in Australia*, which was to become an art magazine of considerable authority. At his house I met Leon Gellert, who had just published a successful book of war poems, a fine-featured chap with a lightweight boxer's physique and a nervous tensity of emotion. Norman had illustrated his war book and was going to issue a limited edition with etchings of a long poem, *The Isle of San*, which Leon had written up at Springwood, Norman's place in the Blue Mountains.

About this time George Robertson, the publisher, at B.S.'s hint, sent me a copy of N.L.'s collected pen-and-inks. Here were the early drawings with influences from Dürer and the pre-Raphaelites; the tumbling exuberance of the bacchanals (as Rubens breaks in); the great concentrated power of the anti-Christian manifestos – all plastic in richly built-up tones – then the Petronian pictures with their gay quotidian impact, in which a directly laid-on line, gathering tone and design both in a single virtuoso sweep, is used; the Villon tributes with their gallows-shadowed earthiness; the flowing decorative charm of the final work. At the very lowest valuation here was a skill with the pen that has never been approached. The pictures which touched me on the quick were those in which a philosophic judgement was made: *Pollice Verso* posing the Roman world against the lonely emaciated Christ or *The Crucified Venus* in which the various sects nail a naked woman on the cross.

My reaction was a sharp entanglement of delight and revulsion. I, the disciple of Blake, could not but accept with acclamation the defence of the life values, the yes to the pride and lust of life. But I had now carried my Blakean forgiveness and anger into a Dostoevskian guilt; both attitudes demanded an uncompromising sympathy with the suffering sources of life. Just as I was nearing a fusion of pride and pity, of selfhood in a flame of fire and absolute readiness for self-sacrifice, here came *Pollice Verso* which insisted on setting pride and pity at loggerheads. I was for both the Roman acceptance of earth and the redemption of life from its crucifying greeds and egoisms

– though I was against the Christian church and the Roman state alike. Now I was being asked to choose where I thought the problem of choice was over.*

I could give, it seemed, an easier assent to *The Crucified Venus*; but my divided response awoke here too. To Blake's repudiation of organized religion I could agree without second thoughts; but I felt that one could not properly attack the dark forces that denied life and muddied the spring of sex, unless one also attacked everything that confused and distorted one's sympathy with *all* the victims, with broken Christ as with defiled Venus. Simply, who could this sacrificed woman (drawn in 1912) be but my own mother, whom Norman had cast aside, whose potentialities he had never tried to develop? There must be a flaw in this philosophy of life if the free expression of one's own needs involved an encroachment on the very springs of another life.

So, despite a powerful response to certain aspects of the pictures, I felt that they broke away from the synthesis I was trying to achieve. It seemed that the impure will was confounded with the pure desire, the Roman state and its gladiatorial cruelties with the tragic gaiety of a Catullus.

I sat for hours, repelled and absorbed. Then I was swayed towards admiration, reacting against my aunt's comments. 'Of course he's got a wonderful skill, but it's really all immoral. You know I'm not a prude. I'm the last person to deny that sex can be a beautiful thing, but it should be kept private, inside marriage. This flaunting of it in the public's face is unbalanced, ugly. Norman's not the least like it himself. I always used to tell him so. It's just a sort of showing-off. He's never grown up. We all know that a rose needs manure, but that's no reason for putting the manure instead of the rose on your drawing-room table.'

*I had already been moved by some drawings in old copies of *The Lone Hand* which Mary had – illustrations to a passage from the Apocrypha and to Malory. But these had raised no particular problems in my mind, though they must have stirred the wish to meet the father again. (Now when I look at *Pollice Verso* I see an ambivalence such as I had felt in *The Rejected*; but at this moment it was the Roman rejection of the Christ which hit hard.)

After an hour of that sort of talk I began to feel that Norman must be more right than I had felt. Perhaps he was right to concentrate on attacking the lie of shame and secrecy.

My mother was going through her last revival of interest in things. She had a lump sum of money as part of the divorce settlement and decided that all she really wanted was a nice house of her own. She found a small weatherboard house on Kangaroo Point, almost opposite the Women's College. For weeks she went round looking at furniture and choosing things. Sometimes she asked me to go with her, and I went, though I wasn't interested. She was as light-hearted and hopeful as a girl waiting for her marriage day.

But as soon as we were in the house and the furniture was installed, she didn't like any of it at all. She saw only the drab routine of sweeping and washing and sausage and mash, which she had stupidly brought down once more on herself. She grew more bleakly depressed than ever.

17 · VERY HEAVEN

PROFESSOR P., my uncle's friend, who had gone camping with us several times, enlisted in the artillery half way through the war; and his wife, a fragile-bodied keen-brained woman of German birth, suffered badly during his absence. I became friendly with her and often used to visit her house in one of the far suburbs. We talked of poetry and I learned many things from her fastidious intellect, which had a clear sense of what was shoddy or false. At times I came near to telling her of the other things that now lay close to my heart: my repudiation of the war and my sense of a radical wrong in our society, my confused efforts to make out what were the consequences for poetry. But though I hesitated on the edge of utterances, I never came to it. We discussed some of the side issues. I could not approach the core of the question because it was still a burning chaos in my mind, not yet cooled into definite words. I knew that I must further live out my thoughts, follow the line of their zig-zag movement, before I could speak them.

She introduced me to Witherby, who was in charge of the Workers Educational Association, recommending me for a course of lectures on English literature that needed someone to take them. I was scared of lecturing, which I had no idea how to tackle, but did not resist. Witherby gave me the job and also his queer friendship. I went often to his house and soon to his hut on the Tambourine Mountains.

It would be hard to define why he had such a powerful effect on me, for he did not express many ideas. Yet even by his silences, by his capacity to give a direction to a conversation through small and almost imperceptible suggestions, he brought my own ideas out. He had the teacher's gift, the gift of awakening interest and ensuring that enthusiasms did not fruitlessly exhaust themselves, of developing another's thoughts without seeming to do more than throw in a few passing comments. At least that was the effect he had on me. A tall greyish man, with a touch of gauntness, he quietly conveyed a character of mingled energy and repose, of mild and yet obstinate integrity. It was this questioning and assured air about him, of a man whose mind was open and whose opinions were ready to take new shapes from the impact of life, and who yet rested unshakeably on certain clear beliefs in human dignity and freedom – this it was that made his personality both gentle and provocative, encouraging and stimulating.

Though a clergyman, he never mentioned religion to me; and when I showed any survivals of my phase of ascetic disciplines, he murmured something about how terrible such obsessions were. I soon heard all sorts of tales about his eccentricities, which were mostly true even if a little exaggerated. He had a foible of liking to shock any highly respectable and pious company, and could not resist using the basic Australian adjective *bloody* at the Bishop's table – asking in his extremely aristocratic accents, made even more drawlingly polished for the occasion, 'Will you please pass me the bloody-ay jam?' Once, bored at a meal with two women in a restaurant, he got under the table and started reading. He just did what occurred to him as the most sensible and pleasant thing to do, and with a courteous smile ignored all conventions.

Soon after I came to know him, he spoke at a public meeting organized by some supporters of the Russian revolution, and I was astonished to find how powerfully and passionately the smilingly aloof English gentleman could express himself. After defending the revolution as the achievement at last of a truly human society, he declared, 'I believe in Lenin because I believe in Christ.'

His words seemed to come out of my own deepest self, bringing together all my broodings and doubts, my half thoughts and quarter thoughts, my deepening revolt against the society in which I lived, my conviction that at every minute of the day that society was crucifying life and art. What had been a close and intense personal rebellion was suddenly widened, taking on the whole scope of the earth. A tumultuous daylight poured

in on the little room of my angry meditation. What mattered
was the realization that in 1917 something new in history had
happened and that this event was linked at every point with
the allegiance I had sworn to poetry, the rejection I had made
of the world around me. I knew in the marrow of my bones
what Wordsworth and Blake had felt in the early days of the
French revolution. Bliss to be alive, but to be young very
heaven. Of the political and economic aspects I knew nothing;
I was concerned only with the fact that here I felt a clean break
with the past, a prophetic voice crying justice in the wilderness
and changing the wilderness into an earthly paradise, the
naked truth of man making possible all forms of beauty.

These thoughts and emotions in turn were tied up with my
work in the W.E.A. To talk of English literature – the subject
about which I had thought night and day for so many years
– seemed an easy thing; but when I turned to the job of translating my reveries and intuitions, my complex sense of the
interrelation of things, into talks before a class of individuals
about whom I knew nothing, I found that I had no idea at all
what to say. In desperation I turned to the textbooks which I
despised; and then because I generally disagreed hotly with
what was said, I had at least some glimmerings of an argument.
I filled in with readings from the poets whom I was treating,
and trusted to luck for a peroration worthy of the theme.

I always had the feeling that I lectured very badly. Yet my
class did not fall away; on the contrary it even increased by
one or two. And every time, someone or other stayed behind
to tell me about the 'new light' I'd shed on things. These con-
gratulators could never elucidate what the new light was, and
on thinking over what I had said I was unable to pick on the
revealing moment. I seemed always to fail to say anything at
all of what was hubbubing in my mind, what had been so furiously clear in my thoughts before the lecture as I prepared my
notes. And yet I was finding that I very much enjoyed the
experience of trying at last to put into coherent form my
musings on art.

Through the W.E.A. I was meeting people who were new
to me: the keen though generally inarticulate readers of my
literature class, various working-class fighters among whom

was a sprinkling of revolutionaries. On the one hand was a lad named Cunningham, a carpenter, with a deep hunger for art and philosophy, who begged me to lend him books, talk with him, help him. On the other hand. Jim Quinton, an experienced I.W.W. from the United States, who had known all the trials and persecutions of the devoted Wobbly and who had remained a cool clear-eyed fighter, rock solid. Here was a new world for me. And between these two types there were all sorts of gradations of workers looking for knowledge, eager young schoolmistresses, engineers in neat blue suits with notebooks full of notes on economics, aspiring aesthetes with a cult of Oscar Wilde, an aggressive rationalist who heckled Salvation Army meetings and started arguments on free will and determinism at street corners.

Several of my class were well read, but with a slant to their reading which was quite unlike my own. Through them I discovered a confused but genuine working-class tradition of rebellious writing. There was a strong American element in their choice of books. A few knew Whitman, but Jack London was the main figure, and with him a group of novelists whose names I had not previously heard – Dreiser, Crane, Bierce, Poole (author of *The Harbour*), Norris, Harold Frederick. But there were also English writers who were known and loved – Blatchford, Tressal, William Morris and Ruskin. Wilde, approached from the angle of *De Profundis* and *The Soul of Man under Socialism*, seemed a different character from the aesthete of the plays and novels; and Morris, whose early poetry, *The Defence of Guenevere*, had long meant a great deal to me for its pictorial clarity, its extreme tension of emotions, its bare and relentlessly simple rhythm, seemed a different character when approached through *News from Nowhere* and the later essays and songs.

Gorky too was well known; and though at this time I did not get a chance to read his *Mother*, the image of it was warmly communicated by men who loved it and in whose life it had played an important part.

I still found it difficult to concern myself much with the novel, and I did not read with any thoroughness the authors which my new friends were always ready to lend me. But I read enough to get the feeling of their world. Certain aspects repelled or did not interest me in my absorption with poetic process. I wanted the lyrically revealing image, the drama that cuts to the bone and brings out the essence of good and evil; I shied off from the elaboration of everyday detail in novels, feeling that it muffled the contours of the clear choice, the poetic image. And yet there was something in the problems of the novel that was beginning to exercise its spell over me. How far could one enter into the daily movement of people and things without losing one's grasp on the essential truth and its unceasing pressure? How far could one deal with small and fleeting things, yet preserve an unblurred poetic sensibility and the understanding of what was truly great in human personality?

Witherby had bought some land on the top of Mount Tambourine – about 1,800 feet high, some 50 miles from Brisbane on the south coast. Here amid the luxuriant rain-forest trees and palms, hung with creepers, ferns, lichens, he had a peculiar shack set on the edge of a precipice and built on unnecessarily tall and thin poles. It looked as if it could be blown over and swept down into the magnificent vista at the least puff of wind. I used to go there for weekends with, and various, friends – chiefly with V. Gordon Childe whom I often met at his rambling bungalow in Brisbane. Childe had been flatly opposed to the war and had got into some trouble at Oxford – how public I never knew, for he was not a person who unbosomed himself about his private affairs or whom one asked about such things. I knew that he had done a certain amount of archaeological work and I tried to read some writings of his in the Journal of Hellenic Studies on Aegean pottery. But the subject was then too far from my ken, and I never dared to raise it with him. In any event his main interest was now political; he never spoke of his work, but I think he had some job in workers' tutorial classes at the university. He preferred to slip in a sly and ruthless comment rather than expatiate; I remember him in those days solely as a bubble-pricker, a mildly caustic iconoclast, whose glasses took on an unholy glitter as he demolished somebody's illusions with sardonic kindliness. He was the most detached person I knew, and yet one felt all the while that there was a warm core to his gently spoken and deadly sarcasm. No doubt all the while his strong socialist convictions were being outraged by the insights which he was gaining into the realities behind the façade in the political world – and which he not long after put into his first book, *How Labor Governs*.

My professor, Michie, was often helpful and invariably conscientious and sympathetic, but he was too shy for me to get far with him; and Childe was the first person with wide knowledge of the ancient world with whom I had a chance of conversing. He always listened patiently to my divigatory outpourings, sometimes correcting facts or pointing to facts that had been omitted, sometimes nodding in assent, but also often waiting for the best moment to interpose one of his amiably withering comments, after which I would feel shiveringly bared of all pretensions to understanding of the Greeks. In those days the only way to reach the mountain top, unless one was the unlikely owner of a car, was to walk across the flats to the slopes and then wind one's way up. I recall particularly one day when he had let me ramble on about my conception of Periclean Athens all the way over the paddocks and the rutted roads, and then, as we began climbing up a rocky track lined with trailing vines of purple passionfruit, he demolished my whole picture with some nicely chosen details of the real nature of Greek society and its inner struggles.

He was lean and spare, with something of a stoop, though when I met him again later in England he seemed much shorter and slighter than I remembered. He liked walking and climbing, able to wander on interminably, bent a little, listening equally to the noises of the earth and my meandering hypotheses, never commenting on the scene, but now and then pausing to draw his shoulders back and gaze round with a brooding enjoyment. And looking at him, I was never quite sure if he guarded his detachment as a defence against the bruises which a brutish world could so easily inflict on his too tender sensibilities, or if he wanted to break through it, but halted the moment he felt the cold wind blowing in through a fissure. His odd though likeable face, I felt certain, contributed to his refusal to come too far out of his inner refuge.

I slept a few times in Witherby's rickety shack; but the breeze coming up through its crannies made me too uneasily aware of the possibilities of floating off down the valley; and I preferred the ground below. I can still see Childe standing near the cliff edge, staring with vague intentness into immensity, swaying a little with bent shoulders and sliding his glasses down to the end of his nose. That image was revived with a shock when I heard, as I was in the midst of this book, how he had fallen from a similar ledge in the Blue Mountains towards Katoomba.

I remember too, without tragic overtones, Witherby perched naked on the small slab of a verandah at the back of his shack, shaving himself to the raucous dawn hails of the parakeets and waving politely to some scandalized females from the nearest farm.

Once I went up with Mrs P., the porcelain-fragile wife of the professor, with her birdswift mind, and Mrs S., bluff and ugly and making the most of her looks with witty self-deprecations. We wandered on the paths under the tall silver gums or the giant cycads – the oldest living things in the world, someone had claimed – which, though growing in small patches on various Australian sites, were specially numerous on Tambourine. Mrs P., bird bright on the shaken boughs of my mind, went on challenging me to improvise verses in various styles – Swinburnean for the vast view down the Canungra Valley, Wordsworthean for a nameless tiny wildflower, Rupert-Brookean for our sense of insignificance under the cycads, the macrozami palms:

> And will these ancient palms at last
> into mere Ancientness have passed,
> or will they, as all senses calm,
> spire to the only topless Palm?
> and though it really doesn't matter,
> will our chatterings die in Chatter,
> or, in that blank Ideal Garden,
> into coralline Silence harden?

And in the bitterly cold evenings we sat tranced over a pine fire while she read Goethe in a naiad's voice, piercing the heart like an icicle that killed without leaving a trace.

We were staying in a small cottage; and one afternoon we were all, together with Witherby, on the verandah, when we saw the head of the college coming down the road. He was staying at the farm where we got our milk. 'A bore,' said Witherby. 'But don't bother. I'll get rid of him.' He went down on his hands and knees, ran down the steps and up the path to the gate, yelping and barking. Halting, still on hands and knees, by the gate, he went on barking at the man, who paused with hand on latch and after a while walked sharply on. Witherby barked him triumphantly out of sight; then, rising, he smoothed his hair and resumed the interrupted conversation.

At the university I had met Thatcher, the previous editor of the magazine, who was now working as the Queensland governor's secretary. A devoted man with a face like the wall of a hidden altar. One day he asked me to take on the office of secretary to the committee of social action – or something like that: I forget the exact name. The society in question had been developed I think largely by himself for inquiry into abuses and for action to right them. When I demurred, he told me that he had some plans for bettering the lot of the Aboriginal remnants in the north and far west; so I agreed. Whether or not the scheme was the best thing possible, I had no way of judging; but the point that Thatcher made was that the Aboriginals, thinned down by bad treatment, by wholesale murder (through poisoned waterholes or rifle hunts), by neglect and exploitation, were in danger of extinction; therefore the only thing to halt the process was to demand reservations for them – though reservations in themselves were no final answer; in the end the Aboriginals must be given full educational and social rights, taking their place in ordinary Australian society. The reserves were needed as the only practicable way of preventing things from getting worse; after they were gained, we could find the next step.

P.R.S., a student from Bundaberg, mocked the scheme and called Thatcher a callow idealist. 'Nothing will settle the matter but a proper socialist Australia. You're a victim of

reformist delusions. You want to tinker, not to change things.'
I agreed that in the long run the full liberation of the Aboriginals was bound up with a wider social struggle; but it seemed
to me that P.R.S. was using his point schematically, to avoid
doing what could be done at the moment.

The plan and the knowledge were all Thatcher's; I added
a certain young keenness to give momentum to his coolly determined course of action. We drew up the scheme in detail and
called a meeting to which we asked the public characters at
all likely to support us. Almost at once we found ourselves waiting on the state Premier with a deputation of influential citi-
zens. The Premier was Ryan, an able Labor politician. He
accepted our scheme in its entirety, without equivocations, and
everything seemed settled. We thought we had saved the Aboriginals.

But within a few weeks Ryan resigned his premiership and
entered federal politics; clearly he had known all along that
he was going to resign and that his affable words would be
worth no more than the breath which uttered them. His successor refused to consider himself bound and flatly turned the
scheme down. It was impossible now to work the campaign up
again, to gather the supporters afresh by personal canvas and
letters in the newspaper. The students who had helped had
drifted to other activities. We had been neatly baffled and
things were exactly as they had been.

P.R.S. grinned; and the adroit way the project had been
side-stepped and then crumpled up, did seem to justify his
scepticism.

In the process of collecting information, groups of us had
visited stations on which small numbers of Aboriginals were
working, and we had found out what we could of the religious
missions. The latter often did their best according to their
lights, but the net result of their work was depressing in the
extreme.*

*I have long lost my notes of the period; but here are some details of later
developments. A missionary in Queensland chained young women to posts,
whipped them and turned them into the bush. So said Dr Crookston, reporting in 1939 on the expedition he had made with Dr Thomson to inquire

At the university I now called myself a Bolshevik. I wore a red tie and rose in the debating society and defended the revolution. I had not yet even heard the term Marxism and had no idea that it was the philosophy of Lenin. I interpreted the Soviet revolution in formulations drawn from Shelley, William Morris, and Blake. But I arranged for Jim Quinton to come and address the students in the lunch-hour. He gave one of his steady fierce speeches; and in memory I see him at the end of the room as at the back of a cavern, with the light shafted on his face, and the audience listening intently, drowned in shadow. As he clenches his fists and uses his familiar appeal, 'Get down to bedrock!' he seems to strike and splinter the light; and when he makes his gesture of opening his arms, as if to take all men into brotherhood, he becomes a figure angrily crucified on the fears and greeds of the world.

From my discussions afterwards it seemed that the listeners liked him and felt that the world was enough out of joint to need a certain amount of putting to rights; but what had been for me the message running passionately through every word he spoke – the denunciation of something utterly rotten, the demand for something quite different – all that did not seem to have come home at all. I felt all the more bitterly close to him.

From Quinton I heard many tales of working-class politics in the recent years. The International Workers of the World had first arrived in Australia in 1905 from the States, with

---

into conditions. He characterized the actions of the Queensland government in the employment of Aborigines as a 'slave trade', since the latter were paid only a pittance and the rest of their wages appropriated in a trust fund which had never been used for their benefit. This sort of detail could be much amplified. Conditions have remained terrible. Dr Thomson in 1937 advocated reserves of the kind that Thatcher asked for. Also T. Wright in his *New Deal for the Aborigines* (endorsed by the Labor Council of N.S.W.) 1944. Katharine Susannah Prichard writes: 'Stories of atrocities committed by pioneering settlers against the native races have aroused horror and condemnation. But the conditions in which remnants of the Aboriginal race are now living remain a matter of shame – and we do nothing about it.'

branches in Adelaide in 1908 and in Sydney in 1913. The latter
became their H.Q. Then their numbers had been swelled by
their fellows hounded by police action in the U.S.A. and fleeing from lynch-action during the war. In Australia they met
much the same persecution. On the Sunday after the outbreak
of the war in 1914 they held a Sydney rally in the Domain
under the slogan, 'War what for?' For markets, raw materials
and profits, they declared. They played a vigorous part against
the two conscription referendums of 1915 and 1917, both of
which were defeated. In reply the police framed them on various charges and patriotic groups were incited to beat them up.
The Wobblies went on with their efforts to popularize the project of one big union. Quinton told me about the general strike
in N.S.W. in August 1917, which began in the railway work-
shops; and I was ashamed to think that I had known nothing
of it. The one big union had got some T.U. endorsement in
Sydney in 1918 and Quinton was hopeful about it.

He was however moving away from the rigid syndicalism of
the I.W.W., with its belief that capitalism was heading for
automatic collapse, that all political forms of struggle were useless or corrupted, and that the general strike was the sole revolutionary weapon. The more he thought about Russia, the more
he felt that the Wobbly formulations were too narrow.

My aunt, with her acute sense of what was happening in the
family, had gathered some idea of the changes in my political
opinions, but was too astute to launch a frontal attack on
insecure evidence. She contented herself with comments on the
idiot behaviour of immature people and with renewed abuse
of trade unions – legalized forms of blackmail, bleeding honest
employers and encouraging a go-slow trickery among the
demoralized workers. She said that it was terrible to recall that
she had once entertained the Snowdens during their Australian
tour, and now Snowden had turned out a double-dyed traitor;
if only she had known at the time, she'd have flung him out
of the house.

I smiled to myself and infuriated her, remembering Quinton's low opinion of English Labour politicians such as
Ramsay MacDonald and Snowden. In my spare time I was trying to write a series of sonnets on the world situation. One

appeared in the university magazine, describing the class world of 1919 as a blind man stirring on a bed and unable to reach out to the dawn breaking magnificently round his head. This was meant to refer to the failure of the German workers to break through the barriers and join the Russian. In another, *Memorial for the War Dead*, I tried to say that a product of the war, unintended by those who started it, was the Soviet Union, so that the dead soldiers, however little they understood what was happening, had not died in vain.

> *This mountainous death was not upheaped in vain;*
> *not vain this war. Rather, the crack that ran*
> *through the old war of greed. The battering strain*
> *served in its dark despite the cause of man.*
> *Still the mole Evil, heaving hidden away*
> *in busy lanes of death, had sapped the base,*
> *and all the craggy fears that fenced the day*
> *crashed from the sky and left an opened space.*
>
> *Look, the Memorial stands for those who fell.*
> *The lies, the dreams and agonies, east and west,*
> *helped a deep purpose working out unguessed*
> *by those who conjured up this terror and pain,*
> *who smashed their own closed profit-rings of hell.*
> *Those lives the cost, the soviet world the gain.*

But these sonnets were only jotted notes, memoranda scrawled in a flickering light. I still felt on the threshold of a new dimension of life and art, and could not see what things were like beyond that threshold.

18 · NATIONALITY

My MOTHER grew hopelessly tired of the house. She retired into a sort of bored stupor. She gave up trying to control the mere £5 a week which was all we had. Ray and Phil were now going to a Church of England Grammar School – I forget why they went there rather than the Grammar School proper where I had gone; there must have been some matter of reduced fees wangled by my uncle. Ray took little interest in the school and was already planning to get away and find a job, so that he could buy the materials for painting. Phil was a precocious school rebel, intellectually outstripping the others in his class but refusing to fit in as I had. He read several of Bernard Shaw's prefaces to find arguments against the oppressions of school and family; at home he sometimes lost his temper and was unmanageable, throwing at us whatever he had in his hand, book or table knife, and he gabbled in his sleep out of heavy nightmares. Once, reprimanded by the headmaster for some misdemeanour, he tried to set out the determinist case as a defence. 'I'm not responsible for what I do.'

'That is obvious, Lindsay,' the headmaster replied and the boys bellowed with laughter.

It took him weeks to live the episode down. He was writing short stories of a subversive kind, illustrated by himself. He lavished red ink on the pictures of whipped girls surrounded by Cossacks. For the most part I ignored him as well as Ray, despising their interest in film stars; but at times we carried on a literary conversation. I read him passages from Greek or Latin poets, then asked him what the sounds suggested. I wanted to prove that the sounds themselves held some of the meaning, so that Rimbaud on the vowels might be vindicated.

He patiently listened and tried to say what he thought I
wanted him to say.

I had had to take over the accounts of the family, aided by
my aunt. My worst misery was when I had to go into the local
grocers and say that if they served any member of the family
with beer or other liquors they wouldn't be paid. Even so, with
the remarkable guile of someone whose whole life has been
reduced to devising petty trickeries, our mother succeeded in
getting as many bottles as she wanted – or almost as many. The
strain on the finances was extreme. I had to order groceries and
the like, but was all the while in debt through untraceable
losses. Meals and other housework happened or didn't happen
according to unpredictable systems. Our location directly
opposite the Women's College was finely calculated to haunt
me with the expectation of awful scenes, exposures, scandals.

At last, in consultation with my aunt, I decided to evacuate
the house. We sold the furniture for very little and went to a
boarding-house in our favourite setting, the river. The house
was three-storeyed, wooden, inherited by three sisters from
their parents. The eldest girl was already arid, doomed to
harden soon into a fully carapaced landlady, with hairy wart
and suspicious eye. The middle one was half bleached with corrosive kitchen smells of cabbage and mulligatawny soup; she
powdered her face hastily and patchily before meals, and kept
yawning and patting herself on the mouth in a ladylike gesture.
The youngest was Dolly Vardenish with gay curls and pink
cheeks, petted and plump and twenty-five at the least, still a
flighty young thing to her fading sisters, their one hope, their
one proof of lost days of floppy gentility. They brought down
their rates for us, though they clearly couldn't afford it. The
tired brows wrinkled and the pencil stub from the dresser
scribbled unhandily on the back of unpaid bills and they
decided that they'd just be able to do it. 'Regular guests now,
you know,' said the middle one. The eldest nodded with pursed
lips, narrow-eyed with calculations.

I had been introduced by Randolph Bedford's son, who had
just come to Brisbane after a trip in a lugger round the Gulf
of Carpentaria. How he found me out I don't recall. (R.B. was

a large genial journalist, story-teller, wildcat miner, and lots
of other things; a personality from the spacious pre-war days,
who had now become a member of the Queensland Legislative
Council: a bulkily witty man, 'whose brain, polished in the
shop of Minerva,' said the poet Hugh McCrae, 'sent out sparks
that made me wink'. Rather, perhaps, a generously overflowing beer tankard of a man, with a dangerous glint of mining
shares in his right eye and only bluff humour in his left, whose
sops of laughter made one amiably glow and whose slouch hat
hid a rosy bald dome. Entering the House, he had shouted:
'Which way to the bribery department?')

R.B.'s son was the first person who made me enjoy beer
because he was the first person who insisted on standing five
or six rounds to my one, explaining that he had the cash and
a time would come when the roles were reversed. I admired
his red tan, his pioneering solidity, his journalistic devil-may-
care.

As soon as our residence in the boarding-house was settled,
he slapped Dolly Varden on the plump back and sent her into
squeals; then he rushed away and came back with bottles in
all his pockets. The girls said they never never drank. The arid
eldest pursed her lips and went out; but the middle half
bleached said that she'd never known such a one for wheedling
and cajoling. Under his capacious persuasions she and the
youngest agreed to sip and were soon converted to his thesis
that beer wasn't an intoxicant like some things, only a cheerful
beverage, and so we drank all the bottles and I'm sure the
boarders got sago pudding with their stringy mutton.

Next day we moved in. Ray and I had a tall back room
lighted through dingy skylights, with peeling paper and damp
stains on the ceiling. It was the poorest place we'd yet been in,
but nobody cared. We boys had interests of our own outside,
and our mother had given up caring. But she was much less
miserable, now that the burden of the house was removed from
her back. She even regained a little of her vague pleasure in
sitting still and looking out of a window at clouds or people
or leaves.

Young Bedford introduced me to his father and we went
over the House of Parliament and heard some of the scandals

about the ministers. Then we drank more beer. Why didn't I go north, I asked myself – to the shores of the pearl oysters, the great bush of bunya pines with their three-yearly fruit that the Aboriginals loved, the sandy coast where men got gulf fever and had to be tied to trees to yell themselves out? I recalled the day I had sailed north of Bribie with my uncle, hoping to see the tail of the great Barrier Reef, the coral rosy in the green vitreous depths, the giant clams, the ruffling line of white on the golden-blue waters.

The question of nationality in art had belatedly come into my thoughts. Until I had been drawn into the current of things around me, I had been secure in a European tradition which I translated with unconscious sleight-of-hand into my own Australian setting. Now a split had come. I had to ask myself how the tradition and the facts of the situation corresponded.

My aunt as usual helped me maladroitly to focus the problem.

'Write poems with Australian objects in them,' she urged. 'What's the interest in Australian poems about roses for people in England? Write about gumtrees or jacarandas. That sounds strange and interesting. Make them exotic.'

Against this formulation I strongly reacted; but I knew that by rejecting its crudely opportunist terms I could not settle the matter. There was much more to be grasped, accepted or rejected.

One afternoon I met Gustav and went over to his rooms on the south side. Along a dusty shabby street, with a tom-cat on one sill and a woman lolling asleep on another with her mouth open, with small boys collecting horsedung in a pram. Gustav was one of the bohemians who flittered round the W.E.A. groups, a bad artist who could manage a likeness of a likeness with a pencil and who had made his way over most of the main roads, dashing off drawings of people in pubs or shearing sheds, slab huts or cane plantations. A short semi-bald man, he dressed in a rubbed velvet coat with a large frilly tie in a bow; and he always carried a portfolio. He mouthed the most atrocious banalities about art without a blink of shame.

At the door of his house an old man sat on a packing case, cutting his cracked toe nails with a big pair of scissors. We climbed a ricketty flight of stairs with many steps missing and went down a narrow passage into a barn of a room partitioned with sacking and tin. All the glass was missing from the window; but in the event of strong wind or rain some shutters of deal board could be fitted on.

Producing half a bottle of stout, Gustav asked permission to draw me. I sat to be drawn, sipping the flat stout, while Gustav talked on and on. 'I love my art, I worship it, but even an artist must live. To live he must eat, sleep and drink. The necessity is regrettable. Also at times he must love a woman. That maybe is regrettable too, especially for the woman. No woman can hold the free artist, but every woman thinks she can. However, I am not speaking of love; for an artist can get it without money. Only the philistines have to buy love, in a brothel or in the yet viler marriage bed. The artist has merely to speak with his secret voice and the woman is his. But for food, drink and a bed, money is required. So I must sell my art.' He added blithely, 'Yes, to you, a fellow artist, I admit that I prostitute my art. Not only in the portraits that I make of the common herd, but also in the drawings of criminals in dock that I sell to a sordid Sunday paper. I mean, that I used to sell. For unfortunately I have lost that chance of prostitution, badly paid as it was. The regular artist has recovered from the deetees.'

I suggested that there was no reason why he shouldn't find some interest in delineating the characters of criminals.

'Criminals have no character,' he replied. 'No, I have myself broken the law, and I shall break it again, I trust. But I am not a criminal. I have character. I am not caught out. A criminal is a type over whom the steamroller of mediocrity called civilization has passed. He is flat, a pancake, a mess on the road. But he is not a character. I am sorry to spoil one of your illusions.'

I wanted to ask him more about the secret voice that charmed women to his arms; but a knock on the one-hinged door admitted Will the rationalist, who had one trait in common with Gustav, a deification of Wilde as the superior man stoned by the mob. He studied a small painting that I hadn't noticed on the mantelpiece, beside an alarm clock that didn't go and a chipped china shepherdess accompanied by an ithyphallic satyr in plasticine. 'You're learning the mystery of green,' he commented, and turned to me. 'Do you like green? Psychologists state that it's the colour of abnormality.' He was wearing a greenish suit and went on to talk of a great thinker whom he begged me to read, Stirner, author of *The Ego and its Own*. You only had to read that book and you were freed from all the delusions and prejudices that shackled the rest of the world.

Gustav took advantage of a pause to describe the time he was arrested in Toowoomba. 'I told them that I was married spiritually to the Venus di Milo and that my nationality was Artist, Citizen of the World. Whatever you may suspect me of, I said, I am guiltless of it; for you lack the imagination to know my sins.'

'That was a good answer,' said Will grudgingly. 'What did they do?'

'They took my fingerprints,' said Gustav. 'I told them that someday they would be able to sell the prints at a high price. What would the world not give for the fingerprints of Michelangelo?'

Andy, the travelling friend of Gustav, came in. The pair had worked out a new scheme. All you needed was an impressive camera and a presentable suit of clothes. Then you hired a car and drove round a district of rich squatters. You produced your gaudy cards and explained you were taking photos for an edition deluxe to be entitled *The Fine Houses of Australia*. Then you asked for permission to photograph the rambling bungalow as you wanted to give it a prominent place in the book. You didn't need any film in the camera, you just pushed the button a dozen times with much pretence of finding the best angles. Finally you produced a printed form, which said that the book could be bought for five guineas sub before publication, ten guineas after. That at once brought you in a cheque or banknotes, perhaps for two or three copies. All sheer profit, after paying for the hire of the car.

But Andy, it turned out, was considering a new way of making an easy living. After all there wasn't an indefinite number of fine houses and sooner or later the police would be notified of the book that never appeared. He had wandered into a chapel, intending to take a few prayer books and sell them, but he struck the minister and told him a tale of spiritual upheavals. 'What's the purpose of life?' I said to him. 'I feel I can't go on the way I'm going. I want something different. I can't believe this is the only life. It doesn't make sense somehow.' He winked at us and turned the stout bottle upside down. 'He fell for it, bait, hook and sinker. I was almost sorry for him.'

'You're wasting your time,' said Will. 'The parsons are the meanest skunks ever known. Did he end by shaking the collection box under your nose?'

'No, I really think I'm on to something good,' insisted Andy. 'By the time I'd told him of the stirrings of a sense of sin in my insides and the need I felt of being regenerated, the old boy said I was a natural preacher and would I address his bible class? No, I've got a hunch I'm on to something good.' (Within a year he was on the way to being ordained minister. The chapel had put up the money for his training and he'd found a rich widow with a pious squint in her eye – or so he said at the farewell pub party he gave us.)

Will suggested that we drink to Andy as one of the coming lights of the church. He donated half a crown, Andy a shilling, myself sixpence, and Gustav his good will. Some bottles of beer were bought, partly on the four shillings and partly on credit, from the tousled pale-eyed woman who ran the house, Mrs Hales. Gustav and Andy began singing bush ballads, songs picked up on the road. The one thing I respected about them was their readiness to walk out into the open, the wilds, taking their next meal where they found it. Surely if I were a true poet, I'd join them, I'd walk out without taking thought into the red earth of the sun and the uncharted roads of my own body.

Hurrah for the Lachlan, boys, and join me in a cheer;
that's the place to go to make a cheque every year.
With a toadskin in my pocket that I borrowed from a friend,
O, isn't it nice and cosy to be camping in the bend.

With my four little johnny-cakes all nicely cooked
a nice little codfish just off the hook
my little round flourbag sitting on a stump
my little tea-and-sugar bag alooking nice and plump.

Knocking out the chorus on a box. Good lads. Gone out into the endless mallee scrub, in the yellow-brown cracked earth and the grey boulders, the great valleys of fern and the lakes of blinding salt. Gone with the screech of the parakeet troops of morning, the kookaburra yell, the sweet song of a magpie flock. Knocking at the squatter's back door for the regulation hand-out, a pound of meat and a pannikin of flour, coming in late as a sundowner so as to escape being given a job.

The earth rolls on through empty space, its journey's never done.
It's entered for a starry race throughout the kingdom come.
And, as I am a bit of earth, I follow it because
and to prove I am a rolling stone and never gather moss.

For I'm a ramble-eer, a rollicking ramble-eer,
I'm a roving rake of poverty and son of a gun for beer.

I've done a bit of fossicking for tucker and for gold.
I've been a menial rouseabout and a rollicking shearer bold.
I've shanked across the Old Man Plain after busting up a cheque
and whipped the cat once more again, though I haven't met it yet.

I've done a bit of droving of cattle and of sheep
and I've done a bit of moving with Matilda for a mate.
Of fencing I have done my share, wool-scouring on the green.
Axeman, navvy, Old Nick can bear me out in what I haven't been.

Tremendous oaths of bullockies on the hillroads with iron-ruts, the bullocks tossing their mad bloodshot eyes and slavering mouths. Not even the clack of a whip will save you unless you can curse stinking hell out of a bullock's hide.

O we'll live like fighting cocks.
For good living I'm your man.
We'll have leatherjacks, johnnycakes,
and fritters in the pan.
Or if you'd like some fish
I'll catch you some soon.
For we'll bob for burramundies
round the banks of the lagoon.

A wagon with forty in the team, that's what broke the land in.

Say what you like, a drover can be made but a bullocky's got to be born. You never drove sheep or you wouldn't talk so snake-headed a lot of leary mullock. Just you go staggering through the maze of the drafting-yard with two buckets of water from the hole nine hundred yards off and the heat one-one-seven in the shade!

> First morning I set out
> when the grass was green and young
> and they swore they'd break my snout
> if I didn't move along.
> I said: You're very hard.
> Take care, don't raise my dander.
> For I'm a regular knowing card,
> A Queensland Overlander.

The earth crushed into fine dust by the hammers of the heat, you'd swear no germ of life survived in it this side of hell; and then after the rain the green plush of the young grass. But the sun'd soon shrivel all that back to dust unless there'd been at least a fortnight of pouring water. The earth's so hard that the first torrents slide off it into the gullies and creeks as if it was solid rock.

> It's true we pay no licence
> and our run is rather large.
> It's not often they can catch us,
> so they cannot make a charge.
> They think we live on store-beef
> but no, I'm not a gander.
> When a good fat stranger joins the herd,
> 'He'll do,' says the Overlander.

Following food and water: if you can find it. Maybe what you find is a swamp right across the track in the hollow of the plain and you run and pull your sheep by the horns, and he fights and you shove him on his back and drag him through the slush. And when you get him over you tie him to a tree. If there isn't a tree, you'd better wait till one grows up. You do that for a couple of hours, chasing the leaders. Then at last, if you're lucky, they dash across and the rest follow. Or up in the hills:

'O for a tame and quiet herd,'
I heard a crawler cry.
But give to me the mountain mob
with the flash of their tameless eye,
with the flash of their tameless eye, my boys,
as down the rugged spur
rush the wild children of the woods
and the horse that mocks at fear.

This is my country, with the song in its angry bones. And mixed with the struggle against a vast and ancient nature, the free-for-all with the bosses. Jim's friend from the cane area spins his tales about the management's gang out with shotguns and rifles, trying to pick him off as he dodged among the she-oaks. That's a strike for you, That's Australia, that was. Is it?

But when I sat in front of a blank sheet of paper, the heroic echoes of the hooves on the rocks of the ridges went flying in incoherent images.

Ned Kelly reined up at the edge of the cliff,
he turned and looked at me.
'The crooked world throws a gallows-shadow
on him with a mind to be free.

'O when I knew that Justice is found
on the high mountain-stone,
why did I shout across Australia?'
I stand and listen alone.

I sweated at bombastic stanzas in which I hoped to pack some sense of Blake's aphorism that all that lives is holy.

The sunset-shambles bleed across the waves,
a flower bursts in my heart,
a rose of bubbling blood. Come, Dionysos,
let me not stand apart.
Upwards, in quickening gyres of jagged birth,
now lift me and consume
the windy world that ashes round my feet
in ecstasies of doom.

Then the grey woman huddled on the seat
shuffles and gives a wheeze;
and the stray mongrel, crouching at her feet,
whines, biting for his fleas;
and they are part of me. The furies call,
out of my broken hands the flame-birds leap,
through the dead town the flames of water sweep,
All things are holy, all.

Yes, and the fires shall purge, the fires redeem.
Here, merging, I behold
the girl who looked through lattice of a dream
on apples of reddening gold
and plucked them at morning; this, the thing of scorn,
the tattered rag of flesh; and also here
beyond the Virgin and Venus, burning clear,
the Woman yet unborn.

If that poem was a confused effort to accept a world in which my mother mourned, it also held memories of an early *Bulletin* drawing by Norman, illustrating some verses entitled *The Woman I was, the Woman I am, the Woman I'll someday be.* A plain bit of moralizing, a rhymed temperance tract: the only work of his to be praised from the embattled pulpits of the land. But my triad was different; I had learned from Blake that transfiguration must come from the defeat of the alienating process, the satanic mills – though I still did not know how to find the poetic image for the knowledge.

When I turned to the world about me, I flagged into scattered phrases of rage and defiance, or retreated into a satiric acquiescence without any clear direction.

The men with birds-nests on their faces
frequent the bars in longlost places,
they tread resignedly the rails,
regard their large gnarled fingernails,
and lift their eyelids now and then
across their saddened fellow-men
to catch the barmaid's gladys-eye,
order another pint, and sigh.

At times they take an old blunt axe
and lay out policemen on their backs,
and then return to private life
and never dare to ask as wife
the barmaid who, still swelling, stands
with disillusioned puppet-hands.

I read and reread Aristophanes, and there was the whole secret, gloriously shouted. While I read, there was no problem. The poet simply was Aristophanes, and all the elements of expression, from aerial lyricism to bawdy topicality, were fused in a delighted whole. But the moment I looked up from the Greek text to the world outside the window, I was lost again, without a clue.

This Australia, spread in the clanging sun. Was it inside or outside my poetry? Was my poetry inside or outside it? From the Tambourine I walked alone or with others across country, along the Canungra Valley, towards Beechmont. I came to know something of the signs of the bush, and of the faces of those who lived in it.

Barefooted, or with unstockinged canvas shoes, I wandered along the tracks. Clinging to saplings, bushes, tree-roots, I descended to the waterfall, to a ledge from which I might view its long swinging silver braids powdered with fumes of waterlight, and feel the gentle spray on my feet and hands and uplifted face. Watching out all the while for leeches and keeping on the move as one way of baffling them. Sooner or later however one or two caught on to my feet and legs, and then I felt in my pocket for the twist of salt and soon had them curling obscenely off. If I lingered, my legs would become bloody from the assaults; and if I'd forgotten the twist, I had to race for home. Once in a wet glade, under the lovely soft-green filtered light, I paused to meditate and look round to find a whole host of leeches coming at me, reaching up from the rotted leaves. 'Have you ever seen a great mob of leeches charging on their hindlegs?' I boasted.

With another lad I plunged down the south side, walking till we struck a railway station. Stopping for a meal at the hut of a cockatoo farmer: one of those growing vegetables, maize (corn in Australia) and the like. Cockatoo farmer because the best crops raised are the cockatoos eating up the seeds and young plants at dawn. This one was tending corn on the lower slopes and hadn't cleared the ground for long. A cockie has a hard start; land fit for crops is sure to be in the thick scrub and to need much clearing and fencing. Charley was cursing the corn. While it was being sown, the crows followed the plough and picked the seed up; when it started sprouting, every kind of kangaroo-rat, paddy-melon and bandicoot wanted a taste; if there was one hole in the fence of netting (and there was sure to be lots), in they sneaked. Then the weevil got going. And all the while you had to plough and hoe between the rows. And what was left by God and the Devil you had to pluck by hand; you had to strip the husks by hand; and only then could you put the corn in the machines for shelling. 'Nobody but a German or a Chinaman can make a go of this kind of bloody job.' We tripped over his pumpkins and melons, grown among the corn, and tramped in for tea. 'Come on into the badger-box.'

There was a big fireplace inside, built from bricks of puddled sun-dried clay – the first part of a selector's house to be set up. Round the fireplace go the two or three rooms – three in this case – constructed from sapling uprights and boarding of shingles from the splitter's camp. The rusty iron roof looked full of holes; but inside things were cosy enough, with a canvas ceiling full of bulges and sheets of illustrated papers pasted on the wall-shingles to keep the draught out. The floor was beaten earth; a slab table and gin cases made up the main furniture; the beds were canvas stretched on sapling frames. Lily, the wife, with her red chapped face, welcomed us and two kids peeped round the doorposts.

'You come just the right day,' said Lily, wiping her hands. 'I got a leg of mutton in the oven.' She pointed at the three-legged iron pot sunk in the ashes under the hanging griddle.

'No, just give us a cup of tea, really.'

'You don't think you're going to get away as easy as all that.'

'Come on, tell us the news,' said Charley, sitting on a case.

But we couldn't think of a thing to tell, and Charley regarded us with a quizzical smile. Proper educated chaps, who were in Brisbane a few days ago and who hadn't got a scrap of news for a man lost in the wilds.

'Well, I'll tell you something,' called Lily, who had gone into the next room to tidy herself. 'Mrs Simpson had twins last week and the very same day a death adder stung her cow and a dingo got away with three of her hens. What do you say to that for a chapter of accidents?'

'All the same I could do with a cup of tea,' said Charley. 'And make it real strong. Strong enough to stand a stick up in.'

It was always easy to get lost with the heat waves flickering among the trees and sweat thick in the eyebrows. Stumbling along the rough ground freckled with light through the tangled trees, climbing on soft slippery pine-needles among sharp rocks, tickled by the fronds of harts-tongue ferns and jeered at by triumphal parrots. You think the track is quite clear, then, as you meditate on the *psithyrisma* of Theocritos or look up for the wonga pigeon, you find it's dribbled away to nothing. You don't like to turn back yet, you push on and find another track, then in a few moments it begins to twist unnecessarily and criss-crosses with other tracks that seem just as definite. Before you have gone a dozen more paces, all the tracks are equally indefinite and you realize they are aimless things, made by horses or cattle, leading nowhere. You sit down on a stump and at once you are stung by soldier-ants. And several wallabies bound away, just to show you that it is possible to keep going if you have any bush sense. But if you don't lose your head, you'll come out after a while on a real track or a creek you can follow, perhaps in a dusk of curlew-cries.

A harsh land, but I loved it in its own right, in its particular existence, not simply as the given example of water, air, fire, earth, from which I might draw the poetic essences. Witherby pointed to the lack of variety as compared with an English landscape. Every tree trunk straight as the next, every ridge as stony and meagrely grassed as the next. Tall scraggy trees soaring into nothing in particular, into an indefinite entanglement of thin leaves; ragged broken rocks. Miles and miles of ringbarked trees, killed off to make the grass grow thicker, without any concern for the ultimate effect on the soil, on the climate.

Box-flats with the leaves gone scantily into the sky, the bark hanging scabbily in festoons, the scrabbly undergrowth. Thick scrubland, with odd bunya-pines and criss-crossing creepers. And then a broad vista, where the delicate distance of hazy blue and purple was born from the endless dull green tree tops; and a strange mirage of luxurious beauty shimmers out of the dry gritty earth.

'I like it because man has yet done so little to it,' Witherby said.

I could not appreciate that remark until I had seen England; but I felt the untamed grandeur, the infuriatingly labyrinthine mess, as part of myself. Now I no longer experienced the ecstatic communion of my early adolescence, no longer could slide from the human world by leaving the houses behind me and listening to the tongues of water. Yet I at moments felt myself rooted in a new way, a mere visitor to the seething life of nature but happy in its sufficiency and coming back into it by devious roads, overcoming my exclusion. For the elemental union I substituted a meditative calm, in which the blue distance, the waterfall-plume, the pillared strength of a silver gum, became images so deeply brooded on as to express the whole of reality.

I read Henry Lawson and found many elements of this new self in his work; but still could not see where I next went as poet.

I watched the carpet snake, about a dozen feet long, marked on the back and sides with a pattern of rich brown and yellow. It lay gorged on something that showed as a lump in the middle of its body – maybe a bandicoot or even a whole wallaby. There was nothing to fear in it any more than in the frilled iguanas that looked like baby dragons as they scampered over rocks or ran up a tree. But it made me think of the adders and the brown snake with its iridescent drabness and the snake with the neat white rings and the black snake with red stripes on his sides and a salmon belly. An earth crawling with many horrors. Any stick you leaned carelessly to take up might leap and lash and sting you to a blackening death.

'Death adders, nothing to scare a bloke in those cross-eyed buggers,' said the hairy chap in the pub down on the flats, scratching himself and spitting at a spider on the wall. 'You can catch 'em on the hop any day in a pear clump. When they strike, they hoop 'emselves up and whack their head and tail together, real comics they are. Some bloody fools say they stick you with the horny end of their bloody tails, but they bloody well don't. Many a one I've held by the blasted tail. They can't do a thing in hell then. But when they've got their goddam danders up, they'll come hell-for-leather at you, rearing up like a mad Irishman. But you can knock the buggers silly with a stick and pick 'em up by the bloody tail. I wish I had one here. I'd soon make all you bastards run.'

He spun a coin. 'My shout.'

A hard earth. I began to fear it, but I fought my fear down.

19 · REDCLIFFE BOAT

IN RETROSPECT I liked the crowded scenes; among them I felt lost, with a mild envy, regret and distant enjoyment sighing a dim Debussy music of reed pipes. Today I had brought along a copy of *The Idiot*, with the odd conviction we all have, that travelling is the time for some serious quiet reading; and I opened the pages automatically as the steamer moved out amid shouts and whistles. But my eye refused to focus on the type. I stared at Kangaroo Point sliding by, the furrowed waters, the squat ferry, the people boisterously packed all round me; and as I stared, I thought only of Dostoevsky. But the moment I returned to the book, it was the people, the breezy sunlight, the veering gull, that mattered. My book slipped and was retrieved with difficulty from interlocked boots and shoes, pram-wheels and suitcases, scrambling small children. Someone had already spilt gingerbeer.

I forced myself into the Russian scene, but a gap widened in the sentence that I read, and mind could not straddle it. I felt lost like Myshkin of the book between the impulsive Aglaia and the proud embittered Nastasya, but unable to grasp why even a Dostoevskian fool did not delightedly stretch out his hand to either girl. And yet, more than half my hope that a girl would fall in love with me was derived from summoning up the moment when I would renounce her, renounce everything that bound me in any way to the world. For how could she be the Impossible She who incarnated my rejection of all bonds and offered a union that was elementally free, beyond all echo of the lamentations of the Daughters of Albion? I heard the leaves of the novel flap and many laughters scratching on a metallic surface of consciousness. The whole ship seemed breathless with anticipation, though jarred with turning noises like those of a record murmuring towards the sonorous release of the first chord. I waited for an apocalyptic music, which would make me one with the festival day, which would mate Myshkin with both his lovely girls.

I was looking into two eyes, into a single eye, the Cyclopean sun. Not an eye at all, but some liquid point of light carved on a blue immensity. And then, as my distraction deepened, I was aware only of some vanishing joyousness beyond the light point, a crystalline intensity which no colour could shape.

The ship swung and rolled. Mangrove islands rushed drably by. A child gave a peacock scream. My thoughts collapsed giddily down the cavern of vision as if I had been looking through a reversed telescope which was rapidly shut up. For a moment the kaleidoscopic sunlight expanded with a wild variety of truncated episodes: people snipped into pretty little bits and stuck together again by the winds of chance, spectacles riding a pair of rosy nipples and a baby with a scruffy beard, a nose growing from a bald head and a lionfaced maiden emerging from a luncheon basket with a sausage for her nether limbs, a gilt bird carrying off someone's false teeth and a weeping fish in a clergyman's collar. Then the world was its strange normal self once more. And there she was, my Aglaia-Natasha, a blue-eyed girl only a few yards away, barricaded by a family of seven children that all seemed the same age except the fat-jowled baby.

She was fair, if corn gold is white and if corn white is gold, and the cheap muslin betrayed the precise circumference of her young nipples. She was fresh as the sea breeze, certainly the very breeze that wafted Venus up from the foam in her own scallop shell. Surely her gusto was what blew her hair sideways and frilled the muslin. So perfectly she matched the easy exuberance that it seemed the day had been expressly invented for her, out of the myriad of possible other days. This day on which the sea pranced and tripped with practised exhilaration, as though the bosom of Tethys moved pneumatically in deliberate beauty exercises. On which the holidaying sun beamed and bounced, a commercial-traveller sun who slapped you with gold, an undampable familiarity of jostling light, and muttered smutty tales in your ears about girls with cornflower eyes.

Aglaia-Natasha breathed and the waves rose and fell with the charming unbalance of a rocking-horse; and the smoke from the funnels reminded you of those illusions of fatly painted tin attached to a toy locomotive, so suavely cut were its curves. I listened for her heart, but heard only the beat of the boat's engines. I knew that it was the restless energy harnessed in her slight frame, which drove the boat along.

Now that the day had a definite and warmly coloured image, I was happy. The maze of various forms revolved around a single face and had meaning; the niche of the sky had its goddess; the noise made up of many voices and of the sea-wind had become a slow undulating song. I could even read, in snatches. I went again through the drunken lick-spittle Lebedev's denunciation of utilitarian ethics. Now it all seemed ironic, fool-mockery, perhaps because I felt there was a deathliness, an hysteric zone, in Myshkin, I found myself watching the juice of an orange that ran down the chin of a fat woman, it dripped gently off, one drop delayed for a moment by the long hair of a warty barrier before it joined its fellows inside the discoloured edge of the corsage. I was saved again from nausea by remembering the girl, the glint in her eyes which reflected her golden hair curling round a finger of the sun. Here, surely, was the source of joy undefiled, or what was the use of living on into the decay and compromise of time? I was desperately keen that she should not notice me, should not ever know what a debt of gratitude I owed to her. She smiled at the lad seated by her. Her mouth curled slightly back with an effect at once tender and cruel, though with her eyes she gave herself unreservedly. And so I saw in her both Aglaia and Natasha, and wanted to weep for her and for myself, for the beautiful thing that would be broken.

People pushed between, on, past, over me, making for the lavatories or water taps or long lost friends. Children trod on each other's hands and bawled. A blind man with a deal wood and tin violin squeaked disconsolately, with a label in his hat: This man is guaranteed blind and a family man pity me. A woman afflicted with modesty put up an umbrella while she breastfed her baby, and was accused of blocking the passage by a man with a twisted walking-stick. A child found his hand caught between the planks of a seat and howled, obsessed by the horrible idea of a life fettered to an excursion-steamer seat. Around me lay the trippers in their determined holiday swoons.

I felt entirely with them in their aim of enjoyment, their surrender to the wind, of sunlight and the cradle of the deep; and in the ikon of the white-golden girl I had my Venus of the annunciatory moment. But I wanted more than that. I wanted the cry of the wind to become the hymn of a multitude adoring the elements, I wanted all movements to become rhythmic and obedient to the central pull of the image of Venus. Without the earth ritual, what could enjoyment do but become a dopey inertia, a philistine daydream?

The small boy named Dan Dan the Baker's Man was given a blown-up brown paper bag to burst; but he hit it sideways and it tore with no magnificent bang. In consolation he was presented with a lemonade bottle to throw overboard at a clear loss of the penny claimable on returns. It plopped in the waves, an offering to shark toothed Neptune, and yet I was still unplacated: a part of the gay throng, an accusing outsider. The idiot also had double thoughts; so he confessed, boasted, collapsed, a high motive coupling with a base one: himself torn in half, no pure fool but a narcissistic eunuch, finally one with the murderous Rogozhin, seated with him on the floor of degradation. Did Dostoevsky want to suggest the secret kinship of good and evil, the underhand compact between renunciation and the murder that is ownership? A little of the superfluous milk from the young mother's bountiful breasts had stained her blouse in two mauve circles, and a few white drops welled through and fell to her lap. She noticed, and with a scared glance around she turned seawards with one arm thrown awkwardly over the front of her blouse, diligently following the leisurely curves of the seagulls. So are we all afraid of the fullness of life.

A delicious torpidity, as though I had drunk several bottles of Burgundy, was numbing me. I too was one of the pleasure-racked, the stupefied. Dostoevsky merely gained his subtle effect by not being sure what he wanted to depict, Christ or a weakling who incarnated the contradictions of life in absolute terms. And thus, one way or another, all meaning was fabricated, injected painfully into the unprepared body of things, a serum of festering dreams and toxins of rigor mortis. Suddenly I seemed wholly inside my body, aware of every pore, every cell, filled with an unholy warmth of fermentations, sprawled in giant power and quite fearless. I had only to put out my hand and take; I was alive. Here and now. And yet so heavy that I wondered the boat did not sink, and so locked in the completeness of the moment that I felt unable ever to move again, to lift a hand or flick an eyelid. A Gulliver swollen uselessly in a universe of pygmies, impotent with a plethora of power. And yet all the time the gross sensuous satisfaction kept brimming over, and a voice went on saying: All things are permitted.

We were now well into the Bay, passing Sandgate. Someone struck up a song I did not know. A boy's cap blew overboard. The whistling foam sounded like the sharp-edged overpowering Song of the Sirens, lulling me in a dangerous noon coma. The smoke was torn from the funnels in ragged patches, vanishing into the blue dazzle. Now a mouth-organ had taken up the accomplice tune. My book closed of its own accord. The moral problem was fraudulent; the sun and the sea remained. I felt entirely in accord with the people around me.

Then we were slowing into the wharf; and amid the hullabaloo of arrival, the packing of pannikin and basket, the shrill questions of children, the shuffling release, I too stood up, breaking the spell. The corn-white goddess was on her feet, oddly dumpy and plump, no longer the radiant heart of the day, merely one of many girls. I clutched my one piece of luggage, Dostoevsky.

Slowly the thick procession waddled up the gangway, to disperse rapidly along the jetty. I remembered a return from Manly Beach when I was about seven. For some reason the three of us – Phil a baby in arms – were alone with our mother after a day by the sea; I think that Harriet had been there and gone back ahead. The crowd was excessive, noisy, considerably drunken, ready to storm the boats. Our mother had difficulty in saving us from being swung against walls, trampled on. I feel her still hugging Phil and turned aside protectively over

Ray and myself, while the mob surged by with hoarse shouts as some barrier was lifted. (I hear still the clattering of the loose pier timbers under their feet.) Now I could realize my mother's terror, though at the time I knew only her calm shielding presence.

At last I reached the gangway and saw my two cousins waving. A few more steps and I would be free from the nightmare pressure that enclosed me. Like my mother, I might be able to protect someone else, but never myself; and who could that someone else be? A sudden jab sent my novel jumping from my arm into the water below. A woman screamed. With a final wrench I reached the splintery beams of freedom and did not look back; but the moral problem remained.

20 · LETTER FROM OLYMPUS

I HAD come on Freud and eagerly took many things from him
– his feeling for the dynamic force of the whole self, his capacity
to unravel complicated strands of meaning in a single image,
his identification of the process of self-knowledge with the pattern of tragic movement in ancient Greek drama. What
attracted me most was his analysis of the condensation activity
in a dream, where several ideas and emotions were fused in one
symbol, and his grasp of the unity of the life process which with
its inner conflicts gave a vital meaning to the least element of
experience and made knowledge of that meaning possible.
Also, I felt drawn to his thesis of a desire cored in every dream
as the organizing energy. Many other aspects of his method did
not interest me – his mythology of the components of the self,
his geography of the unconscious, and so on. In any event, at
this time he had not moved to the worst of the rigidities which
cramped his thought; his tendency to see reality as a projection
of an inner conflict or desire did not worry me. In many ways
it harmonized with the subjective bias in my own positions –
though I was now trying to correct that bias and move to a
fuller understanding of the forces moulding a man.

Quinton was chafing for action, his eyes turned more and
more on the Soviet Union. I listened to him and his friend,
another Wobbly, discussing the goings-on at Cloncurry and its
copper mines. Cattle-thieving in a big way. Posses of vigilantes,
revolvered, trying to nose the raiders out in the twisting gorges
and hidden flats of the mountain range. The cattle-thieves
shooting the horses under them and burning their camp equip-
ment. 'It's a sort of rebellion.' The District Court refused to
convict any of the men rounded up. 'Sounds like Texas.'

The man with a cabbage-tree hat, a shepherd, blinked his red eyes. He knew Cloncurry, a town set on the fringes of hell, with gutters built so wide to take the storm-waters that they needed foot-bridges across them every now and then. Rows of saddle-horses, with sweat zig-zagged on their dusty flanks, tied to the hitching rails. The giant mountain-line. 'I saw one of the boys lay out a bastard of a stock inspector in the police paddock. That'll teach him, he said.'

Jim C. was trying to memorize all the arguments in Bergson's *Time and Free Will* in order to defeat the determinist Will. But every time he started a discussion he forgot one of the steps in Bergson's involved exposition and was floored by Will's mechanistic sledge-hammer. One evening in the W.E.A. building he took me aside with grave animation and told me that he meant to rescue a girl from a brothel near Breakfast Creek, close to the Chinese joss-house. 'It's an unusual sort of place, the madam's got a bust of Wagner and a piano in her room.' Jim had a romantic eye for culture and felt quite excited at the conjunction of Wagner in his lollopy velvet cap and a Breakfast Creek madam. 'I'd like you to meet the girl. Her name's Jessica. She's not an ordinary sort of tart. I saw it the moment I set eyes on her. I'd like you to meet her. There's a sailor that beats her up if she lifts an eyelid.'

'Why can't she go if she wants to?'

'She owes the madam a lot of money. I don't know exactly how much, but it's a lot. She was crying.'

He was going to meet Jessica in half an hour near the Bridge. I went along with him and we waited, kicking at the kerb, but she didn't turn up. 'They must have locked the door,' he said. We didn't have the price of a pint, and anyhow the pubs were now shut. We wandered along the river bank. Jim wanted to know all about the Socratic dialogues. Also, what was a semi-tone?

That was the sort of thing that went on happening. Talk, talk, and a feeling of emptiness, which arose in considerable part from nothing more mysterious than a shortage of money. We went to a two-up school behind hoardings in Albert Street, but the speed and fury of the betting discouraged us from losing our few bob.

One day Dudley came out of my boy-scout Sydney past. He was now a banana farmer down the coast from Brisbane, a good steady quiet young man whom I was overjoyed to meet again and to whom I had nothing to say. He had nothing to say either. We drifted about Brisbane for a couple of days and then he returned to his bananas, having failed to find whatever he had hoped to find in Brisbane. His visit seemed to ratify my break from the society around me, into which he had hardly fitted; but I still awaited a knock on the door from Life, the opening bars of Beethoven's Fifth Symphony become flesh and blood.

Then one day as I went into the common room at the university I found a package addressed to me. Inside were a dozen etchings by Norman, with a letter. I had only time to push the opened package into a locker and glance over the letter before I rushed into a lecture on metaphysics. All through the hour I kept reading bits of the letter; but I was friendly with the lecturer, who had introduced me to Freud, and I didn't want to appear too rudely inattentive.

At last the hour was over and I could hurry back to the common room, tear off my gown and discard all ideas of work for the day. Terrified at the thought that someone might have carried off the etchings, I rescued the package from the locker and turned its contents over and over, unable to stop at any one of the sheets, wanting to see them all at once in a single superimposed image. The changing figures fell into a complex design composed of snippets from all the etchings; and then as I set off for my aunt's house I found that one work stood out sharply against all the others. *Who Comes?* A naked panic-stricken woman, surrounded with other shrinking revellers, turns to look beyond the curtain at something not depicted – what?

As I was leaving, I struck one of the arts students and hastily showed him the etchings. 'My father's work.'

'Eh?' he said, uninterested, 'Oh yes.'

Then, as I went across the river in the small chugging ferry that served the university, I hugged the etchings under my arm, afraid that they would fall in the water. And suddenly, horribly, I felt Death, not as an idea, but as a possibility implicit in every pore and atom of my flesh. Someday I should have to die and lose these works of art. Death presented itself as a darkness of privation, a void in which the vital image of art was banished, not simply as my own fall headlong into nothingness. My life was in the art more richly than in my own body. Apart from books, precious but replaceable, I had never owned anything before, anything that I thought of as mine, utterly mine. I discovered the loss of self, the moment of sheer self-alienation, in discovering property.

The letter was charmingly placatory and suggested that the time had come for us to know one another. (Bertram Stevens, the well-meaning owl, had reported favourably and indeed done some nagging on my behalf. That I was making my way in education without any calls on the paternal purse also spoke in my favour.) I wrote back a long incoherent letter of delight. More etchings came, and a copy of *Thus Spake Zarathustra* with an account of what the book had meant for Norman.

I read it through. At first I was not much attracted. The attack on poets as liars who fished up bits of old gods from the sea affronted the Keatsian who held to the creed of Truth–Beauty. The attitude to war seemed the sheerest barbarism, vulgar as my aunt's snobbery. But after a while I began to warm to the idiom and found my ideas again falling into turmoil. Much of what I made out seemed to deny the positions that I had been reaching through Witherby and Quinton, my synthesis of Blake, Keats, Dostoevsky and the idea of revolution. And then at moments it seemed that here was a rich new viewpoint which I could work into my insecure concept of revolutionary poetry, adding something that that concept badly needed – a philosophy of history which would objectify the structure of Blake's prophetic books and then yield a revaluation of all values. An acceptance of tragedy as the highest yes-saying to life; an irreconcilable demand for joy. 'To have run through every chamber of the modern soul, to have eaten in each of its corners: my pride, my torture, and my joy. To transcend pessimism effectively, and in short a Goethean regard full of love and goodwill.' Above all, the conception of joy as the deepest creative dyamic won me over.

Norman did not want me to visit him at Springwood till

after Christmas. I did not know the reason at the time; but the fact was that after many years he was about to become a father again. To fill in the time I agreed to go to the W.E.A. camp on Tambourine.

21 · LOVE ON A MOUNTAIN

I WENT up a few days before the camp opened, to help with fixing up the tents, settling the kitchen arrangements, and so on. With me travelled Birt B. (who in the 1930s, as Reuter's correspondent at Athens, wrote a good book on the concentration-camp islands in the Aegean). At this time he was a rather prim ever-so-socially conscious worker – employed, I think, in a brewery where as a rampant teetotaller he went about with a spiritual peg on his nose to save himself from the smell. In the train we began an argument about poetry. It was a mere bourgeois luxury, he said, an opiate only a little better than religion: something the working class could, should and would do without as soon as they stormed heaven and took over political power. I told him that all language was decomposed poetry and that he couldn't ask for a mutton chop or a kiss without stirring the bones of a myriad dead poets. He replied that he was a vegetarian and had strong views on male chastity. So I gave him up and handed him the book I was reading, Masefield's *Everlasting Mercy*. After a few disapproving snorts he became absorbed and refused to return the book; before the camp was over, he was spending all his spare time in writing octosyllabic couplets of a highly moral character. He had decided that poetry could be used to wake up the workers as well as to lull them in demoralized slumbers.

The camp, arriving on the eve of my momentous journey to Springwood and the regained father, was a strangely lighted affair: a gathering of the elect six thousand feet above space and time, at which the destiny of man was to be determined. The holidayers who joined us, coming with a shout into the noon or suddenly showing up in the red campfire, were all remarkable characters chosen for some necessary role in the ritual drama of death and resurrection, the mystery play of redemption. The mountain that I knew so well as a solitude was being peopled with the images bringing unknown gifts and the shepherds seeking the star of the new life.

I finished erecting a bed in the tent – threading saplings through a sack and then sticking the result over two inverted Vs made by driving forks into the soil and leaning stakes against them. Throwing aside the tent-flap, I walked across to the campfire where the newcomers were grouped, helplessly warming their flat hands – a score or so, standing at odd angles like pieces set down carelessly on a chessboard. I saw a girl.

Pale gums stretched up into dark misty skies, into clouds of gloomy sandstone. A fire-scooped cavern of the night, with the tree supports lost to view before they passed through the cracked clouds. Our small world of rosy light was left cosily and cleanly far beneath. Tent-flies, mostly hung too high, made warm blank windows among the scraggy leaves. A swollen burst bole reared over the crackling fire. The newcomers all stood there with the lost waiting air of folk coming on a savage unknown place after dark. And the girl.

She was turned towards me. But I did not believe that she saw me. The world had stopped still and no one saw anything but I. The others were closed inside the derelict moment, awaiting a signal to come alive. The girl was a tall phantom of burning dust, a sweet mummy of pillared fire with eyes of lapis lazuli. She couldn't see me; but I could see her. I stared until she turned away with a light laugh to speak to her sister.

The spell broke. Everyone was moving, everyone was at home; and I was one of the bustling welcomers, one of the ancients of the camp (having been there already two days).

We were introduced and I kept near her side. She turned and gazed straight in my face with clear accepting grey eyes. She said nothing and I could talk to a girl only when alone with her.

'Will you be here all the two weeks?' I asked at length.

'Yes,' she said, and then as an afterthought, 'All the two weeks.'

'It's rather cold tonight, isn't it?'

'Yes . . . I thought it was rather cold.'

You felt that she used your words not out of mockery or vacancy of mind, but as a carefully premeditated tribute to their peculiarly just summing-up of the situation. She did not answer at once; she considered; then she presented you with your own words as though she were adding a profound contribution of thought to yours. As though she were speaking extraordinarily well in a foreign tongue or making an abstruse mathematical calculation. With a touch of amiable distance, of dollish condescension. As though a picture awoke suddenly with bell-like echoes of your thought, startling your difficult meditation with a dialogue of enigmatic clichés.

Another girl approached us, wild-eyed under a heavy fringe of dark hair. 'Bessy, come and help us with the wash-up.'

Bessy turned to me her large mute eyes as though making up her mind whether it was really worth while trying to explain or whether I could possibly understand if she were rash enough to attempt an explanation. Then her lips formed the words in trial and she determined on the one adequate formula. 'Excuse me, I must go and help with the wash-up.'

I lay in my sack bed awake for a long time after the other two in my tent had become (omitting the scandalous complexity of possible dream lives) stertorous corpses out of whose lungs sleep, methodical as a life-saver kneading a half-drowned man, was discharging a regular wastage of breath. A silence was breaking in slow waves on the reef of the trees. An underswell of silence that caught the mind in a tow of danger. Silence beating in tides of sap, in crumbling earth. The fist that slowly crushes the withering leaf, the tiny crackle of withdrawing life, the filtering stain of colour, the busy shuttles of a spider.

What was it that I wanted? I felt a deep grief come up out of me, a moan that mingled with the slow sough of the night. I felt a pity for all women; and as I clenched my hand, it was fitted with a steel gauntlet of anger and devotion. I felt myself one with the ebbing night, in a melancholic eagerness, an endless recession of planes like a gate that moved forwards as I entered it, along an avenue of swaying cypresses.

When I awoke the subtle gnawing mice-teeth of quiet were all gone. Instead, I banged my head on the solid brass wall of locust shrilling. A swerving billow of sound that never broke.

Disturbed by the bird whistles as if a composer were vainly trying to introduce melodic themes into a surge of polyphonic
semitones which had got beyond control. Listen long enough
and you became the mad musician striving to convert the vast
wind of fine-edged discord with a thematic chirp.

As if the abrupt change, the leap from the purring night-
hush straight into the shrill of castanetted light, were a moment
of furious decision altering my life for eternity.

I hurried down for a swim in the pool below the little fall
and lounged on the big wet rock, looking out for leeches and
pulling up pleated waterweeds. The morning sky consumed
the leaf edges with a corrosive dazzle. The leaves rubbed away
against the molten lump of light and the sky pressed in lower
than the tree-tops. Lianas like the cords of a magnificent hussar
criss-crossed the packed bosom of the woods. Palms waved
their topknots, plumed coiffures fixed on lofty stands for the
giants of the dawn. The pranking wind tied bits of sky on the
tail of the trees. The leaves jingled out of tune. The big ferns
had rolled-up shoots like the things that boys blow out in each
other's faces – like the shavings curled from the plane of some
forest carpenter, some satyr craftsman. Mixed with small fern
traceries like hairnets dragged from ravished spinsters in the
midst a midnight dream. Plump spiders mended their lines
which the sun tautened. Water-beetles skidded with busy
aimlessness over the polished surface of the pool, dinting but
not breaking the skin of light. Birds screeked and squealed, a
host of lories, rosellas and other diminutive parrots, hanging
upside down to wink at me with naughty black eyes. Sentimental fruit-pigeons cooed insinuatingly as if they wanted to sell
something, sweet-tongued gerygones fussed about tiny nests in
a leaf-bunch, and a long-runner peeped sagely from behind
cover.

Small tadpole nastinesses nibbled my toes. I shuddered. Was
a spider swinging at me from behind? Was a water-snake dart-
ing at me across the pool? The shadows rotted all around, full
of ugly squamous life, and ticks sprang for my genitals. Oh,
I should have to enter the horrible brown water again to reach
my clothes.

Birtles and someone else were coming down as I removed

the leech from my bleeding ankle and towelled myself. 'Splendid in the water,' I said with British sincerity.

I had promised to fetch some things from the station. She smiled a farewell smile, which would have done very well as a smile of welcome. All the way there and back I thought of others interrupting that lucid smile, pouring out tea for her, asking her how she had slept, showing the way to the sackwalled privy which Birtles and I had built (WOMEN, the notice, with a bony finger painted by myself – the board having now slipped, the finger pointed the Women heavenwards as if they were expected to climb the tree and expose themselves on the yard-arm bough). I thought of her going about her duties and pleasures, wiping her nose, pulling burrs off her stockings, smoothing the crease in the back of her skirt, wondering which pullover to use. All my thoughts of her were of plain everyday matters; but she seemed a dryad trapped inside her unnecessary clothes, uncertain as to the use of suspenders and too shy to ask anyone.

I arrived back as the discussion about milk-getting was on. There were two buckets to be carried. She, Birt and another girl volunteered. 'I'll show you the way,' I said, and she smiled with her slightly puzzled deliberation, encouragingly.

We went down over the creek burbling on worn rocks. Past the ruined sawmill, its tumbled wood furry-green with bright delicate moss distributed as evenly as from a brush, the circular saw still standing between an oblong frame like a dismantled guillotine. Up through tunnels paved with decaying leaves inches deep and showery with dew, while I kicked before us the shell of the giant snail, *panda falconeri*, big enough to serve as a bullocky's beer mug.

A bronze wing pigeon went crashing up, its wings speckled with brown feathers of a fine metallic lustre. 'A bronze wing,' I said.

'Yes,' she remarked, 'yes, a bronze wing.'

We saw the lower parts of the tree-trunks as if we were underground. Tall smooth silver-gums glistened where the crowbars of light broke through the roof of leaves: luminous as the track of a snail, their bark fallen away except near the roots, so that they showed like women stepping out of a fallen chemise.

Damp silence goblined our laughters. Lawyer-vines with their concealed fish-hooks caught in our sleeves and high orchids made holes of warm colour among the birdnest ferns. Bessy and I had loitered behind, both holding the same bucket. My hand slid along and touched hers, and the touch sufficed for conversation. In the bowels of the bush quiet, pitched to a harsh low key like the grating roar hushed in sea shells, the voice was daunted.

We obtained the milk from the small farm and started back over a field wet with flowers, into the soft shadows. Layer on layer of dimness like dusky gauze sinking down and down. 'It's very ghostly about this time,' I said at last.

She leaned a little to one side; then she confirmed my words. 'About this time . . .' She was thinking hard for the inevitable phrase. 'Ghostly . . . very.' She spoke diffidently, as if she expected contradiction; but I told her she was right.

The other pair spilt a quarter of their pail where the path sloped treacherously to the creek. We didn't spill a drop. We were proud of this and felt drawn together.

Next evening several of us went for a walk. Dusk was beginning to blur out of the bushes. Sound became removed as though windows had been closed all round the soul's habitation. We emerged on the open mountainside, into sudden depth of space, like a jump in a Beethoven scherzo, beyond the moon and back. The deep scene was already filling in with edgeless night, but for the moment it was traversed with a faint liquidity, a transparency slightly out of focus, which was neither night nor day. Then the veils shifted imperceptibly and the tones were darkness. Lights were turned on deceptively near and a train engine made little glowing puffs of gold through the gloom as if a man, quite near and yet out over the immensity, was drawing at his cigar as he walked on the ramparts of the world. Silence is always flowing away from or towards a collapse into sound, a fidgeting of patterns in the wallpaper or a rustling of the threads that hang from the stars.

The others talked.

'But,' said the youth with the halfcast in his eye, who, when excited, bored with his forefinger into his ear as if hoping to extract the wax of an idea, 'we must decide if Aldous Huxley is a serious thinker or just a poseur. Everything depends on that.'

'I think,' said Miss Cruicks, who had hair the colour of mulligatawny soup (that favourite soup of all the boarding-houses I had known) and a dyspeptic nose, 'the teaching of birth control should be made compulsory, even if Archbishop Mannix has fits.'

'It was the personal genius of Lenin that built the bridge between the Mir and Marx.'

'But is he a serious thinker? really serious?'

The talkers lacked a sense of reverence. O temple of the great Australian night, encrusted with stars, you need no god to be holy; but those who grasp the world with their senses, not with ready-made patterns cut on their deadened brains, have no words in this moving vastness which comes down to rest on the palm of an outstretched hand. What shall I sing you, the hymn of Alkman in the silence of the jewelled dusk of the ancient Aegean or the ballad of the rollicking ramble-eer, the son of a gun for beer? which comes more truly home to this young prehistoric earth?

'Can't we get away from all this?' I whispered.

'Can't we?' she inquired doubtfully. Then, as though I'd forced a heavy responsibility on her, she stopped and stared at me through the dusk, like someone trying to remember a telephone number. As if she wanted to ring me up but couldn't remember my number, and besides, she didn't know where the nearest telephone booth was. I counted the ticks of the hush. At length she gave the slight pout which showed she was formulating her thoughts between her lips. 'Let's hide.'

She had made a suggestion all her own. Let's hide! We were already hidden in the circling dusk-glooms. The only way to stop hiding would have been to light the lantern I held in my hand, for which neither of us had any matches. But the proposal of hiding made us a thousandfold more hidden, with magical fern seed in our shoes. We shadowed the others down tracks of slushy dark, under tangled skies shaken every now and then by the voices into sprinkling waterdrops. Hand in hand at last, too shy to let go though our palms were sweaty and our fingers cramped: if we ever let go, we could never catch hold again.

And then we had to let go. For a barbed-wire fence loomed up before us and I had to stretch the wires apart for her to step through. But miraculously, on the other side, our fears were proved false and our hands found each other again. Despite the darkness I could see her face. No night could have put out her face.

The others turned to go back. Their clear irrelevant voices hung as solid as blasphemous copperbells in the buoyant air.

'I think the marriage ceremony in a church is positively indecent,' Miss Cruicks was saying. 'I could never submit to it.'

'That's an interesting point of yours, but I can't think it's proved that he's a really serious thinker.'

'Already a structural degeneration of the female pelvis . . .'

'But Russia is primarily a peasant country.'

They passed the spot where we stood peeping, hand-in-hand, hiders after all, behind a bush that lighted up with a myriad tiny bulbs of water, yet did not betray us. The motions of the lantern cabined the walkers in swinging cages of frail light. Then the group was gone, still talking, aliens in the homeland of the night. Still in an aloof courtesy of laughter, we followed. Fugitives of blowing star and the sloped dark, going lightly in gathered secrecy, in confidence of wonder, into the risky heavens.

As we went over the ploughed field near the camp, I tripped and pulled her down. She put out her hand to save herself and lay across me, making no effort to rise. I kissed her on the shoulder. When she moved, it was to bring our faces closer together.

When we reached the camp, we went up to the others expecting to be asked where we had disappeared. But no one had noticed our absence. Birtles was arguing about self-expression in the labour process. Miss Cruicks had a battle gleam in her eye; she had found one of the women who was inclined to be anti-feminist. J.D. the lecturer from Sydney was telling the squinter to read *South Wind*; it was a key book and 'most ironically serious as well as seriously ironical.' The squinter looked baffled.

I watched with benevolent bewilderment. Was it really possible to talk about such things?

She sighed. Her eyes were always closed now and the smile alighting between her eyes with a bird flash was always there. But now it was like a light behind dense water: a fading smile that never retreated beyond the warm lowered eyelashes, a smile that smoothed with a slight tension the calm contours of the cheeks. Doll of a kiss. Toy with indelible smile; toy found at the back of a drawer, suddenly compacting all childhood's memories; indefatigable doll of a kiss, always giving a sigh when pressed on the navel. Drowned Venus floating in the faint tide-cradle below the coralline shadows. O unexplored country of the kiss, O girl unknown.

Nothing mattered, nothing but that. In the dark I put my hand out and caught hold of a poisonous stinging-tree. It pained me savagely, but I made no sign, did not even twitch, and said nothing about it, then or later. But next day I went and chopped the bush down. Then, from a remark of her sister's, I gathered that Bessy too had been stung and she too had said nothing.

Nothing mattered, nothing but this. The storm didn't matter, catching us under a tree where the branches consolidated the raindrops into large streams like roof spouts. The thunder came with a sharp rattle and the lightning kept up a steady flicker, shooting in long streams across the sky, then snapping into a network of thin clear lines, jangling in all directions. A beautiful tree of lightning spread over half the sky, smeared with torrential rain. Then a shattering crash that heaved up the ground under our feet. And all the while we kissed. Sullenly the storm retreated, defeated.

Now when one of the great tree-candelabra of lightnings was held up quivering in a titanic hand, the face of each leaf around us glistened broadly, the spouted streams were full of twisted silver coils, we glimpsed the tight cotton threads of tapestried rain. Fences and undulating earth rushed drably up, still clotted with fungus of the dark, and then collapsed. The water was pouring down my neck, trickling under my belt and filling my shoes. But we were warm where touched.

I saw iguana-faced gargoyles in the tree, reaching out, and then at the next flash boughs of lashing snakes. Nothing mattered.

As I awoke in the morning, words buzzed round my head like flies. I sat up and felt in my coat for a used envelope and scribbled some lines before I had time to feel the need of breakfast and the sight of her face again.

> *I used to wonder how to kiss and what words should be said,*
> *and whether first I'd kiss your mouth or kiss your golden head.*
> *I wondered how one started and just how to hold you tight.*
> *I was so very shy, you know, and anxious to be right.*
>
> *Yet when at last we leaned and looked within the unbidden spell*
> *and all the fears that hid between us broke away and fell,*
> *I did not need to think at all, I did not need a sign.*
> *Our arms went round each other and I found your mouth on mine.*

I had forgotten all my high imagic ambitions, I wanted to write a song for singing, a cry of the morning as plain as the shadow of the bird swung across the canvas of my tent. And the single uplifted emotion carried on through all the days ahead of us, the measured days that went round in an unbroken circle of sweetness. Playing parts in Shaw's *Doctor's Dilemma*, fetching more milk, discussing the rebellious literature born of the war and the economic consequences of the U.S.S.R., exchanging smiles in the tall windy air. Lying in my tent in the soft silted light, sighing, turning as the earth turned, only the mouth of a kiss.

Going back to Brisbane in the train, I sat opposite her. We didn't speak, but smiled reassuringly. After all one cannot talk quietly through the racket of the wheels. And what can one say on a railway platform? One can only shake hands and say, 'Hope we meet again,' and then hurry home, making up couplets:

And on another's lips you'll find
the kisses that I left behind –

yet feeling an emptiness at the heart of the bountiful memory, an ache that comes near tears as midnight strikes, a restive need to walk the pointless streets.

I met her a couple of days later by accident. To see her in the ordinary street was an incomprehensible shock. 'I'm going up country this afternoon,' she said. 'There's my sister waiting at the tram-stop.' Not knowing what to say, I showed her the notebook with my poems copied out in it. (I always carried my notebook in town: not to show people, but to complete my identity.) She glanced at the pages a few moments.

'You have had these,' she said, and for the first time I couldn't look her in the eyes. 'Goodbye,' she said.

She moved off to join her sister. I wanted to stop her and ask a thousand questions. Suddenly she had become a woman, a person with past and a future, with a rich life of thoughts and feelings, a person about whom I knew absolutely nothing. But she was gone. Then I realized that I had said no more to her all that time than she had said to me.

22 · SPRINGWOOD

NORMAN HAD sent me the proofs of his book, *Creative Effort*, which I read through for the tenth time as the train took me through the prosperous wheatlands of the Darling Downs. I wanted to agree with it, but I couldn't. And I told Bertram Stevens about my reaction when I saw him in Sydney. 'I can't accept this rejection of history. Perhaps it suits Norman and what he needs to get out of life. But even if it were true that the earth exists only as a mud-flat for the generation of a few geniuses, I still wouldn't accept it because I don't want to and it isn't true for me. I still believe that I ought to be ready to give my life for freedom, for the people. I can't accept some special ticket of exemption from Olympus.' Though B.S. felt that I was too highflown in my idiom, he approved of my position in his own dim way; he had himself once been an ardent exponent of Bimetallism.

So, still uncertain on what terms I was going to meet Norman, I awaited him in the hotel on the slope up from George Street near the Quay. I felt so flattened out in anxious uncertainty that I was aware of nothing worse than an inner dullness and a vague bother about the right tips for the waiters. At the back of my mind hovered a faint steady gratitude towards Bessy, as though there had been only one possible pathway to this moment – through her sleepy kisses. As though I had gone up to Tambourine knowing that she would be there to initiate me into the only experience which could carry me safely to this moment of shadowy encounter, of entire recognition.

Suddenly a slight eager man, tipping everyone half crowns, rushed into the waiting room and grasped my hand. I was speechless with confused emotions, but he talked enough for half a dozen, though I hardly marked what he said. With his

large head on a long craning neck, his mobile lips and express-
ively modelled face, he suggested a Renaissance sculpture of
Julius Caesar.

We drove up to Springwood in the mountains by car; and
now at last I could hear and speak. By the time we had reached
his house a few miles out from the township, I was charmed.
When I went to bed that night on the broad verandah, I was
a sworn disciple.

All my previous antagonisms and criticisms now served only
to strengthen the bond; for they constituted something to
atone. The halo of genius, apparent enough to myopic
strangers when once Norman let himself loose in talk, had a
peculiar force and attraction to me, who had never before
found anyone to whom I could speak outright as poet. I again
read *Creative Effort*, and now I accepted it all. I accepted the
thesis of a creative power in a few poets, artists, musicians,
which lived and worked on a level of qualitative being above
that of the mass of the people at every phase of the circular
process labelled history. I accepted the thesis that only the creative image was dynamic, concrete, able to hold the universe
together.

This step was possible for me only because of the enormous
inflation of my ego by the father's recognition. Abraham and
Isaac went out to enact the rite of murder and the angel of the
lord stayed the hand of the destroying father. The father-in-
the-father stayed the murderous hand which submitted in all
things to his will; and the son was saved. His life was thenceforth a dedication. He had nothing more to fear. Nothing to
fear as long as he kept intact the sacrificial relation. To do that,
he had to surrender the earth, history, and the mother; nothing
less would content the jealous one. For ten years the dialectic
of that surrender was to obsess me; and then the son's revolt,
all the more violent for its long damming-up, was to burst forth
– defending the earth, history, the mother.*

---

*Part of the childhood drama was the conviction (based on much fact) that
the children had come between the parents, sundering their embrace and
finally driving them apart. In such a situation the loyalties are divided. The
son feels that he must now defend the mother whom he has taken away,

But that revolt lies far ahead, outside the scope of this book. At the moment I sit in the lower studio and watch Norman etch. He is making one of his finely stippled plates, working through a magnifying glass; he is putting a finished plate in the acid bath; or he shows me how to use a burin and gives me a Hokusai print. Then I stroll about the gardens among the cypresses and the life-size statues of satyrs and nymphs – silver-thighed statues in concrete, which had to be finished in a day. I slip off to the bathing-pool built half-way down a gully, with a concrete nymph shading her unimaginable face as she peers into the pale green water rippling at a fallen gum seed. We sit in the dusk in the new large studio for water-colours and Norman reads with abrupt boyish shouts of laughter one of his Fanfrolico fantasies. Or we drink tea under the gnarled apple tree, while a belated tourist, who has come miles down the bush-track, looks over the outer fence in the disappointed belief that N.L. has troops of naked wenches galloping all over his grounds and extruding loose legs from every nook of sun. (Perhaps the imbecile catches a coy glimpse of one of the leaf-fanned nymphs and retires to spread the tale.)

And we talk, talk, talk. As though my mute years are being repaid. I explain Freud and try to outline the technique of Plato's arguments, the facts of ancient Greek life, the development of the Elizabethan stage out of medieval bases, the *Golden Bough* and Cook's *Zeus* and Jane Harrison's *Art and Ritual*. But Norman with his piercing sky-blue eyes speaks as if from the Apollonian tripod. In the sweeping flood of his eloquent idealisms nothing remains except the pure relation of father and son. The shock which the war gave him has taken the form

---

or must meet and overcome the father by becoming the latter more than he is himself – i.e. must absorb the essential qualities that make the father, and carry them to a position of yet greater power. Thus surrender masks a rivalry, which itself holds a contradiction. The son cannot in fact go beyond the father while imitating him, for imitation cannot become creation; in so far as his effort to imitate drives him in fact into creation, he becomes different from the father. This was the conflict now in embryo, but later to become acute.

of a total contempt for society; he has abstracted Art and Spirit into an autonomous sphere unrelated to earthly process, a sort of Gnosticism retaining Nietzsche's lonely defiance but not his acclamation of the earth. I try a while to argue that something different has happened in Russia – but for him it's only the old revolt of the slave, breaking what he cannot enjoy and create. I am overborne.

A Beethoven record is played. And Elioth Gruner turns up, with dark saturnine face, silent before all Norman's explanations of his art. He has been painting in the wilds, stripped naked for days on end, and is tanned almost black. Again we play Beethoven. All voices are silenced.

23 · BRISBANE AND NIETZSCHE

RAY HAD resolutely left school. He wanted to paint, to do nothing but paint; but Mary found him a job on one of the dailies, which he detested. Overnight he developed into a swashbuckling beer-swiper, with foul pipe, taking at a stride barriers at which I had hesitated for years. True he had a weekly salary, a meagre one but still a salary; and that helped a lot. He wrote the most astonishing reports of cricket matches and sailing regattas, all full of the wrong technical terms, either invented on the spur of the moment or adapted from Rabelais. Every week he had a fresh escape from being sacked. But, as he wanted to be sacked, he was repeatedly given a second chance.

Jim and I were still impoverished, for Jim was always out of a job at the wrong moments or preoccupied with rescuing the girl from Breakfast Creek. Once he was shut up in her room with the sailor battering away like a mad elephant. Somehow or other the girl never got rescued, and she never turned up at any of the trysts where he said he'd introduce her to me.

One night we were roaming along the river front talking about Sappho, with our pockets turned inside out, and we ran into Ray at a corner. He flung out his arms to embrace us and smashed a bottle of beer. We danced with a dirge round the broken glass and the beer smell, stricken to the heart. I can still smell the beer running into the gutter.

Jim found a girl in Fowles's pub (where they sold banana liqueurs), a girl who had read Keats. A barmaid who knew the *Ode to a Nightingale*! The girl with black ringlets immured by the Wagnerian madam receded in importance. Jim rushed up to me in the street and jostled me along to the bar.

She was quite a pleasant-looking girl, round-faced with a

small chin and a vague eye, but well built and businesslike. I didn't know what to say when Jim had at last caught her eye and loudly ordered two half bitters. We shook hands and her eyes kindled. Her hair was a forest frondage under which the brown pools invited to a discreet plunge; but could one say in a noisy bar-room, 'Glad to meet you, so you read Keats, do you?' I said nothing, as the next moment she was called off to serve someone else. Jim and I drank our beer slowly as we hadn't the price for a second glass. The girl gave us a shadowy smile in passing; but we couldn't secure her for a conversation at such a busy hour. And what hours weren't busy at that pub?

Biding our time and saving our sixpences, we managed to have several brief chats with her. Yes, she did read poetry sometimes. Yes, it was nice to read. Yes, she had a mistress at school who read it lovely. Yes, she'd had to learn the Nightingale Ode for a competition at school and she kept it up, it was useful to have something to recite at a party, though you couldn't give an Ode like that at any ragtag gathering.

Jim the romantic persisted. He found that Jane the Keatsian lived with another barmaid, the fat kindly one with smudged blue eyes and the big loose mouth; and he suggested that I should show them Norman's etchings one Sunday afternoon. So we were asked to tea.

They lived at one of the riverside boarding-houses not far from us. Ray came along too. Jim insisted on talking about Dionysos (whom he pronounced *Dionishius*) and launched into an account of Paganism and its superiority to Christianity, bewildering the barmaids who were on their best behaviour. Ray and I couldn't help smiling; and the fat barmaid noticed it and thought the whole thing was some sort of leg-pull. So Ray and I did our best to get away as soon as we politely could. Jim grumbled afterwards that we'd let him down by not intervening with more enticing details about Greek gods. He had some grandiose plan of making the barmaids' room a sort of intellectual salon. They could have got us beer at reduced rates, he said in shocked tones.

He was a man of many plans, which at the least encouragement he put into action. Ray happened to mention that he wanted a model. He had read Murger's *Vie de Bohème*, swore by Rubens and his mistress, and couldn't feel himself a real artist until he'd drawn from the nude. Jim promptly said he knew a cinema usherette who would certainly be pleased to pose for an artist, and she probably had scores of friends as ready to oblige. So we arranged a ceremony that was to be both Ray's initiation into a professional art status and a revenge on our aunt. She was going down to Redcliffe for a day on the following week; once she was aboard the boat, she couldn't possibly be back till late in the evening. J. was away on one of his quarantine inspections. We were perfectly safe in appropriating the house for the day and in using it for ends of which Mary would emphatically disapprove.

I saw her off and then rang Ray up. She was now living in the new house at the side of the old bungalow; and I had a room of my own on the cramped upper storey. The key was therefore available to me. Ray hurried across, cutting some routine job on the daily, and we waited. Jim had told us that the usherette was delighted to pose. 'She's awfully proud of her instep,' he said, 'and hopes you don't mind she's got a birth-mark on her left buttock.' And she had asked if she could bring a friend along – but we weren't sure if she wanted protection or if she was a kind-hearted girl liking to share a good thing.

At last, as we were giving up hope, they arrived. Jim ushered in two nice ordinary somewhat skinny girls, who tittered. He made things worse by standing back and remarking on their better points. Ray and I produced tea and Mary's best cakes, and we all talked. The girls were impressed by the gaudiness of the house with its lion-skins and oriental glitters, and turned shy. We talked of the weather and the advantages of being a cinema usherette, seeing programmes as often as you liked. 'It's too dark,' said Rita. Her friend worked in a shop. 'That's when I'm working, but I'm not working at the moment,' she said gen-teely. 'I really don't know, you know.' But we never found out what she didn't know.

Jim however had no compunction in introducing the subject of models. 'Both of them are going to pose, Ray,' he said. 'Rita in her birthday suit and Rosie stripped to the waist – I forget which half of her. Top or bottom half, Rosie?'

'The top of course,' she said primly.

Ray took the girls and his paintbox into Mary's bedroom. Jim and I stayed in the front room and played a Beethoven sonata on the pianola. Suddenly there was a yell and we ran in through the study. But nothing serious had happened. The full-length model was leant against the wall nudely laughing and the half-length was straddling a chair with her blouse and chemise off, also shaking her slight bosom with merriment. Ray was picking himself up from the ruins of his home-made easel. Somehow or other he had managed to slip and fall on it. We shut the door chastely and retired.

My aunt remarked next day that someone seemed to have tampered with her powder-boxes, and I did my best to look as if I didn't understand. She scowled with angry suspicion and clearly came to the conclusion that we had staged some riotous orgy in her absence instead of the respectable party which had been brightened only by Ray's accident; his slightly blackened one eye. Having found that he lacked the skill to make a worth-while sketch with his newly bought paints, he had tried some charcoal drawings, which were not very promising – bony and flat young ladies which he might as well have copied out of a book or his head. Jim offered to find more models; but we declined for the moment with thanks in view of the lack of studio space.

When Jim next came along, he had been studying Confucius and wanted me to go into some of the Chinese laundries to see how much the inhabitants knew of Confucianism. Perhaps Chinese didn't pronounce Confucius the way we did; for the one man we asked was so puzzled that we lost heart. Jim returned to the study of Bergson.

My mother made no comment on my visit to Norman, did not stop my going and asked no questions on my return. But I knew she was deeply hurt. She was more contented generally, how-ever. She sat looking out of windows with her finger under her chin or told the fortunes of servants or of other boarders by means of tea-leaves – uniformly gaining chirps of awe. 'Oh, how could you have known that!' She seemed to have some telepathic powers. Her eyes had turned greener and she wore a velvet band round her throat; she had grown painfully thin and wore any threadbare drab clothes. I still had to control the money; but it was easier in a boarding-house. Once, when she had made her tea-leaf prophecy and evoked a scream of delighted terror from the servant girl, I suggested that she might tell my future. But she flushed and shook her head and left the room.

The groupings of the last year had largely broken up. Jim Quinton had left for Moscow. Witherby, as a forthright Christian defender of the Bolsheviks, was involved in petty troubles and persecutions. Only Jim was left to me of my W.E.A. following. I largely lost my interest in the university and cut most of the lectures. I was living very sparely. A small boarding-house breakfast, probably a piece or two of dry toast; no lunch at all or at most a few tomatoes taken from one of my aunt's bushes, a mango or an apple from one of her trees; afternoon tea of bread and butter and a slice of cake if I stayed on at her house, reading or writing in my small cubbyhole. (I had taken also to drawing and had several dreams in pen-and-ink techniques.) As I hated returning to the boarding-house, I would probably wander about with Jim or by myself, have a beer, and end near midnight at the coffee-stall outside Roma Street Station, where I bought a mess of pease pudding for a few pennies.

The three sisters of the boarding-house were in financial difficulties, the eldest more tight-lipped than ever, the second with sagging jaw, the third with tear-blotched cheeks. We moved to a two-storey wooden building in George Street opposite the Treasury. With the fatality that accompanied so many of our boarding-house moves, the proprietress, whose hair was always coming undone, announced within a week that she was going bankrupt and everyone had better move out. Meals could not be guaranteed after Saturday, she said. Most of the boarders promptly departed, but we stayed on. Why not? One could always buy an apple and a tin of sardines, especially if one paid no rent.

Somehow or other the place ambled along. The meals always turned up if one waited long enough, and they weren't much worse than the other boarding-house meals we had known. Now and then they were much better, some unexplained affluence having flowed in on the untidy proprietress. And an odd new boarder or two appeared, unexpected faces blinking blearily at the overdone breakfast. A tall red-haired girl, Maisie, was the one permanent servant, tackling any job from cleaning to cooking as required, and swearing copiously – sometimes sitting weeping on the stairs, sometimes going on strike and shouting insults at the proprietress through an upstairs window. The house, once a wealthy squatter's town residence, was built round a courtyard.

The place suited us. Its air of extreme instability, its ricketty condition, its happy-go-lucky ways, everything about it seemed to emblematize the breaking-down family, the lack of any shared aims.

Ray brought home a lad who was working on the same paper and needed somewhere to live. A stammering frail lad who wrote poems, drew pictures, composed music and was expecting a fortune from an eccentric uncle. For a while we treated him with much deference. But the second poem he showed me, and which he had had printed in a weekly, was a transcription of one of Donne's poems. Ray set to work and found that the drawings were tracings from old magazines. The music we never tested out, but we assumed that if produced it would have borne a close resemblance to the first cheap score which Peter could lay his hands on. The uncle, a few questions made clear, was a feebly sustained invention.

Still, Peter was certainly hard-up. Within a week he lost his job and declared that he was studying for an examination. For the next week or so he lived on a case of oranges eked out with lumps of cornbeef given him by red-head Maisie. As he had never paid any rent, the proprietress prohibited him from the dining-room, but couldn't bother to throw him from a miserable little bedroom that nobody else wanted.

By the time he had eaten all the oranges I discovered that he had paid for them by stealing most of my best books and pawning them at my favourite second-hand bookseller. He had also bought a pair of green carpet-slippers and a broken flute with the proceeds of his theft. I sympathized with him, but didn't want someone in the house stealing all my books. So we wrote a letter to the home address that Ray had found out from

the newspaper office, and then put him out in the street, allowing him to keep the slippers and the flute.

Daily the boarding-house grew more like our casual rebellious thoughts. The proprietress, yawning at midday with her
hair in curling papers, let the ground floor rooms, which opened direct on to George Street, to prostitutes. These latter, as
a tribute to the higher moral status of the boarders, were not
allowed into the dining-room. One of them had a striking
deadly white appearance. Her hair was a pale straw-gold and
she powdered her face rice-white and wore all white clothes
and shoes; the only colour was her scarlet mouth. She walked
with a bend, as if someone had kicked her in the stomach, and
was extremely thin and bony. I once asked her if she had read
Dostoevsky, but she merely stared at me. No doubt she had
promised not to speak to any of the boarders.

Mrs W., the unlaced proprietress, dropped her hairpins on
the stairs and said it wasn't worth while picking them up. Once
she asked me to slit a pair of shoes, which had become too small
for her. 'Why don't you all go?' she asked. 'I really can't give
my time to running this place. After next Tuesday there's not
going to be any more breakfasts.' But the breakfasts went on.

'Don't take any notice of her,' said Maisie. 'She just wants
an easy life. I keep telling her she's stupid.'

I kissed her. 'No, you don't,' she said. 'Not that I mind it.
But respect that mother of yours. Go on with you.'

I was reading Nietzsche, all of his books that I could lay hands
on. There was much in him that I could not accept at all, much
that seemed in accord with Norman's positions, but also much
that supported my pre-Norman outlook.

True, there were many abstractions of blood and will and
the like, which could be used for the system of *Creative Effort*;
there were the places where Nietzsche parodied himself and
seemed to identify will with violence; but there were also the
places where he cried, 'My brothers, remain faithful to the
earth, with all the force of your love. Let your great love and
your knowledge be in accord with the meaning of the earth . . .
Give a meaning to the earth, a human meaning.' He wrote at
moments as if he preached only to an élite, but Zarathustra

with its deep grasp of the process of creation, was named a Book for All and None. 'I shall give back to men the serenity which is the condition of all culture.' He spoke of the future in which 'no highest good or highest joys exist that are not the common property of all. The odium attached to the word common shall be abolished.'

I did not at this time distinguish the contradictions inside Nietzsche's thought, nor did I see how much of him clashed with the positions now reached by Norman. I sought to find those elements which harmonized with *Creative Effort*, but at the same time I was absorbing willy-nilly the other elements; and in due time they were to assert themselves ever more strongly in my mind.

For the present the effect was to build an existentialist universe, in which the conflicts were resolved solely in and by the creative image; to seize on to the dialectic of an agonized spiralling withdrawal into the lairs of the wounded self, echoing all the complex overtones of irony and bitterness thus educed, and yet at the same time affirming joy. Joy was the transcendent leap, the acceptance of all things, which moved qualitatively onto a level outside the sum total of the given universe, thus creating a new universe. I hesitated yet to embrace Norman's concept of the creative image as a transcendental unity outside the nexus of given relations and moving beyond this world, and yet I saw that by basing myself on his logic I must come to it.

I was torn by the intense conflict of my various universes, those of Keats and Shelley, Blake and Plato, Dostoevsky and Beethoven, Nietzsche and N.L. It seemed impossible to find the forms of poetry which could harmonize these conflicting universes and modes of thought. I read Baudelaire and Beddoes and Beardsley (his prose and verse).

> *Amid the breakers now the starbuoy shakes*
> *O Moreton Bay where gulls swoop down for pearls*
> *of scattered foam, the sun-armada wakes*
> *and waves go shelving on a reef of girls*
> *under the clouds of silver bellying stone*

I composed a long poem on Moreton Bay in terza rima. I composed fables in alembicated prose.

The Witch took out my Heart and put it in a round navelled Pie and I watched the Clock with such heartless fear that after a while I was looking out from its Face on to the dominated World and the Children were trying to make out my Time.

My Heart, which they had eaten, was beating ticktock in their little bellies and no castor-oil would dislodge it. The flaxenhaired Girl came back and looked at me with such infinite sadness that I loved her, poor Clock that I was.

Give me back my Heart, I cried to her Intestinal Canals. Bring me forth in a new life so that I may come down from this bleak and lonely Mastery. Then O then my tick will·be one with your tock, Ophelia my urgent Ophelia naked as a Bone.

But in vain, we still look into one another for what is not. I am remorseless and she is mad: we wag in shameless unison. By tick and by tock.

And then as I leaned over the blank page, I sneezed with the blood rushing to my head. Venus in noon-plenitude of revolving nudity, the bunch of stars teasing her pert nostrils with their mercurial scents:

Like a young hunter buried underneath
the body of the lion he has slain,
who drives his dagger back into its sheath
and, rising, laughs again:
O eagle-thought aimed clearly at the sun . . .

Guided by Norman, I read Hugh McCrae's *Satyrs and Sunlight* and found the idiom that I had been vainly seeking in my own swarming tumult of opposed and mated systems. But it was Hugh's not mine.

24 · DAISY

WE SAT eating gingernuts on cold benches in the entrance of
the Trades Hall and trying to read the notices pinned on the
board. I had somehow lost Jim, who was arguing with a printer
whether Julius Caesar was a greater general than Napoleon;
and I had gained Henry instead. Daisy was the one who suggested a visit to the Hamilton breakwater for no reason at all,
dropping a piece of biscuit down Henry's neck. Ruby, Henry's
plump-shouldered girl, smiled drowsily and pulled up her
dress where it had been slipping from the shoulder. Looking
back as I rattled down the stairs, I saw the clock, like a moon
painted over by some enterprising advertiser, go spinning
through skies of stormy whitewash.

Daisy and I sat in the front of the tram. The wind of our
speed was chilly and we pressed close together, her small body
a bundle of suppressed laughters under my arm. She was so
busy seeing jokes where they weren't that she sometimes missed
them where they were. Her small oval face had a creamy tinge;
her nose was turned up, just an impertinent mark of interrog-
ation under the heavy brackets of her eyebrows and the
changing grey-green-brown of her eyes; her mouth pouted
coarsely and her chin retreated; her ears were tiny and her hair
embowered her in masses of little curls that were dry to the
touch.

The driver looked round, so she let me kiss her. He
applauded. The lights flying past hissed in the cold wind or
rocked like buoys in the flickering waves. Round the warm spot
where our foreheads met, we felt the fringe of cold. The stars
were frayed with the glassy wind. The heat was driven under
the skin and a stodgy mask of cold numbly formed.

'Can you see through the smudge of cold?' I asked her.

'As far as I want to,' she answered in her small harsh voice, with a very slight lisp.

'How far is that?'

'I'll tell you when I get there.'

I was surprised that she had let me kiss her in front of the driver. She was sturdily independent, a worker in a chocolate factory; tonight was the first time she had at all encouraged me.

We jumped off the tram and turned to the right, lingering a few moments at the wharf, listening to the leap of some fishes. I dropped pebbles into the river, to watch the splash of moonlight.

'Why do you do that?' she asked. 'The law of gravity's long been proved.'

'We can all fall faster and deeper than we think.'

'It's women who fall, men bounce.'

I felt her drawing away from me again, but she let me take her hand. We stepped cautiously along the stones of the breakwater, followed by Ruby and Henry, who talked with smothered laughter. The tide was out. Over the mud, riddled with crab holes, every now and then a slime of silver rippled and broke. Oyster shells with the top half shorn away by hungry fishermen ran with moonlight like wounds in the dark rocks, an ooze of mucous fire. Henry produced a bottle of Australian burgundy and we drank in turn from it. The wind had died or we were sheltered. A clouded warmth suffused my flesh, the bushes of straggling moonlight, the garish sand.

Henry explained how he was going to make a fortune out of racing bets, while Ruby nipped off the grass-shoots at her side, blade by blade, meticulously searching with her nails for the point closest against the roots before she bit into the succulent resistance. Catching my glance, she tucked her dress more primly round her stocky legs.

'Walk,' said Daisy. We rose and walked on. After a while she sat on a dislodged stone. 'Why are you so conceited?'

I didn't know what to say. I sulked, trying to look miserable, unfairly judged, hurt.

'That's what I mean,' she added. 'I wish you could see your own face.'

'Well, I can't. I don't carry a pocket mirror.'

She fumbled at her handbag and tossed me a small oblong glass. 'Have a good look while you're about it.'

Instead, I tried to catch the moon in it. 'Pierrot Lunaire. But you're right about self-pity, Daisy.'

'I know. But it's easy, isn't it?'

Stung, I asked her, 'Why did you suggest coming out here?'

'I thought you might know when we got here.'

I leaned over and tried to clasp her, but she moved quickly away. 'That's not the answer, big boy.'

She's a vulgar little brat, I thought. I said nothing.

'I like you,' she said.

'Thanks for telling me. I wouldn't have known.'

'Same to you and many of 'em.' I caught her broad grin and laughed against the grain.

'You're a guttersnipe, you're a silly rude little girl, you're a class-conscious proletarian, you're canaille and I hope you're sansculotte.'

'Meaning that I see through you.'

'And what do you see?'

'The other side.'

'Clear as mud.'

We sat silent a while. She leaned back with her hands behind her head. 'You're all keyed up. I get the feeling that if I pulled out the right pin, you'd break up into little bits.'

'Yet you like me.'

'I used to.'

'Not now.'

She didn't answer, leaning further back. It was easy to give her a tickle in the ribs and make her fall right over. I leaned and kissed her on the throat, which was small and wiry. She laughed and pressed my face closer. Then she rolled aside and sat up. 'No, big boy.'

'Did you bring me all this way just to say that?'

'I suppose I did.' She wriggled round, kneeling, and caught me by the shoulders. 'You're hurt, aren't you?' She stared into my eyes. 'Tell me what you want me for?'

I put my hand flat against her chest and pushed her gently away. 'Baa baa black sheep.'

'I know you want to lay me,' she said harshly, and I shrank. 'But that's only the first step. What do you want after? Really I'm curious. I can't make you out. Sometimes I think I can, then I can't.' I refused to answer, staring away across the river. 'Honest, tell me one thing. If one of the shop window dummies got up and talked and fell over backwards with admiration, could you tell it from a woman?'

'When one of the dummies gets up and talks, I'll tell you.'

'Well, I feel like one of those dummies sometimes, after I've worked my guts out . . .'

'But you don't fall over backwards with admiration.'

She stood up. 'Perhaps that's what I did mean to do. Only you got in first with the admiration.' She shook her mop of a head. 'Oh don't let's quarrel. Let's have a race.'

She ran off over the uneven ground, springing lightly from clump to clump, then almost fell. I sprinted, but not in time. She regained her balance and ran on. Ruby was quietly dozing against a stone and Henry was finishing the bottle. 'Why on earth did we come all this way?' he asked. 'Now I've got to take a tram back across the Bridge to the south side . . .'

'It was my idea,' said Daisy, 'wasn't it, Jack?'

Now she smiled without any urchin malice and took my hand. I wanted to wrench it away, but didn't. How small and hot her hand was, how hard, a small solid fist. 'Yes,' I said, 'your idea.'

She shook her head. 'I like you, really I do.'

Ruby awoke with a snort. 'Where am I?'

'These blasted love-birds lured us all this way,' said Henry, throwing the bottle into the river. 'I'd like to throw 'em in too.'

After we got off the tram, I walked home with her. We chatted about William Morris. She said her father had known Francis Adams. 'He's got a signed copy of *Songs of the Army of the Night*.'

'I'd like to see it.'

At the gate she stood on tiptoe and offered me her pouted mouth that looked so large in her small face but was small and soft against mine. She seemed mutely and stubbornly apologizing, saying: I'm sorry, but I meant it. As I held her, I was aware of the small weatherboard house behind us, raised only three or four feet on its supports, with its sleeping windows, a lattice at the side overgrown with roses, a neat little garden of shrubs and stocks, the house-name hanging on chains over the porch: *Heather-brae*, the worn mat beneath, the torn envelope with a message for the milkman. I felt it as something compact and cosily menacing, a family lair ready to open its door-maws and engulf me. And Daisy, small and sturdily pliable in my arms, was also compact and cosily menacing. For the first time, outside the rejected arguments of my aunts about waiting for a 'nice girl', I confronted the thing 'marriage', not merely as an institution that corralled in my fellowmen, but also as a cataclysmic imprisonment that might happen to me also. The thought of living with a woman was one thing; the thought of an institutionalized relation, involving money-earning, homebuilding, child-getting, compromises and fears, erosions, atrophies, dry-rots, mouldinesses, conventional routines and depersonalized adaptations, cankers, corruptions, adulterations, debasements, prostitutions and the brutalizing rest of it – the thought of all that laying a mutilating hand on me was quite another thing. I realized how profoundly the family had become for me the canalized and concentrated form of the forces pervasively blemishing and warping the world in which I lived – which I had come to call under Quinton 'class-society' and which Norman called 'man.'

I patted Daisy on her small tight bottom and turned away, waving my hand and saying, 'See you soon, dear.'

I had about four miles to walk home, and all the while I pondered fearfully on the vision of fetters. Not that I thought for a moment of Daisy as specially matrimonial in outlook; on the contrary she was the most *gamine* of all the girls I had ever known, skylarking, boyishly given to sparring and tumbling, using no cosmetics, frank to an excess. Perhaps precisely for this reason, demanding to be accepted as a person, she had forced me into the rational daylight. Did I want anything on the other side of her hasty kisses, her down-to-earth enjoyment of the moment? The blue-eyed girl of the boat had used my eyes as a mirror in which she admired her narcissistic self, her mirror-double, and the contact had evaporated in a vain search for someone who was neither the girl nor her double, an anonymous wraith of the city streets. I might as well have sought her in the glossies, the elegant robots of the advertisement hoardings. Bessy had been my pure counterpart, mysterious because never entered beyond the confines of the kiss. But Daisy had restlessly insisted on a girl being a person in her own right, just as I was struggling with the Normanesque idea of woman as otherness devised by the artist for his material, formlessly the stimulant of all form, the material universe taken into the womb of the imagination and reborn as the creative image.

I did drop a line to Daisy, but her mother was ill. I felt rather relieved, though I wanted to meet her. My mind was moving in a direction that she would have impeded. I did not want to see her charming impatience become shrill.

25 · EVANGELICALS

SELMA DECIDED to convert me. She was a Catholic, a science student at the university in her third year, the eldest daughter of a squatter in the north. And so, after she had announced her mission, my only retort was to attempt to turn the tables.

I met her first at an afternoon-tea reception
on hedged-in tennis-lawns
lolling among young trees and eating cakes.
'You don't really mean the things you write,'
she said in merry earnest.
I was standing up, nervously trying
to keep my hair from my eyes and swallow tea,
talking all the while
with a splay-enthusiasm, in icing-lights,
talking and watching with a happy despair
the sun's boisterous approval of the girls,
striking bits of beauty like medals on the air
then snatching them from eyes which longed for life
to offer an unmelting wife,
to freeze the forms in sculpture of pure fire:
talking and remembering as I talked
to keep the best part of the cake till last.

Blouses pinned with showy nipples
for the voluble wind of fun
blowing open the blossomfaces
for that hairy bee the sun.

'I do,' I answered, 'I do.
Poetry alone can justify Ethics.
Bylaws of Venus nakedly obeyed

would yield more civilized communities
than any Religions vermined out of the East.
Wars should be decided by conflicting Epics.
Politics should expire in a low Farce
ambusht with tintacks and fat mothers-in-law
or else a Melodrama with bombastic moustaches
and snow made out of torn-up Bluebooks.'

'O, you'll get over it someday,' she replied.

'Never. I am bitten by the tarantula
of verse, and I must dance
until I drop down dead,
until the weary maenads
reel from the coverts of my heart,
leaving Death a trophy of trampled tambourines
and the frail white bones of perfect singing-birds.'

She looked at me so nicely I saw at once
she had decided to reclaim me. Then
I knew that she'd be mine to unbutton soon.
Wait till I get you near the Moon that bawd,
wait till I find you powdered by the Moon,
Virgin consuming tea
in bowers of sunlight. Wait till you meet the Moon
arm-in-arm with me.
'I'm sure you're really nice at heart,' she said
and put the teacup down.

The poem was written a couple of years later; it catches the scene except that it makes me more confident a riposter than I actually was. It opened:

> *'When I was young I used to drink port-and-lemonade and think*
> *it had an alcoholic taste . . .'*

Selma had said that she'd make a Christian of me; I answered that I'd paganize her. When we got down to arguments, she had only one point to reiterate: 'I don't believe you can really believe all that nonsense.' And then she laughed her deep contralto laugh, her warm and maddening laugh, which made up for her short heavy body, her square chin, her lack of anything

like an easy grace in movement. Another acceptable quality
was that she provoked me into talk by her mocking tenderness,
her pretence at inscrutability which masked a disregard for
everything which did not touch her senses. I talked of sex, politics, Apollo, the Greek hexameter, Milton, Hoccleve, Cheru-
bini, Piero della Francesca, Nennius, Ebenezer Elliot,
Leonardo da Vinci and Mimnermos, all in one burst. She
made no effort to follow what I said, since it was all equally
erroneous, heretical and wicked. She simply said that she
didn't believe me because she was sure I was good at heart;
and she laughed. When she laughed, I started all over again.

I told her that I despised marriage and that the only thing
stopping her from fornication was the terror implanted in her
by a false and oppressive ethic in which she didn't really
believe in the least. She laughed. She found it hard to stop
laughing.

I kissed her. That time we were walking down the main
street after a dance in the common room. She was wearing a
scarlet silk handkerchief on her head, and she watched herself
in the shop windows which the street lights dimly glazed. The
street was quite empty except for a policeman implacably
tunicked in floating shadow. I had forgotten that I wore a
yellow paper cap serrated like a cock's comb.

She asked me politely why I wanted to kiss her. I said that
it was the obvious thing to do, so obvious that I had so far not
done it. She asked what was obvious about it. I pointed out
that we belonged to opposite sexes and that ever since Aristophanes any educated person knew we were imperfect while
apart, wandering halves hoping to become a delighted whole,
a globe of pleasure. She said with a smug air of triumph that
we weren't animals; there was a difference somewhere. I
agreed. I said that was the whole point of my argument. Who
ever heard of a dog composing a *liebestod* or a goat painting a
nude goat-bitch? She said human beings must control themselves; that was the difference. I said that the true control lay
in making love and writing poems about it; that was the difference. She said that there was no reason for writing poems; she
had never written poems, none of her other friends had ever
written poems, Father James had never written a poem. I said

that she and her friends were insufficiently human. 'Go on,' she said, 'make up a poem and prove you're not an animal.'

I chanted: 'The Moon once bent to kiss a shepherd-lad; and you in turn could bend to make me glad. The reason for our various limbs is this: They add together in a single kiss. No rooster ever sang a lyric song. That is my faith, and you can't prove me wrong.'

She replied that I had now composed my poem and so I didn't need a kiss in order to be pricked into music. I said that was her mistake.

Her happiness was flagrant; she shone as if she had just emerged from the River Jordan, washed all over with the soap of a good conscience. The clock of the G.P.O. let out its melodious squabble of midnight birds.

'Heaven will come to pass by an improvement of sensual enjoyment. Surely you can see that, or smell it, or touch it, or taste it, or hear it?'

Her small nose had no powder left on it; it gleamed ungreasily with a healthy pallor. Her eyes had their mischievous twinkle. 'But there must be something in religion. Even you can't deny that?'

'Give me at least one reason for your statement.'

She paused in her step and looked up expectantly, her face milk-bright with laughter, her eyebrows narrowed with thought.

'Look at all the churches.' She laughed aloud at her own cleverness.

'But there are also Turkish baths for the homosexuals,' I began patiently, 'and clubs for those with spiritual gout.' Some loafers jeered at my hat. I took it off with as dignified a gesture as I could manage. 'Deep in a dump with melancholy hat, John Ford was rumpty-tumpty-tum begat.' I coughed. 'You as a scientist –'

'I dissected a frog yesterday, better than anyone else. I caught it in the Convent garden; we were told to. What a funny feeling frogs have, just like a wet glove, a skin glove I mean, not one of cloth. I boiled one once by mistake and it shrank up like a baby's . . .'

'You know those pea-green frogs; they used to crawl all over the house we had for a few weeks south along the coast.'

'They've got suckers on their feet, they can crawl up the wall. At home there's one who always sits in the spout of my water jug in the morning and looks at me.'

We turned the corner. In a barber's mirror I saw my mouth sickled in a grin. We were in long grottoes of tailors dummies, stalactites of iron and wilted confectionery. The late tram cantering past was a centaur questing for a brewery. I looked her squarely in the eyes and found the twinkling lights were quite faraway; her pupils were icily coated with a thin echo of music, a veneer of remembered pleasure. The lightness of her body came from the tentative dancesteps she made instead of walking. She wasn't thinking at all of what I said or what she said; she was intoxicated with bad music, tin cans rattling, saxophones wheedling, all the pennywhistle birds screechy in the rubbery machine-made jungle of jazz. I decided to test her. 'Do you like asparagus?'

'Oh, yes, don't you?' She was unaware of any unexplained turn in the conversation.

She had her own system of honour. Thus, if I succeeded in kissing her under the left ear, she considered she had henceforth lost that ear; I had the right to kiss it whenever I pleased. But the right ear had yet to be won. Every inch of herself was defended with all her ample muscular powers; but once lost it was lost. And so the slow well-resisted encroachment went on, night after strenuous night, with intervals of bun and cocoa in cafés of blistered glass in Fortitude Valley.

We lay in open ground near the river, down New Farm way, among bamboos and mosquitoes. Wrestling in arduous silence between our stereotyped arguments, we watched the prawn-fishers raise nets of intricate gold streaming against the candles. The nets were on fire, they gushed with orange-gold, then only a few tattered sparks welled from them. Hidden in spikes of grass, we heard the small sodden bumps of the prawns on the woodwork of the flat boat. We lay listening, still panting a little, my hand locked in her damp armpit.

The poem put it like this:

The Sweeter-than-Port Era of my life
is dedicated aptly
to a girl who sang warm contralto.
Only when asked, however,
to an accompaniment of sycophantic chords
from the anxious piano.
Never she bloomed into reckless laughter
seeking to vocalize the sinuous rhythms
in those reaches of the moon.
Never the isolde-sob took the pitch of my kisses
shelving through semitones of anguish
into the release
of trombones heraldic of eternity,
dumpy delicious moonchild.

For a month by a river of gurgling silver
on the steps of an old ferry-house
I sat and talked and saw the dovebreasted moon
amid spilt seed of stars
move pouting to her nest.
That enormous tree,
dewy with stars and housing half the sky
still floats a dabbled mass of daedal darkness
flitting
to bunches of vanishing little blossomfires,
fastidious rococo of the moon.

Once when it rained I propped up a fallen advertisement board against a fig. Her back was soon sopping. 'Oh, the stuff won't run,' was her only comment.

I was now engaged in converting her to Wagner from Mendelssohn. She was interested in music. Music and my conversion were indeed her sole passions; and one day, while my aunt gloomily listened, I took her over to Kangaroo Point so that she might play on the piano and sing. Her voice was rich and with a strange edge to it, a tone that one felt ought to be unpleasant, but wasn't.

She turned out incomparably more pagan than I was, though I made no dint in her creed. She simply put it away when it happened to be inconvenient. I was outraged at such unprincipled opportunism and found myself trying to stimu-

late her sense of guilt in order to make her consistent. 'You
don't understand,' was all she said. Nothing could disturb her
gay serenity; and continually I had the feeling that she wasn't
listening, that she was caught up in some distant music or
embosoming memory. I wondered if Father James felt the
same, and something of sympathy for him came over me. 'You
do take things seriously,' she said.

She still boarded in the Convent which was also a girls'
school, and was supposed to come in early every night unless
she let the nuns know beforehand. I forget the time when she
should have been in; for she never kept to it. But, perhaps
because she never arranged anything in her mind beforehand,
and perhaps because she didn't like to face a nun with a kiss-
swollen mouth, she never said that she was coming in late.
Instead, she was let in illicitly by one of the boarders, generally
her sister, who came down and opened a side door while I
lingered in the accomplice shadows. In the Convent the only
class she attended was the art class. Once she took me to a pre-
view of an arts and crafts show by the girls. She herself had
been working at a copy of Millais's *Bubbles*, painting it in careful green slime, with highlights of almond-smelling icing. A
nun, framed in her formal enclosure of stiff black and white,
looked on in benign mistrust, with folded hands. I had a few
words with her on art and found that she had good taste; she
wasn't Selma's teacher. I felt as we spoke that she knew all
about the New Farm nights and that she blessed them. Selma
insisted on taking me upstairs when nobody was about. I went
hastily down a shadowy corridor, glancing in at small rooms
with narrow beds. 'That's my room,' said Selma, and, reluctantly pausing, I stared at a statuette of the Virgin and a large
photo of a man with a wiry beard and furious eyes, her father.
The photo stared back. 'You know, you're rather like him,' said
Selma, catching my eye.

When we had left the place, she referred to her painting. 'It
was bad, wasn't it?'

'Terribly bad.'

She gave a gurgling deep under-laugh, as if only now she was
quite clear how bad the thing was, and the knowledge
reassured her. 'You're so funny.'

'The others are almost as bad, but not half as big as yours.'

'Yes, I didn't mean to buy such a big canvas.'

'It's remarkable how slimy you managed to get the paint.'

'Yes, it took me a long time.'

She looked me slowly over, with quarter-closed eyes, as if she still couldn't quite believe in me and in the nightly results of our arguments. As if the whole relationship had something obscurely yet irresistibly humorous. We went to our favourite blistered café where the cracked marble tabletops were mended with sticky paper and string, where the one-eyed waitress complained of bunions, and the card on the cash register, *Credit loses Customers Trust in God Alone*, jumped whenever the drawer shot out and the bell rang. The waitress brought our buns and cocoa without being asked. 'My bunion's giving me hell,' she confided. 'I'd marry a toothless lion-tamer if only he'd promise to take me away from this bloody job.'

'Poor girl,' said Selma, 'on our station there was a boundary rider with bunions, and he cured them with horse embrocation.'

'I've been lots of things already,' said the girl, 'but not a horse. Still, a woman can't choose.'

While we sipped our cocoa, I asked Selma what sorts of things she confessed.

'My sins of course; the wrong things I've done.'

'But what wrong things do you do?'

She seemed puzzled. 'Oh, I lose my temper sometimes. Things like that.'

'Is it wrong, what we do?'

'Oh, yes.'

'Then you ought to stop it.'

'But you won't let me.'

'Am I as strong as all that?'

She smiled. 'You're strong enough.'

'But you agreed with me that the body was the source of all values – was humanly divine.' I began reciting Blake and Nietzsche on the body.

'Oh yes, of course.'

'Then it isn't wrong.'

'If you put it that way, it isn't.'

'But you said it was.'

'It all depends.'

'On what?'

She was puzzled again. 'Oh well, lots of things. The point of view, for one. I don't see any sense in worrying about things we can't solve or change.'

'Do you mean that it seems right while you're with me, and wrong when you're not.'

'To a certain extent, yes. But it works out quite well. You see, I don't think about it when I'm with other people.'

'You're a hypocrite, darling.'

'No, I'm just happy.'

I was admirably silenced. But as we were leaving the shop, two girls ran by, holding their breasts to stop them shaking too much, and laughing. 'Will you confess about us?' I asked Selma.

The lads with check caps dashed past us after the girls. 'Not in so many words,' said Selma.

'Why not?'

'You said it was different, didn't you? I don't know what words.'

She had no words for it all. There lay her pretext, her safety.

I took her out to tea
I took her out for walks
and with a dangerous smile of pity she listened to me talking.

We absorbed expensive creampuffs
we ate the cheapest buns
filled with the raisins of yesteryear
and dried by chaffy suns

and all the while
all the dreaming while
in air moted with music we sat.
For a dark music, cymbals of grating silence,
shook about her;
and I liked the way her hair showed in the front
under her hat.

Do you remember the simple and lovely world,
believed-in because incredible,
which cushioned us?
do you remember its queer unquenchable suns,
its moons we pitched as quoits?

Sunlight was queerer space.
It turned everything into
flowers of porcelain
hard as gems yet crumbling to a blaze
of gyring gold unpetalled steadily
in a slow motion film.
That gave us the illusion of mastering Time.

All light came through flowerfilters ere it graved
your subtle cheeks that I most liked to see
sucked-in as you pouted a kiss to me
looking-up under your lashes as you poured out tea,
holding the teapot lid on with the tip of your forefinger,
charming conscientiously:
the shifting cloud of sculptural colour laving
your face's mischievous beauty.

And in this underlight of flowers
waded our afternoons
among the wavering houses and
the undulating trees,
tendrils of swaying light, and lamposts
antennae of green fire
stuck to the ribbed pavement
but twisting their iron jaws about
to catch the minnow stars
and swallow their wandering shoals.

I was so filled with a suppressed energy that one fortnight when she was staying with an uncle some fifteen miles out from our boarding-house, I saw her home on the last train and then walked back five or six times – arriving in George Street between three and four in the morning. With what delight I had welcomed the sight of the moonlight crumpled on the joss-house at Breakfast Creek, the long stretch of the Bowling Green, the silent shop windows of the Valley, and at last the fire-escape stairs at the back of the house, up which I clumped – passing the youthful juggler who was sleeping in the bit of square verandah on a camp-bed. In the room next to mine the two actresses, both in their twenties, who by day were heavily made-up, were continuing their jealous quarrel which only seemed to pause for refreshing endearments. I had given up trying to bore a hole through the wooden partition so that I might see as well as hear them; my only tool was a penknife which broke half way. Now switching on the light, I quickly turned back the clothes, killed all the sleepy bugs I could find, then returned to darkness and slept at once.

I went to my first orchestral concert with Selma. I forget if it was some Brisbane orchestra, or a visiting one; I had noticed only the music announced on the posters. The Tannhäuser Overture and Leonora Three were being played as well as some lighter items. Selma bought the tickets. She didn't have much money, though her people owned a fairly large station, I understood, near Cairns; but she had more than I. We were long past the situation where I had to pretend to be the moneyed male.

I didn't enjoy the concert much. I had been so used to listening to music either alone or with one or two others – Norman, Ray, Jim – that I found it disturbing to be in a large hall (with bad acoustics) among a crowd of people, with the players before me making all sorts of uncouth movements. I wondered how Selma, more musically sophisticated, had taken it. She said nothing till we had walked for several minutes, then she murmured 'It was wonderful. All you said of Wagner was true . . .' Later I found that she had had an orgasm during the Tannhäuser Overture.

We climbed into a park which was closed for the night, finding a quiet spot not-overlooked, and lay near the river by a flowering shrub. Henceforth we made this our nightly lair, abandoning the unkempt grasses near the prawners.

One afternoon we went to see our nook by daylight. She ran down a slope and stumbled near the bottom. Her legs were too short for nimble running, though she was a keen rider of horses. I picked her up. On the new white silk dress, of which she had been so proud an hour before, there was a green stain; but she wasn't put out. It was I, always uneasy at a clumsiness in myself or another, who was anxious to pass the matter off. 'Oh, clothes can always be given away,' she said carelessly and sat down.

Now we never discussed religion or morals. We were just happy. She never showed the least qualm, the least interest in the future. Her sister, younger, tall and dark, seemed to consider me severely, I thought, on the few occasions when we met.

'You're still happy?' I said to Selma as the end of the university year was nearing and I knew she would have to return home.

'Yes, aren't you?'

I wanted her to say that she would miss me; I couldn't make out if she looked on her departure as a final break or a brief temporary dislocation of a settled relationship. But the last thing I wanted was a discussion about it. Never once had I said that I loved her; never once had she asked me if I did. There was still a mocking tenderness in her attitude to me, but she was docile and the tenderness had deepened without dislodging the humorous detachment of her smile.

Still nothing had been said when the night of her going was upon us. I got into the train and went with her to the first stop. We hadn't arranged this; I did it at the last moment, suddenly afraid of losing her. Tears were in my eyes. She was grave and yet a faint glint of her indomitable smile lurked in her eyes.

'You'll write to me?'

'Yes, and you'll write too?'

'Yes.'

She wrote me long letters in her flowing hand, about the weather and the crops and her horse, about people we had known, about music. But only once she implicated the future. 'Everything's all right, you'll be glad to hear. I was relieved too, though I knew everything would be all right and of course it was. Still, I thought I'd tell you. I know you're a worrier, aren't you? So don't worry. There's nothing to worry about. The weather's lovely. I wish you could see the birds. I've been riding all day, but I'd much rather I was with you.' Then she added, her script at a different slope, 'But there is more, isn't there?

You know what I mean. More to be done. It isn't everything, is it? You know what I mean, everything. Please tell me.'

But I didn't know what she meant, or not for sure. Perhaps I did know. But what wasn't clear was whether she was expressing a hope that we should come together again and explore that *more*, that unrealized region of body and soul, that fragment of absolute rapture which after all we hadn't captured.

Instead of answering her question, I countered with one of my own. 'Have you confessed yet?'

She answered with the anticipated truth. 'Yes, I confessed to the priest a week ago, after I was sure that everything was all right. He was so kind and understanding. I've been riding all day. I have a new horse, father gave him to me, I'm not quite used to him, but he's first-rate. Sometimes when nobody's with me I call him Jack, but I'd rather be with you.'

26 · NIETZSCHE IN AUSTRALIA

NIETZSCHE IN his own way had forced me into the open, into the need to keep on grasping at history, analysing it. By his attack on Christianity he gave guts and immediacy to the Hegelian schema on the moral and cultural levels, however many his incidental aberrations. He restored to European culture the concept of a single stream of development, broken after the Renaissance and unrestored by Spinozistic pantheisms or Newtonian theisms, by positivist abstractions or fideist reactions against positivism. (I could not yet see how Marx had done the same thing, on surer foundations, because I knew nothing of his work. Apart from the lecture on labour value, of which only the phrase 'socially necessary time' had come through to me, the sole exposition of Marxism I had heard was in a debate on the theme: Is the belly a more progressive force than the mind? The self-dubbed Marxist there spoke with a crudely mechanistic materialism that infuriated me.)

This storm voice alone seemed capable of mingling the elemental song in poetry's forest with the staccato street corner oration of Jim Quinton; it seemed an answer of many voices, all the voices in history. Now in Christianity I could no longer see a set of images, one of which I selected according to the whim of the moment – a medieval Christ with bones like the broken girders of space and time; a tree of angelic voices in the silence of Palestrina; a snub-nosed-jesus Blake; a Galilean revolutionary; a bowed figure sending the antique world grey with his blighting breath. I was compelled to confront Christianity as a vast historical force to be valued in its entirety. Life was a unified stream, despite all its inner conflicts, because of its inner conflicts. A single struggle, a single arena, where the abstracted observer or the esoteric aesthete had no place except as a bad joke.

Let us look at our Australian Nietzscheanism in a wider perspective. At the time when Norman was reaching his first effective expression, round 1900, the first cycle of Australian development was ending. The songs and tales of the pioneering independent, the damn-all ramble-eer who had driven the rocky roads and tamed the plesiosaurian continent, were ending. They might echo on, but their central position was gone. Over the sardonic self-reliant pioneer closed the money-net of the squattocracy and the banks. I wish to stress the turning-point reached about 1900. Though still predominantly agricultural (as she was to be till the 1940s), Australia had her handful of overgrown cities dotted about the continent; and now they were increasingly important. The pioneering struggles could no longer provide the central material for literature, as they had till Lawson's day – though he was by no means simply the poet of the tale told by the bushfire or in the bush pub; he was already well aware of the city and its significances. He deromanticized the country-toils:

> Yes, I heard the shearers singing WILLIAM RILEY out of tune,
> saw 'em fighting round a shanty on a Sunday afternoon,
> but the bushman isn't always 'trapping brumbies in the night,'
> nor is he for ever riding when 'the morn is fresh and bright.'
>   . . . We cursed the fire in turn
> till the atmosphere was heated and the fire began to burn.
> Then we had to wring our blueys which were rotting in the swags,
> and we saw the sugar leaking through the bottom of the bags,
> and we couldn't raise a chorus, for the toothache and the cramp,
> while we spent the hours of darkness draining puddles round the
>   camp . . .

And he saw the struggle gathering in the industrial street:

> They lie, the men who tell you in a loud decisive tone
> that want is here a stranger, and that misery's unknown,
> for where the nearest suburb and the city proper meet
> my window-sill is level with the faces in the street –
>   drifting past, drifting past,
>   to the beat of weary feet –
> while I sorrow for the owners of those faces in the street. . .

But the sudden deepening of the issues needed a poetry with the subtle tissues of Brennan's. At the time of the Boer War that poet was writing *The Burden of Tyre* (not published till 1953) in which the conflict is plumbed with imagery that has all the weight of the great romantics and symbolists behind it.

> ... *Was this your faith to them whose trust*
> *urges within your flesh, your bone,*
> *compulsive, moulding, – which ye must*
> *obey, or madden, all unknown –*
>
> *to them that in the rearward dark*
> *bow'd them above the clod and fed*
> *the brooding earth with dream, with stark*
> *sweat, and with sorrow of their dead;*
>
> *and laid them in her lap, content*
> *to pass, if so her sacred morn*
> *might show some time the grave-clothes rent*
> *around the Saviour, Easter-born:*
>
> *and that high sorrow of the stars,*
> *long-sunder'd, suffering, shall it help*
> *nothing against the hate that mars?*
> *and this, your street-long bloodhound-yelp,*
>
> *shall this be all the note our earth*
> *sends outward to the night to greet*
> *her sisters, bound in mutual dearth?*
> *– Is Eden nought but the loud street? ...*

In this profound poem, of which I cite only a few stanzas, he realizes that the imperialist moment, gripping Australia for the first time, defines a problem of choice which goes as deep as the heart of life, the pulse of death and renewal. The pioneers with their stark sweat and their faith in the deep transformations of the life-process through productive labour, are now no longer the nation-builders. *Eden* – a symbol partly derived from Mallarmé, but having much the same significance as Blake's Jerusalem – can no longer be kept alive in the old way. Is the human situation nought but the loud street, the industrialized class-town, which is now fated to dominate the situation?

In such a crisis of the spirit the old forms could no longer suffice to express the conflicts and needs and aspirations of men. Australian culture entered on a new phase – heralded by the poems of Brennan and O'Dowd, and by the drawings of Norman. This new phase proclaimed the death of all provincialisms, all the parochial philistinisms which had been previously redeemed by a candid comradely crudity and a desperate struggle with a prehistoric nature. By a naked violence of revolt, running from the Eureka Stockade to the yearly strikes of the shearers ready to down tools at a flicker of a threat to their common interests or independences. Australia must realize and absorb European culture, world issues, history in its fullness.

But all that was easier said than done. On what basis was the new universal structure to be erected? How could the nation leap from the bush ballad to the subtle *symbolisme* of Brennan and to the passionate pastoral of N.L. in which Theocritean Sicily fused with the Flemish *kermes*, using types from Woolloomooloo to express the Nietzschean revaluation of all values? There was nothing in our nineteenth-century culture in any way corresponding to Europe's. Only a feeble imitation of the superficial aspects of the great romantics in Kendall and Gordon. Nothing of the real fury, joy and inner conflict of those romantics; nothing of Beddoes and Baudelaire, Meredith and Mallarmé, Ruskin and Rimbaud, Morris and Verhaaren. Brennan and O'Dowd were trying to extend the coastline of a poetry adequate to the modern world, but at the cost of ceaseless struggle against the erosions and pounding breakers of a philistinism unvitalized by pioneering curses and bawdiness. The sharp issues of collapse and re-integration posited by Picasso, Apollinaire, the *fauves* and futurists, the dadaists and surrealists, could have no relevance to us. Yet by demanding that provincialism end and Australia enter the currents of world culture, we were bringing ourselves into alignment with these issues. We seemed doomed to fight a hopeless double battle against local philistinisms of a deadly kind and decadent disintegrations washing in from without.

We wanted, not any sort of futurism, but a new grand art linked with Praxiteles and Rubens, Rembrandt and Turner, Aristophanes and Shakespeare, Catullus and Keats, Rabelais and Blake.

This was the dilemma that Norman had come up against after his first excited absorption of Dürer, Rubens, the Greeks, and the others. He alone in Australia had plugged away steadily since 1900 at the task of transforming our culture to the broad new level in which the great achievements of antiquity, the renaissance, the romantic epoch, might be taken in and built on afresh. In the process he became enraged, wounded, embittered, ironic; but he never lost his faith in the need to continue this work, to hit back, to compromise in nothing. However, the cramping aspects of the situation, after the first vigours of youth, drove him more and more into abstractions of his purpose, finally into the transcendental revenges of *Creative Effort* – the moment when I irrupted on his scene.

How could I not respond to the unceasing moral struggle he had carried on, seeking to vindicate the life-values against a corrupt life-denying world? Though he was entering the phase where he was to deny any concern for 'reforming' the world and where 'freedom' was to take on a purely sexual and artistic colouration, he had in fact in his earlier years been to a considerable extent stirred by social injustices and cruelties. He himself told me of his anger at the way that unmarried mothers were treated in Melbourne and his conviction that the civilizing impact of art must break down all such things. Without political ideas – though drawing political cartoons for the *Bulletin* according to editorial policy – he yet responded to the simple needs and indignation of the common folk, proud of his friends among boxers and sailors. Till 1919 the people in his drawings have a rich and vital tang of Australian common life. His Petronius illustrations have the Roman world authentic to its very smells, but they are also expressions of Australian toughness, roughness, gusto; they are set equally in Pompeii and in the sailors' quarters of Sydney. Bill Dyson was his close friend.

In his exhibited pictures, which attacked the ideas of sin and pollution, and which affirmed the joyous ruthless fecundity of life, he continually risked prosecution and imprisonment. Again and again the bishops and the whole pecksniffian press shouted for his suppression. He could easily have kept his drawings quiet, sold them direct to collectors, but he insisted on public shows. Though often suffering from bad health, he never wavered one inch in his moral convictions. 'Do you tremble, vile body? How much more you would tremble if you knew where I am taking you.'

Now I began to understand something of his indomitable character, the profound gaiety of his art, the single-handed struggle he had waged against a perverse and pitiless world. He had affected Australian culture in such a way that it could never again return smugly to its parochial wowserdom, its sugar-coating of cruel realities. Brennan's essential work was done by the early years of the century (he even wrote a booming dull poem on the 1914 war without one flicker of his earlier insights); but there was Hugh McCrae emerging as a light-hearted *franc tireur*, skipping out of the thickets with glancing lyric missiles that he hurled at the rhinoceros-hide. The more I grasped Norman's courageous loneliness, the more I felt drawn to his side, impelled to champion his philosophy.

Perhaps now the special significance that Nietzsche held for us will be becoming clear, the strengths we could draw from him, the distortions we could add to his distortions, the way we extended his thinking in a society with many radical differences from his European world. I have explained why we could not see what was correct in his statement that nihilism must be both fought from without and transformed from within, but we found in him something that European thinkers did not find.

Lancelot Whyte has explained this, I think, though he did not have Australia in mind when he wrote in 1944: 'The subjective tradition of Europe restricted further development, and its decay was inevitable. The isolated subject had to die before being reborn as part of nature.' Nietzsche carried an active subjectivism to its limit in the discipline of his loneliness; but at the same time his intense need to dramatize the conflict swung him into the middle of the historical arena. The subjective approach trembled on the edge of a new objectivity: or rather, a new dialectical fullness, a fully realized structure of drama. Despite all his confusions, contradictions, delusions – because of the struggle put up against them – Nietzsche was facilitating the patterns which made for the overcoming of the hopeless tension. As he said: You will find me best when you reject me.

His arrow for the further shore can only be followed by those who stand outside their own failure. Europe cannot accept Nietzsche because he represents the death of the European tradition. He is the last despairing cry of the European subject, humanistic individualism outreaching itself in an isolated and dissociated genius, forerunner of the rage with which Europe would turn its sadism on itself, his man-god as much an illusion as the god-man whom he rightly repudiated. Until European man had expressed this despairing rebellion in this ultimate challenge, the resources of dissociated subjective thought had not been exhausted. (Whyte)

One may consider that 'Europe' appears there too simply as a single bloc, a purely individualistic tradition, and that the 'ultimate challenge' of Marxism is an aspect of the situation that cannot be ignored; but there is an element of truth in the formulation – an element which took on many new relations in 1917 but continued to assert itself. The words certainly illuminate powerfully the reasons for the fascination we found in Nietzsche.

We considered that European man had reached an impasse; we saw all *modernismus* as nihilistic and disintegrative. Within the focus of the Nietzschean critique we sought to refound the grand tradition of concrete realistic and beautiful imagery on Australian soil. We rejected 'nationalism' in art because we identified it with the parochialism that we correctly felt the need to fight. The *übermensch*, the beyond-man (vulgarly called the superman) whom Nietzsche saw as the revaluer of all existing values, the man in whom a new centre of living had been born, we interpreted wholly as the hero-artist, the bearer of the creative image. This narrowed Nietzsche's thought, but saved it from many of its vulgarizations. With *Creative Effort* we cut the umbilical cord of the *übermensch* with earth. Earth, the woman, became only a passive material or object for the plastic and vivifying imagination and embrace of the hero.

Our individualism in fact had many roots in the pioneering tradition that we saw outmoded; it was elemental, not urban; it was driven to fight against the hydra-headed monster of bourgeois egoism, refusing to recognize its blood-kinship. We drew on the 'pre-capitalist' elements in our society in order to affirm something that went (we knew not how) beyond capitalism. By a lonely tour-de-force we wanted to create the realistic and concrete image of beauty which in fact could be born only out of a popular culture with a vital relation to nature. So, denying our Australian links, we proclaimed an Australian Renaissance.*

Zarathustra announced himself in Springwood. We saw that, but we failed to note his Australian accent.

*I have a few times used in this book the convenient cover-term *alienation* though I did not know it at the time. But, under such terms as the omnipresent, lie or self-division, the disintegrative process, I meant precisely what is covered by alienation. The point is that I was not concerned with incidental or peripheral distortions or flaws in my society; I felt a central and ubiquitous distortion. But, failing to see that in the productive process life' was created and recreated for men, I did not see how the creative and alienating forces alike met and struggled there. So I saw the creative defeat of alienation only in terms of art and sex. Linked with this was a whole series of contradictions which have been brought out or implied in the analysis of this book – a key one being the way in which the demand for a full humanity (the beyond-man of a way of life that overcame the alienating process) was flawed by the conception of woman as pure otherness, passive object of man the supreme subject, the active creator. The art-image in turn became transcendental, cut off from earth, the mother, deriving in the last resort from some pure (male, paternal) essence, which in the platonic terms of *Creative Effort* retreated beyond the sum total of the existing relations in the universe. Thus the effort to vindicate 'earth' was flawed at the heart. And so on.

27 · TYING UP LOOSE ENDS

MAURICE INTRODUCED me to the daughter of the owner of a large-scale ironmongery store. A well-built comely girl of Australian proportions, she aspired to be a second Sappho – though the role of a second Corinne, Ninon de l'Enclos, Charlotte Corday or Mrs Bloomer would not have been disdained. The main thing was fame, a beam of light picking one out as one walked and playing one's signature tune on a violin or a fog-horn (whichever was loudest). For an ambitious, high-breasted, strong-legged girl of Brisbane, with enough money to be elegantly bored, the obvious solution was to become a world famous poetess. In her lavishly tasteless boudoir, brooding among pink flowers and pale-blue ribbons, she composed the necessary poems, in which every line was correctly scanned and the sentiments impeccably noble. Then, having read Zora Cross, a sonneteeress who at that time was achieving fame through her ringing lines of fiery blood, she tried to introduce a daring note of passion; but her mixture of virginal timidity and day-dreaming frankness failed to out-zora Miss Cross. Vaguely aware that the few poems, for which her father's ironmongering prestige had obtained entry to the local newspapers, were not likely to bring a golden shower of glory seductively through the plaster ceiling of her tower of spiritual brass, she worked out a splendid series of past lives for herself. She found by certain though indescribable means that she had been Cleopatra, taking a score of lovers in a night and decapitating them before breakfast. As she did not know much history and thought it a bore to read long tomes in order to discover some more marvellous ladies, she fixed on a mysterious white Arab princess as her other main incarnation. What a white Arab was I never found out. The geography of her adventures

214

was mainly bounded by gorgeous palace-walls, minarets and tinkling fountains, though once she fled on camel back behind her lover across the sands of the desert, from oasis to oasis. The account of her Arabian otherlife went on with interminable dullness.

We drove in her Ford car along bumpy country roads, passing cornfields and pineapple plantations, and a few times going as far north as we could in a day. I looked out on the Queensland scene; Rosalind, facing straight ahead, told me of the life she used to lead in Lesbos some 2500 years ago and the drinking parties with Antony in Alexandria. She considered that Shakespeare must have been the incarnation of her court poet at the time of her barge journey, he had described it so exactly in his play. But she was quite put out when I mentioned that Cleopatra, though a Macedonian, had been married in the Egyptian fashion to one brother after another. 'Oh yes,' she said at last, as the Ford car bucked and jumped over a great hole in the road, 'there were some quaint pieces of court etiquette in those days.'

Lying on the white Indian carpet of her Watteauesque bedroom, she described her days and nights as a nun in the year A.D. 1000 Then she rang me up at my boarding-house at midnight to continue her account of the white Arabs.

All the same, she was no fool. She had her father's shrewd business character which had raised him from a small shop in a side-street to the emporium level of city fathers. She had simply fixed on a line of sales talk which seemed to her full of profitable possibilities, and she was trying it out on me. She found me a more amenable listener than Maurice, who could not resist making sarcastic remarks. 'Do white Arabs wash their feet? And how often? Would you talk a little in the various languages which Plutarch mentions Cleopatra as conversant in?' She was hard-headed and her heart was cased in a tough leather-case and her intelligence would have rapidly developed if she had had something to use it on. Aware of the calculating commonsense that stuck out through her worst excesses of daydreaming, I treated her with the utmost respect and never once tried to kiss her, sufficiently rewarded by the spectacle of her small tradesman's mind seeking a romantic enlargement. Even when we lay under the wild honeysuckle, I merely admired her silky ankles and talked about white Arabs. Listening to music, she became rigid and closed her eyes, emitting small gasps of ecstasy. Once I had to chafe her hands, her feet, to restore her to her wide-eyed self. 'There is no Time when I hear music,' she exclaimed. 'I am all my lives at once.' We played Mendelssohn's *Song without Words* on the gramophone in her bedroom, and she said that she felt roses growing out of her breasts. 'Another minute and I would have thrown off all my clothes and danced.'

I took her to my aunt's and she caused a number of uncomfortable silences, which she did not seem to notice. She stared at the roses on the table and forgot to eat her lunch. 'Oh, doesn't Beauty hurt?' she cried, clasping her left breast. 'Oh, Mrs Elkington, please, may I put the roses somewhere else? They hurt my soul, they are too beautiful.' She removed the roses and sighed. 'I feel too intensely. Beauty makes me suffer. It's a white flame under my eyelids. Oh, if I were only more thick-skinned, more ordinary.' She shot a glance at my aunt to see how her raptures were being taken.

Our relationship, briefly absorbing, was suddenly ended. I had dined at her home. Her sister, a pleasant warm-faced girl without the least nonsense or hardness, was soon to be married to a country doctor. I had with me as usual my notebook of poems, which I put down unthinking on a side-table. During the evening Mr W., a small bearish man with a gimlet stare that he tried to disguise by a whimsical smile, picked the notebook up. With sinking heart, I saw that he had fixed on a ribald ballad concocted with Maurice a few nights before; and I expected to be thrown out of the house. However, after carefully reading the poem, he closed the notebook and said nothing. But two days later Maurice rang me up to say that he had shouted after I left and had forbidden Rosalind to meet me again.

We did meet a few times, in the Botanical Gardens, on a sloping bank of grass or under the drooping scarlet poinsettias near the bandstand. But somehow the saga of incarnations had lost its verve. Rosalind weakly took refuge in saying what she really felt, the confinement of body and spirit that afflicted her in Brisbane, the readiness she felt to do anything, however temporarily menial, if she could break out of her domestic jail. I was tempted to say: Let's buy the cheapest gold ring obtainable and go off to the ends of the world, equally homeless. But one glance at her handsome set face deterred me. (Our lives were destined to cross unimportantly later in Sydney and London; and she finally married a statesman with an ignominious place in history. At least she escaped a Brisbane fate.)

Everything was falling away, becoming insubstantial. My aunt, the one definite point in my life, the touchstone of opposition, was soon to go off on a long trip in Java and Malaya. Her absence had the effect of unravelling my world; by removing the knots she tied in my thoughts and feelings, it seemed to remove all connecting links. I felt continually closer to a crisis-moment in which I'd have to make a fundamental decision – not just one more spiritual jump, but a combined operation of action and thought.

Maurice introduced me one day outside his shop to a slight pretty-eyed plain-faced girl in muslin. 'Fifi . . .' I realized that she was the girl I used to play with when my aunt had her house straddling a gully; but there was nothing in the present girl to fuse her with that delightful naiad-image, the wild-haired creature coiled with bare legs in a nest of grass. We exchanged a few polite inanities and parted. Afterwards, Maurice told me that she had pestered him to make the introduction; and for a moment I almost arranged to see her again. Then I realized that she had been as disappointed as myself, and I said nothing. But our encounter for the moment turned the figures of my childhood into dusty ghosts, its flowers into things of scentless wax and cloth, its birds into overwound toys which couldn't be stopped in their jingling song and which then burst. There was only the meaningless litter at the bottom of a drawer, cards with indecipherable messages, ribbons from forgotten heads, broken collar studs and badly developed photos that had faded out of all recognition. I felt more rootless than ever.

I seldom went near the university and had quite fallen out of the Starry group. Instead, I talked at furious length to the dazed but undefeated Jim. 'You'd better take care,' said Ray, one night in the park as we looked down on careering trams,

'you want disciples. There's only one end to that – crucifixion.'
'Naturally,' I replied.

My last expedition with the Starries was on a launch that took a score or so of us down into the Bay, to a small island, where we swam. On the way back, on the packed deck, I lay with Cynthia lightly reclined over me – though her attention was all for Hoskins, a square-built chap who was going to be a surveyor. I had written some sonnets to her eyebrows (taking up the Elizabethan challenge because there she had a definite eyebrow charm: a long thin face with slanted eyes and clear nicely curved brows); she had read the sonnets, smiled, and said nothing. Now, by not moving or twitching despite my cramp and the certainty that all my limbs would be racked with pins and needles as soon as I rose, I endeavoured to give the effect of being no more than a couch agreeably constructed so as to take lithe dreamy girls. She would thus have no reason for moving. Besides, it suited my desire for stoical endurance, for *apatheia* in the face of any bodily stress. I liked to stay under water till I nearly burst, and in listening to music I never moved throughout a piece, however long, no matter how a fly might torment or a posture threaten to petrify me in an awkward pain.

At the boarding-house the proprietress's prolonged bankruptcy went on its eventless course. The flour-white corpse who prostituted herself nightly on the front ground floor had developed a listless cough; she walked past me like a somnambulist, dropping a small bone-button which I cherished. Maisie the raw-boned red-head had a regular, a bullet-headed lad with an eye of frenzy, who turned up between business deals to carry her straight to bed in his arms. Looking out of my window, I saw through the fanlight of her room on the ground floor opposite a momentary entanglement of limbs, a Laocoon of complicated delight. While he stayed, our meals suffered; but he never stayed for long. Taking a fancy to me, he kept on trying to lure me into his way of business without divulging what the way was. Certainly, if it was not directly criminal, it verged on sharp practice; and his habitual caution made it hard for him to explain it in comprehensible terms. 'Aw, you don't want to be squeamish,' he said, jogging me with his elbow and buying me another beer. 'To get on in this world, you need your topknot screwed on right. Give as good as you get. Not that I believe in doing anything cronk. It's just a matter of being quicker on the uptake than the next. You know we could make a fine pair. What I need is someone with a gift of the gab like you. You know you look so honest it's a scream. Drink up and have another. But let's get this clear, there's nothing I hate more'n a shicer.' Then after a while he smoothed his hair; he was always very neat. 'Back to the good old saddling paddock' – by which he meant Maisie's bedroom.

Next morning he'd rush away. 'Off to the Woop-woop!' Somewhere in the backblocks that meant.

Odd characters kept eddying into the place and out again. More loose-limbed loud-voiced girls from a stranded theatrical company, all smiles and headaches, asking my mother to tell their fortunes in a tea-cup. 'It's gospel,' said Maisie in hushed tones. Chaps from way-back sidled in, bringing remarkable moustaches, shy manners, bitten ears, and drinking large cups of boiling-hot tea in a breath. Spruikers and smart-alicks, with magnificent silk mufflers and an inability to talk except right up against your face, breathing beer and onions. More stranded actresses, sitting on band-boxes and biting their lips. And once a bald clergyman with a tic. How they all got to know of the place, I never found out. The proprietress told them that she was closing on Friday, and Maisie found them a room in the rambling house.

I had never prepared for exams till about a fortnight before their date, when I hastily made a digest of all that I was supposed to have studied. I worked about eighteen hours a day at the digest, read it through a dozen times, and then went into the examination room, where I wrote my answers at a breathless pace. (This method of work has stayed with me, determining all my approaches to composition.) With doubts, I tried the same scheme yet again.

At last the date of the finals came. The night before the first paper I went out with Ray and we spent all our cash on beer. The main thing I remember is the difficulty I had in persuading Ray not to climb over some tall brick wall; what lay on the other side is lost to me. Perhaps we didn't know at the time.

During the following days I wrote in a state of hypnosis and had no idea how I had done. The result was first-class honours in both Latin and Greek.

That relieved tension in part. But new worries arose. What was I now to do with my life? The three-years scholarship had been a barrier against all the questions that I most feared. Now it was over. What the devil did the world care about how much Latin and Greek I knew, or didn't know? Without my aunt to argue against I felt myself in a void.

About this time for a few weeks I took over a job of teaching at the technical college, which stood close by the university; a fellow classics student who taught there had to go away for a while. One large mixed class gave me special trouble: there were some girls in it who demurely refused to bother much about work, and I was quite incapable of compelling them. The subject was algebra, at which I was very rusty, and for the blackboard I always used sums that were worked out in full in old textbooks which I found in a cupboard. The steady secretive smile hollowing the cheeks of one girl, Lyra, expressed an amused contemptuous sympathetic awareness of my algebraic incompetence: or so I felt it. Lyra never did a stroke of work, not in my class anyway. Even when I stood behind her and commented on her lack of interest, she merely looked lazily up, slightly stretched herself, and said nothing, smelling of caramels and cheap violets, a girl with a long thin face and very wide mouth, ungainly hands and elbows, a scatter of mauve freckles. I meant to ask the student for whom I stood in if she behaved with as defiant a silence when he was teaching; but I never did.

One day I received a message from a visiting musician Arthur Benjamin and went along to the hotel by the Parliament House where he was staying. Norman had worked out a sketch for an opera libretto, *The Faun*, and had been recommended to try Benjamin. He had sent along his draft with a suggestion of getting in touch with me if a verse-text was needed. Benjamin however didn't want to do the opera. He chatted amiably and took me out to the concert hall where he was rehearsing a programme. A shortish young man, he fitted admirably inside his shirt, something I had never been able to achieve; and his comments on music, which assumed a much higher level of technical understanding than I had arrived at, were flattering. Also, his questions after he had played a work of his own. Did I think the end effective? Had it seemed too sudden, inconclusive? I tried to find an answer which could be interpreted in several different ways.

The encounter, however, had the effect of making me want more than ever to get away from Brisbane, whether to Sydney or Oxford. There still remained the visit to the oracle of Apollo, Springwood. I went there. The simple outflowing delight of the first visit was lacking. A note of anxiety had intruded, a feeling that I needed somehow to prove myself, to make myself worthy of my discipleship. My poems were more confused than ever; my views on poetry had dulled to a mere echo of *Creative Effort*. And I was hurt by Norman's refusal to advise me for or against the Oxford project. In part I wanted to go, though my aunt's vehement support of an Oxonian career had made me veer suspiciously away; in part I wanted to go to Sydney and link my future indissolubly with Norman's.

Norman was no doubt perfectly right in refusing to influence me, but I couldn't help feeling that he might look on a disciple in Oxford less embarrassing than one in Sydney. I didn't want him to help me in any way. Such help would injure my conception of the dangerous luck of poets, the necessity not to arrange life in any way. But at the same time I wanted to feel that he had some sort of need of me.

Perhaps to expedite my departure, he came down to Sydney with me and we stayed at the hotel above George Street. His main purpose was to attend a concert at which Beethoven's *Fifth* and Vaughan Williams's London Symphony were being played: the *Fifth* specially put on by Verbruggen (then doing much to lift musical appreciation in Australia). I did not care for concerts, but was compelled to recognize how little I understood of instrumental colour: stirred by the winged subtlety of Beethoven's violins. The *London* we felt meanly naturalistic, hearing the title rather than the music. Afterwards Benjamin and some of the players came for a drink; and B. mildly rebuked one for bragging he could break wind silently at any orchestral moment.

28 · MORE LOOSE ENDS

AT CHRISTMAS in the boarding-house we had an improvised party. The place was unusually full. The dining room was cleared for a dance and nothing was sacred. 'Musical chairs' gave excuses for sitting in the laps of the girls or for watching them pushed over on to the floor in screaming delight, with a flourish of sleek legs. The game then developed into 'follow-my-leader.' The leader was Maisie and we traipsed all over the house, into every room. We pulled a headaching chorus-girl out of bed in her torn chemise and found a bottle of whisky, half full, in an empty room. Little Miss S. with the cork-screw curls and the knitted openwork blouse got hiccups and was held by the ankles over the banisters: which cured her. The chorus-girl in a pink kimono did the splits on a table and someone recited *Dan McGrew* in sepulchral tones. The small stocky man from Longreach turned out to be an expert in juggling tricks; he broke three glasses and a cane chair. The proprietress said it didn't matter as she was closing on Friday, the furniture would all go to heartless creditors, so on with the fun. The laundry basket had a prop stuck through its handles and was balanced on two chairs. I sat in it with an actress who had feathers in her hair, and we smacked each other with pillows, simultaneously falling out.

Then I made the mistake of trying to smoke the pipe I had bought some while ago in emulation of Ray, who sat in a corner, mixing his drinks and steadily puffing. Within ten minutes I felt stomach qualms and retired to vomit in the backyard, slapped in the face by wet washing.

Suddenly we were in a launch chugging down the river under a thin drizzle of stars. Maisie was on my knees, tousling my hair. It seemed that a triton kept handing bottles of beer up over the side of the boat from the riverdepths. The songs were like gramophone records caught in a crack, endlessly croaking a tuneless phrase. The barge she sat in, like a burnished throne, burned on the water. Maisie, as heavy as a knobbly sack of potatoes, broke my stoical endurances: I shifted my position and almost threw her overboard. She clung to my ear and muttered, 'I like you. Why are you so shy?' I kissed her and she said, 'Hoopla, who cares?' But something went wrong with the engine near Breakfast Creek and we never reached our unknown destination.

We came back soberly in a tram and resumed our drinking round a bonfire in the yard. Maisie lifted me off my feet with a kiss. 'Honest, I wouldn't mind, but I got too great a respect for your mother,' she said as if apologizing for something disgraceful. This time the words altogether lacked conviction; but the effects of the pipe on my stomach had removed all powers of initiative. She took the small man from Longreach off to see if he could find out what was wrong with her alarm clock. I sat on the mouldering wooden steps and watched the leaping antlers of the flame. The police were quite polite when they called.

I entered for the travelling scholarship. Only one was awarded on the arts side. If I won the dice would be cast; I'd go to Oxford. Thus the decision was in part at least taken off my shoulders; for I had a fair idea as to what would happen. I had craftily arranged for fate to send me in the direction I most wanted to go.

I filled in my time by trying to teach myself to play the piano with the aid of a metronome and an old book on the theory of composition – Berlioz seemed the latest composer cited; but that suited me. The piano I used was in the house of Mrs Jay at the back of the boarding-house. Mrs Jay had a daughter at the university who was a friend of Selma's, a girl with the map of Ireland on her face, blurred a little by kindly bog-mists. Once Selma had stayed with Mrs Jay for a few days and we had clasped on a lumpy black sofa outside the large kitchen, listening for footsteps and watching the moonlight move like a dim oily stain over the linoleum.

Mrs Jay was a middle-aged woman married to the oldest

man I had yet seen, who emerged from his disinfectant-stinking cavernous room only on days of strong sunlight, for an hour about noon. The proximity of such physical decay repelled me. Mr Jay with his clammy white skin and his shrunken, hairy, swollen-veined blotched hands, his eyes sunk beyond the light of day in a ferocious skull, was not a spectacle to overcome my aversion from a body already coffined in a senseless resentment. But I avoided his hour and saw him no more.

Mrs Jay made no pretences. 'I married him for money and it serves me right, though twenty years ago he didn't look so bad. But he can't help being what he is, and I don't see how I could have done otherwise, being my parents' daughter. Think of the jobs that nurses have to do, my mother said. Think of the mortgage on the farm, my father said. And I didn't say anything. I was brought up to honour and obey. I obeyed, but I soon gave up honouring. And I don't see how I can be blamed, either for doing it or not liking it.'

She had a son, a year or so younger than myself, who worked in an export firm and who was wrapped up in horse-racing. It was on him that she concentrated her sense of repulsion. 'He's not interested in the things of the mind. I can't understand him. I'm ashamed to be his mother. Look at his coarse lips. The one thing I can't bear is coarse lips. It gives me the horrors. It's so animal-like.' Her daughter was working at chemistry, a quiet industrious girl who seldom smiled.

I practised energetically, rocking the metronome. But my fingers refused to become supple. I moved them about in imaginary scales wherever I was – reading in my narrow bedroom where I paused now and then for a bug-killing, or talking with Jim about a world in which Rubens's ladies burst from their foam of silk in any thicket and barmaids chatted like the heroines of Shakespeare, it seemed quite feasible, if we thought and talked long enough about it, if we kept our faith in poetry intact. But no amount of twiddling made me any better as a pianist. However, I began to try writing music on a system worked out by myself. Then, knowing that I would never dare to show my music to anyone else and that I would never be able to play it myself (a scheme for cutting lengths of wallpaper to fit in a pianola having miscarried), I decided to write poems on music – on Beethoven as a musician, on particular works of his – and to try to get the music into the poems, not merely by the harmonics of vowel and syllable, but also by transposing the structure of music, its counterpoints and methods of transition, its opposing phrases and variations. I wanted an image in which the sensuous essence was musical in its very mode of grasping the world, feeling it in the special system of time-sequences which were musical form, the concentrations achieved by chord and the movement of chords.

Ray similarly wanted to paint poems.

We now had Norman's *Curate in Bohemia* to supplement Murger as a textbook on etiquette, and we decided to wear black silk bow-ties. A small decision, it may seem to those who know not Australia. There the slightest oddity in dress, most of all anything that can be interpreted as the fashion of a queen (homosexual) is liable to bring about assault and battery from the tough Australian – at least it was in those days. A month or so back a visiting pianist suspected of queenery because of his coloured shirts, had been beaten up along the river walks. So our silk bow-ties were a genuine gesture of defiance. But though they often drew insults from passing lads, we were never put to the test of fisticuffs.

Ray and I went painting, and I used up his good paints to little purpose. Once we were in a field by a creek and thought we'd paint the willows. In our assiduous efforts to translate the brilliant values of noon into Gruner's subtly shimmering dawn-tones, we failed to notice that a huge herd of cows had surrounded us from the rear, morosely regarding our pallid canvasses. For a moment of terror I felt that the cattle of our Saturday ordeals, the visits to the meatworks, had gathered round us in a silence of death-judgement; and I needed all my courage to walk through the impassively horned herd.

That night we arrived home late, having paused for beers in wayside pubs. We passed along the riverside and came in a moon-instant on two girls leaning in the nook of an opened gate. They were ardently embracing, locked in a busy kiss. We halted and they undid themselves, muslined with moon-gauze. We looked at them and they looked at us. We said nothing and they said nothing. Their eyes reminded me of some Babylonian fear, phosphorescent in their shadow-masked faces.

'Going home?' said Ray at last. 'Let's go with you.'

They said nothing, still staring, touching shoulders.

'It's a lovely moonlight for a walk,' I said coaxingly.

They said nothing.

'Do you live round here?' Ray asked.

They said nothing.

'We live in George Street,' I added desperately, as if by local-izing ourselves we might cease to be objects of fear – or was it repulsion?

They said nothing. We all stared.

Finally Ray and I walked on. Ray whistled and felt for his pipe, though he had no tobacco left. As we turned the corner, we looked back. The girls didn't seem to have moved. Some-how our dignity had been upset and we didn't know what to say to one another. Suddenly I recognized the image that had been evoked – that of the woman huddled on the benches near the Botanical Gardens. Perhaps the panic I had felt in looking at the cows ranged in brute judgement drove me to note the likeness. And now it seemed that I could recall the same fear, stunned or reproachful, in the eyes of all the women I had ever seen.

'I wouldn't like to be a woman,' I said.

Ray grunted. 'We used the whole tube of white.' Then he added, putting his pipe back in his pocket. 'Silly little bitches, they could at least have told us to mind our own bloody busi-ness.'

Suddenly the closure did come upon the boarding-house. Maisie wept. The commercial traveller said that he was any-way on the point of leaving for Gympie; the belated chorus-girl said that she'd had a letter from a friend in Perth; the two spielers said nothing and left hastily with what remained of the knives and forks. I had noticed a few days before that our pre-vious place on the riverside was still functioning, so I went along there and found the three sisters still in control. The youngest girl had gained an admirer, a tallow manufacturer who had left his nagging wife and wanted something plump, harmless and biddable. We moved back on the old terms. More plaster had fallen from the ceiling of the room shared by Ray and me; otherwise things were unchanged.

Sitting on the ricketty bamboo furniture of the front verandah I scribbled a poem: *To the Unknown.* .

> *You too are looking out upon this night,*
> *you lean against the sill.*
> *Somewhere, behind a silence and a flight*
> *of scattering doves, you are still.*
>
> *You too are looking out upon the moon*
> *that threads the dangerous maze;*
> *and we shall come together, late or soon,*
> *by twisted faltering ways.*
>
> *This moment, with a kiss, I seal you mine.*
> *The moon your proxy bends*
> *to take it; and you'll know the shuddering sign,*
> *though at the world's closed ends.*
>
> *And so each careless step will bring more near*
> *the inevitable kiss.*
> *O listen deeply now, beyond all fear:*
> *our tryst we shall not miss.*
>
> *Walk down the casual streets and hold this troth*
> *clear like our harvest-moon*
> *globed in your heart. I cannot fail my oath*
> *to find you, late or soon.*

By the dim light of the moon and a candle in a chinese paper-
lantern I read over what I had written, with various discard
lines: Stroll from the myriad world of women slowly. Gaze in
the moon unitl your face is etched in gentle acids there . . .

I listened to the bell-like laughter of the tallow manufacturer's beloved; the copper of her bell had been adulterated
since Bedford junior tickled her fancy. Why had I written these
lines? Did I believe in the unknown like that? Someone fated
to complete my fragmentariness? A particular person? Or did
I believe that any girl not a shrew or a cross-eyed simpleton
could provide the inflammable material of the creative image?
Why hadn't I made any efforts to keep in contact with Selma,
with Bessy, with Daisy?

A crash, followed by bell-like laughter. The girls were washing up and the dolly-varden was developing a propensity for breaking things. Another cup gone; we'd soon be drinking out of celluloid. Abruptly it seemed that I had really said no more to Selma than to Bessy; but whereas Bessy remained shadowed in the niche of her pure otherness, Selma had been playing a game all along exactly as I had. Her naivety was only part of her sense of humour, her refusal to be deeply implicated. She knew as well as I did that we could never find a lasting relationship; she needed a spacious stability. She'd marry a squatter's son and have her generous hospitality and her horses and her contralto songs and her children (whom she'd bring up admirably, without either dominating or neglecting them); and all the while she'd smile, keeping the world and her husband at a respectful and unjarring distance. And part of her smile would be the memory of the game she had played with me.

I felt pleased and a little discomfited at this realization. As if the discovery of Selma's active unimplication somehow belittled as well as relieved me, robbing her of all depth. What qualities then would the unknown possess, to hold me? Cruel vanities and treacherous narcissisms? Candour and intelligence to break down the self-conceits in myself of which Daisy had complained? I didn't know. I didn't want to know yet. The time would come. The tryst was laired in my unwritten poetry. The conflict would be worked out on Zarathustra's mountaintop and in the loud street crucifying Eden.

The dolly-varden laughed again, this time definitely with a crack in the bell – a crack that was near a sob. By the lamp inside, the tallow manufacturer crackled the newspaper where he was reading the reports of cattle prices. I felt sad and thought of the lot of women. But such broodings were forbidden under the heading: self-pity disguised as pity for women and others exploited, a failure to grasp and accept the totality of things. It was pleasant to have a dogmatic system. I looked out into the peaceful night.

I didn't get the travelling scholarship. Eric Partridge, since become lexicographer of British slang, was the other competitor; he rightly gained the award and went to Oxford. My professor told me that Eric, a returned soldier, would not have been eligible next year; but I would. So I was expected to stand the second time, when there was little doubt I'd be chosen, etc.

However, I had sworn my oath to Apollo that I would go to Sydney in the event of failure. I decided to go.

At last things were settled. I hadn't the remotest idea how I was going to live in Sydney – except that I knew I would refuse under any circumstances to take a job, that is, a regular job with set hours, or anything that limited what I considered my poet's freedom, or seemed to make me an accomplice of the buying and selling world. But this uncertainty agitated me far less than any voyage to Oxford with a guarantee of income. I had wanted all along a good excuse for going to Sydney, within reach of Springwood.

Luckily, my aunt was still in Java, in what was for her a marvellous world of blazing green and of slave labour. I lingered in Brisbane, needing some definite sign or compulsion for my exit. Suddenly half a dozen reasons for departure came up. My aunt arrived back and through some delay of letters I didn't know she had come. I saw her unexpectedly near the Bridge and shrank back into a shop entry, from which I peered out along the street. The place wasn't far from the law courts and two detectives noticed my suspicious behaviour. They swooped on me and asked a lot of questions before they let me go. This inquisition coming while I was still uncertain whether I had seen my aunt or not, shook me considerably; and I was left wondering what crimes I had committed and how soon it would be before the detectives caught up on me.

I went over to Kangaroo Point and found that my aunt had in fact returned. Soon we were arguing in the old way, but more vigorously. She was sure that I had ruined my life and said so in a number of vociferous ways. I replied that I hadn't, but if I had it was what I wanted to do. At last I told her that I absolutely rejected her world of careers, hypocrisy, money-making and nice marriages. I preferred Marlowe's murder, Beddoes's suicide, or Blake's anonymous garret crowded with silly angels.

It went on for days.

Then came the episode of the university magazine, now

edited by P.R.S. I contributed an essay attacking academics as eunuchs of mechanism, plus several poems. One of the poems, derived from an etching by Norman, was excoriated as obscene; and the issue became a scandal. Mrs P. in patiently hurt tones asked me why I delivered such a blighting attack on academics when I had so many good friends on the staff, from whom I had certainly learned a lot? I tried to explain that I had intended no ingratitude to such persons, whom I respected. I had been attacking – what? I had known it clearly enough as I wrote; but before her intelligent helpful face I lost all the clues. I began trying to explain what Blake meant by spectre and abstraction, and felt myself as abstract as Urizen himself. I stammered and was sure that I had indeed been stupidly ungrateful and that the poems hadn't been good enough anyhow for a scandalous explosion and suppression.

I waited outside the ground-floor room where P.R.S. was arraigned before the Students' Council, hoping that I'd be called in. It seemed humiliating that he should have to take the rap, while I, now a graduate, was ignored.

Still, with mingled pride and regret, I felt that now I was better equipped to depart for Sydney, my poet's apprenticeship concluded by the minor defiance of the essay and the poems. With a valid triumph – no more dubious than were all events in a self-contradictory world – I could face the journey into the unknown. Further, I at last had somewhere in Sydney to go. A lesser German sculptor, Pillig, who professed anthroposophism with a melancholic enthusiasm, had been visiting Brisbane a short while back to hold an exhibition. His sculpture was laboured and unoriginal, but at least professional; his paintings were crude in the extreme, daubed for cheapness in shiny house-paint. He complained that he couldn't paint from nature as then everything came out green. However his nudes were also yellow and red. He said it was expressionism. To help him, I wrote a cautious article in the *Daily Mail*; and he asked me to stay at his huge studio on an upper floor in Elizabeth Street, Sydney, where he made plaster casts for barrow-sale. (A couple of years later he committed suicide.) His mistress was an unscrupulous woman with green promiscuous eyes and a flattish nose.

And so, with a suitcase and several brown paper parcels, I left Brisbane at last, never to see it again. My mother had accepted my decision, wondering, hurt and uncomplaining; my aunt sulked; I paid a farewell visit to Redcliffe and went for a long walk with my cousin Nancy, wondering why I had never sounded her deep interest in poetry. But now as the train rattled over the Indooroopilly Bridge and the iron girders switch-backed by, I felt at last that I was rising into a new dimension, with £5 6s. 3d. in my pockets and baggage composed of two shirts, two singlets, a razor, three odd socks, a spare pair of trousers, a penknife, *Thus Spake Zarathustra*, Blake's poems, and *Creative Effort*.

Ray had already lost his job on the newspaper by writing up a council meeting which never took place. He had rung up the clerk and had the agenda read out to him. Then, knowing the councillors in question well from previous reportings, he concocted an account of the proceedings, which was duly printed. But somebody's death had caused at the last moment a postponement of the meeting.

Within a few weeks he had perfidiously sold all my books, which had been left out at our aunt's house, and had bought a ticket to Sydney. By that time I had a garret of my own and a new life had begun; not the new life of our reveries, but something quite unlike our Brisbane years. The inner conflicts and contradictions of this life had yet to be worked out; but that, as one says, is another story.

THE ROARING TWENTIES

CONTENTS

1 · THE FREEDOM OF THE ARTIST

PILLIG WAS out, touting for orders. On the rough shelves of the outer half of the vast top floor of the warehouse stood his plaster-casts, some still white, some half-painted, some garishly completed. Boys and girls in peasant costumes of a fabulous German principality, rosily rotund nudes admiring the soles of their right feet, A.E.F. soldiers grinning in khaki dung. In mid room lay dismembered moulds and brown paper packets of plaster, while overhead were belts running round large wheels, the remnants of a small bankrupt factory that had preceded the plaster-casts, draped with spider-webs. The dry mouldy smell made me aware of my blank fear, my lack of money or prospects, my obstinate and fruitless isolation. The statuettes in the splintery desolation mocked me with the threat that the artist, even when as lachrymosely high-minded as Pillig, was required to produce some sort of orthodox rubbish, if he wished to survive.

I went into the inner half. Kitchen, bedroom and picture gallery. In fact two bedrooms. Mine made of an uncouth wooden frame with sacking, some seven by four feet oblong, and eight feet high; and P.'s, where old velvet curtains slung from the rafters enclosed a damaged fourposter. All round were hung unframed paintings, hundreds of them, excruciatingly bad, daubed with ordinary house-paint from tins on cheap cardboard. Pillig said he couldn't afford better materials; but in fact he liked the slimy paint on the coarse absorbent surface. He couldn't paint from nature; too much green, he insisted, his eyes saw only green. Certainly the few landscapes were a block of hardly differentiated verdure, with a few purple cows or yellow clouds. For subjects he preferred to draw on old books of German academic shows, studying the small reproductions through a magnifying glass and then transforming them into the explosive caricatures he called an emotionally free version.

I went over to the window and looked down at the traffic through the dust-grained pane: the careering trams, the pedestrians threading the opposite pavement, the rattling carts, with cars jostling an occasional hansom cab. A drab veil cut me off, making the vehicles and passers-by look monstrously spectral, imprisoned in a dully echoing vault of grey daylight, menacing and yet impotent. Able to do no worse than run one over or starve one to death. The deadly city of thriving commerce. I was five storeys up, and feeling cold. I fingered the few coins in my pocket.

I returned to the rickety table to find Calydon on the map. What was the point of reading the Fifth Ode of Bacchylides? Only to prove to myself that I didn't belong to the world on the other side of the dirty veil of glass. I expected something exciting and important to happen. Latitude 38, longitude 22: that brought me to the borders of Arcadia and Achaia, but I still couldn't see Calydon on the map of Ancient Hellas (*Everyman Classical Atlas*). On the inside of an unfolded envelope I had scribbled a literal translation: 'The Maid sent/ a boar to the fair land of Calydon/ ... widely devastating/ shamelessly fighting.' Uninteresting stuff, except that shamelessly fighting was an amusing epithet for a boar, it did give something of a picture. I found Calydon at last, across the gulf, in Aitolia. Somehow I hadn't expected it there. And anyhow I had very little idea what life was like in Calydon of the fifth century B.C. when Bacchylides stopped writing and scratched his nose with pleasure at finding that excellent epithet for a rampaging boar. Red rust in the crops, wheat scarce, barley no better, beans only a handful; as for almonds, you know what almonds are, breaking the boughs one year, then not a peck. And don't talk of olives, the snow withered them up. The one sure thing was Phylilla lying with half the village lads under the scraggy vinerows. For a moment I saw the flinty glitter of the hills, the broad lake of rippling milky light. All gone, no matter how the horny peasant hands clung to the dugs of life. Death snapped their bones, shamelessly fighting. I longed to be at work hoeing the olive-fields, to hear the songs come up from the enclosure of Artemis.

I began writing. This time a poem of my own. 'The dryad with her leafy hair unghosts . . .' But I kept sneezing. Every time the image burst in my head, I felt that irresistible impulse to sneeze. I put the pen down and the blood ebbed and I had no need to sneeze. But the moment I felt the Calydonian girls crystal naked in the pool of the hill-spring, I sneezed again. I was being deprived of my one chance to write a good lyric by the dust tickling at the back of my nostrils. All the while, too, I was aware of the dull rumble of traffic, the dingy windows of apprehension through which I kept the chaffering world at a distance. A fly buzzed round my head. Outside, the great blowfly of the world was buzzing. I closed my eyes and felt my head turning like Keats's Grecian Urn of frosted dance patterns, but faster and faster. I sneezed again.

Pillig came stumbling up the stairs, small and fattish, with shining bald head and eyes of pale dissatisfied blue. Any luck? 'No, there is no such thing as luck,' he replied irritably, blinking and tightening his lips. I tried a soothing word and he cried out, waving his heavy arms, 'Isn't it enough that I prostitute my art? They want to get the last drop out of me? It's too much.' His mistress Rahel had previously done the bargaining; but they'd parted just before I arrived from Brisbane, and now she was living in a room over an arcade in Elizabeth Street with the child, which wasn't Pillig's. 'I'll buy a tray and go round selling direct to my public,' he went on. 'Though these casts are a prostitution of my art, yet they're far superior to the Italian trash Kroeker is selling, things done in slimy marble, of low sex appeal. My casts may be mere commercial art, but they're the work of a sculptor, a man who respects his hands.'

From the boarded-off kitchen he produced bread and cheese. His small clay models, tinted to look like bronze, were at least far better than his paintings. Somewhat over-muscular and ponderously allegorical, but with a mild academic competence. He had left Germany shortly before 1914. I think he'd had some trouble with a wife who wanted a regular income, and perhaps he had scented the coming war. He was really a timid kindly soul, his father a small baker. He liked to drink lager and talk endlessly and vaguely about the need to return to nature and the anthroposophic ideas of Steiner. Today, however, as we ate, he continued abusing Italian sculpture; he hated marble of any kind but especially when soft-grained or glistening. 'Cheesy,' he said, squashing a lump of cheese under his strong workman's thumb, and gave a half-hearted imitation of a Neapolitan tenor strumming on a guitar and turning up the whites of his eyes. Then, boiling a kettle for tea on the gas ring, he summed up. 'The world's in a bad way and we must suffer.' Exactly what I was afraid of, myself. In a few moments he'd start afresh the never-completed story of the Baron who'd been his patron.

I had the impression of a hard struggle to acquire a sporadic art education, bronchial illness, and unhappy marriage, an unreliable Baron and much nature-culture and melancholy amid the red pinewoods and the Munich beer mugs. But I couldn't fix my mind on his problems, I had too many of my own. I studied his latest picture, Othello incompetently strangling Desdemona in sickly oranges and scarlets, hell in the harem. I wondered about writing to the amiable clergyman I'd met at the summer school in Victoria, who'd had some connection with adult education at one of the Sydney colleges; perhaps he'd find me a W.E.A. class. I needed very little to live on. Pillig, appeased by rye bread and cheese, took up his zither and played; his peasant hands strummed a light tune and he sang dreamily.

'Well, what have you been doing with yourself?' he asked at last, averting his pale hungry eyes.

'Translating some Greek poems.'

I knew that'd impress him and he'd forget to ask what use I could make of such translations; he had a naive respect for learning. He sighed. In his kindliness he didn't mind my staying with him, but he worried for my sake about my lack of any future. And though he didn't even hint that he hoped I'd interest Norman in his work, I knew he kept thinking about it. But I didn't have a high enough opinion of his modelling to take examples of it up to Springwood; so I had an uneasy feeling that I enjoyed his hospitality on false pretences. Usually he gave me advice in the form of phrenological disquisitions. He fingered my head, consulted charts, and said my bumps reminded him of Beethoven's. 'Ah, I'm sorry for you, my friend,' he repeated mournfully, 'so much suffering I see.' He shook his head. 'You have the true soul of an artist, but the world is not made for such. The bridge of your nose shows a deep break between emotion and action.'

I was flattered and uncomfortable; his remarks seemed a diabolic parody of my Zarathustrian aspirations. 'I can look after myself. Beethoven didn't suffer. Not in the ordinary sense. It's a question of the overfilled heart.' I quoted: 'The pang of having so much to give and no one who can take. The lightning pang of the summer cloud.' I could talk like that to Pillig, who was so simple, so naturally decent; who should never have left his ancestral bakery.

He sighed and woke a thin flutter of notes from his zither. 'It is all very true, my good friend, but you must study the philosophy of Helios and find your rightful place in the universe.'

He was setting up the moulds and preparing to make yet another Teutonic schoolboy with tasselled cap and dimpled face. Whatever he said, he liked the manual work of casting. I went off down the steep stairs. The floor below us was rented by a company packing something in cardboard boxes; and the other floors were the usual sets of neat-looking useless offices. I crossed the road and made for Hyde Park. The excavations of the underground hadn't yet begun and I sat awhile on a sunny seat. I felt a raw wound in my mind, round which the flies were hovering. Two sailors sat beside me, half drunk, and I lent them my matchbox, listening vaguely to their altercation. Did you see where she got to? I haven't got eyes in the back of my pants. Then where have you got 'em? What does it matter? I don't like her thinking she got away with it. She'll think that anyway, you can't stop a woman thinking. Aw, can't you? I went on conjuring up Calydon, but couldn't recall the unwritten poem except as an oracular sneeze. The suave rippling of a girl's flanks deepened my despair before the intractable world of words. The lankier sailor returned my matches and suggested I might know somewhere worth going to. I didn't.

I walked down Elizabeth Street and ascended the circling steps in the arcade. If the door's open, I'll go in. The door was on the latch and the fuzzy-haired woman was phoning. As soon as she heard me, she began patting the untidy hair over her nape, then she put a hand over the earpiece and turned. 'Oh, it's you. She told me to tell you she's moved up the street. She wrote the number on an envelope somewhere.' She yawned capaciously and held her stomach from wobbling. 'I put it somewhere. Look under the cushion, will you? No, it wasn't there. I remember, I stuck it behind that picture.' I found the envelope. The woman returned to the phone and found her caller had rung off. 'They'll ring again if they've got anything to say,' she remarked with another yawn.

I went back up the street towards the point where the trams swung round the side of the park. Rahel's numbers were continental, 5s and 3s looked the same and 7s had strokes across. But I found the probable place, behind the street front. To my relief there was the podgy small boy Willy playing with a stick and some string; he looked up and said nothing. 'Where's your mother?' He pointed to a French window. I knocked and entered. She was in bed and raised her bare arm across her head as if she expected a blow. A shapely arm. Her wavy brown hair was spilled on the pillow and her green eyes were long and cold; she had a hard out-thrust chin and slightly flattened nostrils; her body was wiry, lascivious, and somehow dead. I knew now that one couldn't trust a word of hers. The room smelt musty, dank, with a tang of iodine.

'I've got a bit of a chill,' she said heavily.

I sat on the stool by her littered dressing-table. 'What have you been making?'

'Only something to wear, silly.'

What I had wanted to ask was where she got the expensive material from. Medicine bottles and combs full of long hairs stood by the sewing-machine. I looked curiously round and refrained from comments that might suggest a right to intrude and claim her as my property; I had begun to learn caution from her. I disliked the room, but was flattered at being in it.

She asked how Pillig was getting on. She had now lifted both her arms and twined her fingers behind her head, sitting up a little. I wanted to ask why her nightgown had been torn down the middle since Tuesday, why she had moved from the arcade, and what was really wrong with her. 'Tramping round for orders. Mixing plaster.'

'You know,' she said, widening her long green eyes, which momently were hazel, then green again, green as a muddy pool full of woodland shadows, 'he's really a good man.' I nodded. 'But he shouldn't listen to lies.' I nodded. 'You haven't kissed me yet.' I kissed her, filled with an increasing fear but determined to do the right thing. She pulled at the coverlet and it came away from the bottom of the bed, baring her small feet. We laughed. She threw the coverlet away. The boy was singing to himself in the damp courtyard, with its sooty wistaria, a low wavering song that never ceased. 'You're very young,' she said, 'I don't think you know how to take care of yourself.' She had long thin fingers that refused to stay still.

'To respect women is to earn their contempt,' I replied devoutly. 'But I don't mind.'

Afterwards her words made me more suspicious than ever; but at the moment they merely made me want not to appear the callow fool I was.

As I went out I handed the small boy a penny, which he took with a weak smile and hid in his knickerbocker pocket. In the street, without bothering about my direction, I went on towards Central Station. But as I neared the first corner, I glanced across the road and noticed someone dodging behind the line of taxis. Pillig. The next moment I was uncertain. I turned the corner and halted to look at the heaped windows of the shop, where they had installed the first escalator in Sydney. With my mother there on Christmas shopping expeditions I had wanted to go on endlessly ascending the moving steps. Now the shop looked more alien than a patch of Congo jungle, with all stairs leading down to the repetitive hell of money values. 'And with arithmetic go down to hell,' as Cyril Tourneur put it in Jacobean days. I turned the farther corner and walked towards the building where Pillig had his workshop-studio. I wanted to find him at home and prove I hadn't seen him dodge behind the taxis. But I passed the door.

I lingered before the second-hand bookshops. Even without a coin to spare I couldn't pass a cheap booktray without turning it over. Then I went up Hunter Street, making for the basement wine-bar. Down the narrow steps into the cool dim low-roofed room where an elderly man was talking to himself in a corner. I knew him a little; he liked to push against one, dribbling about liturgies and choir boys in a fluting voice. I ignored his call, though he'd have bought me a drink, and went to the bar where the fat kindly Italian served me with a Frontignac. Somebody had suggested a Frontignac the first time I visited the bar, so I always ordered it. It was green and I liked the name. Nobody had been in yet. I took my glass to a table under the street pavement, the high heels of girls click-clacking on the thick glass cubes. I resolved not to see Rahel any more. As I closed my eyes, I seemed to be sitting on her bed with the half-drunk sailors, who tore her gown and tossed her in the air. I scribbled on the table-top. Where are they now, those friends of mine? With rip of silk and whistling flame, the tavern night, the bubbling light the red wine sheds, men who could lift big naked girls, up over their heads.

It wouldn't come out. I sipped the heavy wine and drew a meander pattern round the words. I'd look like a poet at work (design after Manet) if anyone peeped round the pillar. Overhead girls were walking on the arch of cool dusty light of my Frontignac grotto. For a moment I struggled up out of my stupor. I had no idea how I was going to stay alive. Any settled job that tied me in with the damned world would mean a total failure; an odd spot of journalism however would be acceptable, any temporary occupation that came out of my obsession with poetry and did not link me with the money system. Now that I had accepted Norman's *Creative Effort*, I had to find if its terms applied or didn't apply to myself. Norman's philosophy, fused with my earlier decision not to compromise in any way with money values, worked out for me as a belief that if the body of my unborn poetry had any virtue it would act as my fate. It would somehow find and determine my way of life and a means of subsistence that I could not myself devise. I must suppress my own will, strive to liberate the creative image, and leave the rest to the Muses, the Fates of Poetry.

The others began to drift down, the journalists and bohemians I still expected to talk brilliantly, though so far I had encountered only the small talk of scandal and shop. At first I had held myself nervously taut, waiting for my chance to strike in with an epigram compact of wit and knowledge, which would establish my position. The chance never came. If it had come and if I had achieved the epigram, nobody would have noticed it. Hart, a lanky good-natured commercial traveller, was arguing with Panzer, a large-faced Czech, who drove a taxi. They wanted to found a Club. Panzer liked easy dancing, Hart liked easy drinking. I listened with a certain interest as they canvassed the costs, the police-squaring, the amenities. The idea was a good one. I'd be able to sleep under one of the club's tables on indefinite credit. All the while I kept my eye on the pillar at the bottom of the steps. I knew that Phyllis wouldn't be likely to come down; she was no winebibber and if I really wanted to chase after her I should have gone down into Mockbells. But I also had a stubborn hope that someone like Leon Gellert might look in for a drink. Licking the last smell of Frontignac from my glass, I went to the Gents past the rows of large casks, a long damp cavern journey where the shadows became medieval if one had had enough Frontignac.*

*Ray reminds me: 'I do not know who the original Pelligrini was, although the place had been a centre for artists, writers and musicians for many years and is referred to in Louis Stone's *Betty Wayside*. When we used to go there it was run by a fat jovial Italian named Truda. It was quite like a club, and any casuals, especially women, were discouraged. About five o'clock in the afternoons the place used to start filling up and the company was always pleasant. Gruner, whenever he was in town, would be there, and other regulars were Leon Gellert, Flozellas, Percy, Dulcie Deamer, Les Robinson, Jack Quayle, Hugh McKay, Hugh Brayden, Margot R., Denis Driscoll, etc. It was not long, however, before the bar was closed down by the energetic police for the simple reason that it was conducted in a cellar basement. Wine-bars in Sydney generally had a very bad reputation in those days (though it's not much better now: they are generally known today as plonk

Then I drifted to Mockbells, only a few minutes away, pleasantly jostled by home-hurrying typists. Phyllis wasn't there. Only some smoke-framed domino players. Outside the Hotel Australia the limousines were rolling up and plump society women out of bad novels were trotting up the broad steps between the flunkeys. I wandered back along Elizabeth Street, pausing at bookshops and restaurants, and fingering my coins, which seemed to lessen every time I counted them. How long before the tarts began to promenade or fill door niches along the front of the park? My interest was purely platonic. Even if I had had money I should not have contemplated picking one up, such procedures being forbidden by my interpretation of the Muses as Fates. But I felt a certain companionship in any outcasts who detested the police as much as I did.

Some hours later I went up the dark stairs, risking fires by lighting matches at the difficult corners. Pillig wasn't in. As I undressed and lay on the creaking camp bed in my cubicle of sackcloth, I had a conviction of carrion death, of a body rotted within and ravaged from outside by eagle beaks of malice. My chest a frail bone defence against the cruel edge of time. I had been wearing only a thin shirt under a loose coat, and the marble tables over which I had leaned now seemed frozen grave covers that exhaled a breath of dissolution. I tossed feverishly.

'What is it?' asked Pillig, staring out of a splash of candlelight, in his pink flannel nightgown.

'I'm all right,' I said, tightly closing my eyes.

---

shops), and I recall quite a few where the girls used to work, selling drinks, only on a commission basis. But the police got tough and no women were allowed to work in them unless they were the owners or related to the owners. Thus it was automatically assumed that any conducted under street level must be haunts of vice. But Pelligrini's was then, without doubt, the best behaved in Sydney. Truda later opened another wine-bar at the corner of Dalley and George Streets, near the *Bulletin*, but it was never the same as the old place.'

I awoke with dawn light seeping in a faint green glow through the dusty windows, the fever squirmed with maggoty violence in my brain, and then I saw the world unchanged and abominable. All things coated with a bilious slime of light, confessing the putrefaction of the powers that ruled the bought-and-sold souls of men. But I heaved myself up, and to Pillig's grunted and worried questions I answered that I was feeling a bit of a strain. 'Got an idea for some new work.' That shut him up. The tireless imitator in wall paint of tenth-rate academic paintings, the laborious caster of chubby peasant boys, had a touching belief in inspiration. Besides, he wanted to see me earning something.

I recalled Rahel's remark about my not being able to look after myself, and now it seemed more menacing than ever. I pondered her words, her tones, her gestures, trying to understand her nature and its motivations. Incredibly stupid appeared my verses about her as an inscrutable Helen bringing the glare of burning Troy into Hyde Park trees smouldering in the dawn. But I couldn't bear to stay shut up. With aching bones I evaded Pillig's advice about Helios and water treatments, and went out to sit in the park, coughing and oozing phlegm in sunlight blearily weighted with dust, amid sparrows whose chit-chatter was the voice of the world's rambling madness. Though I had taken a resolution, written out in ancient Greek, not on any account to bother Norman with my problems, I scribbled him a note saying that I felt ill.

On the way back I halted before the building where a brass on the door announced Adolphe Beutler, Second-hand Pianos, French Polishing, Tuning and Repairs. After some hesitation I went up. The works were on the second floor, packed with pianos in various stages of coming to pieces and being put together again. Beutler in his shirt sleeves was puffing at a cigar stub and tuning a reconstructed piano, leaning now and then over the exposed strings. An employee was polishing the top of a baby-grand. After a while Beutler noticed me and grinned. 'Tea in a minute, take a seat.' He went on striking notes and turning his head sideways, like a thrush that pecks the ground and then listens.

I had met him shortly after my arrival from Brisbane. One

day he called on Pillig, who brought him in to where I was scribbling at my broken deal table. There was something about him that at once impressed me. Not the lion mane flung dramatically back, but the concentrated energy that rounded his eyes and lifted his scalp as he spoke, the smile that broke through and played about his finely moulded lips. Pillig effusively remarked that I was a poet. I lugged out the copy of the varsity magazine that had been suppressed because of my poems, and Beutler read them carefully through without comment. Then I showed him Norman's etchings in my suitcase. He looked them carefully through without comment, stared at me with rounded eyes and lifted scalp a moment, and shook hands. I must come along, he added, with Pillig to their next concert.

The concerts were evenings or Saturday afternoons spent in the piano workshop, both men smoking cigars and drinking lager. Beutler played a series of sea songs from Heine and Pillig sang them in a thin, correct voice. Now and then Beutler joined in with a squeaky, erratic composer's voice. I knew little of songs, which I had always considered sprats in the symphonic ocean; but I was ready to admire Beutler's and I tried to recall the little I knew of Schubert and Wolf, to whose tradition his work clearly belonged. Wagner he disliked, Schoenberg and Scriabin he despised, and he turned a deaf ear to my inquiries about any works of his own that weren't lieder. But his thoroughly worked-out theories of the relation between the structure of poetry and the melodic curve, the thematic development, of music began to fascinate me. I saw his work as carrying Wolf's method to a new lyrical precision. Besides, there was a remarkable gaiety about the man, a jaunty panache that justified his careless lion mane and gave his broad Beethoven-mask its pose of dignity.

Now, watching him, I decided that he had in him the root of true musical form and that therefore my going to Pillig had had a fated aspect, an Apollonian guidance. Pillig had been the mild sheepish emissary of the gods, bringing me to a man whom it was necessary for me to know, a man who had fought his way through to an essential clue, a grasp of the art image, which defeated the disintegrations of our world. He put his cigar stump down on the edge of the keys and turned to me. 'You look ill,' he said in surprise. 'What are you doing about it?'

'Nothing,' I replied obstinately. 'It's near closing time. Perhaps you'll play me those last songs of yours. They'll do me all the good I need.'

He grinned and took me out for tea and sandwiches. Then we returned and he sat at the tuned piano, taking the MSS of the songs from his jacket. As I listened, I felt sure I was right and that his Heine settings were all that songs should be; he had caught the wit, warmth, clarity of the words within the deepened dimension of a unified musical image. I felt better and insisted that I was cured. Refusing to go home with him, I made my way back to Pillig's workshop; and the moment I sat down there, I felt worse than ever.

The next day, the next two days, I spent in a dull effort to keep the feverish mists at bay. As long as I could read Theocritos or Zarathustra I felt I had dominated my body and proved my poetic worth. Then the fiery weight of the rebellious flesh was too much and I slumped into misery. In fitful moments I attempted to think things out, but my mind trudged round its lame circle. Trust Apollo and the Muses, and live. Trust them, and die. I looked out on the swarming world and saw its denizens as inhumanly adapted to an alien thing, money, so that every breath they drew was at someone else's expense. Somehow that alien thing had become the feverish chill agitating my bones, had become my body itself; there was a traitor inside me, with whom I wrestled as with the enemy of all life.

I had gone out to sit in the park in order not to bother Pillig too much, and as I turned the corner on my way back I saw him coming down the opposite footpath, Rahel with him. He was holding the small boy by the hand, and was dressed in his best clothes, looking very roly-poly and pompous, with stiff collar and magenta bow. So they had made things up, though he had repeatedly told me that he'd never speak to her again. Perhaps he'd been meditating the reconciliation for some time; and the uneasiness in his manner, which I'd been feeling, was derived, not from anxiety about my future, but from a guilty feeling that he'd soon ask me to vacate my hut of boards and hessian. He needed his hausfrau, his privacy rank with cheroot-smoke, and the evasive Willy as a substitute for his own lost children. But he'd been ashamed of admitting to me that he meant to take Rahel back; and when he'd watched me with his pale eyes, perhaps he'd been wondering how much I knew of the reasons for their quarrel.

I turned back into a shop entry and waited for the trio to pass. Then I hurried down the street, filled with a sense of impending disaster. I climbed the steep stairs and unlocked the outer door. The door leading into the bedrooms and gallery was padlocked. Never before had Pillig locked it up, and I had no key. Looking round, I found my books and clothes on a shelf by the plaster-casts, and on the door was a note: 'Back about 8.' No doubt it was meant to pacify me, to indicate shame-facedly that my bed would be shifted into the workshop after they returned. No doubt Pillig had taken Rahel out for a cel-ebration at the Austrian restaurant and had no intention of hurting me. But all I saw in his act was an intimation that I was turned out from the living quarters and would have to buy my own meals if I were poor-spirited enough to hang on and doss among the plaster dust and the whited cobwebs.

I found some fibre rope and tied my books together, put on my spare shirt and tucked my spare socks in my pocket. Then I wrote on the note: 'Thanks for all you have done. I never for-get favours, or injuries either.' I think this was the only time in my life I have indulged in a blatantly melodramatic phrase. Let's hope the fever was to blame. I took up my books and the suitcase with the etchings, and went downstairs, leaving the outer door open. I knew that would upset Pillig, who was fussy about locks; he seemed to think he was beleaguered with bur-glars after his plaster nudes. As I reached the bottom of the stairs, I recalled the figure dodging behind the taxis and knew it was his. Obviously I had no further place among his domestic sanctities, Rahel sidling viciously about with jutted lip and long fingers, waiting for him to go out. I wanted to return and tear up my fustian and quite false note, but I felt too tired.

Where was I to go? Whatever happened, I could not return to Pillig, and I lacked the money for even a cheap room. The weather wasn't altogether suitable for a fevered poet to sleep in the Domain in a coating of newspapers. The only thing was to call in at the wine-bar, buy a Frontignac, and hope that someone like Panzer would lend me a few bob or tip me off about some really low-down dosshouse. Then in the wire letter-box I saw a letter and read my name. I fumbled a long time before I got the envelope open and read Norman's message. He had written to Percy, his elder brother, who lived up the North Shore line at Roseville, to say I'd be coming to stay with him for a while till my influenza went.

2 · Woolloomooloo

I HAD several quiet days at Percy's suburban house, lounging in the back garden or sitting in the shed where he drew. He was a man of indomitable and imprudent cheerfulness, liable to drift off on a sea of beer for uncharted destinations, amiably unambitious and quite lacking in Lindsay disputatiousness. Perfectly happy if he had funds to go on painting his gently perceptive landscapes between the beer pints. A worry to nobody but his wife, he did his best to make ends meet by rather bad illustrations for the Bookstall series and other such cheap booklets. No more comforting presence for a poet wrecked on the first slight rocks of his career could have been found. Once when he came home full of beer in the late afternoon, he paused to rest on a seat in a public garden after getting out of the train, dozed and woke up beneath a reddening sunset-sky. Lord, it's dawn, he thought, and hurried home with a story improvised to explain why he'd been out all night. Another characteristic tale comes from the later years when his wife had died; she took the precaution of leaving the house to their son; and in some resulting altercation Percy remarked in bewilderment to the latter, 'Here now, don't you realize you're talking to a man old enough to be your father?'

Did I take this chance of a momentary haven to take stock of my situation and search for some way out? I did not. Then, as I was feeling about as well as I was ever likely to feel, a letter came to say that my mother was arriving with Phil and that she wanted me to find her a boarding-house. I went to town and wandered about in Darlinghurst, which Percy had suggested as a possible area. I took rooms in a house in Victoria Street and went to meet the train. Phil, now about fifteen years old, has recorded the moment in his *I'd Live the Same Life Over*, though I think he has confused the image of my untidiness at this moment with his memories of the following weeks:

On our arrival, Jack had met us at Central Station. I was appalled. Signs of his sartorial degeneration had been apparent in Brisbane; but they had now become so evident that he looked more like a tramp than the neat undergraduate of Aunt Mary's garden-parties. I was almost ashamed to climb into the single-decker bus beside him; but my worship was keen again immediately he began to talk, and then I criticized no further.

Up the curl of Oxford Street near where later I was to work, to the Darlinghurst jail, went the bus. From here it swung left into Darlinghurst Road, along which we sped until evacuated at Kings Cross, that hub which I was to learn so thoroughly in all its dirtiest windings. Down Victoria Street, past the cinema show that straddled into Darlinghurst Road, arching the corner behind the dago fruit-shop, we walked to our boarding-house. And there Jack left us, after making certain that everything was prepared and our mother at peace at last with the knowledge that her firstborn had not been murdered. I have no idea where Jack lived, or rather lurked, in the months that followed, existing in some miserable fashion on freelance journalism.

I tried to arrange for Phil to continue his schooling; but he was obdurate. Neither our mother's tears nor my furious arguments had the least effect. He merely repeated, 'I'm not going, I'll educate myself, school's waste of time.'

Not long afterwards a letter followed from Ray, announcing that he had lost his newspaper job in Brisbane, collected my books from Aunt Mary's house, and sold them for his train ticket to Sydney. Determined to be a painter, he was setting out with even less luggage than I had. About this time I met Pillig in the street. Neither of us made any reference to our bad-tempered parting; and when I told him of my mother's arrival he offered to take Phil on as a sort of apprentice. Phil, more set than ever against schools, had no objection to any employment connected with art, and he agreed to help Pillig in his casting and in the transport of his products.

Breathlessly Ray turned up, with brownpaper parcels, spilling paints and socks in all directions, shouting down the platform and waving his foul pipe. The time was mid-morning;

and with all the adventurous day before us we considered what to do. Ray remarks, 'We went to Pillig's studio in Pitt Street, where I left what scanty belongings I had, and where Phil was supposed to be working and helping Pillig. (All I remember of Phil's activities there were some small plaster statuettes he made of lugubrious reclining dogs à la Landseer, which cluttered up various flats we had for years afterwards.) You and I then went on to lunch at a small Hungarian café in Castlereagh Street, run by Julia Rasborsek, which was very popular with artists and journalists in those days. (Now an enormous David Jones department store stands there.) After lunch we walked through the Domain to the Art Gallery. A tremendous event for me was the impact of Ford Madox Brown's immense canvas of *Chaucer at the Court of King Edward III.* I was still enthralled by the Pre-Raphaelites and Rossetti had actually posed for the figure of Chaucer. (It is a painting that I still love and the only one in our wretched gallery, sad to relate, for which one can have any respect.) After that we went up to the boarding house at Victoria Street.' He took a room for a few days there.

Now that I had a fellow in hardship, everything seemed easy. I thanked Percy and returned to Sydney with a few pounds from Norman in my pocket. What we wanted was a very cheap room, preferably an attic, but the cheapness was the main thing. Moving towards Woolloomooloo, we read all the cards outside the stationers' and barbers' shops, and discussed the many useless but sometimes enticing objects offered for sale. Rooms within our means were not so evident. But at last in William Street the very thing came to light, an attic as derelict as an attic could be, at five shillings a week, some five storeys up. The owner was a deaf and irascible old man with poached eyes and a scaly bald head, who after several delays was produced from the interior of the ground-floor shop, with a wuffing voice. He dealt in scrap iron and I had the impression that he was tearing down most of the basement and ground floor and selling it without much concern whether the upper storeys fell down. Through crashes of stone and old bedsteads, I made myself understood and was taken up through landings full of buckets, mops, scrap iron and kerosene stoves. The top floor consisted of two rooms. The back one was heavily padlocked, the front one looked as if a small tornado had recently blown in through the shattered shutters. The owner, after considering all the litter, began to wonder if the room wasn't worth more than 5s. weekly, so I closed with him.

The room was thick with dust and strewn with oddments of furniture, several score green blind-slats, the table of a sewing-machine, sections of a cast-iron bedstead, assorted bits of chairs and about half a chest-of-drawers. No glass in the gable window, not even cardboard. The wuffer clattered the bits of bed together with a pretence that if one was ingenious enough one could make a sleeping-place out of them, and surprised himself by pulling a drawer out of the chest. 'You see it doesn't stick.' I paid him five shillings gratefully and asked for the front-door key. He told us that we could borrow any of the backyard scrap-iron that would be handy in furnishing the room; for washing there was a tap at the turn of the stairs.

He went off. I had a feeling that he wasn't the owner at all; he was a thief carrying off the scrap-iron, who hadn't disdained a small cheating act. But after about ten minutes he came panting back with the key. We set to work tidying the room and scraping the worst of the dust and soot on to the landing. We propped and tied slats against the empty window-frames; they could be nailed as soon as we bought nails. Then we tried to put the bed together and found it consisted of the parts of three different beds that didn't fit. After some crashing failures we gave it up; anyone who had tried to sleep in the precarious structure would have been liable to death or maiming. But we stuck the wide-meshed mattress on to two broken chairs and an old box, and though it rocked it wasn't lethal. We had no bedclothes, but found several pieces of linoleum and dirty carpet that we put on the wires. I decided to use the mattress while Ray composed a sleeping-place on the floor out of bits of carpet and curtain. The drawer that didn't stick was used for our few shirts and socks; the second drawer had no bottom; the third wasn't there.

In the backroom lived a clock mender with a huge number of clocks that rang at random moments, a small shuffling man who never spoke and who lived among whirring springs behind a bolted and padlocked door – there was a hole in the door through which he could unlock the padlock from inside. When met on the stairs, he stood flattened against the wall, slipping his spectacles to the end of his nose and suspiciously staring. Below, a family lived, the tired woman cooking by a battered lead sink, in smells of rancid bacon fat relieved only by cabbage pongs.

High in the sky, we had peace, together with the small sum left from the sale of my books. Lacking anything better than a broom stump I never succeeded in properly cleaning up our room, but I felt something of pride in it. I put some boards and thick cardboard and slats on the sewing-machine table, to cover the hole in the middle. The thing was difficult to sit at, but after a while I found one angle at which I was least uncomfortable. Getting into bed and out of it was always a touchy business; and as the carpets settled down, I woke each morning with the lozenge imprints of the wire on my body.

As the clockman's clocks rang at all times of the day and night, we couldn't rely on them to tell us the hour. And we had no clock or watch of our own. Ray records, 'As soon as we awoke in the morning we used to rush to the window to see if the hash house of a restaurant, which was almost opposite, was still open, and this would give us some indication of how early or late in the morning it was. Its name was the Cambridge Café and it was in a dilapidated building which had not yet been demolished; if it was still open, we would go there for breakfast.' He might have added, 'if we had the money'. 'We used to have our regular evening meals at a pleasant little café in Park Street, the Moana.' He goes on (1959):

The building with the attic is still standing, and on my way by tram down William Street I often cast a sentimental look at the old attic window which peers out from behind a splendid new facade covering the activities of Electrical Engineering Merchants. William Street is now a very busy thoroughfare (it was in process of being widened at the time we were in the attic, the opposite side of the street being then half demolished) and is the centre of the retail motor-trade, being flanked by resplendent window displays of all the newest, most luxurious, chromium-plated motor monstrosities.

In Mockbells I sat over my eked-out coffee and dozed amid the pseudo-moorish decorations almost obliterated by smoke, age, damp and their own insignificance. I blinked up to see, not Phyllis, but her husband Jacques, who gloated over me with his intelligent sheepface, then withdrew into his own thoughts, drumming on the table. He addressed the waitress distraitly – I always held against him his careless capacity for charming waitresses – drawing himself up with his hands on his knees and arching his bushy brows over his soft brown eyes. But he thawed with the coffee and leaned forwards to tell me of the mnemonics system he had concocted by the simple device of getting a friend to enter two different correspondence courses on the subject. 'I scrambled the pair of them and added a few condiments of my own fancy. The result: the Goldston School of Memory Building and Character Consolidation. All I need is the money for advertising. As a friend, I won't ask you to invest your own money, but maybe you know someone fool enough. Actually, the service is the best on the market.' He regarded me with mingled pity and scorn. 'Come on, thumb through the tattered Who's Who of your memory. No money refused, however tainted. Think of the chance for your million-aire friends to lose their money. And profits, however small, will indubitably find their way to my pocket.' He laughed, a small baaing laugh. But it was all a pose. He knew I had no friends with money; he knew I knew he knew he was no businessman. And yet he was genuinely convinced his system was better than the others. What really interested him was sainthood; while living self-indulgently, he desired asceticism; and while a sceptic, he read James's *Varieties of Religious Experience*, as hypochrondriacs read medical textbooks, hoping to find some symptoms of faith in himself.

I asked him about Phyllis and his eyes filmed over. 'Oh, she's somewhere about, she looks after herself remarkably well.' He began talking of the Unaniste poets and their effort to express oneness with the industrial masses, smoking all the while and turning up his eyes to watch the smoke rise to the fretted ceiling. 'You should try to grow up,' he said, 'it's quite an interesting experience, you'd find.' He mused. 'One day, after all, we shall have to be mankind.' Knowing that he despised my verse,

I did not take kindly to his advice. In the end he offered me some copying work and pressed ten shillings on me as an advance.

Half past six when I climbed back into the street: the bottle rush was over, though a couple of broken beer bottles in the gutter remained as its memorials. I walked down Castlereagh Street to the Hungarian restaurant, ordered goulash, and half hoped that Pillig would come in. The girl at the desk was a softly bulging Saxony blonde with misty blue eyes, the sort that melts creampuffily on the palate, at least when watched at about ten feet distance. When I went out upbuoyed by the soft memory of that milky hand lifted to transfix my bill on a spike, darkness was spread over Sydney with a wide glitter of crusted stars and trams leaping in the denuded streets. I stood a moment outside the *Sun* offices, then went round the block to see if anyone I knew was going into the Press Club.

No matter how dull it was, I had a consuming sense of purpose. I made notes for a ferocious essay on Baudelaire under a lamp-post. Gone was any gratitude for the angry sense of loss I had once extracted from his poems, his imagery of the city-desert and the damned cityfolk under the pleasure lash. Corrected by *Creative Effort*, I saw him as the type of all who built up an idealist abstraction out of the mud of disgust; it seemed dreadfully important I should expose him as the renegade of beauty. Unless he was demolished, and by me, in an elaborate subtlety of dissection, in a vehement contempt of paradoxical insights, the rebellious joys of earth would be swallowed up in the night of horror. *Je me tournai vers elle/ Pour lui rendre un baiser d'amour, je ne vis plus/ Qu'une outre aux flancs gluants, toute pleine de pus.* This denial of life, I scribbled, by the angel of renunciation whose wings are a brothel-screen; this obscenity of the concept that there is only a choice between soulfulness and necrophilia. I saw a policeman coming, pocketed my notebook and walked on; he'd probably think me a bookie's runner. A few doors past the hotel, a café was open and I went in. To my surprise, Phyllis was there with a girl I didn't know; they were talking intimately, heads close, smoking. Phyllis had light golden hair, a whitish daintily moulded face, a slight but firm chin and china blue eyes. For all her effect of graceful fragility, she was compact in build, with a nervous laugh, a fluttering bird manner; she liked a cigarette in her fingers, for gesturing and playing about with; she got rid of the ash by holding the cigarette high and tapping with her forefinger. The other girl had a small glistening face, ugly in a pleasant sort of way, with a large mop of small curls. She, I noted, liked to push about with her cigarette in the ashtray; she took little puffs with half-closed eyes.

Phyllis looked across and saw me studying her, looked across a rippling of slender white hands, a tremolo of long soft eyelashes, faintly reflected in the glass of the table-top. 'Fancy meeting you,' she said with a light laugh that sounded false, as if we'd arranged the meeting. She introduced me to Yvonne, who had large clumsy hands. (Later I found she was having an affair with Jacques, and Phyllis hated her.) 'Have you seen Jacques?' I said I'd seen him in Mockbells as sublimely stoical as ever. 'Tell me after,' she said, and returned to her low-voiced conversation with Yvonne, whom she hoped to draw into giving herself away.

I lit a cigarette and got some smoke down the wrong way, choked and spluttered, to my annoyance. So I found another used envelope in my pockets and began jotting down notes on the failure of poetic drama in the nineteenth century.

General readiness still to stage verse plays. Read Macready's memoirs again. Also study Byron's relations with Covent Garden. Byron and Shelley, the failure to find the necessary diction (i.e. relation to life). Byron the clue. His weakness in drama impedes the young Browning from picking up the trail at the right point. Where does Beddoes come in? Close relation to Byron as well as to Jacobean drama. The abstract element in Byron and Shelley, different in form and effects, has a common element. (Look at Goethe.) Any connexion with the incest complex in both men? (Too inturned, off balance, to find point of self-revelation in drama?) Also the huge abstraction of 18 C. poetry, still crushing. Link with Milton, Puritanism and money power.

In all my theses I took for granted a pre-established system, a given structure of potentiality, which the poets and artists lived up to or failed. I felt it my job to track out the reasons for inadequacy in any of the fated creators and to take on myself the task of providing the lost elements in the vast creative synthesis I was to build in my own verse. Now I grew so interested in Beddoes that I forgot I was posing for the benefit of flutter-lashed Phyllis and her ugly-charming Yvonne. Looking up, I found Yvonne going and Phyllis beckoning.

'Is the magazine coming along?' she asked as I sat down.

'It needs a lot of preparation,' I said, sorry I'd ever talked about a magazine to impress her and give some appearance of purpose to my indefinite activities. 'You see, I suppose I'll have to write it all myself, under different names.'

She gave her tinkling laugh, which stirred her small firm breasts, and went on turning over the sugar lumps in the bowl with a teaspoon. I knew she didn't believe in my magazine but all the same wanted to make sure of getting an article on her dancing in, if anything ever did eventuate. I felt that my sole hold on her.

She smiled without looking at me, and I felt in her smile the disdains of the Irishman Barry, who had migrated to help a chest weakness, who lived by teaching English at a language school, who was very friendly with Phyllis and knew much more about music than I did. She made a few more covert attempts to find out if I really did know where Jacques had gone, then she stood up with a miniature yawn and said she must be going. We walked down to the Quay. She talked lightly most of the way. On the downward slopes I had the feeling she'd lose her mincing balance on her high-heeled shoes and held myself ready to catch her. Then, as we stood in front of the wharf, she kept swinging round on her left heel, still prat-tling, with her bag behind her back. I tried to think out some way of being wounding about Chopin, whom she adored. Of course, you know, his *legato* is emotional onanism. But I feared she wouldn't know what the word meant; and I knew that if she forced a cruder synonym, I'd spit the word out with an embarrassing overstress. Theoretically I believed in entire frankness in discourse; in practice I was lamentably chaste. I never had managed to tell, or even remember, a single smutty story.

'There's my boat.' She ran through the clicking turnstiles,

throwing her pennies down, and flitted along the wharf through the rush of disembarking passengers. I turned from the chocolate slot machines: was the electric-shock machine we had bravely tried as children still in operation? or had people got beyond that stage of shock? I confronted the Quay's confused amphitheatre, the scurry of lights rocketing on the edges, the maze of arriving and departing trams. On the left I glimpsed the name of an important firm of wool dealers set above their warehouses. About the age of eight or nine I had known the grandson of one of the founders, who lived near us in North Sydney. His mother, a beautiful woman, drank gin. What I remember is the marvellous silkiness; the gin drinking I knew of from the gossip of our cook Harriet with my mother. One day the son Colin and I found some jewellery in the street and hid it under loose stones in a wall. The things must have been valuable, for prolonged inquiries were made. Colin, an insolent cocky lad three years my senior, insisted that we should say nothing. So I said nothing, dominated by his lord-of-the-earth assurance. Then I forgot. But now, catching the family name lofty over the warehouses, I felt sure that Colin remembered and that he was doubtless already an honoured pillar of society, making his battering-ram way in the world. I dodged a car and heard the brakes scream.

We were atticked on the edge of Woolloomooloo. Squalid terraced streets falling to the docks of work, ragged with children whooping, slitted with the famished eyes of scandal, stocked with old-clothes shops, and echoing in the night hours with policemen pacing two-by-two. One evening as I listened to a street organ I felt that my aesthetic had betrayed me and that the words at my disposal were less even than the wheezing tunes that raped the desolate soul with the incomparable banality of their love gags. A strangled and halting voice taking in the street noises as necessary counterpoint while it spouted out everything most weak, shameful and self-pitiful in one's gutter-heart. In retort I tried to compose a lyric that would mingle the hurdy-gurdy babble with the notes blown from the flute made out of Sheba's thigh bone, the tinsel stars of Sydney's slum night with the sweat glittering on the bones of the

driven dead in hell. Someone crying out on the other side of
the bobbined curtain and the aspidistras; a girl with a head
of rat-tails listening with wide-open mouth, fingering a medal
of the Virgin Mary; an old woman sitting on a doorstep and
feeling her toothless gums. I saw the image as clear as a deer
of the moon leaping with updrawn hooves over the crystal
foam-ferns of a valley stream; but it flashed past and left only
the thick soggy tune beating and bleeding out of the red hole
in the world's flank. My verse, I realized with dismay, had
heavily deteriorated since I became a full-time poet.

Another night, when I'd been out with Panzer and someone
else, I came back late after Ray had gone to bed. He had had
the key. But beer had sunk him deep, far beyond any noise I
could make by banging on the door or throwing stones up at
the gable window. By this time I was feeling tired and drowsy
myself, so I went into the ruins of the house being pulled down
opposite, and found a fairly pleasant nook of dust and plaster,
where I slept. In the early dawn I was rudely poked out and
found myself blinking frowsily at two policemen. Luckily, I
had the envelope of a letter that Norman had written to me
in the attic (I always kept envelopes for making notes on) and
I was able to convince the policemen that however dusty, beery
and frayed, I was no homeless vagabond. They told me to go
easy on the beer and moved on. After yawning through a few
more hours on the wreck of a wall, I managed to rouse Ray
and stretched out on my lozenge-patterning bed.

The woman on the floor below was cooking bacon as I passed,
dressed in uncertainly bunching petticoat and blouse. Overcome by an outburst of modesty, she slammed the frying-pan
down, spilt fat over the matchbox, kicked out sideways at little
Nell, tossed her untidy hair back out of her eyes, and pushed
some more blouse through the string round her waist, disordering her petticoat. Her nuggety husband with a perpetual
frown, wearing socks, trousers, and braces over a collarless
shirt, appeared in doorway with a newspaper. 'For Cri sake,
where's that bacon?' He nodded malevolently and I paused.
For the tenth time he asked me what rent we paid. 'Don't let
him do you down,' he vociferated. 'Tell him to go and stuff

himself. A man's got to take a stand,' I knew he wanted to push me into doing what he hadn't himself done. 'The place has been condemned, we oughtn't pay a penny, we could sue him, we could put the old bastard in jail, he ought to pay us for staying her and scaring the rats off, otherwise the whole bloody caboose'd fall down.' A small girl with prettily insolent face thrust her head under his arm and he played with her tousled hair.

'Good idea,' I said and went on down. Almost opposite was the cheap eating-house. I stared at the curled-up sandwich and the spotted bun in the window, and entered. At the desk was a swarthy girl with a sore on her lip, which she kept licking. Only a cup of tea. All right, she said, the rush was over. I sat at a table smeared with the egg, tea and bacon of many breakfasts. About half a dozen wharfies were still eating in dogged silence. A foxy-faced fellow brought me some dark tea in a heavy chipped cup and I drank it slowly. I felt at home. It wasn't that I had a taste for dirt and stale air; I had a distaste for the sort of people that went with cleanlier surroundings. I had nothing to say to the wharfies, but on the whole I preferred their chewing noises to polite conversation. I relaxed. As I went out, the desk girl said I could get 21s. breakfast tickets for 18s. 'I might come into a fortune some day,' I said, and she wasn't sure if I meant it. 'Kidstakes?'

A couple of nights later Ray and I went into the fried-fish shop a bit farther up the road. We were wearing our black crêpe-de-chine ties, as we did now and then as point of honour, though we knew how dangerous it was. Seven or eight local lads were chewing the lumps of white fish and the chips, and they made rude remarks at our appearance. We went on talking about Rubens and took no notice. Then as we rose to go out, some of the lads went up to the counter for more chips; we had to pass them in the narrow exit. They resumed their taunts, sure that only queens could wear such unorthodox ties. I reached out and punched one of them on the jaw. As I moved on quickly, I was out of the shop before he realized what had happened. Swinging round, he struck at unprepared Ray. The next moment the whole band of them had poured out into the road after us. I had a brief glimpse of the proprietor jumping over the counter, shoving out the last of the toughs, and locking up the shop. We went on slamming away at one another. I found that I couldn't put my full weight into my blows, I somehow didn't believe the whole thing. A larrikin came up out of the shadows, with cap pulled low over his eyes, slipped behind me, and gave me an uppercut under my arm, which almost stunned me. We retreated across the road, but the others didn't follow us. A whistle blew somewhere and we managed to get on the other side of our door. Ray was infuriated and told me what a bloody fool I was; now we'd have all the Woolloomooloo pushes looking out for us.

It might have worked out that way, but it didn't. A few days afterwards I was coming down from Kings Cross and met four of the lads lounging round a lamp-post. One of them said something. I stopped and stood looking at them, clenching my fists. They said nothing more. After a while I walked on and they didn't call out.

These were the only episodes in my life in which I have acted with physical aggressiveness. Perhaps I objected to the particular insult at the moment when I was trying to stand on my own feet; perhaps I was suffering from the general desperation of our position and my dried-up poetic vein; perhaps I felt that I had to assert the honour of poets and extort at least tolerance from the tough lads. Anyway, we won. I had lost a tooth in the brawl.

Ray was now going to the Sydney Art School, under Julian Ashton. 'It was situated in the Queen Victoria Markets building in George Street, near the Town Hall,' he says. A hideous pseudo-Gothic building with myriads of rooms and passages, echoing hollowly under its huge dome. 'It still stands, but there is frequent talk of tearing it down. Old Julian was a damned good teacher with a splendid personality. George Lambert, J. J. Hilder and Gruner were his star ex-pupils. He had always been enormously generous to Norman in his early days, and, being a man of great courage and integrity, had led many of the onslaughts on the wowser attacks on Norman's work. However, I used to quarrel a lot with him in the school. I was a terribly bumptious young bastard in those days and used to try and get the other students to paint with glazes, etc. (methods of the Old Masters) that Norman had instilled into me, instead of using what was then the approved manner, à la George Lambert and Orpen: the direct approach with the brush. Finally I walked out of the school and took a studio with Fred Finley over an old junk store in George Street North, near the Quay.' He had also quarrelled with Julian for not being let paint at once from the model. Julian had taken him in gratis.

His main friend among the students was a large fellow with a lazy sense of humour, Hubble, who had a trick of making tiny satirical drawings full of swarming devils. Hubble felt his likeness to Michelangelo's David and 'gazed at the world,' says Phil, 'through a deliberately supercilious mask, smiling ever sideways, and would sicken me by going outrageously cross-eyed, suddenly.' A devotee of Velazquez, he languorously bickered with Ray, the swashbuckler of Rubens.

Pelligrini's wine-bar and Mockbells. In the latter I resisted the offers of cross-eyed J.W. to go into business with him. I'd met him first at Pillig's where he was trying to sell a pile of battered frames and a pianola attachment. He was all too well aware that his script was illegible; and his old clothes and general rubbish business needed the writing-out of a large number of descriptive cards. I wrote some cards on the spot and did my best to damp his admiration by demanding a small fee for every ten done; but that merely led to the offer of a regular job. He attempted to glamorize the old-clothes business by telling me tales of the fabulous quantity of bored wives who were seducible over cups of tea; then to sell me an imitation diamond ring wrapt in several layers of tissue-paper and kept in a small cardboard box in one of his capacious waistcoat pockets. 'For a nice girl,' he said with a lascivious glint of his wall-eye.

That evening I met Anna Brennan, who, despite her careless amiability, oppressed me as too luxuriously blonde and strong minded, despite her angelic smile. Perhaps I was also overawed by her being the daughter of Christopher, poet and scholar; and the fact that she was buyable hedged her round, as far as

I was concerned, with an inviolability. Not that I ever tried to find out the exact line between her caprices and her finances. Now she was celebrating the removal of her fallopian tubes.

Besides, there was a party at someone's rooms in Elizabeth Street; I think Panzer asked me. It was there I met Janet. The party was rather an awkward one where few of the guests knew one another, and Janet asked to be taken round and introduced. (She told me later that she did it to make sure of meeting me.) That was how we shook hands. She was a tall Scottishly handsome girl, generous in all things, in build, character and purse, with her light brown hair parted in the middle and a pleasant voice, clear and warmly modulated. I liked her at once and didn't know what to say. She passed on. I talked instead to Dora because Dora talked to me, a gentle lisping girl whose dress was always coming undone at the back and who thought everything was lovely and funny, even Dvorak's *Humoresque* played on a violin with steel strings. It's wonderful to be alive, she informed me. I said, Yes, but are we alive? She laughed and clapped hands, spilt some wine on her left breast and said I was ever so funny. Her bosom was so creamily soft that I spilt some of my own wine on it. Don't, she said, it's a waste and it tickles. She was Clancy's girl. Clancy was a fierce Irish lad with cropped hair and corrugated brow. I didn't notice that he was at the party till I took Dora out on to the narrow cast-iron balcony over the street. He at once joined us, producing a revolver. 'Look at all those blasted fools,' he said, pointing the revolver, not at me, but at the trams. 'Thinking of races and beer and pictures, not how they're duped and bloodsucked. You're a poet, aren't you?' He lurched against me with claret breath and stubbled chin. 'I'll give you a phrase, something real this time. A broom of bayonets. We'll come sweeping the streets up yet, we'll swab 'em out. Only one way to clean 'em. A broom of bayonets. Put that in a poem, will you?' He was squinting with anger and drink.

'Isn't he funny?' cried Dora. 'Fancy trying to sweep up with bayonets. They'd catch in the floor. Such ideas.' She hugged him. Grasping the rail, I looked down on the bobbing hats and caps below, and was pleased that someone else felt the world had gone wrong. But, purely in terms of poetic imagery, I didn't think much more of bayonet brooms than Dora thought of them in terms of kitchen competence.*

I walked home with Janet. As we strolled through the park towards her flat, passing the statue of her grandfather (Australia's first Privy Councillor), I discoursed on moonlight. Moonlight making shapes loom in strange solidity, yet sucking all weight from them. Splashing the world with leprous white and softening the drifted glooms. At full, casting such clear shadows the earth has the starkness of a dream, with buildings cut like stage flats: the world a stage scene, therefore the right place for lovers. Corot, I said, painted a moon effect in daytime, a liquid simplification of tree-mass plus a subtle tone gradation, a feathery implication of light rather than a reflection and refraction of light by hard surfaces. I was so carried away by the idea that I ended by describing a painter of moon trees with little relation to Corot, but who'd have been an admirable painter if he existed. Besides, surely it was obvious I was talking about my own poetry, or one slight aspect of it. Janet said little and my claret inspiration weakened. But she thanked me at the door of her small flat and suggested I should call on her some time.

*As I was correcting the proofs of the hardbook edition of this book, I chanced on the Russian of a poem by Khlebnikov written about the time of Clancy's remarks: "The broom of guns hot with money's graveyards sweeps the streets . . ." So Clancy had more poetic rightness than I admitted.

3 · ON THE MOVE

WITH A WRENCH I got through the window. My cracked shoes slid over the grey-blue dust with its fragments of crockery, glass, burst cigarette butts, paper. I felt giddy but the rail of scabby yellowish stone secured me from falling. The narrow gutter was an awkward place to walk on, sunk between steep roof and balustrade. My shoe-welt kept catching against the edge of crumpled lead, my knees knocked together, and I fell sideways on to the roof. But in my daze I felt I had fallen the other way, into the growling canyon of William Street where the trams were leaping through the hoops of early morning quiet. I lay a moment and watched the faint dazzling blue of the skies, which my eyelashes almost touched. Then, twisting round, I thrust my head as far as it would go through one of the balustrade intervals, and watched a tram curvetting down the street. The trams always descended from Darlinghurst with a dash, a charge, a gaily rocking sweep, the overhead cable waving and smacking back into connection, the driver stamping on his dingdonging bell.

Yes, the world was there. I extracted my head and lay back. Useless to go on looking for the meal tickets on the roof; and yet before I climbed out, I had a precise picture of them lying by the cover of the discarded notebook I'd thrown out. Three meals lost because a scrap of paper was lost: soup (gravy), sausages and mash, jam tart triangle with thin yellow custard, and tea, a big cup of strong tea. I groaned. Then with smarting eyes I stared into the lucid sky and forgot my hunger. A great solid silver-lilac cloud floated almost above me, a magnificent architectural cream puff, an Australian cloud. I had seen no other sort (save in paintings or on the cinema screen) but I was highly patriotic about our clouds. Ray too. He had recently declared that he'd be happy painting nothing but clouds for the rest of his life. Probably, somewhere in the country with Hubble, he was painting them at that moment, unless, as was more likely, he was pledging them in beer.

I closed my eyes and pondered afresh various moments: when Delacroix tried to link the Constable shower of light, broken-up colour, with the heroic Rubensesque scene. When Turner let light sweep full blast on to the earth becoming industrialized. (Why oh why did the heroic have to fade then? the delicate serenity of infinitely involved perspective, as in *Crossing the Brook*, have to fold up?) When Cézanne brought space structure back as volume in definite recessions. (Why did this hardening of planes have to end in Cubism with sharp edges mangling the curves and tensions of organic form?) I felt the world around me as an arrested kaleidoscope of the life-denying intellect. Look instead at a Rembrandt canvas, at the slow permeation of light, the sense of skin after skin of space removed as you stare, the forms stirring from within with an endlessly slow breath of gold, warming, expanding, the revolving energies of space becoming in turn the very pulse of time and the passage of time like a tenderly brushing bird wing, a penumbra of pathos, an embrace of proudly bosoming light. In the gentlest canvas of Rembrandt was a passion and glory of movement and form that all the geometries of abstract art could not come within measurable distance of rivalling. I wanted to give my life in his defence, nothing mattered but his vindication, and it was an urgent matter, needing to be done here and now, here and now.

My mind turned over like a turning page and I couldn't find the place again, probably there wasn't one. I leaned with hurt elbow on the hot metal, smiled and twitched. Hunger makes you jumpy, memories grow peculiar irrelevant too-relevant, you smile on the edge (of all things, of nothing). Not because of courage, but because you've found them all out, found what they had up their sleeve all the time. I was born, fed, caressed, washed behind the ears and sent to school, etcetera, for this. You can't fool me now.

I shuddered, then felt in my pocket for something that wasn't there. The world swung slowly round in my head like the tune of a scratched gramophone record, then grated to a standstill. The lost meal tickets. Life had stopped and would go on stopping till they were found. My only entry ticket to the cinema, repeat performance, of life; my only password through the enemy lines. I opened eyes again on the majestic clouds of silver and lilac, hewn in clear air, unmoving. Can a starving man appreciate beauty? Slowly I recalled the debate, out at Clayfield, Brisbane. Is sex or food the deepest instinct? An adenoidal clerk quoted Napoleon on motherlove or was it the stars? God among the stars, fouling his own nest; no, motherlove among the tigers. Someone, speaking from the window-seat, with the pawpaw tree like a Gauguin sketch in the red light. How good life is, how abysmally sweet, pawpaw slices with lemon juice squeezed over them, very thin slices. The chap by the window saying: Would a starving man prefer to copulate (pronounced with earnest emancipation) with the most beautiful woman in the world or to slake (yes, slake) his hunger with a loaf of common bread? Debating point, duly knocked home with fist on palm. Well, now I know, or do I? Hermes, bring me the Most Beautiful or a Common Loaf, here I am all stretched out, on Mount Ida, William Street.

In the gabled attic on the right lived a barber who held spiritualist seances, attended by Woolloomooloo workers whose wailing hymns, getting the right atmosphere for immortal spirits, could be heard on Sunday evenings. Suddenly the burning isolated height on which I lay was a place of temptation, murmurous with a myriad devils. Jump over and end it all, take your revenge on the world, shame the world. Against my closed eyelids I saw the balustrade with its row of short fat pillars quivering like the calves of a line of dumpy show girls. It was easy to feel myself crawling towards the edge, heaving slowly up and over, dropping into the first crumpling release and then going down as fraily as a petal of smoke that shreds itself out into the lap of opening air.

I pushed myself up onto the window-sill, got one leg through and stuck in endless dismay, with pain knocking behind the eyes. Then I was all through, tearing my trousers under the crutch, swaying in the hot room, filmed with dust. Wearing a shroud of debility, with weighted eyelids and silly hand, a seething edge of heat on the raw outskirts of my uncertain identity. Unable to distinguish myself any longer from the room so hot, so dusty, so foul that I had a conviction of having invented it all myself.

But after I had sat awhile in the park, I came across a kindly Austrian, Flozellas, generally called Flo – a particular friend of Percy – whom I'd met at the Press Club. He bought me a meal and took me back to his room to show me his inventions. 'I only need capital and my fortune is made,' he explained. His room was strewn with the gadgets he'd devised, labour-saving oddities and abstruse children's games. His latest contrivance was an unspillable ink bottle and a parlour game half way between chess and snakes-and-ladders. 'You're run down,' he kept saying in a puzzled way, standing back to clasp his hands and consider me. Then he had an idea, nodded reassuringly, and rushed out, leaving me alone with his life's work. I tried to wind up a toy train. Something whirred inside but the train refused to move. So I put it away on the highest shelf. Then I spilt some ink from the unspillable bottle. That distressed me most of all; for clearly Flo now reposed all his hopes in the bottle, which he had declared foolproof. Lacking a handkerchief, I took off my tie to mop the ink up, and meddled with no more devices.

After a while he sprinted up the stairs and came in breathless, brandishing a huge bottle, which, when stripped of its wrap, I found to be labelled Malt Extract. 'That'll set you up,' he cried with a hey-presto gesture of confidence. 'Nothing like it.' He recounted some of his cheerful bad-luck stories, then took me out for a drink. He had an unshakeable belief that it was correct in English law to urinate over the wheel of any vehicle, even in the most public places; and now, after showing his faith in the law, he saw me all the way home, frightened that I'd drop my malt extract. 'That'll set you up,' he said and squeezed my hand.

It kept me alive for a while, a tedious but a setting-up food. To defeat my anxiety I composed an essay, on my sewing-machine table, to prove that (a) fear of women or (b) inability to develop his sensuous imagery in true dramatic form or (c) mixture of (a) and (b), which coming first I wasn't sure, had killed Keats off, thereby tying the poetic consciousness into knots at a crucial moment (all moments being crucial, especially the present one) and bringing about the calamitous shame, greed and distortion of the Victorian era, the death of the Poetic Body. 'If Life is Form, and if Poetry is the highest consciousness of dynamic Form, then Poetry creates Human Life (as distinct from the repetitive round of mere Existence) and is the Directive Force.' (*If* in my writings at this time meant *Since obviously and irrefutably.*) On rereading, I cut down the capitalizations, but felt the argument conclusive, and turning to Blake, I added the quotation, 'By Laws of Chastity & Abhorrence I am wither'd up, Striving to Create a Heaven in which all shall be pure and holy In their Own Selfhood.' Then Ray came back and something or other turned up.

Jacques had taken offices down near the Quay and floated his mnemonics system on some shadowy capital. Phyllis had rooms in the same building for her dancing and piano classes. I met Jacques carrying a load of circulars to the G.P.O. and he asked me to call and do some small jobs. I found him in a corridor-like room trying to detect where the main draughts came from, and reading *The Liberator*. 'All I need is cash for advertising,' he said wistfully, 'and the money would come rolling in.' He showed me adverts he had drawn up. 'Is Your Memory Failing?' followed by suggestions that you were bound for the loonybin if you didn't at once take the Goldston Course. Or else: 'You can make your Memory a Magnificent Instrument' and within a few weeks double your salary and advance to managing positions. By playing on fear and greed, he insisted, you ran through the whole gamut of human weakness and only one person in ten thousand could resist you. Then he took up *The Liberator*, read me some Negro poems and reports from the Soviet Union, adding that like Michelangelo he did not believe anyone had the right to personal happiness in a suffering world, a world of power-madness and exploitation.

However, he had circulars to send round. So I addressed envelopes while he went on reading from *The Liberator*, adding his own caustic comments on a society of fear and greed. Then Phyllis came in, swinging her bag, in a flowered cotton dress.

Her face, it struck me, could seem either dollishly round and pretty or delicately charming in its clear bone-structure, according to the way the light fell and the way one was thinking about her. But what I felt most at the moment was the cold doubt in her eyes, the gleam of calculation. The high heels of her shoes, the strong brand of her scent, her slightly affected voice, all cheapened her. Even the curly glow of her wheat-gold hair couldn't rouse me. 'When you've finished that nonsense,' she said, swinging her bag, 'come in and have a word with me.'

'Leave the poor fellow alone, you Messalina,' said Jacques. She gave her tinkling laugh and moved off. 'Fancy you,' she said to him, but stopped herself and went out. Tartish in an anaemic sort of way, I thought, with her small nose sniffing hypocritically at her advertised breasts.

'When she's going to have her concert?'

'When some moonstruck fool puts the money up.'

She was playing some Schumann; I could just catch the notes. That seemed a friendly gesture, as in our last conversation I had belittled Chopin's concerto. The warm harmonies she was now playing implied a more sympathetic attitude to me; and so, conjuring her into thought, I found nothing vulgar in her finely agile leg, the lovely pivoting of her hips (spacious as an earth turning on its heavenly axis), her small unharvested breasts, her white face with its embellishing eyes, her turned-up nose smelling at the posy of an eternal spring. Jacques wanted to talk about a man he'd met, who'd known Flecker and told odd tales of the poet, consumptively doomed, in Paris. But as soon as he paused, I stood up. 'Well, if you must be polite,' he said. He always kept up an assumption that no one could possibly find anything in Phyllis worth bothering about.

She was as delightful as I'd imagined; more radiant still, warm with the beams of song and on her head the tousled fleeces of the sun. I kissed her half-open mouth. She stood up and shivered, with eyes wild and wide. Even her cheap scent was now of forest violets, her powder an orris of the moon. But she remarked in her precise agitated tones, 'There's a letter I really must post, at once'. She looked in her bag. 'Let's have coffee.' I followed her distrustfully out.

Near the G.P.O. we met Beutler, who shook our hands heartily. 'I've been wanting to meet you.' He took out the MS of a song. 'Can you come along?'

I looked at Phyllis. 'Shall we have coffee first?' Then I saw that Beutler was hurt. 'What about your hearing the song too?' I asked Phyllis. She bridled a little, but acquiesced. I asked Beutler how Pillig was doing, but he was taken up with belated compliments.

'And how are you?' he asked Phyllis. 'I can see you're as charming as ever. What a nice new frock. Like the world reborn. You are the eternal female.'

'I'd rather be myself,' she replied with the childish intonation which expressed extreme annoyance.

But he thought he was doing well. 'Is she not charming?' He dug me in the ribs. 'What was there wrong in my words? Am I not judicious? Then accept my profound apologies.' He beamed.

As she made no reply, I remarked that he was in high spirits.

'Yes, I had just sold a Bechstein Grand to a woman with a voice like a parakeet I knew in Western Australia. You have very talented birds in your country,' he cried enthusiastically. 'I've heard a bird of yours that sings a full scale.' He whistled.

'The bird's flat,' said Phyllis.

'I'll get it next time,' Beutler rounded his eyes, brushed his hair back and thrust out his jaw. Whistling, he made ecstatic clown faces. 'Just like that. A remarkable bird.'

'Indeed,' said Phyllis with demure chilly sweetness. Beutler, delighted, squeezed her arm.

'Come and hear the song. The words are Bierbaum's. A hammer song. Listen if I have not the anvil in it, and the beat of the heart. It is a song of pain, a very good poem for music. You will agree.'

In the show-room he sat at the Bechstein and played. Phyllis's distaste had made me grin mockingly at him as she shrank under his confident chatter; but I ceased to think him a comedian after the first chord, even though he fumbled the second bar and had to start again. I didn't think him funny even when he gave us the melody in a painfully cracked voice. The clang of the notes splintered in sparks of dew and the

strokes were on the anvil of my heart. The strained voice like
the crowing of a benighted rooster could not spoil the clean
fury, the acceptance of the ultimate challenge. He ended,
turned his broad face with its clamorous smile at us, and felt
in his waistcoat for a cigar.

'I'm rather tired of this cling-clang stuff,' said Phyllis,
'though you've done it neatly enough.' I hated her, though at
the G.P.O. I had cursed the clumsy Beutler and seen her as
a Mosman Dryad bowered in her own lilylight. She went on,
'X would sing it quite well. It's not in my line. If you like, I'll
show it to him.'

'He's too soft and dead. A hard strong voice is needed, hard
and clear, like yours but a man's.'

'I think he'd do it very well.'

He returned the MS to his coat, then made snorting and hinnying noises that startled us. 'I detest all snoring basses and
goatish tenors.' He grinned with pleasure at our discomfiture.
His aproned assistant produced tea and biscuits. Finishing,
Beutler patted his stomach. 'Now I'm a finished artist.' Again
he grinned round for applause. I smiled but Phyllis didn't.

Nothing original in his work, she said to me afterwards.
Diluted Schubert and weak Wolf. But I had decided otherwise.
After weeks of wavering I now made up my mind to write and
tell Norman. And thinking of the letter I was going to write,
I remembered her excuse for leaving the office. 'What about
your important and urgent letter?' I asked.

On leaving her, I hastened to Mockbells and wrote to Norman. As I posted the letter, I had a sense of being Apollo's
emissary in a Cimmerian world. One of the verifications of *Creative Effort* would be the gathering of a devoted company of
poets, artists and musicians in Sydney, all pledged in the face
of the stock exchange, the churches and the police force, to
bring about a fresh Graeco-Roman Renaissance.

Round the corner lived Margot, a remittance woman from
England. Australia had more than enough of remittance men,
mostly Harrovians, who, after disgracing the family, had been
sent out with a quarterly allowance on condition of no-return.
But Margot was the only exiled woman I ever met. She had

married into a very rich family, famous producers of horrible
Christmas cards and the like. Her husband, according to her
lurid and garrulous accounts, had been one of the neutrally
sexed, limp-handed, vaguely artistic members of the upper
middle class. He'd taken to her because he hoped, I felt, to gain
through her some of the contacts with life that he could never
achieve for himself. 'And I looked different then. He said he
married me because I had a face like a boy, a Florentine profile,
no bottom worth speaking of, and didn't like chocolates. I used
to have a page-boy haircut. I was a cute little thing. Not like
I am now.' She puffed out her chest, caught some of her
superfluous stomach flesh in her hands, and pulled her dress
over her knees. 'Hard to believe, isn't it. But it's gospel.' For
a while they'd been happy despite the family's sniffs and snubs.
'Afterwards I began to answer back. A wicked animal, she
defends herself.' I gathered that she took increasingly to the gin
bottle as she found the difficulty of infusing more than a tepid
glow into her husband's refined existence. And he began to be
overborne by her omnivorous vulgarity. She grew too broad in
the beam and he acquiesced in the family plot to banish her
to Australia where she'd seem just like everyone else. She too
felt it as good a way out as any other. One of her many tales
about the bricks she dropped on high-society toes concerned
the marriage of the Pitt-Rivers, who lived next door but whose
house was too small for the reception. They borrowed Margot's
place. Margot got drunk and forgot to hand the keys over. Pitt-
Rivers couldn't get in for his own reception, so he collected an
axe from somewhere and chopped his way in. The tale was
quite convincing when told by Margot with a toss of her ringlets and a ladylike belch.

She still had much charm. Ray remembers: 'She had very
dignified manners, was very beautiful, although then rather
faded, with a lovely oval face, heavy eyelids and aquiline nose
of a Sir Peter Lely portrait; she even wore artificial ringlets in
the Restoration manner. In reference to those ringlets, I recall
her telling a story, in her alcoholic way, which was typical of
her. One night she had been dining with a very amorous
gentleman who kept on referring to the beauty of her curls. She
stood it for a while; but, after more and more drinks, she grew

so tired of his repeated admiration of her curls that, with a hic-cough, she pulled them out, threw them at him and told him to take the bloody things if he liked them so much. She was a colossal dipsomaniac and lived in a sly-grog shop in Crown Street, one of those streets that cut William Street at right angles through Woolloomooloo. However, she was a wonderful cook and used to insist upon us visiting her every Sunday, when she would give us a first-rate midday meal.'

One weekday before Easter I met her in the street, and when she found I was hard-up she asked me home. The mistress of the house dabbled in painting; I recall some peculiar-looking flower pieces and the like. And at the moment there was also an ex-jockey and a stuttering blind man in the place. Margot was in fine fettle, having recently received her quarterly allow-ance. She had redeemed the more useful or ornamental of her pawned clothes and wanted to celebrate. The flower painter asked if I thought she was a true artist and her flowers were lifelike. 'I know I've never been really taught, but if you've got the feeling you've got it, and money can't buy it.' I nodded sev-eral times and she said in gratified tones that she had wanted to have my *real* opinion and was ever so pleased to have had it. The blind man preluded each remark with an ear-splitting stammer, a tormented cachination, a thunderous and pro-longed sneeze. Margot talked of long-past high-jinks and I studied her admirable Florentine profile, damaged but iden-tifiable. The ex-jockey malevolently produced bottles of beer from under the stairs, suspecting me of designs on the flower painter.

In the course of the evening, others drifted in and Margot remembered that she had suggested a party. Yvonne, who failed to recall meeting me with Phyllis, came in with her gamine face on its long body, and Anna Brennan. Yvonne con-fided to me that she was a sort of honorary member of a group of male homos. She liked them because they had refined man-ners, helped her in making and choosing her clothes, and were so much more understanding than proper men, who just wanted one thing out of a poor girl, then went off. Dressed as a boy, she attended their most intimate conclaves. (Later I found that she was that unfortunate thing, a nymphomaniac who was terrified of finding herself with child; she lived in deadly terror of the activities without which she couldn't sleep. Without which she felt herself going dotty.) Anna, who had already acquired a whisky breath, kept on announcing her deepest aspirations. 'A house on the edge of a cliff and holly-hocks and old-fashioned flowers all round, and good books, and God's own wind coming up over the sea. Nothing of all this sordidness. Hollyhocks and God's own wind blowing cleanly over the waves. Facing the sunrise. That's the only way I can be happy. Drink your own wine, you bitch.' (I omit the adjectives which underlined the dream-escape by counterpointing it with the present squalors.) Yvonne found that there was a peacock's feather decorating the wall and almost fainted with fear.

After this party in which beer had been copiously mixed with wine, I awoke late and found that someone was hammering on the door. Ray had gone off to spend the holidays with Hubble at Sans Souci, a pleasant seaside suburb, near the mouth of the George's River where it enters Botany Bay. With some other lads they were moving up the George to its tributary the Woronora, where they meant to camp. For a moment I thought the hammering must come from Ray, returned so drunk that he couldn't find the door-handle. Then two men entered and started sticking numbers on the odds and ends of lumber in the attic. I watched them idly through a hazy pane of half-sleep, then realized the outrage. 'Instructions,' said the small man and stuck a number on the frame of the etching by Norman I had selected for the week's meditation. I protested that the work was mine, and the man said I'd better get my things out if I didn't want them sold up. 'Eleven o'clock,' added his tall sad companion.

I pulled my shirt and trousers on over my ragged pyjamas, and hurried below. All the way down, the stairs were packed with black tin trunks and bulging baskets on which sat disconsolate children. The landlord was standing on the ground floor amid bits of the ancient machinery from the backyard. Men were tossing bars and wheels about with the sole aim of making as much noise and dust as possible; the air glowed with the clanging clouds of rust. To my shouts the landlord, cupping hand to ear, replied, 'All out yet?' I yelled that I'd had no notice, but he shook his head and confirmed that my rent was paid up. On my return journey I learned from the woman on the floor below our attic that the house had been suddenly condemned on account of rats and other horrors. (In 1900 bubonic plague first invaded Australia and wasn't exterminated for nine years, Queensland and N.S.W. being the worst sufferers. Now another attack was threatened. A rat with Indian rat-fleas, the plague's intermediary between rat and man, had been found, I think in Woolloomooloo, and the health authorities were acting with speed. Our rat-infested house was a danger-point. The plague did break out, though not as badly as in 1900.)

The evictors were now trying to get into the workshop-home of the clockman, who flatly refused to surrender. The tall man followed me back into the attic and pointed to a charcoal study by Ray of a nude model. 'Did you take that?' I nodded. 'From a real live woman?' I nodded. 'And she sat like that while you took her?' I nodded. 'That's rough, all right, but she's got a nice face.' I nodded. 'What I wanted to say, would you tell me where she lives? She's got a nice face, she has.' I gave him the address of the Goldston Mnemonics Institute.

I took stock of the attic, the torn curtains of green baize hung on string over the window, charred on one side, my uneasy bed, the shutters of now neatly nailed slats. The slope of stained ceiling was scrawled with drawings, addresses, insults, lines of poems and other memoranda. Pulling out two blankets, I dumped there Ray's drawings and paints, our books and papers, the love-letters of Selma from my Brisbane days (very solid because she wrote in a large hand on foolscap), our few spare collars and socks. I roped the two bundles and threw them over my shoulder, one in front and one behind. Remarkable how even in our poverty we had collected about twice the bulk of things we had entered the room with. My pockets I crammed with overlooked oddments. Ray's pipe-rack and stinking pipes I managed to push into one of the blanket bundles. Norman's etchings were in the suitcase.

The clockman was still gruffly refusing to surrender, backed up by an alarmed clock. I went on down the stairs with their lessening population. At the street corner I wondered where to go. Margot's was the nearest place, but I didn't want to return there, to meet the headaches and groans of the morning-after. Then I recalled Janet, only a little farther off. I arrived just as she was on the point of departing for the weekend. 'Can I leave at least the suitcase?' I asked. 'What happens to myself or the other things is not so important.'

'You can leave yourself too,' she said gaily. 'I shan't be back for a couple of days or so.' She let me into the neat clean compact little flat. I had forgotten that living quarters could be so neat, clean and compact. 'I'm sure you'd like a bath,' she added.

4 · A NEW START

'WHEN I RETURNED, late on the night of Easter Monday,' says Ray, 'there was not a sign of you and not a stick of furniture in the attic. I was naturally amazed and at a loss. There was not any clue or sign of what had happened to you. All I could do was to stagger up William Street to the boarding house and dig Phil out of bed. He told me the story.' So we got together after Ray had gone off to put up with some friend and I had found another room, in Yurong Street, closer to the Park. A first-floor room, empty of all but dust. We used a few shillings in hand to buy two second-hand stretchers at a market somewhere in Surry Hills. Ray also somehow acquired a primus. Later, I think, lent by the landlady, there was a table with chair. No more furnishings were needed by rational beings, we decided.

And so we were installed in a plain three-storey building, with the trams crashing outside, a loud noise after the sunken traffic of William Street in our Olympian attic. I was sorry in some ways to leave Janet's ground-floor flat (in a building named Cambridge like our breakfast hash-house) where I had slept on the sofa in the living-room; but on her Wednesday return I evacuated. Ray was expert with the old leaky primus, which made threatening blurts and now and then vaguely exploded. He used to crouch round one side of the projecting chimney piece with the primus held near the grate; in this position, which would have afforded no protection in the event of a major explosion, he used to light the thing gingerly, regardless of splutters and grumbles. I refused to have anything to do with the contraption.

Ray records that after I left, he made himself quite at home, 'a kindly landlady gradually adding to the limited furnishings till I was very comfortably settled. The place rapidly developed into a home-from-home for passing drunks and other friends, such as Tom Hubble, Hugh McKay and Jack Quayle (a sporting cartoonist and *Bulletin* joke artist, a delightful companion now flourishing as a racing cartoonist on the *Sunday Telegraph*). A curious fact about the Yurong Street building was that a sly grog shop was conducted there; but during the many months I lived in it I never suspected it. I found out much later, and quite by accident. Next door there was a brothel, where the proprietor, finding out somehow that he had an artist near at hand, commissioned copies of amorous Japanese woodcuts. 'I remember his outraged horror once at my suggestion that some of his girls might pose for me in the nude. As if *his* girls would do such a filthy thing, etc, etc! Well, many months after I had left Yurong Street, I was prowling through Woolloomooloo one night with a fellow drunk on the hunt for somewhere to buy beer. We ran into the ex-brothel owner, now a taxicab driver, and I asked him where we could buy some booze. He told me to go to my old Yurong Street residence, and was astonished when I told him that I never knew drink was sold there. However, he was a better psychologist than I, and said that naturally they would never admit to me now that they were sly groggers. So he directed our footsteps elsewhere.'

One afternoon in Pelligrini's a man I hardly knew gave me a card and told me mysteriously to go next day to the address on it. 'Take them a ready-made dummy of a weekly magazine and they'll finance you.' Then he went off without further details. Is he a madman, I thought, or a messenger of Apollo, well disguised? Has it at last come, the chance I wanted? I drew up a general draft of what seemed to me a possible literary magazine, and went to the firm, an advertising agency with printing connections. I interviewed the man whose name was on the card and who didn't seem in the least interested, left my draft, and heard nothing more of the matter.

A well-brushed solicitor's clerk had somehow wandered into the wine-bar and kept turning up. Finding who Janet was, he began wooing her (or the statue of her grandfather in Westminster Abbey), and asked her to visit his mother in a villa up the harbour. I thought she smiled too tolerantly on someone who was by definition a louse, and sulked. I had however no claim on her and had not kissed even her fingertips. Myself, I had become friendly with a fat girl, who played the flute. Once I met her outside the Conservatory, and as dusk was coming on, she put her full weight into my arms and brought me down on the rather exiguous space of grass at the side by the Gardens, where I expected a policeman at any moment to stamp on us. Besides, she was so fat that I felt raised to an undignified height into the view of any passers. She found out where I lived, and visited us in the room. Ray thought her of an admirable size for a model; he wanted to try sweeping brush strokes. But I pointed out that she was volubly sentimental, tediously bent on marriage, and far too large for us to feed.

I was getting nowhere at all. My verse had shrivelled. My denunciations of Baudelaire and my inquiry into the failure of English poetry after Keats filled some notebooks, but what was I to do with them? I had made a large number of acquaintances, but only Beutler roused my respect. I didn't really like Phyllis, whose one strong emotion was ambition tempered by jealousy of Jacques. Her talents as musician or dancer seemed slight; and my main interest was to plumb her obscure relationship with her husband.

I thought all this out with lucid melancholy one Saturday afternoon, as I wandered along the barrel passage at Pelligrini's to the dank urinal. The more I clung to poetry as an all-sufficient purpose, the less purposeful I became. I had sat for an hour with a single Frontignac, unable to compose one line of verse and watching anonymous boozers enter and exit.

But on my return I found Ray and Janet and Anna and half a dozen more familiar faces. The lights were twice as bright, the bottle glints twice as many in the loud friendly voices. Poetry was again possible, despite Fanny Brawne. The next few hours were loud and friendly enough to damp down any doubts. Then several of us were on our way to Janet's flat for tea. I had left the suitcase with the etchings there for safety and freedom from dust; and we had a look at them. Suddenly I was the only visitor left. Janet lay smoking on the couch in the long dark-red single-piece dress that fitted with a pleasant sinuousness. I sat by the window, feeling bitter about the universe but less eloquent than Ivan Karamasov. She smiled with superior wisdom, her voice deep, slow and husky, her remarks provocatively sensible. I recognized that if there was anything fated in my dusty meanderings in Sydney, here it was. The warmth of understanding, the finesse of intelligence, the breadth of social experience, for which I had vainly looked under the tables of Pelligrini's, did exist, and in the pleasantest collocation. I had been bellyaching because my daimon-of-poetry was perishing for want of sustenance in a barren philistinism, and here all the while Pallas Athene had been smiling at me. Now I felt aggrieved that she hadn't made me notice the obvious fact sooner and was mocking me sympathetically from her niche of heavy-lidded amusement, sleepily alive in every pore and speaking French as I'd never be able to speak it. I'll rise and go, I'll go at once. But I didn't. And after a while she took pity on me, asked me to be a pet and find the matches and light her cigarette.

A few nights afterwards I admitted to myself what had happened. Anna had promised to call on a musician (Arthur Benjamin) who shared his flat with a languidly good-looking medical student. The musician had heard rumours about his way of living, and to refute them he had been dining with Anna as a golden and buxom alibi, irrefutably female. He had even managed to please her; 'I'll sign a testimonial,' she said to us. But she didn't fancy an evening alone with him discussing music, so she bundled us both into her taxi. We had a charming evening, and over our whiskies the musician tried me out by playing various bits of music (mostly impressionistic scores by Debussy and the like, with specific titles) and asking what they suggested. My score was quite high. We left Anna at the flat and I saw Janet home. As we kissed on the doorstep I knew I might as well say 'I love you' and have done with it. But those weren't words so easy to say, so I didn't say them for a while.

My marriage with Janet brought a stable point into the aimless life I had been living out of a strenuous sense of duty. And her Scottishly sturdy common sense did much to amend the fanatical abstractions that swayed me. But it could not overcome them, and she never fought them directly, through a sense of humour, a sceptical tolerance, and perhaps a certain folk-respect for the possessed. So the element of conflict in our harmony was never brought out into the open and our relation did not develop as it might have. Only later, after our marriage was broken, did I begin at all properly to sound the wealth and strength of her character, and the liberation she could have brought me. And yet, it then seemed, her humorous sanity had somehow affected me through the years of our companionship and had helped to undermine the abstractions – though their crash arrived too late and in too devious a way for the happy coming-together of us two in a complete marriage. A sad matter, for which in due time I paid heavily enough.

One of the obstructive abstractions was Experience. The Poet had to accept Experience, submit to it, be drowned and lost in it, so that he might arise on the third day and find his life afresh in the Image born of his suffering and joy. The Image was his sole enduring love, the Woman its chance begetter. And so there was a ceaseless split in my being: the Love which was in fact central but which was visualized as a sort of daily companionship, and the Sexual Response as myriad as the forms of beauty. As a result, though the Wife appeared as a sort of refuge and haven-of-return, she was only one of the consuming forms of Venus. Janet's tolerant and ironic intelligence in a way helped the perpetuation of this conception of the torn Poet, since she seemed so ideally the detached and yet loving companion. The abstract idea of Experience insisted that married love could go on without the effort to concentrate and canalize in it the scattering-bright impulses.

Also, the idea, however defined by me in a complicated thesis of Dionysian god-rending, had its affinities with the common Australian attitude of the male as the wandering, tough man-of-action and the woman as the fixed point, holding a home together against the return of the lordly male. The attitude that in so many ways brought about a segregation of the sexes, not merely excluding women from pub-bars, but keeping firmly alive the convention of a totally different set of responses for men on their own and for men let loose among the female of the species.

I stated plainly my anarchist orthodoxy. I explained that I had no respect for marriage and that I should consider myself more bound to a woman with whom I wasn't married; for the bond would then be one of honour. Once the state was brought in, the sanctions of law had taken the place of personal honour, and the woman had replaced the infinite delicacy and variety of an endlessly renewed compact (of wit, delight, beauty) with her rights. I considered that I myself had no rights of any kind, since I did not recognize the law except as the instrument of greed and power-lust. I despised anyone who wanted any rights. Nothing but the direct and immediate bond of love, friendship, honour, had any validity in my eyes. All the same, in view of the many problems of living according to one's ideas and ideals in a mad world, a police world, I saw the point of going through the vile and meaningless ceremony, etcetera.

We moved first to a larger converted flat a short way off in some cool lane, I forget why; perhaps the lease of the other had run out. Here we had a reminder of the abhorred law. Late one night we were larking in pyjamas and ran out into the ver-andah just as two policemen were passing. They shone their lamps up at us, came and banged on the door, and were abus-ively threatening. As Darlinghurst had a large proportion of brothels and what not, no doubt the police were on a sharp look-out for any disorderly houses. For us however it was an unpleasant reminder of the dirty world we inhabited. Soon after we moved to a flat overlooking King's Cross itself, the heart of Darlinghurst: in a building called the William.

The problem of a stable point had been overcome. Janet, who had quarrelled with her mother and left her Macquarie Street home, had a small allowance, just enough for us to live on without discomfort. To this was added the few pounds I made from time to time, mainly through articles, stories or poems for the *Bulletin*. For a while I wrote articles for *Art in Australia*, and I did the art criticism and some reviews for a weekly, *The New Outlook*, in which Jacques was interested, as well as occasional journalism. (In *The New Outlook* someone composed my epitaph: Sic Transit Gloria Lindsay. And Har-old Monro, writing from London about some matters I had raised in a review, complimented the periodical in having more informed comments on poetry than anything his publi-cations could get in England. Maybe he was just surprised to find that we could read and write in Australia.) But the basis was Janet's allowance; and here one touches a deep flaw in my sort of revolt against money values. All very fine to repudiate any form of money-making that turns you into an accomplice of the system of alienation and degradation; but the inevitable result, unless you migrate to a virgin spot and keep yourself wholly on your own products, is to parasitize on someone or other and to obtain the fruits of injustice and inhumanity at second hand. For the time I was not aware of this contradiction; I felt myself true to my Apollonian oath as long as I personally took no hand in iniquity. Earnings from your own writings did not come under the heading of Crime because you assumed that anything you wrote was one way or another aimed against the system and amounted to an extortion from the enemy at pistol-point, an act of poetic Robin Hoodism. If I thought further about the matter, I took for granted that if I were true to myself I'd extort enough to save us from the gutter or would come on some windfall of the charitable Muses.

Years later I was amused to find that my attitudes, which from one angle could be defined as the last-ditch resistance of the petty-bourgeois in blindfolded revolt in the post-1917 world, were by no means my sole property, but were shared by large numbers of similarly placed young rebels in Europe of whom I knew nothing. Among the surrealist inheritors of the Dadaist repudiation of the world of war and money, very similar positions were present. Thus, Aragon declared on 18 April 1925 at a meeting held at the Residencia des Estudiantas in Spain:

Ah! bankers, students, workers, functionaries, servants, you are the *fellateurs* of the useful, brandishers of necessity. I shall never do a stroke of work, my hands are pure. You senseless pack, hide your palms from me, and those mental callouses on which you base your pride. I curse science, that twin sister of work. Have you never gone down to the depth of this black well? Have you never found this gallery into the sky? All right, I wish you only a great explosion of firedamp to restore you at last to the idleness which is the sole homeland of true thought . . . We shall master all things. And first we'll wreck this civilization dear to you, where you are imbedded like fossils in schist.

Despite a few differences in idiom, the emotion is identical with that which dominated me in these years.

I thus did not have a strong moral position when my mother kept appealing to me, and I did my best, to persuade Phil to go back to school. He scornfully went on refusing. After learning how to make plaster-casts and trundle them round with Rahel to the shops, he had managed to get into Julian Ashton's art school. For the rest he was taken up with the excitements of King's Cross, which had not yet become Little Paris with awning'd cafés under plane trees, but which was already an odd area of larrikins and flat-dwellers. Phil has told in *I'd Live* how he became a member of one of the last city pushes.* He also drilled in the cadets there, among the lads who threw an officer in a sewer because of his English accent and went on strike because they didn't like the uniforms. He saw the arrival of the gangsters and flash molls, ousting with their guns and razors the larrikins used to fists and boots. Only once in our school debates did I put him out of countenance. He had been talking with hectic admiration of the leader of his push, one Jumbo, and he suddenly pointed out of the window at the turmoiling scene of the Cross. 'There he is, that's Jumbo,' he cried in awe. I looked out and saw a fattish lad talking with some of the paper-sellers. No doubt he looked from above even squatter than he was; but through the panes of Phil's awe he seemed ridiculously unimpressive and I roared with laughter. Phil was hurt and reduced to a sullen silence. Mostly however he answered back with a shout or even threatened to bring the push up and wreck the flat. I gave up arguing that as he wanted to be a writer he might find a little education of use later on. 'I'll educate myself,' he repeated, adding, 'but I don't believe in education anyway.'

One day in the Cross I struck the spruiker I had known in the George Street boarding-house in Brisbane. Madder-eyed than ever, he pressed me to join him in his (unnamed) business. 'We could make a go of it, us two.' Another day I was taking

* *Push* is Australian for gang or group; *spruiker* in the next paragraph means a platform speaker, but with an extension to any plausible speaker or patterman. *Bonzer*, used later, means excellent.

Percy home in a taxi. I had struck him in town at the end of a few days' booze and as he was in cash he insisted on the taxi; but he had no wish to go up into the flat, and when I tried to pull him across the road, away from the pubs, the paper-boys, members of Phil's push, thought I was a homo dragging home a well-screwed client. They surrounded us and struggled to rescue Percy, who thought it was all a great joke and who made things worse by escaping at the last moment and throwing coins from the kerb into the midst of the traffic, to watch the boys dodging among the wheels and hooves to grab them. At last, when all his coins were gone, I got him upstairs and he went calmly and blissfully to sleep. (Only a few years ago, when Percy must have been well into the seventies, Ray mentioned in a letter that he had seen and slipped aside, not wanting to be drawn into a booze-up of some days' length, so unquenchable was our uncle's spirit and so magnificent his stomach.)

About this time Ray's Yurong Street period was ended by an attack of yellow jaundice. We took him into our flat for a couple of weeks till he recovered. He then made an effort to return to Yurong Street, but again was knocked out by jaundice, this time nursed by the landlady. When he was better, he came out to us in Bondi – a movement of ours which I shall recount later.

5 · POETS AND OTHERS

THROUGH JANET I had met Kenneth Slessor, who was a close friend of her brother, an intelligent fellow maligned by his nickname Gaga. I was somewhat prejudiced against Slessor through an article of his I had read in a newspaper, which said that the modern Byron went back unrecognized in the rush-train to his suburban home, etc. It was meant doubtless to pinprick illusions, but for me it upheld philistine positions. However, when we met, I was quickly charmed and felt that here at last was a fellow poet speaking the same language. We first talked in a flat he had on the North Shore, right over the harbour's waters, and he was fiddling about with a small crystal set, the first I had seen. Coaxing music out of the brilliant air, conjuring up spidery voices from nowhere, and then losing them. The waters of the harbour briskly moving in regular scalloped lines like a child's painting of the sea – if the child were working with a brush dabbed in blue fire. Enclosing us with a busy tangle of reflected lights. At the moment, with the unfamiliar and erratic instrument, he seemed a poet picking up the music of the spheres and finding it slightly out of tune. An intently smiling face, gingery hair parted in the middle, toothbrush moustache, and Teutonically oblong head.

I found out in a few moments that he had read widely. His own poetry was still rather heavy, tight, and laboriously tinted, e.g. *Kubla Khan, Pan at Lane Cove*, and the like. But he was struggling to break through the too compacted and worked-up form and achieve a *felicitas* that was less *curiosa*, a fluidity that broke up the deliberate colours. He was doing well as a journalist and had nothing of my hankering for hardship as a test of devotion. Yet at the same time he was already chafing against the journalist yoke, afraid that he would never be able to liberate all his powers with the daily grind of reporting. There was in him something of the fastidious touch of the amateur (or rather the eighteenth-century dilettante), with an enthusiasm for mah-jong and the collection of ivory chessmen. He dressed well, a Byronic dandy wanting to be almost (but not quite) undistinguished from the upper levels of the suburbanites of the rush-train. Whereas I, then as ever, suffered from a refusal/ inability to achieve even a minor tidiness or to wear a hat that didn't look either ridiculous, sitting on my head as if it repudiated its owner, or limp and shapeless as a wilting cabbage leaf. Still, we got on very well together, feeling no more than a mild amusement for one another's idiosyncrasies and united in our love of poetry.

His wife Noela, slender and elegant with pretty ringlets, did not seem particularly to belong to his world or any other except that which she inhabited when offering us afternoon tea in a cup of bone china. Herself owning a porcelain fineness, which one felt would ring with as true and subtle a note as the cup if one was rude enough to *ping* one's fingernail against her. She and Ken moved over to a flat somewhere in the Darlinghurst region, and we visited one another in family through the following years.

Another poet, less talented but closer to my own way of life, was Hugh McKay, who had come back to the literary world after some sort of scientific work, as a chemist I think, in Western Australia. He had a wide general knowledge of science; and after some months of dire privations punctuated with quickly used-up windfalls, he steeled himself to becoming a regular writer for *Smith's Weekly* on marvels and anything scientifically sensational. He was in love with a small dark woman, Rose, whom he married. Tall, ungainly, odd, with a lean and hungry look, he was a charming fellow with his croaking humour, wearing an almost impenetrable armour of sardonic nihilism. Only in an occasional poem, written against his will, did he reveal the strange world he inhabited – a world that was suddenly found to accord with his beloved Rose and his cats:

> *The black world of her brain swung in her skull*
> *Like a dark spider in a web of dreams . . .*
> *To wander blind at dawn through the streets of waking,*
> *An alien land . . .*

Returning always to the image of star-bees, the girl 'in a green-sea-net, with silver bees in her hair,' or 'loosened from the net, soft arm sea-ripple-wet, and bee-starred hair.' The forest shadows tolling like angry bells, the moon coming back to the earth and filling the whole great arch of the sky.

He had an acutely analytic mind. I had read some years before a masterly essay of his in which he discussed the crafty fear of life and the egoist neutralizing of the flesh that limited Shaw as a dramatist. But now he refused to write criticism. He had consciously withdrawn from ordinary life, obsessed by his conviction of a dark world on the other side of the everyday surfaces; and this dark world he feared and desired as his lost self, as the human reality that the busy day denied. Yet there was in him an immense power of enjoyment and of concentration in friendship. The purring pleasure with which he could put a bottle of beer down on the table or watch the liquid guggling out into a glass was something all his own. And when enough beer had flowed, the cruel edge between the inner and outer world broke down. He had a single term of denunciation, which he pronounced with such merry vehemence, such variety of loathing, that it never seemed stale or inadequate: *Insects*!

When enough beer had flowed, I used to try to instil into him a faith in himself and poetry – that is, my kind of faith: I could conceive of no other. He listened with a grateful and bitter smile, and now it seems that he was too kind-hearted to prick my Platonic bubbles with the sharp ironies that he never lacked. But at the time I thought I was drawing back to the fold a strayed poet of our star-fated Renaissance, and pressed my point with all the callow cruelty of which in my good intentions I was capable. I see his sunken gaunt face, his keen dark hidden eyes, his hair which he kept black by combing it back with a leaden comb, his profile harshly outlined for a moment against a golden light of beer and a snatch of music, as he lifts his mug and pledges the one comfort he had found secure.

Generally I went on Fridays to the *Bulletin* office to collect my mother's allowance for her. There I often met Henry Lawson, whom the *Bulletin* generously paid something every week for old times' sake. Infinitely mild and amiable, bent and showing the signs of his nearing dissolution, he began an interminable conversation which continued next week from where it had last broken off. Unfortunately very little of what he said was intelligible. In his extreme deafness he seemed to have no sense of what was or wasn't audible. He smiled with his gentle, warm, brown eyes and talked on, now and then exciting himself and gesticulating. Certainly among other things he described the problems he had in getting a drink, so well looked after was he by the capable-faced woman who soon emerged and kindly took him home. I gathered that he had many hiding-places for a bottle, but none good enough to deceive his benefactor for long. I gathered too that he was expressing some sort of goodwill.

Only about fifty-five but looking much older, receding out of life greyly as one gazed, waving a dim and desperate farewell as the tides sucked him out. His obscurely agitated smile, his restless broken gestures, seemed to express a doomed attempt at a last communication, a humble benediction, before he went under. That was all he had got out of life, this yarning poet whose work summed up an epoch of our national life. Only the dogged desire to break through and say something friendly. All his life had been like that, all his work had been like that. Struggling with a love that made him reach out despairingly, happily, into a good world of men, a good earth. His death was the desolation closing round him once and for all as he tried vainly to borrow the price of a drink. What could one say? At moments I thought he knew I was a writer and wanted to say something encouraging to the whole breed of young writers through me. At moments I seemed to hear an echo from his living past, as he slipped away from the bare *Bulletin* office with its counter and its glassed-in waiting-room, down past Lambing Flat, past the Pipe Clays – take care or you'll slip – past Gulgong, over the rickety plank-bridge where the drunken Irishman broke his neck, past Home Rule and the old-timers squatting on a mullock heap and crumbling a lump of clay, talking of the great days when the lads used to light their pipes with five-pound notes and weighed out the gold dust with a certain lady's ring, down past the whole roaring lot, the bark huts and the sly-grog shanties, down to the small shed where a lanky kid lay in the red dust and plaited a length of stringy bark and watched, always watched. All his life in his eyes, his yearning melancholy eyes, now much dimmed but still liquidly alert, revealing in their weak moments the anxiety of a hungry dog uncertain of its master, then in their strength the whole of the mateship he sought to define in his work.

'You should have known him in the old days,' said Bertram Stevens. 'I introduced him once to a man who'd been asking for a long time to meet him. "Here," I said, "meet a great admirer of your work, Henry." Henry held out his hand in that friendly way of his, and they shook hands. Then, after the shake was over, Henry still held his hand out. The admirer looked at it. "Can you lend me half a crown?" Henry asked. And he got it.'*

John Dalley suggested that I try my hand at topical verse. I began browsing through newspapers (at which I had not looked since the breakdown of my interest in politics). After despairing of a theme, I struck a paragraph that made me smile and turned out some satirical verses, which the *Bulletin* printed. After that I wrote quite a lot in the same vein, under signatures like Panurge. Though I had a low opinion of the exercise, I enjoyed it and the work helped in loosening up the muscle-bound state my verses had got into and gave me something of a new start.

Many tales of the pre-war literary life floated nostalgically around the *Bulletin*, among contributors waiting to be paid in the front office, or in the near pubs, especially the Star – tales

---

*Lawson certainly had his not-so-pleasant side bred in part of many hardships and devious tactics in keeping alive with the price of a beer in his pocket. Ray reminds me of this in writing, 'The image of Lawson as the Spirit of the Bush, the Rebel, the Standard Bearer of the Spirit of Mateship, the Picturesque Storyteller, one whose alcoholic weakness was really only due to a rather charming and eccentric Bohemianism, was well and truly built, long, long before George Lambert finally fixed it, sickeningly, in bronze in that awful statue which now stands in the Domain. Actually *Bulletin* old-timers who knew Lawson well have told me that he was a thoroughly unpleasant character with as much feeling of "mateship" as a crab walking frontwards.'

about Henry, Victor Daley, and the like. Daley near his death, answering the Sisters of Mercy who tried to coax him into eating mutton chops, 'I'm sorry, Reverend Mother, but I couldn't eat them even if they were off the Lamb of God.' A. G. Stephens with his magisterial beard, like a bedroom fire, said Hugh McCrae, mouthing some tremendous rebuke ... Eric Bedford gives me the words of a conversation in the Star between his gargantuan father, my uncle Percy, and the fluffy *Bulletin* poet McKee Wright; they excellently raise the ghosts of those bombastic days:

'Welcome back, Randolph. What's it been this time? A new company on the Tiber with the Pope your chairman of directors, or a plan to bottle moonbeams?' asked David McKee Wright.

'I've formed a Poet Union. You're chairman, David, and I'm treasurer. We'll corner the market in good poetry, which means you and I just have to down pens, march to the pub, and dispatch yards of garlic sausage and beer. Come along, we'll commence to spend the Union fees. Ah, Percy, is Lionel in town? The Lindsays ought to paint a huge canvas with real Australian light to act as a backdrop for the London scene. It would cheer the English up no end. Come, Percy, we're about to tread the sacred boards of the Star.'

'Randolph, you're like a sunrise on the Hawkesbury after a heavy night,' said Percy, his mischievous face dissolving into the familiar warm grin.

'And where is our D'Artagnan, our Lionel?'

'He's away in Melbourne.'

'I wrote to him. The silver-tongued Apollo should be here.'

'It's as well he isn't. When you two get together, you're like a couple of priests in conclave on the sins of the poor.'

As the beer went round, the top of the bar became a battlefield on which lay the slain. Pigs-trotter bones, cheese rinds, garlic sausage skins and crusts were there as evidence of the human locusts' devastation.

'Ah, you drinkers of soda-pop and eaters of buns, who fill yourselves with wind and self-righteousness, pull your long black hats over your heads and shudder at the sight of men who enjoy the gastronomy of the tavern and not the gas of the bilious mind.' The man in the big hat was now the centre of a large group as he anecdoted, talking in broken accents of the Australian musician who bought a milch-cow during the depression of the 90s, or of happenings on a dozen outback Australian tracks, or of the night and its stars.

And long, shy Henry Lawson came in to lean on the bar and drink beer, and wipe the suds from his long moustache – sinking further into his Norseman's isolation, as though the last Viking's ship had sailed away and he was upon a desert island.

'And what else, Randolph?'

'I've been trying to form a company for the largest cattle-station in the world in the Northern Territory, but the money-men, or the men that can get money, can only think of a cattle-station like some farm in Sussex.'

A. G. Stephens with his beard-broom spread over his double-breasted suit of blue was still prowling along Castlereagh Street with fierce eyes under his big felt hat. He had been the critical power on the Red Page of the *Bulletin* from 1896 to 1906, in strenuous years of building up a well-rooted national litera-ture. He had begun his *Bookfellow* in 1899 and had gone on issu-ing it in various forms. (It died in 1925.) My ignorance of such literary traditions as Brisbane possessed was shown by my having no idea that he had been born at Toowoomba, Queens-land, sub-edited the *Boomerang* in Brisbane in 1891 and edited the Cairns *Argus* next year; and that in 1894 while working in London he published *A Queenslander's Travel Notes*. (At my prep. school there had been a long gangly lad, son of Brunton Ste-phens, whom I heard described as a poet's son; I approached him with some respect, but found him uninterested in poetry. I later read some of his father's galloping verse-tales and thought them pedestrianly insufferable: which did much to put me off looking for local literary traditions. I heard of Adams, but never located a copy of his *Songs of the Army of the Night*.) A.G.S. did good work in fighting for the dignity of Aus-tralian literature and the writer's right to base his work on national conditions and needs; but I had never more than glanced at his essays. Perhaps I can suggest why I resisted him and his teachings by citing a few of his words. Despite the hard struggles of pioneering, he wrote, 'there are not wanting adumbrations of the beauty of Australia – glimpses of the secret enchantment in which this strange, feline land – half fierce, half-caressing – holds those who have listened to the gum-trees' whispered spell or drunk the magic philtre of landscapes flooded by Nature's opiate-tints.' No teaching in such a style could rouse anything but resistance in my breast.

Still I called on him once in his room of littered books and papers, and he surveyed me suspiciously but without hostility across the table, from under his bushy brows, an intruder from a new and unsurveyed region of letters. We sparred vaguely, but nothing came of it.

Let us look a moment at the literary and social scene of those years. Lawson and Furphy had matured the pioneering phase, but with many limitations. The approved novelists, with large circulations, were still minor romantics like Ada Cambridge, Tasma, and Mrs Campbell Praed. Important new novelists were soon coming up – Henry Handel Richardson, K. S. Prichard, and Vance Palmer – but as yet they had not begun or had effected nothing. Two poets, Hugh McCrae and Christopher Brennan, had broken through into a new dimension of Australian experience, but their work was still eccentric in terms of the general literary life. At the turn of century Australia was as yet weighed down with multiple feelings of colonial inferiority, and many of these feelings still persisted in the 1920s.

Life had sprouted in its native soil; it had vigour, but it was like a bracken frond trying to uncurl beneath the weight of a boulder. Assumptions that today have vanished, or at worst are merely fighting rearguard actions, held the whole front. No native-born Australian was considered eligible for a responsible post in government or business; if a Britisher were not available, then one must be imported. It was seriously doubted whether the native-born would ever be fit to take political control of their own country; it was questioned whether they could ever acquire the necessary crafts to engage in local manufacture. It was even seriously doubted that the native-born had the physical stamina to make 'old bones'; and as for art and letters – as late as the early twenties the idea that these were integral to a country's development was far from universal acceptance. Press articles pointed out in a superior manner that there was no occasion for all this anxiety about Australian art and letters when we had Europe's – and particular Britain's – accumulation of centuries to serve our every need. (F. D. Davison, *Meanjin*, VII, I, 1948.)

This background picture must be borne in mind throughout the story I have to tell of our effort to proclaim an Australian Renascence. In repudiating nationalism (by which we meant, in effect, a repudiation of the limits and weaknesses of Lawson and Furphy, of the philistinism that wanted nothing but loping narratives in verse), we were defending the national pretensions on the level that had previously been considered on almost all sides as forever barred to the lowly colonial.

There was a further aspect of the situation of which we were less conscious. Our period was one of intense growing-pains in the political as in the cultural sphere. Francis Adams had noted in Sydney in 1884 'the brutality of the old slaving families administering hideous and unrepealed statutes,' and 'the rule of a squattocracy as voiced in the hopelessly subservient and corrupt legislation'. That the first decades of the new century saw little essential change was revealed by the Report on the Administration of the N.S.W. Land Department in 1906, which was one long tale of corruption and bribery, perjury and chicanery, theft and extortion; millions of acres were shown to have been dishonestly gained; the undercover rule of the big landowners or squatters had survived all legal attacks. The scandal went on for two years, but nothing was done. The state Parliament, cynically passive and unconcerned, merely bided its time till the arrival of the White American Fleet, which I recall, gave them a chance to shuffle the whole matter out of public sight. The scene was still that of hanging judges like Docker and the raucously ranting journalist Norton, a blackmailer who survived prosecution after prosecution. There was definitely something, as has been acutely said, of an eighteenth-century atmosphere. Norman, Brennan and McCrae had come up through the years which Adams succinctly describes. By the 1920s, various factors (including the rise of the Labor Party) had changed much of the situation, but many elements of 'the brutality of the old slaving families' still survived. Our confused reaction against them played its part in our complicated attitude to national pretensions.

One more visitor to the Kings Cross flat, or rather a pair of them. Jim Emery, draughtsman and drunks-friend, and Dave, who had married into the family of the most important politician of Australia in the days before the latter's rise to power. 'Do we intrude, Jack?' said Dave, shuffling and goggle-eyed, in his throaty voice. 'Send us away if we intrude. I won't pass the threshold unless I'm sure that I'm welcome. I'm not the kind of person who sticks his nose in where it's not wanted. Only say the word. We know you're a busy man.' Blinded with his own eloquence, he orated on, with large gestures; he always gave a long speech of self-depreciation before he entered anywhere, but he outdid himself at our flat.

'All right, Dave,' said Jim, 'let's go down to the pub and he can join us there if he likes.'

But though Dave was too humble to venture in without an extended explanation of his position in the universe, he objected strongly to being prevented from making that explanation in all its nuances. In the days when his father-in-law had been a mere stump-orator, he, Dave, had been a good catch for the daughter, an etcher of line-blocks in a big firm of art printers. But now with the family's grandeur he was a drag and a nuisance. He had taken more and more to drink, and, denied the drawing-room of home, sang in his fruity tenor in any bar or grog shop where the proprietor failed to eject him. 'No, no, Jim,' he said, struggling, 'I won't let Jack think I've got no manners. Lemme go, Jim. I must explain things to Jack. I won't have him thinking I'm a bloody boor without company manners. I may be a nobody. I may be disliked and trampled on. I may be a worm. But a worm has his feelings, as nobody knows better than me. I refuse to go, Jim, till I put the case to Jack. He's a real good cobber. He won't kick a poor bloke when he's down. He won't say he isn't fit to kiss his own daughter, and what's more, he won't set a poor innocent child against her own father and make her despise him.'

'Come on, he's busy,' said Jim, giving up hope of a drink in the flat.

'When Jack says go, I'll go,' answered Dave, rolling his eyes and clutching at his hair. He had a retreating chin; when he sang and tried one of his long-drawn sobbing notes, it disappeared altogether into his neck. And his nose was coppered with beer. He waved his arms. 'Lemme go. Nobody will ever say I stopped a moment where I'm not wanted. I'd spill my blood rather than stay a moment more'n I was welcome. Whatever you can say of me, you can't say that. Let's all be good cobbers, Jim.' He clasped his hands in appeal. 'I dunno what the world's coming to. It's money that goes to people's heads. No, Jim, the trouble with you is that you're not outspoken like me. You don't look a man in the eye and tell him to turn you out if you're not wanted. Cut my throat and tear my guts out, I wouldn't stay where I'm not wanted, it's not my nature, I just couldn't do it.'

'That's well known, Dave,' said Jim.

'Put it here, Jack,' said Dave, stepping unsteadily forward. 'Put it here and I'll go without another word. Let's all be good cobbers.' He held out his hand. 'I know you think I'm in the way. I always know what people are thinking. But I don't bear no malice. Live and let live is what I say. I know I'm not your sort. But put it here, let's all be good cobbers.'

'Come on, Dave, you're being a pest,' said Jim.

'Lemme go,' Dave insisted. 'I won't go till we've got it all clear. Jack's a good scout. Jack and me understand one another. I won't go in because I know where I'm not wanted. Is that understood?'

'If you won't come in when I ask you, I'll go down with you to the pub,' I said in desperation.

'Now don't get me wrong,' said Dave. 'It's best to have things out and then nobody can't say nothing. Put it here, Jack. Let's all be good cobbers.'

'He's had a bit,' said Jim as we went down the stairs. 'They're going to divorce him, he says.'

Well, I thought, Australia's the only continent where a world-famous politician could have a son-in-law like Dave. That's something.

Janet wrote poems too. But they were almost all in free verse. At least the best ones were, and it was one of our dogmas that free verse was incorrect, decadent, a turning-away from the difficult techniques from which alone could emerge the bright-edged image of beauty.* I did my best therefore not to recognize the virtues of her writing, which was often fresh, direct, strongly felt, and which included many anti-war poems. She gave up writing.

---

*A student had forced his way into Springwood and read wads of Ezra Pound to Norman, who thought the poems pretentious and scatterbrained. At N.L.'s request I read what of Ezra's I could get and confirmed his opinion; but I did not strike *Moberley*.

6 · DELPHIC SPRINGWOOD

I HAD BEEN keen not to implicate Norman in my difficulties;
I fell down over my illness at Pillig's place, but that was the
only time I directly appealed for aid. No doubt he had been
afraid that my descent on Sydney, followed by Ray and Phil,
would mean an infestation by penniless, untidy and pestering
sons. But he hid his panic well, and our occasional visits to
Springwood were decorously managed. The needs of his work
and his stomachic inability to absorb beer saved him from any
disrespectful attempt to draw him down to the circean sties of
Sydney. I took Janet up and he confided to me that he thought
Rose and her the only intelligent women in the world: which,
translated, means that he thought them those rare birds, suitable wives for Lindsays.

He had already told me a little about his spiritualist convictions; now I learned more. His mother at Creswick had had
a shattering emotion of a message from her young son, Reg,
who was serving in the A.E.F. She spoke of the shock at the
time and later found that its date and hour coincided with the
date and hour of the lad's death in battle. Norman was already
in a violent state of emotional crisis on account of the war. He
had produced conventional war posters and had tried out some
satirical jokes of his own on the unimpressed *Bulletin* editors:
Jesus seated on the Right Hand, asking, What did you do in
the Great War, Daddy? Underneath he had been badly hit by
horror and disgust for a world that could suddenly drop its
mask of civilization and let such fathomless brutalities loose.
He told me of an argument he had with Bertram Stevens who
for long had acted in various ways as an agent of his. Stevens
made some patriotically callous comments about the war and
Norman burst out, 'Do you know what you're talking about?

The war isn't something over there, in Europe. It's here in this room. There's blood everywhere, all round us, on everything, on us. Can't you smell it?' Stevens blinked in dumb dismay. In his world, metaphor was a thing which, if sufficiently diluted, could be segregated in the poetry column of a respectable periodical, but it had no right to speak out in ordinary life as the accusing witness of unrealized relationships, of the hidden murders and ultimate hopes that linked men in guilt and in revolt.

Here was the first great point of moral choice that Norman had to confront since the achievement of his anti-Christian life-affirming positions in early youth. He could either extend his social consciousness and deepen his art, or build abstractly on his sense of horror and isolation, and cut his art off from the sources of renewal. He took the second course, halting at the moment of overwhelming horror. His Nietzscheanism, which he had used to concentrate his love of energy and fertility, his contempt of other-worldliness and of the lies by which men shrouded cruelty and repression, he now inverted and fabricated into a transcendental philosophy. If all that he had dreamed of joy and sensuous fulfilment was denied by a world of maddened war, then he would deny and defy the world by lifting his dream clean out of it. He clung to the dream, but felt he could sustain it intact only by locating it outside time and space in a new dimension. In this volte-face he was aided by that side of Nietzsche which, unable to see any basis for a sane and life-affirming society in the world around him, had turned to plans for brotherhood groups and had shouted in lonely rage at the driven mob of the nations (in fact the bourgeoisie blindly controlled by the system of exploiting controls they had themselves devised). Hence the scheme of *Creative Effort*, which saw the art image as autonomous, living in its own unity, its own higher time-space, and which saw the artist as a member of a sort of Apollonian secret society or blood-brotherhood spread over the ages and redeeming the hungry chaos of matter by the stabilizing Image. A sort of Neoplatonism cast in the focus of all that was most lost and exasperated in Nietzsche.

In his anguished revolt against the war, against a society

which professed Christian love and yet was propelled by its
deepest nature into war, Norman sought to preserve his faith
in the image of joy and love by alienating the image entirely
from the earth – whereas, before, he had been attacking his
society for its alienation from the simple pieties and fecundities
of the earth. The passionate force with which he made this
reversal drove him to need more than a mere aesthetic conviction; he hungered for an actual proof of the image's reality in
a dimension beyond our time-space. Hence the importance to
him of his mother's experience. It gave him a definite point
on which to re-erect his faith. The death of Reg, of whom he
was very fond, experienced by their mother in what he decided
was a contact outside our time-space, became for him a rebirth,
a second setting-forth from the maternal womb. And the mechanism for extracting his own 'proof' of the other-worldly
dimension was provided by David Low, who came up to
Springwood with a ouija board.

After Low went, Norman, considering his visit a guided
event, set to work with Rose, attempting to get into contact
with what he believed to be his own art dimension outside
earthly time-space. He worked out a simple form of spirit
board (the alphabet written on a piece of cardboard which was
hung on the wall). Two persons grasped a stick with both their
hands, taking hold alternately. The tensions of their grasp gave
a nervous movement and direction to the stick, which pointed
out letters that formed words and resulted in a message. Thus,
with Rose's aid, he felt sure that he had come in touch with
the blood-brotherhood to which he belonged, Shakespeare and
Rubens, Dürer and Apollo, Rabelais and Beethoven.

He was rather shy in telling of his experiences in detail; but
once he had properly begun, he found a relief in so doing it.
For in my devout discipleship I believed as raptly as he did
himself. Only once however I participated in the board business. Norman believed that in Rose lay the force which
brought the messages into our time-space. He asked her if she
thought I might hold the stick with her. I had the feeling that
she wasn't pleased, but she agreed.

That evening in the water-colour studio we held the stick,
which pointed out various letters, words. Nothing very

impressive happened. It seemed an off-evening in the spirit world, with the more important characters gone roystering off into some yet remoter sphere. However, I asked various questions, to which I did not receive illuminating answers. For instance, I asked if the Homeric hexameter was much older than scholars suspected and if its roots lay in the Mykenean world. (I already had a notion, on general grounds, that the Greeks had much earlier origins than the textbooks said and that their culture had close links with the Mykenean and later Minoan societies, as has now been proved by the reading of Linear Script B.) If there was anything one would expect Apollo to be well up in, it was such matters. But I got no clear reply; I was told that the subject would have to be gone into.

However, there was no second time. Partly a sense of taboo, partly an obscure sense of shame, prevented me from ever suggesting it.

At some time before my arrival in Sydney, Norman had gone through a bad phase. Rose I think was ill, and he was left by himself in Springwood. He suffered at being cut off from the board and devised a spelling-out mechanism that could be operated by one person. At first things went on much the same as when Rose presided over the seances. Then there was a slow and subtle change. The spirits began deliberately to disorder and demoralize him; and finally they revealed themselves as emissaries of evil, intent on breaking his will. By this time the contact had become so close that he could not stop the messages, could not avert the process of disintegration he had touched off. Clamorously the voices lacerated his mind and one night all but drove him to death – over the edge of a bluff in the wide grounds of Springwood. He was however able to break the spell in time, and then Rose returned. (He wrote a story based on this experience, which at the time I thought a powerful work.)

Only once in Sydney did we have a shot. Ray and Hugh McKay were in our Kings Cross flat, with a considerable beer supply. Janet, in a moment of enthusiasm for myself as an Hellene, had made up a chiton of some soft fabric and insisted on my wearing it. Stimulated by the beer, I did so, to the unquenchable laughter of Ray and Hugh. I recall Janet's kindly sheltering embrace. As we consumed more beer, Hugh with all the resources of his caustic wit ridiculed all the suppositions of spiritualism. The results, when not fraudulent, were merely produced by unconscious muscular tensions, minute but compelling, on the part of the wand-holders. As for the directing power, only think of what had been shown of the multiple personalities of certain hysterics. Perhaps the direction came from some level of the unconscious in one of the performers, perhaps from a fusion of unconscious levels belonging to both. That was the only interesting point raised by the silly thing.

We decided to have a try and improvised a board. We took turns with the stick and soon had roused a spirit who declared himself a Dublin jarvy-driver, who swore in the best possible Irish, and talked like a Sean O'Casey character. He made a particular set at me and called me a Dinner Pig. Whoever's unconscious worked out this odd fellow had the makings of a good dramatist. After a while however he grew repetitive. We lost interest and let the old roarer return to his whoreshop in eternity.

But a year or so later there was an episode with Phil which was much along the same lines as Norman's dangerous experiment. We were then at Bondi. Phil had been working hard at a novel; he was rather run-down, drinking too much and generally feeling at a loss. One night he and I had been printing at Kirtley's house (as I shall recount later), and on our way back he came in with me instead of going straight home. I had noticed that he was distracted and subdued all the evening, and I now asked what was troubling him. He found it hard to tell me, then blurted it out. He had been playing about with automatic writing, first using an alphabet and pointer, then, as the spirits became more familiar, suspending his wrist at the end of a string and letting the pen run along at their will. He had invoked their aid for his novel; and at first they had given him excellent advice on construction and dictated whole passages. The writing was better than that he had been doing unaided. But now the voices had become so definite and close that he didn't even need to suspend his wrist and take the weight away from his hand. They changed in character, dictated page after page of Joycean puns and complicated free-associations, and at last announced that they were going to drive him mad and kill him. All the evening, he said, as we'd been printing, the voices had threatened him, trying to force him into doing something idiotic and dangerous. Now he felt at the end of his tether.

I gave him a long talk, as encouraging as I could make it. With Norman's tale in my mind, I couldn't try to convince him that the voices were the echoes of his own anxiety; besides, they now existed for him in such detached virulence that he was sure of their real existence. I talked instead of creative will and love, and walked on with him to the house he shared with Ray and our mother. Next day Ray came to consult me about the way Phil had been behaving over the last weeks, doing very odd things, getting into the bath and talking to himself there for hours. (Phil had told me about the bath. There was some sort of test involved, of which I have now forgotten the details. What scared him most was that voices would drive him over the cliffs as they were trying to do.)

I told Ray not to be upset and explained. For a week I kept Phil with me, playing Beethoven records, reading Rabelais or the Greek poets to him, and talking our philosophy of Nietzschean joy. Woe says: Hence, go! but Joys all want Eternity. The present made eternal by being realized as joy and beauty.

Anyway it worked. The voices became bored. They slowly slackened their grip and Phil felt secure. Promising abjectly to try no more automatic writing, he dared to take up pen or tap his typewriter again.

Norman had quarrelled bitterly with his brother Lionel over the spirits. Lionel saw nothing in his obsession but a moral breakdown, a surrender of pagan gaiety and earth-faith before the ghost of their missionary grandfather. Till this point Lionel had been the intellectual leader; and recently he has given me his own version of what happened, together with many details of his and Norman's early years. 'I was devoted to Norman, very fond of him as a kid, and always as big brother protected him against the bullying of state-school kids. After my spell of enthusiasm as pupil assistant at the Melbourne Observatory,

I returned to Chiswick; and when I was about eighteen or nineteen went back to Melbourne at the behest of an old actor who had seen my youthful drawings, which were very bad, to start a paper, which was stillborn.' He was about to return downcast to Creswick when the old actor came along to say 'that there was a split at the *Hawklet* (a sort of crime-rag) and a chance of work. In three weeks I had ousted a rival, who wanted to do the bushranging holdups, and with 35s. a week I went to the Gallery School, to learn to draw. The supposed stigma of drawing for a police gazette I have always scorned with a laugh, and said it was the best thing that ever happened to the Lindsay clan, as it taught us to improvise designs – however disreputable in the eyes of the good and the just. None of the students could design anything at the school. Norman fell into my shoes when he married, to be followed by Percy. I used to tell Brennan the delightful episodes that distinguished this crapulous weekly, and he said to John Quin, "Think of it, John. Lionel was living when we were swotting Greek participles." '

Again he says, 'It has always seemed to me that he has never forgiven his mother for keeping him in, when he was a delicate boy and suffering from some skin ailment that necessitated confinement to barracks. You will be surprised to learn that when I insisted on his coming to ghost the *Hawklet* while I did the *Freelance* work, he was the quietest and most amiable boy imaginable, who talked little but observed everything.' (That acute power of observation, with sense of character and gesture, marked his work up to the time of *Creative Effort*.) At my request, Lionel elaborated the points he had made about his brother's youth. 'Olive Westcott, a handsome girl, dominated her cousins and Norman, ruled them like a queen and distributed her favours as she wished. She comes into his early writing. Apropos his writing of *Saturdee*, infinitely better in the *Lone Hand* text, he was as slow at writing then as he later became too fluent. He would ask me if I remembered various details and what the boys said characteristically. I wasn't much help except in elucidating events and characteristics, but digging into the wells of memory he unearthed conversations that are exact. Creswick haunts him still, and I am sure that his late bitter attacks on our mother are due to the fact that for his health's sake (and the 'spots' as this skin trouble was always called) he had to be kept indoors and not let rush about like other kids. So, like R.L.S., he saw life through the window for some time. His remarkable powers of observation were undoubtedly quickened and increased by this imprisonment. I was always fond of him and taught him to read.'

He goes on, 'From a termagant playing and rebelling against all restraint, when he came to me in Melbourne, there wasn't a quieter or more satisfied lad on the globe. I encouraged him, told him to study, draw from himself, make armour and study costumes, from the time I had started on the model. He made astounding progress, and though Percy wanted to come I had my way as the first to earn a living in the family. Percy never could draw – only, like most landscape painters, 'map' an outline, he had no sense of line. When the *Freelance* was killed by two traitors who sold out their shares, I took Norman out to Charterville and with Ernest Moffitt he set up house. He listened whilst Moffitt and I talked endlessly on art and poetry – you know that great stage. He was under the spell of Frederick Sandys and Theocritus and very happy.' (Moffitt made careful Pre-Raphaelite drawings of foliage and landscapes. The work of Sandys that Norman knew was his woodcuts.)

Lionel, with his indefatigable curiosity and ardent scholarship went on feeding Norman with ideas and interests over the years, introducing him to the Greeks and Romans, French writers from Baudelaire and Balzac to Villon and Rabelais. It was inevitable no doubt that sooner or later Norman would be driven to assert himself; and when his spiritualism developed, he made strong efforts to convert Lionel, who found his ideas infuriating. 'Now for the quarrel,' Lionel says, 'not of my seeking, but which set me free from an abominable oppression. I had suffered the long wearying letters on spiritualism, which to one who had hated all mysticism, Christianity *et hoc genus* since boyhood – and still does – were as obvious as they were *eitel schaum*. Then *Creative Effort* and a diarrhoea of letters which I answered though bored stiff, and then was rewarded by being told that I and poor Bert Stevens were mere chopping blocks, and that our opinions only confirmed him in his *knowledge* that we were completely wrong. Grandpa Williams *redivivus* – but worse. The book completely bewildered the public, and when I was over in Melbourne with a small one-man show, I was asked by Shirlow to lunch with Ellery the Town Clerk and Cross, both intelligent men, to explain what N.L. was driving at. Which I did as well as I could. The talk was quite above Shirlow's head. (He was a bad etcher who hated both of us.) He put it about Melbourne that I had said Norman was mad. I received one of the most damnable letters possible threatening me with action for libel. I at once, and without any pressure, wrote to Ellery and Croll to ask if, in the course of our discussion, I had stated or suggested that Norman was mad, to Shirlow (frightened) also; and all affirmed my innocence.' Later he presented all the correspondence to the archives of Melbourne University, to be kept there till the death of himself and Norman.

He adds, 'The break was inevitable. I had been so long devoted to Norman that he had reached the stage of petty tyrant, obsessed by what Renan called "the horrible mania of certitude". I suffered with the breaking of a lifelong friendship and devotion. Well, it was a relief for me and I have never been forgiven my London success.' But the causes of the break clearly went deeper than any incidental clash or conflict; they implicated deep differences in the whole outlook on life.

Norman said something briefly to me of the threat he had felt impelled to make to Lionel. I did not press for further details. On the one hand the idea of taking police action against anyone, let alone one's own brother, was against all my convictions; and on the other hand I had always assumed that no one could possibly be bothered about statements of his nearing madness unless he was himself afraid of such a fate.

I did not see much of Lionel at this time, though once or twice I visited him at Wahroonga. Though I respected his scholarly interests in art, my position of discipleship to Norman made any serious contact impossible. His daughter Bingo, whom I had met on my previous Sydney trips, was remarkably beautiful, but had shown no interest in me. I recall once at Wahroonga citing to Lionel Nietzsche's definition of decadence as the ability to resist stimuli. Now this is the exact opposite of what Nietzsche said, but it fitted in with our view of the romantic sensibility of the artist passively submitting to Life (specifically visualized as a woman, Madame Life) and recovering his active dominance only as artist, giving birth to the creative image. I mention this error of mine because it throws some light on the function of memory, the way in which we distort something to suit our needs or to rationalize our positions, and the way in which at the same time we keep somewhere in our minds the awareness that we have made this distortion. Otherwise, why should this trivial matter have stayed in my thoughts forty years later while so many much more interesting remarks or discussions have evaporated? I recall even the moment I said it, going into the bathroom; and for this reason that room is the only part of the house I remember at all clearly.

Now I agree with the interpretation of Hugh and Lionel. The actual experience of the spirit-wand is disconcerting; the magnetic tensions are strong and one is quite unaware of the involuntary muscular effort one must be making. Or rather one is aware of it as a sort of resistance on one's part. Presumably some sort of magnetic field is set up along the wand between the two holders, a flow of obscure electrical energy, in which one feels acted on rather than acting. (It is the same with a water-divining fork. I once tried one and was surprised at the feeling of an immense and gentle force flowing through one.) Exactly how the 'personality' of the answerer is formed is an interesting psychological problem. Hugh referred to the cases of personality-layer in certain hysterics. There is also an analogy to some extent in the momentary projection of a character by a novelist, which in the act of creation seems to assume a reality of its own, to act or speak out of the core of its own definite being, not at the writer's conscious dictation.

Our philosophy, as I have said, was Neoplatonist, with a Manichean or absolute sense of division between good and evil, matter as chaos and spirit as the formative principle. It was other-worldly, but at the same time claimed sensuousness as good and creative, as the emanation of the art-image which stabilized earthly space-time despite the efforts of evil to disintegrate, to abstract and devitalize the body. Earth was a battleground, a point of reduction below which lay chaos or hell, and which provided the basis above which lay the dimensions where the art-image was the free organizing factor. Into Norman's universe of thought, derived almost wholly from his own broodings merged with certain aspects of Nietzsche, I introduced more orderly and traditional concepts, derived from Plato, Hegel, Blake, and, among living philosophers, Alexander (who had been born and bred in Sydney), not to mention Croce and, later, Gentile. At the moment I was using these elements only to strengthen and expand Norman's conceptions; but there was inherent in them lines of thought, of dialectical apprehension, which were in time to aid me in breaking through our Neoplatonic other-worldliness and bring me back to earth. The Neoplatonists, we may recall, also were fascinated with spiritualist devices and strange phenomena.

There was a close affinity between our ideas and experiences and those of Yeats with his medium wife. Yeats himself thought so when we discussed the matter in 1928 – but that is an aspect which does not come within the scope of this book.

7 · RAY AND PHIL

WE MOVED from Kings Cross to a bungalow at Bondi, in Blair Street, which we called *Idyllia* after McCrae's book of poems. One large room, with a fireplace which winter was never cold enough to drive us to use; a front bedroom, two smaller rooms, one of which I used as a study, kitchen and bathroom. Not much ground: neither of us made an attempt to grow things. There was a hydrangea by the garden tap, with a hoard of nails to turn its flowers blue, nothing much more. We never bothered to lock doors or close windows, and never suffered from thieves, though one night a peeping-tom lurked in the front garden and threw earth in Janet's face as she ran out to find who was there.

Bondi was still undeveloped. Only in the last year of my stay did the first modest modern flats begin to rise. Opposite us were rambling sand dunes, which led up to the wild ground along the top of the cliffs, and, by thin tracks, to the Gap with its lighthouse and its barbed-wire efforts to deter suicides. (All the same Pillig, unable to bear the slings and arrows of a world that bought his plaster-casts and ignored his clay figures of workers striving against heavy burdens, went over her to join the many other broken-backed skeletons.) Here I rambled and lay in a hollow of the sun, watching a goanna flash like a miniature dragon up a tree or listening to the drowsy sough of ocean, scribbling now and then in penny notebooks:

> *Come by broken fences and shadows pocked*
> *along the blunted flanks of dunes*
> *come with the neat and rickety wagtail*
> *over the stream that the wind scallops*
> *by the stricken pine with a clot of resin*

under the flickering stone of the lizard
into the breadth of heat

Bondi.

Here where the wave wallows
in a trough of spangled seaweed
out of the skyline of windy ocean
here where the billow drives
with a long flap of whiteness over
turning and briskly turning over
to our deliberate feet

O these were nereid fingertips
that burst the bladderwrack
and there beyond the crinkling haze of glass
the pubtower squarely lifts its clock
with letters advertising BEER
instead of numerals for Time.

We bathed on the beach amid great billows, with the shark-watcher on the headland. Often in the early morning we saw several sharks hauled up, but we bathed, now and then startled by a flurry of underwater white that turned out to be only the disturbed sand, with no sudden teeth. At times the beach was so hot that it stung, and the sturdy brown girls in their grooves of sand looked as if being cooked in some crystal oven of Venus. At times the summer breeze came flowing, damp and sticky with sea-salt out of the north-east of the Pacific vast, gently at its full in the late afternoon and fading with the rapid sunset.

More violent was the southerly buster. One afternoon I noted the violet-darkening sky rushing up over rooftops to the south. I hurried to close the bathroom window and could not have had more than a half-inch left to bring the window in when the wind struck. The whole pane was shattered in fragments in my face. This wind came on us with an express-crash, with doors banging, tiles flying, and trees bending flat on all sides. The rubbish-tin went clattering half a mile off.

At the corner was a barber's shop where I listened to workers discussing races and the form of the horses. I computed that the intellectual effort put into memorizing the facts and figures about horses would have enabled each man to master a couple of languages or lay a solid basis in any one of the sciences; but one can only learn what one is interested in. And in Australia the Horse was the one great symbol of sudden riches and of events that carried one outside the deadly round of daily toil. Opposite the barber's was a dentist where I spent some hours of hellish pain. (Apart from hangovers and some chills I had no illness these years, or the thirty odd years to follow. Which I attributed to my decision not to succumb to any bodily weakness, illness being only a form of cowardice and inner division.)

For the rest of my time in Sydney I lived in Bondi. There were occasional trips, apart from the Springwood visits. We honeymooned at the National Park despite my intense but mainly dumb objection to the proceedings. There, in a large vague guest-house, I was annoyed further by a telegram from Ken and Noela that enabled everyone to know we had just been married. But the walks were pleasant and there was water to row on, with cool lush shadowy winding ways, just the place to read Keats in. I read *Endymion* carefully and found that it had a clear and powerful under-structure. The sort of discovery that gave significance to the moment of drifting change, of entry into a new warmly enclosing life. We went somewhere down the south coast too, in rooms where a piano was handy and I made my second efforts to write music – something rather difficult for a person with no sense of pitch and no knowledge of theory. We wandered on the hills. Once, as we lay among bushes at the height of noon, in a wild place, a shepherd came upon us, as abrupt and silent as Pan, standing sheer in the sky. He said nothing and went off as sharply as he had come. And one midnight of the moon we came on an out-of-the-way playground of children and swung in the swings, embraced in a garden of Fragonard delicate bawdries. Both scenes left a deep impress.

My mother with Ray and Phil had moved into a small house farther over among the dunes, with a companionable terrier Garbage. Ray had taken the studio in George Street North near the *Bulletin* offices. Phil, after a mild clash with the police, had been finally extracted from his Darlinghurst push, and was seriously grappling with the novel.

In *I'd Live* he has described Ray's studio at length and its

Friday gatherings, the giant easel Norman had given, and the hole Ray made in the wall to let in the street-lamp's light and save on candles. On the side away from the Quay one came into a disordered and gloomy dockland, with twisted streets, gasworks and timber-yards, with wool and wheat as the obvious lords of the world. And sailors thronging the pubs nearer the Quay. Ray was on the top-storey of a marine-store. He had begun by sharing with Fred Finley, an ex-student of Julian's, who had returned from studying in Paris. Fred smoked a curved pipe and wore no socks as a simple sign of his repudiation of the bourgeoisie. A fine draughtsman instinct with indignation for all the oppressors and repressors of the world, he had much influence on Ray's painting at this period. 'I have still got a good portrait of myself which he painted out at Blair Street. However, he went broke and left the studio, his place being taken by Jonah, another ex-student of Julian's. Jonah's real name was Lloyd Jones.' A fair, good-looking chap, rather inarticulate, but filled with a passion for music. I was at the farewell party, when Ray at last abandoned the effort to catch up with rent arrears. He managed to get his beloved easel out through the shop by persuading Hubble to claim it as a purchaser; the shopkeeper-landlord was placated by being told that Ray was sacrificing the thing in order to meet the rent. Less ponderous belongings, meanwhile, were dropped in bundles from the side window into a lane. We had a meal at the Italian joint across the road, where the favourite dish was called Harlot's Rump, and surprised even the familiar waitress with our high spirits and our rum-aided appetites for chops and poached eggs. Then we sat or reclined in the studio and began the serious part of the evening.

A while back Ray had taken pity on a pallid lad whom he found derelict in one of the sailor's pubs. This lad sat in a corner of the studio, entwined with a stool, and smiled in a sickly way when addressed. 'Don't bother about him,' Ray said when asked what the exhibit was. 'He's been sleeping here and living on lard. That's why he's a bit run-down. Nothing but lard. He says it's cheap and nourishing, it's cheap anyway. He's come from New Zealand to see the world, so I'm shipping him back again. He thought he could do it all on lard, but you see he can't.' The lad grinned feebly, probably stupid with fear and starvation.

Surrounded with bottles, we talked. You could tell how drunk Ray was by the angle at which his upper lip stuck out. He quarrelled with someone and insisted on a duel; the weapons were cutlass and eighteenth-century sword. The duellists slashed and clashed and bashed alarmingly while we shrank behind our chairs. Then we grabbed them and removed their weapons. Jim thundered out his laudations of beer, which redeemed men from a foul world of business-hounds and women. A policeman called from the lane. Ray wanted to throw something at him, but was restrained. At last the beer stunned me with distended belly. Some boozers trickled off. The rest of us went down the passage, broke into a store-room and took out several bales of sacking. In the studio we unwound what seemed hundreds of yards, and improvised couches. After I had been lying awhile under a spinning plaster-sky, I retched into the hessian, folded the bit over and found a new place. Next morning when we bundled the hessian together again, the vomit went into the store-room with it, plus various other articles lost by uneasy sleepers.

One day Ray and I were on the way to see Beutler. Ray had had more beer than I had. Suddenly there poured out of some hall in George Street a horde of parsons in dogcollars; some church-meeting must have been held in the hall. Ray, amazed and delighted at the sight of such a congregation of clerical black, ran up and down the gutter, shouting with laughter and peering into the faces of the men, pointing them out to the rest of the world. The clergy shamefacedly dispersed as fast as they could, and no policeman interfered.

We had another drink in an arcade, while Ray vociferated his tale. 'A marvellous sight. Thousands and thousands of bloody parsons like a plague of black beetles. There they were, crawling all over the place. And can you believe it? Nobody taking any notice, nobody rushing up with disinfectant and brooms.' He was most of all astonished that no one else seemed to think the spectacle as funny as he did. 'That was what got me down. Thousands of black beetles dressed like men and nobody taking the least bit of notice. It's a mad world. Now, if it'd been a few thousand girls with no clothes on, everyone would have been horrified. Can you believe the world is so mad?'

'You won't go to heaven when you die,' observed the broadly based barmaid.

'Haven't you read *Aucassin and Nicolette*? Sizzle with me in hell, my dear. You'd look charming in a nightgown of flame.'

'Don't talk of such things.' She wriggled. 'You make me hot all over.'

'Let's see.' He leaned over the counter. 'You don't know what colours there are in human flesh, especially in the tender portions of lovely well-fed women. There's the red of lust and the green of corruption and the gold of lickable honey. The slime of the abyss and the sun in glory.' He gave up reaching for the barmaid and tried to tell me how he'd looked at the Bondi bathers from the headland and had had a vision of colour, had seen the universe as a torrent of colour. 'No form at all.' He hammered on the counter. Form as colour, colour as form. Only the flowing of precise colour like a new world. 'Then must thou needs find out new heaven, new earth. And new hell. Shakespeare forgot that. I went one better than he did. The crisp and piercing flames.' He lunged at the barmaid again. 'I want to paint you, beautiful. I want to paint you more gigantic than a nude by Titian or Renoir. Do you know how big women are? Mountains, beaches, plains, whole continents. Enormous lumps of splendour. Everything inside them. Not only babies. Oceans and valleys, apples and birds like balloons.'

'It don't sound polite to me.' The barmaid polished a glass aggressively. 'I'm not a menagerie.'

'Fiery whoppers of women,' he enthusiastically persisted.

'Sssh,' she replied, yawning with the teeth of decay.

I was very moved. At root my notion of the Australian Renascence was Ray, Phil and myself tackling all problems of art, under the aegis of Norman-on-Olympos – just as later my revolt was to be a revolt of the sons under the golden parasol of my Mother Venus, Alma Venus of Lucretius.

Norman had shown Ray how to work in washes like Titian,

and Ray was building up a picture with neutral tints, rather heavily modelling with the paint, then washing over with transparent reds and blues. 'But how can a poor bloody boob learn to paint here without a single good picture in the art gallery? If only there were a Titian or a Rubens or a Rembrandt or a Delacroix to study and analyse.'

A while later a rich gin-sodden woman tried to take up the role of his patron. But she was mean and only on drink was she ungrudging in her outlay. She had a mysterious chauffeur, Arthur, of whom she was afraid and who controlled much of her movements. Arthur would suddenly appear in the room, wherever she was, and say in a sepulchrally lordly voice, 'Time to go, Mrs B.' And she'd go, however drunk she was. We thought he might be acting on the husband's order. But the latter, a successful bookie and speculator, was often away from Sydney, and Arthur, working on a system of propriety known only to himself, continued to act in the same way as Mrs B.'s inopportune conscience. We decided he had some blackmailing control over his dimpling, loud-voiced and rollicking mistress in her tight, well-cut dresses.

Phil was living deviously, having decided he wasn't cut out for an artist, changing from poems to stories, and stories to novels, and reading unsystematically. He was already a formidable lover, as fickle as faithful. That is, he threw all his eager self into his admiring eyes and caressing voice, and deceived himself more than the girls. Once I went into the midst of a dance given by some art students, taken by some beer drinker. The room was long and thick with the turning couples, a hundred or more of them. And there, at the heart of the maze of dancing, seated on a chair, Phil was weeping hopelessly and copiously, totally blind to the gyrating world. The dance stopped and the couples retreated to the walls and the end of the room, but Phil still sat there, in the middle of the floor, weeping. Someone had turned him down and the world was dark. This capacity to adore, however briefly, made him on the whole, then as later, a success.

In his papers after his death in 1958 I found a worm-eaten note from these years, which, though not his, has something of the emotional tone of his woomngs. By what chance he kept it, I don't know. It was the only letter he had preserved of the whole of his Australian life:

Dear Dot, Would you mind giving enclosed letters to my late dearly beloved and oblige me. Don't you think that was a rotten thing to do, what she did last night. If you were in my place what would [you] do, go back to her or keep away from her as I am doing. I'm damn sure I'm not going crying to her for another chance, it will have to be the other way about. Yours sincerely Val (1/10/24).

Perhaps Val's late dearly beloved had upset him by turning to Phil and handing over his remonstrances.

ALL THIS while there hovered before us the will-o'-the-wisp periodical in which we were to set out our ideas. Norman made some efforts to bring about a reorganization of *Art in Australia* with more space for poetry and essays, and had some hope of seeing me its literary editor. At the time he told me nothing of the discussions, probably so as not to disappoint me if things fell through and not to seem unduly pushing his son by involving him directly in the negotiations. However, after a while he dropped me a hint. Bert Stevens, who would have had to be dislodged as editor, had a good idea of what was in Norman's mind, and he fought back with all his considerable wire-pulling powers. The changed format came about and went on for two issues, with long essays by Norman and myself, and poetry by McCrae. But Bert successfully clung to the controls. Not long after he died and Leon Gellert took over his position, an incomparably better choice than myself, since I was too intolerant as Apollo's advocate for any magazine needing a broad front. *Art in Australia* lapsed back to its original nature as a magazine primarily concerned with the pictorial arts.

I had met in Dymock's bookshop an assistant named Frank Johnson, a very good-looking dark-haired young fellow with a slow persuasive voice, who was ambitiously interested in literature and who made something of a club out of his corner of the shop. There I struck several odd characters, including a sly Catholic priest whose main reading was black magic and pornography, and who liked to say lewdly blasphemous things close against one's ear. I disliked him, considering that if he was a priest he should act up to his position and if he disbelieved he should unfrock himself as publicly as possible. I discussed the possibility of a magazine with Frank, and was introduced by him to John Kirtley, a stocky brusque chap who worked for a stock exchange firm and was very keen to do some fine printing. He had bought a press and asked for some poems. Thus appeared *Fauns and Ladies*, my first book, which in more than title followed in the rear of McCrae's *Satyrs and Sunlight*. My versifying had still not recovered from its setback. Above all, an all-too-faithful admiration of McCrae's work and the feeling that it was duty to translate Norman's visual efforts straight into words had arrested my development.

It must have been in April 1922 that Frank told me I had just missed D. H. Lawrence, who had come into the shop, and asked if I'd like him to arrange a meeting. I said no. For D.H.L. was one of the writers on N.L.'s index of art villains. I had yet read little of his work, but had just glanced through *Twilight in Italy*. The powerful essay on the Tyrol Christs I had scamped, and I had been annoyed by what seemed to me a facile and superficial playing-about with Shelley's dome-of-coloured-glass and white-radiance image. Otherwise I had only a crude idea of D.H.L.'s exaltation of the blood as a resentful primitivism. Later I was sorry that I did not snatch at Frank's offer. A confrontation of D.H.L. and N.L., if it could have been managed, would have been a remarkable event. For N.L., faced with a living person, was always infinitely more supple and responsive than his absolutes on paper would suggest. And in much the same way D.H.L., who would have felt an ineffable scorn for N.L.'s paper-ideas, would have found much of himself in the discoursing man, or at least something against which to explode brilliantly.

I talked the magazine project over with Ken and Norman, and we agreed to muster our resources if Frank could provide the mechanism. How Frank raised the cash and paid the bills, I never knew. He made no complaints and we were only too glad to avoid such matters. Smilingly he agreed to all our propositions. N.L. did a number of line-decorations and gave us stories, as well as our title, *Vision*. Ken, though he did not at any time share our fanatical universe, in his own way drew a certain sustenance from our ideas and enthusiasms. The impact loosened up his form and extended his range just at the moment when he needed to grow beyond the packed mosaic-efforts of his somewhat static early verse. And in many of his new poems, *The Embarcation for Cythera* or *Thieves Kitchen* and the like he ventured into the Lindsay world though keeping his eighteenth-century touch of tact and courtesy even among the 'good roaring pistol-boys, brave lads of gold'. While in *Realities*, dedicated to N.L.'s etchings, he made the direct tribute, as in *Earth-Visitors*.

A preliminary bout was tried in the February issue of *Art in Australia*, 1923. There an essay by George Pitt-Rivers (who had broken Margot's doors down with axes) set out the thesis that primitive art was sexless or at least not 'of an inciting nature' and had its most important function in defining clan-badges; clan-badges led on to heraldry, which as a chivalric expression could be opposed to the modern world of money values; art last flourished under the Ming Dynasty. A more confused and narrow expression of the social function of art and its integrative effects could hardly have been made. Norman, who had already had an encounter with Pitt-Rivers over the dinner-table at Springwood, replied in the magazine. 'So we are to turn away from *Antony and Cleopatra*, the frankest revelation of sex ever uttered, and the Seventh symphony, the greatest saturnalia of god-drunken happiness the earth possesses, to a Papuan fetish because its sex reticence could be safely introduced into a suburban drawing-room.' He rejected a social purpose which was to maintain 'a crude symbolism to define ruling-class caste systems'.

In the same issue I had an essay on the functiion of lyric poetry in the same vein. The poetic image gives form to experience and rhythmically organizes the sensory basis of consciousness; so poetry is spiritually the body. Lyric poetry must be most sensuously definite and hence cannot deal with abstractions like humanity or justice; 'such concepts are the furthest removed from poetry which expresses the highest humanity when it finds the highest image of beauty.' I also had an essay on music, which I shall deal with when I come next to Beutler.

The first issue of *Vision* appeared in May with a Faun leaping after the butterfly psyche on its cover. I was enchanted at first sight; surely this would do the job. Then I noticed that my translation of two epigrams by Plato had had their lines messed

about, and I was filled with a rending sense of failure and confusion, all out of proportion to the minor mishap. Looking
back, I think what I secretly felt was a mess up that involved
everything in the magazine. The private illusion, kept warm
by our endless discussion among ourselves, was hard to sustain
when a comprehensive appeal was made to the outer world.
Janet guessed that I was upset. She suggested going to the new
local cinema. We went out; and as we neared the place, I felt
an immense revulsion from contact with other people, even to
the extent of sitting among them in the dark. To buy a ticket
and go into the hall was an ordeal I could not face. We quarrelled over some point so irrelevant that I cannot remember
what it was. At the last moment, as we stood before the box-
office, I walked off and let her go in alone. This sort of petty
squabbling was very unusual for us; I cannot recall anything
quite like it before or after. And that all the more underlines
the wordless yet violent upheaval that was going on inside me
and that I had managed to dispel next morning when I gratefully woke at Janet's side.

The press reception was kinder than we deserved. 'Naked as
Manly Beach in December,' said the *Bulletin*. 'Its founders
think that the world is ripe for a renaissance, and that Australia
is the most likely place for it to originate in. *Vision*, which is
certainly not lacking in exuberance and the joy of life, is to be
its official organ,' *Sydney Morning Herald*. 'Australia has its first
quarterly worthy of the adjective "literary". Its pages embalm
some of the glorious madness of youth,' Sydney *Daily Mail*.
'Unlike anything else previously printed in Australia. To file
Vision in 1923 is a surer speculation than to store whisky in
1915,' *Sunday Times* (Sydney). 'Written from the standpoint of
the Dionysian intoxicated with life, and drunken with the glory
of youth and its relatively simple pleasures. The literary pages
will prove a delight to many, a source of irritation to a few dis-
cerning souls, and a source of annoyance to a few undiscrimi-
nating prudes,' *New Outlook*. 'An important and welcome
venture in Australian literary development,' *Evening Sun* (Melbourne). Not that the expected wowser voice was unheard.
Typical was the plaint of the Melbourne *Age*, 'It is doubtful
that there are enough readers in Australia suffering from satyri-

asis and nymphomania to add sufficiently to its circulation. The contributors wish to vindicate the possession of youth, but some of their work will most gratify the pitiable senility that smacks its Paphian chops at the voluptuous representation of sex, and assumes the leer of some of the satyrs in the illustrations.' Several readers wrote in to ask why we had omitted the Biblical quotation about a People without Vision being doomed to perish; and all copies sent to England were strictly ignored.

It was certainly something new for Australia to have a literary magazine that thus discussed itself:

Vision; 'The First Australian Quarterly worthy of the adjective "literary",' *The Daily Mail* (Sydney).

Geographical Note: – The area of Australia is 2,974,581 square miles.

Can we lend you a pair of spectacles?

That depends. We may not like you. *Vision* will not lend spectacles to anyone.

But if you are tired of glutinous chatter about Chelsea artists – or reports from passionate spinsters on their souls – or studies in the rectangular nude by futurist tradesmen – or the poetic dropsy of the weekly Celts – or the smacking honesty of the monthly sea-dogs – or the album-cleverness of the young ladies and gentlemen who write *vers libre* –

If in short you are tired of being modern, and want to be alive –

Then take heart. *Vision* may help you yet. *Vision* is the only magazine in the Continent with a definite literary standard. *Vision* will show you what is true and what is false. *Vision* will bring you gaiety and indignation. You will probably not like it – at first.

But keep on. Thousands have succeeded. In six months, *Vision* has a circulation higher than that of any other quarterly of its class in Australia. That proves there must be a large number of strong and determined persons able to resist it long enough to like it. Keep on. You will like it, too. *Vision* will lend you spectacles to see.

Vision is published on February 1, May 1, August 1, November 1, except when they fall on Christmas Day, Good Friday, or days of national penance and humiliation.

What wit we had, however, came principally from Slessor.

We attacked all forms of Modernismus and abstraction in art, and set out our creed, in each of the four numbers. But we did not effectively recruit new strengths and tended merely to repeat ourselves.* I feel that the effect must have been weaker after the fourth issue than after the first. But in fact the publication was so successful that Frank halted the quarterly form with the intention of turning the thing into a bimonthly. As usual when this sort of thing is done to a magazine, the result was fatal; he did not manage to raise the necessary capital in time.

As examples of our criticism I may cite some of N.L.'s writings. He attacked James Joyce as a Christian Father, the anti-Rabelais, the voice of blind sex-repression, 'not an emancipated intellect,' but 'that cramped and fettered thing, the automaton of evasion himself,' discrediting the art-image which by arousing the conviction of beauty vitalized all images of passion and action, and thus stabilized and expanded life. What we meant by beauty, passion and action, he set out in his gay fantasy of the Land of the Hyperboreans, the Free Spirits (in the last resort, his patrons and the buyers of books by Ken and myself), who responded to the art-image, as compared with Man, under which term he subsumed

Those which make a pretty pretence that robbing and slaying, and an insensate greed for goods and gold, are expressed by him in a noble zeal for patriotism and progress. They are those which give the name of Purity to that picketfence which encloses the studbull within him and which allows him to protest in public that he never does that sort of thing in private ... It is because he looks so tame, so meek, so much a good fellow, that we are sometimes deceived into accepting this disguise, and believe the world secure from his destructive lusts. But we have only to turn to his actions in mass; his collective impulse expressed in his commercial greeds; his activity in manufacturing implements of destruction, his last war, and the war he is now preparing for, to realize that this animal, for all his rituals in religion, his

---

*Looking through the issues, I find Dulcie Deamer, Louis Lavater, Colin Wills, Les Robinson, Blamire Young, Dorothea MacKellar, Andrew MacCunn outside our close circle; but they are hardly enough to balance things.

conventions in sociology, his prattle of humanitarianism, and all the surface effects of civilization in city streets and civil life, is just as savage and dangerous as he was a million years ago. It is not *he* who faces this truth, my friends the Hyperboreans; he is too imbecile and complacent to realize a single evidence of his being. Its weight and depression of knowledge fall upon us, who know that beauty and happiness exist as an inner spirit we call joy, and which we seek always to express by our response to the passion which recreates life upon earth.

I quote here at some length to bring out how strong still in N.L. (and in myself) was the violent revulsion from the war and how deeply this underlay our position. Also it shows how profoundly social in origin was the repudiation of a social message.

The best things in *Vision* were Norman's stories and Ken's poems; I was nowhere in comparison. 1923 saw also a *Vision* anthology, *Poetry in Australia*, with a preface written by Norman, except for the remarks about English poets which were mine. The preface declared that poetry in England had lost its way. Then, while denying nationalism in art, it stated that England had become historically the home of poetry in the post-Roman world, 'a locality in universal consciousness'. There, poetry was the 'governing symbol of Mind', the underlying force of Order. If English poetry collapsed, all that England stood for would also collapse – unless Australia took over. The ambiguous use of Order here identified, at least from one angle, English poetry and the English state (including its imperialist phase); we see then the confusion nullifying the rejection of war and greed in the Hyperborean fantasy.

The collection added little to *Vision* except that it did extend the scope of acceptable expression by drawing in poets like Brennan and Shaw Nielson – though not in a way to disturb our stated positions. The reviews were the usual mixed bag. 'Abounding vitality and vigour . . . sticklers for form,' and all that: 'something like a renaissance in Australian poetry', *Sydney Morning Herald*. 'The most important collection of poems which Australia has yet seen, a milestone in Australian letters . . . Gone are the days of the poems of the gum trees, the kookaburra, and the stock-rider,' The *Daily Mail* (Brisbane). But the protests tended to swell. 'Dwells in a morbid way on imaginary episodes of sordid types,' The *Argus*. 'An otherwise charming volume is spoilt by the fleshly poetry of two men, Kenneth Slessor and Jack Lindsay. The youthful indiscretions of Swinburne pale before the determination of these two to be improper,' The *Register* (Adelaide). The excluded poets came out strong. 'Infernal loftiness towards men who knew and know this land ... Mind is merely fleshly matter,' Dora Wilcox in the *Daily Telegraph*. 'Ring the changes on the one theme of animal lust ... No book of verse so dirtied with the paws of the primitive beast has ever before been published in Australia,' McKee Wright in the *Bulletin*. 'Laborious literary dungbeetles. Sydney City Council employs youths with brush and pan to remove ordure from the streets. Why employ youth to preserve the odour of ordure?' Bert Stevens in the *Bystander*, getting his own back. We reprinted the attacks in our columns. Another joke (of Slessor's) was to use up a spare page at the back of No. 3 by printing the opening of Chapter One of Casanova's *Memoirs* with the statement that we meant to print the whole, as well as various other classics. We calculated that we should have to run several hundred years to complete the serial.

May had seen the appearance of *Fauns and Ladies*, 'the first book printed on the Hand Press of J. T. Kirtley, at 28 Burton Street, Kirribilli.' At least I was happy to have this handprinted book of my verse on handmade paper, with N.L.'s woodcuts. Despite my suppressed qualms 1923 seemed to be marking a large advance.

This year also N.L. was working on his last important pen-and-inks, a series of large and complex compositions, each about 30 by 21 inches. In these elaborate works he showed his extreme virtuosity with the pen. I watched him fill in the darker spaces by skipping the pen across the paper while chuckling and talking. There was still something of his sense of direct character which had given force to his pre-1918 work. After this, turning more and more to etching and concentrating on decorative effects and textural refinements, on suavity of bounding line and odalesque luxury, he receded from the earthy tangs, the roughnesses and the immediacy of character, which made his pre-1918 work essentially Australian despite the range of his subject matter through the centuries. For me then this last set of drawings is the climax of his work. Not that

I thought that way at the time. The etchings (abandoning the dramatic effects carried over for a while from the pen-and-ink world into works like *Who Comes?*) seemed to me then the pure expression of beauty, even though my own bias was drawing me towards drama.

But I would falsify the experience of those years if I stressed these elements of dawning dissidence and did not testify to the extraordinary happiness, the idyllic fullness, of the weeks spent at Springwood. Swimming in the dam with its guardian naiad, wandering in the gulleys of gums, watching N.L. at work on a plate. Mostly he scratched with a fine needle on the wax coating, looking through a magnifying glass. He had given up rouletting or such devices as too coarse and set down at needle-point each of the myriad dots with which he built up his tones. The strain of thus staring through a magnifying glass at a copper surface which glinted back at him with each removal of wax did not affect his eyes. Sometimes I helped him put a plate in the acid bath or pull a proof. (All the editions were printed off by Rose.) He had still not lost his interest in, or respect for, nature. On a walk he carefully noted colour effects and showed me bits of bark with delicate harmonies which he studied for his water-colours.

In the evening we sat in the water-colour studio, and often he read a story of chapters from one of his many novels in MSS. To get a sense of the pattern in a novel he used to arrange the chapters on the floor, noting the positions of those with related aspects of the theme, the thickness of the piles, and so on. He read, for example, *The Cautious Amorist*, which he had written in part to assuage his unending hatred of curates and in part to parody De Vere Stacpoole's *The Blue Lagoon* which someone had lent him as he was convalescing from one of his recurrent illnesses. Reading with shouts of laughter and an excellent mimetic energy. (Years later he must have turned this MS up in a drawer and decided he might as well make a few pence from it. Published here and in the U.S.A., it sold in millions; and when Hollywood made a film of it they did their best to turn it out like *The Blue Lagoon*. When I was in the army in 1941, I wrote to N.L. that he was one of the two most popular authors read by the soldiers.)

I used to put against the wall the works he had done since

my last visit, and study them for hours. Hoping a poem would leap out of the deep-sea waters, a curving anadyomene. He gave me one in faint blue-greens of Aphrodite uncurling from the foam with attendant sirens, for which I had written some lines that we printed in *Vision* and *Poetry*. The poem was in fact my best effort to define the N.L. image coming up out of Sydney Harbour and winging to Springwood, as I made explicit in a revised version:

> The dimpling harbour rolls with frills of foam.
> Light's finger drills in water's navel-rings.
> The seagull sinks beside his Pinchgut home
> with folded wings, and, watching, gently swings.
>
> Then in a sun-pulse scattering breaks a shower
> with delicate ferns of mist, and, as it clears,
> through spinning wheels of blue uncurls a flower,
> her wave-eyed face, and each long limb appears.
>
> The reluctant veils drift downward. Arms are seen,
> wringing bright hair. The ivory face at last
> securely poised in wings of gold and green,
> and tilted nipples, as more veils are cast,
>
> down to the loins and long loose opening thighs
> with dainty seaweed worn for virgin badge:
> O bubble of fireburst, down I drop my eyes
> to small feet feeling for the foam's frail edge.
>
> The shift of blossoms at length subsides and lies
> heaped at her feet, and with her head thrown back
> she turns her gaze towards the silver skies
> and rises tiptoe on the wind's thin track.
>
> When, look, to guide her straight to Springwood's height,
> come sirenwomen broadwinged from the South.
> They cluster round; and as they start their flight
> I saw a birdgirl kiss her on the mouth.

Thus set in its proper time and place, with Springwood substituted for Olympus, the poem seems to me to attain a certain value; but it was of the essence of my confusion between experience and the image, between national or other roots and the universal element, that I did not then make even this simple correlation, thus leaving the image wandering in a vague inane.

Now and then I found in a drawer or lost at the back of a shelf, say, Hokusai's print of a Wave, one of Blake's Thornton woodcuts, or a Rembrandt self-portrait etching, which Norman promptly told me to take. Such things represented the period when Lionel's art interest and ideas had been a part of Springwood; now there was nothing that aroused N.L.'s scorn more than the aesthete admiring a Ming pot – a figure that keeps popping up in his writings as the type most patently evading the realities of art and life (i.e. Lionel).

At times I slept on the verandahs of the main house, at times in a small room attached to the large studio. Under the bed in this room was a large tin box. One day I asked what was in it and Norman said it held the wash-drawings illustrating Casanova. He lugged it out and I eagerly went through the careful and vigorous drawings that brought the eighteenth century to full and detailed life. He had lost interest in them and was unmoved by my insistence that something ought to be done about them. They had been left in London after his return with pleurisy, and somehow they held for him the stigma of 'failure' in assaulting Europe, a defeat that rankled and underlay much of his rationalized accounts of European decadence and surrender to primitivism or abstraction in art. The fact that the art world he had encountered in London was the dull and foundering one of Orpen and Strang and the rest of those directionless academics did not matter for him; to have conquered that world would have been a pointless triumph. The forces, from Cézanne and Van Gogh to the Cubists and Futurists, whom he saw as coming up over that dead world, seemed to him to have no elements whatever of revitalization; and so he turned utterly away, as from a monstrous thing.

Once a bushfire came swinging our way, blown by a westerly out of the dusty continent. An orange-red haze on the horizon, darkening with smoke; rustling, as it came up, like a great waterfall. We hastily began burning off as much as we could of the dry grass and undergrowth all round the house and studios. Then rushed round with leaf-switches to beat out the flames as they came leaping and creeping towards us. A swirl of grey-black and a ghostly fire of transparent red sparking and bursting and going out with an acrid whiff of smoke. The sun shrouded and lost or showing momently like a burst and bloodblown insect that cleaves to the wall it dies on. In Sydney the tar would be melting and nobody would want to leave the bars of cool beer.

Afterwards we went in and played the *Siegfried* fire-music, noting how true it was. Noting too the likeness of fire and water in their sweeping and gushing noises.

9 · FITZGERALD AND MARLOWE

ANOTHER POET met about the time of *Vision* was R. D. Fitzgerald, who was training as a surveyor, a tall, somewhat clumsy fellow with an engaging humility and a ready mind. I liked him, and perhaps it was only my liking that made me feel sure his verses would get better. At that time they were rather tame. He did quickly develop, and so he was one of the few cases in which a wish of this kind came true. We used to meet in Mockbells, and Bob himself has written about this drab and useful place, with its fly-specked waitresses emerging from vague screens. 'A gentleman named Mockbell established a line of coffee-shops in Sydney. They were mostly cellars dignified by the title of basements; and though they were lit by murky electric globes, not gas, I feel sure it must have been these haunts that Kenneth Slessor had in mind when he wrote of "the gas-lit cellules of virtuous young men." Certainly we were all virtuous enough then (our pockets demanded it); and Mr Mockbell encouraged virtue by charging only fourpence for a tin jug from which you could squeeze two, or with luck two and a half cups, of passable coffee. And you could stay as long as you liked at the marble-topped tables, at ease in good chairs or on leather-upholstered seats with backs safely to the wall, quite unlike those stiff tightly packed little cubicles that constrict you everywhere today. Did everything good like that go out in the twenties, or was it only youth? At any rate it was to one such cellule (in Castlereagh Street, near King Street) that Jack Lindsay invited me early in 1923 to meet Slessor (for the first time) and himself (for the second or third) to discuss the newly projected and now memorable journal *Vision*. They had considered (with some misgivings) that I might perhaps be admitted as a contributor. Thereafter it became habitual for me to frequent the place between 5 and 6 o'clock in the afternoon. There was always company.'

Phil has given a picture of Fitz that I cannot better. 'Impatience is his keynote, an impatience with flesh and bone that withholds the luxury of dissolution, the return to earth. In life, too, was he impatient, boisterously thumping his fist on the marble-topped tables of Mockbells, or the linoleum covering of a bar, while he insisted that *Vision* found a new school, the pre-Kiplingites, escape from the modern mathematics of verse, from the intellectual cottonwooling of emotion. Huge, lean, gaunt Fitz, with his bright dark eyes and tousled hair, striding down Pitt Street – I can see him now – a theodolite tossed carelessly over one shoulder, roaring suddenly at sight of a friend, and swinging round, theodolite and all, so that had he been of ordinary height, he'd have brained at least a dozen passers-by; Fitz bellowing in the Angel or some other pub, or trying to fold his long legs under a restaurant table.'

Phil himself had been helping to pack, post and deliver copies of *Vision*, 'to oversee printing and binding, and to try and cadge advertisements. It was exciting, but I made no money, except an occasional quid from Frank when I grew desperate.' Frank himself had started a new bookshop with Malcolm of Gilmour's.

Fitz, after Phil's death in 1958, described his meeting with him at Mockbells, when he himself was just short of twenty-one and Phil about seventeen. 'Four years is a big gap at that age; and he seemed very much younger than the rest of us and a little subdued – it must have been the only time in his ebullient life such a thing could have been said of him – in the company of his eldest brother's associates. That did not continue for long, however. Ken and Jack had *Vision* matters to see to and left early, while Phil and I, at loose ends, both stayed on; and then from a mind packed with literary ideas and knowledge of books, and faster than anyone I had ever heard who yet articulated every syllable, Phil began to talk. He had had very little schooling, I should say; so the years which most of us had wasted loafing through school, he had occupied in reading and living. He talked fascinatingly and confidently, yet I would not say precociously; for his views were already very much those of his more mature years, his outlook formed.' And he notes Phil's charm. 'It arose out of his complete unselfconsciousness in conversation, and it won him the widest and most varied collection of friends it would have been possible to have.' He cites an example of this charm at work:

In 1926, having qualified the previous year as a land surveyor, I set up in a private practice; and Phil found my small office in Pitt Street a convenient city headquarters, whence in my slack periods – they were chronic – we adjourned often enough to the Angel or still, it might be, to Mockbell's. Then in 1927 a sound, quiet man, Athol Blair, joined me in partnership. Phil came up to the office one morning after some all-night binge to borrow two bob. Broke, as we all were, he was generally a bit shabby; so was I; but this time he was also dishevelled, unshaven, beer-eyed and even dirty. Blair was shocked – concerned too about the possible impression on clients (if any). 'You must get rid of that hobo,' he said. 'All right,' said I, 'I'll take him down to the pub.' But something called me away for half an hour; and when I came back Phil was talking animatedly and Athol was listening engrossed. It was Athol who lent him the two bob; the hobo's visits to the office continued.

On one later visit Phil invited Athol to a party and Athol accepted; so I had to stop him from going; telling him in concise terms just how the party might finish up. I always dodged those parties myself; Bohemia, beyond the sea-coast, had no attractions for me. The beer, girls and poetry which composed Phil's Bohemia were well enough, but a pinch of squalor thrown in seemed to me an ingredient to be avoided. Perhaps I was wrong: Phil, I think, found it a necessary part of experience; so Athol could be right in never (I suspect) quite forgiving me.

And he adds, with genuine insight:

'Magnificent!' was his favourite word. 'Magnificent!' he would exclaim of some verse; 'It's a magnificent piece of work!' of some new or old book or a painting at a show. Your lukewarm critic can damn or commend half-heartedly, and either way the best in the writer is damped, while mere uninformed praise stultifies; but confidence and enthusiasm are infectious and a spur. Zests for life, laughter, art, all came to the surface of his personality; and if underneath there were

certain grinding torments and apprehensions, his natural exuberance
overcame them. He hated the fact that he was not of better stature
and physique, so he neglected bodily health and needs almost venge-
fully. He suffered inarticulate jealousies and rages against fortune,
then punished this weakness too by building it into drama. (*Meanjin*,
3, 1958.)

Fitzgerald and Slessor were the poets who were to carry on in
their own ways the impetus begotten by *Vision* and in the 1930s
to dominate Australian poetry, lifting it definitely to a new
level of intellectual responsibility and ending once for all the
reign of the slipshod, the pedestrian and the emotionally inchoate.

I have said that my own verse had gone backward. In one
respect, however, 1923 saw me gain a new start. I felt an
impulse one day to try some blank verse and scribbled a few
rough scenes, one of which I liked till I noticed that its keyline
('to cleanse my bosom of the perilous stuff') was lifted straight
from *Macbeth*. However, in the scribblings I did feel the perilous
stuff being cleansed from my bosom, and so I persisted. The
result was a short verse-play *The Death of Marlowe* (based inevitably at this date on the early interpretation of his end.) In the
verse here I got something of the wild bar-talkers from Randolph Bedford to Ray in his rhodomontades:

> 'You cast your treasons where the world's pricked ear
> is stretcht to catch the echo.'
> 'Ha, there, stinkards,
> mark you my words, for I am Moses' son
> prophesied by the Muscovite heretics,
> foretold as coming on the roundpaunched moon
> then hooped and ribbed alike malmsey-cask,
> I sitting astride; and from a spigot unstuck
> drench all the earth in wine, till everyone
> drown in that bounty. Men shall float facedown
> as sign they died still drinking, but the wenches
> on their backs as they were wont to do in life.
> Virgins shall, nay but I forgot, that time
> there shall be no more virgins.'

'Come away.'
'John said: There shall be no more sea. But I
say that in heaven there shall be no more virgins,
I'll see to that myself . . .'

In comparison with my other work, there was a direct and assured note, which showed me where my bent lay. The seed of all my best coming work, in verse or in the novel, lay in this playlet.

Also, as a result of my topical verses, my song-writing for Beutler, my sense of relief through *Vision*, in May 1924 I wrote a large number of lyrics (some of which were collected in 1928 as *The Passionate Neatherd*), which though showing derivations from McCrae and de la Mare as well as Herrick and others, had a note also my own. I cite here *The Sleeping Beauty* because it expressed our sense of liberating anciently lost essences and recapturing the grand tradition detested by the moderns:

I shut my eyes and kissed. The dark place tingled
with a thin twitter of strings
turning the silence edged with glamour,
a harp's twinged mutterings.

I kissed. The quiet was brayed with sound,
life clanked with buckled stride,
and faint with twitching past the centuries,
women's voices cried.

The hoarded silences crashed in my ears;
but ere her breath returned,
her lips, in that cold body alone alive,
on my lips burned. *

*It is hard to find any European or American analogy for our *Vision* positions. Emotionally we were close to Dadaism and early Surrealism in our violent rejection of the society that had begotten the 1914-18 war; but aesthetically we took the opposite viewpoint. In Europe it was possible to identify the bourgeoisie with effete 'traditional culture'; in Australia that was impossible. On the contrary we identified it with a total ignorance of tradition. (The still embryonic state of industrialism in Australia must also be taken into account. The 1914 war had given a stimulus to heavy industry, but not till the next world war did this become decisive.)

10 · HUGH McCRAE

THE NEWS that Hugh McCrae was coming up from Melbourne stirred and excited us. He arranged to meet me one afternoon outside the *Bulletin* office. Though I had seen only a few snaps of him, at some distance I recognized the poet magnifico picking his way through the plebeian street as though dodging agilely among trees. No doubt I saw him through the transforming prism of his poems; but I felt that he came in a sort of flight along the human pavement and was himself one of his cloven-hooved satyrs, afraid that the drab beings around would blink and see him for what he was, turning with jealous bitterness on his ear-pricked woodland-self.

Norman had described him as Roman-looking and had given me a snap in which he stood draped in the toga of a blanket, changing a suburban backyard into a garden of Julio-Claudian Rome. Certainly in face and build Hugh had much of the grand manner; yet the image of the street-bewildered satyr persists. Hugh was tall and straight-standing, but as I remember that straightness it seems rather of a wild creature startled amid the bushes and suddenly coming up with lifted head and sensitive nostrils to look into the shadows for a dangerous presence. Yes, with his long Scottish head he looms up with a sharp slitted vigilance in his eyes and with pointed ears; and the sudden smile lifts his eyebrows in angular circumflexes of satiric whimsicality and lengthens his intrusive nose. I see him sticking his head out of myrtle thickets, anxious to retreat from the strain of using words in everyday small talk triviality, without their full sensuous weight and their possibilities of explosive fantasy being explored – anxious to bound off to his pals the sweaty centaurs biting the dryad's splendid knees, the lord of everything except the deadening sphere of money.

With a hearty laugh that first day he scooped me up from the rackety street and carried me into the shadowy refuge of the nearest pub, into a grotto of bottles inhabited by a properly plump barmaid, into the rumbustious asylum of his gaiety. We arrived by the last train at his house in the mountains, below Springwood, still laughing.

He told me later that he had been terrified of the meeting; and well he might have been. I was portentously an admirer, ready to pour on him all the lavish generalizations in which I then splashed. Hugh hated abstractions and generalizings with all the intense 'negative sensibility' (in Keats's sense) that made him the poet he was. He loved Norman as man and artist, drawing deeply from both aspects, but Norman's theorizings made his hair stand painfully on end and increased intolerably his itch to bolt into the green places of intuitive thought. Once I met him in the street with a notebook under my arm. He took the notebook and casually opened it, then shut it with a bang, afraid that the vipers of the glimpsed prose might strike out at him. 'How on earth can you write such things?' he asked with a mixture of awe and derision. How on earth indeed?

I didn't come to know him as well as I'd have liked, despite many happy and uproarious meetings. Those cursed abstractions stood between us with their flaming swords. But though Hugh was a thousandfold right in sheering off from our domineering ideas, there was that in him which shrank from any conscious effort to grasp the principles of art. Therein lay both his strength and his weakness. His way of pulling a hood down over his revelling mind as soon as anything like general principles threatened to look him in the eye, had its use. It enabled him to carry on despite his many difficulties and above all to evade the crushing impact of a philistine society on his lyric gift. It enabled him to conserve that gift in an art of remarkable purity, but at the same time it inhibited his development.

That is why my first image of his rapid movement as a flight had its rightness. He was indeed a creature of shy wildwood sensibility, for whom laughter was both a cavern of secrecy and a bridge over which he could venture in momentary safety among men. He was only really at his ease with women, preferably with one woman, and a lovely one at that. But a woman, any sort of woman, even a plain one at a pinch. In everyday life, apart from his uncounted love affairs, his fancy peeped from coverts as among the leaf-sheens and moon-drifts of his verse, and then hid itself. Fleeing alike the burden of a conscious purpose (which he took as an imposition on life and art) and the vulgarities of a world of petty greeds, he felt that his only safe course was the small island of many delights on which he was finally marooned.

But if he feared the larger issues, he loved to brood over and discuss all the incidental felicities of verse, and gave much thought to delicacies of texture and components of imagery. Once he told me that the lines he liked best as music in his writings were those about the melancholy brook murmuring below th' harmonious pines. He brought many enduring things into Australian poetry. Technically, with him as with Brennan, it came of age, ceased to be parochial and shallow, achieved a complex unity of form and content, and found the rich relations of sound and rhythm that utter the vital patterns of the life of man, the organic life. Part of this new unity was a deepened grasp of the pictorial image, to which he gave a sensuous fullness, aided by both his own art studies and his enjoyment of N.L.'s work.

He had gone up the Blue Mountains, to Blaxland, to be near Norman, but things did not work out particularly well. There was still a good distance between them; and N.L., while pleased with a companionable visitor now and then, did not like to feel crowded in by a friend some dozen miles away. Hugh's cottage was a humdrum place in a lost wilderness of gums, dry and stony. On the morning after our first arrival there he took me behind the galvanized-iron water-tank and asked me to be careful what I said in front of the family; he did not want too many bacchanalian echoes of our pub-crawl to upset them. Nancy with her worried face certainly had enough problems of her own in making ends meet and wondering whom Hugh had last embraced. The girls had a remote charm, but lacked the vivacity I had felt sure would belong to McCrae's dryad daughters. Mahdi was given to spasms of poetic inspiration whenever washing time came near. But they

had a close friendly feeling for their father; and when he pur-
posely wheezed as he sat down, they chorused, 'You're getting
old, Mac!' It was a family ritual.

At times he could not control the fear aching in his bones.
Once, after walking down an avenue of trees, he was limp with
sweat and could hardly stand. He had been afraid all the while
that the trees would fall on him, and even more afraid of
admitting it. A friend told me how he was once sitting with
three or four chaps in a pub-corner. Hugh came in and ordered
a drink without seeing the others. Then he turned, saw them,
and bolted in panic from the bar. Later, meeting my friend,
he told him that he hadn't had enough money to pay for a
round of drinks, and so had hurried off. But I have no doubt
that he was at that moment unprepared for being drawn into
the everyday net of personal relations and succumbed to an
uncontrollable impulse of flight.

There was also an element of suspicion in him, linked with
the fears. Norman asked me to correct the proofs of the very
costly edition of *Idyllia* he printed, with several original etchings, to help Hugh's finances. I queried one of the lines in *Pan-
tera*: 'If once a phantom . . . I or you?' *Is* seemed a more likely
reading than *If*. Hugh decided that I was trying to rewrite his
poem, and was in a rage with me for a while. (I had probably
deepened the offence by printing *Is* in *Poetry in Australia*, unable
to find out from him in time what was correct.)

There could be a momentary hardness in his eyes, as if he
felt overbearingly his aloofness and wanted to take his revenge,
a claymore-whirl round his tall granitic highland figure. Then
he gave his great head-thrown-back laugh, his thigh-slap, and
no one could help joining in. As I have said, he felt at full ease
only with women. I base this statement on what more than one
girl has told me of him. One for instance, with whom Phil later
in London had an affair, provided many stories of his delightful companionship. After making love to her, he used to leap
about the room, beating down the spirits of unborn babies spilt
from his seed and making sure that they didn't invade her.

His whimsicalities in writing were at times pointless except
for some excessively private joke; but in many of his letters he
was almost as much himself as he was in his best lyrics or in

his games with a girl. In later years he brought his verse more and more down to the world around him, but lost much of his sensuous pictorial clarity by surrendering to the zig-zag movements of his attentive processes. In 1939 Fitz had reviewed a book of his, which he praised at the expense of the earlier satyr poems, referring to the centaurs as rocking-horses. Hugh replied in a letter which remarkably reveals the odd movement of his mind, the definite line of thought under the nervous leaps and tangential reactions. We see here both his powerful poetic faculty and the almost-terrifying anguish of his uncertain loneliness:

When I began writing all verses wore bustles over their arses and skirts down to the earth; so it became easy for me to cause a stir with my Cupid and nymphae who'd give you the collywobbles to see them stripped. In this way it wasn't hard to make a rep., and my Dad said so – unhappily – becos he feared blots upon his 'scutcheon which eventually arrived fast and thick.

My rocking-horses too, which you imply, stop in one place, while flesh-an'-blud nags flash like Hell to the post. You have winners to prove it, Ken Slessor, the same . . .

The worst is the bastards keep on rocking . . . They keep on rocking millions of hours after the race has been won. How would you, loathing them, like to see them tippetty-upping and downing all thro' your life, in sunshine or rain?

When I get letters from people I don't like, but which must be answered, I turn the envelopes face-downward. Promptly forget 'em.

But rocking-horses! Nightmare images! fastened in the brain.

One has to serve one's apprenticeship – learn to manage the pen. It took me all my young life to graduate half-way; and still, I'm 'flummoxed in a ditch.' Can any of us grow tall enough for our approbation?

Sometimes I imagine myself an elephant, washing my royal body with moonlight and never getting any forrader. In Mauretania, I think? But I mustn't say Mauretania. I mustn't postulate a classical education even in yourself.

Actually I'm the ignorantest, most un-universitied creature on earth.

C. J. Dennis admired S[atyrs] and S[unlight]. I saw him, alive, for the last time (looking like Dante reflected from a distorting glass) in a hutch of the Melbourne *Herald* office against a passage with a door constantly opening and shutting. He said, 'Why don't you do the stuff you used to? Once upon a time, you were on top.' P'raps he only wanted me to vail my crest . . . truth or no truth.

And so on. Deeply hurt, Hugh uses the images of repetitive hell, which Fitz had imputed to his poetry, in a fierce rejection of the charge. With Dennis saying the exact opposite of Fitz, he brings the nightmare repetition-image down to its real place, in the newspaper world of lies, sensationalism and money values. He could make a ferocious statement in this veiled and intuitive way, but he would never had dared to face consciously what he was saying. Dennis (the sentimentally successful poet) is a denizen of hell, with his cheap envy, but the reflected Dante is Hugh himself, with that noble face which could go wooden or crinkle into a mad smile.*

As an appendix to this chapter I am able to add some notes, and verses that were made by Hugh for a girl he was in love with in the 1920s. As I was writing about him, I recalled her, sent her a letter, and received back a notebook full of his drawings and scribbles, poems by Heine copied out, a passage from Beaumont and Fletcher's *The Captain*, Act IV, a money order sent her at the Moulin Rouge (when she was in Paris) for a million pounds, signed Hugoest McCrae, and many charming fooleries. He writes her *The Deserted Lover*:

> *I have not died, nor withered yet:*
> *And, if thou shouldst return,*
> *There's fire enough to still beget*
> *Young giants, when we burn*
> *Tall flames together, fiercely thrown;*
> *Until the final gust*
> *Wafts us, immortal, from our own*
> *Too perishable dust.*

'Hugoest to Huguette.' Or he parodies Poe's *Raven*:

---

*In 1925 I sent a copy of *Satyrs and Sunlight* to Walter de la Mare, who replied appreciatively; I believe that he also wrote to Hugh and that they corresponded quite frequently.

> *It is twelve o'clock:*
> *I shall hear her knock*
> *In the worst of a storm's uproar*
> *I shall pull her through the door*
> *I shall have her evermore!*

The notes are mainly made up of small humorous sketches, so that they need to be reproduced in facsimile. Thus, he writes, 'Nobody loves me . . . Even the Pubs run away from me at six o'clock' – with a sketch of a chuckling pub in flight from a wildly pursuing Hugh. He often calls himself Needleface.

I still love you, and can never stop loving you. I see your eyes constantly; and, sometimes, they come between me and the pages of the book I am reading. At other times, I hear your voice, which is different to everyone else's: and, in my dreams, I weigh your black hair in my hand, *constantly adoring you.*

He was living at Darling Point at the time, with Will Dalley not far away. Will, with his trivial obsessions, was the kind of person Mac liked, for there was no need to be on the defensive with him.

Child: *Only one letter from you today*; but a nice cheeky one, which I was especially glad to get, because my spirits were at 40 degrees below zero.

Being without you for a whole year has had a depressing effect upon me; and I really believe I am the loneliest man in the world.

Bill [Dalley] is off his drink too; so, when I visit 'Glenrose', I have whiskeys all to myself, and stare like a bloody lunatic at the chairs you once sat in and will never sit in again.

But Bill is such an unconscious humourist, that sometimes the dear old thing makes me laugh in spite of myself. Today, he asked his lady-neighbour (who, by the way, doesn't wear stockings) to come and get a tansy-plant, 'excellent for salads'. So off went Bill, in his shirt and trousers . . . Miss Johnson, in her bare legs . . . and Hugoest, exactly as you have always seen him.

After crawling over various muckheaps, and crashing into broken bits of window-pane hidden in the grass, we arrived at the tansy-plant; and Bill gave a lecture on its virtues, squeezing up leaves in his fingers and making us smell the stuff in turns.

'Don't you know Tansy? . . . Surely you know Tansy? . . . Hughie, you do; don't you? . . . Well, I'm astonished! . . . *Tanacetum Vulgare* is the Latin name. It's seldom found truly wild in this country; but is often grown in cottage gardens, and is prized by poor folk as a tonic, ferrifuge, vermifuge, etc.'

Then he began to explore among the roots of this particular specimen; and, while he was doing it, I decorated the back of his trousers with nasturtiums and marigolds; so that our homeward journey attracted quite a lot of attention in the street.

The next business was to replant the tansy in Bill's backyard; everybody, by turns, digging under W.B.D.'s direction. I was the last one to use the shovel, and I was sixteen feet below the surface-level when Bill discovered he had lost the plant. He suggested we should walk back to get another cutting; but, when he said that, we all gave him the bird and ran inside for gin and palato.

While we were sitting in the dining-room, a puff of dust came along the passage, and Bill got in a real rage and exclaimed 'Bugger Albert! That's his man beating the mats on the yacht! . . . I'll write a letter to the papers!'

In the evening he bought a fish, and took it for a stroll along the jetty, where we met your friend, an evil-looking dog if ever there was one. Worse than Phipeon! But with rather a nice voice. He is living now in the flat below Phil—— (who by the way is engaged to be married to a Lieutenant Commander in the Australian Navy). After a few walks up and down with Bill and Me and the Fish, S—— said he had to 'take his spouse to the theatre' and disappeared. Then we had tea with the everlasting Shiela; and I managed a couple of drinks and came 'ome. So now I have told you the whole of my uninteresting career since I wrote to you last.

Another letter, written after moving to Camden, says:

Here am I, buried away in the country, among cows, and ants, and beetles, and things; and they've all been HORRIBLE to me!! But, *really*, I'm having the time of my life . . . quite by myself, with my books and papers, on the edge of the bush. Three nice girls live across the river; and, now the moonlight nights are on, we exchange visits, or go for drives to COBBITTY, NARELLAN, FISH CREEK, and PENNANT HILLS . . . Although it is August, the days are quite hot, so that I can draw my stick across the rays of the sun, just the way I used to do with

iron fences at Darling Point, when I was DUMB! DUMB! DUMB!! Had
turkey and boiled leg of pork, washed down with long draughts of
Volnay, at Bill's house, just before I came here. A nice Frenchie,
(friend of Judy's), sat beside me. She adores Clive Brook, and said
if he ever asked her ... she would say 'Yes; PLEASE!!!'

Glad you've met D——. She's a darling; not a bit 'UR'. Comes of
a good family, and is full of wit and kindness. I like old Phil too. Give
them both my love.

You don't say anything about the fate of the drawings I sent you.
Did they *all* go sqokk? I hoped you might have been able to get yourself some money through selling 'em ... but evidently I'm *the* champion dud of the Universe.

Congratulate the new Baron, for me. How's dear little Wink-Eye
Virginia? Tell her Paul is bearing up bravely. Yours always, and
always, Hugoest.

I adore you ... Don't I, old stick-in-the-mud? Must go to bed now:
my possum's calling me.

Will Dalley keeps on reappearing. 'Bill pumped whiskey into
me and hung me up in front of the fire.' (A sketch of Hugh
hung on string over the fireplace.) 'The "Yellows" chase each
other lasciviously from one side of King's Cross to the other;
and even old Bill Dalley cocks his hat an inch higher seeing
Pola Negri's picture outside the Cinema.' (From the sketch the
Yellows seem to be dogs.) 'It always rains like this when I want
to go down to Bill's!' (Hugh facing a solid wall of rain.) 'Perhaps I'd better cut it out!' (With a saw he cuts a doorway
through the rain.) 'Where there's a Will (Dalley) there's a Way
...' (Hugh crawls through the cut, leaving the removed section
labelled: *Don't Touch. Wet Rain.*)

And here, finally, another of his little poems:

> *If I could step inside the sun*
> *And sail across the sea*
> *To come at length to London Town*
> *Where —— waits for me*
> *I'd have kippers for my breakfast*
> *And she would pour my tea ...*
> *Or shout an English view*-halloo!
> *A'ridin' on my knee.*
>
> *Hugoest*   *(pretty drunk)*

11 · ADOLPHE BEUTLER

I HAD KEPT closely in touch with Beutler all this while and had taken him up to Springwood, where Norman also thought he had in him the musical root of the matter. He had changed his premises for a larger floor and had a couple of workers, though he still did much of the work himself, the tuning, the relining of the keys with green felt, even the French polishing. He took pleasure in his hand-skills and his expertise in evaluing what an old piano, remade, would fetch. He had a frank simplicity of manner, which clearly uttered the man; his puppyish gambols and trite jokes could be forgiven for the high spirits which were anything but childish. There was a happy solidity, a deep reserve of force in him; and as soon as he sat at the piano, his skittishness went.

He had been in Australia since before the war, having migrated on account of lung trouble. I gathered that he had first worked in Western Australia and had had a difficult time during the war; that there had been an earlier Australian wife, a temperamental musician with nerves of anguish, who had also given him a difficult time; and that he had almost died in 1919 or so with double pleurisy, but was now regaining his health. He seemed determined to write nothing but songs, though I kept trying to push him towards larger forms. Why? he asked. I can say all I want to in a song; there is no need to say it all over a dozen times in an extended form without adding to the main point, the essential thematic material. I replied that the larger form would be a poor thing if it showed only a thinning out of the elements concentrated in the themes; but made little headway. Bach he loved and knew thoroughly; Beethoven he admired but didn't want to talk about; Wagner he detested.

We lunched at the near Greek club, eating fried octopus and drinking sweet gritty coffee; and he went on asking me to write song lyrics for him. He had a good sense of the sort of poem that had a clear structure capable of musical transposition and development, but to the colour and imagery of the poem he turned a deaf ear. If at all emphatic, they merely got in the way of the colour and imagery of the music he wanted to conjure up out of the words. 'A poet ought to be able to write that kind of skeletal poem,' I said, 'but he can't stop at such a level. You can't halt him at such an embryonic phase and forbid him to absorb music and light into his textures.'

'Hasn't Heine both form and colour, wit and fire?'

I argued that Heine emerged from a particular phase of German culture, a relation of folksong, poem and music, which couldn't be repeated. He wasn't interested. Why should the poet bother about colour and richness when the music could add all that? It was no use arguing. I accepted the position in his eyes that my highest function could be to act as librettist for his special needs. Outside music he had little taste and would have liked a Wagnerian pomp, velvet drapes and seignorial display. When I attacked all glossy surfaces, he defended French polish for pianos; but one night when we were dining with Norman at the Australia and the theme of 'What I'd do if king' was raised, he pondered, gave his round-eyed stare, and said passionately, 'I'd abolish linoleum.'

We kept on coming back to the question of musical form. He took some of his progressions and insisted that they were compressed in a new way, the only way that mattered, a way that didn't seem original unless you could think in music. He wasn't much interested in orchestration. 'There is my novelty, there is my concentration of voices and instruments.' But if there was such dynamite in the harmonies, I said, why not explode it? why not expand and explore the world of colour? He didn't listen.

Still, there was interest in trying to write quite bare verses that satisfied his idea of orderly emotional statement and movement. I composed small lyrics that I thought poetically penurious and he thought masterly since he could set them. But there was another aspect of his theory I found fascinating.

He insisted that all valuable music was in effect song and that every interval had a definite relation to the emotional intonations of the voice. He took songs by Brahms and showed me how false and arbitrary they were in their relation of words and sound; he took songs by Schubert and Wolf and showed how they rang true. I raised the question of Wagner, and rather reluctantly he admitted that here too was a right relation of word and sound. Song should grow out of the words, he said, taking the rhythmic shape precisely implicit in the rise and fall, the leap, the curve and cadence of the voice stirred to its richest potences of emotional expression; harmonies should echo the intertwining voices of experience, enrich the basis in intonation without deforming or confusing it. Any notes added to fill out without such a definite need and meaning were bad art. Where there were no words, the organic relation of melody and harmony, of contrapuntal or polyphonic movement, to the voice was still essential. Good music had it; bad or trivial music lacked it.

'But can't you see the implication: that the most complex development of the voices – the sonata or symphonic form, the Beethoven type of variation – is the fullest and highest form?'

He shrugged his shoulders and ordered more turkish coffee. We sat in a corner of blistered mirrors in the front room, looking at the counter with its coffee urns, its glass case of honey cakes, its swarthy proprietor with discontented swollen-lidded face. Beutler held his cigar tilted at an arrogant angle while I flipped the ash off a wilting cigarette. (I didn't really like smoking and smoked only as a social duty.) 'All the same we will conquer the world,' said Beutler as a casual and obvious comment. 'Not that it matters. What matters is that our thematic development is true.' My interest was mainly taken up by watching if Phyllis came up the stairs with or without the long-faced Barry.

Once Beutler stripped to the waist in the shop to show me the marks where the pumps had been in his back. I looked unwillingly at the blue cavities. I hated all talk of sickness, all wounds; also I feared someone would open the door and come in. Often he expatiated now on his early years. He told me preposterous tales of the large sums of money he'd won then at gambling, and of the invariably successful amours of his youth with bankers' wives, servant girls, actresses, or mysterious beauties on trains, in pine-forests or behind the piano. Then he turned, convincingly, to his boyhood. His father had played first violin in some town orchestra; then he'd taken to drink and let the family fall into extreme poverty. His mother had been the strong character; perhaps her strength had been of the kind that drove a husband to drink. In any event she now fought against heavy odds to rear her children. Adolphe the eldest bore the main brunt, running errands, begging, stealing in the market. He had stories of the hard winters, the lack of clothes and food, his mother's calm, grey courage, his father's wheedling, broken good humour. 'In his last illness they shaved him. When I saw his chin, I knew how weak he was. He had hidden all his life behind his beard.' He summoned up the picture, the flattened defeated man with his big brow and slight jaw, his pitiful eyes, and the wife, worn hard by her griefs, with her grey hair tightly drawn back in a bun; the children pressing in awe and curiosity round the bed. All like an early U.F.A. film, and, I am sure, quite true. Beutler grew excited by his own narrative and wanted me to write a novel about his life, giving him the name of Rabenflug. He dictated lots of details in a disconnected way, but the task was outside my powers or wishes.

Then he set his chin, his eyes narrowed, he leaned forwards and began again on his music. He had an impossible idea of getting an artist to make drawings in which the pattern illustrated exactly the rise and fall of his melodic line. I'd write the poem, he'd set it, N.L. would do the drawings. It was a sort of reduction to absurdity of his subtle perceptions of thematic development. Art as a sort of comic-strip to the text.

'There's a real relation,' I said. 'The structure of a musical piece, taken as a whole, and the rhythmic design of a picture, taken as a whole. *King Lear* and the Fifth Symphony. Forms of an equal breadth, depth, height. But you can't superimpose them.' He wasn't interested.

He persisted, and N.L. did some drawings to be printed in a light colour under the musical text. But on consideration it was found that the result would be merely confusing. Still, *Art in Australia* (May 1923) printed a drawing by N.L. which attempted to represent broadly the main pattern defined in a song *Love and Hate* (words by me). One page of the music was given and I added an essay in which I set out Beutler's philosophy of the melodic interval and stressed the close relation of musical rhythm to physical motion, impulse, the contractions and expansions of the body reflecting emotional tensions or releases. I said that the modernist effort to supplant the major and minor scales by abstractly worked-out systems showed a failure to grasp the 'basis of musical form in the development of a modulating emotion as defined by the interval.' In understanding that basis lay the only real novelty. At the same time I admitted that the composer could not now simply revert to the classics. He had to find his way forward to new form and its development by a deepened consciousness of 'the exact emotional burden of the interval.'

With regard to the relation of the art-image and physical motion, Norman once remarked to me that it was impossible to draw an angry face if one were smiling, and vice versa.

At least once a week I went home with Beutler to his horrible suburban house at Marrickville near the station. His second wife was a small glossy-faced woman whom I assumed to be domestically empty-headed, but whom I found in time to have her own shrewdness and penetration. He had met her while conducting some group of suburban amateurs who were staging *Les Cloches de Corneville*. (He still eked out his earnings by taking such groups one or two evenings a week.) She could sing and play a little, but now her time was thoroughly taken up by their growing family, three young children I think it was at this time. I have never been good at counting the small children of my friends. Soon there was another, named Jack Lindsay Beutler.

His first wife, in Melbourne, had been an expert pianist. He said that he had slackened in his own piano-playing through having her on the spot to run through the fugal and sonata work on which he seemed mainly then to concentrate. He hadn't been able to hold her mind or her heart or banish her migraines, he confessed with a shame-faced grin. He grinned too as he showed me the MSS of some early works. The sheets had been torn across and then stuck together with transparent gum-paper. In his rage, after the final quarrel with his wife, he had torn everything up, swearing to write no music ever again, and had then buried the MSS in the back garden. Not long after he dug it all up again. I told him of Rossetti's remorsefully buried poems, but he didn't listen. He opened his eyes wide in the way that showed inattention, cut another cigar, and fidgeted with the ruler on his music-stand.

He liked composing in my presence. Sometimes I worked at verses with a pencil, mostly I sat and watched and listened. He hammered away at already-written bars till the emotional force thus generated carried him on into the next phrase. Then he wrote the fresh bars down on the music paper in the stand above the keyboard, scowling and grimacing, returning to the keys and thumping out more notes to make sure he had got things right. Then he laid down his pencil, made a triumphant snout of his mouth, took up the cigar left smouldering at the end of the keyboard, and calmly played the piece over as far as the new notes.

At first I was surprised. 'I don't believe in composing out of my head,' he replied. 'I could do it, but I wouldn't get the music I want.' He needed to test at every moment that he was getting the desired weight and resonance. To work without the piano was like an artist painting without a model; after a while the forms drawn from memory grow thin, formalized.

The Beutlers were a happy family. I enjoyed the peacefulness of the evenings with them. Even the meals that ended with B. patting his stomach as a Finished Artist, the silly games and charades played when his sister-in-law was staying with them. The steady hours of composition and the final tea and biscuits, as we discussed the evening's gains. The rush across the road, over the railway bridge, along the cindertrack, to catch a late train. From the carriage I lay back to look at the box of a house, the window-light, B. at the backdoor with a cigar to wave or returned to his stool, hunched over the keys. Mrs B. in the parlour dining-room with its cheap furniture, sewing the children's clothes with her shining warm face close to the light.

Once she tried to make a new hat for herself; and B. the

craftsman swore that he could handle a needle better. She challenged him and he sewed the hat. That night in the train he said he had a great surprise for me. His wife was made to come into the music-room with her new hat on, a close-fitting thing of red silk, with much sewing involved. She blushed girlishly, no longer the calm hausfrau, and I noticed her charm. B. was smoking his cigar, puffing out complacent rings. 'What do you think of that? A Paris model. Where did you ever see such work?' He pulled the hat off her head. 'Look at those stitches.' Minute and regular. But he had insisted on reconstructing the hat according to his ideas of fashion, adding more and more things to make it difficult. His wife didn't feel at ease in the elaborate construction and would obviously never wear it in the street, but B. was enchanted.

The only thing they disagreed about was the way to feed babies. His principle was that whatever a baby was ready to eat must be good for it. 'Otherwise it wouldn't eat it. That's how I was brought up, and look at me.' She wanted to keep to a more usual diet. 'I'm not giving it cheese,' he insisted, 'I'm only seeing if it will eat cheese if it's got the chance.'

Before he began composing, he turned to the heap of MSS songs on the piano and flicked their sheets over. 'What would you like?' I told him and he played my choice, singing the parts, whether bass or soprano, in his cracked and rumbling voice. 'His playing is getting better,' his wife said, 'you're keeping him up to the mark.' But he played his earlier fugues and preludes patchily, and only after much pressure from me. I felt that his revulsion from all but songs derived at least in part from his experiences with his first wife. He felt safe with his songs, his apple-cheeked hausfrau.

Then one day I found him at work in much excitement. He gripped my arm and drew me to the Bechstein. His hair was standing out in dense, curly masses, showing that he'd been running his fingers through it. Behind his ear was the pencil of composition; on an ashtray smoked the cigar of reward. He pulled out some MS and played. He had begun on a work that wasn't a song. The opening movement of a piano and violin sonata. I didn't like to tell him, but I was disappointed. The writing was clear and lively, but seemed rather of the Mozartian world – while I took the later Beethoven chamber-music for granted as the basis from which any serious musician should seek to launch himself into a new dimension of grand form.

These days saw the highest level of the *Vision* union. One day I was talking with Beutler in a wine-bar opposite Pelligrini's and Ken Slessor came in. We had reached some exalting moment of discourse and I felt the signalling flash in my eyes as I looked in welcome at Ken. A few days later he shyly gave me the poem he had written on the moment, *The Mask*:

> *The rout stamps by – now beards of copper*
> *Dance in dark breasts – now music smites*
> *With horns and bells to the candelabra,*
> *Shaking their waxen lights.*
>
> *Plumes rock – the masquers plunge and riot –*
> *Heat in a steam has drowned the floor –*
> *Dumb with old fears I lurch bewildered,*
> *Beating upon the door.*
>
> *How came we two to this hot chamber?*
> *What painted marionettes dance here?*
> *It is in vain thy dreams to remember,*
> *It is in vain to fear . . .*
>
> *But suddenly out of the clang and tumult*
> *I saw thy mask descend,*
> *And knew thy face revealed for a moment,*
> *And knew thy speech, my friend!*
>
> *And words we cried that were not mortal,*
> *Whilst burning in eyes that were not eyes,*
> *There shone the star that shines not ever*
> *In earth's dark skies . . .*
>
> *O traveller, greeting! O merry meeting!*
> *O strange disguise!*

The high-pitched note was not too high for the level of ardent discovery and companionship we then inhabited.

12 · ELIOTH GRUNER

I HAD MET Gruner several times at Springwood and Sydney, but I came to know him well only after I wrote a notice of his large *Valley of the Tweed* in the *New Outlook*. For some reason he was pleased with my remarks, but he somewhat damped my response by several times treating me as if my profession were criticism, citing Wilde to prove it an art of its own. Even without Norman's imprimatur I should have admired his paintings of trees caught in delicate dawn-mists of light; with it, I considered them to hold an apotheosis of earth consumed in lilac and crystalline fires of the sun, the tree become phoenix. Small and wiry, often burnt dark from his long sojourns in the wilds, he could never forget his years in a draper's shop. He rarely mentioned them, but when he did, it was with bitterness. As part of that bitterness he wanted to cut a figure. When not in the wilds, he dressed carefully, but as a nemesis never quite outgrew the effect of a dapper draper's assistant. He wanted to get into 'society', but never felt at ease there and deeply resented its smug denizens. Once, at a highly select party, a kissing game was held. When his turn came, he gave a really passionate kiss, to assert himself, and the blindfolded woman cried, to his infinite shame and rage, 'Oh, I know that was cacky Gruner!' Once, somewhat drunk, he was arguing with a man who tried to impose some view on him through his superior social position; and Gruner said in clear, savage tones, 'Who do I think I am? Whoever I am, I'm Jesus Christ to you.'

But these stories are liable to give a wrong impression of the man. With those whom he liked he was as quiet, kindly and retiring as a man may well be. Indeed it was the reserved and retiring element that made relations with him difficult. He found it extremely hard to articulate his thoughts in words, the thoughts that mattered to him. At times when he had had enough drink, he imagined that he was overcoming this tongue-tiedness, this failure to find the right words for the intensely meditative inner life that accompanied his activity as a painter. But he was then more inarticulate than ever, relying on repetitions and heavy gestures, labouring with the idea which he could not bring forth into the light of day, and fiercely smiling to himself. I have spent hours in that confused exchange of thoughts which seemed all the while hovering on the edge of an important revelation, but got no further, and which yet at the end did leave a feeling of deep communication.

Now and then however he succeeded in saying just what he wanted to say. 'Inspiration,' he remarked once in reply to some vague comment of mine. 'I'll tell you what underlies each picture of mine. I go round looking and observing, interested but not moved. Then suddenly, off my guard, I see something. See it only for the flash of a second. It's there, and there it isn't. Only a pleasant landscape arrangement is left, the sort of thing any well-taught art student would select and paint. And yet I know that what I want is there, I saw it in that flash. So I stay and study the scene, looking and looking at it, analysing it from all angles, painting too, experimenting, till at last I manage to grasp analytically what I saw in that first flash, and then I struggle to get it down.'

'The momentary marriage of your mind and nature,' I said. 'The inner patterns of your creative processes and the outer patterns of nature. The two come together, then fall apart. You struggle till you mould the facts back to the inner vision.'

He smiled his saturnine smile. 'I only know what I feel. That's how it happens.'

Like McCrae he had a deep scepticism of high-sounding art principles, but unlike McCrae he did want to think out the principles that determined his steady and disciplined struggle as an artist. What he could not accept were any short cuts, any tendency to regard the struggle as solved by a rapid recourse to generalizings. Norman's praise, while gratifying and encouraging him, was always met with that brooding silence, on which an enigmatic smile hovered. For the same reason he had a harsh distrust of his work and subjected it to cruel self-criticism. One felt at times that if he had no money problems he would paint and destroy, paint and destroy, concerned only about getting closer to the vision stirred in him by the Australian scene. He had no tinct of Norman's transcendentalism, no notion of nature as something that was only crude material. He blamed himself, not nature, for the evanescence of the moment of vision. He knew that what happened in his work was not a mere selecting of certain aspects of a scene; he knew that he added something out of his spirit and his hand; but he suspected any theories that suggested the imposition of patterns on the infinite richness of nature. His sense of being born with a different face might lead him at moments to outbursts of pride before the complacent wealthy who were his patrons; his normal self was one that claimed no privileges. There was a sense in which he was the most humbly anonymous man I have known.

This aspect came out clearly in his reactions to the 1914 war. He enlisted without the least shred of ordinary patriotism, but because he did not see why he should be safe while others faced death. He had no intention whatever of fighting. He told Norman, 'Oh, I'll just go wherever I'm sent. I don't intend to do any killing. I couldn't, anyway.' And so when Norman and others kept pulling strings and stopped his embarkation for Europe, he refused to help them and protested all the while that he must not be gazetted as a war artist. Norman says, 'His intense aesthetic consciousness insisted that he could not do that sort of work. But we ignored his protests and were still hammering at the military authorities about it when the war ended.' That comment is totally wrong. It was a moral, not an aesthetic, consciousness that dominated Gruner in this matter, and indeed in all things. Not that he felt any distinction here. *I am not a war artist* meant many things. It meant: I will not paint war in any shape or form, I will not kill, I will not lie, I will not claim a destiny different from the others, I will paint only my own vision.

In 1915-16, knowing he would soon enlist, he went to the Emu Plains to paint; and there, with the hell of war and his coming enlistment beating in on his mind, he first found himself. He felt that he must somehow achieve his marriage with the earth before the end came. He sought to use Corot's control of tree-mass against sky with the utmost immediacy of light impact: painting straight into the light and choosing the dawn-moment for its explosive diffusion of light. He was after more than a light effect; he wanted to paint the sudden permeation of the dark earth with a universal lucidity.

The weak side of the man appeared in his house at Tamarama Bay between Bondi and Coogee, where everything was of extreme refinement and ended by quite lacking character. Fastidious pale greys, a suite of dark blue, an early nineteenth-century chandelier, silver candlesticks and chippendale table. Flowers arranged with tactfully unobtrusive taste. I disliked the place, but forgot about it when I was there and we listened to the gramophone or sat outside looking at the changes of the sea. In his Sydney guise he was neat with bow-tie and expensive shirts, his palette and his brushes meticulously cleaned, and his friend Lecky like a ghostly butler, never daring to say anything above a discreet side-whisper, coming home after work (surely in a draper's shop) to tidy up and cook with mute efficiency. No wonder his lively old Irish mother, with her cameo-closed spacious dress of black, complained that she had nothing to do in such a house, and was frowned on if she touched a saucepan or moved a vase. Yet Gruner roughing it in the wilds was a very different person; and there were times even in the genteel house when he forgot to play the Sydney part, or was bored with it. Once, having to look after himself for a week or so, he kept a huge pot on the stove and threw into it anything that came to hand. He called me into the kitchen to see the simmering mess, and we ate there. He was carelessly dressed and enjoyed the camp meal as he didn't enjoy a fine dinner, boasting about the length of time he could keep a pot going on the hills. Once or twice he asked me to go camping with him, but it never happened. Perhaps I was a little doubtful of the ambiguity in his sex relations. His mother had dominated his early years and he never outgrew that situation. He could not achieve a settled love relationship and remained at an uneasy bisexuality. Once when I surprised him on a couch (where the girl was certainly taking the initiative), he followed me out into the next room, put his arm round my shoulder, and said, 'It's you I love.' But another time a young married woman who lived in one of the few blocks of flats rising along the beach front confided to us her overwhelming passion for him, we introduced him to the bonily slender, brilliantly browned-all-over and well-permed thing, and thrust him one afternoon on her lewd mercies. He seemed pleased.

I missed him when he went off to England in 1924-25. There, among other things, he took charge of the Academy Exhibition of Australian Art.* Orpen attacked the *Valley of the Tweed* to him without knowing it was his work and gave him much bad advice about painting, some of which had a temporarily deleterious effect. Norman cites some of these adages: 'Paint can't be too thin, no subject should be bigger than two by three feet, style is more important than subject, paint should have a dry pastel-like surface.' But from a quiet study of what he found valuable in Cézanne, Van Gogh and even the Cubists, he came back to Australia resolved to tackle the problems of structure and volume with a new thoroughness, to seek out the harmonies of colour that corresponded with the rhythms of a landscape where men were only beginning to affect the forms and movements of surfaces.

He had already been pondering these matters before he went. Indeed the search for solidity and underlying structure is apparent even in his most light-drenched dawn scenes. I remember his excitement after he had gone up flying over wide stretches of landscape in order to study the layout and the movement of forms from above. He felt that he had gained an enhanced sense of rhythmic relations. He was already feeling out for the breadths and reciprocities of forms locked as well

---

*Two anecdotes told by Gruner of the effect of N.L.'s pictures on royal personages are perhaps worth repeating. The first, on sighting them, stood back, ejaculated, 'Gad, what wenches,' and strode briskly forward. The second, after her equerry had tried to bar the way and refused to accompany her into the wicked room, made a thorough survey and then remarked with truly royal innocence, 'But why has he put stockings on some of them?'

as flowing in a characteristic substructure with shadows used to underline the slants and diagonals of space.

I felt that he had made a considerable step forward when he showed me *The Pines* shortly before I left Sydney. Here he had taken only foreground and sky, but his changed outlook showed in the simple mass of the short length of earth, path, grass, with the dark weight of the pines either side, and the sudden break into an immensity of pure light on the other side of the hedge. As we looked at this work and talked of it, something of his new concern for weight of pattern and for colour absorbed into rhythm was brought out. He was keen for landscapes of broad bare mass, with undulant and receding movement of lines.

Norman mentions that he and Gruner met little in later years, and then only by chance. At one of these meetings Gruner said, 'The only thing that interests me is the anatomy of the earth.' He carried this anatomization to a certain fine point, defining the Australian earth in its first phases of transformation by man. But he had no point of faith or love outside the momentary visions of transfigured earth, which he laboured with such single-hearted purpose to set on canvas.

He drank himself to death, broken on the philistinism of the only world he saw on the other side of his canvases, and gave up the ghost at fifty-seven in October 1939. Perhaps the outbreak of the second world war had been the last straw.

He was not a man with whom one could carry on a personal correspondence; his moments of self-revelation were too hardly fought for, too difficult to put into words except at the rare moments of intensely realized friendship. I wrote to him a few times from London in the later 1920s and had some brief replies, and I tried to express my gratitude to his art in a poem on landscape painting printed in the *London Aphrodite*, 1928. That was all.

13 · ASPEN OF LIGHT

MY VERSE was gradually developing. A longish poem in octosyllabic couplets, *The gods are all abroad tonight*, had a slight charm, if I remember correctly. And I followed up *The Death of Marlowe* with three other Elizabethan scenes, Greene at his boozing with Nash, young Donne wooing Anne Egerton. I sent them to Constables, as Michael Sadleir was arranging to do a book of N.L.'s etchings in reproduction. M.S. replied that he liked the set and would do a book of them if I wrote three or four more. It was an excellent chance and I should have taken it. But I had moved on to a two-act comedy called *The Masquers* (Renascence setting), and replied that I didn't want to return to the sketches. I sent *The Masquers*, which was turned down. I was pleased. At this stage my recognition made me feel I must be on the wrong track.

I recall of *The Masquers* that at the crucial point in the second act I remarked to Norman, 'The essential thing in dramatic structure, in character definition, is to find the point where an emotion turns into its opposite.' But how I applied this dictum, I have forgotten. (All my early work in MSS, that I could lay hands on, I destroyed in 1930).

I had for some time been concerned with trying to catch light effects in verse. N.L.'s etchings, often organized round a light burst, and Gruner's dawn paintings, conspired to make me brood more and more on the relations of light and colour in the poetic image. But the moment I felt that I had decisively found the clue was down the South Coast where we had gone to stay with Dr Francis Crosslé, who had become a friend of Norman's. Francis had migrated from Ireland with an elderly woman whom he had championed in some way, a large bossy woman who seemed rather an oppressive mother to him than a wife. He was handsome, high-coloured, with oddly slitting eyes and swollen underlip, an in-turned man, passionately seeking a cause to which he could wholly give himself up. The cause of Ireland lost its force in his far exile, and not even such a willing martyr as Crosslé could get indefinite satsifaction out of being hag-ridden by the large woman. He fell under Norman's spell; and when I introduced him to Beutler, he was again spelled. Beutler, with his family burden, his continual oscillations of fortune, his doubtful health, his flamboyant and boyish charm, appealed strongly to him; and he devotedly tended him as his troubles increased. More than once he dragged Gruner back from death in the latter's miserable alcoholic last years, till even he decided it was best to let him die.

I liked him, but the odd element in him, something lost, secretively unhappy, weakly inexpressive, came between us.* However, Janet and I were staying down at his big rambling bungalow at Bulli, a town with the ocean boisterous on one side and the hills soaring greenly up behind. Crosslé was very attractive to his female patients and had many botherations from them. One day as I went out with him in his car on the rounds, he told me the village scandals. A few nights before the butcher had gone off his head and charged down the road stark naked. The woman he was first visiting was a rich amorous hypochrondriac who had nothing wrong with her; she'd be lying in a fine silk dressing-gown that would easily come undone, etc. I asked him what he'd do when the gown slipped; he said that he'd tie it up and give the woman some draught that would provide her with something else in her innards to think about. I think he got a strong pleasure out of baffling the advances of his flock. He mentioned also that a fairly common task for the doctor was to extract things like eggs which women had lost inside their anatomy; in a panic about getting them

*The failure may well have been on my side. Ray remarks of Francis, 'He died, suddenly, in 1947 from a heart attack. If ever there was a genuinely noble character, it was Francis Crosslé, and his death really devastated me, as it did many others. He was someone who could never be replaced. Without doubt he was the finest man I have ever known, and the good turns he did for me could never be repaid.'

out they had to curb their blushes and call the doctor in. I don't know if this habit is restricted to seaside towns with attractive but severe young doctors in attendance.

He left me in the car, in the bright windy morning, and I looked around for one of his eccentric patients. None obliged. However, I noticed a poplar tree, not a lofty one, but sufficiently leafed to twinkle continually with bells of silver light, to cast off endless coins minted by the sun, to tremble with lascivious sequins, to sweat with mercurial drops of starlight. I went on seeking adequate phrases for the lovely glitter. A fountain sparkling up out of the earth, a nymph scattering the gold dew from her wild hair and her lean flanks.

Crosslé came back, duly having administered his draught to the lovelorn wife of an incapable businessman. We drove on. But the image of the tree shaking its tambourines of metallic light, with a thin scraping rustle in the wind, remained with me. It came up again as I dozed after the large lunch, and again on the edge of sleep, merged with the image of the lovelorn wife vainly letting her silks slip and gaining only a purge for her pains.

We drove into the hills, among the cool shadows of great ferns, into a scream of lorikeets, and along the ridge, looking down to where the flattened sea crawled to the foam-frilled sand. I tried to make out the poplar among the trees dwarfed below in the toy township, and saw a gleam, a puff of silver. We were standing on a wooden platform let out over the cliff-edge, with a sheer drop beneath us; and for the first time in my life I felt hopelessly giddy, with a sick emptiness under my soles, and had to grip the rail, then as quickly as I could, without betraying my mortal fear, retreat to where the car waited.

Back in the house, we discussed Yeats and the Irish Movement. Mrs C., with her stern grey eye on Francis with his slow meditative voice, described the first night of *The Playboy of the Western World*. (Her nympholept sister, who played Chopin all day, was elsewhere, to my disappointment; I had wanted to see her eyes. To watch the strain between the large woman and her young sister, with Francis dreaming chivalrously, but not without resentment, between them.) I remembered the tree spiked with light, the valkyr-tree with bosom as big as our

364 · THE ROARING TWENTIES

hostess's bursting through the chainmail of the sun. The flight of countless doves out of the body of Venus as silky-milky-white as plumply-crumpled as flickeringly dimpled as the shimmering Flemish flesh of Helena Fourment.

> *Pillars of light that colonnade*
> *the temple of the afternoon*
> *The tree, helmed with gold, the metal leaves*
> *burnished and tasseled with clashing light*
> *The spring ties ribbons in the trees*
> > *ribbons of fluttering light*
> *Flags of the sun, tattered*
> *The tree dissolves in tinkling light, the nymph*
> *trails her blue film of nakedness along the shade*
> *The tree upbabbles, a swerving fountain of light*
> *sprung from the loins of earth*
> *Baubles of light that chatter in the breeze*
> *The tree sways to the anchor of shadow*
> *tugs but cannot float away*
> *The brilliant dragon of the tree*
> *scaled with grinding light*
> *tussles with the leaping wind*
> *The sun's bells jangling in a tree of wind . . .*

Not long afterwards I picked up *Facade* and *Bucolic Comedies* in a bookshop, turned them idly over, and was captured. The mastery of colour imagery struck me in the midriff before I tried to see the poems as wholes. I felt at once at home in this time-space where colours like a parakeet shrilled loudly in the chattering heat and the beewinged warm afternoon light roved gilding someone's hair (wooden nutmegs and cloves), cocks and hens in the kitchen fire, each flame shrieking cockie-do-do (with cock combs flaring high) . . . Here, I was forced to realize, was sensibility tuned in the same key as my own, the key I sought. In *Vision* we had condemned the Sitwells as well as Van Gogh, anything that N.L. had labelled disintegration or primitivism on the scantiest of investigations. But now I was driven to admit that if I were to be at all true to my own senses and their poetic impulsion, I must learn to drink at the spring I had placarded as muddy and polluted. Not that it was only a matter of imagery. The rhythms of Edith Sitwell came home as strongly, folksong dance-beat nursery-rhyme mingled with traditional forms to achieve a note of delight in the earth, a scorn for those who had bartered the bright life of the earth for the mumpish darkness of hell, the repetitive round and the money curse. For a while I tried to hold out and pretend I wasn't as centrally affected as I was. But I bought the books and returned to them. Also, later, *The Sleeping Beauty*, and Sacheverall's *Hundred and One Harlequins*, with the lovely various flow of a poem like *The Neptune Hotel* or the glancing fantasy-mode of narrative in *Dr Donne and Gargantua*.

It seemed I had found the poetic earth in which my poplar tree had its roots. I rechristened it an aspen, as that suggested more the shivery-shake of the light-jangle. But a formula was needed to hide my divided allegiance. I declared to N.L. that there were many elements after all in contemporary experimental verse that could be used for our purposes. He took my word for it, as he wouldn't if I had come to say the same of Van Gogh or Picasso. But a split had been born in our concepts that was later to have important effects for me.

About this time I met a young fellow, Laurence, who was working as a conductor in one of the touring companies run by Williamsons. He had a blithely responsive manner and the face of a villainous cherub. We took to one another over some beers and I showed him the MS of a light-hearted prose-play on a Roman theme (drawn from Plautus), over which he chuckled. There was a reckless element in his make-up, a wind-blown daredevil headlong approach. If my motto was 'I can take it' (in the stoical sense), his motto was 'I can take it' (in the brigand's sense). He had come out a few years ago from England. His father had been glad to see his rebellious face disappear over the horizon. He had trained both in London and Leipzig, and owned a considerable musical knowledge – at least about the composers who awoke his enthusiasm. Wagner above all, Mussorgsky and Rimsky-Korsakov and so on following a fair way to the rear. Beethoven he looked on as old stuff, and this was the only point on which we bickered for long. He was desperately in love at the moment with the young leading lady of his company, and after we had sent her several telegrams I took him to see Beutler. They didn't get on well at all. B. saw L. as an unstable modernist and L. saw B. as a stick-in-the-mud. 'It's all been done, done a thousand times,' he insisted to me; and such advice as he offered to B. was not kindly received.

We continued our argument on and off in hotel lounges at all times of the day and night. He knew all the pubs where drinks were illegally served in the evening at enhanced prices. Or we invaded the bedrooms of actors or singers in back-street pubs and allowed them to share our drink while baffling them with our discussions. One actor had a roulette-wheel in his wife's hat-box; some of the actresses were pretty. But we sat on their beds and talked. Talk was the most entrancing occupation in the world.

One night we sat in a lounge among palms and discreet lights. Waiters always succumbed to L.'s English suavity and air of sophistication, even with the disadvantage of my shabby company. George Lambert the artist was running through his usual gamut of tricks to lure and impress clients. A very capable painter, of the generation and breed of Orpen and Strang, but more talented than the others, he always seemed a very lost and unhappy man, uneasy with others and twice as uneasy with himself alone. We often struck him drinking in one of the better-class lounges, restive and uncomfortable, like an incompetent fakir who was bored on his bed of nails. Giving the worst imitation of a man deep in thought I have ever seen, clasping his hands or thrusting his gingery beard at the ceiling. When he saw anyone he knew, he floundered in relief and made unashamed efforts to flatter them into commissioning a portrait or a pencil sketch. Tonight he was telling a blank-faced man what remarkable hands he had, how full of character. Hold them out, let me see them, yes, hold them like that, put them together, yes, hmmm. I don't know if he bribed the waiters, or if they had a natural sympathy for a high-class flunkey, but they liked to halt and overlook any drawing he might proceed to make. They glanced from original to drawing, nodded wisely, went off and came back, as if overcome by the wonderful likeness. When we left, George had still failed to convince the half-drunk shrewd-eyed sheep-owner that his hands should be immortalized.

Laurence had a thorough knowledge of Wagner, a grip of his architectonic basis. We went over the scores of the Ring and *Tristan*, especially *Tristan*, on the piano, while he analysed the structure. After which, we went into one of the large gramophone shops and listened to records of orchestral performances, under a thin pretence of sometime or other buying something. Then, having impressed the assistants with his professional position and his general air of owning the world, he borrowed the records, twenty or thirty at a time, and handed them over to me. So, though I had seen no operas at all, Wagner's or anyone else's, I felt that I grasped the whole basis of Wagnerian form.

I could not, of course, for a moment take his contempt for Beethoven, but otherwise some of his arguments affected me, and, added to my new admiration for Edith Sitwell, made me feel all the more that modernismus could not be lumped together in a block of disintegration and abstraction, but must be scrutinized, each individual expression, for what was blind alley and what was a road, path, or even meandering forest-track, leading somewhere. (T. S. Eliot I disliked for his literary allusiveness, his sniffy fear of life, and his effort to arrest the fertility rite at the point of death, winter, loss.)

Leaving the Greek café, with Beutler already gone, I stood a moment on the landing, watching the animated faces in the coffee room, leaned over the rail and saw Phyllis with Barry in the dim entry below, come into each other's arms. Dingy drift of light from the street-lamp some way off. She drooped in his arms as never in mine, her head fell back with a helpless surrender, a splaying of the lips over the teeth, as never with me. I didn't want to go down and pass them. I returned for a second coffee and scribbled in the penny exercise book I always carried and never lost whatever the exigencies of beer.

> *This garden latticed with the light of stars*
> *brims with dim sighs of lovers every shadow*
> *shakes with a skein of kisses and the glow*
> *where netted Venus flutteringly unveils*
> *a lantern breast a snow of light that sifts*
> *under closed eyelids of delight*

With a feeling of colour-intoxication, I wanted to work *littered* in, to pull the sounds further together, *garden* and *stars, latticed* and *light*, the soft hiss preparing for *sighs, shadow shakes skein* taken up by *kisses* centring the s's, *snow closed, littered* linking *netted* and *fluttering, closing the eyes* (the i's), the *lantern* lighting up the latticed garden. I was gaining a new awareness of the interrelation of sense and sound: not analysing the separate details, but conscious of glitters caught up in a single glow. The swish of her clothes passing my table echoed my innermost delight, my desire to affirm life. I rose and went out in a clumsy exultation. Down in Elizabeth street I heard the clack and clatter, the muffled exclamations of dismay, of the whores in flight. A police raid, the girls looking for somewhere to hide. One stopped by me and said, 'You don't mind taking my arm, do you?' I took it and saw her as far as the neat handsome colonial church lost in the modern city dump and left her there, but still felt her heart beating against my arm.

Beutler had a concert at which his violin sonata and several songs were given. He heartily enjoyed the preparations and the rehearsals with a girl violinist where I sometimes turned the pages. Now he listened to me when I talked of N.L.'s idea of an opera *The Faun*, and after a while he asked me to write the libretto. The concert was neither a success nor a failure, nobody attacked or praised with any intelligence, though Barry said to me it was pleasant but without relevance to the existing world of music. I disagreed, but was not unaffected. So I decided to use the libretto to push B. as much as possible towards the same position in music as I was reaching in poetry. He refused to look at scores or listen to the music I thought might be of use to him.

'I know most of the works are of no lasting value. But you can learn things from them. Perhaps learn is the wrong word. Find yourself to some extent in the contemporary dimension they represent. Even if in so many ways it's a bad dimension. It's what we have got to take in and overcome.'

I'm not clever,' he repeated. 'I couldn't write a good jazz tune to save my life. Just as little can I imitate Stravinsky and all that.' (We had just been playing the *Spring Rite* on a pianola.)

'I don't want you to imitate.' I began to get tied up in my own arguments. 'You have the Beethoven ethos. Why not at least consider Sibelius?'

'If my work is new it's because it's emotionally true. No other newness is worth having.'

My own coin was being paid back to me with a vengeance. Anyhow, I agreed substantially with his claims, though I felt he was in part misapplying the truth in them. So instead of arguing further I wrote the verse of the libretto in as strong an experimental style as I felt he could take, using the imagery of explosive and integrative light. The more brightly sharp-edged the words, the more he would surely be driven to a new harmonic outlook. To my surprise he did not object, and I felt that indeed his music was taking on new freedom and limpidity.

The question of orchestration now came up. Beutler had only a book by Berlioz, which he insisted was adequate for his problems. Laurence was drawn into it at my insistence. This time he was impressed, but still critical. He thought B. had at last broken through into a significant style, but was being held back by all sorts of technical weaknesses, particularly in the translation of his ideas from the piano to the orchestra. This time B. did not disregard some of his counsels. On our own, Laurence told me that the orchestrating was pedestrian and muddy, and needed to be wholly redone. He however repeated his praises of the general direction of the music. I on the other hand was beginning to feel that as the work went on Beutler was falling back on Wagnerian methods, unable to sustain on such a long sweep his own lines of thematic development. The likenesses to Wagner were what now reconciled Laurence, but I felt they went too far.

How anyway was an opera of this kind ever to be performed in Australia? That was impossible to imagine; but with our belief that artwork created its own fate, the problem did not seem important.

Laurence lost or gave up his job. I think the chase of the leading lady had something to do with it. Besides, he wanted to stay on in Sydney to continue our midnight conversations in the hotel bedrooms of bewildered actresses. He took a job playing some sort of ghastly organ that came up out of the floor in a big cinema, with him already ensconced on the seat. Sometimes I turned the pages for him. There he grew fond of an usherette named Lola, a slender, dark girl with enough sense to know that if she said very little she would seem twice as alluringly slender. She walked in a way that made one believe in the dryads of willow trees with long legs and singularly elastic waists. (In this cinema, too, I met the dancer who had charmed me in Brisbane, a bacchante violet-eyed in a Hellas cut off by garish footlights.)

One day Laurence said he had the evening off; he had been lent by the management to a Roman Catholic Reformatory for Fallen Women which was putting on the film *The Ten Commandments* (which was running at the cinema and for which L. had the musical accompaniment). I agreed to go and turn the sheets and have a look at the troop of prostitutes who had become repentant enough to slave in a laundry for the good of the church's purse. After some wanderings in the wrong streets we found the large brick-walled building with its hall and installed ourselves at the piano on the platform. Busy nuns hurried in and out and verified that we were harmless musicians. Then the plainly dressed and mostly hard-faced troop came murmuring into the seats, well behaved but staring. Darkness was switched on and a sigh of immense anticipation rustled across the audience. The film began.

All went well till the section dealing with the orgies round the Golden Calf arrived. The women manifested a slight excitement, but no more. The priest in charge, however, lost his head. He rushed shouting on to the platform, unintelligibly rebuking sin. Then he dashed up the aisle and made for the projector. He put his hand over its shaft of light and immersed the screen-revellers in a most suggestive darkness, through which (between his fingers) an amorous leg or a leering face momently escaped. The women were in an uproar, half in protest against the effort to eliminate the orgies and half in excitement over the hasty slabs and slits of debauchery they glimpsed, which were far worse than the full shots. Now and then the priest removed his hand, feeling sure that the orgies must have sunk into debilitated slumber; but every time the revellers leaped up out of the darkness into unabated embraces. Even I, who had seen the section several times at the cinema and found it little more inebriating than a schoolgirls' display of eurhythmics, was astonished at the remarkable effect of vice which the priest had manipulated into being. The uproar was now terrific. The women were standing up and jumping about. The show terminated with full lights and perturbed nuns shooing the screaming women out down the aisles.

But such treats were rare. Then Laurence had a lucky accident. One afternoon as he was hurrying over to ascend the seat of his American monster of a piano-organ, he slipped, caught his foot in something, and found that he had sprained his wrist. Dr B., whose consulting-rooms were not far off, wrote out the certificate of his incapacitation; and now we suddenly had all the time in the world for going over the scores of Wagner. We even hired a room in a rehearsal building for hours on end, and with the aid of a whisky bottle ran through a whole opera without pause. The unity of *Tristan* was a tremendous discovery and affected henceforth all my ideas about organization in play or novel. L. analysed the music, particularly here and in *Siegfried*, for its fundamental structure and interrelation of parts, and for its dramatic expression, showing how the notes did not only characterize, but also described every movement of body and spirit alike in the people.

Dr B. was an amiable gynaecologist. Once L. acted as his assistant, duly dressed in white overall, handing him the instruments and much interested in the proceedings. The doctor suggested that I too was curious about female anatomy. I agreed, but took care not to have any dates fixed. I didn't like unfair advantages. 'Such a nice girl this morning,' said Dr B. 'The third time she's been here. Why do you do it? I asked her. I don't want to, doctor, she said, but when a man looks at me in that suffering doggy way I feel so sorry for him I can't refuse.' We laughed doggily.

The doctor was a small man with baldish head and watery eyes, and with two passions, his unfaithful wife and the stage. He impartially liked anything and anyone connected with the theatre, but above all Gilbert and Sullivan light opera. Unaware of his wife's industrious adulteries, he thought her a wonderful woman, only a less-prized possession than the array of autographed photos of minor stage celebrities lining his study. He liked giving parties, on which he expended much of his ill-gotten gains as a doctor, growing ever more incoherently amiably shortsighted, while his wife cuckolded him upstairs, downstairs and in the back garden. At one party he burbled for hours about a great surprise for his guests. He had had a wireless set installed, a fairly rare thing still, with a loudspeaker hidden behind a sofa; at a signal, as we all assembled for the surprise, it was to blare forth. But the secret soon leaked out and some drunkard fiddled with the set. When Dr B. waved his triumphant hand before the gathered company, nothing at all happened. Bursting into tears, he was led from the room, while his wife tickled my hand.

That evening, before the fiasco, Dr B. had suggested various games, one of which involved improvisation of verse. I reeled off several octosyllabic couplets and was accused by my runner-up, who had managed a pair of rhymes, of reciting verses from memory. Mrs B., who didn't know rhyme from reason, championed me; and my opponent, who had discovered various lethal weapons of surgery in the study was disarmed. In the back verandah I heard Janet recite one of her poems to a group who were discussing the war; and I shrank away. For the scene reminded me, as I disliked being reminded, that I had imposed my literary views on our marriage and made no effort to help her in developing her talent.

14 · BETSY'S AND BRENNAN

MICK PAUL with his one eye slept in the Domain among the other dossers who covered themselves with newspaper shrouds. He was drunk and someone stole his trousers, pulled them off while he snorted and failed to wake up. In the early dawn he discovered that he had cold legs, scratched himself, and then started off to run through the streets in a newspaper kilt for the nearest studio. Good-natured as he was, he felt that someone had gone too far in pinching trousers from a harmless drunk. If a down-and-out couldn't be respected in the Domain, where could he be? 'He didn't take my coat, he didn't take my shirt. Why not? was it out of decent feelings? I ask you, would a bastard with decent feelings inveigle the pants off a poor drunk? It was some stinking lousy Pommy.'

Mick was an expert in living without visible support, but always ready to share his methods with deserving drinkers. He knew how to stuff into his maw a maximum of counter-lunch under the eyes of the most obnoxious barmaid – with one beer, or even no beer at all, producing voluble and plausible accounts of the friend for whom he was waiting. Thus, catch some chap with marked features coming out, go in and ask if a chap like that has been in. Yes? Oh he'll be back in a moment then, he owes me a fiver, he swore he'd meet me here, the fact he did turn up shows he means to keep his word, he'll be back in a moment. But it was hard to work these tricks in the pubs with the best counter-lunches. (Phil, I find, with reference to his shrewd friend Mervyn O'Hara, records the high-class pubs with chicken sandwiches and curried eggs, sausages hot on grills. In the swell houses the chef cut slices from a roast while you grabbed bread; in the more plebeian, you stuffed yourself with curry and rice. This pub habit of freely feeding the beer-hound was an Australian thing.)

In restaurants Mick in hard-up moments was not above putting pepper, salt or vinegar into bottles kept in his pocket, following the example of Domain habitués who wore under their coat a long string with many bottles attached for this purpose. But his most famous exploit could hardly be emulated. He grew tired of catching mice and putting them on an almost-finished plate under the potato, so that he could haughtily summon the waitress and shout, 'Take this to the manager, look what you feed to your customers!' The device was getting too well known, so he removed his glass eye and put it in. 'I'm taking this plate to the police.' Then he walked off with the remnants of the meal and a plate in addition.

In the Domain, in front of the Art Gallery, a meeting was being held. A man stood on a soapbox under a naphtha flare. To keep out of the fight, I stood on the outskirts and couldn't hear very well. The speaker was describing the wrongs of the wharf-lumpers and seamen. 'This job-control issue will come to a showdown,' he repeated, hammering his fist into his palm and giving figures to prove that the growers of wheat and wool had made huge profits out of the war. The war committees had functioned efficiently, to ensure the profits of the interests they represented. Not content, the bosses had tried to corner shipping by their Overseas Shipping Bureau, a disguised company union. 'Bust it, or it'll bust you. Always them or us. No common interest, never was, never will be.'

'What about beer?' someone shouted.

'They don't drink beer. Whisky or champagne, chum. And let me tell you that bad jokes don't fill empty bellies. But they keep attention off the real issues. There'll never be a lack of dope while the boss-class is on top. Dope for breakfast, dope for dinner, dope all the while. The one commodity the bosses don't grudge you.'

I was always stirred by this sort of thing, however much my theories now discounted it. I had written in the *Bulletin* about art passing over the heads of 'bankers or wharf-lumpers.' Something like that. A T.U. leader of the wharfies wrote in to protest, and I answered humbly. I had been using emblems of opacity (N.L.'s Man), but when faced by a challenge from the wharfies I found that I didn't want to hold by my words as

I would have if the challenge had come from the bankers. What had I meant then? I recalled my earnest working-class W.E.A. students in Brisbane; they had their weaknesses, but not ones to insult.

About this time I was coming home to Bondi in one of the still uncommon buses. A drunken returned-soldier was swaying on a strap and cursing the world, cursing the war and cursing the profiteers and cursing himself for a fool. On reaching home, I wrote down his words as they rang clearly in my memory, and intended to quote them in a *Bulletin* article. But the more I looked at them, the less I saw how I could make a journalistic use of them. There was too much in them that I agreed with.

Eric Bedford turned up again, full of sunburnt energy, newly married and saying how much he had liked some verses of mine in the *Bulletin* against a U.S.A. judge who ordered the burning of the *Decameron*. 'And tear down passion's house from floor to rafter,' I recall of the rhetoric, obviously a line that rhymed with *laughter*. Eric took me out to visit Fred J. Broomfield, a grey-haired Labor fighter, who had been on the *Bulletin* Red Page and the *Worker*. A big tumbled barn-like house, in Marrickville, with a feeling of patriarchal life without the Jehovah side, loud with the fighting traditions that I knew little of but always respected. Reminded of the time, Eric remarks, 'You always had a look as though you were on some B.C. Grecian Isle when I was talking to you, and as my talk was more of revolution than the arts, I don't think I interested you much apart from my zest for living.' True, in the sense that then nothing much interested me but the arts, but I always liked to see him, though I could have got more out of his zest than I did. His wife Jessie, he says, remembers the visit to Marrickville 'because we did not get home until 2 a.m. next morning, and we were just married, and Janet said she ought to leave me, and Hugh McCrae made passes at her, and, in fact, she remembers it very well.' At Broomfield's place, as well as the beer and the anecdotes, there was a daughter of his, a tall comely girl with calm eyes, whose image has remained clear and important to me till this day.

I began to feel the need to write a drama in which I could pack something of my disquiets, fears, angers, hopes. Suddenly I had the idea I wanted, the conspiracy of Marino Faliero, Doge of Venice, against the state he represented. Byron and Swinburne had treated the subject, but not I thought with sufficient penetration. In my version Marino, driven by a fierce sense of outrage and blind to his wife's infidelity, attempts an act of revenge which is also his tribute to an idea of justice that he does not believe can be actualized. His conflict is between these deep contradictions in himself, which corresponded even more closely than I understood to my own inner division, where a revolutionary impulse fed aesthetic convictions that turned it into abstract forms, leaving it only the concretion of the art-image rejected by the world.

My experience with Phil and the strong feeling we had of a coming war, a convulsion that would leave 1914-18 far behind, also gave me a sense of deep-going contradictions in our world, which men would not realize in time.

When I reread the play a week ago, after not having looked at it since I passed the proofs in 1927, I was surprised to find much more in it than I had expected. There seemed a genuine mounting tension of anguish and anger, but at the same time a disproportion between theme and form which was never overcome. The strength and weakness of the play centre in Marino. On the one hand he represents a sort of Urizen, a sheer force of hate and abstract construction cut away from all contact with the processes of change and union. At its height, in the waiting scene, his anger breaks into fear and momently he realizes that the murders he plans are only the final form of evasion from the truth of self and humanity. Yet in his outbursts I sought to express both the blind evil of egoist power and the uncompromising resolve to bring about a totally different world. His final words utter the fanatic madness of suicide; and yet his lonely pride, in expressing a contempt for things as they are (and so, above all, for the egoist power he wants to canalize in himself) have the ring of my own sympathies and in the last resort expose the untenable nature of my own positions. Hence an ambivalent element throughout the theme, which gives something of a tragic tension and yet prevents its full working-out. For this reason the various conspirators were

reduced to lesser aspects of the divided impulses in Marino.
Here is a passage from Marino's first outburst:

MARINO: *O, I am half mad*
           with seeking for that word in my mind
           which can dash a storm of waters on this city
           and kill me with fulfilled vengeance. That I ask.
           Death for myself and death for all the world.
           The whizz of death's sword through a moaning air
           of dizzy slaughter would be time enough
           to know that earth had shrivelled. Let it die.
           Myself and you and you and everyone
           that's carcassed for its maw. Let air grow ice
           and choke each throat; and a stone of silence
           freeze on struck man, and trees wrinkling with sunlight,
           and all the fields blotchy with flowers, and fruits
           like blistered rottenness blown on boughs, hot sores
           of earth's rank blood spotting fiery green
           and all the harlot seas leprous with foam.
           But chiefly man.
           For him the sweating sun bleeds and the gashed moon
           ulcers night's flesh, but have no stratagem
           to unfrost his face of lies and beneath show
           whimpering hate, his soul. Then what flat leer
           of blind grey sea-shapes, and a night of bats,
           skurrying glooms puffed from small white dead things
           that the touch loathes, lice shook from the moon's hair
           to bead in eyes, the wide-jawed gobbling fish
           that lip the pallid glass of the eyes' cistern,
           risen from depths of slime –
BERTUCCIO: *This is intemperate,*
            all things have remedies.
MARINO: *But this has none.*

The imagery, I found on my rereading, is throughout organized on the conflict of opposites. The sea imagery in the cited
passage, with the yet more violent one in which Marino sees
the waters turning to crush the insect-ship in the mangy foam,
are, for example, counterposed by an earlier speech in which
a lover asks his girl:

> *Are you wearing the mirrored garters that I gave you,*
> *to preserve in their bright veils of metal*
> *white secret shadows of huge embraces*
> *like lilies bubbling through time's vague water?*

And so on. The wreck theme (parodied in the merchant Andrea's complaints) is developed in love terms by Michele:

> *those tangled seas of flouncing flesh and linen,*
> *billows of bolsters, rearing storms of arras*
> *and runaway fingers, rudderless mouths and crests*
> *of falling kisses and dark foam of hair,*
> *islands swimming on a reeling keel*
> *and unknown boats fluttering down past mermaids,*
> *the crew wondering what's the crystal port,*
> *and narrow estuaries of madcap tides*
> *swashing backwards and forwards, up and down . . .*

Or to take a smaller example. Bertuccio in the waiting scene:

> *. . . drizzling shadows*
> *that hang their inaction on the deed*
> *that leans beyond them like the beckoning lip of a star*
> *trembling through leaves and a blur of wind –*

is opposed by Michele in a love scene with:

> *luxury of breathing kisses hung*
> *on trellises of sleep like stars fondled*
> *on the broad laps of roses.*

There is the same pictorial opposition. The second last scene ends with Michele and a girl:

> MICHELE: *You are wise. Discourse in kisses. Think in kisses.*
> LAVINIA: *Mind my hair.*
> *I did it carefully.*

Thus the scene fades out with Michele kissing her on the throat as she shakes her lazy head and tries to draw it away – while the final scene ends with Marino bidding the executioner, 'I am ready now to see you all die. Strike and sever earth from my mind,' the crowd thronging in, and then:

EXECUTIONER: *Behold the head of a traitor.*
(holding up
the head).
VOICE FROM
THE MOB: *Look at the blood running down his arm.*

The girl's kiss-sleepy head and the severed head of Marino are
contrasted thus, life and death. And the rapid sentences at the
end express in succession Marino's absolute scorn and spiritual
death, then the actual death and the triumph of the state, with
the voice from the people bringing together and wiping out both
those statements by its realism, its different sort of acceptance,
its drawing down of the exalted tensions into the earth that drinks
the blood. (The image came largely from Delacroix' painting of
the execution with its dramatic placing of the tensions.)

I wrote the last part up at Springwood, the waiting scene in
the etching studio while Norman dealt with some visitors who
had arrived, the sound of animated voices coming down to
them as I sat in the stone-built room that seemed bursting both
with all the figures resplendent in the etchings and the dark
presence of his planchette ordeal.

In Wilmot Street, not far from the Central Police Courts in
Liverpool Street, there was a wine-bar run by an Italian named
Amendola. Ray sums up our memories of this place. 'The bar
was in the ground-floor front room, and in a back room just
off it there was a dining-room where we used to lunch every
Saturday afternoon. A group met regularly there and had
formed themselves into a sort of club, portentously named
I Felici Literati. In the chair was always Sam Rosa,* a most
repulsive-looking man, completely bald – although I believe
that in his younger revolutionary days he had had flaming red

*Samuel Albert Rosa, born in Australia in 1866 but brought up in England,
had become by the age of eighteen a member of the executive committee
of the Social Democratic Federation under Hyndman. He returned to Australia with violent anarchist ideas. Expelled from the Socialist League in
1892, he announced that he'd form a League of the Just – see his *The Truth
about the Unemployed Agitation of 1890*. In 1919 he was expelled from the
N.S.W. Labor Party and formed a brief Socialist Party. At our club he
indulged in ornate oratory, but not of a particularly political kind.

hair, with brigand-like moustaches – with evil-grinning flashing skull-like teeth. At that time he was editor of Sydney *Truth*.
Others who used regularly to attend were Hugh Brayden, a
charming, intelligent Irishman, then schoolmaster, now
retired; A. L. Kelly, then music critic of the *Triad*, an amusing
chap with a rather ponderous sense of humour; George Gould-
ing, a likeable fellow, then in the Public Service, fat and grey-
ing. There were other regulars who were mainly of a political
turn of mind and did not interest me. Among the casual customers were George Finey, then *Smith's Weekly*'s most brilliant
cartoonist, Mick Paul, and various other journalists. The custom was, after spending most of the afternoon eating, drinking
and talking at Amendola's, to adjourn to the Greek Club, then
in Park Street, where one pulled oneself together with enormous draughts of rich Turkish coffee; and then, if one had still
enough strength, to go to Campbell Street, then as now Sydney's Chinatown, and dine on Long Soup and the Duck for
which Percy had a rhyming but unprintable epithet.'

Amendola's, Ray says, will always remain in his mind as the
place where he first saw 'that fabulous beautiful bitch Annie
Brennan. I will never forget how, one Saturday afternoon, she
came in drunk and danced among the bottles and glasses on
the table. It was an old stunt of hers, but to my goggled still-
adolescent eyes it was the most spectacular event I had ever
seen. I whispered to Hugh Brayden, "Who is she?" "Annie
Brennan," he said. "How beautiful," I sighed. "You should
have seen her a couple of years ago," he replied, bored. I was
horrified at such blasphemy. But that bitch. How she dominated all that crowd in those days. Leon Gellert was inspired
to write *The Isle of San* by the thought of her downfall. Everybody was in love with her, even Gruner, although everybody
knew what a slut she was. I always think it was a sad waste
that her particular choice piece of feminine bitchery has never
been immortalized in paint, so many artists were in love with
her. But I do not know of any who would have had the ability
to record her unique charms. He would have had to possess
the bravura of an Augustus John, the sentimental sensitivity
of a Greuze, and the bitch-insight of a Toulouse-Lautrec. But
her beauty, vivid as it still is to me, was very subtle. Her small

delicate features with the Germanic colouring inherited from her mother, her slow smile, the soft cadence of her voice, her grace of movement, were all factors that went to disguise the Queen of All Bitches.

'At that time she had a flat in Victoria Street, on the other side of Kings Cross, not far from the Fire Station. I went back with her there that night after I first met her, and I sat there entranced, just gazing raptly upon her beauty, my bladder near bursting point with cheap wine, but too coy to ask where to go and ease it. I'll never forget my relief when I got outside against the wall of St John's Church. I used often to go up to her flat in the mornings and sit there bemused and dumbfounded as I watched her dressing and titivating herself after a night's debauchery in expectation of another to come. But the idea of doing more than gaze never crossed my worshipping mind.'

At this time Phil too often went to her flat in the mornings and tidied it up, just for the pleasure of gazing at the goddess. I confess that I never felt quite this magic in Anna. I found her a notable spectacle, but one that moved me only at a certain distance, as if I were watching her on the films. But one more anecdote of Ray's is worth giving as an example of the way Anna could spell people with her queenly Teutonic presence, which in repose seemed often to have an air of nobility and virtue.

'Despite all her bitchery, her selfishness, her utter unscrupulousness, she retained an extraordinary and uncanny ability to arouse love. As an example of this, I remember sharply an incident of some years later. One Saturday night I went to an Italian café, the Roma, then popular with us all, accompanied by a girl I was getting around with in those days. To my surprise, there was Anne seated alone at a table, looking very tired and ill. I had not seen her for some time; I believe she had been in Melbourne. As we passed her, I wished her good evening and she replied with that slow, grave, sweet smile of hers. When my girl and I were seated, she excitedly asked who Annie was. I told her and she exclaimed how beautiful she was. "You should have seen her a couple of years ago," I replied, unconsciously quoting Hugh's remark to me when

I first saw Anne. But my girl could not take her eyes off Anne and said that I must introduce them as she wished to kiss her! (My girl was perfectly normal, let me say.) I was horrified and told her not to be silly, not to dream even of doing such a thing as Annie was by that time rotten with T.B. and God only knows what else. However, when we had finished our meal and were leaving the table, she rushed over to Anne, introduced herself, and asked if she might kiss her. I looked on, stricken but entranced. Annie, with all the dignity and grace of a princess, gave that irresistible, beautiful smile of hers and accepted the kiss as her rightful homage. I never saw her again.'

But to return to Amendola's bar. The place was taken over by Betsy, a red-haired woman with a limp, who had been married to a very capable I.W.W. speaker and organizer. The marriage broke up in 1920, and the husband, Rudolph, was said to have joined a circus and become an animal trainer. Betsy did not take over Amendola's licence but rechristened the house Café La Bohème, and it certainly became, as Ray says, 'a meeting place for all the madmen in town. It seems to me somewhat amusing, when one realizes how close Betsy's was to the Police Station, that the dumb-headed police took so long in raiding her, with all the uproarious carousing that went on there day and night. The site has been absorbed into a hideous bastard Spanish-American architectural monstrosity of a picture show with entrance in George Street. How clearly I remember Betsy herself, limping and staggering up and down the stairs with her tubercular hip, her untidy, gingery curls dangling from under the lace of a grimy boudoir-cap, and her screeching, birdlike voice vibrating through the place – a voice that could dominate a room full of obstreperous drunks. Many a time have I seen a cantankerous boozer cower in a corner or slink from the room under its lashing. But she was really a very generous and kindly person, and many are the times when I and others have been grateful to her for a meal when we did not have a penny in our pockets. The quality of her cooking was very variable and her menus erratic. Typical of the reaction of her customers as to what they might expect to be dished out to them was what happened one night when Betsy announced in her piercing voice that the main dish was Spanish Pie. I noticed the eyes of a fellow art student who was sitting next me flash expectantly, and, when the dish was placed before him, he whispered to me with genuine disappointment that he had thought it was to be Spanish Fly.'

Betsy was abjectly afraid of thunder. She remarked, 'I get under the bed at once or whatever's handy. It makes my head crack.' But she didn't seem afraid of much else. Among the many journalist frequenters was David McKee Wright, then editing the Red Page, with his shaggy mop of blown white hair, white face and pulled-out nose, a face rather like his own mellifluous faceless poems. He hated catching the train home to Glenbrook and always managed to find excuses for delay so that he just missed it. Then he'd sit back and say that he mustn't by any chance miss the next one. Which he missed. He was married to Brisbane-born poetess Zora Cross who had had a brief period of fame with a series of sonnets full of sonorous terms of passion (a long way after Rossetti's *House of Life*). The literary world had been highly excited to find a woman saying over and over again that she was passionate; and David had been proud of carrying off the many-adjectived creature. But he still didn't want to go home.

One night, as he was denouncing poetry that didn't sing, lilt, chirp, pipe, carol or warble, I pointed out that he'd miss his train. 'I wouldn't miss that train for anything in the world. Zora's waiting at home for me, watching the clock, listening for the train-whistle, God bless her, there's nothing like a cosy home and a loving wife to welcome a man at the end of a hard day.' But as the time neared, he remarked hopefully, 'It isn't far to the station, is it?' At last we pushed him out. He grasped my hand. 'Come and see me off?' he begged. 'We can have a last one at the station bar.' We got into the tram. He watched his watch all the way. 'It's no use,' he said as we got off, 'we're too late. I feel it in my bones that we're going to miss that train. We can't fight against fate. What a misfortune. I wouldn't cause Zora a moment's worry if I could possibly help it. You're my witness before God that I did my best. Let's have one at the bar.'

'You'll catch it all right if you hurry.'

He couldn't find his ticket when he came to the barrier.

'I can see it's going. We're too late.' As soon as the train started steaming out, he found his ticket and made a dash along the platform. 'I knew I'd miss it,' he said, as he came back panting. 'Well, you saw I did my best. Fate's against me.'

We went back to Betsy's and he drank some sour claret, praising the Irish for writing with a lilt. I reminded him of Joyce, but he said Joyce was a renegade, only a true Irishman in his capacity to pull the wool over serious people's eyes. He sank into his claret-cup of maudlin amiability and I left. Later I heard the sequel. Having missed the last train, he slept on a chair, and woke the house up at an early hour by screaming that he'd swallowed his false teeth and could feel a murderous lump on his chest. They rushed him off in an ambulance. At the hospital he was hastily given sandwiches of cottonwool to chew, and was X-rayed. No sign of false teeth anywhere in his anatomy. He was told that 'the great pain there is in my stomach' was no proof of nearing death, and he walked back to Betsy's, ruminating.

Someone must have stolen his teeth, he insisted, and was given some porridge to eat. Then, after he had remembered several times putting his teeth in places where they weren't to be found, Betsy began sweeping up and rattled out his teeth from behind the piano. Then he remembered that he'd thought behind the piano an excellent place for hiding one's teeth.

Ray had even more experience of David's dislike of home-going than I did. Betsy used to ask him to take over the job of getting David aboard his train. 'He would continue to gesticulate wildly with his long arms and lean fingers, reciting more poetry and blandly resisting my efforts to get him on to the train. Then as it moved out of the platform, he'd watch it disappear into the darkness and suddenly pull himself together. "There," he'd say, "you can see I've done my best, but I've missed it. There is only one thing now to be done. Back to Betsy's and some more beer." Thus it went on until one night I actually managed to get him on to the train, on the promise of going home with him. In my ignorance of Sydney, I imagined Glenbrook to be in the suburbs, not realizing till the hours passed, with David's lanky figure parading up and down the carriage, still reciting poetry, that it was well up in the Blue Mountains. When we finally got there, Zora Cross emerged through the bush to meet us, carrying a lantern and looking not unlike Holman Hunt's *Light of the World*. It was a crazy house, with what appeared to be hundreds of children.'

In the pub near the Press Club, a few minutes off closing time. All around the bar a heaving mass of men elbowing, pushing, trampling on each other's feet, and shouting their orders. Reaching over shoulders, waving pound-notes, dropping irretrievable coins. The one time when even the most pugnacious of Australians had no time to pick a quarrel, intent only on attracting the attention of those floating goddesses, the pink-bosomed pneumatic barmaids with sweat in their curly-haired armpits. The daily rush scene in every Sydney pub. And when the door was at last shut and bolted, the retreating beer-swipers would drop bottles at the tram junctions as they pushed and jumped on to the packed trams, or fell off them.

We retired with our drinks to a window-recess and leaned. No good Australians stand when they can lean. Up came Malcolm, a deadly metaphysical Scot, who had an inturned almost blind look behind his thick glasses, especially when he remarked, standing square with feet wide apart and one arm behind back, raising and lowering his head sharply, 'Now what is your opinion of Kant's concept of the moral law?' Not that he waited for any answer. He merely went blinder and bleaker, and suspected all attention till you had finished any ill-advised comments; then his eyes glittered and he launched his prepared sermon. 'In my view the moral idea of Kant is a highly spiritual conception, and what the world lacks today, particularly Australia, where materialism reigns supreme.' He was a first-rate journalist, a bloodhound on the trail of any skulking news item, particularly those without a moral idea. He reserved his metaphysics for leisure hours, and took a special delight in fastening on to me. I'd first met him at the Press Club where he buttonholed me for an hour with the declaration that Carlyle was a moral idealist, a true Scotsman, badly needed by the world today, particularly by rampantly materialist Australia.

Now he said that next day he'd be driving up the Blue Mountains on a secret assignment, and, as he knew I'd like to accompany him, he'd call for me early in the morning. Learning that he'd pass Springwood, I agreed. The season of the year was mid-winter, cold enough for a few days to make us decide at *Idyllia* that it was perhaps about time to light a fire, though we never did. If I'd had to meet him somewhere, I wouldn't have turned up; but he drove to our place and blew his horn till I appeared. We drove away without breakfast and stopped at a wayside pub on the outskirts of Sydney for bacon and poached eggs. Malcolm produced a bottle of whisky. It was cold driving, especially after we began ascending the mountain road. At Glenbrook we stopped to see David.

He welcomed us in and I met Zora, a plain woman with the brick-red face of someone looking often into ovens. Malcolm had calculated the right moment to call. We ate the food of the married poets and looked at the pictures that David had painted in rather heavy forms and cloudbursts of colour, with titles like *Zora Cross Watching the Birth of the World* or *Spiritual Eclipse of the Life of a Nation*. Zora figured largely in all of them. I was touched and looked again at her. She wasn't so brick-red after all, much softer than she'd seemed, and tranquilly remote. David then wanted to take us on a three-mile walk to a spot where a recent murder had been committed. Malcolm busily computed whether any more blood could be squeezed out of the stones of the murder spot and decided there was no news value in the walk. To my surprise he didn't ask Zora what she thought of Kant and Carlyle.

We drove on in our rickety Ford. The air grew colder. Malcolm now divulged the goal of our journey. Snow. There were rumours of a snowfall not far up in the ranges and his paper wanted a photo. We looked down into the great gorges, the blue bush sweeping with subtle gradations into horizons of intense violet, the canyons filled with a rich smoky azure that seemed exuded rather than inherent in objects, lying in a soft dust of light over the miles of dwindled trees. The eye, used to the cramped spaces of town, or at best to long paddocks and the restless creeping expanse of ocean crumpled on to the sky, was unable to cope with such an exuberance of distance. The

panorama of blue amplitude, cleft into magnificence and toppling through depth after depth of teeming light, made the
watcher dizzy. Nothing moved or could move in the enormous
valley of majestic silence; and yet one felt the precise form of
it as an outpouring, a swinging-to-glory, like a Beethoven
rhythmic change which in two bars conquers all space. Only
the luxuriance of blue, the effluvium of a gorgeous complexity
subdued to a single pattern. Hard to credit that even all the
rays sent out by the sun, decomposed into brilliance by all the
spectra of the world, could produce such a weight and wealth
of harmony.

We couldn't drive on for ever. Malcolm had a one-day
assignment. No sign of snow at all. Yet it was unthinkable for
such a capable journalist to return and confess that snow had
beaten him. If not findable, it could be manufactured. Noting
a stretch of limestone, he halted the car and walked about till
he struck the angle at which the stone platform glittered plausibly like a thin snowdrift. The few shreds of grass and bush on
the stone would show up like survivors of the vegetation that
the snow had trampled out.

We turned back; and nearing Springwood, Malcolm took
the side-road for Norman's house without asking me. He had
had it all worked out. Norman received us with some surprise
and produced a whisky bottle to relieve our chilled state,
though he didn't himself drink. Malcolm rose in his usual
stately way, and remarked in guttural tones, 'In my view the
moral idea of Kant . . .' Norman was polite enough to say
nothing. When we left, Malcolm confided to me that he'd
always wanted to know what N.L.'s opinions were on fundamental morality and he was very pleased to find that they were
so like his own.

Rose asked Janet and myself to dine with her at the Australia
and suggested she'd like to look in at one of our haunts. We
took her to Betsy's, where someone played the piano and a few
couples danced. Les Robinson, a lesser Kafkaesque fantasist,
sat hunched in a corner, gloating and remarking of any passable girl, 'Wouldn't she exhaust a fellow nicely? Oh wouldn't

she?' Rose paid for everyone's drinks and sat queenly in another corner.

Anna Brennan like the others came now and then. And suddenly one night her father Christopher arrived. We had all assumed there was no contact between the two since Anna left home to live on her considerable wits and her ample charms. I had not met Brennan before, though he was a close friend of Lionel's. Norman did not think much of his poems and for this reason I had not read them closely after an initial attraction. Someone whose word I trusted had told me that one night over his cups C.B. had talked about Anna in the days before her flight and had expressed the most ferocious jealousy. C.B. declared that he waited up at nights behind the door to leap out on her when she came home late, smelling too warmly of kisses and wine and dance music; he was determined, he said, to stop her before she went to the bad. From this account I felt sure that his too-heated anxieties had played a strong part in driving her into the extreme step she took, and that he was an example of the domineering father unconscious of the roots of his jealous furies. Anna herself told Ray of her girlhood at Newport: how C.B., when in liquor, used to force her into a corner and abuse her intolerably.

There was certainly between Anna and her father both a sharp antagonism and a deep bond. And clearly the bond had become twisted and lost inside the antagonism. What happened at Betsy's, though in part obscure, showed both the irritated attraction and the inability to live in any sort of lasting accord. C.B. installed himself at Betsy's, in a little room in a courtyard at the back, and drank steadily. He was rather heavily turned in on himself, silent, but not unfriendly to us others, only rarely coming out with one of his ripely opinionated comments, saying that the piano didn't disturb him, music being no more than a vague background for entangled bodies and minds or a stimulant for those too poor in purse or spirit to buy liquor, tolerable anyhow if bad enough and not played too loudly. 'Every night,' says Ray, 'he used to appear in the room upstairs which was reserved for Betsy's more intimate customers. He would seat himself quietly in a corner with his own bottle of beer and appeared to take little interest in the drunken cavortings around him. Actually he was a shy man, did not mix easily with other people, and had no small talk.' He was sunk in a prolonged and unrelenting crisis. He had given in. No longer could he bear a life of domestic respectability and university boredom. (I have been told that he had given up marking exam-papers, let them accumulate and lie on his table, then at long last ordered them to be taken out and burnt; the students he allotted places according to what he knew of their ability.) He wanted to get down into the gutter where Anna had taken refuge. She had proved stronger than everything else in his life, and with morose determination he tossed his prestige, his scholarship, his peace of mind and his assured income into her wide and insatiable lap. But Anna won only because she had as her ally his poetry, the pressure on his mind of the poetry he had once written and didn't want to understand, the poetry which accused his society, his civilization, of a total dereliction from the human path, the human dream. His poetry, devilishly nestling between Anna's breasts, proved stronger than all his rationalizations about it, all his studies in so many languages of verse, all his hopes of a definitive edition of Aeschylus. (Only a few scraps found at his death: 'It's all here,' he said, tapping his brow.) Anna and his poetry became one, the defiant whore and the song that would accept nothing less than Eden in a world of money and the fragmentation of men, the reduction of men to things.

Brennan was the only genuine *symboliste* poet in the English language, deriving in large part from the work of his master Mallarmé, but owning the rages of Rimbaud and the vision of the city of alienation that was Baudelaire's. The overpowering vastness and the ancient bones of desolation that litter his inner landscape have however their Australian basis; and *A Burden of Tyre* brings out fully this Australian rebirth of *symbolisme* in his work, its relation to our national development and the crisis of imperialism: for Australia the decisive changes linked with the Boer War, federation, and the movement into modern nationhood.

It is one of the great regrets of my life that I did not even try to say one intelligent word to him as he sat brooding with his quick eyes dulled, sucking at his great curved pipe and bending over his beer mug with his magnificent beak of a nose and his mane of rusty black hair brushed back. A strange predatory image, a defeated eagle, too lost even to wave his pipe argumentatively. When he stood up, he stooped more than ever, his more than six feet broken. Anna too, very hard up, was taken in by Betsy; and she and C.B. drank together and quarrelled bitterly. Whatever brief emotion had flared up in the gutter-meeting was dissipated in the chafing animosities of a pair whose love had irreparably become envenomed. To save the fallen woman, to go down and become part of her, purging guilt by a deeper guilt, repudiating the burden of a consciousness hopelessly divided against itself . . . Anna, already suffering badly from T.B., hammering on his door and demanding money for her medicine, shouting foul things; Brennan slumped inside his clothes, opening his mouth to speak and unable to speak.

But after a while he was joined by a woman from New Zealand, Violet Bird, of pleasant but not striking looks. They were fond of one another; perhaps the bond went deeper than one thought. Once or twice, seeing him glance at her with a half-smile, I felt that we were underrating her, that I was prejudiced in my youthful down-at-heel scorn for their ageing seediness. Underneath she had had a sweet bright light careless quality; and I had the conviction that with his feeling of a foundered world and the confused anguish of his hell-descent after Anna he had become emotionally dependent on her. Their relationship had begun before he took the Avernian Road to Betsy's. They used to drink, Ray says, in wine-bars and pubs around the university, and C.B. was warned not to make a show of himself in full view of the students. In any event, she turned up at Betsy's soon after the collapse of the reunion with Anna. Then one night, after she had been on a visit up the coast to Mick Paul's place near Narrabeen, she thought the last tram had gone; it crashed round a bend and knocked her down, killing her. Brennan was badly hit. I saw him in his crushed misery; but what could I, who had never known him, say? Then he faded from Betsy's and I did not see him again.

I have cited the story that I think was most prevalent about Violet's end. But my faith in the folklore and scandal of pubs was somewhat shaken when I consulted Ray. 'Brennan had returned,' he said, 'temporarily to Newport where he had lived for many years. Newport is on the seaside, about twenty miles from Sydney. Today you can travel there in comfort in modern double-decker buses direct from the city at Wynyard Square and over the Harbour Bridge. But in those days you had to take the ferry to Manly, a tram to Narrabeen, and then an antiquated bus to Newport. Well, somewhere on that stretch between Manly and Narrabeen, poor Vi (drunk of course) was hit by a tram one night and killed. Chris went into great poetic attitudes of drama at his mistress being thus killed while on her way to see him. His beery eyes becoming more and more goldfish-like and distended at the thought. However, my approach to the drama became rather cynical when I heard Mick Paul, who lived at Dee Why, about halfway between Manly and Narrabeen, bewail, with tears in his one eye, how Vi had been so tragically killed while on her way to see him. Then a drunken Scottish architect named Armstrong who lived at Manly (several years later he jumped off Manly ferry in a state of alcoholic ecstasy), told me, with his bloodshot eyes more bloodshot than usual, that on that awful night Vi had been on her way to visit him.'

Perhaps it was out of a rage against her father that Anna acted perfidiously towards Betsy. She brought in a couple of police pimps and had the place raided. Betsy managed to survive this, but a second raid put her out of business. She was already in difficulties through another piece of duplicity. She took in out of the kindness of her heart a White Russian named Theo, who, after living in the house for some time and paying nothing, opened up a rival café at the corner of Campbell and Pitt Streets. 'I remember,' says Ray, 'how Betsy used to limp round her place and screech in that awful voice of hers, "That bastard Theo! The skunk only made up to me to learn how I cooked spaghetti, and now he's trying to put me out of business."'

As for Brennan, he had entered irretrievably on the broken life he kept up till his death in 1932. Forced to resign his associate professorship in 1925, he survived on contributions from various friends (including Anna after her marriage). It seems to me that he was himself unable to face the complex of emotions that had driven him into his pitiable revolt. The events I have narrated have been hidden away, but there are many accounts of his later picturesque career as a fallen giant. However, I give Ray's memories of those failing years. 'He was certainly a complex and frustrated figure. I remember him well up to the time he died, when he had become quite a figure around Kings Cross. He was always amiable enough, but quite lacking in personal charm, with his watery bulbous eyes, great beak of a nose, and a characterless mouth disappearing into chinlessness. He was usually very dirty, smelling like a stale brewery, given to wearing black shirts, which in those days were usually worn only by engine drivers, hob-nailed boots, and quaintly shaped hats, the brims of which were always so twisted as to remind one of Robin Hood. He was not a good conversationalist and was only at ease when he could pontificate in a Johnsonian manner. After his collapse at the university he had a rather tough time and used to drink in the lowlier pubs at the bottom of William Street. But as conditions improved slightly with him, he moved gradually up until he reached the heights of the Mansions Hotel at Kings Cross. There he used to hold court, seated in the saloon bar; and he could be quite entertaining with an audience, quoting bawdy passages from the classics. You could approach the Presence as long as you bought him a schooner of beer; and after an afternoon's homage from admiring university students, or others like myself who knew him so well, the old boy would be left at closing time with more beer than he could drink . . . Poor old Chris Brennan, at least I had the privilege of literally being sick on his head when recuperating, drunk, one night at Betsy's.'

Is it worth while bringing up all these details about Brennan? I myself hold to the simple faith that the truth is always worth telling and that if there is any spiritual depth, any positive value, in a man, it will come out in spite of and because of the pangs, ordeals and shames to which he is brought by his inner conflicts. Brennan, if not a fully great poet, had many elements of greatness; he represents the most complex and penetrating point of poetic vision in Australian culture up to the present. For this reason all the significant details of his life are of the utmost interest. He is big enough to need and to demand the most searching light on all his deeds; and his collapse is integrally related to the conflicts defined in his poems, his social and his poetic insights, his grasp of the divided and alienated nature of man in the post-Baudelairean world of the cashnexus and the city-desert. His relations to Anna help to reveal what he is really getting at in his poems, and to distinguish its genuine *symboliste* vision from its vague and emptily idealistic elements. And so Anna too has her meaning in this world of the 1920s, when the conflicts that Brennan grasped or intuited were coming to a new head, baffling us and yet driving us forwards. Rightly enough she keeps on reappearing in this book, an emblem both of desecrated life and of the beauty that survives desecration and stirs our hearts against the desecrating forces.

15 · MASQUERADING VILLON

ONE EVENING, with Janet holidaying in Melbourne, I was with Ray and Phil and some others, Unk White and George Finey, in a restaurant. Someone ordered beer. A normal though illegal order. Suddenly some hatchet-faced roisterers, who had been setting the example of loudly calling for beer, rose to their feet, blew whistles and moved to the door to make sure no one escaped. The police poured in. All the diners were rounded up and shoved into Black Marias which were waiting round the corner. A recent regulation had declared that not only proprietors but anyone drinking on unlicensed premises could be arrested. But why our restaurant was unlucky I don't know. Perhaps the police had to raid at least one place; perhaps the proprietor had annoyed them about something else, had fallen behind with his contributions to the constables on the beat. Anyway there we were in the huddled van. We hastily conferred and decided that we must not give away our relation to Norman. Otherwise he'd be embarrassed by headlines next morning:

NORMAN LINDSAY'S SONS ARRESTED DRUNK

or something of the sort. Even though we happened to be stone sober. We hadn't even drunk the beer bottles that had arrived under our table. At the police court the drab details were quickly taken. Then we had to pass along between rows of detectives who gave us a once-over to see if our faces were known. I have seldom known such an unpleasant feeling. Those smug-ugly faces with their vicious eyes and clumsy cynical jokes as we ran the gauntlet. One detective is enough to make any honest man want to vomit; the effect of twenty to thirty of them all together is hard to describe. I should have to call up the curses of Marino.

I was put in a large cell which was tiled on the walls like a public lavatory. The walls were running with water. The only bit of furniture was a wet wooden couch. But I didn't feel like complaining, not after those congregated detective faces. I sat or lay sleepless all night, with the waterchill striking to my bones, and watched the slow dawn come up through the bars which constituted the door. A clammy dawn, dirtily phosphorescent, coming up over a world that had turned utterly hollow, like my chest, and echoed with dull reverberations of boots, snorts, far voices. At last we were herded out into a yard. We stamped about and came warmly to life, not knowing what to say, like friends who have met after years of separation. But the others around us had no such difficulties. Somehow the news had got round that we were writers, artists, and things like that. The tramps, down-and-outs, petty thieves and wife beaters all wanted to talk to us. At once a discussion on Dickens began. The others knew all the novels and had ideas about them. 'What we need is a writer like that who'd tell the truth and help the poor.' But they also enjoyed his work and got worked up talking about the characters.

Then we went in. On account of hiding our identities we hadn't been able to ask for anyone to bail us out, and we owned only a few shillings in our pockets when arrested. However, there were champions duly present to pay our fines when we came up before the uninterested bench. Out in the glorious open street we shouted, embraced, and rushed for the nearest pub; but I had got a bad cold in my kidneys from the cell.

In Melbourne Janet had met Adrian Lawlor, who wrote for *Vision*; and he came up to stay with us, a worried fellow with an odd-shaped head who sat in the kitchen in his dressing-gown and banged on the table, 'Look at him, the dirty dog! He's got no small talk.' I thoroughly agreed with him. Altogether his stay was miserable for him. For instance, when Laurence and I were discussing one of the pauses in Beethoven, A.L. jumped in and said, 'It's a transition from light to darkness.' We disapproved of such simple analyses and began asserting that there was a complex emotional leap, an opposition of elements harmonized in the total conception. A.L. dashed out muttering, 'Why can't I say anything right?' I recall

too when several of us were in the kitchen looking at a photo
of Phil that exaggerated his eyebrows and made him look like
George Robey. 'Not at all like me,' Phil insisted gruffly, and
every moment became more like the photo, indignantly resisting our laughter and (I now see) suffering.

I met Phyllis at the G.P.O. corner, keeping my eyes open for
Jacques, who had a Box Office number at the other end of the
colonnade. We hurried off to drink coffee, then after our usual
fencing comments she took me to see the new room she had
hired for dancing lessons. Nothing in it but a piano and a dusty
light, a window and floorboards. As soon as we were alone, I
grew oppressed and less eloquent; also I feared that my breath
might smell from the bad claret of last night. You can't kiss
with abandon if you are intent on not opening your mouth.
Also, I still didn't know what she thought of me, though I knew
she still hoped to use me to write notices of her dancing. Not
that she was particularly mercenary; her affection for Jacques
interfered a lot with her career. She didn't want me, but didn't
want to lose me.

Worse, I still didn't know what I thought of her, or why I
was with her in the bare room. Of course I was jealous of
Jacques, who had been in love with Janet before I knew her;
but that wasn't sufficient explanation. I kept on trying to
impress her with my reputation-to-be (which otherwise I didn't
think about), and that increased my conviction that I wasn't
and wouldn't be loved for myself alone. Besides, I didn't want
her to love me. In boasting to her, I expressed my lack of faith
in any coming fame, and I wanted to be revenged for the lies
she made me tell (not to her, but to myself). Afterwards I
always felt more a failure even than I was; the topless aspiration that spoke to the bored and scented girl became a bot-
tomless depression when on leaving her I looked into my
notebook.

Now, holding her in my arms in a tiny room empty except
for a hollow and dusty smell and a piano that one couldn't
expect to burst into music of its own accord, I had no desire,
only a strong wish to humiliate her for never having wanted
me and for never having made me want her. Perhaps if she had

wanted me, I could have expressed my anger by turning away, but how could I repudiate her when she took so little interest in me and was not enough moved even to deny me her mouth? (Though I told myself also that if she became venus-alive in my arms, I'd be so enchanted that I'd forget all my resentments and uncertainties. Another illusion.) True, it was only her vanity, with a faint mixture of contemptuous kindness, that held her quiescent; so I could indeed hurt her if I really wanted to by a blow at her vanity. And yet a hurt of that kind was too small, too feebly base, to satisfy. Surely I'd have risked my life to save her from the slightest rebuff to her good nature. The hurt I wanted to give, the hurt alone capable of salving my self-pity, was a blow that both woke and broke her essential femaleness. If somehow I could make clear that I rejected, not the rather silly and dear Phyllis, but Woman altogether, how happily I'd have made the gesture. Phyllis the person, the tinkly laughter, the dance-dreamer, the lithely legged, the lost soul, I wanted to treat with all kindliness, with fostering concern. And yet again, if she awoke, how should I tell the particular girl from the whole sex that she concentrated? (These insolubles remained, since I would never be asked to deal with them. How could I expect an offer of her entire self when I was offering only a fragment of a poet? only the cigarette butts of café-boredom, the jingles of vanity? What I protested against in her was only the shallowness of my own response, which was determined, not by what I had to offer, but by the narrow philosophy of my art.)

The passion was there, I insisted to myself, the central force. In poetry. Theoretically that persuaded me, but I still felt personally stultified.

'I think I'll put the piano at the other end of the room,' she sensibly said. We pushed it along. I blamed the daunting room. The floor was damp and warped, the piano could not even be sat upon. She prattled of blue curtains to be bought. We considered the view from the window: a brick wall and a sooted tree. A photo-peeling hung from the rakishly angled lid of a rubbish tin like an arch curl over the ear of the handle. Her face was expressionless.

I had not yet read Stendhal's *Le Rouge et Le Noir* or I might

have learned something about myself in the character of Julien
Sorel. I was in fact obeying a drastic sense of honour, an adolescent test or ordeal. In the last resort, a conviction that the
world of women was suffering from a lack, a void, a chill, which
it was my duty to offer to fill with warmth and purpose whenever the chance turned up. Not that I was quite so vain as to
look on myself as the sole person capable of saving women from
a dull life unredeemed by the Blood of Dionysos; but since I
could only be myself and could only exist at the spot where
I existed, I had to take the challenging chances as they came
along, and treat them as the crucial moment when earth hung
between life and death – just as every Christian of the medieval
world had to treat his particular moment of temptation or
grace as something on which the fate of the universe depended,
with all the angelic hierarchies circling the point of his individual needle. If I had been thinking of anything so paltry as my
own happiness, I would have been at home or meeting the
Pacific breakers. But I had to 'submit to experience' so that
I might control the art-image of beauty.

Donne's *Elegies* provided an idiom for rejecting the abstract
Laura of contemplation and for finding the centrique part of
all experience lodged in every woman aware of possessing legs.
To love the Petrarchan Laura was to submit to the tyranny
that arrested life and falsified it with a rigid balance, a virtu-
ously dead symmetry. For poetry and love, the individual girl
evaporated into puffs of colour from outside the spectrum, into
circulating contours, yielding an inexhaustible sweetness and
asking only to be pivoted afresh on the centrique part, the life
axis. After that she became an individual girl again. The two
aspects fused and yet were quite distinct.

It seemed as simple as that in theory. Yet nothing could
worse accord with my wish to be wanted for myself, which pre-
supposed a point of pure self somewhere inside me – and like-
wise in the girl who was asked to appreciate this melancholy
core. So I hid from the contradiction in a banal bitterness.
Women belonged to the obvious brutes of the world, the stock-
brokers of the confidence trick, the baboons of business and the
thugs of trade. With their miraculously tender bodies they gave
themselves to the sugar daddies with gold rings hanging from

gouged noses over blabbering lips, the shop-window dummies of standardized neatness, the nitwits of patent leather hair, the good timers with a repetitive gramophone record of slang for brain, the gigolos of jazz, the shaven gorillas of the old-school ties. But to those who laboured by starlight to provide their venus-toilet, the mirror of delighted consciousness in which, amid the roses and lilies of the blood, all proper girls stared themselves into beauty, they turned up their noses. I powdered your tits with orris of the moon, I repeated, watching Phyllis coyly take the curtain measurements.

Glad when we left the room and the gawky silence. We walked up to the Public Library. The silver sky was breaking with silent bombs of glory, lightnings of my bitter exaltation. Phyllis wriggled her plump shoulders and I asked to see her hands. She gave them with an apologetic smile. But they weren't the hands I wanted: as if she had unwrapped them from a parcel, not slipped them from her muslin sleeves. Still, I kissed her palms. Pleasantly she crossed her arms and placed the hands palms down over her bosom. I thought perhaps I had misjudged her. An old man with bulbous nose coming lordily out of the Union Club, retired banker or wool-merchant, turned to look at us, then went off banging his stick down. We laughed at his spats and were suddenly quite friendly.

Another drawback of hypostatizing adolescent confusions in a theory of tests and trials, ordeals and submissions – a perpetual calling up of chaos in order to impose a precarious order upon it – was the haunting emotion that somewhere, unknown, missed, was going on a fabulous scene of enjoyment. Somewhere, just round the corner, was the party to end all parties, the impossible She who was both Laura and Gutter-Venus, the rose of all roses lolling to be plucked. One heard the music momently creeping down some alley, saw the abrupt light aureoling a girl's head in an attic, watched the meeting shadows on a curtain, and was certain of the tryst, the invitation, the chance collision of mystery and naked delight. Working or reading at home, wandering on the cliffs or diving under the breaker-crest, I felt nothing of all that; but after I left those refuges, the lure of the fabulous scene increased as

I neared the town and the familiar dens where nothing happened but everything seemed always about to happen.

I felt sure that an important event would be encountered at the Artists Ball in the Town Hall. How anything worthwhile could happen in a vast building overrun in every nook as wide as a girl, in every cupboard and narrow staircase, by roaring revellers, I do not know. To talk in its maze of din would be as hard as composing a poem on asphalt with a road-drill. No one could clasp there without having flashlight photos taken with the most unbecoming foreshortenings. I was going in character of Villon because hose could be borrowed from lady friends and I could wear my own battered hat without ceasing to be medieval.

We dressed, undressed, dressed, at the house of the good-natured boozer who managed somehow to draw a draughtsman's salary. Toreadors, gitanas, pierrots, bears, and someone almost as bare as Truth. Our amiably rotund host with dark sweating face said that he could carry whisky flasks most comfortably under his inside-out dressing-gown, tied with old rope as girdle. I told him that I could change Villon into Panurge without the police being any wiser; surely Villon had been one of the Panurgean prototypes. And he, Jim, could be Friar John. We swigged whisky to gain courage for a tram journey, taxis being voted down as pusillanimous as well as consuming money better kept for bottles.

We smuggled drink in, though there would be a bar. We mistrusted the bar's capacity. 'The price will be hellish too,' said Jim. We suspected that the cordoning police would search us. Malcolm, pessimistically dressed as a Chinaman (having been lent the costume), insisted that there were rumours of disreputable characters planning to gatecrash and the police had instructions to watch out for whisky smugglers. But when we flourished tickets, the police let us in; perhaps they thought that the real disreputables would have disguised themselves better. We were among the first arrivals in the big resounding space, and everything was tedious and tawdry. Lots of music was needed to polish up the decorations, revive the flowers, rub the stale air and make it sparkle. Lots of determined girls with bright faces were needed. We went down into the basement because the bar was there. No drinks were yet being sold, but we felt more at ease near an unopened bar than an unfilled ballroom. We went into a telephone box and took a nip of neat whisky in turns.

Things began moving somewhat more rapidly, though we still hung round booths where photos were to be taken or fortunes told. I was wearing a scalloped curtain as a cloak, a blouse-doublet, hose and an ancient felt-hat trimmed with a parrot's feather. She had said she'd meet me at the bar at half past ten and I had no near future but drink. I knew that when we did meet, she'd say in a weak voice: You've been drinking, really it's too much. Slowly the basement-night accumulated noises, a dust of uproar blurring the senses. Ray was there as his pirate self, already berserk with a dangerous sword, Phil as burly Pierrot. I tried to feel like my relevant heroes, Villon, the Archpoet, Hugh Primas, the Monk of Montaudon, the reckless filchers of song under the gallows-shadow, the wind rattling in the chained skeletons to fill the pauses of the stanzas that were a testament on the brink of the grave.

'You see the aptness of the Will-form in Villon?' I asked Jim. 'The insecurity, *timor mortis conturbat me*, the yellow shadow of the pest.'

'Insecurity? What do you call it today? You were too young for the war, you lucky sod. Rickety kids, war, hell and bananas.'

Villon wrote the *Little Testament* after committing his first criminal act, the first one anyway on a grand scale: December 1456, breaking into the Chapel with the other rapscallions, picking the locks of the chest, getting off with 500 crowns (500 golden girls, 500 torrents of golden wine). And the terror of death came on him in the icy dawn and he needed to pack his doomed young life in a ballad, so he became a great poet. Out of the shivering stinking terror. Listened to the bells, death a tremendous light that outlined life with a new hungry significance, picking out each little detail of the foul world with an acclaiming glee, netting the bruised breasts of the snoring sluts in a flowerglow, in a pathos of desire. And here was I, 400 years too late, still lost, but never having gone robbing amid the midnight cobwebs, never having written a great poem.

The crowd was gathering, the music beating in a froth over the churning voices, the feet shuffling. And this was revelry, O sweep and tumble of a Beethoven scherzo, forgive me. 'For the purpose of art we must experience all things, booze and girls and this, whatever you call it. And so gain the material for the image that transcends the broken senses, yet holds them together in the orgiasm of rhythm.' Beethoven's poisoned veins breaking into moonflowers of infinite tenderness, in gay rondos of desire perfectly gratified. 'We find the insufficiency, but unless we unreservedly give ourselves we lack the recoil.'

'Am I to understand,' said Friar John, 'that you belittle booze? that you fail to see it as a sublime end in itself? that you cheaply compare it with the windy excitements of art? My poor bloody friend, have some whisky.'

The pressure was already extreme. The dancers pushed slowly round the heaving floor. Over the packed gyrating mass reared the stalactitic organ pipes, like the bared teeth of yawning monsters that inhabited the cavern of heavy noise and furry lights. A Juliet turned my thoughts to Verona's Renascence festivities, a heroine from Balzac with high Empire bosom made me think of Beethoven rotted with such a freight of joy in his derelict body. How many girls here had primly thumped out the notes of the *Appassionata* without hearing one note of its cry of loss, without feeling the pus of anguish trickle down their suburban fingers? (N.L., on first hearing this sonata, without knowing anything of Beethoven's life, exclaimed, 'He must have had syphilis.') 'They think they're civilized,' I remarked, 'because they've been taught to wash.'

'Sure thing. I've unlearned all that, myself.'

'Saint Jerome said that he who was washed in the blood of the lamb did not need to wash again.'

'Not that I object to other people washing.'

'The multitudinous seas incarnadine.'

'What about coming down to the camp at Narrabeen?'

'I wrote a poem about tonight yesterday. I mean about Verona. I believe in anticipating events by looking backwards. You know they used to dress naked page-boys in gold leaf, which closed their pores. Pretty while it lasted. See how the little gold-leaf cupids gleam, they'll die by morning but they're charming now. The one thing I hate is cruelty.'

'Have some whisky.'

'A ghost flaps vanishing with a peacock-scream, and orange moons smell nicely on the bough. Horrible.'

Ray roared and swung his sword. A woman fell over a bench and showed her milky legs. The band played, *Yes, We Have No Bananas*. Jim tackled Ray from behind and took his sword, which he hid in a phone box and Ray was pacified at the bar. Half past ten and Phyllises everywhere. Time to end this nonsense. My poem disturbed me. Beauty and Joy did not need Inhumanity as their base. 'The contrast is false.'

'Don't you think it. A man can't remember and he can't forget. It's just hell. Do you know what cruelty is? At Victoria Station, that's London, Aussie. All the women calling out to us: Stick those dirty Germans, one for me please, Jack. Licking their blood-red lips. There's nothing but hate, only you weren't at the war, and so what do you know about anything? Dog's bottom.'

Were children dying at this moment to make possible a tumult of worthless junketing? The only difference between Sydney and Verona, perhaps, was the hypocrisy that hid the sacrifices and talked of uncontrollable laws. Can I accept a beauty married to such an antithesis? I accept the world, evil and all; I rejoice in it, evil and all. What does that mean? Beethoven, Man help thyself. Blake: Cruelty has a Human Heart, the Human Dress is Forgèd Iron, Pity could be no more, if we did not make sombody poor. I accept because I do not accept.

The dancers swung past, looped on terraces of light. The faces faded fierily in groves of the moon. In whose whispering world, no barriers now deter but farthingales, and spangled hair come dewily uncurled, while the cool grass jerks back to tell no tales. On these coffin-boards.

I met her on the stairs, lisping, a buxom columbine, whiter than ever, tinkly laughing, and forget that I didn't want to see her. She took my arm.

'I'm going to write a poem for you,' I confided, shouting

above the noises. 'On Titian. An evening at Aretino's in all the colours of a Venetian dusk-garden, with lute notes from the little summer-house as unimplicated as your laugh. The evening earth seen across a slow kiss and the smell of dark red wine spilt at your feet. The breadth of Titian's forms. No one else can model such a sensitive rotundity. The flow of contours is hardly discernible, yet as subtle as if there were a million gradations. Flora's bosom, fine as a single rose petal, broad as the earth.' She said nothing. I felt that I had the right to hold her while I talked of Titian. 'Danae's court painter. All his girls are Danaes ravished by gold, drenched in seminal light, the whores of Zeus. A sliding flux of gold shutting out the world, all but the small landscape tranquilly remote between the crimson curtain folds.' Titian now seemed to explain everything, to redeem the little gold-leaf boys, to silence even Aretino's cruel laugh and harmonize all experience. Yet Aretino's advice to his friend Dolci came into my mind: Strive to become a sculptor of the senses, not a miniaturist of vocabularies. Just what I was trying to say. A vast neighing laugh seemed to rise above the hall's babel, a fierce rutting neigh of cruel triumph. 'In beauty I trust,' I cried aloud in fear (as sleeping out alone on the mountains I had summoned up an image from one of N.L. pictures on the edge of sleep, and felt secure from all snakes and vampires.) She smiled unknowingly at me, a dainty consumer of rump steaks. 'I am Villon,' I told her in desperation, the wings of death fanning my eyes, the police after me, the blood price on my head. One of my hose started coming down. The costume didn't really suit my scraggy legs. 'Lend me a garter.'

Everyone laughing. Swaying bells of buoyant delight, innumerable laughter, *anarithmon gelasma*. I wanted to find Brennan again and argue whether *gelasma* meant laughter or sea-glitter. The ancients saw movement as light-flicker, colour as light effects: dogs were *argoi*, bright rather than swift. See the flashing dogs. The world spinning on the axis of the hall, the axis of my thudding temple. I was not so much learnèd as out of place. I knew that Phyllis was not for me. Besides, I didn't want her. 'My hose is coming down. Who gives a damn?

I'm a sham medieval. Got no codpiece. Can't be medieval without a codpiece or the Virgin Mary.'

The waves of the sea, the merry-merry waves, the going-around sea, the pool-whirl of my musical consciousness. We floated off on the sedate curves of a waltz. I could dance at last, being drunk. The world revolved in spirals of intensifying sweetness. Andante of the Fifth. Soon we'll storm the barricades. Flow on, life; you can't stop anyway. Wagner, after that long tramp and diarrhoea exhaustion, dropping dead into a dream that unwound the Rhine theme. Out of fear, death, anguish. What does not kill me, strengthens me. Smash the cymbals, Baccha with medusa-curls and enamelled face. Yes, we have no bananas. 'But Joyce is wrong,' I assure her, 'the flow is not a dissolution, it is a flow into the power and the glory, into a new concentration and clarity of form and meaning. The Rhine motive growing broader, more sweeping, as it grows from the small earth-springs. The Arietta dreaming securely into a deeper graciousness. Joyce is just damned, poor fellow. Some nice jimjamtin effects, Djin jingos jingling gingerly and all that, you know, twiddle-riddle silvergasht oyster. But life is the flow to more life. That means greater simplicity, greater richness.' I am broken, I yield.

With a rally of trumpets, with a swoon of nearness. We end against pillars, listening to hammering. Yet I could not say I loved her. The one lie I couldn't tell. I didn't know why. I simply didn't think of it.

'Of all the bloody skunks,' said Jim.

'Who pinched my sword?' Ray bellowed, melancholy as a cow, down aisles of reverberating loss.

Whisky in a phone-booth.

'Room at the end of the passage where they're laying the tarts. Shall we go? What happened to your sheila?'

'That is the question. Slings and arrows.'

Ray fell through some canvas. When last seen, he was beating his hands on a stone wall. 'Why doesn't someone play the organ?' I asked. 'God, for example. A terrific blast.' Villon sat in his attic with the bitter wind ribboning through the crannies. Too hungry to think, he coughed and the world swung seething below. Pity me, brothers. Then the many Phyllis became one Phyllis. Now I had the chance to see her home, stay the night. Now the ground was crumbling under my feet. I walked through the dark fumes of my fever. They will throw me into the cell under the graves and the winter, and I'll cough up my lungs. I saw Barry and Phyllis together. The opening notes of the *Appassionata* were now one with the thudding in my head, louder than all the jazz in the world, more powerful even than *Yes, We Have No Bananas*, the only tune that the band knew. I fell with the three notes down down and down the terrible depth of those three notes. Not the unimportant cracks of darkness between the stars, but the vaster space between and under those three notes. Nevermore. So I passed out and didn't see the fights when the crowd thinned and toughs raided the basement. People who didn't know me carried me up and down the aisles on their shoulders and set me out on various biers. So Jim told me next morning, fishing some beer up from under the bed. Jim the unfailing drunk's friend, frying bacon, indestructible. When the smell made me retch, he was on the spot in time with the pot and a word of useless encouragement, Jim the drunk's friend, advising beer.

16 · TWISTS AND TURNS

JOHN DALLEY, who was doing editorial work on the *Bulletin*, had decided on marriage – after an illness, I think. He and his wife were living up the northern line on the coast. John was keen to develop himself as a novelist who would catch the changing flavour of Australian life with an upper-class focus. A dapper small man with rounded face and suavely jaunty air, he had made himself as like an Englishman with an Oxonian background as any Australian could, with well-tailored dark blue suits and bowler hat and cane. Called to the English bar in 1901, he practised in Sydney a few years, then turned to *Bulletin* journalism, to which he stuck, apart from serving in Egypt and France in 1915-18. He had done much to draw N.L. into upper-class society, its ladies and its horses. N.L. was too busy an artist to succumb to this snob world, but it had its effect on him and the élite theses that underlay the god-fantasy in *Creative Effort*. The N.S.W. squattocracy has always been the most overbearing and self-assured; and something of its conception of society as simply divided into a very small élite and a faceless bad-mannered mob seems to have played its part in helping N.L. to build his picture of a small hierarchy of artists set over the masses who are passive except when destructive.*

*Two tales, N.L., commenting on how one at times can repress even familiar names, mentioned how he once had to make out a cheque to J.D. in repayment of some loan, and couldn't recall his name, went on gagging in a desperate effort to find some time and allow his paralysed memory to function. J.D. once purloined a number of letters exchanged between two very fine society ladies (I think he was having an affair with one). The larger part of the letters consisted of normal gossip, but suddenly in the midst of sentences the ladies interpolated obscenities, then went on normally again. Apparently a simple way of working off their more inhibited emotions.

John's correctly routined life was soon to be disrupted by the breakdown of his recent marriage. He had moved to a bungalow along the North Shore, where he hoped to find a quiet retreat. Unfortunately the place turned out to be all too quiet for his wife, who was left to her own resources when he went up to his Sydney offices. As a result it was not long before, despite his deafness and his dislike of sordid details, he found himself compelled to institute divorce proceedings against her, naming as co-respondent the house-agent assistant who had found the bungalow for them.

The lad had lost his job up the coast, but found another of the same sort in town, married to the ex-Mrs Dalley at Darlinghurst.

The pay was poor, or at least insufficient to keep the rent and liquor bill paid up; so he took a second job playing some instrument at a cinema – he was ardent on saxophones. Poor chap, he did his best to keep up with the unsteady and hurried world into which he had romantically jumped, a world that sill held a hectic glamour. But how could he hope to be a satisfactory husband, politely available all day as an estate-agent and blowing sadly most of the night in a stuffy cinema? He was slowly wilting and pimpling. He tossed back his lank hair, swallowed whisky, and increased his indigestion.

Naturally by this time we knew almost everything there was to know about John. In recording one of his peccadilloes I am swayed by three motives. First, I stubbornly hold with Terence that nothing human is alien to me – or ultimately ridiculous. I recall saying to Norman about John's idiosyncrasy, 'He'd be petrified with shame if he knew we all knew, but none of us likes him the less for what we know. On the contrary we like him better, for it makes him more human and washes out the last of the spiritual starch with which he collars himself. But so obtuse is self-love that he'd never see the positive values of the revelation.' Secondly, John once played a jape on Henry Lawson by sending him a fake cheque for £50. His upper-class arrogance made him quite unable to realize how cruel this was and how wretched must have been Henry's disappointment after finding what was for him an impossibly princely sum evaporate in his hands. For this he deserves no mercy. Thirdly,

the revelation plays such havoc with his gentlemanly demean-
our and is such an excellent period touch. This final aspect convinced me that I must bring the detail in. The following
passage in the *Times Literary Supplement* on Havelock Ellis's
Undinism and Urolagna, read as I was debating the matter,
made me realize the social background:

. . . Havelock Ellis's own view (and that of his sister) [was] that their
mother's behaviour had been sufficiently unusual to constitute a form
of erotic flirtation with her son. This matter has never been much
written about, and it is not easy to write about it with decorum. It
may, nevertheless, be suggested that the principal incident upon
which Havelock Ellis aligned his own sex-life for so many years was
not in fact unusual at all before Edwardian civic plumping and later
short skirts, and that, indeed, its probability was the great determi-
nant of women's fashions for many centuries. The remarkable thing
was the importance that an exceptionally shy man allowed one
moment of vesical incontinence to assume in his own mind throughout a long life. (Feb. 2, 1959.)

John was not so shy, but it seems that he had the same sort
of image at the core of his love responses. Like Ellis, he found
his deepest satisfaction in a urolagnic release.

He was not without boldness in his editorial policy. He told
me once that he held there were some people who couldn't be
libelled and that he kept this journalistically in mind. Another
aphorism of his was that the moral guilt or innocence of many
acts were (legally) determined by social situation. If a navvy
visited a friend's wife for tea, there were grounds for a divorce;
if a gentleman visited a friend's wife in the same way, it was
just a friendly visit. He put many odd jobs my way. Once he
asked me to write an advance critique of two visiting American
pianists, who played César Franck to me. I wrote a lot of nonsense about Franck being not so bad once in a while as long
as we had Beethoven regularly, etc. (In fact we had either of
them very rarely in the Sydney of those days.) John patiently
rewrote the notice and had me paid. (He was swept out to sea
when fishing, in 1935, and drowned – I think near Bondi.)

An imperious dowager relation of Janet's descended on Sydney from England, trailing a limp son who talked about his

dear friend Noel. Janet could meet her on her own level and remain human. As for me, I hovered, with unspeakable hat and ready-made suit, on the edge of her vision, too odd a specimen I think to call up her obvious powers of shattering the lesser breeds.

Will Dalley, John's elder brother, was also small; but at the other end of memory's telescope, he appears wizened and monkeyish, yet lacking the expression of infinitely suffering wisdom that would have shown on the face of a chimp his size. He had bought two old geography globes and installed them on either side of his flat's fireplace, where he admired them with side-cocked head. We had old brandy in ballooning glasses while he intoned on the aroma and then on the special soup with which we were to be regaled, the crowning glory of his epicure's career. For a week it had been gently simmering. He retailed the ingredients. And at last we sat down to dine and awaited the arrival of the incredible soup. When it was brought in its silver tureen, he took a spoonful, gave a tiny sip, flung the spoon down, and wiped his mouth several times with his napkin. 'Spoiled,' he groaned, 'a foul mess, utterly spoiled.' We timidly tried the soup and found it rich and appetizing. 'Can't you taste the sage in it?' he wept. 'Sage of all things, a vulgar herb like sage. I can't think what went wrong. Don't say you're going to drink the foul stuff. No, I protest, politeness can go too far. Take the foul stuff away,' he called to the attendant. 'Pour it down the sink, pour every drop of it down the sink.' He sat plunged in gloom. We tried to save some of the excellent soup, but feared to seem too vulgarian if we praised it.

After the meal he revived enough to remark that nobody after Addison had written prose that a gentleman could read; and he grew animated over a scheme for arranging dinners by colour harmonies. 'What could be more barbarous than to eat things with clashing colours? Use your brains, use your sensibilities, my dear young things, if the young are born with such disabilities nowadays, as I rather doubt. Surely there's some operation used to remove them, like tonsils and appendixes and other unfashionable organs. Just look here at this composition with a dominant yellow. I've made some good ones in green, but that's almost too easy.' After a while he turned on me. 'Young man, I read an article of yours the other day. You used the beggarly word *which* five times in ten lines. Have you no ear nowadays, no sense of values, no respect for the concinnities?'

But he didn't read only as an Addisonian censor of manners. At the Slessor flat, where we were dining, Ken remarked that Will had been saying of *Vision*: 'It seems to have some delusion that there's a conspiracy to oust Beethoven.'

'Well, in a sense there is,' I said.

The others laughed me down. 'Do have a sense of humour,' said Janet. So I too laughed. But I didn't have a sense of humour.

Despite the qualms of my flesh, the code of submission to life continued to control much of my outlook. Woman as the active principle in life, Man as the active principle in art or thought: a sheer dichotomy that was momently overcome in the embrace of love and the birthpang of the image (psychologically coincident moments). Inside these formulations I built an unending dialectic of the sort that delighted the Renascence Libertines or Free-thinkers to whom the young Donne belonged: the praise of constancy in inconstancy, of stability gained through submission to change, of unity gained through acceptance of the Dionysian rending of the flesh. Woman as the image of life's wholeness, known only in act, embraced and lost in an endless series of discoveries where the circle of repetitions was momently contracted to the point of new realizations, new intensities of integrated sense. Woman as the image of wholeness in conflict with Woman afflicted with the mirror-vanities of Laura, with Woman the social animal conspiring to trap a man in family responsibilities. And the long series of truths and lies in the Man's oaths and pleas as he spoke to one aspect of Woman in terms proper only to another aspect. With the moments of achieved harmony when the various aspects came together, thereby making all the more confused the conflicts of everyday relationship, in which the masquerade of fragments of the self as the complete self went on in both the Poet and his Muse.

The thesis was not simply drawn from *Creative Effort*, which is more Napoleonic in its notion of commanding artist and accomplished lover. The colouration was mine, drawn in part from Donne and Keats, Catullus and Propertius. By providing in sexual imagery a concentrated symbol of all union, fusion, change, growth, movement, development, it stimulated my poetic processes, but at the same time limited them. Despite a belief in the Cyclopean hammerings of all creative activity, in the need for an equal intensity of conscious and unconscious elements, it inevitably laid stress on spontaneity in expression. And so, working with my discovery of the explosive colour-image, it drew me to see my writing more and more as a free or spontaneous exploration of the complex emotional associations which an image touched off – a sort of oscillatory process, each swing drawing in further variations of the given image, then starting off in new tangential constellations, until the criss-crossings and accumulations fused and burst out in a new direction, a new central image.

In fact the submission to life, the drinks and the voyages to Cythera, took up only a relatively small portion of my time, which was mostly spent in sober and domesticated study. But they had a determining effect on my whole attitude to life and art; or rather they summed up certain aspects of that attitude. On the lines of Robert Burns's defence of drunkenness, I believed that the disruptions prevented one's spiritual and bodily system from falling into static patterns. In Burns's phrase, they defaecated the standing pool. They brought up a deep rush of fear from the unconscious and thus dictated the lines of movement, provided the chaos which the creative faculty had to turn into cosmos. An essentially romantic position, in the narrow sense of that term. While stimulating the imagery-explosions, it narrowed their sphere of value, and, in my personal life, prevented me from reaching a mature married relationship – a failure for which I was solely responsible. Because of my preconceived ideas, I failed in art and life alike to realize and develop the rich possibilities before me.

And so there I am, turning up from Martin Place. I take a look at the *Sun* office, with newspaper boys shoving papers about on trucks but I don't really expect to see Ken. I go left along the street. A limousine has drawn up outside the Hotel Australia. The commissionaire bends in portly uniformed magnificence, the blue-tunicked chauffeur leans forward, the door opens. The traffic noises of the blundering street are cloven, the two walls of the Red Sea of confusion stand up quivering and foam-tasseled, glob-eyed with puzzled fishes, and the Chosen march across to the promised land of cocktails. A lily-white hand appears, feebly waving and lost, a more than white milk puffy bosom appears, laired in fur. Deeper the commissionaire bows. Now is my moment. If I walk quickly, I'll slip up the broad stairs before the procession begins, before the bosom of pampered cream floats across the pavement, throwing small wreaths of false smiles left and right, and the spacious carpet of flunkeydom is laid under the swollen-ankled feet in their too-tight shoes. Before the damned commissionaire turns again and has a good look at me. For I still wear the same hat. He wouldn't dare, quite, to bar my way, tell me to hop off, mention that the Hotel isn't for the likes of me. I'm a borderline case as I don't give him time to sum me up or betray my cringing emotion. At least that's how it's been so far, and I expect my luck to hold and my trousers not to fray right away in the seat. But as I dodge up the steps into the vestibule, I know his gimlet-eye is fixed on my left boot sole where the leather is all but worn through to the sock. I know he guesses my braces are fixed with a safety-pin at the back. I know he scorns my dark blue herringbone suit, bought under duress in the shop of an unquenchably optimistic Italian, the coat of which is cut tighter at the waist than I like and isn't as long as I'd like. The shiny threadbareness of my behind makes me feel vulnerable. Also my hair is badly cut and I try to walk with my coat collar up and my head thrown back. Also, even when I've left the steps, I try to walk without showing the soles of my shoes to anyone behind me. And my hair is falling into my eyes and a notebook bulges in my side pocket. But I feel better now I've removed the hat with the sweat marks round its band.

Nothing inside daunts me like the large commissionaire outside. Not the cool girls at the counters, since I do not even exist for them. Not the small impertinent page boys with costumes even more bum-freezing than my own. Not the well-dressed loiterers. Not even the bored and insulting waiters in the Winter Garden can make me feel such an interloper as that horrible huge ex-soldier with his cod eyes and his mulligatawny moustache.

Into the Winter Garden I go, from one spacious scene of gilt and guilt to another. All hips and haws, in one of my favourite puns. A buzzy chatter fills the room, ascending past the empty balconies to beat on the lofty ceiling and drop back, a drizzle of dead echoes, on the heads of the buzzers. I savour an odd pleasure as I step into the buzz. First, because I have managed to get in at all. Secondly, because I feel such an absolute hatred for all the buzzers. The vicious vixens, the voluble viragos, the vermiculated virgins, the varicosed vamps, the vivacious vampires, the varnished venereals, all voraciously vulgar. They virulently buzz and I vertiginously hate them. They sit ventrally at the little tables, smoking the cigarettes of ennui, with males of two varieties, the handsome youths as interchangeable as playing-cards and the pudgy-handed seniors whose faces are grills through which greed looks monotonously out. In the heat of the place, which begins undulating with the bilge of sound pumped out by the discreet band, the many eyes are poaching and bubbling. I hope that I look more romantic than shabby.

Mrs B. isn't in her usual seat. And she told me to come. Only because I'm sure of her raucous welcome and her large purse, have I dared to enter. While looking round, I shrink behind a palm and a supercilious waiter almost knocks me down, without a word of apology. His nose merely becomes longer as he takes two gins to a square man, mahogany-faced and jutting-jawed, who talks to a girl so plump, so tightly clad, that each flick of light seems a gash in the material. I hope to see her luxurious flesh ooze out, burst through increasing seams of gold, into a soft and meridian nudity. 'Hell, Maud, you've got a nerve,' he says as he pays the waiter without looking up, screwing his mouth sideways as he propels a folded note with his thumb on to the tray.

'It's not nerve, it's gin,' she says coarsely. 'Cheerio.'

He's worried about something. He isn't a strong silent man at all, or not with Maud, or not with Maud just yet. 'You've got to think of others, Maud,' he says.

'When they think of me. Like hell I will.' She tries to take his gin. But that's where his wrist of hairy steel comes in, he catches her hand and holds it. He's feeling good at last and she pulls so hard I feel sure she'll break something essential. If she lets go, she'll fall over with a fine crash, waving her satin-shod shoes and lots more. If she doesn't let go, she'll do something rash. All ways it's interesting. 'I want a drink, Jim,' she says in a thin mean voice.

'Not mine,' says Jim, within his rights.

'Jack, Jack,' breaks in a voice sweet and harsh, harsh and sweet, and saves me. A flutter, a handwave, a lowered eyelid, a woman resting inside an open coat like a sheep's carcass in its half-ripped skin, in the welter of hot lights, wasp-buzz, and music bleeding from some wound in space, all mixed with my fear. She is smallish, not so prepossessing at first view (or second, or third). Her eyes are shifty with a blurred yet glassy look, the effect of mixing a Catholic upbringing with sin-wallowing. The eyelids are a little swollen at the rims, the eyebrows are plucked, the face is small and unsymmetrical, very smoothly cosmeticked cream and rose. The marble consistency over a lax skin makes her look both dead-rigid and softly dissolving. Her brown hair curls as nicely as money can make it.

I sit at her table. 'Fancy meeting you here,' she remarks for the benefit of her companion, a lumpish woman with buck-teeth and chapped skin, who gives a disbelieving sniff. The sniff flops the woman's bosom up and down. She is some relation of the doctor, down from Googalong where her husband has a station.

'I thought I'd look in,' I answer unconvincingly. Another sniff and bosom-flop from Googalong. The lump doesn't like me; and having ascertained that I am an impoverished poet, she has no qualms in showing what she feels.

'Maggie dear,' says Mrs B. who had wit at least in malice, speaking ever so sweetly, 'you've got hiccups.'

'I haven't,' replies the other in a deep contralto. She gathers up her parcels.

'If you're in a hurry, you needn't wait for us.'

I'll wait,' says Googalong, changing her mind.

I remember Maud and look round. She leans back with her

bag held open in front of her face, doing herself up in a mirror.
The white-coated waiter is setting down two more gins. Jim
watches Maud puckering out her lips, with one thumb thrust
in the armhole of his waistcoat. 'Something interesting you?'
asks Mrs B. too sweetly.

'I thought they were going to quarrel.'

She smiles coldly with small even teeth. 'It's easy to quarrel.'
She taps my hand.

'We'll go when you're ready,' says Googalong.

The band is playing a waltz, which wreathes its flaccid lines
through the heat-buzz. Maud has her long legs outthrust as she
goes on studying her pleasant over-ripe face. Mrs B. is waving
to some theatrical people. I wait for her to buy me a drink. She
leans over. 'She's going the day after tomorrow,' she remarks
in a whisper quite loud enough for Googalong to hear. She has
high ideas of herself as an intriguer and imagines that she has
only to make a show of secrecy in order to bring it about.

She was a bore, but firmly and stockily present, producing in
me a sense of fatality, as if the only way I could walk forward
was through her fissile body. She had no taste for art, but was
eager for studios in which pictures were actually painted and
models briefly sat between more important engagements on
the floor. So, at her promptings, I took her to Ray's new studio,
which was excellently stacked with canvases and had its huge
easel, plus a three-legged chair and an all-too-collapsible camp
bed. She remarked confidently, doing up her easily damaged
face, 'Oh, wouldn't we soon kill ourselves if we could take our
fill of love!' I felt that I had had a privileged glimpse into what
she considered her real self of purple passion. In fact she had
no passion at all, only a gin-oiled belief that she ought to live
a life of abandon and go places. No doubt she got a kick out
of doing or talking about things they had told her in the convent were sinful. I blushed at the disclosure of the phoney day-
dream that warmed her. Also because there was nothing
between us to warrant such a comment from moronic fiction.
Her remark indeed sounded as a sharp satire on my inability
to give even a tenth-rate imitation of an amorist in her presence. Yet it was clear that she believed her words as she said

them, believed herself Madame Bovary in the role of Cleo-patra, ticking with the wounds of a great heart, defying the world rapturously on moonlit balconies, a deboshed schoolgirl. The less that actuality reached her standard of passion, the more she felt the need to supply a commentary of dazzled del-ight, excused from noting all crudities and failures. Maybe there was even a touch of kindness, a wish to console her part-ner for his incompetence. But mostly it was, I think, a mechan-ism of evasion adopted to excuse her first aberrations, when her Catholic conscience still vaguely worked; now something she couldn't drop even if she wanted to. In any event I couldn't answer. To speak in the same tone or to say something dep-recating would alike put her falsity in high relief.

I pulled out a big canvas that Ray was painting on a theme from early Australian history, and propped it against the easel. It slipped and an arm of the easel went through it. I felt a cold fury. I knew Ray could paste something at the back and paint over the L-shaped tear; but damage to an artwork through the hypocritical situation in which I floundered was the last straw, unforgivable.

Sitting in a pub lounge with whisky provided at her expense, I still felt coldly enraged. Recalling her sham ecstasy, I recog-nized that it had been spoken in a matter-of-fact voice, with less emotion than she'd give to the critique of another woman's hat. Her words had been a kind of politeness; also an effort to show herself, if not young, youthful in passion. She wasn't a person with much backchat or small talk. The thought made me feel almost tender towards her, and she patted my hand, 'Dear.' God help me, she sounded sincere.

At a party in some North Sydney flats, someone put the lights out and there was a grab-and-kiss. That was how I met Mrs B. and why she considered I was fated to love her. Luckily however she forgot for periods, then turned up again. One night she arrived at Gruner's place with a supply of whisky, having somehow found out I was there. We sat on the terrace overlooking the sea, watching the stars drown in the lazy waves, while Gruner grew more tight-lipped. I yawned, think-ing of phrases for the dusky foamwreaths. But Mrs B. felt her-self a success, mixing with poets and artists. Yes, she was the fit spouse for her husband with his unassuaged sense of footlight glamours. And now and then she met her match. For instance, once she took in a handsome Harrovian with light curly hair, a most superior accent and a Rugger physique, who had been selling vacuum-cleaners in the suburbs to women who already had vacuum-cleaners. He decided it was easier to drop the vacuum-cleaners out altogether. She declared that he was very sensitive as well as an absolute Apollo, not made for the rough-and-tumble of our colonial world.

It is well known that anyone who harbours a Harrovian in Australia gets what he deserves. Mrs B. got it and deserved it. But before that happened, she opened her purse and her person wide to the gallant remittance-man, whose tastes were crude and who liked spending money. One night, she, the doctor and Apollo went with some squatter friends to a newly opened and expensive restaurant. Apollo hadn't been told that the males were expected to pay for the festivities, and for some reason his Harrovian soul shrank from touching the doctor for another loan. Perhaps the doctor had intimated that no more loans would be made. Anyhow, Apollo said that he had an important phone-call to put through to Melbourne and must slip out to the G.P.O. What he did was to taxi home to the B.s' house, let himself in, and then smash the cashbox open in the yard with a meatchopper. He did not even bother to remove the debris, but returned to the restaurant with all the doctor's petty cash weighing down his pockets. When the time came, he paid his share of the dining costs like a gentleman. I gathered that he had been struck by a sheep-heiress, to the displeasure of Mrs B., who was on the whole philosophic about such backslidings but who didn't get Harrovian Apollos every night of the week.

When next morning the demolished cashbox was found in the yard, suspicion fell on other frequenters of the much-frequented household. No one thought of the honourable Harrovian, who had been at the dinner. The B.s decided that one of Mrs B.'s discards, a frowsy fellow whom even Mrs B. had tired of, had done the burgling; he knew where the cashbox was, and had come in on the previous afternoon to ask for a loan. The Harrovian said that he had always thought there was something criminal about the frowsy one's ears, and told some stories to his discredit. Indeed, he played his part too well. Mrs B. was all for hushing the matter up; but Dr B. was so worked up over whiskies by the Harrovian that he called the police in. 'Circumstantial evidence is often deceptive,' he said, 'but here is a case which I pride myself is completely watertight. I can forgive anything but ingratitude.' The police however had had considerable experience of Harrovians. Instead of acting on the doctor's carefully worked-out case, they took the elementary precaution of looking for fingerprints on the cashbox. The prints were there, and were the Harrovian's. The taxi-driver who had brought him home picked him out at an identification parade.

All the same there was no court case. Mrs B. smoothed things somehow out. But the Harrovian tactlessly gave away his relations with her; he blamed everyone except himself, though he admitted he shouldn't have left the fingerprints. Dr B. wandered disconsolately in pyjamas up and down the stairs of his home, with a revolver in his hand, trying to find someone, even a housemaid, who would take his threat of suicide seriously. The revolver was rusty and unloaded, a stage effect, but Dr B. was doing his poor best to act the part of a deceived husband in a melodrama. After a while he lost his cues and couldn't remember which play to fit into. Mrs B. disarmed him and put him to bed with an effervescent drink. They staged a moving reconciliation, and it was agreed that Harrovians were so villainous that they couldn't be believed even when confessing to villainies. Some time later the doctor decided to accept an offer somewhere in the South Seas. What a perfect pair for a sweltering tropical port. Surely they must have found their way into the works of Somerset Maugham.

So much for Mrs B., about whom I relate only the less scandalous details. Let us take another symbolic exhibit, from the other end of the female scale. Marjorie, who aspired to be a novelist, had written to N.L., and her letter was sent on to me. I wrote to her in a wary style. 'Publishing is of course difficult in Australia on account of the absence of publishers interested in anything but bushranger yarns, south-sea romances, or studies of flying-foxes.' She promptly replied in firm schoolgirlish script with date and hour for a meeting outside the Mitchell Library, as she would much appreciate counsel from a more experienced author. I wondered what I was more experienced in. However I went and watched the sparrows chirping round the statue's head, with a covert eye on the slope up from the Quay. A tall rosily lovely girl appeared, but took no interest in waiting poets. Then a woman in a veil, who seemed to be champing something. But she too went haughtily past. A man with bloodshot eyes from the Domain lurched near, turning back to announce, 'I been stung by a horsefly, got a fag, chum?' A large woman with the bouncing bosom of haste came round the corner and I gave myself up for lost.

'Mr Jack Lindsay?' asked a small pleasant voice and I looked down to find a diminutive figure with merry brown eyes regarding me. I hadn't seen her approach. Descending the steps, I removed my battered hat. 'Miss Lawton?' Her smile confirmed the obvious. I was disconcerted. She reached only to my armpit, but otherwise was not unattractive with her round softly clear unpowdered face, her shapely mouth, her slightly dumpy but unpadded frame. Voice and eyes were the nicest things about her, with a merry warmth that I hadn't expected. But she was so small. I thanked Venus that we had met close to the Gardens, where we could walk in the decent obscurity of the afternoon avenues and where it was most unlikely I'd meet any of my friends.

I led the way across to the gates and we went on. There was no escape from expending the price of afternoon tea in the kiosk; she'd look less tiny when sitting down. 'Shall we have tea? It'll be quiet there.'

'I'd love it,' she replied with a faintly mocking note of demureness. I liked her a lot, but her smallness daunted me and went on daunting me every time I looked at her.

We sat in the almost empty tea-rooms. I talked of the nature of form in the novel. 'The question of form in my opinion, is one of mass. Not of telling a story in the ordinary sense. Dickens is a master of form, so is Balzac, so is Dostoevsky. They proceed from the mass to the configurations of the individual. I'm against Flaubert and the well-made novel. It deadens and flattens. It's a coward's attempt to find a substitute for being alive and in the midst of everything. As for modernist methods of dissecting a trivial mood, a passing nexus of sensation, a flow of meaningless thought, all that is just disintegration, the death of grand form. We must look to Dickens . . .'

She entirely agreed. Her novel told the story of a defenceless girl in Melbourne and in the Queensland backblocks. Yes, she herself had been in Melbourne and the Queensland backblocks. She had the MS in a brown paper parcel and gave it to me as we parted. I opened it in the tram and found it written neatly in her young hand, correctly punctuated, grammatical and serviceably composed, though with a sort of sentimental sincerity dimming its direct picture. Without a doubt, capable, and owning a certain genuine pathos. Not what I had expected. The heroine, smallish (though not as small as her begetter), sensitive and sensible, seemed to me, as far as my brief knowledge of M.L. went, an excellent self-portrait. Against my will I admitted that she had expressed, without undue self-pity, something of the lot of an intelligent girl thrown on her own resources in hard circumstances. I posted back the MS with a complimentary letter, but still denied I was any help for a novelist.

At the last moment I added a postscript suggesting another meeting. We had tea again in the Gardens. Certainly she didn't look so small at the table, though at a glance she must have seemed a young niece being given a treat by a disreputable uncle. We had met at the Conservatorium end and passed the reproductions of Canova's Boxers. 'I adore the Greeks,' she said. 'How beautiful the male form is.' In her demure way, deadly serious, with a reserve of humour in her eye. I repeated that I thought her novel had a good chance of success if published, but who would publish? After tea we went across past the monkeys to the Art Gallery and spent an hour talking of the art or letters, with a quickly averted glance now and then at the paintings. A water-colour of a Punch-and-Judy Show however interested her. Then, to test her taste, I led her before Gruner's *Morning Light*; but as the work was small, she didn't notice it. I asked her if she were still a Catholic. 'Not altogether,' she said with a twinkle, seriously. We parted at the gates in Macquarie Street after walking down the avenue of figs. I said I'd write to her. Never again, I told myself.

But I did write. She lived, I had gathered, with a disapproving aunt. We met on a bright breezy day. The blue-white sky was drizzling with a fierce light and displayed some superb mauve-silver hulks of cloud to the east. The waters of the harbour were a filmy blue skipping and wrinkling into foam glints, stippled with quicksilver. The green banks of the gardens, striped with red and white and yellow, sloped to the dancing waterlights. A gardener turned on a hose-ring and the sparrows bathed in the lustrous spray. Statues offered us the world with outstretched hands. Amid the dry lisp of leaves a naked woman of marble remarked that Hellas was not dead and a butterfly settled on her wrist, a flutter-pulse of yellow-red. The ferries, neat as toys, slid about the harbour, trailing cottonwool of smoke. The scene took its cues from the brisk windy sunlight, and the urns above the steps were there to catch our overbrimming delight. Down the gravel paths, down the broad stairs of stone, along the curve of the little bay, we made a victorious progress acclaimed by every clapping leaf, every handkerchief of sprigged light waved from the bowing trees, every murmur of sweetness blown from the crowding flowers. How beautiful that slope of garden falling to the spacious waters under the blaze of blue. All distances crumbling in a lilac haze, all shapes picked out with lapidary clarity, all flowers tenderly graven on the limpid air.

'Mystery does not lie in things hidden, but in things wholly declared. Not in veils, but in entire nakedness. Not in ignorance, but in full knowledge. Not in God, but in action. Not in death, but in life. We announce war against the obscurantists, aesthetic as well as religious, intellectual as well as moral. No mystery in Scriabin's tortured nerves, only torture. No mystery in Schoenberg's elaborate constructions, only elaboration. But mystery in a Beethoven scherzo, because there is an inexhaustible spring of joy, recognition, union. Our beauty must have this bright candour, this unashamed edge, even though the edge is flower-fine, molten with the sky.'

She unreservedly agreed with me.

We had tea and buns, served by a waitress with a hairy wart. Marjorie was so small that her feet didn't touch the ground when she sat. I dropped my pencil to make sure. She wore low-heeled shoes with squarish toes, and white cotton stockings. I approved.

We went out again to meet the cymbals of summerlight clashing in the intense sky, the curtsying trees with their fluttering wind-ribbons, the broad sweep of unquiet waters, the happy day of Sydney. Down to the water's edge and on to the gate where the gardens ended. We wanted to reach the headland. There we found a seat and watched the slide and foam-scatter of the lapping waves, the gulls wheeling round Pinchgut, the small yachts tacking in the wind, the portly ferries. Nursegirls with perambulators, dawdling and mute lovers, went by. An old man looking at the world for the last time. Then we had the headland to ourselves. The mauves darkened, the haze closed in, the lightsoaked skies drained into heavy blue. The quick dusk came down. A whistle echoed in sadness and the cry of the gulls wheeling over Pinchgut. I kissed her, and she said, 'Thank you,' in the most dutiful and grateful tones, abashing me.

We went back in darkness through the Domain and the long avenue of Moreton Bay figs that reared skyhigh, sparkling with a few reflected lights. Then we had a hurried pie and tea in a Sergeant's café. I was wondering how to get rid of her, but she made no claims of any kind. If I had got up and walked out, she wouldn't have said a word of protest, even to herself. To cover my confusion, I scribbled some verses on the back of the menu card, and with a slight demure uncertainty she offered me a snap of herself.

We parted without an appointment, but I wrote. We met several times and set out on a series of hasty and undefined expeditions. She asked me no questions and I asked her none. She remained charmingly outside everything except the Australian weather. We went somewhere by ferry or tram, and I talked all the while about poetry, to which she listened meekly, with her twinkle, serious and agreeing. We took a ferry up the Parramatta and went across a bridge and wandered in a scrub of gum saplings and bull-ants. We took a ferry to Mosman and had a rapid look at the Zoo and strolled to the farther side from which we could glimpse the Heads and the billows beyond.

There we inspected the temple which the theosophists had built for an Advent expected to come from the East across the ocean, bang for the opening of the Heads; and talked of Bishop Leadbetter whom one saw at times in doddering patriarchal gravity amble across Circular Quay with a bevy of pretty acolytes. We took a ferry and went to Manly and the Fairy Bower. We went to Vaucluse and walked on the cliffs and sat on sand-dunes amid sparse tussocks of grass, above the champing ocean.

What perhaps gave a zest and even significance to our journeys (at least for me) was the sense of flight, of adventurous secrecy. For I dreaded any acquaintance sighting us and spreading the tale of my raiding the cradle. As we strolled among gum trees or kicked our legs on a wall, she was a guaranteed nymph come in her divine silences from a gum-tree bole, a rabbit-hole, a gush of wattle gold, to inhabit my daydreams. I wouldn't have had her an inch taller. Her smallness at such moments indeed was the delightful thing that made our expeditions worth while. For only then did I really look at her. The intrusion of a full-length woman on the idyllic landscape would have been disastrous, a crude breaking of the lyric spell. But once we left the secluded sunlight, I grew furtive and ashamed, expecting at any moment the derisive comments of my friends. I liked her very much and didn't want to hurt her feelings, but however I disguised my reactions I felt sure that she must recognize my perturbations, my haste to embark on tram or ferry, my haste to disappear after our return to the city. She listened to my jumpy talk with her calm deprecatory smile, with that faint humorous glint. And I never had the least idea what she really thought of me, what she expected. It was clear that she liked me; that was all. Our relationship did not end, it faded out. And as though she had been a Cheshire cat in an apple tree, the last I saw of her was that serious and yet infinitesimally comical smile. I lost her address in my notebook and after a while couldn't remember it. Then I recalled the heroine of the novel, the lost and defenceless girl in a world of strangers. It might be asked where all this got me and what I learned from it. From Phyllis I learned – what? That I really was quite incapable as a philanderer and didn't enjoy it. From Mrs B.? That suburban vice was repellent. From Marjorie? Heavens knows what. Perhaps that if one is afraid and guarding oneself all the while from an attack that isn't being made, one learns nothing of the other person. But I wasn't hoping at any time to learn a lesson that could be put in words. If cornered with the point, I should have retorted that I wasn't a minor novelist. What I sought was confusion and shock. Only, according to my aesthetic, it was wrong to seek such things; one must however accept them when they sought one out themselves.

A few more of the pictures that slip into my mind at random as I stare at the blank page. The girl who was ambitious of becoming a writer and who confessed that she sent in some of her works to children's competitions, giving herself out as a seven-year-old, but only once won a prize, two-and-sixpence. The girl who, in a discussion about women's inability to describe their sensations as women, insisted 'I can', and, on being challenged to describe an orgasm, remarked after a moment's thought, 'It's like white rabbits running out of your backside.' (She was voted the first woman poet since Sappho.) Somebody saying, 'We can get drinks in here,' and knocking, late one night, at a high-class dress shop: we were let in by a slim girl in tight black and drank surrounded by unclad shop-window dummies: 'Not fair on a girl,' said Z., 'having to compete with all these hussies.' Two larrikinesses picked up by Y. and brought along to have tea; my one with a cheeky smile and tousled hair, exclaiming 'Cri-Almighty,' when told I was a poet, and pulling me on to her lap. (Y. said she went on ringing up, but I lacked faith in my capacity to keep on impressing her, a brown-cheeked chubby wench with a hoarse slum accent and a smile as broad as the smile of one of N.L.'s satyresses.)

Rosemary, whom I had known as the daydreaming reincarnation of Cleopatra in Brisbane, turned up as a journalist on a weekly, determined to make her way in the world. She earned our indignation by going into a chemist's shop, staging a faint, and extracting some prohibited drugs from the poor man. Then she went and wrote him up in an exposure article.* Still, she didn't last long and drifted off to London.

*Another journalistic villainy, which specially upset Phil, occurred when a group of both sexes late one night went in bathing naked at Bondi. One of the bathers wrote the episode luridly up for a weekly.

17 · BEUTLER AND WORLD-END

BEUTLER HAD been doing well in his business. He decided to expand. He said he was getting in capital to open a shop with ground-floor windows on a main street. 'I only need the capital to make a big corner in the piano business.' He was so confident that I accepted his claims, though I demurred at the amount of time he spent with local businessmen, with whom he drank whisky. I found him several times absent from the shop, and the foreman, a good craftsman devoted to him, corroborated about the whiskies and the bowler hats. He didn't criticize Beutler outright but he spoke with an Australian sarcasm about his master's business friends. As for Beutler himself, he became rather secretive about his manoeuvres; and as I wasn't very interested, I didn't press him – though I once strayed with him into the bar of the bowler hats. No business was talked. Only smutty stories and rose-culture. These ruddy men, champing to tear the guts from their fellows, were ready to chat endlessly about the best ways of making roses bloom, manure them, arbour them, save them from aphides or whatever were their own equivalents in the insect world. Beutler even seemed to have built up some wild ideas about going higher and higher in the business world and inducing its denizens to help in founding an opera-house. 'Feudalism can produce mad kings,' I replied, 'but you can't convince me that the Australian money jungle will ever produce a gorilla aesthete.'

With Phil's aid I was at this time writing a long essay entitled *The Worst Man in the World*, about Henry Ford. This was done entirely for our own vituperative satisfaction, as the work was libellous in the extreme. Ford we saw as the supreme expression of the repressive stereotyping forces of the world about us, his conveyor-belt systems the final horror of labour division that

426

fragments man. His social attitudes perfectly applied this horror outside the factory.

Once Beutler was sure that a fortune was coming his way.
We set on a crazy cross-country journey to a strange old house
where an old woman had just died. The old woman had been
impressed by B.'s music under circumstances never clear to me,
and was expected to leave him something substantial. We
found the large ugly house, crammed with Victorian knick-
knacks, satin sconces and spindly legged what nots. Outside
were giant rose bushes, gooseberries gone to wood, and a pond
where the broad leaves of water plants were turned up round
their rims and a plaster cupid mourned the loss of his arms.
But someone else interested in the will had turned up, a pink-
faced parson with mad eyes, who obviously had a stronger grip
of the situation than B. had. He and B. held a long hostile conversation while I studied the photos of bearded and bonneted
Victorians, a race far more distant and alien than the
Pharaohs, or loitered under the lichened apple trees. How
much, if anything, B. got out of the estate, I never knew. I felt
that the episode was rather too typical of what came of B.'s
high hopes, and my feeling was all too correct. Not long after
I found him striding up and down his works with cigar
clenched between his teeth. At last he admitted that things
were going badly. I learned a little more about his business
downfall than I did about the will, but not much more. He
hated to discuss a defeat. Clearly however he had let some of
his business friends invest in the firm, sure that he could use
them for his own purposes. But as soon as they knew enough
about the way things were run, and had him in their control,
they proceeded to squeeze him out. 'I'll beat them yet,' he
ended with assurance. 'Anyway it doesn't matter. This is more
important.' He sat down at a piano and began playing the
latest bits of the *Faun*.

Before long he lost the workshop altogether. The ring of
bowler hats closed in and ejected him. But he wasn't long
downcast. In a few days he had taken over a small shop in Hunter Street and stocked it with all sorts of cheap musical instruments and novelties, banjos, mouth-organs, even kids' whistles
and trumpets, as well as a few gramophones. At much incoher-

ent length he told me how he was going to sue the bowler hats and iron grey moustaches. They couldn't do it, he'd wipe the floor with them in court, they'd double-crossed him, he'd get the workshop back. But there was no case and they kept his premises. The dream of a big shop selling both new and second-hand pianos was ended. What I couldn't make out was why, in view of his genuine expertise with pianos, the evictors hadn't wanted to keep him on as manager. However, I helped him to fix shelves and curtains in the new shop, which was badly placed. Anyhow, what could he hope for with his stock of junk? He succeeded in making enough to pay the rent and his fares, little more. Indomitably he refused to admit the blind-alley.

One day I dropped in early and found a silently grinning Jap there, a sailor from a visiting warship. He had some records and an old gramophone he wanted to change for something better. B. smiled at me and gestured to show that he was going to get the better of the simple Oriental. Patiently he went on arguing. The Jap heard him out, grinning politely all the while, then briefly repeated his proposition, quite unmoved. I stayed for about an hour, at the end of which B., though refusing to acknowledge defeat, was looking exhausted. When I came back two hours later, the Jap was still there, briefly restating his proposition, while B., wilted, was leaning on the counter. We went across the street for a beer. The bar was conveniently situated, as from its door B. could see if anyone entered or left his shop. On our return the Jap was still there. He briefly restated his proposition, which hadn't altered one syllable. B. agreed and gave me a sickly smile as the pleased Jap courteously retreated.

He still kept his jaunty humour. Set on paper, many of his jokes would seem foolish, many of his remarks pontifically dull. Yet such was the vivacity of goodness in the man that his buffooneries were irradiated with a love of life, a gentleness and a serenity; and his comments had a core of shrewdness and insight despite his limitations, which included a wide ignorance outside the few matters that interested him. He was thoroughly German in that he had worked out a windy philosophy from scraps and ends and bobtails of metaphysical thought (with Steiner bulking large), and was ready to accept anything heavily pretentious as inspired doctrine. (Not that I was in a position to throw bricks at him for all that.) German too in the pedestrian and flat funny stories he sometimes told. When he laughed, I laughed as loudly, but at him, not at the story. One morning he turned up early at *Idyllia* while we were still abed, puffed cigar-smoke all over us, and vaunted his moral superiority as a dawn-riser, a lark of industry. His geniality was extreme, and yet, when necessary, he owned a calm commanding manner. His goodness was an aspect of what I felt as greatness in him – though how far I should now find greatness in his music, even potentially, I cannot tell without re-hearing it. He could do all the simple acts of kindness, talk to a child in the street, help an old woman across the road, sit up with a sick neighbour, and so on, without the least sense that he had done more than bite the end of one of his unfailing cigars or narrow his bushy brows as he picked up a rubber to erase the last bars written with stubby pencil.

One day he came into the shop where I was waiting, and sat down with a smile. A few minutes before, he had been crossing the street and found a motor-car bearing down on him. There was no time to get out of the way, so he leaped on to the bonnet. 'Not so easy to kill me,' he smiled.

One afternoon I went with him and his family to Brighton-le-Sands, Botany Bay, where a fair was in noisy progress. He delighted in the whole thing so much that he couldn't stop his joy-riding and throwing rings and shooting at bottles, not even when the children were peevish and tired. I see him stand grinning on the big spinning circle of the merry-go-round while the music coughs and chuffs and spanks along. He holds the eldest boy in his arms till the wearied child bursts out bawling, and B., surprised at such lack of stamina in enjoyment, has to leap off and spend the next half hour in coaxing the boy back to contentment in a hurdy-gurdy universe.

Yet that afternoon saw our first important disagreement. B. declared that the andante of Beethoven's Seventh Symphony depicted a slave-girl dancing. This seemed to me a hopelessly poor and wrong-headed interpretation, revealing an inability to recognize the significance of Beethoven's use of rhythm or the interrelation of parts in one of his symphonies. A blindness to the blessed release and recuperation of the spirit in the andantes of the sonatas and symphonies. The dreaming of a fighter between two episodes of struggle, the quiet fountains of the unsealed heart, the gratitude which in the midst of pain rises above pain, the strange depths of bodily tenderness which become a new source of moral strength, the sweetness of renunciation in the spirit vowed irrevocably to struggle, the triumph that is as beyond triumph as beyond defeat. What words can utter the subtlety of the broad flow, east of the sun and west of the moon and closer than breathing, in a Beethoven andante? And to reduce it to so banal and naturalistic an image as that of a slave-girl dancing!

Perhaps I made more of it than I should have. Beutler often spoke in simple terms when his thoughts weren't simple, using a conventional image to correlate his thoughts. He may have wanted to stress the strangeness of the song, specially plangent after the energy of the first movement. He may have felt the dream-spirit inhabiting the song to be a lovely woman, whose cry was of freedom-in-captivity, and so on. But I saw only a shallow comment. Perhaps I wanted to see only that.

Some days later, several of us were lunching in a first-floor little café in George Street. Rahel was there with an elderly chap, drink-sodden with an English accent. Someone spoke of the poem in *Hermes*, which had brought about the suppression of that issue of the university student's magazine, or at least the confiscation of the page with the amorous poems. The poet was the B.B. whom I had initiated at the W.E.A. camp on Tambourine with *The Everlasting Mercy*; he too had come to Sydney, an earnest teetotaller, but oddly determined to follow in my footsteps. He thus repeated my clash with the university authorities and published at his own cost a book that followed the format of *Fauns and Ladies*. (After this, he sensibly decided I was no model and developed as himself.) The horsefaced Englishman with a neighing laugh observed in a superior voice, puzzled and contemptuous, 'But why does he want to *write* about such things?' The morality of the lie was succinctly expressed in his sly lecherous smile: Brothels in the back streets, Female Virtue prominent in the shopping centre, and Cash the Lord of the World. I was infuriated. Laurence and another chap were baiting Beutler, and instead of taking up his cudgels I led him into a discussion of rhythm as a unifying force. He started showing the different beats as if he were a conductor and we all laughed. Then Nietzsche came in. Laurence, who had heard me expatiate, asked B. jeeringly, 'What do you think he meant by Eternal Recurrence?' B. couldn't explain at all and looked at me for aid. But Laurence went on pressing him and I was silent. B. flushed, at last aware that he was being laughed at. Then I took pity on him and intervened with some comments on Zarathustra's *Midnight Song*. Yet even when the jeerers were having everything their own way I felt only the bigness of his mind and the triviality of the others. I felt base, but couldn't help it.

About this time he managed to arrange a holiday for the family up the mountains, and I stayed with them part of the time. Of the train journey I recall only a woman who was worried by the immense amount of stones on all sides and asked what would happen when they grew out and blocked the cuttings – she couldn't be convinced that stones didn't grow. Of the township I recall only a triangular strip of sparse grass with a war memorial. Ray too came up for a few days. The cottage was secluded in a gully of gum trees and we walked out along the ridges and down the stony slopes. Hoping in vain to come on a lyrebird perching low in the scrub, but seeing a cockatoo nibble a beetle and a wedgetailed eagle show above the rocks. Meeting a man in quest of parrot-pie. 'There's no bird that'll carry off more shot in him than a parrot. You've got to hit him hard.'

Once I went for a walk with Mrs B., down among the thick-set trees, along a twisting track. 'Less snakes than in Queensland, but more than enough, all the same.' I kicked a locust shell. 'I've seen hardly any lizards too.' At last near a bubbling spring we sat on the bare ground and she told me some of her worries; and I kissed her on the back of the neck. I was fond of her and she was fond of me, but nothing more. I was merely driven by my Julien Sorel curse of fearing to fail a challenge, even when the challenge wasn't there. Alone with a young woman by a woodland spring: how could I look Theocritos in the eye again if I didn't do something about it? I knew that she devotedly loved B. and was absolutely incapable of being unfaithful to him in the least respect. In a way there was a close bond between us, but the whole basis of that bond was our entangled love for A.B. It would indeed have been hard to find the adequate word or gesture for just that warmth of liking, in a common interest, we did feel. It was easier to do the wrong thing. Particularly as I felt that time was passing; in a moment we'd have to rise and return for the lunch preparations. The challenging pressure increased. Perhaps there was a certain tension between us at that moment and she was feeling out for my help in her difficult circumstances – Beutler more ill than he thought, and his finances worse than ever – and I should have sought for a way of securing more strongly our friendship, of showing that I realized and felt for her as a person, a woman, as well as the hausfrau, the cipher attached to my beaming and bustling friend. By ending the tension with the maladroit and unemotional kiss on the nape of the neck, I escaped the problems of the moment, the real challenge, but made myself feel and look a fool. She said that she hadn't been kissed since her marriage by anyone but Adolphe. I said that that was surprising.

So we got up and walked back, chatting again about the bush and spotting some small green birds. Something had been spoiled, and yet I had a feeling of inevitability. Perhaps the overstrain growing between B. and myself had to find some such expression. It seemed for a moment that I had been protesting against all Germanic acceptances of the hausfrau as the role of woman, against the suburban wilderness of drab repetition in which the family lived, though I had no idea if she was aware of a lack in her life, of a surrounding deadness. No doubt, with the children to care for and Adolphe to tend and support, she had no time to look at the suburban void at all.

It didn't strike me at the time that she would tell him; but I suppose she must have done it. And I suppose he resented it, despite his own cajoling flirtations which did not for a moment impair his warm and solid sense of family-oneness. (On my behalf it may be mentioned that if my Dionysian ethic rationalized adolescent instability as a 'vital readiness to respond to the changing demands of life,' it had at least the consistency to give the same rights to woman as to man. I was far too fanatically logical in my theses and their working out to make a one-sided application.) On thinking the episode over with sinking heart, I felt sure that A.B. would not see in the incompetent peck at his wife's neck only a wish to crystallize the unpassionate warmth that linked me to her, to make us both at least more magnetically aware of one another's existence by the momentary contact and the consequent separation into our distinct selves. And then I felt that I was making a lot out of nothing, trying to justify my (partial) withdrawal from the Beutlerian universe.

Rose had driven me into Springwood station after a visit to Norman. She was also collecting a rather lymphatic model for transport to the studios. Someone hurried up with a wire addressed care of Norman. It was for me. 'Found Beethoven, Laurence,' I read, smiled evangelically, and handed the paper to Rose to show Norman. On my arrival in Sydney I found that Laurence had been in Palings, and while waiting for some other record had idly put on the scherzo of the Ninth Symphony. The colossal swing and antic surge had bowled him over, and now he marvelled at the blindness which had denied him the Dionysian harvests of such music. He tried more and more Beethoven records and was overwhelmed.

Beutler was in sore straits. The oddments shop had gone to pieces; and I don't know what the family was living on – savings, I think, which Mrs B. had been making for the future needs of the children. Crosslé probably helped in various ways. Beutler was depressed at moments, but often he was uplifted in grandiloquent schemes. He'd resuscitate the orchestra that had gone down after Verbrugghen's departure; he'd find wealthy and intelligent patrons; he'd found an Australian Bayreuth; he'd write bigger and better operas. We sketched out the libretto for a vast set of operas that would outdo the *Ring* and last at least a week. The theme was Atlantis. We would show the collapse, not merely of a nation or of a civilization, but of a world, through its inner forces of corruption, hatred, greed, repression, art-abstraction, powerlust. I had my Platonic thesis of Atlantis, Beutler had a concept born somewhere in his anthroposophical reveries.

All my interest in his music was rekindled. It seemed that we would express in our opera sequence what I had put into *Marino*, and much more, on a grander plan:

MARINO: *What did you see in my eyes?*
ADMIRAL: *A brave intent.*
MARINO: *No, you saw mounded stars some pestilence*
bleared with a lichen of clammy light
that slew them in an hour; and ghastly moons,
pale mummies grinning in a glare of dead fire,
hanging in a frozen haze, light decomposed;
and greenish dripping skeletons of suns;
and earths and pismire empires built in
squelchy marshflames, like wheels of red and black.
Man is not there, but only a darkness mired
under the feet of darkness.
ADMIRAL: *Yet you want my help.*
MARINO: *Your help? ah, yes, Gisello, pardon me –*
I cannot yet think steadily on this city.
Some half-forgotten wrong of deluged beauty,
and laughter dismantled, breaks within me
as the thought of this city scarped with dawn
unmists some pillared anger ruined of old.
Forget all this.

(For me, in *Marino*, the term *city* had all the Baudelairean connotations, though I was denying Baudelaire.) For our immediate stimulus we had our settled conviction that the world was driving towards a new war which would be far worse than the last. We based this belief on our sense of the unrelieved tensions of hate and the deep-going repressions in our society; and though we did not use a politico-economic analysis, there were many echoes in my mind from my Brisbane past with its revolutionary formulations by Quinton and Witherby. So we weren't such fools as might seem. Throughout the boom illusions of the 1920s I kept intact a conviction that our society was rent by deep conflicts and discords that could not but explode in war. For the moment the idiom was Norman's, dividing people into Man and Hyperborean (or Fanfroliconian; any terms suggestive of Rabelaisian Utopia or Platonic Mem-

ory would do); but the effect was to enable us to seize on the
elements in our world socially and morally making for war,
philistinism and dehumanization:

He has been to his uncle the parrot, and can rattle off words in such
perfect imitation of the human voice that you would no more suspect
him of wearing a smell of raw meat in his mind . . .

Looking at him we have disposed of him as useless. Listening to
him merely adds a confusion to the sound of trams, and whistle-
buttons and cats being trodden on in the dark. Inspecting him
through bathroom keyholes is also ineffective, for that apparently
innocuous chemical combination of grease and caustic soda allows
him the disguise of soap, and the wisest dog could not detect the
odour of his mental epidermis. Shouting at him suddenly in the
dialect of the Limpopo River is no use; he has forgotten the language.
Nor is it of any effect to wave raw meat at him. He will mistake you
for the butcher, and tell you to call for the bill next week. Indeed,
the smell of boots and bibles and barbers' shops has quite demoralized his olfactory process, and you may see him eating the cooked
bodies of dead animals at any moment by merely glancing into a restaurant; and what grander evidence of his civilized being could you
wish for? In fact, the only raw meat he enjoys sniffing at is that of
bodies mutilated in printed matter, and if no battle is available for
his delectation, two columns of murdered corpse will usually supply
the deficiency. (N.L. 1923.)

There was much cogency in this satirical picture and in our
correlation of the repressed violences and death wishes of our
society with what we called primitivist or abstract art. For in
such art men are reduced to things and deprived of individual
sensuousness. Where we went wrong was in the absolute nature
of our statement of the conflict involved: as if two races of being
were in question, the Free Spirits voluntarily coming down to
earth and ascending out of it on a Platonic ellipse determined
by the art image, and the Dark Phantasms born of the earth
and going back into their abyss of disintegration.

Beutler and I thus felt a terrible reality in the Atlantean
theme, in its relation to the death wish of a decaying and divided society. We even realized that as the hatreds and
repressions piled up, scientists must evolve ghastly methods of

destruction at which we could as yet only guess; for in our erratic way we had a grasp of the unity of consciousness and being, of theory and practice, of art and society. We meant to make our Atlanteans, at the climax of their social and spiritual conflicts, torn by the discovery of the full nature of matter and energy, so that they had a creative and a destructive power beyond anything known in the 1920s; and we were meant to show how the dark forces used the power over the transformations of matter to destroy the earth.

Not much of the opera however was written down beyond the opening passages, but Beutler improvised themes and motives, struggling to define a vast pressure of maddened and cruel forces and to pit against this the luminous image of joy and beauty. We were thrilled, again and again, by the pictures we summoned up in our minds of huge barbaric ceremonials of bloodlust and mass movements of violence: the sort of thing that at the moment seemed sheer fantasy, but was actualized about a decade later in Nazi Germany.

Laurence was having troubles with his Lola. They had temporarily parted. Her husband, described as a rotter, had shown up and was trying to blackmail her. One afternoon when I was alone in the house, she turned up, looking her calm slender self, slinkily assured yet with a lost evasive glint in the corners of her eyes; and after I made her some tea, she asked me for advice. She had decided to murder her husband. 'I can't bear to think of him doing Laurence any harm,' she said in her melodious little voice, perfectly mild and easy, as if she were discussing the price of shoes. She set out her detailed plan for taking her husband up for a walk along the cliffs and shooting him among the bushes. 'If only I wasn't married to him, there'd be no problem at all. I could just shoot him and plead that he'd tried to dishonour me.' She used the word *dishonour* quite naturally and lifted her mouth to me for a reassuring kiss – no, not so much one to reassure as to confirm herself in her sense of wifely virtue. 'But I'm afraid it wouldn't go down with a jury as things are, don't you agree? Of course I could explain that we'd been parted for years and I forgot we were legally married. Do you think it would sound all right?' All right for a death sentence, I thought, though one could never tell when a girl with such an innocent manner got working on a jury's emotions. But then there might be some catty women on the jury. I expressed my doubts about the scheme, but she was hard to shake. 'I love Laurence far too much to let him be upset and bothered. He can't possibly afford to be blackmailed.' She lay back on the couch and adjusted her suspenders. I suggested less drastic methods. If she were set on using a revolver (she had one, though she wasn't carrying it round, I was relieved to hear), why not pull it out and fire it, taking care not to score a hit. Surely that would frighten the fellow. She considered. 'No, it wouldn't frighten him much. You don't know him.' She shook her head. 'No, it wouldn't be safe at all. I don't mind killing him, but I'd be scared to shoot him like that. He wouldn't like it.'

'You'd probably miss him anyway. I think you shouldn't try shooting.'

She admitted she had never used a revolver, and I told her that she'd never hit what she aimed at, revolvers bucked like mad, the most she'd bag was a chance seagull. She considered the objections and admitted I might be right. If she shot her husband, it wouldn't do for her to have carried out revolver practice beforehand; the fact might come out in court and even the most impressionable juryman might be prejudiced against her. The only sign of her agitation was the way she got up and walked about the room. Her voice remained even and calm, and she paused now and then to kiss me, so that she could look straight into my eyes and read my mind. 'Oh dear,' she said, 'it's a problem, being a woman, but I suppose we must take the rough with the smooth. You're being most helpful. I can't talk all this over with Laurence.' She ruffled my hair. 'Don't look so serious.'

She had her own way of defining values and positions. Once, later on, during a period of grass-widowhood on her part, Phil spent the night with her. In the morning as they lay lazily abed, she talked about her love for Laurence and remarked dreamily that she could never be unfaithful to him. 'What about me?' Phil asked indignantly. 'Oh you don't count,' she replied amiably and truthfully, and went on talking about her great love for Laurence.

On the day when she called for my advice, as she left, she thanked me for having calmed her nerves and told me not to worry; she'd find some way out. She did. But what it was, I don't know. Anyhow, it didn't include a normal kind of fidelity to Laurence. One night he rushed into *Idyllia* with a bottle of whisky, unable to sit still or listen to records. After a while he came to the point. He had come home earlier than expected and had seen Lola get out of a car in which sat a loathsome business-type. Questioned she had coolly insisted that she had merely accepted a lift home. 'It's all I can do to keep my hand off her, I know she's lying . . .' Then he astounded me by saying – he, the lover of a host, to me, who sat in an elemental solitude gnawing the fingernails of my poems – 'I only wish I could handle women like you can.' It is clear that what he mistook for my mastery of women was merely my evasive fear of them.

Otherwise we were discussing the problem of rewriting the libretto of *Parsifal* so that Amfortas would appear as Wagner himself and the Pure Fool as the chaste Nietzsche resisting the flower girls of amorous music. That was the content at one level, I insisted; deeper still the clear essential elements of ritual drama. Wagner admitted to Nietzsche that the Germans wanted religiosity, and he wrote *Parsifal* to save Bayreuth. But beyond the opportunisms, beyond the heroic anguish and the failure to win Nietzsche, was it the onset of the years or the effort to purify form that moved in this work to a structure of direct states of being? Anyhow, we must redeem it by the new libretto.

One night, when we were discussing this project and other such matters on which we considered the fate of the universe to hinge, we had begun by drinking in town; then we took the galloping tram for the large pub opposite the middle of Bondi beach with a beer advert for numerals on its clocktower. I must have had more than I noticed, and on the way home I turned a corner too sharply, running right up against the edge of a brick wall. I knocked myself out and don't remember how I got back to *Idyllia*, where I woke up in the morning with the unwashed blood dried all over my face. Luckily I had just missed the eye.

Near the brick wall that almost did for me, there lived a

couple of girls with young families, with whom we became friendly. At a party they gave, one of them, lean, sallow and intelligent, showed me a woman's monthly with a photo of Aldous Huxley, spectacled and loose lipped as befitted a sensuously mild and melancholy man, among the advertisements for corsets and shoes. I had just read *Antic Hay* and felt very friendly to its author. So I drank all the evening to A.H. and Coleman, with an eager desire to convert the silent toasts into witty conversations. That night the resolve to go to Britain was born.

I had picked up a broken-down Albion sort of printing press; Phil helped me in working it. Almost every time we banged the bed up on the type, half a dozen letters or more fell out. Printing was thus a slow business. We produced only one complete work, the title of which I would have forgotten if I had not found it to my surprise seriously listed in the huge bibliography of *Australian Literature* edited by E. Morris Miller in 1940:

The Pleasante Conceited Narrative of Panurge's Fantastic Ally Brocaded Codpiece; its Damnation and a Tricke plaied on a multitude of letcherous twats, by a poeticall Ladie of Paris. Sydney, Printed by the Panurgean Society, Anno Diaboli MDCCCXCXIV.

The date has gone a bit wrong, probably through the letters having fallen out several times as Phil and I banged the press together on the floor of the spare room. For paper we had torn up a notebook and we bound the entire edition (some five or six copies) with needle and thread, cardboard and gum. This poem was probably the only one which the poet has improvised with setting-stick in hand; there was no manuscript. *Fantastic Ally* was a sort of accidental pun; the capitals of the title turned over there, breaking up *Fantastically*.

However we had now become friendly with J. T. Kirtley and were doing what we could to help him at his press, which we reached by the Milsons Point Ferry. Phil came too at times. Kirtley was a quiet reserved chap, who could be jovial and Australianly sardonic now and then; he had a keen appreciation of good writing and a collection of first editions of Conrad, Ronald Firbank, D.H.L., A.H. and the like. His press was on the first floor over a butcher's shop, and at times the machine seemed a bit weighty for the planks. But J.K. said it was safe, and we were never precipitated down on to the chopping block and the frozen carcases. He lived with his widowed mother, a person of homely and shrewd wit, and often expressed pessimistically commonsense views as to the ultimate, and proximate, effects of Phil's and my views and actions. Occasionally we celebrated a run of good work with excellent Australian burgundy and masses of asparagus from tins. J.K. had just done Ken's *Thief of the Moon* and was feeling ambitious. I mentioned that I had translated Aristophanes's *Lysistrata* for my own delight, and he at once suggested that we print it on the press, making it a large and impressive book. N.L. was approached and offered to do full page illustrations as well as decorations. These, as all the considerable work he did later for our Fanfrolico Press, he gave us gratis. We in return did our very best to turn out a fine volume. The skill was all Kirtley's. Phil and I, with an occasional friend of J.K.'s, did a fair amount of the donkey-work. But I was steadily learning the tricks of the trade, from setting to presswork.

About this time a sculptor arrived as an art teacher in Sydney, Rayner Hoff, a stocky dark man with an energetic manner. With my readiness to look for a fated gathering of the necessary free spirits for Renascence, I had hoped he would fit into our system. But though a capable enough craftsman, he was clearly too sensible. Another sculptor however had turned up, a native product, who was more like our man. Frank Lynch (always known as Guy) had been born in West Melbourne and had served five years in the war, then spent two more years in New Zealand working at war memorials. He was now round twenty-six-twenty-seven, practically self-taught, and lived out at Gladesville. Tall, clumsy, excited, with furry hair and a stammering enthusiasm, he was consumed with an eager need to take up clay or chip away at marble and bring out the forms of his fancy, a gaunt Anzac or a satyr smelling of wattle blossom, a surf girl looking in the mirror of Aphrodite. One day in a pub near the Quay he and Beutler discoursed over beer about what could be done with the Quay. Any sane municipality would turn it into a magnificent amphitheatre for he-men to lean against pillars, girls to stroll about, and grand opera to be played among forests of statues. Guy raided the privy for paper to sketch on and roughed out the plan for making Sydney an Hellenic city, with a Colossus larger than that of Rhodes to straddle the Heads. 'We'll outdo Athens. We've got the men, we've got the ideas, we've got the scenery. All we need is money. What's that? Does anyone here know what money is? Let's have a drink and think about it.'

His brother Joe was there, a looser and wilder version of him. A sprawling good-natured lad fired with socialist hopes and ready to fight the whole villainous world single-handed. A few years later he was drowned from a ferry and Ken wrote his *Five Bells* about him – a poem which has justly become famous; for it holds the essence of these years I have called the Roaring Twenties.

> *Deep and dissolving verticals of light*
> *Ferry the falls of moonlight down. Five Bells*
> *Coldly ring out in a machine's voice. Night and water*
> *Pour to one rip of darkness, the Harbour floats*
> *In air, the Cross hangs upside down in water . . .*
>
> *Nothing except the memory of some bones*
> *Long shoved away, and sucked away, in mud;*
> *And unimportant things you might have done,*
> *Or once I thought you did; but you forgot,*
> *And all have now forgotten – looks and words*
> *And slops of beer; your coat with buttons off,*
> *Your gaunt chin and pricked eye, and raging tales*
> *Of Irish kings and English perfidy,*
> *And dirtier perfidy of publicans*
> *Groaning to God from Darlinghurst.*
>
> Five Bells
>
> *Then I saw the road, I heard the thunder*
> *Tumble, and felt the talons of the rain*
> *The night we came to Moorebank in slab-dark*
> *So dark you bore no body, had no face,*
> *But a sheer voice that rattled out of air*
> *(As now you'd cry if I could break the glass),*

A voice that spoke beside me in the bush,
Loud for a breath or bitten off by wind,
Of Milton, melons, and the Rights of Man . . .

In Sydney, by the spent aquarium-flare
Of penny gaslight on pink wallpaper,
We argued about blowing up the world,
But you were living backward, so each night
You crept a moment closer to the breast . . .

'Loaded with bottles, he had been off to some North Shore party with Frank,' says Phil, 'when, tired of the slow progress of the ferry – or, perhaps, of life itself – he had sprung up, saying he'd swim there quicker, and, fully dressed, dived overboard. A deck-hand had leaped in after him, and lifebelts were thrown. They saw Joe, said Frank, wave cheerily and strike out for Milson's Point; then he vanished in the moonlight. Perhaps a shark got him, or a mermaid – as some said – or the load of bottles in his greasy old raincoat tugged him to the fishes: no one can tell, for the body was never found.' Yes, Joe, and the Elegy for Joe, stand out as the very essence of that world. Joe in one way, and Anna in another, were the Hero, the Heroine, of Our Days.

The elegiac element suited Ken's poetry. He had now rapidly matured, in poems like *Heine in Paris* and the little play on Sterne; and he was to use his idiom, conversational and yet highly coloured and concentrated, in his poems on the explorers, the sea captains, that added a fresh dimension to Australian poetry, recapturing the spirit of adventurous voyaging into unknown seas and making this voyage at the same time an exploration of strange dimensions of experience. His inner conflict was between his keen sense of enjoyment and his sense of overwhelming loss. In *Five Bells* and these other poems he finely resolved the conflict and won his full poetic stature. And this achievement of his, I think it will be clear, was firmly rooted in the phase of Australian cultural development which had been ushered in by the wild banners of *Vision*.

At the moment Guy Lynch was full of hope, planning a 1925 exhibition that caused quite a sensation, and getting a commission from Melba. He had an Irish-Australian face, rough and tough and of the wildwood, yet sensitive, the sort of face an Australian faun would have, quick and vivid and visibly in process of forming itself. There seems to me something of it in his satyr sculptures, even when the features are not the same.

Guy's fortunes at this time ran rather parallel with Ray's, and though it just overlaps my Sydney period I should like here to give Ray's account of his Bligh painting. Ray made several large paintings of various aspects of the struggle between Bligh and Macarthur. 'It interested me as being one of the few occasions in Australian history when there was any real drama, with the conflicting personalities of the two men against the rich background of the Rum Corps and all their skulduggery. The main canvas represented Major Johnston announcing the arrest of Bligh to the crowd of convicts, drunks, hoodlums, collected outside the old Government House. I painted it, with the canvas propped up on a rickety old washstand, in a lousy untidy bedroom that Phil and I shared in the flat at Kings Cross. Since leaving Bondi I had had two different studios, one in Victoria Street, Kings Cross and one in William Street – the latter being the one that Phil described as "haunted". However, we had been kicked out of both for generally raucous behaviour, so I had resigned myself to working in the more uncomfortable and restricted conditions of the flat, which was at least more peaceful and free from interruptions. Nellie Melba bought the painting. It was very decent of her, as the gesture gained me plenty of publicity: of which, of course, she also got her fair share. She was holding her last opera season in Sydney and I remember very well going up to meet her at the Wentworth Hotel. She was a rather raddled old bag by that time; but despite that awful cynical precociousness of youth, I was soon overwhelmed by her incredible personality and charm. Then automatically was turned on that tremendous power which could dominate and entrance vast audiences – all upon one insignificant person, who was nevertheless an audience. All my youthful arrogance vanished. My immediate thought was: Good God, to have known you, to have loved you, when you were in your bodily peak of perfection! As you can guess, I was utterly flabbergasted.' *

He adds, 'But the meeting sticks in mind for another reason. Clara Butt had just published her book of memoirs, in which she gave a story about Melba advising her to sing only "muck" to Australian audiences. This story, of course, got lots of space in the newspapers, and poor old Melba, in the middle of her opera season, was doing her damnedest to deny the story and claiming that Australian audiences were the most artistic and appreciative she had ever encountered. So I got a bit of a shock when she asked me in her forthright manner, "What are your plans for the future, young man?" I replied that I intended to stay and study for a while yet in Australia before venturing abroad. She turned on me violently and said, "Take my advice. Get out of this country. It's no good for any artist!" This rather staggered me after her heated statements in the press about how artistic and understanding the Australian public was. But it gave me an opportunity to resume my cynical disguise. I was no longer quelled; I could, so I imagined, be superior in my

*In Phil's scanty papers (1958) I found a scrapbook of Guy's with a press cutting about the show. Of Guy's *Australian Venus*, 'If this girl of plaster were to awake today, from her perch in the galleries of the Education Department, step down with her looking-glass, and brush her radiance upon the crowds that gaze at her, what a scamper would resound in the staid, official corridors.' The writer sees her as liable to come alive to the piping of a water-lover and go running through the flowers, or else to hurry tumbling from the Pacific surf to chat with someone in a motorcar. 'So this is the line which bounds a goddess, from Athens to Bondi.'

He adds, 'Almost the only painting to strike a new note, something more vital, something with a fresh emotion and a new interest is Ray Lindsay's magnificent historical canvas, depicting the resignation of Governor Bligh. For years the Art Society has been stagnating on a pond of middle-aged land-scape and still-life studies, or portraiture which is even stiller than still-life. This year, thanks to Lynch's statue and Lindsay's painting, it has contained more vitality than the last dozen exhibitions put together.' Ray tells me that Crosslé bought Guy's work, had it cast in cement, and erected it in his Bulli garden. When he sold his practice and moved to Bellevue Hills, he trans-ferred it to his garden there, 'where I assume it still stands.'

shoddy arrogance. She told me that my Bligh painting had "too much Long Bay in it." (Long Bay is where Sydney's biggest jail stands.) When I replied that Sydney in Bligh's day was nothing but Long Bay, she exhorted me to paint only what was "beautiful". (How sweet were the twenties.) Still, she said she would give me a commission to do a painting for her home at Coombe Cottage in Victoria when she returned from abroad. On her way back from Europe a few years later, she promised, from Perth, that she would if well enough open an exhibition of mine in Melbourne. But she was a very sick woman at the time, and when she arrived in Sydney it was not long before she died: of what no one knows.'

About the time I was writing *Marino* (September-October 1924) Melba visited Springwood with her secretary Beverley Nichols trailing behind; and in *Twenty Five* he gives, in a chapter entitled 'showing how a genius worshipped devils in the mountains', something of the effect of Norman and his conversation:

He did not walk towards us – he fluttered to us, like a bird. So like a bird is he that I had the feeling, all the time, that I must catch hold of the end of his jacket in order that he should not fly up a gum tree and pipe his distracting arguments from the topmost branch. He was so thin, so fluttering, his eyes were so bright, his nose so like a beak, perched on top of his tiny neck. As for his talk – that, too, was birdlike – the words pouring out one after the other, making one think of when the swallows homeward fly. As difficult to follow, too, as a bird. In the first half hour of our conversation (I say 'our,' although my contribution was limited to negatives and affirmatives) – he had smashed the whole Christian philosophy, set Nietzsche on a pedestal, made at least a hundred genuflexions to him . . . and invited me three times to have a drink without doing anything about it . . .

We went back to the house and drank. I watched him. He talked of wine as though he were a Bacchanalian. One had the impression that he was only five minutes off a bout of drunkenness. Yet, he sipped only a mouthful, and even that was taken with pursed lips, as an old lady takes her tea.

He mentions that N.L. said the two persons in England he'd like to meet were Aldous Huxley and Dennis Bradley. (The reason for A.H. lay in my enthusiasm for *Antic Hay*, which I had carried up to Springwood; and it was because of Bradley's spiritualist experiments, not despite them, as B. N. thought, that this Bond Street tailor, with his chatty adverts in the *English Review* was included.) B.N. ends his account with an effort to dramatize the situation. Norman set out to show him an 'anti-Christian satire', turned over scores of designs, finally picked out one in which a pale-faced figure stood, 'sickly, anaemic, almost half-witted. It was like a patch of fever in the riotous health and brutality which crowded in on all sides. He laughed loud and long. I could not laugh. I felt absurdly, desolatingly shocked. Not, I think, by what Lindsay had shown me of Christ. But by something which he had shown me of myself.' However, at this time N.L. had long given up drawings of that sort, and the loud, long laugh is hardly in character.

Stimulated by Aristophanes, I was again working at verse-plays. I wrote *Helen Comes of Age* about the young Helen at Sparta. I had now found a personal form, but it was over-weighted by my light imagery. The discovery of the colour image and Sitwellian time-space had seemed to free me from all the old disciplines without fully clarifying the new one I sought. Interested in the complex interrelations and confluences of imagery born from light and desire, I felt that I needed only to let the entanglement go on winding and unwinding itself; the spiritual movement would emerge necessarily from the contacts and impacts in the visual and the tactile spheres. As a result there was a cleavage in the dramatic method. A few characters (here, the irritable Menelaus, the young Alcon, the two girls who wait on Helen) had something of ordinary drama existence; but Paris was a lyrical figment and Helen an irresponsible young girl intoxicated with her own charm – the being of these two was defined by the imagery alone, as I shall show later. The tragic element, grappled with in *Marino*, had receded. The conflagration of Troy had meaning only for the strange ominous colours it lighted in Helen's ringlets.*

---

*In retrospect it seems that much of Anna Brennan went to the make-up of the Helen I depicted. I have not dealt with Phil's struggles to become

18 · CIRCULAR PROGRESS

JACQUES HAD got into trouble. He took a job as accountant in a shop owned by a friend; and being more interested in mnemonics than in book-keeping, he forgot things and produced a confusion in his figures that alienated his employer who threatened proceedings. Jacques remained philosophically resigned, ignoring the whole business as a minor nuisance not worthy the concern of a business Napoleon or of an ascetic following in the footsteps of St Francis. Those who knew him would know that his motives were of the best, even if his arithmetic wasn't; those who didn't know him were unimportant. Why worry? I played dominoes in the coffee-lairs and discussed D. H. Lawrence, whom I had still hardly read and therefore disliked. At his insistence I read *Women in Love*, which impressed me beyond like and dislike. I even wrote a few short stories showing its influence, which Phil (my sole reader for prose as Norman was my sole reader for verse) pronounced good.

I visited Jacques next night at Mosman where a game of poker had been going on for an indefinite time. Barry was there, and a fat croaking fellow, and an uncouth enthusiast on Upton Sinclair. The only game that I found exciting was strip-poker; now I played cautiously and withdrew after I had won

---

a novelist, his *Snakes and Ladders*, *Farewell Rocking-Horse*, and *Jesting Venus*, since he describes them in *I'd Live*; I should like to add however that there was an odd charm in these works, which were quite unlike anything of his published works. (His main influences were, apart from Dickens and Dostoevsky, A. Huxley, N. Douglas, Joyce, the Sitwells.)

half a crown. On the terrace Phyllis joined me. The starlight
drifted on the crenellated waves, trees lifted their dark plumes,
the terraces of the night receded regularly below. Inside, the
poker-players in a red glow, behind panes of silence, made
incantatory gestures, blinked, sipped beer, or lowered their eyelids over the lordly cards. We said nothing and perhaps it was
the only time we came close. She was worried about Jacques
and the threat of proceedings which he shrugged away. I murmured the epigram of Asklepiades about Aphrodite snuggling
her cloak over nakedly embraced lovers, which seemed appo-
site except that we weren't lovers, weren't naked, and were very
inadequately embraced. The cool starlight, stabbed by a bird-
cry, flowed down the stepped terraces towards the grey foamwreaths. The ferries, gay with garlands of yellow light, slid on
the sluggishly heaving waters. The city twinkled beyond,
trampling up light dust, a fume of venomous warmth, an
emanation of promiscuous pleasures, a sprinkle of music
churned from the vulgar hurdygurdy, O Baudelaire. I loathed
the city glow, but it fascinated me. Yet here the fragile tissue
of starlight chambered us apart. Her face was delicately powdered with the rays of a myriad stars and the flickering foam-
candles. She sighed triumphantly. Gaudy with its spikes of fire,
the beaming ferry passed behind the headland as if into
annihilation. The waters sighed, with a rustling of ninon. We
were still as far apart. I wondered what I wanted of the night,
of her, of anyone. But such thoughts were forbidden. They
came under the heading of self-pity suitable for naturalistic
novelists and minor poets isolating the ego and finding it a
lonely incommunicado thing. Poetry, poetry pervaded all
things joyously, linked all things in the total defeat of loneliness, ceaselessly begetting new flowers, new rhythms that sustained the universe. The universe as single as my heart or her
face. One thought fills immensity.

Jacques as usual got out of all his troubles. Phyllis managed
with much trouble to patch things up. But now that everything
was settled, Jacques took a serious view of the situation. He
began avoiding us and behaving like a pariah. When unable
to escape, he adopted a cold aloof air. I would have liked to
help him, to reassure him, but didn't know how.

There was another intellectual who had a still worse end. Nicknamed Tinny, he had been a tutor at my W.E.A. camp on Tambourine, a sociologist interested in literature or a literary man interested in sociology: I was never sure which, as it always depressed me to discuss books with him and jar against his bright well-informed sane and absolutely tinny outlook. He had married a pupil and (to please her, I suppose) had become a Jew in religion, even being circumcised. But he failed to consummate the marriage, though he always indignantly denied the imputation of impotence. His bride, a warm and likeable person, was affected by the situation to the extent of being unable to travel in a train. Her home was far away, I think in Western Australia. Tinny tried to escape his problems by going off to England, where he met Ethel Mannin, as she recounts in her autobiography, and committed suicide.

I have mentioned that I was no drinker and that the episodes which stress beer appear here for their symbolical importance, not because they represent my normal mode of behaviour. Often I drank not even a thimbleful of beer for weeks or months on end; then, once started, I drank anything in sight, at any speed, anyhow. In that I was merely carrying out the orthodox Australian way of life, following in the well-trodden tracks of the sheep-shearers or drovers who collected a fat cheque at the end of a season and then blued it on one non-stop spree.

The day after I'd be knocked up and perhaps I'd descend to reading a detective story, which otherwise I scorned as the pabulum of nitwits who feared to face the murder-lust they titillated. Sipping liver-salts. And all the while I suffered an excruciating anxiety, a sense of quaking doom. Then next day I felt better. I had a theory that such an interval of domination by fear was necessary, setting up some of the tensions required for the crystallization of the image, the forging of the structure of tragedy in the groaning depths. Defecating the standing pool and stirring up the demons that had to be defeated.

If the intellect with its abstracting modes was never to be trusted, could one trust even an analysis of its shortcomings and tricks? could one ever be sure that it hadn't falsified the account of its own falsifications, hadn't exceeded its role as the clarifying interpreter of act? Perhaps it was taking revenge for its dethronement when it prompted the thesis of the male existing only in a planetary attachment to Mother Earth, a subservience to the purer intuitions of the Woman. She was the earth; he was the engineer of her roads and bridges – and in the vortices of his loss, the contriver of the artificial madness of speed, criss-crossing and mutilating the earth's surfaces. But if she presumed on her self-sufficiency, he could retort that he had made up the story of her centrique nature, her intuitional profundity and dominance, as a joke to amuse himself, to complicate the simple processes of love, to dramatize the needs of his fear. The goddess could be no higher than her worshipper; but now that she was brought down from her pedestal as a mere invention, a whim of his poetry, he too was belittled. Now it was a weakness that he must go to her for food, a servility that his mind was blank without her body enshrined in a mirror. There was a mock on the face of Venus, he was blindly jealous, and blood dripped from a hidden wound.

So the argument between the Poet and his Muse went on, with a widening circle of unresolved conflicts, with relief only in the images born from the tensions at their extreme point of contradiction and instability. And Woman, who was she? Why, Janet. She was the secure part of my existence, just as my poetry was written in the sober intervals that made up my normal life. The aberrations from sobriety and the day-long night-long obsession with words, when recounted, seem to stand out as the characteristic incidents. But, as feared and accepted jarrings, they gained their meaning from the thing they jarred. They were oscillations over an infernal pit which made me appreciate the return to firm earth, *Idyllia* and the wrestling with words.

I still had seen very few plays. In Brisbane, the Bellow dramas and one dull drama of the commercial theatre to which a visitor at Mary's house, learning of my inexperience, took me – plus *Twelfth Night* at the university. In Sydney, the *Beggar's Opera* and a play by Helen Simpson about Cellini; and then two productions by an experimental group: *Masses and Man* and *The Hairy Ape*. The main actor in both was a very small man who willy-nilly gave an effect of parodying the symbolism. In *The Hairy Ape*, when he ranted in the fo'c's'le, he seemed tolerated as a loon by the other sailors. His rebuffs and misfortunes descended on him as the inevitable result of an animalcule thrusting himself into a world where he could at most be a pet buffoon. Toller's work was similarly reduced to a hilarious caricature. Then for a while Janet worked with an excellent amateur group, in the role of Gormflaith in Bottomley's *King Lear's Wife*; but unfortunately the whole project came to nothing.

I still saw Ken fairly often, though he kept aloof from the more knockabout boozers and maintained his own journalistic routines. I recall however one nightmarish session at the state Parliament House, where he was reporting the proceedings, in and out of the gallery, the bar, the streets, and back again. I have the impression of our having been the last left in the dim corridors, in the large dustily silent mausoleum of lies and empty rhetoric, seeking a beer bottle or a book of notes, continually coming back to the same spot and the same patiently cynical attendant.

Now and then he went off on some journalistic job: for example, to record the federal sessions at Canberra. Canberra, populated entirely with civil servants, had acquired an inbred lunatic atmosphere all its own, worsened when a pack of journalists, with nothing to do but to report politicians whom they despised, were suddenly dumped there. Australian journalists in a pack can always be relied on to consume an abnormal quantity of drink; in the dull unreality of the fabricated town they surpassed themselves. And the civil servants went madder still. I recall a story of one of them trying, at a party, to cut a rump steak off himself for grilling.

One night at Theo's Club I saw Rahel dancing with a yellow-haired journalist and did my best to ignore her. Pillig had painted a frieze of women and baboons along the walls with a depressing maladroitness; his honest heart and hand could not deal with themes of vice, and all he achieved was a travesty of a low Berlin beer cellar (as I recognized when I saw U.F.A. films). Rahel came up as I gulped beer near the green baize curtains. I knew that she had gone up to Springwood, forced her way in, but gained nothing. Now she said that she was arranging an exhibition of Pillig's work in a basement café, with the paintings along the walls on the frieze-line. I agreed to do a note: 'something on modern painting,' I said, meaning to write a few general remarks without direct reference to Pillig. (However, the show never came off. Pillig had impressed the management with his silk tie and some newspaper cuttings; but when the paintings turned up, they refused to hang them. Not long after, he committed suicide.) She lounged at me, arms akimbo, leaning back from the waist, prognathous, greeneyed-greedy. The floppy-haired journalist came over, embraced her and slid to the floor against the wall. 'I wanna tell the world.' He laughed. 'Man overboard.'

The dancers were gliding around, patina'd with a dim glossy light of beer. Giggles from next door. A Dutch sailor, blonde as dealwood, lurched through the curtains and hiccoughed, with a stocking in his hand, a black stocking. He said something and split his wooden face with a kindly grin. Rahel shook herself, jangling with bangles. I leaned on the wall. The sailor held the stocking out to Rahel; and when she didn't take it, threw it round her throat. 'Woman overboard,' said the journalist on the floor, awakening. Rahel helped him up, while the sailor playfully pulled at the stocking. The music wheezed and flagged, an ineffective flagellation of the distraught flesh. To these whips of lackadaisical frenzy the peculiar celebrants danced. I looked round the corner at a pallid girl examining a bite on her left leg. The saxophone, a foghorn speaking through the mist of despair on an iron-bound coast, splashed on me its warm soggy wail. I stepped over the arched ankles and came out on the cubistic stairs, with unsolicited regret knuckling me in the nape of the neck.

We went to a Chinese joint in Campbell Street. Not a two-storeyed restaurant looking like an ornate pub in a decayed seaside resort, but a soup kitchen grimy with rusting light and international sweat and soya sauce. From the whitewashed walls broke dingy mortar and ridges of rough stone dripping cobwebs of shadow. An old Chinaman hobbled in, cross and crabbed, not a nice Chinaman, but then he was old and doubtless had justifiable grievances. In fact he had. There were Surry Hills toughs in the other corner, with caps pulled down; and by the time he had hobbled back to us with the rice and the oddments Jim had learnedly ordered, more toughs came in. 'Jees, there's going to be trouble,' said Jim, recognizing storm-signs that escaped my less objective eye. And so for the second time in a week I saw bottles thrown.

We didn't wait for explanations of what push-feud was involved. We ducked and ran for the back-way out. Jim pushed into the hobbling Chinaman and we dashed past steaming soup-cauldrons in a garish suffusion of belching light, some-one's shadow thrown high on the smoky roof, the squeal of an unseen woman, Dave falling over a clattered rubbish tin, spraining his wrist and getting a cabbage stump in his coat pocket. A hissing cat sprang from the wall top in which were embedded bits of broken beer bottles no longer sharp. The gate wouldn't open. Panting, Jim threw his bulk against it and hurt himself. I found the bolt down near the bottom and we were safe in the street.

We strolled along to the tram shed, Jim giving Dave first-aid for his wrist and Mick distributing an unexplained packet of ginger. Suddenly the whole evening became unreal, a painted backcloth for the lonely dancer in the spotlight of mysterious clarity. Zarathustra, beyond good and evil we found our island and our green meadow, we two alone; therefore we must be friendly to one another. We stood by the hurdled off space where workers were repairing the tramlines, with sagging grey tents, bellows wuffling and sending sparks in showers, a caul-dron of tar smoking. In the acid light of oxyacetylene crouched a man with puffed out moustache (making me think of Nietzsche's attachment of martial bluff under the deepsunk eyes of infinite torture), a welder was spurting green over asphalt. The toil went on steadily, a tiny mouse-twitch under the vast Australian night roughcast with pebbly stars. A glow of cosiness filtered through the rents and eye-holes in the can-vas shelter. Men at toil and men at rest, a piece of chewed ciga-rette hanging from the mouth's corner, men spitting and thinking of nothing. Good to lapse into the small railed off space, like coming home after a long and fruitless journey. A wife's body in the darkness of the bed, taking familiar curves of contact. Only that, the sense of being there in the right place, and safe. A dreamworld halted at the rails of toil, with notice calling on traffic to beware: *Road Up*. Here was no dream, but the touch of hand on hand, hand on tool handle, a hard confident touch. I was aware of a great gap somewhere in my idea of the world. All things else fumbled in wandering tides of froth up to this rock certainty. My beer-tired head longed for this pillow, the hard and confident palm of this strong hand.

And yet, as I tried to take the scene in, the old difficulties intervened, an inability to focus on detail. I could grasp the effect of night toil, the steady workers with the flame of power hissing at their will, but the precise shapes and purposes evaded me, leaving only fatigue and a wound. General aspects and faces in a lightburst, not local interlockings and configurations. The trumpets, but not the intimate gradations of speech that were so relevant to humour or active understanding. When I tried to listen, the world fell confusedly away, these men like the rest of it. That was why I was a poet, and worse, a frustrated poet. Or was I? what was I? What I wanted was the fine details of the network of lights and textures, the exact intonation of the sleepy voices. To know completely what the men were doing and why they were doing it. I yawned.

The earlier bottle-throwing that week had occurred in Anna B.'s flat, or rather the flat of the man with whom she was living in Forbes Street. She had taken up with ex-pug turned sporting journalist, a squat man with flattened nose and cabbage-ears. He still hadn't got over the excitement of seeing his name printed as commentator on the sports page where he used to read the reports of his own matches; and he felt the need to confer, overflowing in friendliness, with a fellow author, someone who ought to be able to appreciate his pride at rising into the intellectual world. 'Jack,' he kept saying as he took my arm and pressed it, 'us authors have got to stick together.' He took out a batch of cuttings and made me read them. 'Now what do you think of that? I know I've got to polish up a bit, but I don't mind saying I've got the knack of it. If you'd told me a year ago, I wouldn't have believed you.' He retrieved the cuttings and read out choice phrases. 'Now what do you think of that?' He was anxious to find if I had any enemies so that he could bash them for me. We had a drink in a quiet pub and he showed me what progress he had made in yodelling. Some of the customers looked round with an intention of saying rude things, but after a glance at his battered face they thought again. 'Jack,' he told me, clutching my arm again and fixing me with a look of ferocious sincerity, 'it's good to meet a bloke that takes writing as serious as what I do.'

Ray was present on the afternoon he met Anna. 'He was a real larrikin, and, with his bullet head cocked on one side, in Pelligrini's bar, he suddenly said to Anna: "I bet I'll have you in a fortnight." ' The term used was rather stronger than that. Will had been impressed by Anna's majestic deportment and tickled by her bawdy complacence of language. To possess her appeared both impossible and easy, necessary and fabulous. 'The extreme bluntness of this attack did not at all move the imperturbable Anna; she merely gave him her sweet composed smile and said, "I don't think you will." Of course he did, if not that night, probably the next; and he continued to do so for some time, anywhere and at any time.'

Anna had been originally seduced by an Italian waster, who was said, as a connoisseur of female plumpness, to have a bed specially made with boards for mattress. But she continued to hanker after him. All the while she was steadily going downhill; but her affair with the ex-pug marked a definite point of degradation. He liked to take his friends home to show her off, being as proud of keeping such a woman as he was of being a writer with his name printed in large type (plus a photosmear of his glowering bull face). The night he took me home she was in a bad temper and he wanted to put her through her paces for my benefit. That started the trouble. She didn't want to be put through any paces, she wanted to sulk comfortably and drink. Also I think she was ashamed at my seeing her installed in Will's lair. Not that she cared for me or my opinion, but I did represent in some sort of way her father's world, and she didn't like to feel degraded before that world. To the end she nourished an idea of writing and being a not-unworthy daughter of Christopher the Poet.

Will couldn't see that she was getting angry. He kept on telling me what a bonzer girl she was, how different she was from the usual pack of blinkblankblonk, and how suited he and she were. So at last she said, 'Hell to all that, go and buy me a bottle of brandy.' He said the local pubs didn't know him yet. 'You go to so-and-so's,' she replied, 'and mention my name. If they don't know you, they know me.' He said he wouldn't wait on no dashdash woman and she said he dashdash might as well get used to it, so start as soon as possible. 'You don't get me as cheap as you'd like to.' They began shouting at one another; and by the time they had really got going, the respectably nurtured Anna was easily a match for Will, who glared at her in a daze, with a punch-drunk sway.

'Give us a yodel,' I suggested with ill-advised humour.

'That dashdash of a woman don't appreciate art, Jack,' he dolefully answered me. 'Not like you and me do. Shut up,' he roared at her. 'You're worse than a roof-full of tom-cats. If only you were a man I'd put my fist through your dashdash guts,' etcetera, etcetera.

'You're not dashdash man enough,' etcetera, etcetera.

'Don't be so dashdash sure of that, you're not dashdash dead, though you soon will be,' and so on.

'Listen to him, Jack, listen to the funny sod, I'll tell you a few things about him.' She told them.

'Listen to me, Jack, you don't know what that woman'll descend to. I'll tell you.' He told me.

He was annoyed when she appealed to me, standing against the wall with her hands on her broad hips, her face rosily lighted with her anger, her eyes flashing with their cornflower blue, her bright hair tossed about her thrownback head. So he started appealing to me too. I felt the danger of the position and tried to mumble words of placation. But they were both at me, insistent that I speak up and agree. I sympathized with Anna; but if I had to choose, I feared Will's large fist more than her tongue. Besides, I was flattered by his liking for me, though it was really only a liking for his own name in print.

She threw the first bottle. There was a number of beer and milk bottles standing on a box by the kitchen door. She threw the bottle slowly, calmly, but without aim. It smashed on the wall some six feet away from Will. He said, 'Cri, I won't stand for that from a woman.' So he threw a milk jug. The milk splashed over me, flecked her big bosom and gleaming face. 'So you would, would you?' she remarked. They spoke without shouting now, in a tense angry coldness. Anna threw the second bottle. He threw a soup plate. They were not many feet apart and could easily have hit one another, but their careful lobs and throws became a sort of ritual of destruction, not intended to damage anything but the walls. I was cut off from the door, seated against the dresser, and didn't know what to do. Someone from another flat yelled below. Anna and Will went on throwing things at one another (at the wall), uttering stereotyped insults in cold harsh voices.

The peltings seem to have been a nightly practice; for Ray records that when he visited the flat, the same thing happened. 'It was their custom to whip themselves up into a frenzy of lust. On this particular night they hurled practically every ornament and piece of crockery at each other, together with such delightful and imaginative insults as . . . (censored). I remember also, at Pelligrini's, Margot R., wiping alcoholic tears of amusement from her eyes and giving a detailed account of the previous night when the loving couple, having been flung out of the flat by their landlord for the noises they made, arrived at her room, pushed her out of her own bed, and installed themselves there. Margot added, in her philosophic manner, that as she herself now had nowhere to sleep, she filled in the time by washing Annie's one and only pair of pants (although, if I remember rightly, bloomers were then usually worn because of the shortness of skirts). After the affair ended, Will returned to his lawful wife, an enormous arrogant woman with cross eyes, and continued his successful career.'

Anna, I mentioned, tried now and then to write. A few times she told me that she'd like to write a novel, though what she had in mind was a piece of self-vindication. She never forgot her father, as he for his part had been unable to forget her; she wanted to show him that despite everything she had some of his creative fire. She had listened intently to his talk and repeated many of his ideas. Thus, he had a low opinion of psychoanalysis, which he liked to describe as a modern conjuration of devils. In April 1924 Anna contributed an article to the *Bulletin* Red Page, in which, writing in an easy forcible style, she denounces the works of Freud as a 'prostitution of science,' a device for peopling the undermind with 'foul-smelling ghosts' and 'unsavoury fantasies'. She attacks the interpretation of dreams about teeth falling out as showing 'tendencies towards sex-perversion'. (One wonders what analyst ever said that, since the normal interpretation of such dreams would be that they showed a fear of impotence or castration, probably linked with masturbation, which did not possess any special intensity unless linked with other symptoms.*) She goes on:

Freud himself tells of a girl of eighteen suffering from those ordinary 'nerve' symptoms which frequently follow shock or prolonged strain – fear of crossing the street, of being in a room alone with the door shut, irritation at the ticking of a clock, excessive fidgetiness as to the placing of things. He works out by a train of reasoning which is screamingly funny or very nauseating, according to the reader's type of mind, that the girl is obsessed by a peculiar and revolting sex-passion; and, in spite of continuous and sustained denials, by persistent pressure he breaks her down to acquiesce. That is to say, he finds her a nervous girl, he leaves her a sex-pervert.

This prim and disgusted statement is made by the girl whom we have met at Betsy's and in the ex-pug's flat. Freud, I think, would have smiled benevolently if he had been given her essay. He would hardly have needed a dossier to diagnose that its author was suffering from a very bad father obsession which was doubtless working out in odd ways. He would have noted the obvious resistances to bringing up into consciousness the hidden structure of motivation. As for us, knowing what we do, it is hard not to see in the fantasy of Freud who 'finds her a nervous girl, leaves her a sex-pervert', the father-image towards which she had such an ambivalent attitude.

Her yearning for escape, her repeated wish to get away to the clean sea, the wind of God, the healing earth, was real enough, and embraced memories of her earlier years at New-

---

*She had the very person before her eyes for a long time in Yvonne who shared a flat with her in Victoria Street and whose exacerbated symptoms I forbear to list.

port. Here too there was an echo of her father's views. Rose in her Notes on Brennan's conversation at Springwood mentions that he talked 'of his home life, his wife's excellent cooking, his love of sleeping naked between blankets, summer and winter, because on hot nights they mopped up the sweat, and in cold they warmed the blood. To sit on a blanket, eat a potato baked in its jacket, and drink red wine at his seaside cottage, was all that he wished for his old age.' That seaside cottage with its simple life haunted Anna too. After her marriage she tried to inhabit it; but her husband was taken by a shark on one of the beaches and she died soon after.

19 · THE PARTY TO END ALL PARTIES

WE HAD some new friends, Ronald and Pat. Ronald was darkish and handsome, except that he wasn't quite tall enough and was beginning to put on weight and had an uneasy eye, a peevish brown eye. With a small pouted baby-mouth, he had a grouch against a lot of things, but mostly not the right things. Pat was a buxom tall rollicking daughter of a publican, with a large hearty voice in a comely face, a hooting laugh, and an unquenchable thirst. Ronald wanted to be a musician and was writing a *Darlinghurst Suite*, which never got much further than his midnight ambitions; he worked in a family business near the Quay, a small mercantile affair, and had an uncertain feeling that by buying me a drink now and then, but not too often, he became an intellectual or would at least be recognized as such. Pat had no aims beyond enjoying herself, which she did extremely well, as the drinks seldom ran out.

After a while however she grew impatient with Ronald and his inability to make up his mind to marry her or to become a starving composer or to turn into a rich merchant or indeed to do anything that entailed hard work and a stand-up fight with the family. She considered me a sap, but was tolerant.

One of the friends with whom she lunched was a large oily lawyer, supposed to have a considerable importance in the background of the Labor Party. I have been told that he was the main model for Kangaroo in Lawrence's novel, and perhaps D.H.L. heard some of the odd tales about him. He owned a bland demagogic manner, a bumptious and wily persuasiveness, a breadth of gesture; and prided himself on his taste in wines. I disliked him very much, and was only once drawn into lunching in his chambers. Throughout the lavish meal I said nothing at all. Afterwards we sat in the flat of some kimono'd vaudeville artiste who was ironing out her underclothes. The image of the egregious lawyer with his pig-eyes behind intellectual spectacles was still with me, and I remained silent, feeling crushed, enclosed in a chilly armour of isolation. Pat in her chitter-chatter had come round to dealing with some acquaintance who was as dull as ditchwater, a dummy without a word to say for himself, an absolute bore, my dear. Then, noticing me, she added, 'Of course it doesn't matter if a person's really clever underneath.' Sweet of her, wasn't it? I still didn't say anything. I existed for the world only as the thin mask of a smile behind which my spirit lay in ambush and anguish. Holding that smile like a frail mask of papier-mâché, the kind that N.L. made in large numbers once to fix on his studio lay-figure. Only, I wasn't as pretty as they were.

Pat talked enough for two or three, anyway. She wasn't malicious, she simply thought that friends existed for the sake of the funny stories she could tell about them. She noted their oddities with a quick eye; and the more she ridiculed them with her sly Irish tongue, the more she liked them. Even behind my precarious mask I felt something of that heightening of the ego that comes from the merciless belittlement of one's friends and acquaintances. Perhaps because the vituperative image is a swollen image of the actual person, bigger and better and even sillier than life, a gigantesque caricature. So, in composing or responding to this image, we are Jack-the-giant killers, twitting the dangerous forces. We inflate the meagre personality we laugh at, giving it a largeness of stupidity, grossness, even of evil, to which it hardly in fact aspires. We inflate and then puncture. The giant lies in a flat rubbery mess on the ground, harmless. We take a deep breath and inhale back the virtue of power which we had blown into the adversary. For what is comic is something we deeply fear twisted into a joke and deprived of menace. Look, it's only a guy, a pumpkin with a candle in, a sheet over a tree. Also, we make a vicarious scapegoat of the absent person, laying on him our own fears and malices; and by driving him out into the desert of our illimitable scorn, we momently delude ourselves that we've got rid of the curse.

So I meditated while Pat rambled on.

One night at her flat there was a slight earthquake (as we learned from the papers next morning). 'And we never noticed it at all,' she remarked. 'Just shows you how good it is to drink whisky. Now I think of it, I did feel something, but I thought it was Ronald hiccoughing.'

Through Ronald we met Lilith and Johnny, both of rich pastoral families, who were nonchalantly engaged. Lilith had her own flat, looked after by a young housekeeper-companion. She was fair, svelte, expensively dressed, with an oval face in which the small regular features never, in my view, registered the least emotion. She said little but lapped whisky as a kitten does cream, and without apparent effect, except that she said even less. One night we ended a party at her place by going out to wander in the streets, looking for some club that Johnny had dreamed about. I happened to be with her. Seeing a street sweeping cart approach, she hailed it, remarked that she would like a drive, and was invited up. I joined her; and on a lofty seat we moved on, with the brushes turning and sweeping behind us. After a while we came on the others, who watched us in astonishment. We gave them a regal salute and swept on. I went back with Lilith to her flat and was given a mat and some cushions to sleep on.

It was Johnny, however, who brought things to a climax. He decided to sell his sports car, invest the whole of the proceeds in crates of whisky, and hold a month-long party. Meanwhile, things weren't going well with Pat and Ronald. Several times in a few weeks she had hysterics in the middle of a party: 'the hoots', she called it. An excellent description. I have never heard a lustier hooter, or one who began hooting with less warning. Ronald's parents were getting more difficult, threatening to cut off his allowance unless he did more work at the office; and Pat herself couldn't make up her mind whether she wanted to marry him. As for him, he hungered for a life of married respectability and feared it, especially with Pat. He was extremely jealous, not of the present, but of the past. He had fabricated a theory that the first man impregnated a woman for all time with his particular kind of blood or seed. In this he anticipated Nazi biology. I later found a Nazi ideologist declaring:

Male semen is absorbed immediately and completely into the blood of the female in intercourse. Therefore a single contact between a Jew and a woman of another race is sufficient to corrupt her soul for ever. With this alien albumen she also acquires his alien soul. She can never again, even if she marries an Aryan man, bear pure Aryan children.

Ronald, it is true, wasn't concerned whether Pat's earlier lovers had been Aboriginals or pure beer-swilling Aussies; he was concerned only that they weren't himself. But otherwise his paranoiac obsession corresponded with that of the Nazi maniacs. As Pat had had previous lovers, he tearfully insisted over his whisky, she could never bear 'his children', even if her albumen-acquisition had occurred years before she met him. 'It's a scientific fact, Jack, and it proves that women should never have more than one man.' I knew little at the time about biology, but I knew enough psychology to know that he was veiling some persecution delusion behind his grief at never being able to beget his own children on the woman of his choice.

In fact he was bothered about more than the seminal ghosts of Pat's past. She was being honourably wooed in the present by a pumpkin-headed chap from North Queensland who had never realized that he could only beget someone else's children on Pat's sturdy charms. Unable to face the fact that, unless he soon pulled himself together, he'd lose Pat, Ronald preferred to concentrate on her harmless and divulged past. The shadow-fight suited his indecision; it also unfitted him hopelessly as a lover – which increased Pat's divided state and led to more 'hoots'. Both partners confided in me at length; and my advice that they should do whatever they wanted to do, had a consoling effect and intensified their confusions.

Ronald hunted us up for the party to end all parties. 'Come along, Johnny's asking for you. It's going to be an historic event.' Already he looked bloodshot and heavy-lidded. Johnny's flat was in a mansion with a large court over which some of his windows looked. We arrived as the festivities were hardly started, with less than a crate of whisky consumed. There was however even then a certain lull, a torpidity, setting in. A few recliners flourished bottles in welcome. Johnny came up, immaculately dressed as usual. 'Been sending telegrams all over the world for you. Hurry and catch up. Take a crate or two.' He knocked the top off a bottle. 'Finish this up at once. No time to lose. Serious matter. Hurry.' He spoke urgently, as if we were all on the point of departure to another world. Waving his hand generously, he knocked himself over backwards.

Lilith was there, cool and collected as ever. After a few drinks she said to me, 'I think I'll visit the lavabo. Come and hold my hand for me.' So I held her hand. And as I heard a tinkle of water, she began reciting my poem on Aphrodite rising from the foam. To my surprise she knew it right through. 'That is the loveliest compliment a poet has ever had paid to him,' I told her. She looked a little more blank than before, and I repeated my words, which didn't sound so good a second time. She still didn't understand and I didn't understand her misunderstanding. Then she guessed. 'Do you mean you wrote that poem? I never look at the names on books or anything like that.' She was really animated for the first time since we'd met.

The party gurgled on and on. Snatches of sleep and snatches of song. Ronald babbled about the need to keep women faithful to one man from the age of puberty. 'We need a moral society. If it won't be moral of its own accord, it must be forced. It must be taught with whips.' He scowled and closed one eye, watching the handkerchief drop out of his shirt cuff. Pat took me aside and told me once again of his shortcomings. Poor girl, she couldn't decide between pumpkin-headed cattlemen who knew what they wanted, and clever cosmopolitans of the big city who didn't. I said that it all depended.

Now and then someone remembered a new story or had the energy to tell an old one, rising up as if from the bored dead. All limericks had run out. Now and then a couple floundered round in a foxtrot, but tripped over the first obstacle of legs. Then suddenly the flat was thronged with unknown faces. All sorts of bums had heard of the whisky crates and had come to pocket a bottle. But nobody had enough interest to ask them who they were, or to throw them out. Johnny passed out and came to again. He had some undefined plan with an undefined object which it was necessary to expound without the least delay. Pat remarked that she'd rather marry a dog's lamp-post than a man who said she was poisoned with alien albumen. Ronald tried to whistle the tune that represented Kings Cross in his *Suite*, and had a fit of coughing. Pat asked if he were trying to give us a bassoon tune. Someone kept on frying bacon. Two gramophones were playing with cracked records. Lilith sat perfectly calm on a chair in the balcony after having had her third bath.

Finally, after three or four indeterminate days, it was found that the crates, as a result of raiding outsiders, were almost empty. Johnny had donned aviator's clothes (he owned a small private aeroplane) and decided to jump out of the window without a parachute. At last, it seemed, he had found out why he held the party. He cleared the front room and stood against the wall opposite the window, swinging his arms. 'Make way there, I'm coming, I'm coming.' Someone looked out of the window and noticed the pointed iron-railings below. However, Johnny had sunk to the floor in a stupor. Then the police arrived, extremely polite, and we went home. The party to end all parties had itself ended. What now was left to do?

Besides *Helen*, I had completed several lesser plays: one in the Restoration manner, but in blank verse, in which I worked in practically all the amorous dodges of Wycherly, Congreve, and the others; a shorter play on an episode from Casanova; two one-act plays about Titian and Rubens, in which I sought to keep throughout to imagery of light and colour in the key of the painter in question; also a play on Catullus, of which I recall only one line directed at Clodia ('and all your boasted fierce frigidities') because Rupert Atkinson singled it out and quoted it a number of times. This last play was thus the first step to the trilogy with two companion novels which I was to write in the 1930s around Catullus and his world. There was also a long and hasty poem *Between Two Kisses*, in which a girl, awakening under an apple tree at her lover's kiss, dreams through a series of adventures set in periods from the ancient world on to the present, each section being written to some extent in the style of the period it treated. All these works (apart from the already-printed *Helen*) I burned in 1931. I regret the little plays on Rubens and Titian (to which I had added one on Rembrandt by that time). There was also a play set in the seventeenth-century tavern, to which Norman did a water-colour. All these works, and many lesser ones, were written in 1925.

My unconcern with the existing theatre did not mean that I looked on my own plays as closet dramas. I considered them poetic dramas in which the essential thing was the words, but I did not regard the words as divorced from action, from visual pattern. On the contrary: but the stage I had in mind was a mixture of the Attic and the Elizabethan, without scenery but with the words and the visual pattern determining the system of production. In idiom and method alike I was starting from a point in my head, derived from Greek and medieval tradition indeed, but flatly ignoring the proscenium arch and the naturalistic systems ruling in the existing theatre, ignoring too what I considered the broken up naturalisms of modernist experiment. The fact that I had no apparent point in actuality from which to proceed did not bother me in the least. It merely made me more obstinate. (In England the only ally I had was Gordon Bottomley, though I meditated starting a theatre in 1929-30 – but all that must wait till the next volume.)

I had a sense of pressure, as if I realized that a stage of my development was nearing its end, a sense of purpose and a sense of distraction. It seems now that many of the inner tensions and contradictions in my being were coming close under the levels of consciousness, though they were not to explode till 1930-31, in England. The *Creative Effort* fantasy world still enclosed me, both stimulating and crippling; and within its given space I had gone about as far as I could go. I walked the streets of a dull loneliness; and my preconceptions, my word-obsessions, wall-papered the four-square dungeon of time-space in which I scribbled. Did I see the sprags sitting on a half-rotted post by the shore-line? did I chat with the friendly wagtail among the bushes? No, but I saw Alkman's ceryl winging over the flowers of the foam, the sea-blue bird of spring, saw it with praeternatural clarity. Phyllis was a wraith glimmering in the great shelving waves of ecstasy that engulfed Isolde. This was not the literary life, no. To see the ceryl in all the precise beauty of its movement that gathers in all the observed flights of sprag and seagull, to swim in the Isolde Sea, is not literary. It may reveal many fears and evasions, but is a form of intense living. As a flower might burst with a new force of scent and unfolded petals, cut from its bough and set in a vase, flaring richly out for death. Yes, moments of anxiety and exaltation, seeking for the sensuous essence by short-cuts that led away from living. When the Beethoven banners swung from one end of space to the other. When the pyre of the wrecked universe was too small for the celebration of the dead hero. When Danae, glowing with the seed of the sun in her brazen tower, spread out her flesh of lily-grain, spread out her breasts from which spurted the milk of light, spread out her flanks suavely flowing with the fire of marble.

But Oh, also, the dullness, the ache of shapeless days, the knock of the void. The aftermath of fear, of smothering doubt. When thought goes quite out of focus and words lose their body, the weight of their momentum. The inability to keep one's mind clear, especially with others, even to listen at all. Stunned into a deafness of isolation and watching the others talk behind the bright veil; feeling oneself lost and unable to answer for fear that one hasn't heard straight and the others will gape and laugh. Yet alone, returning to the thought process that works with pouncing brilliance, with a sudden burst and simplicity of relationships seen like the lines on one's hand. Riding the storm again, with the manes of the wind flapping in one's face and the valkyrie-breasts stabbing with paps of bronze against one's back.

The voices end, the hand draws away, and there is only the crevice of silence and the missing beat of fear. Look on the known faces and find in the familiar smile wrinkles of the eyes the mark of the beast, the alien cruelty. Feel in the uneasy shift of limbs in a creaking chair, in the nail that scratches with unwitting impatience, in the tilt of a listening head, the omnipresence of death and his engines, the huge distances of fear. In the beat of the hearts, in the beat of one's own heart, the scuttle of crabs under the rotting roots, the suck of mangrove mud, and the white ants gnawing in all the wood of time, dribbling a white dust.

Let it go. It becomes an exaggeration when put into words,

because the words hold so little of it. They hold only a tick, a crumb, a shiver; and because they concentrate on that detail, swelling it up to look like a whole moment, a whole emotion or act, the wholeness is lost and only the ungainly magnification of the detail remains. No, it wasn't like that. It wasn't like anything you or I can say. Who has ever read a book in the least like life, even remotely like life?

Yet we keep on trying, and rightly. The world is real and we are real, and the words are part of us and our changing, our oneness, and we must struggle inside the words or reality begins to desert us altogether. Everything leaves us but the omnipresent death. So, though you say, and I say: It wasn't like that, it was really quite different; yet, as you finish reading the words, as you've half-forgotten them, you may suddenly find that they have conveyed a truth. You may say: Yes, that's it.

There was a lot of happiness too, and a quiet as broad as the sky at dawn over the Pacific. We bathed often and lay on the beach together. The great breakers coming up out of endlessness with a slap and a bang of skidding foam on the golden beach, and the depthless Australian sky overhead, gave a ceremonial importance, as if I knew that I was soon to leave this magnificence for ever. The stretch of furious gold, the carpet of light on which we lay, lifted and carried us away dazed into immensity, into the droning summer heat. A routine of peaceful communion. Enough contact with the restless world in the breakers; suddenly heaving up out of indeterminate silver-blue perturbation, the purlers bringing in a venturesome swimmer or a glistening girl on a surfboard, her torso braced strongly against the oceanic force, the beer froth of the unseen tankards of tritons whisked along the sand, the sinewy broad-chested life savers with their tackle, the girls with long lithe legs, each moving like a Victory against the wind, the pompom band in the diminutive bandstand and the promenaders in their cheap new suits. And if the shark signal was given from the watch-tower, there was a life-hallelujah in the successful dash for the shore.

20 · CONFLICT AND IMAGERY IN THE POEMS AND PLAYS

A GOOD starting-point from which to consider what I was trying to do in my verse is given by the critique of the plays in *Australian Literature*, 1940, which was written, I believe, by Frederick Macartney:

In them he reveals the self-creative tendencies in action and shows woman as a dominant energy in love. His Nietzschean philosophy of life characterizes these plays. The individual, who is himself and not another, is his own authority for what he does; correction is not to be externally imposed but springs from within. He is his own critic. He has cast out fear. Each acts within the limits of what he can energize. Through poetry, then, may be unfolded the creative expression of the individual as absolute authority. And drama is a fitting means for the manifestation of the poet's creed in action.

In Lindsay's verse-forms imagery and symbolism are highly complicated. He has been so accustomed to turning the abstract into the concrete that it is not easy for him to realize adequately the difficulties his readers have to overcome in order to follow his meaning or get any meaning at all. An object in the world of his imagination takes on the form of what is organically alive and makes new associations out of all ordinary settings. Sensations cease to be abstractions and become living things capable of movements beyond the limits of the rational; they can take on new shapes and work in smoothly with their opposites in a way that leaves the intellect staggering. It happens at times that the imagery becomes so complicated that the thought is, as it were, lost in a maze and cannot get through. But generally the meaning comes forth somewhere through an apt or direct expression.

Despite his egoism, which springs from his philosophical outlook, Lindsay's poetic dramas cannot be lightly passed over. They do not achieve all that he aimed at, and they are not likely to win extended favours. But they are among the good things he has accomplished. Some of his scenes shimmer with poetry. The symbolism is oft-times rich and delicate, and the imagery graceful and light. But there is an undue tendency to overdo it, and the general effect is an unevenness of handling. His material is not sufficiently malleable to his touch . . .

Helen is as changeable as the winds and all too conscious of her charms. She joys in awakening jealousies in her womenfolk and rousing ardours in men whom she willingly leaves floundering. Her lovers scarcely come into contact with one another.

His strictures seem to me just; his interpretation is certainly along the lines of my intentions in writing the works. I would like to add that the ceaseless imagery developed from the embrace, with the centralization of this imagery inevitably in the body of woman, has a much larger implication than might appear. This imagery is conceived (a) as defining the continuous creation and recreation of the universe by the act which merges the sensuous essences and the enjoying consciousness, (b) as embodying the energies of the mind which are present in all sensuous realization and are 'transcendent' (my idealist term at the time) in that they help to create new dynamic unities of sense-and-mind, (c) as expressing the processes whereby men enter into the world of nature, processes that surpass all contemplative or analytic methods of apprehension, and that merge the enjoying consciousness with the organic movements and cohesions outside man, (d) as revealing the unity of the organic processes inside and outside man.

Take almost any lines from *Helen*:

> *. . . build a city for love with names*
> *for every street of trodden and broad laughter,*
> *every lane of mazy touch where spirit,*
> *dazzled at last by dull torches of guttering sense,*
> *faces on walled darkness hinged with no postern*
> *of kisses left afar for joy to creep through*
> *and throw up new moons into the dim trees*
> *of secret gardens trellised in my hair;*
> *and then comes trudging sleep.*

The breathless movement of the metre (its collisions 'new moons . . . dim trees') and the continual use of appositions are aspects of the image-series making Helen one with the world around her: not by imposing her on that world, but by merging natural and human process in the special intensities of harmony that we call beauty. She becomes the garden of her own trysting. More, she becomes the whole city of daily life – love and beauty thus transfiguring the city of alienation and the pleasure lash. But the contrasts (gathered most directly in the opposition of the light-of-love-and-life with the sudden darkness, the cliff-edge of world-end) bring into her image, into all it implies in its out reaching, the very conflict of life and death cored in the senses, the body. (The contrasts include the opposition of lonely lovers with the populous city, the sensuous with the social.) The structure of the sentences (an aspect of the rhythm) carried the death-darkness, which seems about to swallow the lovers up, into its opposite. The moons come up into the darkness, which has become her body, in death's defeat.

The movement of thought, which I here clumsily translate into analytic terms, was present in my mind all the while, but immediately transformed into concrete images. I consciously opposed the dialectic of changing and fusing images, opposites ceaselessly clashed into unity, to analytic logic. That logic with its syllogisms that stated equivalences and could not express contradictions or the union of opposites, I identified with blind repetition, social and political tyranny, a machine society based on the division of labour and wage slavery.

To return to the cited lines, note how 'trudging sleep' completes the movement by bringing the imagery back to the trodden streets. The dangerous cliff-edge of death-darkness has been met and beaten; through the labyrinthine lanes of the embrace safety is reached, darkness becomes sleep. And the extension of the Helen image (the alienating city absorbed into the image of beauty) is not surrendered.

Note also the lines before and after. The transformation of the sensuous image into the social, and back again, was thus prepared:

> *We must deck ourselves*
> *in every jewel of devoted joy*
> *forged from our nipples; we must fully assess*
> *bed-empires and the limit of a kiss,*
> *greedy; build a city of love with names . . .*

The metaphor from labour (forging) leads on to the concept
of state and city, with the idea of limits taken alike from the
image of a forged form and that of city-boundaries (the limits
of power). The limit idea further links with the following image
of the cliff-edge or wall between light and dark, life and death;
and further, in connection with the whole changing relation
between Helen and the nature that encloses her and is
enclosed, it raises the question of the relation of self and otherness (both in nature and in other people): the limit of self.

After 'trudging sleep' comes:

> *So to the eventual kiss we force*
> *tarrying pleasures, take the measures of*
> *imperious laughter and the huge kingdoms*
> *of tousled darkness, till we wake to find*
> *our royalty of enfeoffed kisses chartered,*
> *but the dear lover gone.*

Here the images of light-dark and the power limit are brought
together – 'eventual kiss' suggesting both the end of love and
death – with a revival of the state image in expanded form:
sleep and love-fulfilment being equated. 'Waking' then inverts
the whole series. The limit contracts and the daylight stands
for the rule of mechanical logic, egoism, the state asserting its
irreconcilable nature of division. The individual is enclosed in
a loveless self-assertion, an effort to impose demands and external rules on love, so that the living body of experience vanishes.

Now, I am not arguing that this use of imagery is good or
bad, well done or ill done. What I am demonstrating is the way
I thought and the form that my thinking took. I did not believe
that valid thinking (that is, poetic thinking) could work any
other way. The unceasing transformation of the abstract into
the concrete was for me the sole pledge of truth; and the love
image, at its most active form in dealing with the embrace, had
for me both the obvious significance and its wider philosophic

value as defining the relation of man and nature at its most intense. It was not that moon and tree existed only as metaphors of Helen; it was that in terms of her I felt them realized most fully and dynamically as real things, as parts of a universe that man was humanizing.

Let me take one more passage at random:

> *If my kisses humble thus your mouth,*
> *I will repent of leaning down so far,*
> *down, down, a lily's length, my own thigh's length,*
> *through vast air tunneled with a kiss, to come*
> *on your low spirit reached at last by me*
> *under the trailing sunlight, by me leaning*
> *out of the marble heavens down to you;*
> *as though you put a hand up into air*
> *and closed your fist about a luscious cloud*
> *rolled in the sunset,*
> *and it came loose in your grasp, that spray of light,*
> *that branch snapt off the blossoming sunlight.*
> *For I'd not wish*
> *to tread your pride down with my sandalled love,*
> *or make you dizzy*
> *by the stars that preen their fires within my hair.*

There, the primary aim is to conquer space by a series of movements, partly expressed in the continually extending sentences of the rhythm, partly by the way in which the images of girl and flower are fused. We begin with the lily-thigh length, and move, via the dizziness of the excited moment of contact, as high as the sky and then back again, merging heaven and earth, girl and flower, sunset and flower-bush. In the coda of the last four lines we return to the actual scene, her foot which concludes the lily-thigh movement, swing back sky-high to the stars now setting securely within her hair (with the bird image inherent in 'preening' to maintain the flower-branch image).

The movement, rhythmically and imagically, thus depicts the immediate sensations of the lover at the girl's feet (or of the girl looking down at the lover – he and she are merged in the giddy moment). But it also meant for me a conquest of space-time, a creation of the image that fills immensity. An affirmation of human centrality and significance against the vastness of space, which is dead and meaningless till the image of man fills and controls it. Once it is filled, it ceases to be vast and inhumanly terrifying; it is no longer than the distance between Helen's head and her feet.

In my mind I was opposing this aesthetic conquest of space-time to the scientific conquest, which seemed to me valuable only in so far as it echoed, obeyed and clarified the poetic mas-teries. By itself I saw it as a mad instrument of destruction and murder, the bloody anatomization of the living joy, the abstraction of Urizen (which was also that of the state).

I have spoken above of space-time rather than of space; for I considered 'space' one of the dead abstractions that had to be defeated. Space could not be separated from time unless one wished to arrest and annihilate process and development – to put a dead mechanism of balances in place of irreversible his-tory. Poetically, this meant that the rhythm must at all points echo and express the movement of imagery. The clock, the reg-ular beat of the metronome, was Time in abstraction. I identi-fied dead time with mechanism, labour division, wage slavery, money. Poetic rhythm rejected abstract time; it was supremely concrete time. And so in living terms there was no time or space, there was only time-space.

But in the expressions defining the unity of time and space there could be a stress on one or other aspect of the concrete situation. *Helen* aimed at filling all space with the sensuous image; *Marino* with its mounting anguish underlined the con-flict of abstract and concrete time. Marino knows that it is his own death he plans as he waits for the moment when the others die; he is devoured by the pang of time because he is quite cut off from other people, the conspirators he wants to use or the wife through whom he feels his own honour flouted:

> *Then let us leave it. O, are there no ways*
> *of bribing Time, that tinkles in the mind*
> *with tedious jestering, a chatter of bells*
> *over the dull booms of great drums of fear*
> *spread taut in the blood: the ominous bird*
> *that from the unexplored thickets of the soul*

> *drags thudding threat across every silence,*
> *like touching unknown faces in empty darkness –*
> *Time, that obstinate huckster of stale wares,*
> *how can one buy him off from the mind's doors? . . .*

And so on. (The thudding bird, by the way, is the Australian mopoke.) Mechanistic Time cannot be bribed or bought off; for in its essence it belongs to the world of money and alienation.* To bribe or buy it off is thus merely to accept and intensify its alienating nature.

Politically, this meant (though I did not phrase it so at the time) that justice was impossible in a world where the gap between abstract and concrete time persisted.

I did not phrase the dilemma like that at the time, for, as a disciple of *Creative Effort*, I had given up hope that justice could be actualized at all – except in art. That is, I had accepted the very division against which I was struggling every hour of the night and day. That was the unrealized contradiction in my position, against which I chafed, but which I could not bring into consciousness.

But to return to my imagic method in these days. I am not advocating it now; but I believe that it did hold an important truth, which I pushed to a violent extreme because of the unrealized contradictions in my outlook. Above all, I now find the concentration on sexual imagery to be fatiguing and unnecessarily narrow. But I hope that I have made clear why I thought otherwise at the time. I found in it a satisfyingly intense way of expressing man's living position in nature.

The main weakness can perhaps be detected in the concept of the limit, which I glanced at in the passages from *Helen*. The underlying idea there is existentialist. The self is seen as an entity, though a dynamic one, and the limit is the fluctuating line between it and otherness (in other men, in society, in nature). The dialectic of the limit – of the incessantly changing

---

*So the conspirators must express the limitations of that world: one is a trader, talking liberally, but concerned with freeing trade; one wants a chance to ravish; another, to kill; one wants revenge for his dead children and their privations; another, the money owed him by nobles. The 'human' outlook can only appear in a crazed form, in the apocalyptic Antonio.

relations between the self and otherness – lies at the heart of existentialism; and I consistently held to it and worked it out in everything I wrote at this period. I saw spirit as the active formative force, finding its highest expression in art, and moving through an unending series of choices and self-affirmations, shaping the world by its inner needs. In this idiom, the experience to which I submit is that which I have willed out of my wholeness (not selected by some partial decision); my apparent submission to event or woman is thus an acceptance of the fatality I have myself created by my deepmost inner necessity. Hence the considerable insight of the phrases that Macartney uses to characterize the plays.*

It follows from my theory of the importance of the word image that a large part of the dramatic action and conflict in the plays is in the imagery itself. The imagery it is that makes Helen more than the slight girl intoxicated with her mirror beauty, whom the action depicts, or Paris more than a pastoral phantasm. I could elaborate this point at length by analysing passages in detail. But I have said enough to give a general idea of my poetic method.

As to the style, there were still some archaizing elements; but I can claim that with *Marino* I had arrived at a personal idiom and at a blank verse which suited my purposes, generally conversational in intonation, but moving in long shelving rhythms, often of units set in an accumulative upsweep.

It seems then to me that in the poems of Ken and Fitz, and in these plays of mine, we were validly building on the ground cleared by Brennan and McCrae, though only on part of that ground. We were unaware at the time how the novel was breaking into a new dimension through H. H. Richardson, K. S. Prichard and Vance Palmer. We should have needed to go much further to develop the many-sided unity that the situation needed, a fusion of the gains from Brennan and McCrae with the maturing national sense expressed in the new novelists. In certain ways Ken and Fitz, who stayed on, did carry on the struggle along these lines, and did help towards over-

*As far as I know, he and Gordon Bottomley were the only persons who grasped what I was after.

coming the conflict between a national literature and a literature fully absorbing the world heritage. But, leaving when I
did, I turned my back on this problem, which is still rending
Australian culture as I write, in 1959. In many ways I regret
that I departed and ceased to play my part in the struggle. But
by 1926 I had reached a stage, I feel, where the work I was
doing had been carried to a point beyond which it could not
fruitfully develop in Australia. If I had stayed on and continued to write in the same sort of way, I should have been a
mere nuisance to myself and others; and, given my fanatical
positions, it is hard to see how I would have found the sources
of renewal. By turning to England, I turned to a different
world, far from N.L., when it was easier for me to come the
necessary croppers and begin re-thinking things out from the
ground up.

21 · DIONYSOS AND A LAST POEM

THE BREAK between our conception of high art and that of national expressions was only one aspect of a whole series of breaks – between art and people, mind and matter, man the image-bearer and woman the child-bearer. And so our struggle for wholeness and integration was betrayed before it began. Not that it could be simply reduced to its unresolved conflicts; there were positive elements in our ideas of poetic integration and our opposition of this process to all oppressive and repressive forces, all money values and mechanistic implications. Our main failure was to see that the life process involved productive as well as artistic activity and that there was an inviolable bond between these two aspects. Because of this failure we staked everything on love, on sexual activity, making it do the work both of itself and the productive sphere, labour process. If we had realized this limitation we would have found the bridge between our ideas and the life of the people, between Grand Form and the national tradition, and would have begun to purge our ideas of their Platonic transcendentalisms.

In my last Sydney year I made an effort to restate my ideas in a book, *Dionysos: Nietzsche contra Nietzsche* (later published in London). The thought was essentially that of *Creative Effort*, but the style was quite different. In accordance with my hatred of the abstraction I attempted to write in as dynamic and imagic a style as possible. This seemed the only correct way to carry on Nietzsche's work, since he reached greatness as a thinker in his lyrical works and often produced in his non-lyrical works the stupidities on which his disciples built. The only way to express his position: an anti-metaphysical view of the universe, but an aesthetic one.

Dionysos began: 'The purpose of thought is not to solve the riddle of the universe, but to create it.' And attempted to snatch the concept of Will from Nietzsche's vulgarizers by saying on the first page, 'Will is the persistence of a unifying harmony through conflict. Will is that imponderable point of unity where the essential duality of all energy is simultaneously reconciled and yet vitalized into deeper discord. This is what Nietzsche meant when he defined the Will to Power as the Will to more Life.'

These positions were maintained consistently throughout.

We must, therefore, ask, not: What is Mind? which at once abstracts the category of substance from the universe of energy – but: What is the function of Mind? . . .

Once then it is granted that life is a process and not a sum in algebra, it is clear that you can never make it stop long enough for you to cut it up into nicely differentiated and isolated blocks. Any analysis which forgets that it is dealing with a thing in perpetual motion is vitiated at the core; and the creative function of mind assumes supreme importance, for it is that which keeps the process spinning by putting the symbol of unity into actual conflict with the flow of Becoming.

Philosophy too much has thought that by poking its finger in the spokes of the sky it can halt that vast wheel with all its eddying stars. Even when a serious effort has been made to see life as a flowing tumult, there has been little or no understanding of the relation of that flux and the creative self which is at once a fixed rock on which the tides foam and batter in vain, a sieve through which they sluice, a floating buoy tossed on their surface, and the moon that pulls them along. We now realize that no one has a static point from which to clap a foot-rule to the fluctuant universe, for his mind is in motion also. As in physics, this does not result in anarchism, but in the necessity for a more complex, quick and comprehensive instrument of thought.

It also results in narrowing the universe down, with a crash of ruining God, into the curve traced by the individual will.

For it is there the juncture of Being and Becoming assumes its visible and strenuous significance, since it is there we perceive them mingling, and for that flash reconciled in a third thing, the dynamic self, the creative act. In that act their antithetical nature is formulated and destroyed, so that the forces which seek to separate them and those which seek to compel them together are both vitalized.

I had a firm grip of the idea that reality was made up of opposites bound together in a vital unity which led to a collision and fusion from which a new level of conflict was born. But I had isolated the creative process of art from the organic world and the productive spheres alike, in both of which the conflict and unity of opposites went forever on; and therefore I idealistically saw only the art process as embodying this structure of growth. It was easy then to declare that the universe was kept in movement only by the creative intellect with its 'symbol of unity'.

I argued that the natural development of the world after 1914-18 was towards 'another Dark Age. There are signs enough of it'. I equated American Service and Marxian Justice as 'God equally distributed among the members of the group – the abstraction of the machine dominating the life of the individual.' And went on:

No wonder man does not want this passionate discipline, this concentration of effort which can carry a clear and glittering essence of individuality through all the protean shapes of experience in sensation and emotion.

> I stand in the tides, and there is nothing there
> except a tall light fumbling in the water
> and coral-polyps snapping from the foam
> as it comes sliding down the loins of light –
> coralline moonlight drifting into flesh
> and between every pore interstices
> where the moon sets.
>
> I shall arise and walk upon the waters
> and battles will be fought in my open palm.
> Night will be my other hand clapped over
> the stricken armies; and in the foam of tides
> Desire will make the moonlight arch to coral
> and the long upward legs and the beautiful body
> and the deep seacave where the wet moon sets.

No wonder man does not want to wade in these thoughts. They are not puddles.

What will be the prerequisites of a mind that will face this problem?

A new mixture of scepticism as to every human emotion and belief, with a quick faith in every impulse of the imagination. The power to think in two dimensions at the same time: to shudder with a deep scorn of self and yet give oneself with a child's credulity to all the exaltations of imagic fantasy: to be psychologically a brutally subtle realist and spiritually a climber on aerial laughters: to see life as monstrously trivial and yet infinitely exciting: to trace the flesh's tendrils in the most rocketing ecstasy, to have a bitter contempt for one's most splendid thoughts because they are one's best, and yet out of that contempt gain a sharper faith in the life whose unknown beauty can breed such evident contempt: to know that action does not exist, and yet that at no point can one disdain action: to despise all external formulations and yet be involved with them wherever possible: to act in time and think in timelessness: to feel life always as an evasive dualism yet bound together by a continuing delight as if the clash of sound were that which drew the cymbals together and then flung them apart again – just as in *Tristan and Isolde* the lovers in despair and in passion seek to become the music and yet must remain two always: the music is the escaping unity, outside time though penetrating it, while the kisses twist and throb through time's insufficiency. Let us strive always to be an embrace of energies escaping into music . . .

The eternal moment alone exists . . .

We are all then Mozarts, to whom an intricate and lengthy succession of notes swirls into a single design of clotted and instantaneous beauty. The eternal moment alone exists.

The moment when the individual spirit stands up and views the relations of life, the tumbled muddle of facts blasted into significant coherence by the unifying mind.

And to achieve this purpose is not to complete it. That is merely to find a new starting point for the achievement of a more difficult co-ordination.

Along these lines I attempted to sort out the contradictions in Nietzsche: that in him which was true to the idea of the eternal moment (which he called Eternal Recurrence), and that in him which impatiently built up fantasies of power, fantasies of cleaning up the huge mess of modern life by an imposition of order. That in him which saw the Beyond-man as a coming stage in human life, achieved from a comprehensive grasp of the dialectic principle of unity, and that in him which gave an élite interpretation of the *Ubermensch* (vulgarized by Shaw as the Superman). Not that I myself was clear about this latter point; I too gave an élite interpretation in accord with the anti-metaphysical aesthetic view of the universe; but at least I saw that the vulgarizers were wrong.

I will not here elaborate these points, except to say that I was obscurely feeling for the ways in which Nietzsche attempted to fill in the worst weakness in the Hegelian dialectic, its definition of the present as in effect a nothingness, a negation of the past which turns into the future. Such a definition is metaphysical and anti-aesthetic, denying the here and now, denying enjoyment. For joy must be of the present, or it is nothing; aesthetic experience must be of the present, or it is nothing.

I stress this point; for in spite of the extravagant terms of expression, my analysis, I think, made a valid addition to the exegesis of Nietzsche and post-Hegelian thought. My main influences in dialectics, apart from Plato and Hegel, lay in Blake and Keats. I had some acquaintance of Croce, whom I criticized in an *Art in Australia* essay, and later of Gentile; but perhaps the recent philosopher who most affected me was Alexander, Sydney-born, with his ideas of body-mind as an example of Emergence, of the arrival of a new synthesis out of the elements of a complex organized in a certain pattern. The new quality in the synthesis results from the total organized pattern. Mind is thus seen as the emergent quality come from the new complexity of the total physiologico-neural processes in the human body, which involves new possibilities of functioning. (I could not however accept Alexander's notion of Deity as the stage beyond Mind, God as the whole universe tending to a new quality – though in its place I put a neoplatonist system of qualities emerging beyond our earthly consciousness.) His idea of the nisus of space-time in many ways harmonized with the ideas I had been attempting to set forth in my poetic imagery (as I have shown in analysing the *Helen* passages).

Also I must not forget the work of Jane Harrison, *Prolegomena* and *Themis*, in terms of which I read much of Nietzsche's *Birth of Tragedy* and from which I had gained an indelible conviction of the earth roots of art – the way in which the significant patterns arose from a social concentration of energy, linked with productive work and the organic crises of birth and death, puberty and marriage, the moments of initiation-renewal. For the time being I tried to over-ride this conviction, but it was there, biding its time for a full reassertion.

Thus, inside my poems and my philosophy, despite the wildly idealistic formulations, there was a strong element which was anti-idealistic and which wanted to bring the whole system down to a dialectic of the here and now, the eternal moment in its purely earthly significances. But a definite rupture of the god fantasy, centred in *Creative Effort*, was needed before this potentiality in my thought could be realized. Of Marxist dialectics I as yet knew nothing.

Before I end, I should like to glance at a long poem which I wrote shortly before leaving Sydney, which was the climax of my efforts to think imagically. This poem was based in my responses to Beethoven's later chamber music and was written after a talk with Norman in which we concluded that it was impossible to put analytically into words what we felt to be the meaning, poignantly realized while we listened, of such works as the C sharp minor quartette. On returning from Springwood, I set myself to compose a poem integrally related to that quartette, which I played over and over on the gramophone till I felt that its rhythms and emotional development were imprinted in my mind.

> *Through flowers hung with ribbons of the bland wind*
> *those beads of sweetness on the bosomed air*
> *comes one so beautiful the flowers burn out*
> *burn only in the shadows of her hair*
> *O lonely garden icicled with flowers*
> *I have walked there . . .*

The first movement worked out these images of wind, cold, flower, and beauty's strange presence in darkness and momentary lights, ceaselessly found and lost. How was the poet to find a stable and clear relation to this dark fiery world of his imagination?

The second movement broke the elegiac note and sent the quest off into a space-time of broken sense, a threatened earth:

> *The flowers frozen on the wind*
> *melt and colours throb and run,*
> *the crystal glaze is thinned,*
> *the last test is begun . . .*

Fear breaks in; but (3rd) the poet feels that if one does not ask too much it is easy to enjoy life and a certain sort of beauty:

> *Dance then dance, pulse of all lightness,*
> *poise of a flower, hear the spring's need,*
> *smear with a cymbalclash that brightness,*
> *soak the juices, spilth of the flute . . .*

But he cannot accept this light-hearted way out:

> *Ballet-maenads jewel-eyed*
> *well you know your cue*
> *I stand upon a harder pride*
> *and say farewell to you my darlings*
> *say farewell to you . . .*

For the moment then (4th) there is only a twilight passage of exploration, an acceptance of loneliness and the privations that the deeper quest demands:

> *Ah not for me the annunciation*
> *of silence softening to doves*
> *a moonlight hallowing flesh with loves*
> *of proud humiliation*

> *Pass where the naiad lilies lift*
> *their palms for charity*
> *Through the marsh of loss I drift*
> *no tear shall sully me . . .*

There is a deepening of regret, a looking-back for what was sweet and delightful in the rejected level of experience (5th):

> Yet it is far and here much comfort fawns
> The moon charted in my ardour fades
> and lilyfountains sway on drowning lawns
> and vein with coralline designs the glades . . .

> O kiss unkissed the lips now lovelier curl
> than curl the lips of any kissing girl
> the flower faints upon the scent's bright core
> to fade and out of memory's gyre be made
> more flowersoft than before . . .

This mystique of loss determines the next stage (6th), in which the quest is renewed, still along the obscure moonlight tracts of loneliness, but with an effort to understand what is at stake, the tears and suffering which in actuality are mingled with the efforts of union and joy:

> amid the deepening glooms the moon will soon be here, hark,
> dark the waters fall and rustle and leaf-harmonies of fear
> tingle in the underdepths the cliff of night falls sheer, hark,
> mark the chime of fear and sweetness in the shimmering lust of
> gongs
> till fear and sweetness piercing merge to integrate our songs
> and pity leers with wanton tears and feeds on maiden wrongs
> O clang the gongs
> till anger throngs
> But why? so pleasantly we touch and fade
> along the lily-track towards the risen moon in trembling shade . . .

A revolt begins (7th) against the struggle for full consciousness which seems to rob life of its alluring penumbras, but the inner conflict gathers force, and with it the sense of contradiction:

> What then is left if I surrender
> the signature of mystery?
> what unveiled face will then be tender?
> what sibyl voice will speak from history?
> how can I still weave star and bud
> in one garland of my blood? . . .

The refusal to give up the quest intensifies the conflict yet further (8th). Anguish grows, and with it the sense of personal responsibility:

> *Did I then leaf with ghosts of fear the night*
> *and in the cauldrons of the sun*
> *venom with pain the fumes of light,*
> *horror and beauty clasped in synthesis*
> *of the creative kiss? . . .*

This level of struggle is accepted (9th) and the conflict extends its range, seeking for the point of resolution:

> *My heart shall lose a dove on high*
> *through all the eagles of the wind*
> *my challenge sweeps the stormy sky*
> *and now the clouds are thinned*
> *the moon in glimmering rings of mist*
> *haloes the leaf-lair where we kissed*
> *and delicately discloses*
> *spilt blood of roses,*
> *the deathscene haunted by a cry*
> *out of the heart of loss . . .*

The persistence in struggle finds a partial resolution in an elemental release (10th), and for the moment it seems that full freedom and union have been won:

> *Sylphdance on time-gulfs*
> *may mote the gold beam*
> *falling a springdream across the dark vigil*
> *of youth hesitating:*
> *in the gleam of that sweetness*
> *the image has truth*
> *it has truth in desire*
> *a promise of mating*
> *a vision of union with nature entire . . .*

But the ghosts of the old conflict regather, 'the redeeming whole' is not reached, and the dancing rhythm fails. Now (11th) the questioning deepens. The entwined contraries are confronted, and the poet again feels that he is deliberately evading the full truth.

> *Past shame O deepest pang the scornful chill*
> *I had not sounded this last guile of smiling hate,*

> *not only scorn for all that thrives*
> *greedy and pitiful in human lives*
> *but scorn for my own pact with fate*
> *Stubborn I faced the accusing voice, the charge myself had laid,*
> *then suddenly I saw the Judas-eyed betrayed,*
> *saw my accomplice will . . .*

A prolonged effort is then made (12th) to understand this inner betrayal, while all the while the poet seeks to find his union with 'nature entire'.

> *Call up the summer's apple-glints once more*
> *Self pity writhes within my bravery's core*
> *spitted upon the barb O swallowdart*
> *O fires of blood and bronze that stain the beech,*
> *for I have failed the lesson I would teach,*
> *seeking reversal of the law*
> *in scorn of those who use the law for snare . . .*

> *O greengraft promisebud, sing robin sing*
> *clear on the burning bough forever thrust*
> *across my night. This song I wholly trust*
> *for when the darkness recognitions bring*
> *proof of all treason, lies, and suffering taint*
> *that very moment as the charge comes true*
> *innocence may be won anew,*
> *a spasm splits the husk. All growth is pain*
> *is happiness again*
> *is union, and absolved the singing pleads*
> *O orchardfires and rattling of the nuts*
> *along the homeward lane . . .*

Finally (13th) a stage of full acceptance is reached, where the self finds a repose in the innermost core of death-birth renewal, in living unity with all mankind and nature. Now, no matter how much conflict and contradiction return, a point of safety has been reached that cannot be undermined:

> *And now the last cold knife has cut, the last unechoing door is shut,*
> *and yet the sweet pure flow goes on O intricate and pure*

the sweetness flows forever, forms that vanish and endure
and nothing else now matters . . . *

I have summarized this poem, with brief quotations, at some length because I feel that it casts a revealing light back over all the years I have described. It comes closest of anything I had written to my innermost conflicts and to a judgement of all our efforts.

The one virtue I claim for myself, then, as at all times of my life since I began as a poet about the age of fourteen, is that I made a continual effort to unify theory and practice, to live out my ideas. If I had been a Christian I should have been a monk. It was (and is) unthinkable to me that people should hold a world view that they put into practice only at selected moments and in a limited range of relationships. For this reason, also, I have tried to show myself as I was, moral warts and all, to the best of my ability and self-knowledge. To bring out the ways in which my desire to unify theory and practice led me into difficulties, contradictions and instabilities. For out of this conflict was being generated the inner pressures that in due time were to kick me out of the level of theory-practice herein described. Because I made no reservations or compromises I was storing up tensions, gradually finding the points of weakness, insufficiency or falsity in my formulations, and concentrating against them the anxieties that would in term break through them, insisting on a new unity of theory and practice, a new world view.

*The poem was published in *The London Aphrodite*. I cite from the revised version that I made shortly after, in which the meaning is clarified and (in the two final movements) taken to a level I could not attain in 1926 though I was struggling towards it.

22 · ENDPIECE

KIRTLEY HAD sent some copies of our *Lysistrata* over to England, where they were well received. One night he broached to me the idea of accompanying him to London where he hoped to continue the Press. I felt that I had no alternative but to agree. If someone had idly suggested a trip unconnected with work, I should have cried off, but a project born straight from Aristophanes had for me the stamp of poetic fate. I talked it over with Janet and she thought it would be a good idea for me to try England out for a year or so. At the time I had no idea that I would take over the London Press from Kirtley; I imagined that I would do what I could to help him launch the venture, contribute some more translations from Latin or Greek, get to know something of the English literary scene and have a couple of books published, then return to Australia where the Renascence was scheduled.

I talked the matter over also with Norman, who approved and who offered to pay my fare. Also to meet the bill for a good suit of clothes.

We were working hard on the press. Phil and I did a book of poems by myself, *Spanish Main*, with drawings by Finey, part of narrative fantasy, and part of a small book of Fitzgerald's poems. Kirtley meanwhile was printing a book of my lyrics, which he completed but which was never bound up in the hurry of departure. Sydney Bridge was about to be built, and one of the first areas cleared was that in which Kirtley's flat was situated.

A slight temptation came my way. At a party I drank with a chap down from the North and we liked one another. It turned out that he owned a number of islands in the Torres Straits. 'Don't to go England,' he said, 'come north with me and I'll give you two or three islands for yourself.' I have always loved small islands, and for a moment it seemed that he was offering me the only possible earthly paradise. But I told him that it was my duty to visit hell, a dull but inevitable place, of which one of the main suburbs was London. The suburbs of itself is hell, I said, citing Robert Graves.

Beutler was ill: how badly I did not realize till the news of his death reached me in London. He wrote me a rather bitter letter, which I read once and tore up. In it he sent me his best wishes and hoped that I would not have too hard a time ahead before I had learned all the wisdoms that life had to teach me. I deeply regret that I did not at once go to see him, instead of stupidly feeling hurt.

At last all was fixed. I tried to find out from Gruner what he thought would be useful to know in England; but all he did was to give me some good advice about food, weather and the like. He presented me with a large well-made overcoat that had warmed him through the English winter, and I found it very useful when I arrived in England. My luggage consisted mainly of MSS, books (for instance, the Petronius with N.L.'s drawings that Ralph Strauss had printed; McCrae's poems; my inseparable Theocritos and *Zarathustra*), a selection of Norman's etchings, and my old university dinner-suit (which I never wore again). Someone had presented me with a silver-headed malacca cane, which Phil in *I'd live* slanderously says I had flourished about Sydney – I in fact had it only on the boat and promptly lost it in London.

There was a good collection of friends to see us off. Phil tells how he came drunk with Mervyn O'Hara in a dinted bowler hat and stood by Hugh McCrae 'trumpeting like a satyr and sweating in the heat'. The coloured papers thrown from deck to wharf lengthened out as the ship drew away, and the farewellers grew smaller and smaller with fluttering hands indistinguishable from handkerchiefs. Kirtley and I paced the deck, and I found for the first time (apart from the moment of giddiness above Bulli and its twinkling poplar) that I was afraid of dead falls such as the drop on the other side of the railings.

When the ship docked at Port Phillip, we wandered in Melbourne and met Ken, who had moved down in 1925 to work for *Punch*. We went out to his house where he lodged in the suburbs and he showed me some prose he had written for a tentative novel; I recall particularly a brilliantly written description of waves breaking on a shore. He was able to use his poetic faculty to hammer out such set pieces; but by sticking to his journalistic career he sacrificed, it seems to me, much of the contribution he could have made to Australian literature.

As our liner moved into a great rolling swell that was coming up from the Antarctic into the Great Bight, I scribbled a poem: *Listening to a Gramophone in the Melbourne Suburbs at Kenneth Slessor's Flat*. I cite it here as my farewell to Australia, and because it brings out clearly my opposition of the integrative image of beauty to the mechanistic city of alienation (here expressed in the electric train which ran at the back of Ken's place and kept crashing through our conversation and some records he played). After the analyses I have made of my method of image-sequence, it should be easily read.*

> *The nail of silence scratches on the mind.*
> *Thought fades in fans of cinnamon waved across*
> *the sunken statue leaded with moonlight, softly*
> *a drunken sigh is drawn across carousers*
> *suddenly drowsy in a house of moss:*
> *the hush entwines us with hands, holds from behind*
> *and folds us blandly blind.*
>
> *Have you forgotten? The lanterns of the wind*
> *were streaming blurred in the slow dusky trees,*
> *lovers and philosophers lay at equal ease,*
> *the sword in the flowers was sheathed and the stars wreathed*
> *the brooding brow as broad as earth below*
> *and on the circling nest the doves descended*
> *a bliss of blessing with no end*

*I may mention however that the first three stanzas, expressing the peacefulness of friendship and communion in art (also communion with nature), have some images with affinity to K.S.'s own earlier poems: to bring out the sense of our union in poetry.

and nothing else was breathing in the briars
only the intent face darkening in wells of light
only the silver eyes in the shadow of silence
going out gently. Thought on thought beguiled
out of the realized centre of our night
beyond the shaken fringe where fruits are fiery
and limited desire

Then through Music's bridal scene
stridently an electric train
crashed with a roar of ruthless power
down the track of the huddled flowers
after the flurry of clouded lovers
after the naked philosophers
the Face went out in a flare of wrath
the trees were felled in the storm's path
the garden of transformation lay
wasted in the blast of day

Then slowly the bruised quiet again retained
the throb of flowers in the secret garden
the lawns of the moon unrolling and the birds
muttering amid the leaves of the crisp stars
and the delicate grain marbling space again.
After the murder, love's small face again.

FANFROLICO AND AFTER

CONTENTS

FANFROLICO

1 · ACROSS THE WORLD

STANDING in the ship's stern, I watched the wake of foam wallowing and twisting behind us, with a few melancholy seagulls swerving above. Western Australia was rapidly fading out into the dazzled east, sinking flatly into the unimpressed waters. I felt a cord of some sort snap and twang, recoiling smartly between my eyes that watered in the stiff breeze. Now at last I realized I was crossing the world in search of a strange place labelled Britain, perfidious land of shopkeepers and breeding-ground of the greatest line of poets known to men. The rope of the knot-registering contraption spun and dragged tensely, as if I trailed one furious strand of resistance into the sundering waters; and I turned with an effort to join John Kirtley in the interminable deck circuit on which we were to prowl for a month and more, passengers caged in a narrow bucketing space of caulked planks and shivering rattling metal. My thrill of fear was dissipated in boredom and I hoped for an albatross poem to roost in the shrouds of my mind; but nothing broke the deadly routine. We walked as if we had to cover the thousands of miles by foot as well as by steam-power.

The tedium of crossing the Indian Ocean at the most sweltering time of the year took its toll of us. After Fremantle all hope of anyone interesting or even personable appearing in the second class was abandoned. There were no girls at all between the ages of five and forty. Never can a P. & O. liner have contained less charm inside its second-class barriers. Not even one ugly young woman. With the handsome girls of the superior end of the ship I now and then exchanged a glance, as on my endless prowl I neared the barrier FIRST CLASS ONLY: a glance haughtily class conscious on my part and unseeing on theirs. After a while, however, we found there was a bulky sculptress who blocked our way by modelling someone's head on a stand, making a thumb slash and then standing back with fine and crushing abandon on any onlooker's feet. I gave her clay only hasty side-looks, but noted to my surprise that her technique was adequate if unexciting. Our only acquaintance, a tough amused farmer, who drank beer with us, warned against catching the lady's eye, as she was on the look-out for commissions. 'She's got a grip of iron,' he said, and pretended that he'd almost succumbed to her sales campaign; but the salesman who could have put anything over on Mr E. was not yet born. We liked him for his instant and absolute distrust of all the things that the world tried to sell us – wives, curios, God, deck games, or newspaper print. He was clearly more than rich enough to travel first. 'It's better this end. People aren't skiting all the time.'

The ship slid on through the vastness, smoothly or in long pitching movements. In the bar you felt the furious turning of the screw, clutched your glass and listened to your teeth chattering; in the cabin the bunks shook with an incessant screech and grinding, and sweat poured down the lines either side of your nose. The great glaucous gliding water masses gave way to dull and dingy waves heaving vaguely after the ship. Heat mists hovered in the sky moted with a heavy mealy light. Then shoals of fly-fishes skimmed the wave-ridges or a porpoise gracefully cavorted.

I read nothing, wrote nothing, did not think. I sweated and watched the hypnotic waters. Some days there was a canvas tank rigged up in which we could plunge and swim a few strokes. The deck games I evaded, though Kirtley, a good cricketer, succumbed to the bat and drove balls into the rope-nets hanging all round the pitch. One afternoon the first-class area amidships and forwards was opened to the second-raters, and I alone refused to pass the barrier into the more commodious, better-furnished, and less screw-racketed quarters. However, I paused long enough by the bulky sculptress to be engaged in conversation; and thereafter had the job of dodging her to make the deck prowls more varied. Apart from anything else, I couldn't afford to buy her gins.

Then at last our oceanic days were over and we arrived at

Colombo, where we stayed three days, waiting for some over-due mail-steamer. With the sardonic Mr E. we wandered along the swarming streets, drove out to the beaches to sip beer or coffee on spacious terraces and watch the coconut-palms against the sky, dark with blue brilliance, while the foam hissed and crisped along the sands. We watched the nimble fingers of girls moving.pins about as they made lace, and strayed into a ramshackle Buddhist temple garishly painted with dam-nation scenes, where an old priest told us either to get out or to pay up. Mr E. chuckled at the similarity of all religions, as he chuckled at the other passengers buying ebony elephants made in Birmingham as mementoes of Ceylon. He enjoyed himself stimulating the shopkeepers to ever-greater exertions of salesmanship and then buying nothing; we enjoyed watch-ing him. We didn't want to use up our money by going by train to Kandy and the uplands.

On to Aden, where we stayed a day and night: a place of shattering sunlight caught between mountains of cinder and ash and a sea of molten silver. A triangle of grass, with Queen Victoria at its centre dumpily defying the heat, was kept almost green by the water-sprinkler going round and round without pause. Except for the post office round a corner on the right, all the buildings were pubs, with equally long and stifling rooms. We dodged across the slabs of heat, from gin to gin, and paid to see the authentic mermaid, who turned out a stinking stuffed sea-cow. Waiting for the boat back to the ship, we threw coins for the arrowy diving boys in the water.

Now at last the ship shook herself and set off at full speed, rushing up the Red Sea and leaving red-sailed fishing craft quickly behind, till we reached the Canal and went leisurely along. We arrived at Port Said by dark, with only a few hours for a trip ashore; Mr E. went off, but we stayed on board, watching the skurry of lights and shadows on the landing-stage, with the sense of a vast starry gateway to Europe opening ahead of us, till Mr E. returned, to chuckle over the way he had diddled the vendors of dirty postcards and tickets for the marriage of lady and donkey.

We came out into a Mediterranean turbid with recent storms and believed that the world was round. For after climbing up a long slope, now we felt that we slanted downhill and smelt a new air. Nearing Crete, we saw a filagree of lofty snow before we saw the earth, a long delicate fretwork of silver breathed rigidly on the sky. Gradually the fine pattern hardened and the lower sky took on the dark blue of a sprawling island. What vision could have better expressed the conviction of a descent into Europe from an eyrie of poetry? I was entering Europe via the sky-gates of Mount Ida, with the metallic pulse of the boat turned into the clashing of the shields of the Kouretes as they danced around the divine babe.

By the time we were close to the western end of the island I was talking to the girl who had come aboard at Port Said, red-haired and pleasantly ugly, who had been visiting China and who assured me that chopped-off heads, hung on a wall there, had turned into stone over the centuries. Everything she had seen was as fabulous as that. And that night, caught by the tubular sculptress, I lay with her on a rug in one of the scanty recesses of our second-class decks and even kissed her rough dry lips smelling of tobacco.

The great rugged hills of Calabria were the first clear forms of Europe, and then the Straits of Messina brought the towns of men unimportantly into the picture, huddled and flattened in the scene of vast sky and water. That night Stromboli was outlined in dull fire, a hulking pyramid against the flattened sky; and later we passed between Corsica and Sardinia, with glimpses of red-burnt barren earth, ancient as a dream symbol. We landed in Marseilles and wandered with Mr E. along the sea-front, drinking *vin rouge* and watching the tarts with blood-red lips and tigerish eyes. Europe at last; somehow looking disordered, corrupt, shabby, and rotten-rich with its unrealized inheritance, beside the rowdy and yet well-run Australian scene still rawly fresh in our minds. Kirtley bought some snails cooked and restored to their shells with congealed fat, which we took back to the boat and finally threw out of the porthole.

The suit Norman had bought me was still fairly presentable, and I had my silver-headed Malacca cane. But my shapeless hat and my shoes worn away on one side of each heel betrayed me; and I can still recall the shame I felt when we exchanged some comments with a steward on the boat. I was leaning flushed and negligent on my elegant cane; and the steward, sharp with all the snobbery of the flunkey, made some sarcastic balloon-pricking remark. I smiled on, but from that moment to this have never attempted to be correctly dressed or to delude myself about any possibilities of even a third-rate elegance.

The furious dock life brought me back to a sense of realities. I watched for hours a gang who had loaded a barge with huge cases before they noticed that they had driven down another barge under one of its ends. They then had to unload again before they could free the second barge, swearing magnificently all the infuriated while. We sailed out on a silvery afternoon, with the harbour and islands burning in soft tufted lights, a magical scene. Then, along the Spanish coast, I saw for the first time the yellow-greens of Europe, a new dimension of colour after the hard blue-greens of Australia. The broad velvety fields gave a soft feeling of abundance, of earthly promise, which I could not fit into my aesthetic where the luxurious image of beauty was bred from the rough-tough bitter soil, a compensating antithesis. We punctually passed Gibraltar, which for me was the Pillar of Herakles, and rounded the easternmost point of Portugal, into the grey and heaving waste of the stormy Bay of Biscay. I enjoyed the floundering decks, the wild waters, the screaming woodwork of the cabin; the change from the steam heat of the equatorial line to the icy and ghostly tumult which hedged Britain, that ancient Land of the Dead.

I began to feel dimly alive. I still had read nothing, written nothing, thought nothing. Kirtley and I did not even discuss our plans; for I had none and he did not want to talk of his, probably they were confusedly dependent on what he found in London. Only the apotheosis of Crete had struck through my bemused torpor. The last days abroad were variegated however by conversations with the idiot girl from Lancashire, who carried a large stone from the Hill of Olives in her handbag – 'for luck' – and by evasions of the sculptress. We hid from her any of our London trails and were distressed to find that Mr E. hid his from us; he didn't believe in carrying on shipboard friendships. No doubt he scented that we would soon be on the rocks and might want to borrow money. The ship's world of six weeks was breaking up.

2 · LONDON AND PARIS

Everything grew smaller as we neared our destination, which turned out to be the Regent Palace Hotel. Kirtley had picked up that name from someone on the ship, and I was ready to go anywhere, the Ritz or a Limehouse joint. The weather was dingy, the docks lacked the spaciously enchanting hurly-burly of Marseilles, the train from Tilbury swung us through ever worse slum backyards. Liverpool Street was a cavern cobwebbed with smoke and foul with the smell of decaying fish. Everything grew smaller and dirtier. We had never imagined that men could live in such a dwarfed and sootied world. A taxi drew us out of the station catacombs along narrow bedraggled streets. London.

We stared out at Fleet Street and the Strand, confirmed in our impression of a grey diminutive world, wholly lacking in dignity or charm, parochial and constricted. The impact of London so depressed us that we did not dare to speak of it for days; above all we felt fooled and humiliated. To have come so far for this. However, at least we weren't refused admittance to the hotel. Kirtley booked two small bedrooms and a porter dumped our things in them. I wrote down Kirtley's number on a piece of paper, which I then lost, and had the feeling that we were parted for ever. The fact that I could find out his room from the enquiry desk below did not dawn on me. In any event I still had an extreme repugnance from even such a mild instance of authority as an enquiry clerk in a large hotel where I felt an interloper, liable at any moment to be excluded by a disgusted management. A poet, with a deboshed felt hat – out with him!

But Kirtley came along to my room, which I had attempted to humanize by putting copies of *Zarathustra* and Blake on the spindly bedside table. We slunk downstairs to a meal, and then went out to look at London.

Our aimless walk increased the feeling of desolation and smallness. The cold wind poured along the Strand with its two-decker open-topped buses and its cruising taxis; the agitated lights merged to build a narrow frail world, lowering the skies and stinging our eyes. In doorways or along the kerbs were puffy-faced tarts with coats pulled tight round their fat legs; their predatory eyes picked us out at once as bronzed colonials and we ran a gauntlet of hoarsely alluring whispers. I felt the power of rhymes stirring afresh in me after the oceanic sleep and demanding a defiance of the impinging world in what was for me a new way. Australian society I had repudiated on the general grounds that, while nothing human was alien to me, the element in people which accepted the state and the cash nexus was inhuman and therefore alien; but here I felt a more immediate shock of rejection. The intrusion of state and cash nexus was pervasive. I felt the persons of the many beggars as the visible sign of an inhumanity that hit me harder than I knew.

> Chimney-pots like decaying teeth in rows
> stick broken into a mumbling sky.
> Street after street, where cleanness never blows,
> goes shabbily by.
> The frowsy beggar at the pubcorner stands
> with bunch-of-carrot hands.
>
> We have known mangy faces and rubble-shacks,
> but not this dingy graveyard where
> the miminy mourners move with mortgaged backs
> and snoffling care.
> Share with the wind a house of stringy-bark slats,
> but not with mingy rats.

I had never felt moved to write that kind of verse in Australia; now for a while I didn't want to write anything else.

We strolled in misty Hyde Park and on principle visited a few pubs. But neither of us was given to drink for its own sake, and anyhow the beer was dull and heavy after the lagerish Australian brands. We were condemned to the grey wintry streets.

Even Sydney, rising on the sheep tracks of convict days, seemed a well-devised city next to London, where, after the fire of 1666 wiped out the medieval bases, only a commercial greed, I felt, had determined the medley of mediocre buildings. The residential squares of the eighteenth and early nineteenth centuries, or the Victorian terraces, could not affect the overall impression; they were unavailing refuges from the prevailing lack of style and civic purpose, or pompous reflections of the deadening cash nexus in the family sphere. Trafalgar Square as the imperial centre was an excellent admission of the lack of human dignity: the Hero hoisted aloft so that all personal features might be lost in the inane, while Landseer's blandly hypocritical lions digested their prey below with an air of poodle virtue. I liked only the statue of Charles I and occasional dusk-moments on the Embankment. However I ventured into the National Gallery and was warmed by the Titians and Rubens, the first originals of those artists I had seen; at last I felt the handshake of friends.

Kirtley arranged to call on W.P., editor of a print-collectors' quarterly, with whom he had corresponded. I went with him to the suburban villa, but took no part in discussions. Looking drowsily at art books, I gathered that on the strength of our admired *Lysistrata* Kirtley hoped to work up some financial backing; but after protracted negotiations nothing happened. I had dropped a line to Walter de la Mare, who at once asked me to Taplow. I spent a pleasant day of late-winter frost there, during which he drove with me to Burnham Beeches. I recall only one comment of his: 'I don't know much about flowers, but my favourite reading is seed catalogues, they're so full of lovely and intriguing names.' At tea one of his sons remarked, with an obvious intention of belittling Norman's work, that Beardsley had had an overwhelming effect on modern black-and-white artists; and as I didn't consider Norman at all influenced by Beardsley, I amiably agreed. However, though I had enjoyed the day, I made no effort to follow it up and never saw de la Mare again; I felt our worlds did not really meet and I was an impostor in his presence.

I felt the same with Ralph Strauss and Holbrook Jackson, to whom Norman had given me letters of introduction. I had a genial dinner with Strauss at his flat, where he insisted on giving me a letter to J. C. Squire. My contact with Jackson consisted of a chat about typography at his office. He sat with scholarly stoop, bored into me with his lively dark eyes, leaned back and chatted with the wary fluency of someone who had editorially met too many young writers. After some hesitation, I sent Strauss's letter to Squire and was asked to call at the offices of the highly influential *London Mercury* in one of London's very few old buildings, near Temple Gate. Squire received me affably; but in the course of his advice to a young colonial aspiring to the London literary scene, he dropped a plain hint that he'd read an article of mine on Abercrombie's *Phoenix* in the Sydney *Bulletin*. (I had praised the play and jeered at Squire for abusing it as disgusting, as an 'abominable and unconvincing farce'.) Nothing could have been more adroit or inoffensive than the hint and the following inference that rash raw colonials would be forgiven if they now showed the right sort of respect and tried to tread in the footsteps of their betters. Perhaps Squire read my stupefaction as remorse; he ended his long and sensible discourse by taking me down for a couple of beers at the pub nearby. His encouraging handshake however was not a token of entry into the hearty world of weekend poets, but my definite farewell to all malingering on the edge of that world. I was annoyed at myself for getting into a false position, for being polite to the man who had attacked the Phoenix Society for their 'bad taste and brazen effrontery' in staging Wycherley, I forswore all letters of useful introduction and decided to abandon myself to my destiny – do nothing, write poetry when moved, and co-operate with Kirtley if asked.

About this time I dropped into the Café Royal, which was in the throes of genteel transformation, discarding its sawdust floor, marble-topped tables, gaudy gilt decorations, and red plush seats. I had a drink in the corner that wasn't being rehabiliated, and heard a young fellow at the next table talking about Australian poetry and insisting that the coming man was Jack Lindsay. This remarkable speech stunned me, so that I didn't introduce myself; but I took it as an omen that I was right in avoiding the respectable literary world.

Meanwhile Kirtley, who paid all basic expenses, decided the Regent Palace bed-and-breakfast was too costly. Though flats and apartments were not then so plentiful, we could have easily found something cheap and suitable if we had had the least idea how to set about it. What we did was to take a bus in Regent Street which had St John's Wood on the front. Kirtley hoped it would take us to Lord's: which it did. We found a house agent close to the churchyard with Joanna Southcott's remains and he gave us a list of furnished houses. We took the first we looked at, in Blenheim Street, a small prim detached three-storeyed brick house, with basement leading out into a neat backgarden. It belonged to Lady Somebody, who wanted to go to the South of France, and was full of muslin curtains, gesticulating bronzes by inferior Italian artists (two of them lifesize), and tiny bric-à-brac. Kirtley's references satisfied the agent and we moved promptly in, spending our whole first day in stowing the myriad bits of movable junk into the cupboards. We left out only large and apparently unbreakable objects like the prancing Bacchante, with windblown frills covering all the more interesting parts of her anatomy, who stood before the front window on the ground floor, shaking a thyrsus tipped with a frosted electric light-globe. She came in anyway as a convenient hat-and-coat rack. From Priory Street we laid in a stock of tinned food, eggs, bacon, bread. Our meals tended to consist of the same items in a different order, but were eaten in a charming room that looked out into the tender intricate lights of the garden with its acacia trees, its lilac and laburnum, where I tried to keep the grass down with a pair of Lady Some-body's scissors. I took the attic room for myself, to be as high as possible above the sour-faced neighbours who peered curiously in at our front window – though we tried to baffle them by draping the muslin curtains round the thyrsus and thus dislodged ancient dust by tugging in vain at the cords of the velvet side hangings of rusty red.

I paused, scribbling angry doggerel, to recall P. R. Stephensen, whom I had known at Queensland University and who had looked in on me at Sydney on his way to Oxford as a Rhodes scholar. I wrote to him at Queen's, and several days later got a reply from Paris; I had forgotten about vacations.

He exclaimed gleefully at our arrival and invited me to come straightaway over to Paris. I went, with Kirtley's gruff encouragement.

P.R.S. met me at the Gare du Nord, running along the platform with his usual zest, chattering in argot to grumpy porters and carrying me off under his arm to the nearest café for *vin rouge*. Norsely fair, clearly handsome, athletic and bristling with a compact energy, he was able to stamp any moment with a casual effect of historic importance. I already liked Paris; but after ten minutes in his company it was ten times more lively and charming, the French girls ten times more attractive, chic, amorously bottomed, and French. The wine glowed with red earth-fires and for the first occasion since we left Sydney I knew that I had done absolutely the right thing in coming to Europe. The taxi we took darted madly through the traffic with a high-pitched squeak of warning, P.R.S. and the driver excitedly discussing the cost of living and narrowly missing the demented policemen. Paris lay all around me, with avenues revolving and flashing away, people actually enjoying life under the leisurely café awnings, girls who were girls whether seen from the left, right, front or back, from below or above, the Seine broadly emerging through leaves and bookstalls, and myself deposited at the Hotel de l'Univers, near the Panthéon.

In a few moments P.R.S. (never called Percy or Reginald, always P.R.S. or Inky) was hauling me out with brisk hilarious gestures and introducing me to the street scene with impresario generosity as if he himself had invented it all only the day before for my special benefit and was gratified that the world was behaving so well. His keen brisk enjoyment irradiated the persons and things all around, merging with the spring sunlight to stress the peculiar momentary individuality of each movement, each pattern of light and shadow, each gesture. One realized that aeons had gone to bring about this magnificent unrepeatable performance, and felt infinitely grateful for the wayward chance and the infinite pains that had come together to produce the transitory vista which seemed struck in eternal bronze. What setting could suit his spell-binding better than Paris, a carefully staged show with all the Renoir colours and the Dégas tones of spontaneity? He was part-French as well as part-Scandinavian; in Brisbane I had met his fine-mannered old grandfather, as French as a gavotte by Rameau. Paris effervescently stimulated the vivacity that companioned his air of trim purposiveness.

During my stay he introduced me to a friend of his, Winifred, with whom he was already in love and whom he was to marry. She was a classical ballet dancer with soft small big-eyed face, incredibly finely bodied and gracefully slight. I never saw her dance on the stage, but can imagine her as the merest piece of thistledown blown charmingly about by the wind of the music, an ondine floating as weightless as the reflection of lilies on the shimmering surface of the tremolo of the violins. In character she was gentle as her flower-face suggested – something not always true of blossom-girls; and as strong and steady as her dance-image was light and swan-gliding. Also there was R. D. Hall, whom I had known as a fellow-undergraduate at Brisbane; he had turned to economics and was already, I think, a Fellow of Trinity at Oxford. For ten days we had a consistently happy time, talking and wandering round, mainly in the Latin Quarter. Heaping up the saucers on the terrasse of the Dôme and sneering at the bourgeois Rotonde on the opposite corner of the Carrefour Vavin with its grill-room and dance-orchestra, which was cashing in on the legends of Modigliani's boozing in the days when it was a humble zinc. Having an apéritif with Baudelaire's ghost at the Closerie des Lilas and then saluting P.R.S.'s swashbuckling predecessor, Maréchal Ney, in his statue outside. Watching the traffic of the Avénue de l'Opéra from the Régence where Napoleon had played dominoes, with the finely proportioned Comédie façade to remind us of the elegant pretences against which the swooning Romantic (de Musset) fell into the arms of his Muse. Or night roaming among the mollshop cafés near the Markets and the Boulevard de Sévastopol.

Once when Hall was discoursing on the economic world-situation, at the Dôme, I put in some caustic comments about Malayan tin, which I had heard Mr E. make on the boat; and P.R.S. patted me on the back. 'You see the poet isn't such a fool. What a pity Michelle is away in the country. She would have been just the person for him.' I wasn't sure in what way

Michelle would have suited me, but regretted her absence. Walking in the Bois de Boulogne, I was overwhelmed again by the radiant yellow-greens, the veil on veil of filtered light. 'I can understand Turner at last. The greys of dampness in the English landscape. The delicate gauzes of light, as here, drift on drift, vane on turning smoky vane, golden flat on flat as in a stage set but fumed in flower crucibles. A strange new world. Have you noticed how low the night-skies are after Australia, sagging with their stars, as if slung only a little above the house-tops. Australian light is a single infinity, depth beyond depth, and yet only one depth.'

P.R.S. took me and two young Russians from the Embassy on an underworld exploration. We visited bars and cellars thick with smoke where throaty singers bawled witty songs of which I couldn't follow a word, and then took a look at cheap dimly lit brothels where stolid workers sipped bocks at splintery tables from the corners of which a huge swarthy tart picked up coins with an unlikely part of her anatomy, a coin-swallowing contortionist, while other tarts, mostly slummocky, lounged about in bits of underwear or less. I spoke to one girl, slenderly muscular, with a faint dark down on her legs and upperlip, and found her of Italian origin, recently come up from the Savoy.

Somewhat dazed by the spectacle of torpid vice at its plodding routine, we came up for night air and found another taxi, making for a more normally somnolent café – for the hour was late. The Russians noticed that the driver spoke with a compatriot accent, and suddenly one of them recognized him as the colonel of the regiment in which he had served during the 1914 war. When the car stopped, the three Russians rapturously embraced, and the ex-colonel was asked to join us in a coffee. A rapid exchange of reminiscences went on; but as my Russian was worse than my French (P.R.S. knew the language not at all badly), I could not make out what was said. However, our Russians did not tell the White that they were Soviet diplomats – though one of them grew too talkative. The other whispered some code word that I was to repeat to the blabber, who sat on my other side; but in my confused state I translated what I took to be the code-word's sense saying, '*Taisez-vous!*' to the dismay of the young Russians and the ex-colonel's bewilderment.

The last episode of the night I remember was an encounter with two bicycled gendarmes who came upon us as we were all urinating against a notice *Défense d'Afficher*. They dismounted and remonstrated, but in a few moments P.R.S. was slapping them on the back and giving them a speech on the superior humanity and lack of prudery in the French nation. They shook hands all round and rode on again. We sang the Marseillaise.

Winifred had asked me to call on her in London. I called and became friendly. She lived in a rambling one-floored weather-board house (with the doors all at different levels) near the 'World's End,' Chelsea, in a lane that was half slummy, half rustic, a remnant of a London now quite vanished. A handsome confident girl lived with her, whom I didn't much like, though I once took her a large bunch of flowers – the only time I think I have presented a bouquet to a girl. Probably Winifred, a kindly, tactful and understanding soul, egged me on into doing it. Anyhow, having blushingly given the flowers, I felt such a fool I avoided the girl thereafter.*

Through Winifred however I met a group of people who were to play a crucial part in my life. This group centred on Young, an Australian musician, who was a pioneer in evoking community songs at football matches and the like, and his ex-wife Edith. The marriage had broken up, and Young was living with a strange and lovely girl Elza, while Edith had turned to a young artist Roe. Among their friends were the painter Ronald Dunlop and Philip Henderson, then trying to

---

* Winifred Edwards had been a member of various classical ballets in America led by such important dancers as Giuseppe Bonfiglio, Sergei Pernikoff, and Ivan Bankoff. In 1924 she retired from the theatre while her young son (by her first marriage) was at school in England. She had a small private income from Australia, and was working hard at private lessons in both stage and ballroom dancing, in the large studio room which her flat in Kensington contained, and was also teaching in a school. (She stayed only briefly at the World's End house.) She even tried to teach me to dance; but her failure in this impossible task was no slur on her expertise.

write poetry. Edith and Roe had just taken over the house in Ebury Street, Chelsea, where Peter Warlock the musician had been living. Shortly before his removal he had acquired the habit of stripping all his clothes at a certain stage of drink and running about in the street. The Ebury ladies still peeped through their midnight curtains in the hope-fear of seeing his white form speed along the pavement, chanting snatches of some relevant hymn or ballad refrain. There were also tales of his having become so obstreperous on one occasion that he was locked in the lavatory for a considerable length of time; he emerged from his dungeon sobered and disconsolate, declaring that he was henceforth dishonoured.

Edith had a slow wondering way of speaking, while she fastened her large, grave and kindling eyes on you, bearing you down with the full weight of her mental processes: as if only that moment she had thought out what she was saying, and understood what she thought – so that you were inescapably involved with it all, half responsible for the momentous discovery she was making, with all its exciting and illuminating implications. You felt flattered, even if in fact she were only asking by what bus you had come. Everything, the bus number or the interpretation you made of Blake's Prophetic Books, was equally remarkable and full of clues to the ultimate mystery. Not that the mannerism was superficial; it held a genuine childlike element, an unslackening sense of strangeness in the revolving world. I found it pleasant to talk over cups of coffee with her and Roe into the early morning, and then to sleep on the couch, with Roe rushing to his office of commercial art and Edith wondering at the strangeness of an early morning, the eerie quality of light, the peculiar way water boiled, and the secret messages in a newspaper.

Young, prognathous, keen and earnest, introduced me to his colleague John Goss. I listened to them both joyously singing chanties. A forceful woman singer, met at Curwen's musical publishing house, gave me a long lecture on the sort of songs I was to write for her, and presented me with some of Graves's poems set to music as exemplars. What I did write, however, were unsingable curses on the English scene – and an essay *Travel Narrows the Mind*, about the girl on the liner with her tales of decapitated heads weathering into stone sculptures. This I sent to the *Manchester Guardian*, which, to my surprise, accepted it. A fluke that gave me incorrect ideas about the ease with which I could make something out of freelance journalism.

Ronald was a Quaker, slow in his way of speaking, but not out of Edith's sense of wonderment; rather he was deliberately rebuking the world and its devils. His irritated wife retorted by throwing things which he returned with dumb courtesy. A portrait he had painted, the whole head a sodden red-purple, uncomfortably impressed me. What I saw was his own pale face of renunciation, large and heavy, flat as a sheep's, hanging against the red lump, the battered face of denied life. I wrote a furious poem of White and Red in conflict, abstraction and dead matter, the driven sheep and the battered corpse uniting in the Lamb of God and defeated by the red cock of resurrection. What I was expressing was my own divided self as I stood in the bought-and-sold streets of London.

However, it was Elza who most interested me, though for the moment I kept warily out of her way and she said next to nothing as she sat in her lonely beauty, lithe and pale, among the chattering others. Dressed always in long Pre-Raphaelite drape-clothes of rich and simple colour. For the moment I shall cite only a few words from the novel *Lisa* that Edith wrote later about Elza and myself. (Lisa Morrison is Elza.)

There was Mrs Morrison with her head thrown back a little wearily, resting against the wall, seeming cast there, I thought, like a shadow ... In her black frock, fitting almost affectionately to her slim body, she looked curiously unreal, yet more real in her quivering evanescent beauty than any of the others gathered round Mrs Dalrymple on the hearth rug – more real in her way than anybody I had ever known ...

Lisa gathered up her body, as it were, and sat lightly on a stool, resting her head on her hand, looking at the ground as though lost in contemplation, alone in her thought-world.

I found myself picturing her with me by the sea. The white waves would be choppy, blown by a following wind landwards, and a gull would wheel in sight suddenly, like a rare thought, to surprise the laziness of our minds as we lay amongst the thyme-strewn grass. The wind would bring colour to her pale cheeks, and those lips, I thought, would not droop so much, might smile, as I made a cushion for her head.

Edith is there trying to depict Elza through the eyes of one who was to be her fated lover – through my eyes; and she does it subtly and truly. All her wondering excitement at the strangeness of things had become concentrated on Elza, who had followed her in her husband's affections. But her intentness was in no way a mere effort to understand what Young was feeling; it was a pure effort of wonderment, without a speck of jealousy or envy.

There was indeed already something of a cult of Elza in the group, and that was one of the reasons I felt wary. They all spoke to me about her with something of bated breath, and she herself said nothing, seemed hardly to notice me at all. I wondered if they were creating a myth in order to give words to a serene and stricken silence as many worlds away as a statue. And then, watching her, I felt that all their comments were a hopeless effort to catch the strange and proud spirit certainly laired in her long supple body, which, when it moved, moved with the sudden and yet effortless gliding of water.

The General Strike loomed up. I still did not read newspapers, but could hardly escape hearing of this event. Mrs Kirtley had turned up with her ironic smile, taken one look at our house, and gone off with her son to Germany; so I was left alone in charge, living on eggs and sausages. The night before the strike I drifted about Fleet Street, drinking in the pubs and trying to hear what people said. I ended among a group of printers and began haranguing them on the need to fight to a finish, to fight for a complete overthrow of the system. They listened with an air of amused toleration till one of the older men said, 'Weren't we told to look out for provocators?' At the note of hostility I drank up and retreated: which was taken as a confession of my guilt by some of the younger chaps. They started hustling me, keen for a chance to knock me down. So I ran for a bus going Strandwards and caught it, pursued by one of the more obdurate lads. Thus ended my first effort to fraternize with the English proletariat.

My mood of revolutionary hope, which ran counter to all the positions I had accepted under Norman's influence, was the first strong revival of the political enthusiasms of my undergraduate days; it revealed the powerful effect of the English social scene upon me. The new leaven was going to take a long time to work out, but it was already present. I continued to fume with a sense of excluded importance as the strike continued. I would have liked to help, but had no idea how to set about it, unaware that P.R.S. in Oxford was one of the few students there working hard under the Coles to help the strikers. I strode about London, now mostly a city of the dead, with a savage satisfaction. Several times I walked across to Chelsea and chatted with Winifred; and I wrote an article, discussing Wellsian utopias and arguing that the strike involved human factors which made really fundamental change possible. In many ways an innocent article, but expressing a naïvely deep-going response to the situation. I tried it on the *Guardian* and on the *Statesman*, and had it promptly rejected; I realized that after all I didn't fit into any journalistic niche in the English scene.

3 · NINA HAMNETT

SUDDENLY the strike was over. I didn't understand how and why, but felt let down; the possibilities of humanizing the deadly world seemed nonsense. I had tried to say in my article that the serious artist could not be moved by reformist tactics, but that every impulse from below to break through the existent vicious circle must at once engage his total sympathies. With the collapse of the strike I simply forgot this idea. Soon after I visited P.R.S. in Oxford, dined at Queen's, was suitably impressed by the college beer, and met S., who had been a student under Lascelles Abercrombie at Leeds. S. had a cool hard insolence of daring; and the three of us drank in small dank river pubs or swaggered into any premises forbidden by the proctors – easy enough for me, but involving some hairbreadth escapes for the other two. One afternoon, at an outlying pub, I felt my anarchist compulsion come on me and exhorted some yokels to pull down the pillars of a worthless world, keeping respect only for art and intellect. I recall the fascinated bewilderment of one lad who continued the discussion in the Gents.

P.R.S. took me barging with Ramsay Macdonald's daughter; and one afternoon, watching cricket, we met a close relation of Sir John Simon, who gave us the inner story of the strike's breakdown. A story that meant nothing to me, but I understood P.R.S.'s denunciation of the right-wing T.U. leadership.

On the last night I returned to my lodgings at a late hour, groped my way into the dark room, undressed, and climbed into a bed already tenanted by an Indian, whose inconsequent explanations I couldn't follow. The landlady arrived in curl-papers and insufficient wrap, asserting that I'd only taken the room till the previous noon. There was nothing for it but to seize my case and wander out into a moonlit Oxford at about 2 o'clock a.m.; but luckily I met a policeman who gave me an address, where I knocked up an uncomplaining landlady and fell into bed.

Back in London, I carried on alone in Lady Somebody's house, which was steadily becoming more dusty. One day Jack MacLaren, a friend of Winifred's, who had been a beach-comber in the South Seas and still carried a whiff of that spacious oceanic existence, turned up with Thomas Burke, then famed for his Limehouse stories. We went for a drink in a near pub, a pleasant miniature place, a toy pub blown out of an illustration to *Pickwick Papers*. Burke, a smallish screwed up man, talked in a literary way, admired by the simple Jack. When I said I disliked London and wanted to get out some-where on my own, he replied, 'No, I cannot live away from people. Unless I am in the thick of them, I feel that I'll go mad. In any solitude the enemy of souls comes too close. I cannot withstand him.' Jack looked respectful, but I said there was no need to be afraid of the enemy of souls: the problem was to use his temptations against him.

We went on into town and ate in Charlotte Street, then tried the Fitzroy Tavern. An automatic piano was clattering. A woman came up and asked me if I were some Danish sculptor who I think was holding an exhibition. She was Nina Hamnett. Not long over from Paris, she had just had a show at the Claridge Galleries and hadn't done badly. She looked rather like the Colonel's daughter at first glance, perhaps a bit seedily down on her luck, but able to retreat when necessary to a Chel-tenham croquet garden, and her voice was as distinct and colourless.* But in fact, together with a fair talent as a

---

*In registering this image I was unaware that she was actually the daughter of an army officer and grand-daughter on the maternal side of Capt. Arch-deacon, the surveyor of Western Australia; educated at the Royal School, Bath, for daughters of officers, before she went to the London School of Art. Her youthful body is immortalized in Gaudier-Brzeska's torso carved on a piece of marble stolen from a Putney stonemason's yard. (I have just noticed that in *Is she a Lady?* she mentions hearing her voice on a recorded broadcast and it 'sounded just like Itma's drunken Colonel!')

draughtsman, she had an insatiable hunger for life – though her mediocre mind prevented her from bringing the talent and the hunger together in her art. I have met few people who had less interest in ideas except perhaps as a tag on which to hang personalities. In the process even personalities were reduced to the most banal level of anecdotage. She was an odd indomitable character: a bohemian snob who collected names. Not that it mattered to her whether the significance of your name lay in a title, a boxing championship, a criminal record or skill in training fleas, an abnormal beer capacity or high achievement in art. Her aquiline blunt-tipped nose, her brow sloping a little back and her chin slightly retreating, suggested accurately enough her eager appetite for persons and places, as if her childhood had been spent with that prominent nose pressed against windowpanes which she now had no compunction about smashing in all directions, without loss of her ladylike accent. Her rather large baggy ears increased the effect of an omnivorous thrust forwards through all winds, windows, and other obstacles.

We had several drinks together and Nina was delighted to add the author of *Limehouse Nights* to her list of acquaintances. Then we moved to another pub, nearer Tottenham Court Road, where were D. B. Wyndham Lewis and others. I sat back, enjoying the scene from a remote distance, over a bellyful of beer. 'At last I have found my proper Hell', I told myself. 'Now I am at home.'

I had arranged to meet Nina next day. I took along some copies of *The Passionate Neatherd* – unbound sheets – which were the only specimens of our printing to hand. She had with her a young American from Paris, Robert McAlmon, who ran his own press and was a pal of Joyce: peevishly handsome, with depressed lines on his longish face. However, I liked his sudden rude remarks about England. I recall saying, 'In Oxford they think it frightfully advanced to put up a Corot reproduction,' but have no idea where I picked up the information. McAlmon looked even more bored, his fine features pinching into gloomy silence, when I produced the sheets. I knew now they'd fall flat, but couldn't get out of showing them. Nina read out a few lyrics and charitably laughed. Over our beers I tried to convince McAlmon that I had a long poem *Between Two Kisses*, which was a sort of surrealist experiment; but he knew that no experiment of mine could interest him and merely grew gloomier.

Nina however wasn't put off. I became very friendly with her and we went about a lot. Passing down Howland Street, she pointed out the house where Rimbaud and Verlaine had stayed and said that she had lost her maidenhead in the same rooms; and she told the anecdote which she was proud of: 'I asked Sickert if the L.C.C. would put up one of their blue plaques, and he said: They'll put up one for you at the front and another for them at the back.' She took me to a party at Augustus John's studio where I met Tommy Earp, who, I found to my surprise, knew Australian poetry well: the work of Brennan, McCrae, Dowd and others. 'If we print McCrae here,' I said, 'you must write the preface'. And Tommy, with his red beaming face, his cropped hair, and his quavering drawl like a point scribbling on a slate, replied that there was nothing he'd like better. I met also Tallulah Bankhead, then at her height as a gallery-girl crush, with her violet-blue eyes and her hot-honey-and-milk voice, with her ash-gold hair under one of the horrible toques of the time, for some reason she took much interest in our proposed press and offered to introduce me to various N.Y. personages, who could help; but I didn't call on her as she suggested. I had a complete scepticism always as to success gained through the right contacts; and perhaps also I remembered McAlmon's boredom. More important was my first meeting, on this occasion, with Peter Warlock, if meeting it can be called. For he had already passed out when we arrived, and was moaning feebly with closed eyes in the bathroom, where various drunks were trying to revive him with doses of brandy or douches of cold water. I regarded his tipsily pasty face, which I revered as belonging to the original of Coleman in Huxley's *Antic Hay*, and took my turn at water-sprinkling. 'He was talking of God and then collapsed,' said Eugene Goossens. I replied, 'It serves him right for such ungentlemanly behaviour.' I remember that not very bright remark because it was the only quip of mine at this period which received uproarious response. Which only shows how drunk everyone was.

Finally I found that Nina and myself were the last revellers left in the studio with Augustus. As Nina was still looking for bottles with something left in them, I tried to tell him how affected I had been in Brisbane by a book of his Welsh land-scapes and pictures of his wife. One painting, which showed the brightly clad woman in a splendid cabbage garden, recur-red to my mind with luminous clarity, and I tried to describe it. 'The rich blue greens . . . neglected beauty . . . I can only recall one poem, attributed to Ausonius, *On Budding Roses: Vidi concretas per gramina flexa pruinas* . . . The clotted hoarfrost on the bent grass, rounded drops rolling together on the cabbage leaves . . . Break up of the classical generalizations, the poet really looking at nature. Somehow you know, looking at those Welsh cabbages, I mean your colours, in sweltering Brisbane. Quite lost. And now I'm here.' I went on a long time like that, and Augustus said absolutely nothing. Only now it occurs to me that he was owl-drunk.

I also went with Nina to a performance of *Façade* and heard Edith Sitwell performing through a large painted face. I had mentioned to Nina that about the only book I could read on the liner had been Sacheverell's *Hundred and One Harlequins*, with its rhythms that suited the continuous ever-changing sea; and she introduced me to him. My expressions of gratitude seemed to make him yet more depressed, but no doubt he was merely shy. Afterwards we went to a nightclub not far from the Fitzroy. As I took out a banknote I realized that I would have to pull myself up. Nina wasn't in the least mercenary. Having decided that I was Somebody, she wouldn't have bothered if I had announced empty pockets and proceeded to borrow from her; but I had irrupted in the guise of a well-off Australian and had been too weak-willed to change my labels. At the moment I was sitting with a superbly beautiful girl who said almost nothing and encouraged me to talk with her ser-enely imperial smile. After a while Nina came back and made some praising comment on another woman. The superb one paused, held her long cigarette-holder away, and slowly turned her head. 'Yes, a handsome lump of meat,' she said in a voice of lucid insolence, but without any stress or even interest.

I admired her inordinately, rose and said good night.

I dropped clean out of Nina's world thenceforth. I had come
to know Tommy fairly well and had eaten at his flat. (The
legend went that he had inherited a large part of a foundry;
and that he had sold hearth after hearth to finance a cheerful
if not riotous flow of good liquor at the Ritz. He had been presi-
dent of the Union at Oxford and at one time meditated standing for Parliament as a Liberal.) I had even found some
pleasure in McAlmon's morose company as long as we kept to
the shortcomings of the English.* But now I decided that I
must pull out, save my cash, and wait for some deeper impulse
to show itself in me, something which convinced me of its connection with my poetry.

I had been seeing little of Winifred and her group; but now
they asked me to a dance, which was to raise funds for some
art purpose. I went, and under the stimulus of whisky I actually
danced. Again the illusion that I was a rich young Australian
came out in some half comment, and for once I didn't object.
There was a lot of whisky flowing. Elza was there; and my confused attraction and revulsion gave way to a simple high-
spirited wish to draw her out of her mystical reverie. As usual
she was dressed in a long clinging dress of rough texture; this
time the hue was dark. And her hair was plainly done,
smoothed down over her ears and knotted at the back. Her eyes
were still uninvolved in the scene, but her lips were slightly
parted with a breath of excitement.

I felt masterful for once. I kissed somebody else, perhaps just
to make sure that I could act as recklessly as I felt. And somebody else. And then I kissed Elza. I was dancing with her and
had guided our steps into a side corridor, away from the large
hall. She did not return my kiss, but she made no resistance,
and afterwards her bright eyes looked directly in on the
dancers, on me. And her lips were a little more opened. Her

---

*I had somehow become acquainted with A. J. Symonds, who was much
interested in fine printing. During a dinner at his flat overlooking Baker
Street, Marrot (of the bookshop and publishers) made an attack on modern
verse and for some reason picked on uses of the word 'bland'. I cited from
Helen, without mentioning my authorship, 'Or the bland fillets of the wind'.
He guessed the lines were mine and was scathing.

slender body felt strong, pliant, but still locked as it lapsed in my arms. Young, I saw, was watching us with a stare that made his heavy jaw yet heavier; but I didn't care. We went on dancing.

Two days later I called on her as arranged; for then Young was away on one of the tours arranged, I think, by the *Daily Express*. She was alone in her room. Let me again cite *Lisa*. Whether the details are exact, I cannot recall; but the atmosphere is exactly evoked. (*Lisa* was published in 1930; and Edith sent me a copy. But though I was then in throes of trying to understand Elza, I did not read the book beyond the first page – as if there was a taboo on it and I must penetrate Elza's world by my own efforts alone. I read the book in the British Museum Reading Room for the first time in 1961, and was astonished at its insights, though inevitably there was much that Edith did not see, deceived despite her sharp scrutiny by Elza's own account of herself at that time.)

My first impression was of strangeness, of being in a sort of bizarre tent. A divan in a corner covered with some sort of scarlet cloth, a chest of drawers, tall and narrow, painted black, and the white walls, white ceiling arching into a concave peak and then sloping down to an alcove over the window, from the window a diffused, rather pale light throwing one side of Lisa's face into shadow – all these impressions, although they came in succession, seemed to come in one glance, as I stepped rather diffidently over the threshold. It is as I imagined, I said to myself, she creates about herself an atmosphere of legend.

As I came close up to her I saw that she was wearing a dark dress fitting close to her body in her usual style, and a heavy silver necklet – of old coins, they seemed to be – as ornament. Her hands moved nervously. She did not look up.

She made tea and answered quietly to my fervent account of what I hoped to do in England. There was never at any time the faintest suggestion of coquetry in her manner; I cannot remember her ever laughing, though she had a gentle and subtly lingering smile. Although I had kissed her at the dance, I felt no self-assurance; there seemed no link between the gravely aloof dispenser of tea and the girl who had sunk with entire passivity into my arms. I talked on to cover my uncertainty and at last stood up to go. I reached the door, still talking, and turned to say goodbye. She had come up close, but without the least flicker of emotion on her pale tranquil face with its fine modelling, its Florentine clarity of outline. I took her in my arms and she stayed there. I kissed her and she gave a faint sigh, closing her eyes.

Afterwards, we went out and ate in a small café nearby, then returned to her room. When I left about eleven o'clock, I felt that I had possessed her wholly and that she was now an integral part of me, and at the same time that she was more a stranger than ever, someone whom I least understood of all the persons in the world. A minglement of rapture and fear. As if at last I had entered the unknown dimension of England, the alien thing which I had been decrying because I did not comprehend its meaning, its reason for existence. Something parasitic and yet beautifully gathering all the pang of lost things, the broken hopes and yearnings of the many centuries. Already I had a fair idea that she was ignorant, lacking any sense of history, perhaps hardly educated at all; and I guessed that her silences were in part protective. Yet I felt in her the unspoiled essence of all art, all poetry, strangely naïve and spontaneous, and also compressing an immemorial wisdom and lore. Whereas the sophisticated wenches in Nina's world had left me at root repelled, since I felt in them only a delectable well-polished surface with nothing individually significant on the other side, in Elza I felt that the surface was unimportant. Her beauty was wholly a projection of a strange inner life for which she had no words, though she found a certain release in the accessories with which she surrounded herself as emblems of her difference, her sojourn in a dim sea-cavern of oracular repose. The only analogy I could find was in the paintings of Giorgione, where each woman, where indeed all nature, is listening – listening to an unheard music. She was a prisoner of her senses, which were tuned to a system of harmonies denied by the world. Helpless and asking me to rescue her – from what? I too was helpless, deliberately rejecting any of the normal defences against a derisive world, an inquisition in which the threat of starvation was the primary and unceasing weapon used to bring about conformity, the acceptance of the mechanism of the cash nexus.

This close similarity which I felt between Elza and myself was one of the elements of my fear. How could I protect her when I could not protect myself, had no wish to? And yet I knew I could not evade the fascination of her enigma; I could know myself only in knowing her.

These ecstatic fears and foreboding filled me in a confused way, and drove me out of the bus, so that I walked some miles home. But they reached my mind only in fits and starts, in fragments of consciousness; if I had known what they really implied, I should have fled from London.

4 · ELZA

I DID not go to her room again, but she came almost every day to St John's Wood. She offered herself simply, without words, with an emotion that could be either complete trust or reckless despair. I tried to sound Winifred and Edith about her. I had no idea if she had drawn Young away from Edith or had been taken by him after his marriage had broken down. I didn't like to ask Edith questions directly, and she always expressed the greatest liking and respect for Elza. I felt however that Winifred didn't quite accept the legend; I let her know how things had gone and got the impression that P.R.S., learning of our relations, wasn't altogether pleased. Also, the MacLarens, I thought, did not like her. I got hints that she was not the immaculate dreamer she seemed. M., a stalwart whom I had known at the Queensland University, and who had been surveying in the Sudan, was now in London and was haunting her place, I found.

Meanwhile in Lady Somebody's house we had our hasty meals and lay in the attic, or had a bath together and wandered naked round the house. She had a gay tenderness, a childlike readiness to lark. What with my careless and anxious way of living, eating little and erratically, I had a recrudescence of adolescent skin trouble and was afraid to strip. But when she saw the carbuncles on my back, she kissed them and said, 'Poor dear.' I felt as if she were a medieval saint who embraced lepers, and at the same time a Thais of the ancient world. But that seemed a *fin-de-siècle* fancy; and despite her Byrne-Jones aspect, she was at these moments radiantly a creature born from the waters of poetic immediacy, without any ancestry, and yet incarnating a dream of aeons, a thing of beauty with humanity perfected. Perhaps it was now that I was finally lost.

Suddenly S. descended on me from Oxford, with his hard wit, his challenging hand-clasp, his cold air of ruthless daring. He gave the effect of having tried everything once already, and of now dangerously seeking the sin against the holy ghost, passionate and bored. We made the round of local pubs and found Kilburn, where he was more at home, restoring confidence to the most draggled of aged tarts by his ubiquitous glance of brazen desire, P.R.S. also turned up, and Elza promised to cook a duck for us. Young was home, but she managed to dash across, produce the dinner, and dash off again. That night we had the conviction of having cracked the rafters of the heavens, and I danced a mime of the Crucified Faun to *L'Après-midi* on a gramophone. S. tried to dance with the prancing Bacchante.

Then things were quiet again. Kirtley came back from Germany and announced that he would have to give up the house at the end of the six-months' lease. Elza went on visiting me, with his caustic tolerance. She and I never discussed the future. She, who used no make-up, gave herself with a calm and eager submissiveness, with open eyes in which there was a questioning look. As though she understood neither herself nor me, and was looking on from afar.

I knew that things were now strained between her and Young, but she told me nothing and I did not ask. Nor did I mention M. to her. I had met him once when I was in Chelsea on a visit that I could not get out of without seeming to evade Young and the others. I disliked his large confident presence, his husky seducer's voice, the way he watched Elza; and remembered acutely how in our Brisbane days he had had Rosaline at his beck and call, a lithe loose wild-eyed girl with long slim hands, to which I had written sonnets in the Elizabethan manner and which, limply, she had let me kiss, keeping the rest of her tenuous self for M.'s complacent devouring. He had come to London, he said, after a touch of the sun, and he seemed a bit queer, huskily lowering his voice and talking suddenly of Sudanese things we couldn't follow.

Young was doubtless worried about M. and myself; but I think that the more he had come up against the power of dead resistance in Elza, and the more he tried to hold her, to impress

himself upon her, the more she coldly withdrew. There is a
passage in *Lisa* where Munt (Young) states his attitude to Lisa,
a matter on which Edith must have been well informed. I cite
it for this reason and because it shows him torn by the same
divided emotion that I was to feel: the wish to make Elza stand
on her own feet, and the fear of using any of the available ways
of doing so:

'You needn't waste pity on her. She's the lucky one.'

'Why? What do you mean?'

'She's the only one of us all who lives apart in her own inner world,
and doesn't feel. She is cold, I tell you. Damnably cold. I don't believe
she has ever felt a real emotion for anyone in her life. You can see
how apart from everyone she is, by her eyes. Her eyes never grow
warm – or seldom,' he added quickly, smiling as he spoke, as though
he had suddenly remembered a pleasing reflection.

'Why are you attached to her, then?' I asked, interrupting his reverie.

'God knows! Perhaps because of her very coldness. I never know
what she is thinking. She doesn't talk very much, but all the time you
can feel her making her observations – acute ones. It is disconcerting.
She is clever, too. No, perhaps not exactly clever . . . Most women you
understand almost at once – what they will say – what they will do
under certain circumstances. You know what it will be like kissing
them, you can feel their flesh under your hands – and know it is flesh
– and while you pet them you know how they will respond – and
it is all so stale.' He sighed wearily.

Turning on me, he said: 'With Lisa you never know, not from one
hour to the next; I often imagine when I come home she will have
vanished.'

'Like fire and air,' I murmured, forgetting him.

'You can never get at her – so you are always left searching. To
Armstrong she is the legendary woman, he says, but he is so full of
literary ideas, I don't take much notice of him.'

'Can she not earn her living at anything? That would solve one
of her difficulties, surely.'

'What at? But I see – you would urge her to be independent – it
would make your problem easier. The heroic girl struggling away at
uncongenial work! You would not advocate her being an artist's

model, I suppose? That would expose her to temptations. Oh yes! Sully the white bird. It would please you, no doubt, to see her struggling with a tray of greasy plates in a restaurant – perspiring – with the young men looking at her calves . . . Do you know I wish I had never seen her . . . Ever since I first saw her at Leo's,' he said, 'I have never had an hour's freedom – not an hour without strain. Sometimes it is almost unbearable.'

To Young, the leader of community song, who had something coarse as well as genial about him, Elza had been turning her cold impenetrable side: the side which seemed to me her lonely pride. And suddenly she told me that she had left him. Told me without the least emphasis or show of emotion: as if she had merely spoken of going to Harrod's to shop. I asked no questions but I noticed that she had a bandaged wrist. From my other sources of information I learned that she had tried to commit suicide by severing a vein. The effect of this story on me was considerable. My fear of her was deepened, and I felt a sharp repulsion. Suicide, like murder, was to me an act possible only for creatures of a low quality of life. But the shock also drew me towards her, driving away all my suspicions that she was a well-disguised tart whom anyone could have; the deed stamped her with an undeniable sincerity and showed her position with Young as one of long-suffering martyrdom.

She told me that she was moving into a basement in Eaton Square. First however the place had to be decorated. I offered to help her. There was a large front room with a kitchen behind. We set to work distempering the walls a faint undersea green. I concentrated on the ceilings; and distemper ran down my arms, into my eyes and hair, as I tried to produce the maze of wavy lines she wanted. Young had sent over a few pieces of furniture and she had picked up some second-hand things. Nothing definite was said about Young, yet somehow she made me feel that he had been incredibly cruel to her: not by any physical ill-treatment, but by a tyrannical inability to understand her, to cease from trampling on all the fine things of her spirit. She infused me with an emotion of passionate resentment against him, a fathomless contempt, which had the effect of binding me all the closer to her – increasing my conviction that I alone of all men could appreciate her, could come in time to find and unlock the buried fountains of her spirit.

The second night I did not go back to St John's Wood. She did not ask me to stay and I said nothing about any plans. I stayed and we slept on the divan which Young had sent over. It was her own property, she said. The next day we went on with the distempering and with the clearance of lumber from the kitchen, then we drank beer at the Antelope – something unusual for Elza, who seldom drank anything but a little wine – and again I stayed. At the end of a week I was still there. In a strange spell of happiness we carried on with the redecoration and wandered up and down King's Road hand in hand, buying vegetables or spaghetti and looking in the shop windows at our incomparable reflections. I carried back to Eaton Square on a wheelbarrow an old chest of drawers that she bought and meant to paint.

One evening Edith called in and smiled on our ménage. She read a poem I had written on the wall:

> *Pull down the blind and bring*
> *this twilight of kisses. Pull*
> *love down over the mind*
> *and shut out people passing.*
> *Pull down the blind.*
>
> *O that this kiss might be*
> *a silence enduring and strong*
> *to shut out for ever*
> *men the faceless noises*
> *endlessly passing along.*
>
> *Give me your mouth and draw*
> *love down over the mind.*
> *Let the world suddenly die –*
> *pull down the blind.*

'How brave you are,' she said to Elza, who smiled her most mysterious smile and said nothing.

At long last I felt an urgent need to write. I began a verse-play with a Norse setting, *Ragnhild*, which was to be a counterpart and contrast to *Helen Comes of Age*. Ragnhild, a wild dreamy Irishwoman, has been captured by Frithiof. She does her best to set his brother Asmund against him, and draws on a bard, Viglund, to fall in love with her. At the end, meaning to stab herself, she stabs Frithiof in the eye. She persuades Asmund to accuse Viglund of the murder, and the bard is killed. The whole point of the play lay in the enigmatic and contradictory character of Ragnhild, in whom I wanted to express all my love and fear of Elza: the element in her that seemed to me strangely pure, gentle, dedicated, and uncompromising, the element that was bewildered with anguish and capable, I thought, of compulsive violences. Frithiof was given something of what I felt to be Young's hostile half insights:

FRITHIOF: *Standing there as if you have been discovered*
in some great act of guilt that you yet were proud of,
as you are always standing
when I come into a room that you've been filling
with an ooze of sullen and thick silence.
What is it you always do when you're alone
that gives you such a sly anger of surprise?

RAGNHILD: *I am not alone. And I have been talking.*
And I am not angry yet,

FRITH: *Go, Ingebiorg.* (She goes.)
Now we're alone. You always seem alone,
and silent too. Even when you've just spoken,
your words remembered in the echo of thought
seem bellnotes that tinkle harshly from your mind
across the dulcet hush of the air
into my mind.
Not noises uttered at me between your teeth;
and when I speak I scrape that harsh silence.

RAGN: *I shall go also.*

FRITH: *Don't go. What have I done?*
I haven't seen you now for three days.
Where have you been hiding yourself away?
telling your sulks to birds looking sideways at you?
dancing to wild cattle in a glade
in hopes to lure the bull-king from his cow?
going for walks at midnight?

Those lines, which start off a long altercation between

Ragnhild and Frithiof, I wrote at Eaton Square. But we weren't there for long. The woman letting the basement saw that I was with Elza, and said the terms of occupation had been broken. So we moved to a room further down King's Road, losing all our hard work of decoration. What we wanted to keep of the furniture, I took off in various wheelbarrow trips. Elza had no money. Young had been going to make her a small allowance, visiting her in her basement; but naturally when he heard I was with her, he dropped this arrangement. Apart from the few pounds earned from the *Guardian*, I had had all this while only the £40 odd with which I had landed; and now there was very little left. I had lost any belief that Kirtley would manage to float the Fanfrolico Press. What with his going off to Germany and my preoccupation with Elza, a rift had come between us. He was having trouble with Lady Somebody or her agents, who asserted that we had broken large quantities of her valuables. Except for a few pieces of cheap crockery and perhaps a dent or two in the Bacchante I denied the damage; but though Kirtley said little in his testy way, I felt that I was blamed.

We moved from our nondescript room to a basement near Baron's Court. I was learning some facts about Elza. She was married to Robert Craig, a son of Gordon Craig, and had a child Robinetta, aged about six. Robert and the child were living in Paris, where he was acting as a guide for tourists. She always spoke fondly of Robert and I failed to get any clear idea as to why she had left him. This definite background of hers relieved my mind a lot; also the existence of Robert made her dependence on me seen less absolute. About her earlier years she was vague. She gave an incoherent impression of having lived in Paris, born in a family closely related to the poet Hérédia; yet she knew French very imperfectly – a smattering she had picked up when living in Paris with Robert for a year or two before her return in 1925. Her mother, I gathered, had been mad to some degree; and as the subject affected her painfully, I made no effort to press it. At least the Craigs were undeniably real.

She was in touch with Mrs Craig (who had long been parted from Gordon). Mrs Craig called unexpectedly one day on the basement and I was shut in the kitchen. I heard her excessively upper-class dulcetly false voice and caught a glimpse of her as she departed in the taxi that had been waiting. Elza was excited by the visit. She had an ambivalent attitude to her mother-in-law, which she had obviously taken over from Robert. Mrs Craig, according to this version, was an extremely charming, well-bred woman, with fine taste in clothes and furniture (she used her knowledge of antiques to add to her income); but she was completely superficial, conventional, and self-centred. She used her charm unscrupulously to dominate her sons and was armoured in every way against the attack of reality, assured of her good intentions whatever she did. There were three sons: Robert, who was intelligent but restless, unable to settle down to any of the jobs that Mrs Craig used her social position to gain for him, secretaryships and the like; one who, badly upset by his war experiences, had been drowned a few years back; a third who suffered from various nervous disabilities but seemed to have found his place in a city job. Elza blamed Mrs Craig for the drowning of the second son, who had swum out in desperation until he sank, though Mrs Craig resolutely treated the episode as an accident. Robert, it was clear, had been very attached to the dead brother, who seemed highly talented; and I felt that the latter's death had much to do with his own inability to accept a role in his mother's world. Mrs Craig, according to Elza, even used her physical charm to keep her sons tied to her suspender-belt, coquettishly allowing them into her toilet with entire 'innocence'.

I felt much sympathy for Robert, who had severed his class connection with a certain flamboyant and insulting verve. I gathered that he had picked Elza up not long after the war and fallen in love with her. Against his mother's bitter resistance he married her and she bore Robinetta. His mother then accepted the position and did her best to groom Elza and fit the couple into her world. Elza was grateful to Mrs Craig for much that she had learned from her, yet had abetted Robert in all his resistances; it was his refusal to take the conventional profitable line, without being able to find an alternative, which seemed to me to have bound her to him. She had made a few attempts since her marriage to earn something, as a fashion-model and as an actress, briefly taking the main role of Law-rence Houseman's *Prunella*; somebody had also wanted her as Joan of Arc in a film, which had come to nothing. Once again I could not make out why her efforts had flagged away. One of her best friends had been the painter Nicholson, for whom she had often sat. (I had an impression that the Craig boys had been embittered at public school by the fact that their father was an illegitimate son of Ellen Terry; they had been made to feel something of a pariah position.)

Mrs Craig's visit proved that the family did not look on the marriage with Robert as broken, and I tried to sound Elza on this point. Something unpleasant had happened in Paris, but whether or not she blamed Robert I did not know; she had rushed away, leaving him and the child. Had she any intention of rejoining Robert if he came to London? what about the child? how had she kept herself before living with Young? To these matters and others of the same sort I could get no clear answer. Not that I pestered her with questions; but at moments she seemed impelled to talk about herself, and I tried to put together the scattered ends, generally in vain.

She had a cult of Epstein's *Rima* and took me to see the monument in Hyde Park; it was clearly important to her to find if I liked it. I liked it. She took me out into Epping Forest via Waltham Abbey, and she stripped in a small copse where, lying quietly, we caught a glimpse of shy deer. She had a passionate feeling for birds and all wild creatures. I tried to put this side of her into *Ragnhild*, using tales she told of herself – how, for instance, she used to search the harvest-fields for nests and fledglings, which she carried tenderly to the hedges. Such country memories rang more true than her vague accounts of childhood in some mouldering park on the outskirts of Paris.

However, on the whole I had come to accept her account of herself. For instance, one evening we were in Piccadilly Cir-cus and she saw Marie Tempest billed in a play; she sent a note in and a pair of tickets promptly appeared; after the play we had a chat with Marie. Then came a blow. I learnt from her dislikers that she had certainly been having an affair with M. about the time she first gave herself to me, and for a while after-wards, and, worse, that M. had been invalided back to London through catching syphilis in the Sudan. For some days I was filled with a cold revulsion, though I said nothing. Then the pathos of Elza's charm overcame me again and I gradually forgot.

London was now a different place, irradiated by our secret delights and revealing furtive moments of a strange poetry. Elza talked of Regent Street and its vistas before the big shopkeepers got together to kill it. With her I rediscovered the parks and older squares, and strolled through the evening of Chelsea embankment. Along the river, here or near the Tower, I could gratefully recall that London was Turner's city and had in many ways made him, at least its docks and watersides, its Covent Garden of spilt plenty. In the full moonlight the blackened buildings with their rain-streaked whites became the flats of a faery play, and we hunched our shoulders under the cloaks of an enormous secrecy. The traffic lights spun in mad patterns of pursuit and flight, and the puddles were scummed with hellflares. We rode in the front seats of the open tops of buses in the rain, drawing the tarpaulins over our knees, visiting fantastic arenas of hoarse activity, Clapham Junction and the Elephant and Castle, under the wet glittering darkness drawn close down like a circus tent. One afternoon we came out of Hyde Park with twined fingers and no weight at all in our bodies, and I felt someone's glance upon us, turned and saw Lord Balfour watching us with eyes of over-brimming benevolence. Only a moment, but the memory remained clear, an old man serenely blessing life.

A working arrangement had been reached with Kirtley. I was to carry on somehow on my own till the year-end, making a new version of the *Satyricon*. Meanwhile he'd go ahead organizing the Press. The first book would be a replica of our Australian *Lysistrata*; the second, the Petronius, re-using the illustrations Norman had made for the pre-war edition printed by Strauss.

At Elza's insistence I was growing a beard. Visiting my bank in Broad Street to draw almost all that remained of my meagre account, I saw the clerk stare with horrified compassion, but did not tell him my unshaven state was deliberate. Then P.R.S. turned up at our basement, full of adventurous spirits and soaking me in renewed hope. All sorts of ways of making money were instantly possible; the only real question was how to enjoy ourselves. Away from London, the treadmill round, the pleasure lash whistling over the backs of the tormented city throng. Why not Brittany? We got out a map of France. I closed my eyes and jabbed a pin down. 'It's landed right in mid-sea,' I said. 'We drown.'

'Nonsense,' he replied. 'It's on an island.' He snatched the map. 'Ile de Bréhat. Off Paimpol. Icelandic Fisheries. Splendid choice. Let's go there.'

'To Debussy's sunken cathedral if you like.'

Having acquired a beard, I needed a new photo in my passport; but as I knew no clergymen, etc., I went to Australia House to ask someone to vouch for me. The official I saw was sympathetic, though concerned to find out why I had grown such a luxuriant beard. He chatted on, and happened to bring up the fact that the Australians were playing cricket at Lord's. My blank ignorance of this world-shattering event must have made him doubtful of my Australianism; however he signed my photo.

Now came the crucial matter. I used my last shillings to cable Norman with a request for £50. This was the only time I ever asked him for money; and he sent the sum by return cable. In the next few years we took his pen-and-inks, old ones or new ones specially drawn for us, without making him any return in cash. But as the Press was established on the basis of propagandizing his ideas, we felt no compunction. Money, however, was a different thing, and I had qualms about the request. I quieted my conscience that otherwise I did not see how I could be sure of finding time for Petronius, which was essential for the launching of the Press.

5 · ILE DE BRÉHAT

WINIFRED had decided to join us in our Breton holidaying, and we set off late in August, sailing from Southampton to St Malo. P.R.S. impressed the *douanes* with his versatile French and we found cheap rooms near the Quai. I don't know what went wrong with our train calculations, but we spent the next night stranded in mid-Brittany at St Brieuc. We arrived so late, with no connection, that we decided not to tramp through the slumbering township on the quest for rooms. We settled down on the railway station, using what rugs and coats we could muster to keep out the early morning cold, and woke cramped and sore-boned. A train turned up before we could find any café, and we made for it, warned by a porter, '*Vous serez écrasé!*' At last we arrived at Paimpol, to drink warm coffee and *cidre bouché*, and to roam about the port with its ancient lugger and its old men dreaming on lumps of granite. There was no launch to the Isle till the next day, so we walked along the coast, and then found a cheap hotel.

That night I felt abysmally lost and scared for the first time since I had left Australia. But with P.R.S.'s cheerful face over morning coffee and with the pleasant chugging across the blue waters to the island, I grew assured. The port was small, but had houses hung at different levels and angles; and the island itself was a perfect miniature, a clump of warm rocks and pine trees dropped with fine precision of tone upon the wavering waters, against a scudding sky. Actually there was much more of it than appeared at first glance. We drank to our arrival at the first café, with nets drying on the wall; and then reconnoitred inland. We decided to put up, not at the port, but an an hotel a couple of miles in, by a small village. It was cheaper: also there were dining-tables in the open under pergolas of vines.

Here we all stayed two or three weeks. I played chess with
P.R.S. at the café down the road and drank *cidre*; and I finished
putting together *Dung of Pegasus*, an autobiographical fantasia,
which was later published serially as by Peter Meadows in *The
London Aphrodite*. P.R.S. in his large way notified the proprietor
that a great work had been completed under his roof; and the
man begged to be allowed to present us with a bottle of
champagne for the honour of having his hotel mentioned as
the address at the end of the book. The champagne was bad,
but its delivery was a solemn ceremony, with speeches and
handshakes, and we drank it seriously under the shadow of the
broad vine-leaves.

We found a small cottage in the open ground facing the
hotel, which was called Prairie de l'Allégoat. The landlady,
Veuve Lambolet, lived thriftily in a lean-to at the back, with
a goat tied to a post. The cottage had one room below, one
above, with a later room tacked on at one side at the front.

The tide was out as the others went to catch the launch,
which had to be approached by a winding track of stones slippery with seaweed. Winifred had bought pottery at Paimpol
and packed it carefully in a large crate. The fisherman nonchalantly carrying this crate on his shoulders, slid on a slimy
stone and brought the pots down with a crash. As everyone
crowded into the launch, P.R.S. took me aside with an unusual
air of seriousness and asked if I had definitely broken with
Janet. Caught by surprise, I could only answer, 'No, of course
not.' What then about Elza? 'I don't know, we've never discussed it, I suppose things will work out, she's married too.' The
questions distracted and disturbed me, and in my confusion
I mentioned that Norman had once called Rose and Janet the
only two intelligent women he knew. P.R.S. rightly made a sarcastic comment, but looked relieved. My perturbation however
went on and lay heavily on me after we had waved our friends
out of sight and were climbing back to the Prairie from which
no sea was visible. I found it hard to speak, until the dusk
smudged out the world with swabs of blue, and I could look
Elza in the eyes again, because there was only we two left alive
in a softly breathing world.

We spent about three months in the Veuve's cottage and

came to know the island and its people well. We watched the men make apple pulp in the rough stone presses, and drank their cider. Watched them working barefoot in the seaweed spread for manure and going home with a song, tramping or riding in the island's one sturdy cart. Watched an old woman minding a cow with a length of rope round its neck, herself dressed in black with a big poke-bonnet tied under her chin and her face as cracked as a ball of crumpled paper. We wandered over the island, which was really two islands joined by a narrow strip, and bathed among the rocks, thinking at every swirl of shadow that we had stirred up the octopods which figure ferociously in Hugo's novel about the Channel Islands. We climbed to the tiny Noah's ark of a church perched on a hilltop and inevitably dedicated to St Michael; and there we found a rock hollow where we might lie out of the winds, read poems, and strip in the sun, unseen by anyone but a floating bird or St Michael on one of his fiery clouds. We strolled among pine trees where lay the mossy ruins of old fortifications, on afternoons with the broadsheets of light poured on the reddened trunks, or at dusk, sometimes blundering into huge spiderwebs spun stoutly from tree to tree. We came out on the shore with its clusters of golden seaweed at ebbtide, the sea-mews wheeling in the amber-tinted air or a soft radiance suffused like gold dust in the distance, a smack's wake glimmering purple on the smooth sea. Bats flickered in the dimness like our own uncertain thoughts momently troubling us.

There was dancing in the cobbled square before the battered thatched Mairie and the small dark stuffy church. I liked sitting on the terrasse with a cider and watching the heavy bodies lightly revolving, the strong shoulders and torsos of the girls with their veiled eyes. An accordion and a fiddle or two provided the music; and as twilight came on there would be moments of brief indecorum in the shadows, a scuffling and a burst of laughter from the lads, a clucking of black-shrouded women, and a rapid thinning of the last lingerers. The warmth of cider in my bones and the blessed mutter of the vanishing world and Elza enigmatically but consolingly silent at my side.

In the café I played chess with a grey-bearded landscape painter who was slightly lame. There was also a villainous-eyed marquis from Guincamp with a fat mistress sewn into a shiny black dress, the seams of which she was always on the edge of bursting wide open with a cloud of stale scent and a dead white flash of expanding globular breasts and buttocks. Her voracious mouth twisted and swelled as she chewed shellfish and other pulpy live things of the sea. Once, when she and the distrait marquis insisted on seeing us home on a dark night, I remarked, as we neared the Veuve's kitchen-garden, *Prenez garde: la forêt des choux.*' She gave her belly-gurgle of a laugh and with her pudgy fingers pressed my hand somewhere deep into her cleft person – the only time she seemed to notice my existence. Another acquaintance was M. Negroponte, technically British (having been born in Egypt) with a son who had served in an English regiment in the war. He wore a peaked cap, a check coat, and a twinkling air as if he were always about to produce a shattering witticism; he treated Elza gallantly, as if she were so fragile that she must be helped over every rut in the road (which was nothing but ruts) and every crack in the café floor. The one local intellectual, the grey-eyed chemist, a Voltairean, who had once been to sea and spoke English, discussed Breton superstitions and expressed a great desire to read Conrad. Vibert, an artist who lived in a vast place with an uncomfortable studio like a church, had taken over the café to have something to do. We spent some dull afternoons in his studio, looking at his excellent collection of pictures. Clearly the artists and the others were ready to put up with my bad French for the privilege of looking at Elza. I translated my pinewood poems into French and typed them out. The lame artist read them with an encouraging nod and turned his gaze back to Elza; but the fact that I was translating Petronius gave me a certain standing. The marquis woke up, pressed my hand, and asked us to dinner at the hotel, with drinks afterwards at his villa.

Gradually, even with our bad French, we absorbed the island's scandals. The marquis took drugs; his mistress, after administering cocaine, cuckolded him in all her seams with a young fisherman. The woman with big eyes in violet cavities and a pasty-face was a lesbian. Vibert looked so disconsolate because he was waiting for his wife to return. Much younger than he, she regularly selected a lover from the summer visitors and went off with him; but she always came back for the winter. Sure enough, she did turn up, a short high-breasted woman with a hard handsome face, thick eyebrows and down-curving lips. The islanders hated her and would have beaten her up if they had had a chance, but she always went round with a leashed Alsatian. She did not frequent the café or the chilly studio-nave, so our acquaintance was limited to acknowledging her curt nod as she strode defiantly by, with a cigarette in her hand and the dog tugging at its strap. Vibert had grown much happier; he beamed on us and praised *l'amour*.

A Canadian girl with red chapped face, earnest and stupid, turned up at the hotel and hung round us as fellow souls. She was hoping to develop the art of cutting silhouettes and made many efforts at Elza's profile. Once she burst in at a moment when we should have made sure the door was locked, and hastily retreated. A few hours later she returned, keeping up a feeble pretence of calling on us for the first time that day. She too had blundered on some of the scandals. 'I really do think you are the only properly married couple on the island,' she said with pious vehemence. We both laughed loudly, and the poor girl blushed and stammered her way out. But before long she was back to ask us what she ought to do if Mme Vibert spoke to her.

One day we were urgently asked to visit some people whom we didn't know at the other end of the island. We went, were given a pleasant meal and much wine, and at last were shown the surprise for which we had been invited. A wireless set, probably the only one on the island, was brought out and tuned in after long delays, volubly discussed breakdowns, and peculiar noises. Everyone looked at us expectantly and I felt that we were letting them down. Finally I realized that we were listening to someone speaking English with an Australian accent; but who he was, what he was saying, and where he spoke from, I never found out. However I was now able to make ecstatic gestures of recognition and pleasure, and our hosts were satisfied.

One of the fishermen was being married and he asked us to the wedding reception in the village hall. Wine was lavishly poured and I even managed to dance with the bride, a broad handsome girl; but stolid as she was, she was obviously glad when I stopped treading on her toes and delivered her over to her man. She excited much comment among the women of the village through having something pink in her costume; and several of them said that everyone knew she was a cracked vessel but she needn't announce it to the world. A week or so later I saw the couple returning from their honeymoon on the mainland. The large comely fisherlad was striding ahead and greeting everyone, while the girl struggled along behind, with a huge portmanteau on her back bowing her down.

Now and then we went across to Paimpol, to cash a pound or two at the bank, an ancient mouldering place that smelt of Balzac. There was a counter with bars in front of it, and notices on curling paper in faded violet ink. After much banging, a decayed clerk with long frayed moustache emerged from some lair, dusty and snuffy, and tried for a long time to find some excuse for refusing to do business. My only defence was to ignore his objections and keep on presenting the notes, with a demand for francs. He at length withdrew to make his calculations, returned resentfully wheezing, and slowly counted out the money, taking back some small sum at the last moment as he thought up an extra charge.

We liked the port and the old lanes in which sabots clinked, the old woman standing patiently in a doorway made of three great slabs of granite, with a dour room glimpsed through the window, a blurred photo-enlargement ringed with the mourning wreath of glittering white and black shells or beads, whitewashed timber joists and wallpaper showing the rough granite surfaces beneath, a pewter candlestick, a fragment of wormeaten carved timber, men in blue jerseys and patched trousers stained with tar and perhaps even wine-red stockings. The stalwart woman serving us coffee in the port café was hostile till I mentioned that I was Australian, not English. Pausing in her sewing, she called in her small wiry husband to meet me. Come from so far away to see France? I ceased to be a foreigner battening on the exchange and was treated as a friend, under the stained photos of ships and engravings of shipwrecks.

I picked up a torn copy of Loti's *Pêcheurs d'Islande* with plentiful small woodcuts more interestingly full of local colour than the novel. To return to the island we usually went by autobus via Ploubazlanec to Arcouest, passing baroquely muscled Christs at crossroads and finding time for a drink in the sailors' bar of the hotel overlooking the sea. The patron liked to tell the tale of his prize-setter having been out-scented by the fat white dog of his wife, and the setter knew he was being ridiculed, apologetically snorted, and put his head between his paws. There was a marvellous moment as the bus came up to the point above the promontory where we suddenly saw the Channel spread in an intolerable lustre and sown with burning yellow-gold rocks. From here the passage to the island was short.

I was working steadily at the *Satyricon* and revising *Ragnhild*. Perhaps the struggle to define Ragnhild forced me to think about Elza instead of evading the ambiguous aspects of her story, as I would have liked to do. I remembered M. and the sly hints made by the others. I tried to find out why she had left Paris. She had moments of black despair when she retreated inside herself and crouched or lay on the floor, unable to move or speak. How can I help you if I don't know the truth? Tell me, what is it? what crushes you down? She told me a broken tale of Robert falling badly ill and their friends in England ignoring appeals for aid: doubtless they were all owed money. She had to do something. What could she do? For the sake of the child and Robert, who knew nothing of it all, she sold herself. There had been no other way.

Mingled with these admissions were obscure and fragmentary remarks about an unhappy childhood, a beautiful distracted mother, a noble garden grown wild, frogs croaking where the lilies were lost in the matted reeds and ivy strangling the mutilated Venus. Somehow she had been cheated of her birthright and all her life she had been striving to find the cheat out, to regain what she had lost. Before meeting Robert she had drifted from job to job, serving in cafés, in a tobacconist's, a draper's, even kicking her incompetent legs up in a third-rate chorus-row. Always victimized, seduced, driven out, making another hopeless start, dreaming of her lost birthright.

I believed her tales, yet felt that she omitted some essential

fact making sense of the scattered details. My heart was wrung
with pity and I was afraid, chilled and repelled. I hated this
entry into the pitiful secrets of another soul, another body; and
yet, if we were to go on together, I must have some coherent
image of her, something I could trust. Suddenly, from a remark
she made about an operation, I challenged her: 'So you had
gonorrhoea?' She paled and nodded. 'Do you want to go back
to Robert?' She made no definite answer. It seemed that she
did not hold him responsible for any of her troubles. True, his
rebellion against his mother's world had made it impossible for
him to find an easy job, but it was the incapable rebellion
which in fact endeared him to her. Though I did not press the
point, I felt sure from her random remarks that on her return
to London, before taking up with Young, she had lived by selling herself.

I ran out of the house and wandered along the shore by the
pines. But I couldn't think. I felt only a horror. It was not so
much that I made a moral judgment of Elza's past; for her personally I felt only an aching impotent pity. What I couldn't
decide was her nature, her character; and unless I decided that,
I could not understand in the least what was my own relation
to her. The horror I felt was a horror of the void, of the dark
void I touched in her. A void in which all personality broke
down and was lost in a faceless anguish. She seemed to have
no distinctive character at all: to be an image of pure beauty
and the wound of ancient wrong. To save her was to find out
how to give her a personality in place of a strange elemental
confusion of terrors and aspirations, which lacked any centre.

I longed for the harsh clarity of Australian light. In Elza I
felt the chiaroscuro of a rich culture which had broken down
under its own weight and which now existed in a dark cavernous penumbra, lighted by unknown crannies and cracks, with
no way out into the unequivocal day.

But from another angle she was a child, a poor lost child,
who could not tell me the truth about herself because she did
not know what it was, did not possess the words to define the
complex outrage inflicted upon her, could not find the simple
line of growth that would have carried her out of the knots and
cankers tethering her to an unrealized past.

When I pierce your secrecy, Time shudders and dies
and your abandoned mouth, curled from the teeth, replies
but Childhood wonders and broods from your distant eyes

Some implacable terror your passion condones
from the other side of language come your small moans
I see you a faint red flame kindled in a nest of bones

And I possess in one moment as I press on
through closing cones of warmth Time-to-be and Time-gone
the ravished Child and the dancing Skeleton.

I came home to find her crouched where I had left her hours before. Nothing roused her, neither caresses nor exhortations, complaints nor tears. Only at last she revived in an embrace, coming up entire from the depths without a word or a sign to express her change from a deathly numbness to a serene liveliness of all the five senses. I was left torn by a conviction of her duality. She had some absolute integrity and pathos, an immediacy of communion with nature and with all things living (except men in their social existence); I watched her eyes as she watched birds. And yet she had something absolutely broken, a submissive fear that attracted outrage and made her the casual prey of any passer-by. Possessed by corruption, she was uncorrupt.

I lay in our engulfing wooden bed, the roof only a few inches from my face, the wind whistling and blurting through the paper where the wood had cracked apart. I appreciated the *houhou! houhou!* of Loti's wind, ranging from a cavernous noise of tremulous rage to the little flutings of an owl; his lovers lying awake and thinking of the dark sea that would one day flow over them. I thought of the dark sea and longed to put out my hand, saying the one unknown word that would make us recognize one another.

For one thing, I could not think of Elza and Janet at the same time; my will was cut clean in half. And this inner uncertainty of mine, about which I was unable to think, could not but react on Elza, increasing her helplessness. To evade my problem, I told myself that Elza belonged both to me and to Robert; she too was a divided being. If only I could have said to her, 'I love you and I shall never return to Janet, my wife in Australia, we are one from henceforth,' things might have turned out differently. But I couldn't say that for many reasons, one of which was that I had no firm image of Elza, only a series of Ragnhild contradictions. Thus the division inside her in turn intensified my own inner divisions and confusions.

Chequered by the abrupt moments of impasse, which ended because we dared not sustain them beyond a point, our days of roaming and versifying went on. I borrowed a wheelbarrow from the Veuve and collected the *boulets* of compressed coal-dust which were the only fuel on the isle, and burned them in the tiled stove, on which we heated small salted fish. Once as I was carefully chopping some kindling on the tiled floor, the Veuve, who could interpret every sound that went on in her one asset, the cottage, burst in to remonstrate, plead, weep. If I cracked one of her tiles, she would be a lost woman. I was therefore all the more worried when a few days later I spilt a bottle of ink abed, on her beautiful linen. (I can't recall why I was trying to write in such an uncomfortable position.) At all costs I had to conceal the linen, for cash had now run short and I couldn't possibly pay her for the damage and also get back to England. As she did all the washing, the concealment was difficult but I managed it.

Suddenly the time was come to return. We departed in a last flurry of the Veuve's reminiscences and found a large number of people come to see us off, ranging from the lame artist and Vibert to the chemist and the carpenter. The fisherman who carried our luggage refused a tip. (Perhaps it was our thrifty way of living that had made the Bretons like us.) We said *Kenavo*: Till we meet again.

6 · WAITING

WE had to spend the night at Paimpol. At the hotel was another marquis, this time an anglophile sportsman from Dinant. We breakfasted with him and his daughter, a puppy-fat girl who sulked on being told not to eat so much butter. Attracted by Elza, he pressed us to stay at Dinant a few days: at which his daughter flounced out of the room, glaring back at us from the doorway. I was tempted, but our finances were too low. We caught the night boat at St Malo. The weather was rough and Elza lay down, but I felt exultant and stayed up all night, walking the decks and watching the wild waters or drinking whisky with a young engineer, who expounded a *mystique* of machines. We argued and then went out again into the wind.

I dozed through the train journey. The sun rose like a poached egg of bleary gold amid spectral trees, in a yellowish mist. Indeterminate England again, full of strange possibilities. We went to a flat that Kirtley had taken, in some suburban area: where, I have forgotten. We were unhappy there. Kirtley and Elza disliked one another. While she didn't mind cooking her simple dishes of rice or spaghetti and vegetables for me, she couldn't fit in with house running on a conventional scale. Within a few days there was discord and she was refusing to cook. Kirtley, who had lived a life of irritable bachelorhood, tended by his mother with her quizzical humour, considered her a pretentious nuisance; and I was miserable as a feeble go-between, trying to keep the peace by placating both parties. Finally Elza drove me to assert myself and to ask for a definite statement of what was happening, what was my role in the Press. Nothing was more painful for me than that sort of thing. I have never had any personal sense of rights and dues, and

547

I had a more-than-Australian objection to woman's (irrational) protests intruding in the masculine world of careless comradeship. But she insisted and at last I gave in.

Kirtley had arranged to take over a room on the second floor at the corner of Bloomsbury Square. Thus the Press had the excellent address of Five Bloomsbury Square, though our semi-circular window looked out into Bloomsbury Way. This Chiswick Press had been persuaded to print an edition of the *Lysistrata* which followed in all respects our hand-printed version. I felt that it was unfair to saddle Kirtley with my problems at this difficult moment; but when I did tackle him with some apologetic comments about the strain of the existing arrangement, he made things easy for me by agreeing at once, suggesting that we had better part, and offering me £5 a week in advance of royalties on Aristophanes and Petronius. I gratefully offered to help in the office.

I sent the Veuve Lambolet a money-order for her linen, and received a letter of amazed thanks; and I sent the chemist some books by Conrad. We moved to a small flat in a converted house near Earls Court, mainly composed of what had once been a corridor; and I promptly fell ill with influenza, with a mild touch of something like brain fever, a feeling of maggoty pressures in a body of heaving heat. Doubtless the effect of standing up for myself. I then started going fairly regularly into the office to do editorial work and the like. Noticing a reference to Blake's coming death-centenary, I felt the impulse to write something about him.

I wrote *William Blake, Creative Will and the Poetic Image* at high speed. The first chapter was a long commentary on the epistle to Butts in which Blake says that his outward eye sees a Thistle, which his inward eye turns into an Old Man grey. I used this to expound my notion of the transformative force of the poetic image and to develop the thesis of the creative act as a negation alike of the processes of abstraction or of naturalistic and expressionist submergences in the material of life. (In the latter category I should have placed both surrealist automatism or D. H. Lawrence's primitivism.) Here is the conclusion of chapter 1, in which I attempted to say that 'the recoil of the senses' and the fertilization of 'an eternally active mind' were alike necessary:

There is no harm in seeking to express the essential dualism inside all unity by some such set of symbols as long as we remember that, like all antinomies, they must be mingled to produce actuality.

Indeed, the only way to penetrate deeper into unity is to clarify and tighten our conception of the married opposites that are its actualization: Being and Becoming, Life and Death, Force and Inertia, Joy and Torment, Individuality and God, Spirit and Matter – there are scores of headings under which we can define various facets of the dynamic synthesis of unity. We shall find when we return to life that instead of being obliterated by the harsh simplicities of the idea, the nuances of thought and emotion which are begotten by the idea meshed in nerves and blood are multiplied mysteriously. Moreover, Blake of all people insisted on a mystical sharpness of thought, and to approach him with anything less than an effort to achieve his own savage and sensitive precision of ultimate values is an insult.

How then is the tree to become part of myself? Only by growing up on the other side of my eyes, still the tree that is there to be photographed, still carrying the peculiar complex of form and colour which makes it different from any other tree on earth, yet subtly smudged by the lights of my imagination and re-etched by the circling forms of my identity so that it sits somewhere into the ever widening, ever contracting, mosaicked unity of mind. Until this is done, it is an undigested unit in my mind, not a dynamic factor in its unity.

This is the only means by which my spiritual content can be increased. And it is a process which, the more it is put into action, the wider and richer grow its implications and potentialities. Just as the trees in nature, though infinite, if tamely photographed in my head, produce no spiritual action and fade into less than the wraith of a geometrical problem, so the tree-in-my-head, the universal idea of a tree, is also but a wraith if it is left to itself, a bloodless corpse hung on the gibbet of God. But once the tree-in-my-head begins its sport of chafing and knocking with its spiralling energies upon the trees of earth, an infinite series of aesthetic combinations is begun, an eternal game of hide-and-seek with Venus.

Infinity ceases to be a mathematical or philosophic counter. It becomes a symbol of aesthetic emotion, that point where the disdain-ful tree-in-the-head, having done its best like a shaping wind with the tree let in by the eyes, fades, and the wind fades off the leaves. The constructive imagination swoops on the material, sinks through it, sifts it, impregnates every element it desires with something of its fire, blasts the rest out, and then curves back to the closing heavens.

It finds a thistle and it leaves an old man.

I cite that passage as a sample of the positions we were to set out at length in the Press – and also to bring out the fact that my method, however erratic and idealist, was always dialecti-cal and concerned with the unity of opposites. (The term *God* was never used for any form of unity; it expressed nirvana, void, the abstraction from the *pleroma* of reality.) The book went on to discuss the crisis in culture represented by Blake, whom I saw as the first poet consistently taking the creative consciousness itself as his material. But my existential dogmas, my lack of any concrete understanding of history, prevented my analysis from leading anywhere. I tried to distinguish form-image from colour-image: the latter expressing the attempt at a new qualitative synthesis following the crisis brought to a head by Blake.

I sent the MS to Benn. It came back with a polite letter from Victor Gollancz, who had not yet achieved his own firm. Having thus proved to my own satisfaction that nobody wanted the work, I put it aside.

Elza now said that Robert was on a visit to London and she wanted to see him. On what terms they were to meet, she gave no hint, and I did not ask. But I suggested that he should come to our flat. He came and I found him much what I expected: a good-looking well-built product of the public school, with a charm of manner in which were merged both his mother's fine taste and the broadened humanity brought about by his revolt against that mother. Except to tell Elza that their child was well in Paris, he seemed to have no special reason for seeing her. He had indeed more to say to me; for he had roughed out an account of his own life, which had grown into an attempt to criticize his father Gordon Craig for not having fought hard enough for his ideas in the stage world. Though the correlation was only sketchily made, Robert had some idea of linking what he felt his father's inadequacies as a family man with the dilettante element in his work; and I felt there was a good thesis in the project, but one needing more knowledge of the European theatre than either Robert or I had. However, I read and criticized the MS in some detail. Robert seemed thankful, but nothing came of the work. As it stood, it was too slight.

We had several meetings, with the MS our main theme of discussion. I liked him and was jealous of Elza meeting him alone, but didn't like to say so. He appeared to accept without question her living with me. The three of us never in any way raised the problem of our relationship or of Elza's future. After a while Robert returned to Paris.

Kirtley meanwhile was building up the Press, though his comments on the English people and climate grew daily more sarcastic. Once he startled me by saying that though there was every sign of a satisfactory response from the book trade he felt inclined to chuck the whole thing. My heart sank. I foresaw an ignominious return to Sydney on more money borrowed from Norman. And what was going to happen to Elza? While I still theoretically considered myself bound-for-life to Janet, I couldn't imagine myself ever losing Elza. A part of me hoped that she'd find some way of living which would remove her from emotional and financial dependence on me (on anyone); and yet I had resisted any return to Robert, the only visible alternative to her remaining with me. In fact I couldn't now imagine life without her and was involved in a set of contradictory needs and hopes. Whether she really wanted to stay with me and was prevented from going to Robert solely by economic problems, I had no idea.

But soon afterwards Kirtley suggested I should take over the Press on his departure, clearing him from all claims on my part or on Norman's for work done. Neither Norman nor I had in effect any claim on him; there had been no contracts or even verbal allocations of profit and loss. As he was shouldering the whole risk, I had felt that the final word in any monetary consideration should be his. Now I at once snatched at his offer, though he warned me that I should have no capital, only such goodwill as the first two books had built up. The proposition was too much like something brought about by the fate of my poetry to be refused; I had no business experience whatever, but that seemed irrelevant.

In any event I soon had a strong ally. P.R.S. had called on us with his usual irrepressible energy; but over a pint it turned out that he was at a loose end. A Rhodes Scholar who had been a Communist at Oxford, he wasn't cut out for an academic career; nor was he the kind of person who could tamely step into some job in business or the civil service. He wanted a position permitting him to display his panache in a stormy wind; and in our discussion about the possibilities of the Press it became clear that as a champion of Fanfrolico he would find just the outlet he wanted. I was overjoyed. Here seemed to me the fated fellow fighter to match the fated battle-chance. P.R.S. did not accept the Apollonian universe of N.L. as I did, but he shared enough of our Fanfroliconian attitudes to take his place in the ranks with unreserved loyalty.

Winifred was now in her large flat, where she let P.R.S. or his Oxford friends use some of the spare rooms. Among the friends was Tom Driberg, who stayed there a while in a hard-up period. He had broken from his family, quarrelled with his mother, if I remember correctly, and for a while was working as a dishwasher in Soho. He had come down from Oxford, the tale went, after giving a Dadaist concert with all sorts of peculiar instruments, such as typewriters. The star piece came at the end. There was the sound of a chain being pulled offstage, then of a water cascade, and someone entered with a notice: Gentlemen will adjust their clothing before leaving the premises. 'There's only one hall in England that can perform the symphony, as it alone has a water-closet almost on the stage.' T.D. was hoping to start a magazine and I wrote him a brief piece on Beethoven. He was a gentle-mannered quiet person, who not long after rose to fame as William Hickey of the *Express*, starting off the modern type of newspaper column in England. I recall a long conversation with him on a bus, in which I tried to justify my writing verse-dramas of the most unfashionable kind. He agreed to each point with such amiable readiness that I felt driven to find fresh and more vehement reasons at each acquiescent nod.

I recall also having a bath in that flat and towelling myself so vigorously that I knocked over a whole glass shelf and its contents. I was so annoyed at my clumsiness that I didn't even apologize except in a vague mumble; and when Winifred divagated into a panegyric on T.D.'s good manners, I could say even less.

7 · FIRST FANFROLICO DAYS

Elza, who was always good at finding places to live in, secured the top floor and roof of 30 Museum Street for 30s. a week, and we moved there. The place was very handy both for the office and for the British Museum Reading Room. There were two fair-sized rooms and an asphalted roof thick with smuts and grit. I still had something of my Australian habit of never locking doors, but was cured of it by having most of my (sparse) clothes stolen in the first week.

Though I had been in close touch with the office during Kirtley's last days there, I went along with much trepidation on the first occasion of my own control. Nothing was changed, and yet everything was changed. P.R.S. was there, happily brisk, turning over the ledgers, devising all sorts of systems and oblique attacks on the book trade; and I felt sure that together we should be inspired to do the books which would both sell and express our point of view. I threw myself wholeheartedly into the work. Now, while the Press lasted, I did all the typographical designing: often a laborious job – for instance I drew out every single page of McCrae's large *Satyrs and Sunlight*. I also corrected proofs, did most of the editorial work, and translated or wrote a number of the books; our line of country necessitated further a lot of research in the B.M., which I carried out. And though P.R.S. bore the weight of the selling and advertising side, I had to make the final decisions as to our financial strategy, which all the while was highly complicated. Though we took over a running concern, we had no capital, as Kirtley had warned; and if the Chiswick and Curwen Presses had not been ready to give us credit (largely against their better commercial judgment), we could not have carried on a week. Only by the most careful juggling with cash and credit, and by getting each

book out exactly on time, did we survive. The slightest margin
of error or accident – a book delayed a few days at the printers,
or the bookbinders (the worst snag) holding us up a few days
longer than we had calculated, and our system was liable to
crash. Also, needless to say, we could not afford any failures.
Every book had at least to pay its costs by sales at publication;
and the main ones had to make a considerable profit.

Kirtley, before deciding to go, had arranged to publish at
15 guineas a selection of translations which I had done under
the title *Propertius in Love* and for which we had a number of
drawings by N.L. Enough orders had already come in to ensure
the book's success; but I considered the price too high. All we
could do was to make the binding costly and so on. However,
though I kept on feeling a bad conscience about the book, it
sold out and the money was a help to get us started.

The original intention had been to follow up the translations
with my verse-play *Marino Faliero* and Kenneth Slessor's poems,
Earth Visitors. We carried on with this plan. Oliver Simon at
the Curwen Press was very helpful; now as always he was ready
with advice and took special care with any of our work under
his hands. The *Satyricon* had been the first book printed in the
newly cut Poliphilus type; for *Marino* Simon got the Walbaum
type and had the book handset. *Lysistrata* had been praised by
reviewers, but *Marino* was ignored or treated as pseudo-
Elizabethan. I encountered John Rodker on the day that the
T.L.S. found the play wanting in every respect, and he
remarked that the passages cited by the reviewer disproved his
point. I gave him a copy of the book and we remained mildly
friendly. An anxious, intelligent man, he lived near the other
end of Great Russell Street and was publishing his own limited
editions of works like *The Arabian Nights* in lively versions by
Powys Mathers.

Soon after we had moved to Museum Street, I looked in at
the Plough, which was only a few doors away. Whom did I
encounter at first glance but Nina Hamnett again? I said I'd
been on Bréhat, thinking the island something out of this
world; and found that she had stayed there a while before us.
She put me in my place by asking if I'd ever seen any salaman-
ders, as she had, by lantern-light. Without knowing it, I had

come to live close to the other main Bloomsbury pub of the intellectuals. Elza did not drink beer and disliked pubs and every form of rowdy or disorderly living in which her peculiar aura of silence could not function. I myself had no interest in drinking for its own sake; but I felt the pull of the group excitement, the chatter, the meeting with new characters who had something to say about art and life. Not that I often spent an evening at the Plough. But there were after-office chats with P.R.S. over a pint, which now and then led to more than a pint or two. Elza never asked me not to drink, never reproached me, but she made me feel that she suffered. If I drank more than a half pint, I couldn't help thinking of her; and though I was near enough to be able always to tell her where I was, I had a feeling of truancy, which I resented. I still held fast to my Australian ethic of the sexes. Beer was a male prerogative; men drank in a bar and wives stayed at home. Besides, if she felt lonely, she had only to walk a few yards and join me.

I was still sending a few brief letters to Janet in Sydney. In them I gave some scraps of news and stressed the indeterminacy of my position. Later I learned from Elza that Janet, doubtless intuiting that something was wrong, had written suggesting that she could come across, taking a job as stewardess if the money couldn't be raised. (I feel sure however that her father would quickly enough have given her the money if she had announced her decision.) Elza intercepted the letter and tore it up; and she herself wrote an anonymous letter in which she informed Janet that I was in love with a very beautiful woman.

I find it hard to imagine what I should have done if I had received Janet's letter. I still considered her my wife, tethered to my rational side and representing the Australia to which I assumed I would return as soon as the commission of the Press, dropped in my hands by Apollo's well-disguised emissary, Kirtley, had worked out in definite failure or success. Yet at the same time Elza was more and more pervading my life. I cherished a half feeling that she didn't need me, and yet did everything to make her do so. I wanted her to stand on her own feet, and yet encouraged only that side of her which kept her dependent. For one thing, because of my uncertainty about her, I didn't want her out in the world, mixing with other men; it suited me for her to grow emotionally attached, cut off from other sources of strength or satisfaction, and thus unable to seek any of the ways out from our dilemma, which I fondly pretended to myself were always open to her. I was deeply aware of the broken element in her, which called out my tenderness and my pity as nothing else in life ever had; and yet I refused to believe that this was the essential thing in her make-up. For if it was, I could never be so callous as to break our union and complete her brokenness. I clung to our romantic concepts. The poet followed the signs of his fated career through delight and anguish to some battle-moment of significant death; the woman, his image of desire, also sought the fate which was the structure of her character, discovering herself in her lovers. What mattered for both was the poetry, the image, the tension most powerfully precipitating the drama in which they recognized their deepest desire and fear; the dualism inherent in experience ensured that the tension operated most effectively at the tragic level, where fulfilment was realized only in the moment of most intense loss, life only in death. I tried therefore to convince myself that, at the deepest level, Elza was using me for her own development and self-realization, as I was using her – though in very truth I wasn't using her at all; I was desperately bound to her by my fears and hopes, my unknown needs. Daily more hopelessly bound and refusing to admit it.

Someone sent in a hand-written copy of Sir John Harrington's *Metamorphosis of Ajax*. I wrote to Jellinek, whose name was on the MS; and he called in a large, genial person connected with the law, who said that the idea was really Philip Heseltine's. I wrote to Heseltine and he in turn called in. We at once got on well together and I decided to do the book, in which Elizabeth I's godson propounded the virtues of the water-closet, defending his invention with multifarious texts and appeals to authority, which were both a serious effort to overcome opposition and a Rabelaisian parody of scholastic method.

Soon after we settled in Museum Street, Elza took me down to Chelsea to meet a friend of hers, Jeanne, the model of Lionel Ellis, a young painter from Plymouth. There was a flush of suppressed excitement about her, a most unusual thing, as she told me of her friend and waited for the bus to deliver us up at the studio's doors in King's Road. Jeanne turned out to be a well-built young woman, with a mop of untidy hair, who dressed in something of a more careless version of Elza's own clothing. She had a small voice, muffled or sweetly piping, part of the effect she gave of a litle girl dressed up in mama's clothes without being quite sure which things went with which. I got on well at once with Ellis. He had a slight beard and one eyelid hung over its eye: which, he said, helped his painting vision. A gentle and withdrawn character, he did not lack tenacity, but was oddly dependent on Jeanne for his plastic inspiration. Though taken up for a while once with drawing the buttocks of large horses, he showed generally no interest in any other theme than her body; at the moment, as a source of income, he was working on the murals at St Stephens. I admired his big nude and his studies of Jeanne. He had a keen sense of humour and enjoyed life quietly from his corner, though I thought he was too averse from struggle and rated his own dignity too high. He remarked that it was oppressive to see a beautiful girl, so he studied her carefully till he found a flaw somewhere in her looks, her limbs, her walking or her talking; then he felt free from her. A delightful companion, he developed light veins of fantasy with his intimates. Thus, tickled by a phrase in *Dung of Pegasus* about childhood games in an old store-room, 'ridiculous crockery of giants', he kept working out all sorts of variants: the one I best remember consisted of references to the snow we had on our heads as a result of our tall stature. What interested him in painting was primarily the values of plasticity; he did not lack a sense of design, as appeared when he did woodcuts for the Press, but his whole emphasis was realistically on volume, his colour was unimportant. I admired the way he had set himself against all modernistic temptations, though I tried to draw him into experiment with colour; and I saw in Elza's friendship with Jeanne a fated road leading us to an essential ally in the field of art.

He had naïve ideas about Jeanne. 'When I first kissed her, she asked me: Will I have a baby now?' In fact her mother had been a prostitute, who sold her at an early age. But despite many harrowing experiences Jeanne remained a most charming and even unspoiled character. Her good nature was genuine, she was easily moved to sympathy, was very kind and never spoke maliciously. She owned a demure steady delight in life despite her deep fears; the smallest and most ordinary things could intoxicate her with pleasure and wonderment. With all her wayward impulses she had a desire for stability which she expressed by paying down deposits of shillings and sixpences on some monstrous Victorian wardrobe or chest of drawers in a junkshop. The more overwhelming and ornate the giants, the better she liked them, though I don't think she ever collected any of these articles. Going down the street with her, as she stepped precariously on high-heeled shoes that always seemed likely to fall off or cave in sideways, I have seen her dart away to some second-hand furniture shop with a muttered excuse, then emerge with a warm smile, relieved at having added a few more pence to the deposit. She felt less a waif if she had such heavy and respectable objects weighting her down. Her desire for security by means of mahogany lumber did not however prevent her from a continual series of ill-managed escapades. Some of her adventures I heard of from Elza; others I noted for myself. Thus, a wild Irishman whom I had met at Oxford, a voluble excited talker who was well-off if one could judge by his clothes, somehow met her and had a hectic affair. A worse actress than she was, I have never met. I soon came to tell when she was wrestling with an acute sense of guilt, about to slip out and meet someone. Her voice grew smaller and mincingly sweeter; she fluttered about, made the most inconsequent remarks, laughed at herself (as no one else could see the joke), and finally managed her exit, swaying with a special lubricity of the spine. At any time she found it difficult to look one in the eye. Sometimes she made a strong effort, braced herself, and turned on one her eyes of tranquil blue in which the most guileless sincerities were melting; her full lips parted moistly and her hands made feinting movements.

Suddenly, for no particular reason, she disappeared and was found to have taken up with a crippled artist, who treated her badly. She was very fond of Lionel and must have been torn between her need to restore his self-confidence and her wish not to hurt the cripple; she may also have had in mind one of the excessively devious plans for success, wealth and respectability, which obsessed her without ever getting beyond the first stages of incompetent application. Lionel was unhappy without her deft and gentle tendings; and after a while he somehow coaxed her back. They were married. But she spoiled things, perhaps deliberately, by addressing him with the name of the other man at one of the crucial moments on their nuptial night. And she could not stop her philandering. Once I stopped for the night and slept in the upper gallery of the long studio; Elza had gone into hospital for some uterine curetting. Lionel had for some time been telling me about the way Jeanne was talking in her sleep. 'It's wonderful. I know everything she does. I say to her: I know what you were doing yesterday at three o'clock. And she says: How can you know? what was I doing? So I tell her and she's knocked endways.' I guessed that Jeanne was at one of her tricks; and that night I wondered how she would carry on. She couldn't stop her night chatter altogether or Lionel might grow suspicious; but I knew that she'd feel shy with me as eavesdropper. What she did was to put up a modified performance, indulging mostly in an unintelligible babble about an old man bearded like Bernard Shaw. This was the period she was meeting the Irishman, and she knew that I knew.

Ellis said he'd like to paint me. I think the result was a good portrait, and I was pleased at what seemed a Dostoevskian touch in features and mood. (Later however the work was offered to the National Portrait Gallery as a portrait of D. H. Lawrence.*)

---

*I lost the work, as will be later told here. In 1958 Harry Moore told me he had been consulted at the National Portrait Gallery about a portrait offered as of D.H.L.; he recognized that it was of me. The picture, he said, had once passed through the hands of Bertram Rota. I went to Mr Rota, who did not know where the work now was, but found and gave me a photo of it. He paid me the compliment of saying, 'We always thought it looked too gentle for Lawrence.'

In the late summer of 1927 the Ellises stayed with us for a fortnight or so at Winchelsea, in a house on the slopes of the north-east approach. At least Jeanne came for a few days, then developed flutterings and pipings, and remembered that she'd promised to pose for some artist and must really return to London; she went, but Lionel stayed on. We had chosen Winchelsea because Elza stayed some months there once, more or less living with Ellen Terry, Robert's grandmother, in her last days; she had been a favourite of the old lady. And there was a friend she wanted to meet, a girl about whom she showed the same flushed excitement as about Jeanne. The girl however had become stupider, rustically lost, resentfully shy, and at the same time flauntingly painted; the reunion was not a success.

We saw children playing conkers with horse-chestnuts, and Lionel suggested a game. We collected nuts and played, grew exhilarated and looked for more nuts. Lionel stripped to the waist and beat furiously and vainly at my conkers. In the end we must have spoiled the game for the local children by gathering in all the nuts, and I proved I was good at one sport at least.

Winchelsea was the first country town I stayed at in England, and I savoured the square with its church remnant and its broad roads running out, the Georgian New Inn with a spectacled phantom of Thackeray and the tree nearby under which Wesley preached his last open-air sermon, seeking once more to make smugglers conscious of original sin; the vaulted wine-cellars and the gate with its drum-towers and portcullised archway where one had a fine view of the sea and also of the huts and coops marring the shingly waste; the ruined castle on the way to Rye. We had the sea to ourselves when we swam, but somehow we were drawn into visiting one of the coop-dwellers, a retired accountant who fervently declared that he kept himself sane by perpetually beating out copperwork.

We walked to Rye over the shingle, the crisply turfed pastures, the sweeps of sea-gravel, the dunes, and watched the medley of trawlers and coasters in Rye Harbour. And we also walked to Hastings, stupidly taking the dusty main road instead of the coast tracks. Our beards, rare ornaments in those days, caused quite a traffic sensation as we entered Hastings. Still, in lounging about on the flats below Winchelsea hill, I got some idea for the first time of the charms of the English countryside; and Elza murmured accounts of it in the spring with a host of larks, with yellow sea-poppies burning on the tawny-red shingle-sweeps and with golden and saffron flashes in the turf-grass.

In a sand-nook I tried to write a verse-parable on Elza as Cinderella, which was also an account of the struggle of concrete and abstract art – the ugly sisters representing both the repressive forces of society and the thingifying death-trend expressed in abstraction. But I got lost in my symbols. Cinderella grew too pathetic, archaically dowdy, and the Ugly Sisters showed sparks of a new vitality. I gave up and considered the moving waters.

At Ellis's studio I met many painters, such as Mark Gertler of the lobster-tinted nudes and lively Whitechapel Jews, who seemed a solid character glowing with many good sensuous warmths, but who ended by committing suicide. Also Edward Bawden, whose humorous drawings I liked and to whom I gave his first commission. A fraily built painter with a wispy tow-beard, whose name I never caught, kept sniffing catarrhally and once remarked in explanation of his lack of interest in women, 'You see I get rid of so much of it through my nose', imagining that he enjoyed an orgasm with every sneeze. Horace Cole looked in a few times to wink at Jeanne, wrapped pontifically in his huge reputation as a jape-deviser: if he put his hand in his pocket, he was expected to take out a baby or a machine-gun – like Fishey Frank the local snake merchant who was liable to produce a live eel from his trousers. Cole had once boarded a battleship as an eastern potentate, had a famous man arrested for stealing his watch, and held up Piccadilly traffic by digging a hole in the road while wearing the trousers of an L.C.C. navvy.

Sometimes it is said that one always accepts the fashions of the time; only in retrospect they appear silly or ugly. But that was certainly not true of the twenties. Ellis, Elza, myself and the others hated the short tubular dresses with their low waists, which made most women (who have short legs) look impossibly dumpy and clumsy, while the toques and kiss curls we thought the brightest stroke of the devil to degrade Eve since the scandal of Eden.

Unheralded, Laurence, my musical friend of Sydney, now turned up to complicate life yet further. Elza didn't like P.R.S., but she did her best to control her feelings, recognizing his indispensability to the Press. But here was Laurence, another incalculable adventurer, who knew how to warm a woman's midriff with his lordly flattery, yet could not altogether disguise his peculiar streak of chuckling recklessness. She resented the spell he could cast over me: a spell diminished since Sydney days, but still capable of making me succumb to his mockeries, his dares. For the first time since I had lived with Elza, there were a few bouts of heavy drinking; Laurence was a whisky man, a restless quester out of the odder and more dissolute drinking haunts. However, all this did not last long. I pulled myself together and resisted. Apart from Elza's withdrawn eyes, the responsibility of the Press made me afraid of losing my grip on things. Poetry could find its own devious ways of rebirth; but our financial tightrope walking demanded a cool head and obedient feet.

P.R.S. and I had now worked out an extensive programme. There was *Aiax*; and we had asked Ellis to illustrate a selection of Herrick made by myself. I was scheduled to translate Theocritos, Catullus, Aristophanes's *Ecclesiazusai*, and many other works of ancient poetry; and we decided to do complete editions of poets whom we considered neglected: Beddoes, Skelton, Wyatt, Webster, Tourneur, Suckling and many others. Some of these we were to succeed in doing; but we were less lucky with a project of contemporary poets (Yeats, Bottomley, Roy Campbell, the Sitwells). We began on Abercrombie's *Phoenix*, for which N.L. did several illustrations. Abercrombie gave a flattered assent; then at the last moment he grew scared of associating with us and said that his publisher would not let him assign the play for a limited edition. S., who knew him well, said that he was afraid of moral censure and had been much upset by Squire's assault on the production of the play, and that this lack of guts was what had inhibited his development as a poet.

One of my ideas was to use N.L.'s pen-and-inks and etching of Tom o'Bedlam to make up a book with the Elizabethan ballad and Francis Thompson's version of it. Browsing in the B.M., I decided to add various seventeenth-century mad-poems, annotate the whole, and ask Graves to write an intro-duction. I wrote to Graves, who promptly called on us. A tall raw-boned slightly gaunt fellow, with a touch of the wilderness about him, like a mountain dog trying to keep his tail up among the city tykes. I liked him at once. He said that he already had ideas about the ballad and would be delighted to write the essay. We had a drink in the Plough and he asked me to go home with him. After I had run upstairs and told Elza, we went off to the flat at Hammersmith he shared with Laura Riding, whom I felt to be a disagreeably self-centred person with a hard discontented face. In reply to her lifted eye-brows, he elucidated his remark that the Press had done Petronius. 'A Roman high-flyer.' She replied, 'Aw.' (I still don't know what a high-flyer is; but I felt an instant dislike for anyone who had to have Petronius explained by such a term. I may add that I am sure she didn't like me either.)

She had been boiling some corn on the cob for us. But when she managed to spear the pieces with a fork and put them on our plates, they turned out to be as hard as the dried corn given parrots to nibble. 'I thought I'd boiled it enough,' she said with a vague helplessness, which I would have found amusing and charming in most women. Robert set about opening various tins that didn't need cooking. After the meal we walked down to see some friends who lived in a houseboat on the Thames. In a comment about some light effect on faces, as we passed down an ill-lit street, Robert made a sarcastic allusion to Yeats as sentimentally soft; and I wanted to argue. I had been read-ing Yeats's chamber-plays, his *A Vision*, and his more recent lyrics, and had been deeply moved; but I didn't like to admit it in the face of Robert's cocksure contempt for his work.

Laura, I learned, slept always on her back in a definite line of orientation, east-west I think; and she had a number of simi-larly stern ideas. Robert treated her with the utmost respect and tenderness.

They agreed to come and eat with us; and for a while we

were all very friendly. I think Robert liked Elza. He offered to give us his house in Wales, which I should have jumped at if it had not been for the Press; and one day he turned up in a taxi with a pleasant old table for us. He was in a generally rebellious frame of mind, keen for gestures against the establishment; but though his breakaway had its roots in a reaction against the war, where he had been left for dead on the Somme, it had narrowed its scope down to the literary world, and a blow against the powers that be now meant a blow against the critics and the rulers of taste. He had published a poem through the Hogarth Press under a pseudonym and was overjoyed when critics who praised Graves dispraised the new poet (who was in fact rather a dull dog). At the moment he was quarrelling with various writers or publishers and evolving elaborate plots to trip them up and get them technically in the wrong on some point or other. The plots indeed were so elaborate that I cannot remember the details, only the general effect of a furiously spun web. Though his methods were not mine, I approved of his distaste for the literary world and its denizens, and was pleased to discuss the fine points of law and discourtesy involved in his feuds. Gradually all his angers had become focused on to a defence of Laura Riding (Gottschalk) against a world that refused to admit her merits; the crusade for truth and independence turned into a crusade for Laura as philosophic poet. But there was a fresh rumbustious element about his proceedings that I liked. Both he and Laura told at length the tale of the break up of his marriage; and rightly or wrongly I gained the impression that Nancy Nicholson had become fed up with bringing forth an endless round of children and had encouraged Graves to invite over to England his admiring pen friend, with whom he rapidly discovered a soul-affinity.

One night when Robert was with us, an Australian, my brother Ray's friend rather than mine, turned up with some gramophone records. He had worked his way across to England by serving in the fo'c'sle; and he mingled lurid tales of shipboard with excited discussion of the fine dynamic control of rhythmic pattern in the performance of Beethoven's Fifth Symphony on the records (Fechtwanger the conductor). Robert said nothing all the while, and I couldn't make out if he disapproved of the crude Australian jokes or of the passion for Beethoven, though I felt nationalistically proud at the mixture.

I had written another play, *Bussy d'Amboise*, drawing on my boyhood's memory of Dumas's romance for the image of an heroic and foolhardy death. Françoise de Montsoreau I based on Elza; not on her wilful and tormented side as in *Ragnhild*, but on her dreaming hopeful side, melancholy and doomed to betrayal. Bussy betrays his Françoise by an inability to resist the call of various life, the challenge to his male vanity, his bravado. I drew to some extent on P.R.S. and Lawrence for his stormy character, but at root the conflict was that of which I was sharply aware in my relations with Elza; I was trying to wake myself up in time, at the same time evading the issues by glorifying a death in which the unresolved conflict came to a head. We decided to print *Helen, Ragnhild*, and *Bussy* in a single volume; and P.R.S. suggested giving the job to George Roberts, who was acting as a sort of freelance printer. A small sturdy man, who looked like the captain of a tramp-steamer, he was reputed to have sat for the trimly bearded mariner who appears on Player's cigarettes. He had known Joyce and was an encyclopedia of Joyce's Dublin.

One night, at a period when we were in rather dire straits in the Press, P.R.S. rang the doorbell of 30 Museum Street and told me that George must have £50 down or the book would be indefinitely held up. 'All right, we'll let him have it,' I said, and wrote the cheque. Before the end of the week some accounts that we'd given up were unexpectedly settled, and the Press was saved.

About this time Laurence came in one evening, looking worried and flurried. He moved about the room uncomfortably, then sat down and said, 'You know they laugh at you, I don't like it.' I laughed back at him. 'Of course, do you think that's news? How could it be otherwise?' All the same, the information wasn't particularly pleasant. So I delivered a lecture on the nature of art responses. Because a generation or two ago there were important painters ignored, like Cézanne and Van Gogh, nowadays anyone confused, obscure or unconventional is sure of being boomed, because all the advanced critics are afraid of being taken for Philistine frumps. The one thing they can be sure to miss and to slight is grand form and the image of beauty. That's what is new in our miserable world, so it must seem old and stale and misplaced to the hounds of the modish and the abstractly original. Disintegration alone now looks like form, deadness like life. The only tribute they can pay the upholders of form and life is to laugh at them as archaic fanatics, etcetera.

I ended by convincing myself, but Laurence shook his head sadly. 'One has to fit in somewhere.'

'That's the one thing I refuse to do.'

8 · WARLOCK HESELTINE

SOON after the acceptance of *Aiax* I took Laurence on a visit to Eynsford. I wanted to show Heseltine the preface I had written. So far he knew nothing of my work and considered me only an eccentric publisher. He was engaged in rendering on the piano a Victorian oratorio with an ultra-seriousness carried into parody; but stopped and read the essay right through. At once his manner changed and thenceforth for a couple of years I was a close friend of his. He resumed his game of giving an obscene slant to the words of the oratorio, something about opening the doors of heaven.* Laurence was charmed, until his tittering hinnying laugh almost exhausted him; he joined Philip at the piano and tried out his own bawdy variations. We drank up all the beer and hurried across to the Five Bells, where we sat at the back on the garden seats by the rickety table, with the leaves of the trees brushing the sweat from our brows. An old fellow with a white beard full of Kentish vocables helped us to consume the beer, and Darkie, another

---

*Parody favourites were J. A. Maunder's *Penitence Pardon and Peace Cantata*, in which a passage was given the words of the limerick about the Old Man from Newcastle; a Victorian duet *The Fairy Queen* frilly with trills; Reger (defined as the roaring-drunk of music) played on a pianola with rude comments. Nina comments, 'Moeran and Lambert played together with very serious faces. They generally had an argument in the middle and one would push the other off the end of the piano stool.' A ribald concert was normally held on a Sunday morning to offset the neighbouring chapel; the congregation responded with prayers for lost souls. Philip's passion for parodies led to score a *jeu-d'esprit* on Franck's D Minor Symphony for a jazz band, his piece being played in a West End hotel. (After the first amusement, I grew bored with all this parodying, but didn't like to admit it.)

ancient, came in with his sack on his back. Then we carried a beer supply home in a huge earthenware jug. (Darkie did not join us this time; but when he did on other occasions he always insisted on eating at a separate table. Swarthy and bushy-bearded, shy and careful-mannered, he lived alone in a small tumbledown hut. Philip once showed a photo of himself. 'Aye, that's you,' Darkie said, then, scratching his head, 'No, it can't be, you're here.')

We are now too thoroughly caught up in the steady crescendo of uproarious laughters which Philip knew so well how to start off and conduct to a staggering blind-drunk conclusion. I sent a wire to Elza and we stayed on a couple of days. We had a bonfire next morning to celebrate our discovery of one another, and moved on to the pub run by Pansy, a lady with a face of brilliant reds and purples. She had been rebuked by her husband for drinking in the bar, and so she kept a soda-water bottle handy, having previously replaced most of the soda-water with gin.

Early the second morning I found out how effective a retainer was Hal Collins (the alias of Te Akau, a half-Maori, who boasted a cannibal grandmother). He was devoted to Philip and watched over him and his interest with a dark and stealthy eye. I had woken early and felt that I would best restore my stomach and head by a cold shower. The house was dead quiet and I walked into the unlocked bathroom without knocking. Barbara Peach, the small daintily made and reserved girl who lived with Philip, was sitting naked in the bath. I muttered an apology and withdrew. Turning, I saw that Hal had come up noiselessly behind me, crouched for a leap if it turned out that I was intentionally intruding on Barbara. Seeing that my action had been innocent, he nodded and went off.

Hal could improvise systematic compositions, but not write them down. A song of his, *Forget me not*, was taken down by Philip and published by the O.U.P.; and he had a knack with the pen. One day Philip looked in at Museum Street and produced drawings in old broadsheet-style that Hal had made to some ballads of boozers. I at once suggested that he should illustrate a book I was editing, *The Parlement of Prattlers* by John

Eliot. I had struck Eliot's book by chance in my B.M. researches round *Aiax*. I had been thinking of the meagre evidence for any effect of Rabelais on the Elizabethans, and by sheer inspiration turned up Eliot's book on French conversation. In it I found a hitherto unnoted imitation of Panurge in the storm for the use of Channel crossers. The work, though missed by previous researchers, was far livelier than the other French-English dialogues of the period. (Heseltine must have been impressed by such finds of mine. For long after, in 1950, Constant Lambert remarked in a pub when speaking of the fortunate find of some musical MSS in a Cambridge college library, 'It was Jack Lindsay's luck, as Heseltine used to say about putting out one's hand and unexpectedly finding something you want.')

Through Philip I met van Dieren and Cecil Gray. Gray, heavy and silent in a seat of the Café Royal, smoking his pipe and acutely aware of all that was going on, despite his look of somnolence: a man whose critical judgments I much respected, and who seemed well balanced till he momently unbared his fierce contempt for women. And van Dieren groaning as he woke in the morning, complaining that he had to put himself together bit by bit – he couldn't get up hastily or he'd leave parts of himself behind; a man with an obviously rich mind, who had long pondered on art and life, but whose music I could not judge, since, despite the reverence in which Gray and Heseltine held it, I had no chance to hear it played. Somehow I felt sceptical about their insistence on van Dieren as the regenerator of musical style. I suspected, with nothing to prove it, that he was too intellectual, too narrow, for such a role, though I was ready to believe his compositions sensitive and valuably exploratory.*

*I think I now have some idea of the part played by van Dieren and Heseltine in the development of English music: their enlargement of the spheres of interest by their fine scholarly sense, their return to early national sources and their sense of European developments, including the contemporary ones – though they rejected many of these. They felt Vaughan Williams to take too simple an attitude to folksong; yet, admirers of Delius and Sibelius, they clung still to a direct nature harmony as an escape from the alienating press-

On my second visit, Nina was there, living with Jack
Moeran. I had seen her often since our meeting in the Plough,
but without the intimacy of our first acquaintance. She always
had some fresh enthusiasm, such as boxing at Camden Town,
to which she liked to lure a crowd, basking in their clamour
as if she were the entrepreneur of the event. For a while she
was full of the Crystal Palace and her adventures in drawing
London Statues for the book she was doing with Osbert Sitwell.
Now at Eynsford she fell flat on her face on the flagged kitchen
floor and damaged her nose, so that she had to be carried to
bed in a stunned condition. There Hal the handyman washed
her nose in gin and restored her. Moeran merely bubbled in
red-faced confusion. The household had tales of a fancy-dress
protest against the selling up of a woman who had foundered
as a sealyham breeder in a near village. Normally a sealyham
breeder would not have attracted Philip's championship; but
he loathed the house owner, a woman combining the sins of
wealth and religiosity. So he dressed as a magician in his purple
Moroccan robe sewn with spangles and bits of glass, and a tall
black hat attributed to Augustus John. With a red-lipsticked
nose he interrupted the auction with lengthy speeches, backed
by Constant in a huge black beard and Nina in a sheet with
death's-head mask. Barbara turned up half way through,
tricked out as a Tinytot with a bright pink face. A small slight
thing, with smooth hair combed in a thick sweep over on to
the right side, she must have made an impressively wicked
infant. As a detachment of mounted police were announced
in the offing, the masqueraders drove off.

I, too, once delivered a speech on the same green. We had
driven across to drink at the pub, and some tale of

---

ures of the urban (industrial) world, which were reflected in work such as
Schoenberg's. (There were thus affinities to our Fanfrolico positions, which
however were cruder and more violent, and at the same time tried to bite
off more. In the last resort the differences were connected with the differences
between the English situation and the Australian, which we imported with
us and then tried to adapt to the English.)

local oppression like that of the sealyham breeder started me
off on my anarchist desire to see the rulers and the foolers of
the English folk taught a lesson. Several yokels were gathered
chatting on the green and I went over to give a John Bull
speech, waving my tankard to prove my points that a free and
happy life was possible, advisable, and necessary. I am sure
that fourteenth-century rustics would have applauded me and
run for their pitchforks; but their twentieth-century descend-
ants merely gaped. Philip listened with an ironical sneer and
then carried me back to Eynsford.

He was rather pallid-faced, but his neat gingery beard,
added to his dangerous eyes, gave him the effect of a waspish
Elizabethan bravo with a courtly air. I argued with him that
if one was to grow a beard, one should produce a peasant Tolstoyan beard like mine, and that there was no point in shaving
one's cheeks. He told me I was a barbarian and that a beard
was a means to an end, not a master given liberty to mat and
bush over one's features.

I knew that Coleman, the ranting ravisher of *Antic Hay*, was
drawn from him, but I did not yet grasp that he was also
Gumbril, the mild and melancholy man beard-transformed to
a daring wencher. When in 1918 he grew his beard, he was trying to change his character, to become ruthless and forcible,
to dominate women instead of being despised by them.* His
musical capacity was linked with a fine poetic sense; in a way
he remained a frustrated poet finding his lost words in musical
sounds. But if he came to set other men's words, he went on
using words to mock at all conventional attitudes and to devise
obscenities which especially delighted him when blasphemous.
The inside of his privy-door was plastered with newspaper cuttings twisted to read lewdly, with bawdy annoucements and

---

*In letters he stated, 'The fungus is cultivated for purely talismanic pur-
poses', and 'it does have a certain psychological effect on me'. 'It is necessary
for me to make use of any little magical energy-saving devices that suggest
themselves.' Gray cites examples of his verse, and stresses the two sides of
his personality, the mild idealist Heseltine and the bitter revengeful Warlock.

limericks. He laboured hard to deserve the epitaph he composed (Munn being his landlord):

Here lies Warlock the composer
who lived next door to Munn the grocer.
He died of drink and copulation,
a great discredit to the nation.

The name Warlock had been chosen to baffle the critics and editors who he was convinced would never do justice to Heseltine, but it also reflected the demoniac character he had decided to construct. One can easily compile a list of the manifest opposites in his personality as it developed under the deliberate pressures he put on himself. The gentle, even somewhat feminine, hater of violence, and the compulsive brawler; the fastidious youth, once a vegetarian, who took steak tartare as his favourite dish; the benevolent lover of the humble and harmless, who told himself that he hated children, liked birds and snakes, and worshipped cats; the yea-sayer who delighted in finding life 'swish', and the sufferer tormented by what already at Oxford he called 'grisliness'. Gray makes much of the extreme cleavages, but with no effort to explain them, as if Heseltine were simply a schizophrene and the attachment of a label did away with all need to understand.

I think we can get behind the dichotomies; and I feel it is important to understand Heseltine as a typical character of the twenties – that is, one who drove the characteristic conflicts to their limit. Though drinking a lot, there were periods when he shut himself up and worked hard; one has only to glance at the list of his works, and to estimate their quality, to realize that. Yet he had set out to build up a legend, and it steadily swallowed him up. He had created, for the public and for himself, the image of the possessed warlock and he could not run away from it. Whether or not he wanted to, he had to carry on with his drinking bursts. Fresh admirers as well as old kept surrounding him, expecting him to act up to his legendary role. Enclosed in a limelight he had himself fabricated, he felt a growing strain.

It came out in the tarantelle that was liable to snatch him up, send him racing naked in the street or whirl him in strange

acrobatic steps and *pas seuls*, without concern for where he was
or what sort of people were round him. Gray tells how he
mimed his own funeral in that witchdoctor's robe and black
hat of his, intoning the chanty *Walk him along Johnny* in a *danse
macabre*. The strain came out too in his way of dropping dead
asleep, in concert hall or train. The train slumbers became a
problem as they often whisked him beyond his station, and in
the end they caused the wild leap that broke his leg. Jestingly
he insisted that he must have been sober as no drunk ever hurts
himself. I cited Baudelaire's *Litany to Satan* as the corroboration.
And he pointed to the fat volumes of a composer: 'At last I have
learned the true value of his compositions.'

The mild man came out in his non-smoking. Myself, I never
smoked on my own, but could not resist the offer of cigarettes
when drinking. I remember how surprised I was one day lunching with him in a Charlotte Street restaurant when he made
a grimace at the olives and said they were too sharp for him.
As the staple food of ancient Greece they were holy things for
me. But his restlessness made him like motor-cycles. Any idea
or liking indeed was liable to become obsessional. He had a
right-minded objection to the chemical defilement of beer; but
once having taken the matter up, he couldn't stop. It not only
furnished an inexhaustible theme for fiery or fantastic conversation; it also led to an endless, angry, and remarkably complicated correspondence with ministries, brewers, and the
Institute of Brewing. Nothing pleased him more than to read
out the detailed letters sent or come in reply.

He told me that he had refused to have any truck with his
cousin who had done the expurgated version of Petronius for
the Loeb. Such an action was not a passing expression of vex-
ation or the excuse for some squib of wit; it usually led to a
strong vendetta. At a concert he heard a critic say what a pity
to spend a summer afternoon in a stuffy hall instead of open-
airing at Lord's; he proceeded to harass the man with a series
of postcards and even sent him a pair of bellows with instructions as to how to get a maximum of fresh air. A proper sense
of fun and independence of spirit thus became unbalanced,
overvaluing the object of attack. Once, scheduled to talk about
some Elizabethan songs which Victor Carne was to sing on the

air, he went round the BBC staff with a petition for the removal of a musical adviser, unmoved (or rather stimulated) by the fact that the man was in the room. Such tactics could hardly hope to succeed and expressed a wish to be unpleasant more than a hope of achieving anything. At the same time we must recognize the sense of persecution and the wish to exact retribution, a genuine anger at injustice, at the wrong perpetually done to life, and a courageous refusal to reckon consequences as soon as mind and heart were convinced.

The same mixture of qualities appeared in his personal relations. Gray stresses his power of giving himself unreservedly in friendship; and that is true. The strange magnetism of his character for those he liked derived from this ability to give himself in a happy fullness. Yet he could make savage changes in his attitudes to people, the outstanding example being the way in which his hero-worship of D. H. Lawrence turned into a ferocious hatred. Understandably he was hurt by the picture of Halliday in *Women in Love*; but he forfeited my sympathy by having threatened legal action and extorted £50 from Secker and Lawrence. And worse even that the action was the vicious self-righteousness with which he recalled it. Though at the time not sympathetic to D.H.L.'s outlook, I disliked Philip's account of him as a mere neurotic scoundrel. (From Gray's book I learn that he behaved even more badly than I then knew. He wrote to the solicitors urging that *Women in Love* was obscene and that Scotland Yard or the National Council for Public Morals should take action. Gray tries to laugh all this away as an expression of Philip's too-subtle humour; but clearly the latter was violently serious and he did all he could to get the book suppressed.)

D.H.L. saw deeply into him, saw his sexual split. Monogamy, he says, is only for the whole man; split men need two women. So Halliday-Heseltine

wants a pure lily, with a baby face, on the one hand, and on the other, he must have the Pussum, just to defile himself with her. She is the harlot, the actual harlot of adultery to him. And he's got a craving to throw himself into the filth of her. Then he gets up and calls on the name of the lily of purity, the baby-faced girl, and so he enjoys himself all round. It's the old story – action and reaction, and nothing between.

The linking of the defilement-need with the cat-passion (Pussum) is a home-thrust. Philip had a graded set of cat values, ranging from Pussum to Mog the supreme cat; and he showed more tenderness to cats than to women. He had a special cult of the self-red cat and obtained one of the breed near the end. His exasperation with life developed in a definitely sadistic direction. A girl told me how once at a party he took her aside and tried to whip her, insisting, 'Come on, you know you want it'. Later, sober, he apologized and swore not to repeat the performance; but the next time he got drunk, he made the same attack. After that she avoided him, deciding that he was mad.*

His split appears strongly in his attitude to religion. Warlock the ranting boozer was highly blasphemous and rejoiced in nothing so much as a mockery of religion. Yet the mild Heseltine had a weakly superstitious side and dabbled in magic. He had a spiritual guide, 'a model of virtue, uplift, and propriety', comments Douglas Goldring, adding, 'I recall a ouija-board seance I attended in Dublin at which the "control" ordered him out of the room because he was pursued by "evil influences".' While in Ireland he gave a lecture in the Abbey Theatre, with musical illustrations: he was clad in his witch-doctor's robe and showing a long unruly beard, his first magical growth: a beard of nature like mine, not an emblem of defiant dandyism. There were green or amber toplights for the stage, and the performance ended with the Old Man of the Mountains, a commercial traveller turned hermit, exhorting

---

*Gray admits that about 1920-21 Heseltine experimented with Indian hemp. Philip himself wrote, 'The taking of drugs may exalt a man so that he surpasses himself (i.e. his normal self) and proportionately they enable him to sink to a lower level than his normal self could descend to. Everything depends on a man's nature.' I had a strong suspicion several times that he and his closest friends did have recourse to drugs in the course of long bouts of drinking; and I was not the only one to think so. But I have no proof.

the audience to go into the hills and live with the Sun and the Fairies.*

In his *Delius* Heseltine makes a furious attack on that composer's *Requiem* because of the materialist attitude to death. Augustus John tells how he drove with him from Eynsford to Stalham in Norfolk, where the local folksingers met on a Saturday evening. They called in at the parish church.

Philip had just given a rendering of Harry Cox's beautiful but profane song *Down by the Riverside* upon the organ, and we were about to leave the building, when, moved by a perverse whim, I proposed to revive the rites of a more ancient cult by there and then offering up Miss —— [Barbara] on the altar.

At that moment a thunderbolt struck the building, with a flurry of smoke and dust, electric crackles and charwomen's screeches:

a vivid impression of Hell being opened and its devils loose! Philip with his peculiar beliefs in 'Principalities and Powers' was the most shaken, especially as he was about to mount the tower of which a pinnacle now lay shattered on the ground outside. I believe he composed, at the vicar's request, a hymn tune for the church 'as a thanksoffering for our providential escape'.

If now we look back at the pre-Warlock Heseltine we can begin to understand what the split portended and why it came about. The material in Gray's biography – Philip's early letters and the account of him at Oxford by Robert Nichols – show that he had early arrived at an overpowering need to break with the whole existing set up. His father had died when he was two years old. 'A moody, vindictive youth,' he calls himself; he hated Eton and Oxford. Intended for the stock exchange, he found himself on a holiday in France, when about sixteen, not far from where Delius lived, and came under the musician's spell. 'Only fit, as I am, for the lethal chamber,' he wrote in

*During his year in Ireland he musically found himself; he projected, perhaps wrote, an essay on *Music as Number* and 'the employment of hypnotism for the direct investigation of musical thought-forms'. His lecture was entitled *What Music Is*. In 1917 he had his horoscope cast.

February 1913, 'my strongest joy lies in expectation.' Nichols describes him as going through cycles of grisliness and hilarity; a vegetarian pacificist, who admired both Nietzsche and Wagner.

He overflowed with expressions of loathing for Oxford. 'At the age of nineteen, the product of Eton and Oxford is worth a thousand times less than the product of the national board schools.' He repudiated the 'love of empire' and acclaimed 'the things that really matter – which are all the common heritage of humanity, without distinction of race or nationality'. He felt isolated, and, taken away from Oxford in a family financial panic, he schemed to start a magazine, the *Sackbut*. Then came the meeting with D.H.L., the uprush of hopes for a new life with a small group in 'Florida, Tahiti, anywhere', the passionate admiration for D.H.L., the episode in Cornwall, and the revulsion. Meanwhile he has dreamed of starting a private press for books and music, *The Rainbow*. London he found afresh 'a subtle and deadly poison'.

One still wastes much energy resisting and resisting, saying No to the sausage machine which gulps down human individuality at one end and disgorges at the other a conglomerate mass of units organized for human destruction – though this vortex is an influence rather than an actuality, something intangible – one feels it in the streets, in the strangers who pass one by, but one cannot lay hands on it – all the while one must skirmish, be fighting a shadow.

Schemes for taking over a theatre and putting on opera and concerts, experimenting with mime-drama. He married and fathered a son; he yearned for a new start. 'Write to me about yourself,' he told Nichols, 'not a word, though, about London, not a whiff of the old stench that still hangs over the dead past. Let us cut adrift and start anew!' The Cornish spring inspired him. 'My head is dancing all day long.' He felt that he saw Hy Brasil over the sunset sea, and went to Ireland.

A May letter to Delius expressed his sense of the need for a choice of the whole man, a breakaway from the entire corrupted scheme of things:

Material and psychological difficulties combined with other things to produce a kind of climax, a decisive point at which it became imperative to break right away from old paths and choose a new direction – or rather pull oneself out of the mud and regain the path one had slipped away from. The English capital, which our countrymen like to call the hub of the universe, is really a great cesspool – more especially where any kind of art is concerned; if one lives in it continuously for a year or so, one sinks deeper and deeper into the mire until one reaches such a pitch of blasphemy that one begins positively to enjoy one's wallowing. Then comes a horrible moment when the truth of one's position rises up against one – and there is nothing to be done except to clear out of all the muck, or else to sell one's soul to Satan for ever and a day.

Ireland gave him a sense of escape from corruption; he began to mature as a musician; and in gratitude he studied all the Celtic languages, including dead Cornish – partly as an 'effective protest against imperialism', and partly through a hope for 'a Celtic rebirth': though he saw Celtic nationalism as anti-nationalism, 'an individualizing movement – a separating one, at any rate'. He still felt a horror at 'the filthiness of the world at large', at 'the Cimmerian darkness which for most of our race constitutes life', and he still believed he could achieve his regeneration:

If only one has the courage to make no compromise and to be ready at any moment to chuck anything and everything that becomes a nuisance overboard, then not much harm can happen to one. And it is surprising, after a little practice at clearing the decks, what strength and dexterity one acquired in the art of throwing overboard lumber – people, things, ideas, superstitions, fears, fetishes – the whole cargo, lastly perhaps the old creaking ship itself! then one develops wings!

Both the strength and the weakness of his position appear in his formulations about art. He sees the creative image as born from 'instantaneous vision', and he realized that life and art are perpetually in movement. The theory of art as 'self-expression' is for him a proof of the failure of the art impulse:

The self is carefully partitioned, and when the surface portion has become absolutely static and completely cut off from its own roots and from everything that, in its drunken diplobia, it considers the not-self, it proceeds to strut about before a mirror and call its vain reflections works of art. The true self can never be static . . .

He sees the true artist as always oscillating between 'the pure mystic and the artisan', but does not arrive at the notion of the dialectical unity of opposites. He denies the divisions of life (into Being and Doing, Known and Unknown, Conscious and Sub- or Super-conscious), and says there is no sharp transition from darkness to light, from the unknown to the known, 'but a ceaseless becoming and intermingling of the one with the other – which is the unity we call mystical – why, God only knows. It is this free passage through the *whole* of our being, this being *not* divided up into compartments, this being open to the infinite (which is within, not outside ourselves) that alone can make us ' $\epsilon\nu\theta\epsilon os$ a term grossly and almost universally misunderstood thanks to the dichotomizers.' The aim is then 'the realization of the central peace subsisting at the heart of endless agitations'.

There he comes very close to a dialectical grasp of unity, but slides away from it at the crucial moment; the conflicts and the variety are lost, not resolved, in the unity; the agitations are overcome by the central peace, they do not earn it. There is thus a flaw of passivity and resignation at the heart of the rebellion's effort to throw off the rags of the old man and find a new birth, an uncompromising clue to the resolutions of art. Philip rightly claims to have arrived at 'a purely mystical conception of the nature of art'. The whole of his *Delius* is based on this conception.

Here then is the weakness that perverted his rebellion and inverted the adventure of the whole-man into a satanic defiance, a Warlockian foray. The defiance was entirely handed over to personal living; no attempt whatever was made to attack or change the world through art. Philip gave up trying to understand what was wrong with the world and sought his refuge in the peace that was given, not created from conflicts faced out to the limits of endurance – to the confines of truth where unity is grasped as the innermost core of married opposites. And so the peace in fact was phoney, merely a faked counter used to deceive himself and to escape from struggle.

But the struggle went on, between the two sides of his split self. The Heseltine dream of oneness with nature fought to the death with the Warlockian masquerade, in which the defiance of the world shaded off into an acceptance of evil and violence. Instead of fighting violence he took it into himself; and there it tore him to pieces.

9 · FRONTIERS OF FANFROLICO

CONSTANT LAMBERT had rooms not far off, in Lower Oxford Street. When I called on him, it was mostly with Philip; and we seem always to have discussed poetry, not music. 'Your father is the best realistic Australian artist,' I said, rather straining the term *realism* to be friendly, 'and mine is the most romantic.' I repeated the phrases a couple of times in the hopes of evoking some response, some admission of our both sharing an Australian element; but he kept on ignoring the remark. Neither he nor his sculptor brother, whose studio I visited, seemed to want to mention their father.

Constant asked Elza and me along to one of the melodramas performed at Collins' Music Hall, where he had taken two stage-boxes. After drinks at the Plough, we piled into taxis and drove out. Nina has recorded the event. 'The play was *The Executioner's Daughter*, and it was a masterpiece of horror. It was played by a stock company and the executioner's daughter was supposed to be sixteen and have a lame leg. She was in reality about forty-five. The villain was a splendid specimen. He had black bushy eyebrow, fiery eyes, and a large black moustache. He seemed fascinated by Constant and in the intervals of murdering people he would pop his head into the box and glare into Constant's face. In the play nine people were bumped off and the General Post Office blown up.' We were near enough to inspect all the dints in the heroine's pudgy knees and hear the hoarse voice of the overworked prompter.

We had drunk copiously in the long bar during the intervals. After, we hurried to a nightclub and the party broke up. Elza and I ended in an underground joint with green lights and a barman dressed as a Hottentot, with an assegai to threaten the rowdy. A girl with big purple circles painted round her eyes was weeping into a gramophone; the scratched record sounded as though hiccuping through a jazz-moan. Bits of ceiling plaster fell into the whisky that tasted of methylated spirits and rust. A snub-nosed girl was proving that she could fit her left breast into a champagne glass pressed against it. I felt wonderfully happy and at home; but Elza was complaining of the bad air and wanting to go home. Generally I was loath to drink more than a pint at the start; but, proud of my Australian stamina and my desire to push all things to their extremities, I found it hard to stop after the sixth round and impossible after the twelfth. However, after scowling at Elza's complaints, I went with a bad grace and never found out if the girl could get a glass to stick on each breast without any support.

We went once again to Collins' with Constant, this time with a less noisy group. Eating first at a Soho restaurant, I asked another of the guests, an old friend of Oscar Wilde, what he thought Oscar's opinion of Norman's art would have been. 'It would have confirmed his worst suspicions. I think,' he said. In the play the seduced heroine trailed round with a doll which now and then leaked sawdust as she rocked it to sleep.

It was in the stuffy cellar of the first night, I think, that we met Basil Bunting, poet. Anyway he called on us soon after, and for a while often looked in. Elza was the point of interest, which may have increased his shyness. Once when I remarked on a letter of his in the *Nation* learnedly commenting on Dante's icy layers in hell, he blushed and stammered that he had only done it because he was after some academic job and wanted to impress. Perhaps he got the job, for he suddenly disappeared.

Among my own friends was Philip Henderson, who later edited Morris's Letters as well as working on Marlowe, Skelton, Samuel Butler. In recalling those days he says:

To me Elza always seemed an elusive watery Ondine-like creature in a long green dress who seldom spoke and smiled with a wry twist of the lips. Perhaps she appeared to your friends rather as Janey Morris appeared to Morris's friends – beautiful, remote and cold. But I used to love coming to your rooms in Museum Street, just to listen to you and the whirl of ideas about Blake, Wagner, Nietzsche,

Rubens, and talk about Elizabethan drama and fine printing and stories of your father Norman capering faun-like in the wake of Bacchus and his pards through Australia. I found it all exhilarating and delightful, and lived at that time in a state of intoxication between writing poems and making love and bathing in long evenings of Wagner and Strauss in Covent Garden, thinking nothing of standing for anything up to five hours outside the opera house for a gallery seat. This period was for me the time of discovery of everything that was to matter most to me in life.

Elza was aware of her coldness, her watery element. She often used to say to me, 'I'm a fish. I live cold and deep down like a fish.' And her favourite picture was Botticelli's *Venus*; she had the head with its blown snaky tresses in a full-size reproduction over the bed, the only picture she ever had. And rising up into the waking day, she seemed indeed that Venus, sea-pure and only that moment sprung from the foam, her flesh made marble with the cold beating of the wind on all its pores.

Roy Campbell was another poet who showed up now and then in the Plough with his wife and who was keen on Nina's boxing parties. I admired his verses for the stark images and explosive colour virtues that marked him as a fellow colonial in grey England; and I wanted to do a book of his in the Press. Nothing came of it and before long he went south. I remember him lamenting, 'Give me a theme.' Which rather sapped my admiration. He felt a strong poetic force, but in something of an emotional vacuum; he didn't know what to exert his sinews against. His efforts to live a tough life, or at least the appearance of one, I always felt, came from an inner void – the Africa which he had left without understanding and which had become a vast spiritual desert that he wanted to colonize single-handed, a small boy with an epical dream.

Round the corner in Great Russell Street was the Poetry Bookshop under Harold Monro. I went several times to hear him read poems; and though I was anti-Miltonic, I especially liked the way in which he brought out the full rolling reach and the local vortices of rhythm in *Paradise Lost*. A soft-voiced wistful-eyed Irish lad, Mike, a Plough-frequenter, had taken up with Nora, a well-built wench of amiably accessible body. They lived together, pleasantly squabbling and using devious tricks of money-making, until some beady-eyed rogue in the Plough, afraid of a police-hand on his shoulder, deposited with Mike his stock of Paris-printed books which described perversions in the flowery prurient way of such stodgy commodities. Nora read them avidly, though one would have thought she needed no further education in such matters; and her anxiety to try every detail of the advocated acrobatics led to a strain in her relations with Mike, who, though totally lacking in scruples of any kind, was a lazy fellow. Nora grew resentful and accused him of cheating her in various ways. He tried his blarneying voice in vain; and one night, worked up by a commiserating tart friend, she stabbed him in the back with a carving-knife as the Plough was emptying. I had passed them about a minute before, as she stood pushing at him, shrouded in a heavy cloak, and he leaned against the doorpost, giving the soft answer that stirs up wrath, when he turned away, she stabbed him. Carried to hospital, he told an improbable story of falling on a knife when trying a circus trick, and no prosecution ensued. But instead of returning to Nora he took up with Harold and acted as his shop assistant. Several times we had drinks there after pub closing. One night, with Mike sitting on his lap, Harold told us shamefacedly how he'd once managed to embrace his wife. He had been out riding, and came in heated and exhilarated, saw her lying half asleep on a couch with disarranged clothes, and was moved to mount her as if she were still the mare he'd been riding. He considered the event remarkable and disgraceful, needing an elaborate psychological explanation, and insisted it had happened only once.

Not long after Mike went to stay with the crippled artist who had lured Jeanne off: in Highgate, I think. There was a press for printing etchings there and he wheedled out of me the set of small plates etched by Norman for Sappho's poems. I knew it was rash to hand them over but I liked his handsome guileless guile. He never printed the plates, and when we needed them for our edition, I had to push my way into the house and forcibly collect them.

Among the Plough dwellers was a tall very flexible Welshman whom we called Sexton Blake, as he was the main ghoster for the periodical devoted to that detective. He smoked a huge pipe, perhaps to keep in character, and was always groaning at being behind with his instalments. Indeed he lived the life of a hunted criminal rather than of a masterly detective; he often had to flee or hide from his editor's emissaries. Once he lurked in the Plough privy till I came to tell him the hunter had retired. At times he worked out the adventures to go into his next instalment, drawing plans on the table with beer-dipped finger and puffing energetically at his pipe as he spoke in his squeaky excited voice. When not in the pub he lived at the Post Office Social Club, where the counter of a dismantled post office on the ground floor served neatly as the bar. At times he gave up being Sexton Blake and impersonated other characters in the endless saga which he both lived and wrote about, slinking in with a Cockney accent or pounding in the bar as he squandered ill-gotten gains. His mania for dressing up infected the other denizens of his odd club, which Nina knew better than I. She thus describes the goings-on. 'In the morning all the inhabitants appeared in fancy dress when the bar opened. They crept down the almost completely dark staircase early in the morning and sat in the dark on the stairs drinking beer. At eleven o'clock they would all come into the daylight of the bar. A Frenchman appeared dressed as an Arab. He wore a face-towel round his head for a turban and his wife's purple dressing-gown. His wife would appear dressed and painted up like a ghost, which was not very encouraging for the rest of the guests, who frequently were not feeling any too good themselves. Sexton Blake would appear about every ten minutes in another disguise; as a criminal, as an effeminate young man, and as a dope-fiend. The latter was the best as he painted his face greenish white and put black rims round his eyes and made terrifying faces.' Never have I known any writer so possessed and engulfed by his material. In Paris he would have been a leading surrealist; in London he was a poverty-stricken improvizer of sixpenny-dreadfuls.

A character as tall, as assiduous in his Plough attendances, as addicted to a pipe, but giving an effect of bluff sanity, was Hanchant, in charge of some art-and-crafts society, the magazine of which he edited. His passion was the collection of street-ballads. I contributed several articles to his magazine (one on Ellis, one entitled *The Artist as Goya*) as well as a series of verse-parodies; and began to feel the need of a periodical of our own. Arts-and-crafts was not prosperous, and Hanchant was a man of infinite resource and sagacity, with shifts that were obviously too good to be true. Sweeping his hair back and nodding at one with his pipe, he explained hoarsely how a fortune waited just round the corner; but somehow the corner was never turned.

Another haunt lay near St Martin's Lane, a club where Hal Collins, familiarly Collie, had served as a barman and where he painted the walls with vast nudes, lumbering or snoozing, against a tropical fury of greens, blues, reds. The speciality was advocaat, made of methylated spirits mixed with sugar and custard powder. (An equally fiery drink was purveyed at the Fitzroy, called Jerusalem Brandy; but what its throat-rasping ingredients were I never found out.) From a piano on a platform the club owner used to sing *Old Mrs Dyer the wretched baby-farmer*, with the drinkers joining in the chorus – among them a rubicund priest with a bellowing belching voice that would have wrecked any Gregorian chant. Nina was proud of having sung *The Servant Girl in Drury Lane* there. Like many of the clubs, it went down in a police raid and the elephantine nudes scaled off from the walls. Most of our drinking was done in a space bounded by the Café Royal, the Fitzroy and the Plough, but there were a few visits to outlying sites like the Prospect of Whitby, where one could gaze out at the passing ships over tankards of meditative beer.

On the street floor of 30 Museum Street was a bookshop, Davis and Orioli, which only later I found had been started off by Norman Douglas's friend, Orioli, in 1913. It was now run by a man with an imperial beard and a calm, capable and desirable daughter, with a Russian husband. I rarely looked into the shop as I couldn't afford to buy the tempting books. But in the basement, amid tottering book piles, there were occasional drinking parties at which Mike sang in his fruity Irish voice, emotion-throbbing, and the mad-eyed Russian in his hard metallic voice, cutting with the sharp edge of aggress-ive melody and the beat of indefatigable folk-feet dancing.

Though I did not much like the Russian, his singing woke something deep in me and I wanted to dance, on a table, a mountain top, the axis of a star spinning out of chaos.

Tommy Earp often looked into our office in the later afternoon, bringing us news in his scratchy scrannel-pipe of a voice about the latest French verse. He gave me poems by Valéry, Aragon, and others; Éluard I knew from *Transition*. I set out to translate the *Cimitière Marin*, but stopped half way. With Tommy I also discussed Hegel, Croce, Gentile, with rumours of Husserl and Heidegger. Liam O'Flaherty, too, had become a close friend of ours. In the Plough or the tea-shop close to the office he sat and discoursed, telling long tales of the Troubles in his persuasive voice, with his blue eyes flashing. These tales were better in the hearing than they ever were when written down. He wrote with sweat and pain, and in addition was having much argument with his wife at home. Keen on horses, he often asked me to go over to Ireland and see some of the small-town races; we even got as far as planning a trip. But lack of funds, the need to stick daily to the work of the Press, and a disinclination to leave Elza for more than a few hours, came together to prevent the carrying out of any such ideas, however overwhelming and necessary they had seemed in discussion over the pint pot. Liam himself was never a drinker; he found enough inspiration for his tales in cups of tea. Such a hypnotic talker also had less distractions to cope with in holding his audience in a café than in a bar.

I had also come to know Dennis Bradley, the tailor of Bond Street, who put eccentric advertisements (common enough now, but then very unusual) in the *English Review* and who had written the best-selling book on clothes, *The Eternal Masquerade*. He was also a spiritualist. At one dinner at his place Austin Harrison talked about the old days of the *Review*, with Norman Douglas on the staff and works like Masefield's *Everlasting Mercy* appearing in the pages, and made *double entendres* to embarrass his young daughter. Oliver Baldwin delivered a pacifist tirade and declared that if the Old Men dared to launch another of their wars he would launch a movement of passive resistance. 'You can enrol me,' I said. Mrs Bradley was worried about the effects of spiritualism on Dennis and consulted me about it –

presumably I was considered an expert on account of my father's interest in spirits. She expected a breakdown and thought she'd get him away on a Mediterranean boat trip. That night a strapping girl with a horse-face drove me home, as the whisky had gone on till the late hours. As she chatted in her hard breezy voice and wondered whether or not she'd ask me into her flat for a final drink and a hasty rape, I asked myself why I hadn't taken Elza along. It wasn't that she lacked presentability, being beautiful and much better-mannered than myself; it wasn't that I was scheming for a life of my own, with culminations in the wooden arms of horse-faced girls. Rather, it was a feeling I had no real place in such a world as Bradley's and was myself there on sufferance, so that I didn't want to include a second person in an invitation which I felt had come my way by some accident. But it was also an admission that my emotions about her were still unsettled, pulling in different directions. And I was afraid of the criticisms implied in the aloofness I knew she would assume, the spirit-damping question readable in her eyes: Why waste time in such pointless activities?

And why indeed waste it? what was I looking for?

I felt Elza as a sort of poetic conscience, which made me feel stupid in my unaccompanied sallies, so that I seldom went to the same place twice. Through Bradley I met a capable but uninspired sculptor Sykes and dined at his flat, which seemed to consist of large rambling stairs and corridors. And I went once to the Belgravia house of a retired Australian governor who had bought one of N.L.'s water-colours of Pavlova. Mentioning to P.R.S. that I had met there a vague young man with the name (I am sure) of Lord Smith, he jeered loudly, 'What, your first Lord! Oxford's lousy with 'em.'

I had written to Norman Douglas saying that I wanted to dedicate the *Satiricon* to him. He replied affably. 'Many thanks: I'll find living up to it *uphill* work.' As a result a steady correspondence developed and I must have had some fifty or more letters of his, many of them long, when I destroyed my MSS in 1931. Through our project of a complete edition of Beddoes I met Sir Edmund Gosse. He was old and tired, but charming. He assured me on his word as a scholar that every possible effort had been made to find anything of Beddoes in German publications and that the texts in his editions were carefully collated. Nothing would ever be found that wasn't in those editions. Except the Juvenilia in the Charterhouse Library, I said. Yes, except the Juvenilia; he hadn't thought them worth mentioning. Then he remarked, 'As one gentleman to another, can you assure me that you have enough money in your firm to carry your scheme through?' Staring him straight in the eye, I said, 'Yes.' But then, as I didn't consider myself a gentleman, the oath was not as religious a matter to me as Gosse had supposed. In any event I felt sure that by hook or by crook we'd get the two volumes out. A few weeks later Gosse gave us a good review of the Herrick book and *Loving Mad Tom* in the *Sunday Times*.

We had the texts set from Gosse's editions – by the Crypt House Press: the right sort of name for Beddoes, we thought. But when I came to correct the proofs by the first editions in the B.M., I found that Gosse had had no respect whatever for their punctuation, capitalization, and so on. I did what I could to repair the texts without running us into ruinous costs; but I had lost my faith in Gosse as an editor. I added extracts from the Juvenilia for which I went down to the library of Charterhouse School at Godalming one hot day, lunching on beer and cheese at a pub not far off; but it was now too late to go chasing for any possible MSS of the later work or letters. However, after the edition appeared, with the Holbein Dance of Death cuts as decorations, I was invited to talk to an Oxford club about the poet. A member of the club was a Beddoes who was descended from a close relation of Thomas Lovell; I was put up at Worcester College and next day the Provost showed me some copies of Beddoes's letters, including the famous last one, in which I recognized at a glance many different readings from those in Gosse's texts. It was my final lesson as to the reliability of genteel Victorian scholarship. However, our edition revived interest in Beddoes and thus led to the correctly edited texts of Donner.

Before the lecturing visit I had gone up to Oxford at the request of the university printer, whom we had asked to print the Beddoes. To my surprise I was asked to stay the night and was shown over the works, which seemed to me ramshackle in their organization – though I enjoyed seeing the seventeenth-century Fell type still being hand-cast from its original matrices. In our after-dinner conversation it became clear that the reason for asking me up was to plumb the delicate matter of Fanfrolico finances. The printer did not have Gosse's downright method of gentlemanly appeal, and asked me many questions. In talking about Kirtley (who in any event was no longer connected with the Press) I casually remarked that he had been on the Sydney stock exchange. I saw that the information was being carefully tabulated in my questioner's mind; and only then did I ask myself exactly what had been K.'s office position. I hadn't meant to infer that he was a full-blown member of the Exchange, but that, I saw, was the way in which my remark was being taken; and obviously on my departure the lists of members would be consulted – and no K. would be there. I could easily have retrieved my words by saying something about K. having been chief clerk, or manager, or something of the sort, in the firm for which he worked; but the longer I put off doing it, and the more clearly I foresaw the process by which I was going to be nailed down as an unreliable boaster with forged credentials, the less capable was I of saving my face. Naturally, about a week later we received a letter from the O.U.P. regretting that owing to pressure of work they could not undertake our Beddoes. And who can blame them?

Eric Partridge, whom I had known well at Queensland University, got in touch with me. He was keen to have a try at publishing, and for a while we discussed the possibility of his coming into the firm. But without a considerable increase in capital there was no room for a third person with full rights; and I at last reluctantly had to say so. However we agreed to publish on commission his biography and selection of the writings of Robert Landor, brother of Walter Savage; he had done a thorough job of research, though overvaluing Robert. But in his determined way he proceeded to organize his own press, the *Scholartis* (for which he later took over our rooms in Museum Street).

P.R.S. used to do a day's work for the *Sunday Worker*. I told him, 'I'm financing your party, since you take off a workday to help the paper; but don't think I'm complaining.' The anti-socialist positions I'd accepted from Norman were being cor-roded, by my anarchist reactions to the English scene and by P.R.S.'s political enthusiasms. Not that he ever tried to convert me. But through him I came to know Charles Ashleigh who, though English, had been in the American I.W.W. and who therefore had a good supply of rebel songs. One night, in the week Elza was in hospital, he and a dozen others came up to our rooms and sang folk or working-class songs till the early hours. Some of the latter I felt sure had never seen print and I wanted them written down so that the Press might issue broadsheets; but I never got the words.* In the moment's excitement I told Charles I was going to join his Communist Party.

Next day P.R.S. disapproved. 'It's all right for a man of action like me, but you're a poet and you mustn't belong to any party.' Yet he knew the poetry of Mayakovsky, which he introduced to me. I made a slight effort at some translations, but could not carry them through. However, with P.R.S. I worked on *The Scythians* of Blok, which we later printed in the *Aphrodite*. I also translated many Essenin poems on my own, putting one into our periodical.

In a small book, *Kookaburras and Satyrs* (1954), and elsewhere, P.R.S. has stated that:

I explored Marxian Communism, having joined the Communist Party in Brisbane in 1921, but discarded it in 1926, when I discovered that it was only banditry disguised as a political philosophy, based on resentment and hatred, and completely lacking in human kindli-ness, toleration and humour.

---

*I responded to these, given straight, as I never did to the parodied versions of popular culture so characteristic of the decade – whether Elsa Lanchester was singing *Sell no more drink to my father*, or Gwen Otter at one of her Sunday parties at Chelsea was reciting Ella Wheeler Wilcox's *The woman is stoned but the man may go*. Huxley might lament the passing of the last stages of a lively popular culture; the intellectuals revived its songs in order to jape them or made slumming visits like those to Collins'. My impulse was always *not* to laugh.

This statement seems to have compressed a development which in fact took several more years to mature. In 1926, however, P.R.S. did leave the Party. He remarks, 'The circumstances of my resignation were, though unimportant in themselves, widely publicized by a question in the House of Lords, a debate in the Oxford Union, and even a leader in *The Times*. My room-mate in The Queen's College, Oxford, at that time, Tom Inglis Moore, is one of several, in Australia, who know the circumstance.' In that year he got into trouble for distributing Gandhi pamphlets to Indian students; and in a letter to me in 1961 he confirms that this event was what made him resign from the Party.

You might also remember that I was actually sent down from Oxford for twenty-four hours by the Vice-Chancellor's Court for spreading Communist propaganda among Indian students. This on the complaint of the Earl of Birkenhead who revealed it in the House of Lords. There was big excitement about this when the Oxford Union carried a vote of censure on the Vice-Chancellor's Court for sending me down. The story made headlines in the London press and a sub-leader in *The Times*. Anyway, as usual, I was right, and where is the British Empire now?

The dispute was then with the University authorities and *not* with the Party. In fact P.R.S. mentions in this letter that he 'wrote many book-reviews in the *Sunday Worker*, applying the Marxist basis to evaluation of bourgeois works'. And in 1929 he was declaring:

Anarchism in immediate working-class politics has long been put on ice, first by Marx in Bakunin's day, and still more recently by Lenin in *The State and Revolution*. The modern anarchists (if any) are a mere handful of die-hard syndicalists with a flavour of Tolstoyan watery 'non-resistance' theory which washes them out from the field of action entirely. The revolutionary working-class movement of the 20th century is and will be Communist ... Exit the Bakunin principle, exit Trotsky. Enter Stalin, up-stage, sits at desk quietly, works.

Strange words for someone who three years previously had

decided that Communists were bandits.* In a note in *Biblio-news* (Sydney, February 1959) P.R.S. fills out the account of his earlier literary activities on behalf of the Party:

My Oxford vacations, before I had resigned from the Communist Party, were spent chiefly in Paris, in company with other students. Tom Inglis Moore was one of my companions on some of these expeditions. We spent most of our time blowing froth in the Café du Panthéon. I had friends there among the students from the Sorbonne. Two of these were Communists – one a Frenchman, and the other a Russian Jew [Michel Zipine]. That was in 1925 and early 1926 ... While I was in Paris, I was busy translating (from the French) two books by V. I. Lenin. These books, *Imperialism* and *On the Road to Insurrection* were published by the Communist Party in London in 1925 and 1926. They were the first works of V. I. Lenin published in English translations. While I was in Paris, I also learned a little Russian from my Jewish Communist Russian student friend. With his aid I translated into English Alexander Blok's poem, The Scythians, which was later published in *The London Aphrodite*. I also translated Mayakovsky's poem *The Death of Lenin*, which was published in *The*

---

*My brother Philip had the same impression as I had; in 1939, in *I'd Live the Same Life Over*, he wrote: in autumn 1929 'Inky was a volatile Communist, with spasms of anarchism, during which he would drink noisily to the memory of the great Bakunin, while he boasted of donnish cabals at Oxford, due to his socially heretical soapbox speeches; therefore it is most difficult for me to realize the change that has evidently swept over him. He is now back in Sydney, having launched into publishing there, and were it not that Lionel occasionally sends Peter, and Peter passes on to me, his monthly, *The Publicist*, I would refuse to believe that that light-hearted, generous Communist, Inky, could have become a vehement cheer-leader for Japan and German political philosophy: pro-Nazi, pro-Fascist, at least in theory. But whatever faith Inky might accept, he would accept it with such zealous excitement that it would temporarily blind him to everything else. Such was his nature, such was his charm. You heard him approaching a pub many, many minutes before he flung wide the door and entered bellowing for drinks all round. Then there would be back-slapping, laughter, excitement that seemed to tinkle thrillingly along the very glasses on the shelves. He stirred a pub to life.'

Communist Review (London). These were the first works by Blok and Mayakovsky to appear in English translations.

The two Lenin works were in fact published in 1926, with no translator named; and though they were not the first writings of Lenin done into English, P.R.S. might justly feel proud of being responsible for the version of such an important work as *Imperialism.** 'With these and other efforts, during my five years membership of the Communist Party, I earned a little niche in the Communist Hall of Literary Fame.'

One of the singers I had met with Ashleigh was a coarsely handsome Cockney girl who lived round the corner in a flat she shared with a Canadian nurse. She was a Communist and worked for Arcos, the Russian trade delegation. And she was having an affair with the representative of an American publishing house: which worried her a lot. Was it right to accept the embraces of someone who was not only no comrade but was also the envoy of a capitalist firm? Her qualms did not stop her from the affair, but spoiled things between the embraces. The nurse had worked during the war with my uncle Daryl, who had turned the family art knack to account by making surgical drawings in a military hospital.

The compressed account of people and events in this chapter may give the impression that we were gadding about and drinking all the time. In fact it covers about eighteen months, most of which was spent in hard work, as a glance at the list of things we turned out will prove. P.R.S. and myself took £5 each a week from the earnings, and never once during this period did we exceed that sum. When things had become more stable, we employed a typist, a plain but efficient girl, so that P.R.S. would be more free to concentrate on sales. At publication times the three of us got down to making up the packages and carrying them to the near P.O. P.R.S. was also working on Nietzsche's *Antichrist*. We wanted to do new translations of all Nietzsche's major works, and began with the *Anti-*

**State and Revolution* appeared 1919 (Allen & Unwin): *Left-Wing Communism* 1920 (C.P.) a couple of pamphlets 1919: *Will the Bolsheviks Maintain Power?* 1922. The passage from Mayakovsky's *Lenin* (7 pages) was printed in the *C.R.* January 1926 as by P.R.S. and M.Z.

christ because there were several of Norman's pen-and-inks that went excellently with it. P.R.S. made a fine job of the text, and we had what we thought the brilliant idea of printing it entirely in Poliphilus capitals, to give it the monumental effect of a Roman Inscription – though it was not easy to read except in small bits. At the same time I was working over my *Dionysos*, mainly revising passages where I could bring in diagrams derived in idea, though different in application, from those in Yeats's *A Vision*. We issued the book with illustrations from Titian, Rubens, N.L., Turner, Blake, Goya. My Blake book we had printed earlier; it at once sold out and we issued a second edition with a new chapter. This was the only book, apart from a collection of my lyrics, which we did not publish in a limited edition.

All the while I was doing research at the B.M., mainly into seventeenth-century poetry on the popular level. Only a small portion of this work went into *Loving Mad Tom*. Among other things I was hoping to produce a critical edition of Rochester, to follow the rather haphazard omnibus issued by the Nonesuch Press; and had sketched translations of several dialogues by Plato, to go with our Nietzsche series. As a preliminary work I collected and published *Inspiration*, an anthology of comments on the creative process by poets, artists, musicians. I was also working on Donne and the metaphysicals, and hoped to produce a series of selections. I had almost lost touch with contemporary writing, and joined Mudie's Library, which was close at hand. The first book I took out was the first volume of *Scrutinies*, which excited me very much, especially the long essay by D.H.L. on Galsworthy. Almost all the essays woke my hearty assent and for the first time since I landed I felt that I was not alone; somewhere there was developing a body of critical opinion with which I felt a considerable kinship. I wanted to get in touch with the editors, but we were so busy I postponed the matter.

In a prospectus P.R.S. outlined our policy, saying that we wanted effects neither 'showy nor stodgy', but 'adequate to express the individuality of each book (not, be it noted, of the typographer, who should be much more in the background concealed in his beauty parlour, than are several too-shining contemporaries)'. He added that 'in fine book production the question is not merely how to print finely, but what to print finely', and defended the use of illustrations. I contributed a credo in verse, which began:

> *Disguised as publishers, perhaps,*
> *We, the last simple trustful chaps,*
> *believing poetry has power*
> *to clap wild heaven for an hour*
> *upon a new earth glittering*
> *with rhythm lacing everything –*
> *we have essayed, the best we can,*
> *to temper prophecy to man;*
> *to tune our trumpets till their rage*
> *fills the advertising page . . .*

P.R.S. had pushed me into writing a novel, *Face of Poetry*, with the aim of entering it for an historical novel competition by Chatto and Windus; but the result was poor, an attempt to translate some of my Elza problems into an Elizabethan setting. However, in pressing me to do the work, P.R.S. showed a good sense of the direction in which lay such talent as I owned – though I was still too far from the everyday world to do much with the genre or to get anywhere near my aim of 'bringing a Dostoevskian tension into the picture of the past'. I unwarily mentioned the MS to Bennett Cerf, a pleasant American, who gallantly insisted on taking it off to New York in the hopes of getting it done there. At a lunch at his flat I met a well-built silken-legged woman who had once been Dreiser's secretary. She insisted that Dreiser's 'bad style' was deliberate. Once a friend revised a whole novel for him, but Dreiser threw out every single one of the corrections; he felt that the 'clumsinesses' of his style were necessary for the psychological effects he wanted.

Foyle's asked me to take the chair at a lecture and reading by Osbert Sitwell; so I went along to the preceding lecture in order to see how things were done there. The speaker was Coppard, who made the excellent point that the short story had a quite different origin from the novel, so that the techniques were not comparable. I liked his lean dark simplicity and later

became a friend of his. Osbert after his lecture asked me to
print a poem in a set of contrasted types to match the variety
of its ingredients; I drew up a specimen layout, but nothing
came of the project. Another friend made around this time was
John Gough, Australian musician, disciple of Delius, a large-
bodied vulnerable chap whom Laurence with his superior
sophistication found pleasure in baiting. One night he took
advantage of John's imbibing an unwonted amount of beer to
carry off all his records, which he handed to me. I thought they
were a loan till John tracked them down and reclaimed them.
But he was too good-natured to bear any malice, though he
was rather short of money and the loss of the records would
have been a sore loss.

With Laurence I had gone to see all the ballets staged by
the Diaghilev Company. As I never went to the theatre, I
should have missed the ballets if he had not dragged me into
the gallery to see one of the performances. After that I needed
no push. The ballets opened a new dimension of art for me;
they seemed a verification of all I had ever dreamed of the
image of beauty. Together with Yeats's symbolic chamber-
plays they made me discontented with all the forms which had
been satisfying me in poetry; they opened up a myriad new
possibilities in my thought; but I could not find how to develop
in words the emotions and impulses they stirred. In the hope
that by direct collaboration in a ballet I might come closer to
what I was after, I suggested to Heseltine that we should compose a ballet of Elizabethan Drunks – I doing the libretto and
he the music. He at once vehemently turned the idea down,
saying that he despised the Diaghilev ballet as an impure form
and the performers as a pack of perverts and exhibitionists. It
was true that he, like Gray, was an opponent of the Diaghilev
Ballet (though he had once written a pot-boiling Chinese ballet
which was never performed, as well as a Pierrot mime-drama
with Rodker); but I think the vehemence of his recoil had more
in it than a dislike of the artificial ecstasy of the dancers. I had
not yet realized the split between his life and his art. Thus, he
hated Christmas, yet set many carols and Christmas songs; the
last thing he wanted to do was to express in music the life he
lived.

One night when we had tickets for the stalls at the ballet, we went to have a drink during an interval. As we stood by the bar counter, I had a sudden panicked conviction of being stared at by a host of hostile eyes, looked round and saw that I was in fact surrounded by several bulky men with their ugly gaze upon me. Then I noticed that I was standing next to King Alfonso of Spain. With my ragged beard I had seemed to his guard a menacing anarchist. Hastily I moved away.

10 · ELZA AND ESSEX

ELZA had introduced me to an elderly benevolent man who, she said, had befriended her years before. She insisted there had never been anything except pure patronage on his part, and I believed her. He had all the characteristics of a middle-class eccentric wanting to save the world but without any idea how to struggle against evil except by helping young women and by proving that Bacon composed the works of Shakespeare and heaven knows what else. All his strong sense of the world's evil, its omnipresent cheat and lie, had been absorbed by his hope of vindicating Bacon and unmasking the paltry actor Shakespeare. He had written several books on the subject, which he backed with his own money. His edition of the Sonnets with an elaborate exegesis was a remarkable work, which I kept for long with me. One had only to read its analysis for a few pages to feel all one's own most cherished and ingenious ideas undermined; he showed so clearly how strangely convincing a fixed idea could be in picking up clues and exposing hidden relationships – even when one knew quite well the premises were hopelessly unsound.

But he was a likeable and solemn man, with whom we lunched several times. He told me how happy he was that Elza had found the protector she had always needed. I winced at such praise, but tried to repay him by saying nice things about Bacon while keeping off the subject of the plays.

Elza had begun writing poems. One day I came in with P.R.S. and she handed me a sheet of paper on which a quatrain was scrawled. I typed the poem out and handed it to P.R.S. We were both impressed. One of the lines – 'or the toning of a tear' – seemed to have an odd echo in my thoughts, and next day I recognized that it was stolen from Herrick. I did not say

600

anything to P.R.S., but I included the Herrick poem in our *Delighted Earth*, and he there noticed how Elza had borrowed the phrase which gave distinction to her scrap of verse.

However she went on writing; and she did not again steal any phrases. She had gained in confidence and let her inner self overflow on to paper. But P.R.S. was unconvinced; he plainly believed that I was writing the poems for her. And so when I put one of them into *The London Aphrodite*, he cut it out of the proofs; I put it back again, he cut it out again; I finally managed to get it back in time for the printed text. This odd duel was carried on without either of us saying anything to the other.

I did not write the poems for her. Clearly she was much influenced by my work, especially by *Ragnhild* which she must have read far more than I guessed. And at first I helped her by discussing what she had written, trying to make her more conscious of what she wanted to say, encouraging her to rewrite, sometimes several times. She found such revision difficult and fatiguing; her natural bent was to 'express herself' and say that the result however inadequate was all she could do. Gradually however she came to build up her own kind of technique. And the result was so palpably a revelation of her own character that no one could have written the poem but herself.

I bound up a little book from paper samples in the office and copied out the poems, adding small decorative drawings. The book opened with the second poem she had written:

> *This is my loneliness, and here*
> *amid the frightened voices hid,*
> *I see the earth, as in a maze*
> *jewelled lamps hung from my mind.*

Certainly a large part of her initial impulse had been to tell me about herself as she could not tell me in daily speech – and by the quality of the things said to make me have faith in her spirit, to make me love her as she wanted to be loved. But after she had started, she found a satisfaction in the writing itself, a happiness that came out of what she proved, not to me, but to herself. For the first time in her life, I think, she had a certain peace and security.

Thus runs *Before I met you*:

> *I see a sky of faces*
> *blown out on the clouds*
> *and bubbles of the wind.*
> *Their plump white mouths are lapping up the skies,*
> *always thirsty, for my tears are so salt,*
> *and they find no rest. Tumultuous are the heavens*
> *and the faces angrily fade across each other,*
> *coming out the other side like anguished moons.*
> *They press their knotted hands upon the wind*
> *and hem me round, beating cloudily,*
> *seeking to tear the kisses from my mouth*
> *and slake their thirst in the immortal sun.*
> *They do not see the gods drifting by*
> *through my tossing hair*
> *which suddenly is filled with wings,*
> *and I am carried far away*
> *while wailings fill the dark forest*
> *where the shadows fade back through their own eyes*
> *and I die.*
> *And I escape the blood of earthly kings.*

That is one of the easier ones. Others were direct transcriptions of dreams, written down in the early morning. The world of the poems is one of elemental change and dissolution, with her lonely spirit pursued and tormented, finding release only in momentary identifications with the bright life of nature

> *trees kissed by the passionate sun,*
> *fountains playing everywhere*
> *between the birdsongs and the gold*
> *and the clouds of my own hair –*

and in momentary raptures of the embrace:

> *Little sprites tripped up the ladder of my spine*
> *to peep at beauty awakening;*
> *from my burning eyes they saw him*
> *leap the skies and moonlight swarming*
> *round his scarcely breathing nostrils.*

My body stood inside my soul
as in a fountain, and through each fingertip
dripped rubies and drops of gold.

Both releases are steadily linked with her discovery of me, with the point of difficult safety that discovery had given her.

The poems moved me deeply, intensifying the impotent pity I felt and yet confirming me in my still-reluctant conviction that we were bound together for life and that my task was to help her towards an increasingly full happiness. Graves saw several of the poems and liked them. That his liking was genuine and penetrating was shown by the fact that he criticized some in detail, disapproving only of the lines where my influence was strongest. Gordon Bottomley, with whom I was now in touch, also liked them very much. I had written to him about his work, and soon a strong bond developed. I met him several times during his visits to London and breakfasted or lunched with him at his hotel opposite the British Museum.

My friendly relations with Graves did not last long. I sent him a copy of *Helen Comes of Age* with a rash request for a frank opinion. He wrote back at courteous length, but his comments boiled down to the statement, 'I have never been able to bear the scent of hawthorn and these works are heavy with that scent. No doubt the best kind of hawthorn scent, but not for me.' A sensible judgment. I should agree now that the style is clogged with that sort of sweetness, the imagery of the fused senses, though I think still there is more to be said of the total effect. But, for all my request for a frank opinion, I was hoping for a more sympathetic response. I had enjoyed Graves's own work very much, though I disliked the intellectualizing attitudes that had come with Laura; his opinion was one of the few I valued.*

*In the *London Aphrodite* I wrote that 'instead of purging a tendency to prettiness by persisting till it turned to emotional depth, he has succumbed to the temptations of the "intellect" '. I did not take into consideration that the intellectualization might in time help him towards emotional depth and complexity of structure. What seems to me the real weakness in Graves I shall discuss later in this book: his refusal to see the social implications of a revolt that was essentially social in origin. Hence the limitation of his world of ideas.

Thereafter our relations worsened. I was the one mainly to blame; for I had tried to extort from Graves more than I had the right to ask. But I think it was something about Laura that caused the final break. Oddly, I can't remember. Clearly the reason is that the break was blurred in my own mind by the disappointment I had brought on myself.

From Bottomley on the other hand I got as strong a response as I could have hoped. In his generous way he stressed the positive aspects, insisted that I was on the right path for the reinvigoration of drama; and when I pointed out that I had unintentionally stolen a line of his ('I love you and I love you and I love you'), he replied. 'I forgive you. Let the omen stand. Marlowe once provided a line for a greater man' – referring to the line: 'Who ever loved that loved not at first sight.' I had many long letters in his clear fine script on the problems of verse-drama, which were burned in 1931. One phrase I recall, about T. S. Eliot, 'He is very talented, but no man can create poetry out of his inhibitions, and that is what he has set himself to do.'

Suddenly Elza mentioned that her child was coming over from Paris and that we should have to collect her at the boat train. The news threw me into confusion; for in my efforts to escape thinking concretely about the situation, I had taken 'child in Paris' to be a sort of remote counter in our relations, like 'husband in Paris' and 'wife in Australia'. I had never faced the fact that sooner or later Elza would want to see and be with her child. I had no objections, except that I could not conceive our relations carrying on with a child in the household. For those relations were so strangely removed from anything domestic, everyday, ordinary; they existed at the level of silence or of Elza's poems.

Robinetta proved to be a plump little thing, very quiet and reserved, seven or eight years old. No child could have been less trouble. I took her for walks and through the British Museum, and liked her in my timid way. I was afraid of children. I was afraid of all the child represented in the way of family and social responsibility. Our idea of art had in it too much of the play-element abstracted from social function; the child in his or her blitheness was a rival who showed up what was false and highfalutin in our claims. Also I think my fear masked an intense but repressed wish to become a father; the fear was that I would repeat my own father's irresponsibility and desertion.

Suddenly Elza announced that she wanted to go to the country. Behind her decision there lay a slowly mounting tension, which the arrival of Robinetta had brought to a head. She made no complaints about me or our way of life; she merely said that she could not bear to live in London any longer, that she needed country air and fare; and it would be better for the child. I talked things over with P.R.S. and we decided that it would be sufficient if I spent three days a week in town; much of the editorial, translating and other work could be quite well done in the country. Elza found a cheap top-floor room for me in Gilbert Street opposite us, and read through *Dalton's Weekly*. I think it was the first house we looked at that we took: at Alphamstone on the Essex-Suffolk border, overlooking the Stour Valley in Constable country, between Sudbury and Bures. The owners of the cottage (or rather bungalow with one room raised at the end) were two elderly tweedy spinsters with a horde of dogs; all their conversation was on the problems of mating bitches.

Elza was deeply excited; and I too looked forward to the change. Elza I think had a hope of some idyllic situation in which all her difficulties would vanish; I felt that the tension between us would end through my being half the week at home entirely at her call and the other half out of her sight, unworried about, free to spend my time as I liked. Things worked out like that for a short while.

We moved and had the happily occupied time that settling into new pleasant surroundings always is. There was a large untended garden, which I dug up. We had bought a bicycle before we left London. I had never ridden and now began to practise. After falling over a few times I more or less mastered the machine, but was never at ease when a car or lorry came at me down one of the lanes or winding roads. I preferred to stop and if necessary to fall off sideways into the hedge. What were a few scratches as long as one wasn't run over? I used to ride into Bures for the train and leave the bike there, to be picked up on my homecoming. The road between the cottage and the station was about as unsatisfactory for cycling as could well be found – all twists and steep ups-and-downs. There was a sharp downhill on the way back, just before I reached home, and almost every time I crashed in the dusk at the bottom into a large stone – one of the glacial deposits, eaten with pockmarks that look like the cup holes of prehistoric sacrificial rites, which are almost the only rocks found in that part of the world. I became an expert at mending punctures. During my days at home I rode about the neighbourhood, which at that time had little traffic, though there must be few stretches of hedge where into which I didn't plunge some time or other. Parts of the Stour valley were delightful and I spent hours lying at fine vista-point, now at last absorbing in leisurely happiness the earth of the English poets and landscape artists.

Elza, with more time to spare in the scattered village, made several friends. An old couple used to call us in to chat over parsnip wine; otherwise I never touched a drink. My Stour musings increased my dissatisfaction with my London life. The Press was flourishing, but I felt myself as poet standing still. In August 1928 I wrote a longish poem *Time Torn to Stars*, which attempted to define what I took as the linked but opposed trends of disintegration – intellectualism and primitivism – to show how the way forward lay in a resolution of their conflict by a new synthesis of the colour image: the image using the fused senses of *symbolisme* with a deepened human content. I wanted to work through a series of broken forms to the triumphant recreation of the Cleopatra image ('burned on the waters, etc.'): to reveal the Shakespearean image enriched by the resolution of the poetic conflicts intervening between 1600 and 1928. In this sense the poem was an anti-*Waste Land*. I was attacking Eliot's use of the Cleopatra image for a flat contrast with the dead present of depressed naturalism, of which his religious formulations were the ghostly reflection; his blank ignoring of the fact that in ritual-myth the Waste Land existed in order to become the Earth of Plenty through the generative energies, through the creative act of transformation. But my protest against intellectualism was itself far too aridly intellectual; my protest against expressionist hastes, itself far too hasty.

Next to us was a countrywoman, whom a stumpy naval petty-officer had married as a widow with several children. She told Elza that the P.O. had never consummated the marriage. 'I dunno what's wrong with him. Many the time I've tried to strike a light or make a lucky grab and find out if he's got anything there, but he always beats me to it. I got an idea it was shot off.' She wanted to leave the useless man; but he baffled her by never straying beyond the vegetable-patch save at erratic moments for a quick one at the pub. As a result she couldn't arrange to smuggle the furniture out; and without the furniture she couldn't go. Almost every time I came home there would be a new story about some effort of the woman to find out just what the P.O.'s physical condition was or to diddle him about the furniture; but he was always too smart for her. The struggle was still going on when we departed.

About this time I read D.H.L.'s *Fox* and *Captain's Doll*, the first of his fiction I had looked at since *Women in Love* in Australia. Though I still felt hostile to what I thought his general positions, I had been much shaken by the essay on Galsworthy, and I found these two tales stimulating. In our Fanfroliconian ethic, the woman had the right, indeed the duty, to mock her man; *The Captain's Doll* made me begin to doubt such attitudes (based as they were on the idea of the spiritual segregation of the sexes, of primary differences between man and woman which necessitated a perpetual sex war) – though at the same time I could not accept D.H.L.'s position that the male as male must be respected.

I had heard nothing of Janet for some time, and therefore had myself ceased to write to her. Nothing definite had happened and I was able to shut the matter out of thought without coming to any decisions. I could not visualize an end of my marriage with Janet (which implied a decision not to return to Australia); I could not visualize an end of my relations with Elza (which implied a turning-back from the path on which I had now set my feet).

11 · THE LONDON APHRODITE

BOTH P.R.S. and myself, having got the Press stable, could not feel satisfied with limited editions alone. We decided that we were now able to launch a magazine without wrecking the firm; and we began preparations for *The London Aphrodite*. The name was a joke, though a serious one. If there was room for a *London Mercury*, why not for a London Goddess of Beauty? (Mercury, we recalled, was a patron of businessmen and a guide of the dead; we wanted a deity who damned all profitable prudences and who guided the quick.) The publicist work of Wyndham Lewis, which was having a considerable success, also spurred us on. A. L. Morton called lankily in at the office, travelling for adverts for Lewis, and we merrily concocted one in which we set out our positions and called Lewis various forthright names. Needless to say, he did not print it. However Morton gave us some poems, which we used.

The first issue of *Aphrodite* announced that only six numbers would appear. In it, as in all the numbers, P.R.S. composed the commentaries:

This periodical may even be epoch-marking because it has nothing whatever to do with the *zeitgeist*. Therefore the Editors invite contributions from the world at large outside the lunatic asylums of the abstract and other official cliques ... Each number will contain a series of exercises in the forgotten art of lyrical poetry ... Do not subscribe, please, if you are quite satisfied with the prevailing standards in literary periodical journalism.

And underwriting my generalities, he added his credo (in a series of his best puns):

that it is amusing to be alive, but that it is a question of blood in the arteries and you cannot get blood from a Stein: that the emptiest moderns make most noise, owing to the Decline of the Best: that modernity, like maternity, is already out of date, owing to correspondence from France and American specialities: that the Transcendental Unity of Apperception (Kant) has been overcome by the Trans-Atlantic Disunity of Introspection (cant); but that Freud means Joy not Joyce; and that consequently there is No Sale for Poetry because there is no poetry for sale, the nigger being in the woodpile of (musical) Time and (middle) Western Man when he (she or it) comes to Europe with a literary aspiration: that the gods whelp whose who whelp themselves, which means instead of Cummings, They Went, because Beauty is (see page opposite *et seq.*) possible.

(*They Went* was the title of a book by Norman Douglas; otherwise I think the jokes wear well.) The contents included poems by Slessor, McCrae, Robert Nichols,* Powys Mathers, and others; a verse-play by myself as well as a long essay *The Modern Consciousness* and an instalment of the *Dung of Pegasus*; a tale *Patsa* sent from Ireland by Liam; P.R.S.'s satirical verse, *Bullets and Ballots*, ridiculing the Fabianism of Shaw and Wells ('Lenin and Trotsky were Up and Doing, and what about Shaw and Wells? They are up and doing some more new books, for Socialism Sells.')

My essay began by stating that one could not discover the nature of the modern consciousness by abstracting some main point from the position of each of the various competing groups. One must judge the totality of the material 'as partisan', seeking 'to be true to one's deepest experience of life and art in every passing criticism. That is to judge the material, not as isolated completed things, but as imperfect aspirations into the whole human future, the eternity of myself.' (The last phrase shows how I still brought down my method in the final resort to an existential idealism; but now there was the emerging conflict with the 'human future'.) 'I therefore take as my

---

*Nichols had become very friendly. After the third issue he recognized who Peter Meadows was and wrote to me, 'I feel sure that this person looking back on his life has a big future ahead of him.' Mathers also had become a friend: more of him later. Among the poets was Stanley Snaith, a protégé of Bottomley, who called in several times.

criterion the concrete universal, the human dynamic.' I went on to define Nietzsche as the great forerunner of the new synthesis, the new creative adventure:

[After the Renaissance] philosophy marched from abstraction to abstraction, the only conclusion of which could be Hume's pertinent use of logic to sever all the knots of divine law, with the Scotch Commonsense Philosophers tying them up again with penny bits of string. Kant, a great destroyer with a disguise of infinitely tortuous terminology, destroyed metaphysics by carrying to a logical precision far ahead of any predecessor the proofs for the existence of God and then calmly annihilating them. Frightened at this vast god-slaughter, he resuscitated the deity with a salve of moral proof; but even then found himself floundering back into danger in *The Critique of Judgment* (which consequently nobody reads) and gave up the task. However his work remained, its stimulus, behind the deadening veils of style, vitally destructive.

Hegel carried on this work, supplanting for the first time since the Hellenes the abstract universal with the human complex: his dialectic bored down into the human process as significance. His limitations do not matter here. Enough that he saw human activity as real.

On to this scene arrived Nietzsche. Absorbing the whole philosophical tradition at a gulp, he intuitively completed the cycle of Plato – Aristotle – Kant – Hegel; and saw in what direction the new cycle must face. He formulated a Dionysian philosophy: a return to the Platonic knowledge of man as the meaure of all things, with a new passionate sense of the constructive essences of man himself.

He fused the opposites of the ceaseless flux and of eternal recurrence (which I defined as the liberated judgment), Dionysos and Apollo. Here, I claimed, were the sources of value by which we might illuminate and criticize the modern world. By the criterion of the Nietzschean dialectic I then examined Wyndham Lewis, Bergson, Freud, Einstein, Blake and nineteenth-century poetry, Goya and Delacroix, and the development of art from Cézanne (seen as mainly disintegrative), Mozart, Beethoven, Wagner, and the development of music from Scriabin and Schönberg (again seen as mainly disintegrative). Returning to modern literature, I praised the Sitwells, Turner, Roy Campbell, Yeats and Bottomley, and attacked

Eliot; saw Stein and Joyce as mainly disintegrative; tried again to pull Lewis to pieces and then turned on D.H.L. and Shaw (as opposed but equally partial types). And ended with a fresh attempt at defining the necessary synthesis:

Yeats, drawing on I know not what astrological mysteries, prophesied some years back that the turning-point, the arrival of the third kingdom of the spirit, was to occur in 1928.

The signs of the Third Kingdom are a liberation of irrational Dionysian force and, simultaneously, a strengthening of the antithetical symbols of the intellect.

We have seen, under the stress of Music's conquest of Time, all expressions wearing through their old garments till, growing more and more skeletal, they became inert. That was in order that we might have as clear a sense as possible of our tools.

We have seen, side by side with this, the storm of nervous sensibility tear minds to rags or send them seeking refuge in the hot primitive mud. That was to make clear for us the dramatic potentialities of the struggle into self-consciousness.

It now remains for us to make this effort, legionaries of the new Roman determination to stabilize spirit – defining a new faith in life and the eternality of self, and at the same time washing our hands, Pilate-fashion, in the coolest of ironical despairs.

It remains for the Third Kingdom – ignoring the efforts to return to the primitive slime or to make life a psychological abstraction – to define this freedom of self-motive energy, deepening from consciousness to consciousness, and, with the imageries of all the modes whereby the human spirit redeems itself from death, constructing the fluid concretions of its love.

I proclaim the Third Kingdom.

Needless to say, the essay was full of wild and indefensible generalizations, but at the same time it was a serious effort to grasp in a comprehensive vision what was implied by art in the post-Cézanne, post-Wagner world. Compared with the simple denunciations of *modernismus* we indulged in in Australia, it showed a real sense of what the criticized persons were getting at, even if it summed up their limitations or one-sidedness in too lordly a fashion. To this extent I was breaking away from N.L. abstractions; and the preoccupation with 'the human future' showed an even deeper divergence, derived partly from my whole experience in England, partly from the impact of P.R.S. and his politics.

I had written several small verse-dramas. *Love*, printed in *Aphrodite*, took a theme from Norse saga. A poet meets a priestess wandering with her goddess in a waggon, makes love to her, fights and breaks up the intruding goddess, puts the bits of the idol together, and joins the girl in going round for alms, singing the goddess' praises. Under Yeats's influence I was simplifying, or flattening, rhythm, and rationing my thick image-clusters. Rhythm had been conceived as a series of long shelving (Wagnerian) sweeps full of local recoils and eddies; now I sought a single clear curve equably sustained. I was in fact in search of a form that discarded *ecstasis* for a disciplined purpose, and *Love* made fun of the N.L. gods, though my only course still seemed to hymn them before the world. In attempting to deepen irony I was beginning to rebel.

Aphrodite One did well. A steady support flowed in, though the critics ignored us or jeered. Our staunch partisans included such diverse types as the Hon. Evan Morgan, an American business-man A. P. Sachs (who wrote us an essay on Heisenbergian Indeterminacy), and a bank clerk who lived at Bromley and bought all our books. Sachs, a large beaming fellow, visited London periodically and took us out to dine. One night we were at the Eiffel Tower run by the Viennese Rudolf Stulik, where the charges were high but one was liable to meet persons like Augustus John or Matthew Smith at its small tables with pink-shaded lights. Sachs took up the theme of a terrible disaster coming on mankind. P.R.S. argued that the spread of literacy made a decline into barbarism impossible. 'But that's just why it *is* possible, and likely,' I protested; 'the next barbarism will be the worst ever.' Sachs seconded me. I argued, 'It's the mixture of literacy plus the degraded level of life that's becoming more and more general; there's the danger. People can be got at as never before.'

We went to the Eiffel too with Aldous Huxley. He had heard of us (as a passage in *Point Counter Point* shows); and came into the office in response to a note from me. Tall, willowy, with lavish brown hair and loose red mouth, with a large hat and strongly lensed spectacles. He was then badly short-sighted and held a book close up against his face. I liked him. He was living near Paris, but was on a visit to London, rather pessimistic about England and its vulgarized dulled ways of life, the pervasive jazz band burbling away and the old kind of music-hall dead. He listened attentively and politely to our expositions, perhaps wondering if we might add some new horror-types to his fiction – though I think he was responsive to much in our attitudes even if he could not accept many of our point-blank positions. He had been fascinated by D.H.L. and wanted to find how to break thoroughly from the negative positions on which he had built himself up. Something more easily hoped for than done. Anyhow I think he was pleased by our strong admiration of the lively elements in his work, which had come out most playfully in *Antic Hay*.

He asked me to stay with him in Paris. I would dearly have liked to go; but the same reasons as had held me back from visiting Ireland with Liam still tied me down. He sent me two sonnets for the magazine and a copy of *Point Counter Point*. I replied, 'I think you are expelling your rationalist devils . . .' And tried to analyse helpfully the struggle inside his work. He didn't seem to resent my remarks. Perhaps our bull-roaring Dionysiac declarations had some effect in drawing him on to works like *Do what you will*. But if you have been possessed by rationalist devils and drive them out, the void is more likely to be filled with the angels of systematic mysticism than with reckless maenads. And so it was with Huxley.

P.R.S. in *Aphrodite Three*, in a dialogue between Point and Counterpoint, worked out these positions:

Counterpoint: . . . Thus the opinion of the critics will merely confirm Huxley's main thesis that Intellectuals frustrate themselves in a centrifugally developing futility and hopelessness.
Point: Huxley himself being *a priori* included; which he at least, confound his self-honesty, recognizes.
Counterpoint: Well, recognition of this particular kind is generally indicative of the desire to get out of the bag's bottom; and perhaps *P.C.P.* has now cleared the way in Huxley's own mind for an affirmatory human synthesis, in which case it will be more than a flash of lightning on a dunghill.

Point: Does he really hate his characters? Are these futile people photographs, caricatures, or sheer fantasy-projections? Why need he concern himself with the dull world of Michael Arlen grown more culpable because a little more self-conscious and erudite?

Counterpoint: Because these are all he knows. He has been round the world without quitting the stateroom of his own mind . . .

Point: Then raise the Scarlet Standard high.

Counterpoint: But he abhors Communism.

Point: Then let him espouse Fascism.

Counterpoint: But equally he abhors Fascism.

Point: Then let him leave the Political Illusion alone. We already have Mr Wells . . . Need he go via. D. H. Lawrence to Dostoevsky? Need he succumb to the modern evil and itch when he, with a few, can conquer it?

P.R.S.'s polemics were among the best things we published. His *J. C. Squire (Etc)* in *Aphrodite Two*, taking up our quarrel on behalf of *Pheonix*, was a first-rate piece of clear-sighted uncompromising attack. It opened the fight in defence of free expression against the dominant Philistine puritans represented by Squire among the intellectuals and James Douglas among the journalists. D.H.L. in a short while was to pick up the theme and carry on his duel with the Home Secretary Joynson-Hicks. But he was abroad, and we were in London. We initiated and bore the brunt, and we were in a very vulnerable situation. We received many anonymous letters saying that Informations were being laid against us with the Police, that our Wicked Activities were being Watched, etc. And the least police action against us would have brought the Press down with a crash. Eric Partridge had no sooner been installed in our Museum Street rooms with his new firm than a reviewer informed against him before his book *The Sleeveless Errand* by N. James was published; the police seized the entire edition. And there was nothing in the least obscene in the book, only the word 'buggers' used casually in conversation. Those who did not live through the period would find it hard to realize the oppressive atmosphere or to understand the power wielded by windy neurotics like James Douglas of the *Sunday Express* who denounced *Antic Hay* as 'ordure and blasphemy', coupled Crowley's *Diary of a Drugfiend*, a luridly moralistic work, with Joyce's *Ulysses*, and called for its banning. He attacked the seriously dull novel on female inverts, Radclyffe-Hall's *Well of Loneliness*, saying he'd rather his daughter took prussic acid than read such a book, and managed to get it suppressed. 'Squire has approvingly commented that the whole nature, objects, and sanctities of morality are involved. There is a solid block between these two field-preachers. Must the struggle for free expression be fought all over again?' asked P.R.S. In making direct and violent assaults on such puffed up characters we did what no one else of the period did, and we did it in the most exposed position possible. Nor did we leave the matter at the *Aphrodite* articles.

A young artist, Beresford Egan, who imitated Beardsley's *Salome* drawings, had come into the office with some caricatures. We did not think highly enough of his work to put the Fanfrolico imprint on it; but P.R.S. got together with him and turned out a poem satirizing Douglas, with another prose diatribe in his most trenchant style. The result was published by P.R.S. as from the Hermes Press:

The Sink of Solitude. Being a *series* of *Satirical Drawings* occasioned by some *Recent Events* performed by Beresford Beresford Egan, *Gent.* to which is added a *Preface* by P. R. Stephensen, *Gent.*, and a *Verse Lampoon* composed by SEVERAL HANDS and now set forth for the first time, the whole being very proper to be read both on *Family* and *Public Occasions*.

The poem was mainly P.R.S.'s work, though others of us added bits in noisy discussions in the pub, the last seven couplets being by myself. We had the difficult task of defending *The Well of Loneliness* from moral attack, while admitting the mediocre nature of its achievement. *The Sink* sold very well, and P.R.S. was stimulated into three other pamphlets: *Policeman of the Lord* (an attack on the Home Secretary) with drawings by Egan; *Leave the Well Alone*, with short poems and a lampoon in couplets; *The Well of Sleevelessness*, decorated by Hal Collins, for the Scholartis Press. Though these had some amusing hits, they did not keep the high standard of *The Sink*. 'A moral tripehound like James Douglas can say what he likes about almost anything because he has the millionaires backing him in any possible action for libel. That gives him the courage to libel people like Radclyffe-Hall and to get away with it, gloating.'

Contributors to the *Aphrodite* included T. F. and Llewellyn Powys, Rhys Davies, Earp, Sacheverell Sitwell, Ivan Goll, Sherard Vines, Edgell Rickword, Norman Douglas, Karel Capek, Frederick Carter, Albert Highet, Edward Marsh – also Philip Owens and Brian Penton, of whom more anon. Robert Nichols gave us an elaborately worked-out libretto for a Hogarth ballet, which may be said to have prophesied the lines on which the best elements of English ballet would develop. I did translations from La Forgue and Essenin, as well as from Blok (with P.R.S.). In a final essay I discussed at length the kind of dramatic blank verse adequate to express the life of our day, and ended by switching into the conclusion of a verse-play I had just written, in which a poet and a girl have taken refuge in a temple of Venus during the eruption destroying Pompeii; Venus appears and they argue about love, life on earth, poetry, as doom gathers. (I chose this setting to express once more my conviction that science would in the near future develop means of destroying the earth: I arrived at this conviction from an analysis of its mechanistic and disintegrative trends – the trends we have seen in our own day arrive at nuclear fission.)

One point worth making is that *The London Aphrodite*, for all its eclectic furies, was the first intellectual effort made in England to affirm a faith in the Russian revolution, while attempting a comprehensive critique of modern art developments (most of which we saw as floundering away from the concrete image of art into the deaths of abstraction or primitivism). P.R.S. in his essay on Bakunin uttered our lament that anarchism was not enough, and proceeded to affirm his belief in the Leninist revolution. I did not have his clear grounding; but I had come round to this viewpoint sufficiently by the sixth number to write:

With the arrival of the proletarian revolution the human horizon has so far extended that we are forced back insistently upon individuality as the sole universal principle (i.e. in the sphere of experience of course, not of cheating). The political variation between Henry Ford and Nicolai Lenin is not the most important one – the chasm in intellect between the two does not need stressing: no one is likely to mistake Ford for even a human being. The true conflict, which however must express itself in the struggle for the control of the instrument of production and distribution, narrows itself down to the question: Which party will centralize its organization on the needs of the individual, his right to experience . . .

The *bolsheviki* are in my opinion a genuine expression of the Roman constructiveness. In any case the Russian revolution displays a huge and happy uprush of the human spirit; and this brimming worldtide of new energy is to be seen even in the reactionary military dictatorships among the Latins and the commercial dictatorship of the United States. England, bogged in the products of its own cunning and so now its own dupe, remains outside this hurry of energy, whether of the constructive Russian kind or the sporadic American. It is among this international expansion that the poet must find his vindication of Force.

The statement is confused. I did not have at my disposal the terms needed for what I wanted to say. I meant I had now come to believe that capitalism could only thwart and cripple the deepened individuations it had once helped into existence, and that the communal control of production and distribution was now the only way to release new individualities. I then went on to argue that the breakdown of the old kind of democracy into dictatorships and monopolies inside capitalism was a symptom of the necessary fundamental changes, which had been carried out in the right way in Russia. By finding his unity with the proletarian revolution, the poet could find the way to harmonize his creative energies with the Force operating through the workers and breaking down the bourgeois system.

I only imperfectly understood what I was saying; hence the muddled terms. Otherwise I would have gone ahead to build coherently on the new-found basis. In a sense my development in the next eight years was a struggle to clarify what I had here said. All the same, I had said it, and I was to be haunted by the problems thus raised, and I had raised them before anyone else in Britain. My debt to P.R.S. does not need stressing.

Both in the final essay and in *Aphrodite Three* I attacked T. S. Eliot as the supreme example of the dessicating trends, the surrender to the fear of death which Wagner had called the source of all lovelessness. I pointed out that in his picture of Baudelaire the Classicist he simply inverted Symons's picture of Baudelaire the Romantic and produced an equally false image of the poet. 'Both points of view of course are unaware of Baudelaire the Individual, or his genuine creative conflict.' Re-reading the Eliot essay with its bad jokes – 'more efficiently spectral . . . in a phrase from Joyce, Imperthnthnthnthnthn . . . absolute pu(er)ility' – I feel how much closer we were to the Continental Dadaists than to anything in England (apart from the early Sitwells). Our irreverences and puns did have something of an intention of expressing a chaos, of being a shocking reflection of the dead-end bourgeois world, as the first step towards the striking out of a dancing star: even if we prematurely announced the star-advent.

As an offshoot of the *Aphrodite* we published a book of my lyrics, *The Passionate Neatherd*, at the low price of 1/6d, and promptly sold out a couple of thousand. This time we had one defender. A long review of the *New Age* welcomed a work of adult verse in a world of beastly adolescents. I forget how many we printed of the magazine, but it must have been round 3500; and after the last issue P.R.S. told me that he had raised the money for a full reprint of some 1500 copies, which we sold bound. Clearly, despite the critics and the trade, we were building up a strong support, and it is a pity we did not decide to carry on. However, we had announced that all magazines soon got into a rut and that we'd stop with the sixth issue. So we stopped and P.R.S. wrote in the advert in the last (July 1929) number:

Having demonstrated by publishing *The London Aphrodite* successfully for six numbers without any concessions, literary competitions, politics, advertisements, or poems by Humbert Wolfe, that there is no reason at all why most of the reviews should exist, the Fanfrolico Press abandons this diversion of its long summer evenings and prepares to assault another popular misconception – that poetry cannot be produced cheaply and profitably in a handsome format for a large public.

We were therefore going to produce *Hereward*, music and all, at 6s. and *Marlowe* at 5s.

One meeting around this time surprised and excited me. A wire arrived out of the blue from Yeats asking me to lunch at the Savile Club. We were joined at our table by some uninvited others – W. J. Turner and an Irishman who had worked at the

Abbey Theatre. The latter told tales of the poet Darrell Figgis whose famed beard was cut off by his opponents in the Irish Troubles and who gassed himself in October 1925. It was my beard that started the discussion, and Figgis's was voted a grander spectacle. According to the stories, he was addicted to Piccadilly tarts, who made derogatory comments on the beard and were always beaten by his quick wit. Turner with a rather smug grin remarked that all men of rich creative power were much given to copulation; Yeats gravely agreed. After lunch he politely dismissed the others and we spent the whole after-noon together, apart from an interruption when Wilenski interviewed him about the controversy on the Lane bequest of paintings. During the interview he was very much Senator Yeats, keeping the art critic quietly in his place. Unfortunately we discussed, not so much poetic drama, as spiritualism and neo-Platonism. I told him of N.L.'s experiences with Rose, which interested him a lot, and he told me of similar experi-ences with his wife, which at that time he had not written about. He seemed pleased at the seriousness with which I took *A Vision*, and we parted with a general agreement about further discussions. But in the difficult time ahead I forgot all such matters.*

By covering in this chapter the whole career of the *Aphrodite* (July 1928 to July 1929) I have hurried on, and must now return to pick up the thread of my personal narrative.

*Other *Aphrodite* contacts were W. J. Turner who used to lunch with us at the pub near the office and argue about music; Sherard Vines; Edward Marsh, who gave me two of his La Fontaine translations and a lunch in his flat with its interesting collection of pictures; Anna Wickham, a roaring-girl (literally so, with her great booming voice) and a plague to solicitor husband, who lived in a grimy Hampstead den, steadily darning socks and sleeping with a dusty floor-rug for blanket. She became attached to P.R.S. and wrote him a poem which began something like 'I've made a bond with Bundaberg'; he'd liked to repeat it and gave me the incorrect idea he was born in that town.

A. J. Symonds once proposed to me that I should do an unpublished work of Corvo's he had found, binding in with each copy one sheet of the original MS; but he wanted too much money down. With his club he inhabited a large room at the back of St George's church not far from us.

12 · BETTY MAY

ONE day in the Plough, not long after our removal to the country, I encountered a strange woman, who spoke to me. We drank a few beers. There was a merry calm about her. She had a broad face, with some grey streaks in her hair, and wore a long tweed coat and a sort of robin-hood cap of green. She was Betty May, who had just left her fifth husband to carry on with his genteel breeding of dogs in the country. Her frank clear fearless face, with its strong sculptural force, had an unsettling effect upon me. As we were walking out, she took up the hand of a whore who sat near the window and held it a moment. 'You're sick,' she said with a friendly sternness, 'you'd better do something about it.' The whore started and stared back, wanting to say something rude and violent, but quelled by a superstitious fear and Betty's calm eyes. She stammered and finally hid her hands under the table.

There was something barbaric and yet gentle about her, a peculiar emanation of beauty and strength which was all the more powerful because she did not use the least cosmetics or show the least element of coquettishness. Her face with its simple breadth of modelling owned a deep self-confidence that had nothing trivial about it. Although we had exchanged only ordinary remarks, I left her with shaken senses and mind. Despite the extreme difference in effect, she seemed like Elza to possess her body, her own piece of space-time, with a dangerous and serene completeness. I have never known other women with quite this fullness, this presence – though in Elza the energies were turned in, in Betty they were turned out. I wanted to meet her again, and was afraid of meeting her.

I knew I would meet her again. Next evening she came into the pub and walked straight up to me as if we had arranged to meet. She hardly smiled. We had known one another a long time; there was no need to say anything. With a mixture of despair and reckless abandon I knew that I could not escape; she had come to me as much a part of my poetry as Elza. We drank quietly and then went back to her room off Charlotte Street.

I soon heard lots of things about her. Betty the Tiger Woman, the Epstein model, drug-taker, nympholept, man-eater. But she remained to me someone I had always known, known through and through, who was as true as my own images were to me. But the time I lived through with her was a nightmare, haunted with guilt like a horrible *leitmotiv* of music thudding up from deep in my mind, and yet in a way as simple and innocent as a game of children. She accepted me as I accepted her, but without the guilt. She knew all about my divided state; I told her at the outset about Elza; she looked on at me from outside as if a little rueful, but not really concerned. While I was ready to be with her, she felt herself to be mine and left wholly to me the problems raised by our relations.

No doubt I idealized her. But not much. I feel sure there was in her a strange sort of integrity, directed by an image of herself as a *femme fatale* (but without any glorying in tragic roles). She dominated me by making no effort whatever to dominate. She was quite 'unfeminine' in the usual meanings of that word; she hardly made up, she dressed neatly but carelessly; she had not the least touch of coyness, of fluttering invitation; she never laid herself out to attract. In all respects she seemed the active counterpart of Elza, taking what she wanted instead of being taken, resolute mistress of herself instead of being a victim.

Till this moment I had always felt that all details of the Press were under my fingers and that I controlled the situation. Now it all slipped away. I left everything to P.R.S. and for the first time cashed cheques for drinking purposes. The days at Alphamstone were a dull dragging misery, in which I tried to hide my distraction from Elza by pleas of illness, of business strain. She was worried, but did not seem to suspect. The small girl was thriving and I found a certain dogged release in digging hard, in pedalling fast along the lanes. Rats got into the roof and rattled thunderously like great dogs, waking me early for the ride across to Bures. Though I dreaded facing Elza, it was a great relief to escape London and the calm ruthless face of Betty. At least I felt happy in the passage between Bures and the cottage, as I wheeled my bike up and down the hills or strolled across the sweltering fields.

P.R.S. encouraged me. Not by words, but by taking over the complete charge of the Press without complaint, slapping me on the back and assuming that all was well. No doubt I should have resented it if he had asked me what I thought I was doing; but deep down I resented even more that he did not try to pull me up. The seeds of our disunion were sown.

Strange driven nights. In various pubs or the Café Royal which still had for Betty pre-war memories. Mostly there was nothing much to show the deep satisfaction I felt, despite my fears, at simply being with her. She never made any pretentious remarks but seemed to understand anything I said. Always with that dark and generous emanation of strength and beauty. I felt it even if we merely sat and sipped beer on a Monday evening in the Fitzroy when the old women and men of the Loan Club filed down the long saloon bar to where the daughter of the house waited to take their sixpennies (which would turn into a magically large sum at Christmas): shawled and bonneted old women, and old men with every sort of bushy moustache, exhaling the hard dry soda-smell of a desperately clean poverty. If we lounged in the White Hart, run by small dark Daisy with her husband Albert, who had once done a turn of acrobatic dancing mixed up with soapsuds and who now basked in the reflected lights of the mahogany bar with its signed photos of forlorn theatrical celebrities and its barrels on high over the bottles. Or if we strayed through Luna Park at the corner of Tottenham Court Road and Oxford Street, among the snorting merry-go-rounds, coconut-shies, peep-shows, slot-machines, shooting galleries, booths of Madame X. A woman wrapped herself in cottonwool, which was set alight; flaring, she dived into a tank and emerged gasping, the devouring red coat of death changed into a soppy mess of dirty black. Her daughter the Seal also dived, glittering only with spangles, and stayed underwater so long that everyone felt sure she was dead or a cheat, flapping her long thin legs or sinking in a lump to the bottom. It's done with mirrors. She lived in the Post Office Club and we knew her, knew the clammy touch of her hand. In ragged lights the clown-faces grimaced, the hurdy-gurdy tune wheezed ever more hoarsely, and young girls licking coned ice-creams fell over tent ropes or stood in the niches of shadow flicking up their skirts to show they wore nothing underneath; whimpered with a sweaty fist clutched full of pennies, an ear bleeding where the ear-ring had been torn off, or screeched as the monkey jumped. Kiss-curls elaborately drawn out and plastered across the cheek to the corner of the eye. Ebony page-cuts under ugly cloche-hats. Cellars in Soho cobwebbed with smoke, dice clicking and a girl peeing in the corner: 'Sorry, but the Ladies' stinks.' Beer in Covent Garden pubs among brawny tender-hearted porters and broken tomatoes, five o'clock a.m.

One night at the Café Royal, as I was talking to someone across the table, she held some ethyl nitrate under my nose so that I inhaled it before I knew what was happening. I was very angry. That was the only time I had any experience of a drug; and I felt nothing from it at all. Another time, in her room, I suddenly woke up in the early hours with a clear image of elephants surrounding me, all standing upright in a sort of hieratic pose. For the moment I did not feel anything strange or frightening or ridiculous in the sight. Then the whole thing vanished. I went to sleep again. But next morning I told her. She said that she had been drawing blood from me to use in a 'white spell' for the help of friends in trouble; the elephants had had some connection with the words of the spell. I could only surmise that there had been a case of thought transference and that in my semi-drunken state I had projected the image. Anyhow, I had learned that Betty was a witch.

In her way she was as typical a character of the period as Heseltine. That is, she showed certain key tendencies in an extreme form. And because of this, and because of the crucial part she played in my life, I shall give here a summary of the tale she told of herself. On the whole I feel it was true. She may have omitted much, and heightened a few points, yet the effect was true enough to her personality.

She was born in the Tidal Basin of coster-folk, one of four kids. Her half French mother was left by her husband while Betty was still an infant. One day Betty rebelled by throwing her brother's shoes, the only pair in the family, into the Thames; and she was sent to her father, who was then living with 'a huge dark Jewess'. Betty recalled that 'his right eyebrow was almost obliterated by a scar which kept the eye beneath it perpetually open. He looked absolutely devilish.' They lived in Limehouse, amid bugs and stench. He had been a gasworks-fitter, but now only boozed. Naturally cruel, he was a fiend when drunk, set dogs fighting or swung cats to bash out their brains. One day he was arrested by his own father, a police-inspector, whose wife took Betty in, then sent her to an uncle and aunt who lived in a barge. Betty stayed in the barge a couple of years, learning to dance for sailors. Then she was sent to another aunt, on a Somerset farm. Here she at last went to school, in the village. She became much attached to the schoolmaster, who gave her her first idea of the things of the mind. But people made a scandal out of it and she ran away to London, ending up in Commercial Road where she bought some grown-up clothes and roamed about looking for a job. A woman in a pub took her home.

She drifted into a pick-up life, helped by a girl named Rosie. Still in long plaits, she encountered a Cambridge student Gerald outside the Holborn Empire and came to know lots of clubs and the Café Royal. She posed for artists. At a club in Endell Street she met the Cherub or Pretty Pet who lured her to Bordeaux with offers of a dancing job. She did some dancing there in a *café chantant*, singing ballads like *The Raggle-taggle Gypsies* or *The Bonny Earl of Murray*, fought the Cherub, and got a place as a professional dancer. Going to Paris, she took up with the White Panther, leader of an apache gang in the Glacière district, and had a fight with the jealous Hortense who tried to knife her, thus gaining her name of *Tigre*. Trouble came when she lured an English undergraduate into the gang's den, where he was robbed. A police raid was made and she was told that she must find the student. After much searching she found him and managed to get him into a taxi with an accomplice driver; she took him to the gang, and, to save him from a worse fate, branded him on the chest with a hot knife. However another raid followed and she retreated to London. (Her account of her life in Paris has a melodramatic air, but may well be true.)

Now she haunted again the Café Royal and the Crabtree Club in Greek Street. She became engaged to Dick a barrister, who tried to reform and educate her by sending her to his father's rectory in Cornwall. She soon rushed back to London, met Dick by chance in the Café Royal, but turned instead to an Arthur, who also wanted to marry her. At an eve of marriage party, however, she decided she loved a drug-addict, Bunny, who was a Cambridge blue. On the way to their Oban honeymoon he introduced her to cocaine.

Returning, they lived in the house of Stewart Gray, who led a back to the land movement. The place was a warren of similar couples, and Betty drugged a lot. When the 1914 war broke out, Bunny put her in a Richmond flat and enlisted. Bored, she found a job in a hairdresser-tobacconist's shop in Buckingham Palace Road, drinking and drugging heavily. She took up with an Australian major, who married her when Bunny was killed. With much devoted care he broke her of the drug habit. She sat for Epstein, who did his *Savage* from her.

She next took up with Raoul (really Frederick Charles) Loveday, an undergraduate of Oxford, whom she married in the summer of 1925. A photo on the afternoon of the marriage in St John's gardens showed an ectoplasmic figure lying above his head. (Before this, he had dragged her to the Egyptian galleries of the B.M. and introduced her to the mummy of a royal priestess of Amon-Re. When he talked of the baleful power of the god to destroy those who offended him, she put out her tongue at the mummy. He hustled her away, then came back alone to prostrate himself with a prayer for the curse to fall wholly on him.) Raoul gained a First in history and they came to London.

One night at a Soho café, the Harlequin, a Mrs E.Z. said she had the magician Crowley with her at 31 Wellington Square. Raoul, already fascinated by Crowley's ideas, went to her house; but Betty, who had seen him at the Café in 1914, refused. After two days and nights away, Raoul returned by climbing up the drainpipe, stinking of ether. Crowley felt that he had found his ideal pupil, his magical heir. Betty moved lodgings, but Crowley turned up in a kilt and a black curly wig, with a snake-coiled wand – a mad-eyed sallow-skinned man with very full red lips.

He decided to return to his Abbey in Sicily, and from there wrote asking Raoul to join him. Despite Betty's protests Raoul set off, and Betty went at the last moment with him. 'One of you will never come back again,' Epstein prophesied. They arrived at the Abbey on 26 November. Crowley refused at first to let Betty in, as she wouldn't make the ritual reply, 'Love is the law, love under will,' to his, 'Do what thou wilt shall be the whole of the Law.' However, she forced her way in and continued her resistance, using even fists and a revolver – though she had to agree to sign the Oath of Affiliates. Raoul was admitted as Probationer of the order of A∴A∴, with the name Aud (magical light). He enjoyed climbing daily a blind buttress of sheer rock to a spot where he considered an ancient town had been; then he intoned the names of God and the Archangels at the four cardinal points to exclude evil influences; read the Gnostic Collects; and spent the rest of the day in talk, chess, and mandoline-strumming. On wet days a sort of Rugby Fives was played with a football. Also sex magic (sex acts) were carried out to the accompaniment of hymns, prayers, and symbolic performances. Betty settled down to doing the housework and looking after two children of Crowley's, one of whom had been a cigarette-fiend from the age of five and threatened people, 'I am Beast Number Two' with magical powers of shattering.

On arrival, all inhabitants of the Abbey were given a razor with which they were expected to cut their arm every time they said 'I' – a word permitted only to Crowley; they were commanded to say only 'one'. Betty threw her razor away, but Raoul covered his arms with nicks. The men shaved their heads save for a symbolic curl on the forehead; the women dyed their hair red or yellow with henna (a sun-aureole) and wore loose robes of bright blue with scarlet linings, hood, and golden girdle. In the refectory Crowley broke food with his fingers while Betty stood by with towel and basin. One day she poured the water over him, but he simply ignored the action. Another day he decided to sacrifice a cat that had scratched him. Betty smuggled the animal away, but it came back and was caught.

The Bloody Sacrifice was supposed to release terrific energy, in a sort of Black Mass adapted from the Gnostics. Raoul was in charge. He failed to slash hard enough. The bleeding cat rushed round the room till chloroformed. Then Raoul completed the sacrifice and drank the blood. Both Crowley and Raoul proceeded to fall ill; the local physician diagnosed an infection of liver and spleen, but Betty thought their condition due to drugs and cat's blood. Crowley cast Frater Aud's horoscope and said that he would die at four o'clock on 16 February (1923). Five days before that a violent brawl broke out. Newspapers were forbidden and Betty had been found reading one by Raoul's bedside; in the struggle bottles, glasses, furniture were smashed. Betty packed up and went down to Cefalu below, writing a complaint to the British consul at Palermo. Next day the Chinese Oracle told Crowley to be charming and forgiving, but to make it clear he'd stand no nonsense. A letter from Raoul persuaded Betty to change her mind; she wrote to the consul rescinding her complaints, and went back to the Abbey. But on the 16th Raoul died. Betty thought he lay in bed in the exact pose of the wraith floating over his head in the marriage-day photo. Crowley conducted the funeral rites.

Betty went straight back to London. The *Sunday Express* of 25 February headlined 'New Sinister Revelations of Aleister Crowley', and *John Bull* followed with accounts of the wizard of Wickedness. Crowley was ordered by the Italian Ministry of the Interior to leave Italian territory.*

*Betty's account was authentic, as is shown by Crowley's diary (used by J. Symonds in *The Great Beast* 1951). Crowley was born in 1875 at Leamington of very strict Plymouth Brethren. His brewer father dinned into him and everyone else the imminence of death and the menacing face of God, indefatigably posted tracts and travelled round preaching. When he died of cancer of the tongue, his wife carried on the work – Crowley then being eleven. The boy loathed his mother ('a brainless bigot of the most narrow, logical, and inhuman type'), but tried awhile to tread in his father's footsteps. When

Betty felt relief at being back in the Fitzroy: 'It seems more of a café than a public house, or at least more like a café than anything I know in England.' She took up for a while with the artist Jacob Kramer. Then, after a wild interlude in Yorkshire, she was back in a Soho attic with only one dress, which she washed and wore wet. A journalist wrote up her life story and got her £500. An odd fortune-teller calling herself Princess Walatka took her to the U.S.A. and Canada, then gave her £100 and the boat ticket when she wanted to leave. Through the journalist she met Carol, assistant editor of a sporting paper, a country type obsessed with hunting and shooting, who married her in the end despite his mother, 'one of those cold drooping ladies who seem more to live because "one must" than for any other reason. Her only hold on life was her fierce love of her son, which amounted almost to mania.' After a quarrel that drove Betty to London, Carol gave up his job to have more time watching over her and they lived in a bunga-low by the family house. To have something to do, she set up a cake and sweet shop in a tent, but grew bored with the rou-tine. One day Carol slaughtered a number of rooks and made her wring the necks of the wounded birds; he ate the rook-pie, which she refused, and fell ill. She tended him till his mother accused her of trying to murder him. She left for London and I met her with the robin-hood hat that was a survival from her life with Carol. 'I believe enormously in the overpowering influence of Fate,' she said, 'which seems to haunt me equally in good or bad fortune.'

I had expressed no claim on her and she made no bones about going with others while I was in the country. She pointed to a large bedstead in a shop-window at the corner of Blooms-bury and Great Russell Street, 'I spent last Wednesday night in that. Y. had the keys of the shop and we pulled down the

---

he rebelled, his mother called him the Beast of *Revelation* and he believed her words. In a mystical experience of visionary rapture (31 Dec. 1895, in a Stockholm hotel) he was convinced of his spiritual power, developing as a Satanist to oppose his parents as fully as possible. (His real name was Edward Alexander Crowley.)

blinds.' She told me many amusing tales of her adventures. One of them about a commercial traveller I wrote down straight after hearing it: he mistook her for an ordinary trollop and she led him into several undignified situations before she dropped him with a bump. She was not herself a passionate person, though she was reputed to have violent tempers when she let go. I never saw her anything but calm, with a certain ironic insight into the false and pretentious, and with much warmth towards the genuine of any kind. Her driving-force was a complete belief in her Fate – which in effect meant 'being herself', living in the dead-centre of herself.

I had met her almost simultaneously with the appearance of *The London Aphrodite*; for in the second issue P.R.S. wrote up a stag-party held in a cellar in Coptic Street, and I remember dodging off every short while to see her in the Plough. I think I remember that so clearly because it exemplified the way in which at a pinch I was always ready to sacrifice the male companionship I vaunted as the poetic and philosophic bond, and to turn to a woman in whom the values I most admired were incarnated. In the same way, despite the strong pull, I turned down not only Liam O'Flaherty's invitation to small-town races in Ireland, but also his suggestion that I should go to Soviet Russia with him – the journey that he wrote up as *I went to Russia*, 1931. I also turned down the invitation from Heseltine to go across to Normandy with him on a visit to Delius. (Perhaps he did not go; I do not know.) This invitation was one of his last friendly acts. In October 1928 he moved to Wales, unable to stand any longer the strain of Eynsford; and after that our relations grew ever more difficult.

Thus P.R.S. described the party:

Upon the appearance of *Aphrodite* No 1, a titled lady cancelled her subscription, one reviewer said he had thrown his copy into a garbage-tin out of consideration for his waste-paper basket, another duly said he was not amused, another said he could not understand Jack Lindsay's article, the *Nation* said 'no artistic value', several women tried with no success to cut Liam O'Flaherty dead; however several minor reviewers welcomed the rash venture, kind friends did not hesitate to backslap, and for instance Charley Lahrs sold 60 copies in his sentry-box bookshop in Red Lion Street. Whereupon the Editors and Liam and Charley Lahrs got drunk in a cellar kept by Louis XVII, other guests being Rhys Davies, who couldn't find the cellar at all; Tommy Earp, who tried to sing *Rule Britannia* at 3 a.m. on a beer barrel (empty); but overbalanced and broke Louis's collarbone; a calm German scholar who had to go early; an Oxford Don who passed out; and ex-member of the I.W.W. with good intentions but a too-small stomach; a bald and cheerful Australian cartoonist; two roaring Irish bhoys covered in tap-room sawdust; two great policemen; and other Bloomsbury intellectuals. At dawn Charley Lahrs and the Editors took Liam home where he irrationally began swallowing raw eggs. Then Charley vanished in a mist, and the Editors sat down in the gutter, together with a pint of (salvaged) whisky to reflect upon the Universe. Hence *The London Aphrodite* No 2, a sincere production, if somewhat melancholy in places.

A footnote in No 1 announced that this periodical is being produced 'not for profit, but for the fun of the thing'. A wondering old gentleman wrote in to ask what Jack Lindsay does when he is serious if he wrote *The Modern Consciousness* for fun? The answer would get us into trouble, we feel sure.

Will Farrow, Australian artist, was one of the guests; and as I was at work on this chapter he wrote to me after some thirty years' gap in our acquaintance and referred to the party, so it must have left a mark. 'I always think of you when I hark back to the wild party we had in a cellar in Bloomsbury with Liam O'Flaherty as the guest of honour. First we lured in the unsuspecting constable, then finished up with a rather ponderous sergeant who came looking for him. I still have a broken thumb, the after-effects of a wild dance we had when I was unlucky enough to slip with 15 stone of metropolitan policeman on top of me.' And even now, when I meet Charley Lahrs, he chuckles and makes comments on that night, convinced that he then begot his daughter.

Among new friends was Powys Mathers, whom Betty was very fond of: a tubby chap of jovial and learned wit, with a pointed beard and a vast black brimmed hat. Somehow I acquired this hat and wore it with a red neckerchief which Betty had given me; my beard was now more than Tolstoyan.

Betty once mentioned having gone to bed with Powys; and when I commented on his rotundity, she said, 'Oh, it's just a matter of patience and mountain-climbing.'

One night in the Fitzroy we met Edgell Rickword, quiet and solidly built. He had lost one eye in the war, where he gained the Military Medal. Ever since I read *Scrutinies*, which he edited, I had wanted very much to meet him. I remember going over to Betty, who did not know him, and saying, 'It's Edgell Rickword, the person I most wanted to meet in England.' Through him I met his friends Douglas Garman, handsomely tall and large, and Bertram Higgins, an Irish-Australian with considerable poetic capacity, which he was too acidly sceptical to develop. Garman had started a publishing firm with his Cambridge friend Wishart, who put up the money (he had married one of the impressively handsome Garman girls – Roy Campbell married another). Edgell came into the Wishart picture through Roy. 'We wanted to publish all the good literature that was being rejected by commercial firms,' said D.G. to me, 'but we found that meant we wanted to do D.H.L. who already had a publisher.' However, they were building up a small but distinguished list, and had issued the *Calendar*, which had recently been wound up.

I now got hold of Edgell's poetry and admired it very much. He had published the first book in English on Rimbaud, and was strongly influenced by Baudelaire and Rimbaud, by the true *symboliste* tradition, but had organically absorbed what he needed, making it all warmly his own. He had a profound sense of the city desert, the pleasure lash, the alienation of man from man in our world of the cash nexus; and in a sense was trying to live out a Baudelairean life.

> And the I retreating down familiar paths
> creates defences from the terrible sun
> and in its figurative way rebuilds
> the altar and brothel of legitimate state
> adjacent, with mean fanes darkening our streets:
> the silver-swimming gutters blench and fade
> to sinks and sewers where tarnished spirits lap,
> obscenely supine, the stale brink of day.

In the Baudelairean ethic the whore has a key place, for by reducing love openly to the cash-nexus she strips the pretences with which society covers up the bargain of marriage, covers up its whole attempt to reduce people to things, bought and sold things. By accepting the whore one accepts her exposure of the respectable and the self-righteous; her degradation becomes the accusation of the degrading powers, who are the real polluters of life. So on, goes the logic, which I thought theoretically inexpugnable; but in actuality I felt only repugnance and fear for this 'symbol'.

About the same time as the *Aphrodite* appeared I also met Philip and Molly Owens. In Philip I felt that I had encountered at long last the fellow poet I had been seeking, the poet who would work with me in refounding a vital and tumultuous verse-drama. His play *Marlowe* was a work vividly intoxicated with words – intoxicated as Marlowe himself and the Elizabethan audiences were. As he and Molly were hard up, with no fixed residence, I handed over to them my room in Gilbert Street, first warning them that it was rich in bugs. They said that in view of the low rent (5s a week), they wouldn't mind the bugs at all. Indeed, they managed somehow to keep them at bay or wipe them out, and were soon comfortably installed. Thus Phil a little later described the place:

His room, inevitably, was at the very top of the stairs, and it was a minute room with, on the landing outside, a tap and bucket for washing, tea-making, etc. The room itself was very small indeed, with space only for the double-bed and a table under the window, against which Blasco could usually be found wedged tightly in, writing furiously, while he tugged at his pipe, being in truth almost unable to get up again, once jammed into position. A kitchen-range made both a fire for heating and a stove for cooking. 'Molly,' was Blasco's invariable command at the sight of a visitor, 'tea.'

Philip Owens, a slightly built chap with a roundish face and an eager look of ceaselessly excited youth, was said to have gained his nickname, Blasco, through a long argument with a Dutchman in Antwerp, during which the latter kept trying to shut him up with the shout, 'Blast you Owens!' For some years he had been on the Continent, having gone first to Hamburg to study chemistry. The inflation of the mark made living easy, and he wandered round, staying in Vienna with a German artist Gungoff (eating orange-peel collected from the gutter and washed with Condy's fluid) and then in Paris, where he fared better by teaching English at Berlitz and doing translations. He had become a Communist. In Paris he met Molly Matthews, a young art student from Manchester, and married her.*

Phil, who became his closest friend, remarks of him at this time, 'He had a passionate choler, swiftly roused and as swiftly doused; there was always half a laugh even in his rage, an impish cock to his head, as if he acted the part of temperamental genius, and not being a particularly good actor, he very soon forgot his part, and the next moment would be arguing volubly about Lenin or Trotsky, for at this period he was often quite a solemn Communist.'

Just before I handed my room over to the Owens I had the excellent but impracticable idea of getting some capital into the firm, and talked things over with Dennis Bradley. He offered me a letter of introduction to his bank manager, who was good about overdrafts and loans; and so I transferred our account to a bank in Bond Street. To my horror as I was chatting with the manager and doing my best to impress him with our solvency and prospects, I saw a bug crawling over my shirt-cuff. I hastily put my hand under the table and shook the bug off. I hope that it wasn't a female and the bank didn't soon find itself infested. Either the manager was extremely poker-faced or he didn't notice the creature.

---

*It was probably of an earlier stay that he told me an anecdote in which P.R.S. figured. The local party office asked him to call in and take an unobtrusive seat at one side when an odd Englishman called. Blasco did as asked and found the Englishman to be P.R.S. with his flamboyant manner. When I published this tale in an Australian periodical, P.R.S. took me to mean that I was accusing him of having been an *agent provocateur*. Of course I didn't mean anything of the sort; I always considered him to be one of the most loyal, open and frank persons I have known. I was merely paying a tribute to his breezy magnificence of manner, his unfailing panache, which had quite incorrectly stirred the suspicions of the dull officials.

Meanwhile I was being carried along on my dark tide of submission to Betty. There were times when I seemed to be riding with miraculous poise on the crest of the wild wave; then came the floundering and panicked fall into the trough of confusion. One high moment came when there was an explosion of a gas main near St Giles Circus. The area was left in a dusty and smouldering disorder, with a stinking sense of world-end. A line from Aeschylus's *Agamemnon* came to my mind: 'This very day the Achaians enter Troy.' I said it aloud several times with a sort of ecstasy.

Then one day, as I felt quite sober, I went to sign some cheques in the office to meet accounts, and found that my hand trembled so much the signature was illegible. That frightened me. And not long afterwards Betty came to me and said, 'Do you mind if I go and live with Edgell? Do you say I mustn't?' I was startled, as I hadn't noticed that Edgell was particularly interested in her. Sorry to lose her and glad to be free from entanglements, I said that of course she must do as she wished and that I had no claim on her. And so my relations with her ended.

13 · A NEW START

ELZA must have guessed something of what was happening. Suddenly one week, after I had been in London a day or two, she turned up early in the office and wanted to know where I had slept the night before. I took her to the room round the corner which I had borrowed from the Davis and Orioli bookseller. I had then broken from Betty for over a week, and managed to convince Elza nothing was wrong. However, I felt a hard and resistant fibre in her – for the first time since the day when she forced me to have a showdown with Kirtley. And she remained restless. She decided to move, and found a small house at Takeley, further west. Then the agitations of removal took up her mind. The house was of brick, but with lichened apple trees and with shady lanes of hazel-nuts running into the Rodings. I took Robinetta for walks, now more at ease with her silence. I had plunged afresh into work and was translating Theocritos. The period of dereliction had taken up between two and three months, and I was back in my normal relations to the firm; but something had happened, a break that couldn't be mended; the first impetus and its innocences had gone.

A bad public speaker, I gave three lectures. The first was on the nature of poetry, before a literary society of London University in rooms off the Strand. All I recall is that when I used the phrase 'the hell of childhood' (coupled antithetically with *paradis enfantins*), a beautiful slender girl got up and went slowly out, staring at me all the while with eyes of burning accusation; and I watched her with such love that for a while afterwards I spoke with eloquence as well as passion. The theme of the second lecture was Greek attitudes to sex for some sex-reform society. Garman tried to encourage me with several whiskies beforehand, in vain; and he, Edgell and some others came in near the end, as they had threatened, to make me lose the thread of my discourse, but I had already lost it. I had been talking about the Platonic concept of desire and not the homo-sexualities which the emancipated audience, behind their serious spectacles, had come to hear me defend in learned detail. The theme of the third lecture was Christ in Blake's poetry, delivered to the Blake Society from Wesley's pulpit near Bunhill Fields where Blake's neglected grave lay. I was rather put off by the serried ranks of parsons smiling with ben-evolent teeth to show their broadmindedness as I spoke of the rival religions of Christ and Dionysos. However, I was pleased to meet old Wright, a patriarchal-looking figure like one of Blake's old men with the wind of eternity flowing through his silken beard – but with a mild distrait aspect, as of a prophet who had stood up to denounce the world and embarrassingly at the last moment had forgotten what he wanted to say. Presi-dent of the Blake and Cowper Societies (and later the first revealer of the truth about Dickens and Ellen Ternan), he had liked my book on Blake and written to me about it. We met a few times and talked of Blake and Cowper, and got on well together, though his deprecatory cough seemed now and then to rebuke God for failing to prompt him at the moments when he was about to rise to the prophetic status.

Norman Douglas had more than once mooted the project of a visit to Florence; but I should never have gone if it had not been for an accident – the arrival of an Italian artist from that town, the protégé of a rich Australian woman who flut-tered in a portly way round our office. The rich woman wanted me to publish a book of his drawings; but though they were excellent in their way, I did not feel they fitted into our Fanfrolico universe. So, though I would rather have liked to gain access for the Press to the rich woman's bank account, I handed the scheme over to Hanchant, who finally produced the book – not very well. I was present as umpire at the depressed meeting, in some arts and crafts dim-lit basement, where the annoyed artist denounced print after print as inad-equate, and I had no course but to agree with him, though Hanchant with reproachful eyes moaned that the cost of the book was going to be prohibitive. The cost went up, and the book was still not all it should have been. And despite my visiting the patroness' lavish flat for tea once or twice, I was further off than ever from the moment when it would be tactful to suggest an investment in the Press. The artist, disillusioned as to English art books, decided to return to Florence with his wife and patroness. They suggested that I should go with them. P.R.S. supported them, saying that it would do me good to have a holiday; and after some doubts I decided to go. I was feeling out of sorts and my under-the-weather condition had been worsened by my lying out under the apple trees to read Greek poets and catching a cold in the bladder from the damp earth (the same trouble as I contracted from my one night in the dripping Sydney jail).

With a wrench I went. We stayed for the night in Paris, where, left to my own resources, I wandered round some of the haunts I knew from my stay with P.R.S. two-and-a-half years before. Then we went on. I remember the unpleasant feeling when, after we had passed the Italian frontier, I made some comment about Mussolini, which reduced the artist to abject terror. He begged me not to mention the name again. I found that Douglas and other English folk in Florence had their various pseudonyms for the dictator, such as Mr Smith.

Douglas met me at the station, tall stiff and straight-backed, but carrying his heavy build lightly; with his close-set ears, strong jaw, expressive eyebrows, large nose, and silver hair parted in the middle, he had a very Scottish look, but more sanguine and overpowering than I had expected. From the back his head had a Highlander's oblong height; and in his tweeds made up by an Italian he had an indefinable air of masquerading as himself, testy and benevolent, impatiently waiting for some enemy to materialize and be knocked down by his lairdly stick. He carried me off to his spacious flat, where the boy of the moment was pettishly doing housework with the pert air of a spoilt favourite, barked at by Douglas in his sarcastic indulgent way. After lunch he took me to a near hotel, where I threw my bag under the bed and lay wondering why I had come.

For a fortnight of fine weather I roamed about Florence,

often with Douglas, or sat in Pino Orioli's cramped shop on the Arno looking out on the Ponte Santa Trinità with a window full of books, engravings, parchment-bindings, bits of medieval music. Pino with his easy, chattering malice was good company, his tales of the foibles of D.H.L., Frieda, and scores of English inhabitants of Florence made all the more amusing by his odd pronunciation of *v* and *w*, *z* and *s*. An excellent mimic, he enjoyed his imitations so much that he was both performer and audience, and imagined his renderings to be so much more exact than they were, that in the end one did not know if one was laughing at the mimings or at Pino's ecstatic ideas of them.

I visited the artist's studio out in the open countryside and admired the cool charm of his fine-toned paintings of women; and had tea with his patroness at Doney's on the Tornabuoni, fashionably filled with hordes of rich useless women, their strident chatter pitched to drown the jingling of teaspoons, their scandal-mongering glances avidly registering anything to anyone else's disadvantage. To shut one's eyes was to imagine oneself in an aristophanic bog on the verge of hell crammed with sex-starved female frogs. Mrs D. pointed out Miss Pincher, the mean old maid whom Pino loved to pillory, withering himself into the meanest of all old maids and turning his shop with a wave of the hand into her apartments in a palazzo, her terrace-garden stocked with flowers wheedled out of other rich old useless women. 'That flower? Oh it's Buggarvilliar —' Miss P. staring with a new respect at the bougainvillia and saying gratefully purse-lipped, 'Where's a pencil? I must write the name down before I forget. How do you spell it?' while N.D. drinks up her show-bottle of sham Strega and grumbles with twitching eyebrows at its vile taste.

We ate, Norman, Pino and myself, at Ristorante Bianca with its trolley of boiled meats, or at Fusi's, where N.D. grunted that the place was at least foul enough to scare off tourists. For a couple of days Faith Compton-Mackenzie joined us. Norman had a special tenderness for her; he told me that she was the only woman who stuck up for him when he had the London trouble that led to his exile. A generously warm person, I could never take seriously N.D.'s squabbles about food or his grave comments on grey truffles, his ritual with the cheap hard-twisted Toscano cigars stuck in the upper pocket of his coat, which never drew however much he cut them or broke them in half, or his topsyturvying of accepted notions: 'Come on, close the windows and let's have some good healthy nitrogen.'

One day Pino, expatiating at his flat on the trials of dealing with a suppressed homosexual like D.H.L., showed me some of his paintings. (Pino's world was composed of homosexuals, suppressed or unsuppressed.) I found the pictures interesting and said there ought to be an exhibition. Pino shrugged. I said we'd do anything to help, and he said he'd raise the matter with Frieda. I had just missed the Lawrence period at the Villa Miranda; and Frieda had looked in at Florence a few days before I came.

Theoretically I approved of N.D.'s hedonism, but in practice found it humourless and tediously amoral; when I came to write of it in the *Aphrodite*, I clothed it in an existentialist thesis of Desire that had little to do with it. I myself had never kept a review or any of my journalism, and I was shaken to find that N.D. had everything gummed up in big books. True, he was now building up an industry out of his trivia, reprinting them through Orioli. Again in theory I approved of the cynical things he said about making a living out of his American collectors; but the paltry details of the procedure seemed beneath the dignity of the man who had written *South Wind*.

Thus I spent my fortnight in a mixture of pleasant idling and enjoyment of N.D.'s sharp comments, and of disquiet and uncertainty, which prevented me from more than cursory glances at Florence, its buildings and galleries. I wrote to Elza saying I felt it had been wrong to come without her; in the future I wanted to live my life out in companionship with her in all matters. Only once, late at night, as we drank in a small squalid hostelry along the Arno, in ragged lights and amid croaks of song from a malevolently tipsy boatman, did I feel N.D. in the flesh coincide with the sort of person I had built up in my mind out of *South Wind* and the early travel books.

On my return I found Elza ill in bed. Later I learned that she had been sure of my departure for Australia. An old woman from a near cottage had been brought in to attend to the house, and though she was doing her best, things were in confusion and Robinetta rather untended. However Elza was soon up when she realized that I had not gone off. For my part, the mood in which I had written from Florence about our achieving a fuller companionship did not dissipate itself. Looking back, I can see that the effect of my change-of-heart was not however to make Elza any happier; from this period she became more demanding and at moments dictatorial. The more I gave in to her, the more this side of her character came up. My yielding to her stimulated her jealousy of me; it did not pacify it. I suppose that her fear of my going off had previously stifled her other fears; now, as that fear gradually went, the others grew stronger and more domineering. If at times I resented her attitude, I told myself that I was to blame for the stress I had put on her during my gadding-about with Betty. I believed that forbearance and gentleness on my part would make amends and bring her to a better balance.

Eric Partridge had happened on a visit at Museum Street to pick up the little book in which I had transcribed Elza's poems. As soon as he started his press, he asked if he could print the poems with my decorations. When *I Saw the Earth* appeared, it was selected as one of the best fifty books of the year. I also did a preface for an edition of Blake's *Poetical Sketches* for the Scholartis Press.

About this time I met someone else who had been in the Cefalu Abbey. Mary Butts had been married to Rodker, then had turned to Cecil Maitland, who was interested in abnormal psychology. They met Crowley in Paris in February 1921 and were invited to Sicily, arriving in time to take part in the rite of the Cakes of Light, which seems to have consisted of the sacrifice of a young cock by Cecil – the cock being baptized Peter-Paul to represent the Christian Church. 'Alostrael [Leah Faesi, Crowley's mistress] then dances against the will of Mary, on my swearing to give to her the half of my Kingdom. She demands P.P.'s head on the Disk. I behead him and the blood is caught in the silver "charger" on the Disk.' Later, Mary (whom Crowley described as 'a fat, bold, red-headed slut . . . pompous, pretentious, and stupid') seems to have taken part in the rite of the Goat's copulation with the Scarlet Woman

(Leah), during which Crowley cut the beast's throat and its blood spilled over Leah's back. Now Crowley praised her clairvoyant powers; she saw blue lights and once 'a huge Assyrian bull demon'. Still, after some three months, she and Cecil left the Abbey. According to Goldring, they said their health was permanently injured and they had acquired the habit of drugs.*

I met Mary in the Fitzroy, where she had come, I think, to see Edgell. She was then about thirty-five. Careless of herself, she was still impressive with her red-gold hair, her white skin and rich blue eyes, her large naked face. In build she was rather stocky. We talked about Theocritos. She had a passionate interest in the Greeks, and every time we met we spoke of nothing else, apart from a few words about her Butts ancestor who had been Blake's patron; she considered that she had an intuitive understanding of the Eleusinian Mysteries. (Cecil had died in 1927 and I never met Gabriel Atkin, an artist, with whom she went to Cornwall.)

Edgell was now living in some rooms near Bedford Square. I saw a fair amount of him and Garman, though after a few drinks I generally had some strong disagreement with the latter, who was liable to suffer from colic. His tight belt was blamed. Once Edgell, Bertram and myself carried him home at a late hour on our shoulders and handed him over to his sleepily irate wife. Cecil Rickword asked me to write the essay on Joyce for the second volume of *Scrutinies*. I recall the moment as several of us were packed in a taxi and squinting out of the window I caught the eye of Eros aiming his bow at some all-too-easy Piccadilly breast. Not long after Cecil was killed in a motor-car accident.

*It is surprising how many people were affected by Crowley. He crops up early in *Laughing Torso*; and Nina introduced Mary to him. W. J. Sullivan, who wrote on Maths and Music, was won over at the same time; he signed an oath 'to discover my own True Will and to do it'. Next day the Beast, sending W.J.S. south after his True Will, carried out an act of sex-magic with his wife Sylvia. A man met at Austin Harrison's paid Crowley's fare back to Cefalu as well as the fares of Raoul and Betty. See also Calder-Marshall's *The Magic of my Youth*.

About this time the Nonesuch Press advertised a coming complete translation of Plato. After writing to mention our plan of doing several of the dialogues, I called on the Meynells at their suggestion. I remember the vexed silence that fell when Meynell carelessly mentioned he lived in north Essex, and I broke in enthusiastically, 'So do I.' I had also met Pearl Binder who did drawings for our Skelton's *Turning of Eleanour Rumming*, which we bound in sacking with XXXs on it; we meant the book to be a try out for a full text of Skelton. Through Pearl I met Tom Driberg's bearded elder brother, who had much of interest to say on anthropology. And it was perhaps about this time or earlier that I met Gordon Craig, with Elza, and was shown his woodcuts; characteristically the book of ours he most liked by far was my little book on Blake. Elza also went with me to lunch at Compton-Mackenzie's flat; but was very offhand and rude. I remonstrated with her on the stairs and she went back with a perfunctory return invitation; but nothing more came of the acquaintance.

One day in the B.M. I had what I thought was an inspiration: to produce a fine edition of Byron's *Manfred* with an introduction giving the facts about Augusta Leigh. Frederick Carter was often in the office, a likeable but melancholy man, who was in correspondence with D.H.L. about *Revelation*. I asked him to do the foreword and make illustrations; but somehow the book didn't come out as effective and lavish as I had hoped the purple-printed drawings would make it.

I had written to Orioli repeating my remarks about D.H.L.'s paintings. At first I had the idea of getting the rights for a book of them; but D.H.L.'s conflict with Joynson-Hicks was increasing and the customs were doing their utmost to find and burn copies of *Lady Chatterley's Lover*. For our Press to print an edition of D.H.L.'s paintings would have been to invite trouble. Meanwhile a certain strain had grown up between P.R.S. and myself. He was not in the least to blame. At root I think I had lost interest in the Press as it had been originally constituted. In *The London Aphrodite* we had turned from the fine-book market and in the process had begun to develop ideas that broke away from the Fanfrolico aesthetic. P.R.S. was in a large part himself responsible for my growing pangs; but in turning away from the Press as we had together built it up, I found myself turning away from him. I really wanted to escape the Press, but had no alternative economic basis.

These changes in my attitude were also helped by the arrival of a young Australian, Brian Penton, who had been at the Brisbane Grammar School like myself. As a junior contemporary there, he had known me by sight though I had not known him. He was a boarder and once ran away, he told me, because he grew scared at the excessive mutual masturbation. An odd-looking fellow with a thin hatchet-face, as though his skull had been pressed in by someone putting hands on either side of his temple, he had dark wiry hair and piercing dark eyes; a terrific talker, very ambitious and amorous. He had brought over the MS of a novel and many letters of introduction into the world of journalism. He disliked P.R.S. and used all his considerable powers of biting sarcasm to belittle him. Not that I consciously took much notice of what Brian said; for I had the feeling that he'd be as biting about myself to P.R.S. or anyone else behind my back. Yet, despite my distrust of his urbanely stinging tongue, I liked him and no doubt his witticisms had a certain effect on me.

14 · D. H. LAWRENCE

As the end of 1928 was nearing, P.R.S. suggested that he should take a business holiday in the South of France, calling in at Nice and such places to sell copies of our books. I was sceptical about the likelihood of Nice buying our books, but thought P.R.S. deserved a holiday, especially after my fortnight in Florence. He went south and took the opportunity to call in on D.H.L. at Bandol. At this time I thought I was the first person to have suggested an exhibition and book of the paintings; much later I learned that the idea had already been mooted by Dorothy Warren. However P.R.S. now stepped in and really got things moving. On 19 December 1928 D.H.L. wrote to Frieda's mother that Rhys Davies had been staying with them.

We also had a young Australian here for two days, this afternoon he left for Nice. He makes those beautiful expensive books that people collect nowadays – he says he will make a book next year of my paintings – of all my paintings, with a foreword by me, to be sold at ten guineas each. It seems madness to me, but it's his money and he will pay me well – if he does it. [Translated from the German.]

D.H.L. had been much agitated during Rhys Davies's visit about the attitude of the young. Rhys records that D.H.L. told him, 'Kick, kick all the time, make them feel you know what they are. Because you *do* know, you're intelligent enough. The young know, they *know*, and yet they let be. Oh dear, it drives me to despair when I see them holding back, letting be. Because your chance is now, the world is all wobbling and wants a new direction.' P.R.S. told me that at lunch D.H.L. got worked up and attacked Rhys for deserting his class, the workers. He bade him stick to them at all costs. 'Don't desert your class! Don't run away from your class!' It seemed to me a case where the speaker was attacking himself and regretting that he had not himself carried out the good advice he gave.

P.R.S. has stated in print:

Penton and Philip [Lindsay] were very anxious to join the Fanfrolico Press, and easily persuaded Jack that they had a stimulus to impart. I left them to it, and stepped out in about March, 1929, Penton then becoming my successor as manager. I had other plans. In January, on a visit to the south of France, I had met D. H. Lawrence and offered to publish a book of reproductions of his paintings; but Lawrence did not want to be associated with the Fanfrolico Press, as he disagreed with the Lindsay Aesthetic. (*Kookaburras and Satyrs*)

I visited Lawrence at Bandol, in the south of France, and stayed several days with him ... Lawrence did not like Jack Lindsay's writings or ideas. He would never have consented to the publication of any of his works in the Lindsay-dominated Fanfrolico Press. But Lawrence took a liking to me, and gave me his paintings to take to London. The agreement for publication of the paintings was made by me with Lawrence's agent in London, L. E. Pollinger, of Curtis Brown Ltd. All this is on documentary record in *The Letters of D. H. Lawrence*, edited by Aldous Huxley. (*Biblionews*)

But in fact, so far from D.H.L. rejecting the Fanfrolico Press, the initial project put up to him was for his pictures to be done by that press, and he accepted. Also most of the paintings were with Dorothy Warren, to whom he wrote on 19 December 1928.

I think you've been a bit cool, keeping my pictures there all the time and merely doing nothing. However, now the men of the Fanfrolico Press, Jack Lindsay and P. R. Stephensen, say they want to do a book of reproductions of my paintings as early as possible in the New Year. So they want to have the pictures photographed at once ... But if you still want to show them, perhaps you could arrange with Mr Lindsay to have the show at about the same time as their book is ready: perhaps in February.

That letter shows conclusively what the original idea was. The objection to having D.H.L. in the Fanfrolico Press came from me, not from D.H.L. at all.

P.R.S. arrived back from Bandol and Nice jubilant, though

I think he had sold only one book: however that was one more than I expected. We discussed the matter at length. Finally I had what I thought a good idea. There was a bookseller, Edward Goldston, in Museum Street, on the corner opposite the Plough; I had often had a casual beer with him and he had more than hinted that he would like to put some money into our Press. I had been keeping him up my sleeve in case our needs ever became urgent. It now struck me that Goldston might well be interested in forming a new press to produce the D.H.L. paintings, which, in view of the publicity gained through *Lady Chatterley* and D.H.L.'s pamphlet against Joynson-Hicks (which I saw on sale in large quantities in Selfridges), could not fail to make a large sum of money. I suggested that he and P.R.S. should float the company and brought the two of them together for this purpose.*

There was as yet no suggestion that P.R.S. and myself should part; but since he now had his own firm, it was inevitable we should go different ways. He gives March as the time of his going off; but he also adds that Phil's desire to get into the Press was one of the reasons for his going – and Phil did not arrive till September! Also, the last issue of the *Aphrodite* did not appear till July, and we were in close contact until then.

P.R.S. gives January as the date of his visit to Bandol; in fact it was then, after our discussion, that he rushed over for a second visit. D.H.L. mentions his arrival in a letter to Rhys of the 11th, saying how P.R.S. 'stirred us all up as usual'. On 18 April, D.H.L. wrote to Pino from Palma de Majorca, during a visit to Spain, 'The Fanfrolico Press has more or less dissolved. The *working* partner was always Stephensen – Lindsay was the literary side of it. Stephensen has joined with Edward Goldston the Jew bookseller of Museum Street, to make the

---

*P.R.S. must have notified Lawrence promptly; for whereas the latter on 19 December writes of the F.P. as doing his book, by 25 Dec. he speaks of the Mandrake Press. (The name was chosen by P.R.S.) It was about mid-January that P.R.S. collected the paintings from the Warren Gallery (Nehls iii 299). About that time the *Daily News* reported, 'My friend is Mr Jack Stephensen (*sic*) of the Fan Frolico Press (*sic*), and he is arranging a special spring show of Mr Lawrence's work at the Warren galleries.'

Mandrake Press, of which my pictures are the first thing done – the reproduction of *Moses* seemed very dim to me.' He was handing on the news that P.R.S. had given him; in fact the Press was far from dissolution yet. (It would seem from this letter that April was the actual date when P.R.S.'s direct association with the firm was severed. I cannot myself recall the exact time, as we continued working together to some extent till July-August, as I have mentioned.)

For one reason or another the production of the book of paintings kept on being delayed; and in the end the result was not very good. ('Oh, that Mandrake – vegetable of ill omen!' D.H.L. wrote in one of his last letters.) Nehls remarks, in connection with some criticisms by Earp:

'Alternately muddy and garish' as a description of Lawrence's colour will not do. But it *will* do admirably – in fact there is not much else that will – for the 'colour-work' carried out for the Mandrake Press 'under the supervision of William Dieper'. The inference seems clear: While reviewing the 'Introduction to These Paintings' Mr Earp sought to refresh his memory out of the Mandrake pictures – and blurred it.

From early April the Gallery was waiting for the Mandrake to return the paintings and deliver the copies of the book. During this period I exchanged several letters with Lawrence. On his December return P.R.S. had hopes of converting him and asked me to send him a copy of my *Dionysos*; I objected that D.H.L. would detest it, but gave in. In a letter of his to Huxley dated Christmas Day 1928 he wrote, 'Lindsay sent me this morning *another* copy of his Dionysos book!' The only inference is that P.R.S. had already given him a copy out of his portmanteau of books, but had forgotten. D.H.L. wrote asking me to read the proofs of his introduction and to check up about his statement of Henry VIII having suffered from syphilis. (He had got this from the book, *Post Mortem*, by an Australian doctor C. MacLaurin.) He added, 'Now don't say you'll do all this and then do nothing about it!' He also sent us some *Pansies* for the *Aphrodite*, but I turned them down; they were among the weaker ones, unless my memory deceives me. In one letter he suddenly burst out: 'Give up writing all this muck about love.

Leave it to the Sashy Sitwells. You're right in what you hate. Stick to that and you'll get somewhere. Stop the love slush. Stick to your hate. That's what's real and good and creative in you.' (I quote from memory, but as I re-read the letter a considerable number of times I can be sure of having the sense right. Why he dragged Sacheverell in I do not know, unless he had been annoyed by my praising him in the magazine.) He also asked me to have a look over the hanged pictures at the Warren Galleries on a second floor in Maddox Street. Despite the concealed lighting and the silver-grey velvet on the walls of one room, I thought the place didn't look enough like a professional gallery; but the pictures were visible enough. P.R.S. came along, and with us was Barbara, one of Frieda's daughters, an Englishly nice but rather bewildered girl. We had tea together, but my efforts to draw her out only made her more nicely bewildered.

The show opened on 15 June and the attacks began. The police raid was made on 5 July. But by that time I was taken up with the problems of reorganizing the Press.

15 · BACK TO LONDON

ELZA was fretting at Takeley and I asked her why she didn't come back to London. Now that the burden of the firm was falling more on my shoulders, it was difficult to divide my time between London and Takeley. Rupert Atkinson, a rich Australian, was in London. A talented writer of verse and of plays in which he tried to define his own tormented split-up being, his sense of living several lives at the same moment, he was a restless disappointed man, printing his own work hastily and unable to settle to anything definite – poetry or whisky or travel, an intellectual or a playboy role. Generous and kind-hearted, he had done much to help the perennially penniless Hugh McCrae, who responded with a vast fund of malicious stories which mainly dealt with ridiculous escapades with Rupert's wife, Marie. She was a dark-haired woman whom Rupert had met as a barmaid and who still bore the signs of a remarkable beauty. I slept a few times at their large flat in Bloomsbury, and now and then Rupert swept into the office. 'What, never been into Westminster Abbey! Come along at once. I've got a taxi waiting.'

One evening the artist Nevinson came into the Plough on the quest for guests for a large party. He asked a small gracefully wriggling model with a slight cast in one eye, whose capacious bottom he pinched and complimented in a loud whisper; and then he included me. Rupert was out of town, so I took Marie along. The Nevinson house was madly crowded, and I chiefly remember a group of students teasing the pianist Mark Hambourg, whose ponderous German manners could not compete with their guerilla tactics of insult. Marie was annoyed that I couldn't recognize most of the important artists and introduce her to them. She was sure that she only needed to be introduced to Epstein to be asked to sit for a bust. But there were too many drunken young beauties kissing between hiccups and charlestoning with lean legs and agilely out-thrust rumps. She had no hope of being a success, even though she kept to the worst-lighted room. I met the model with her black hair braided over her broad brow several times on the stairs, her squint steadily growing stronger as she complained of her headache and her inability to find our thick-set host with his dark resentfully challenging eyes. Marie complained all the way back to her flat near Marble Arch at having been trodden on and elbow jabbed as well as innocently involved in a soda-squirting battle of the students. 'And where were you all the while?' I told her that I'd been listening to old Nevinson talk.

I had written to Freud asking him if he would write an intro-duction to an edition of *Thus Spake Zarathustra*; at the same time I sent him my book on Nietzsche, *Dionysos*. He replied that he felt too deeply about Nietzsche and owed him too great a debt ever to write about him, and referred me to Ernest Jones. He also added that he thought I was quite wrong in what I had written about Frau Salome and suggested that as she was still alive I should visit her in Germany. This comment of his struck me hard. I re-read the passages in my book about Nietzsche and Frau S., and felt how frivolously cocksure they were, how easily I had assumed an understanding of a complex situation, reducing the relationship to a simple pattern suitable for the Fanfrolico universe. (I had forgotten she became one of Freud's early disciples.)

D.H.L.'s upbraiding exhortation and Freud's polite snub had a decisive effect in re-orienting my mind. They continued slowly but steadily working in the depths of my being, though I lost both letters on the same night. I carried them around in my pocket-book: the sort of thing I hadn't done since I received Norman's first letters in 1919. We were drinking at Edgell's rooms and in some argument I produced D.H.L.'s letter. Freud's came out with it and I showed both of them round. Either someone stole them or they were lost in the confusion. That night I also met a strong reprimand which left a lasting effect. I had been talking about Aristophanes. (We were doing his *Ecclesiazusai* in the same format as the *Lysistrata*, with an introduction by Edgell.) Trying to formulate what I felt about the poet's allegiance to life (which in Fanfroliconean terms meant girls and wine), I said something about Aristophanes not really caring what happened to Athens. I meant that his care for Athens was poetically his care for the freedoms that begat poetry, not for the city in an abstract political sense; but Edgell said gravely, 'I think he cared a great deal,' and suddenly I felt that the opposition I was making between the city of poetry and the city of political actuality was a false one. So, if I lost my precious letters that night, I gained something of self-knowledge which was in line with the letters' message, helping to bring me down to earth.

Shortly afterwards, Edgell called on me at the office, and suggested he might be paid for his preface, if we could afford it. We happened to be short at the moment. But Edgell had just handed over his poem on the Lousy Astrologer for the *Aphrodite*. So I went down with him for a cup of tea in the Express below with Betty, and said, 'While we have any money, what's the use of it except for friends?' And wrote out the cheque. About this time Hart Crane was in London; he called on Edgell, who found him very anti-*Aphrodite* and argued with him; I don't know if he convinced him.

Not long afterwards Edgell and Betty moved to a cottage in the south. I paid them one weekend visit. After some games of shove ha'penny in a long shadowy pub at Lewes, we went by bus to a small cottage lost in a ragged rural nook. Betty looked so like a hardworking gypsy in the rough conditions that the place survives in memory rather as a caravan camping-site, smudged with the floating smoke-wreaths of a rich wood-fire, while the crackle of broken-up twigs punctuates the conversation and Betty flinging back the hair from her sweaty face bares her housewifely elbows.

Elza found a sort of flat somewhere in the direction of Hammersmith, and we moved to London. We had had for some months a mongrel dog Whiskers, and as soon as we arrived he lost himself. A couple of days later I found him in a police-lair for lost dogs, and rescued him. The performance went on being repeated. The back section of our flat, which housed a huge jingling brass-bedstead as well as a wardrobe that fell over if one let the doors swing open, was roofed with glass; and we had no sooner moved in than a window-cleaner fell through the glass from an upper storey and had to be removed in an ambulance. Brian Penton found rooms nearby. He was suffering from the frosty chastity of English maidens, or pretending to suffer; for one never knew if he wasn't putting on an act as part of his disinterested belief that life should be as dramatic and exciting as possible. If it was in fact humdrum, one was justified in throwing various bombs of irony or abuse into its midst, simply to enliven it and bring the temperature up to the point of simmering merriment. So his sarcasms often had a purely comic aim and were meant, not to belittle their object, but to blow life up into oversize caricature dimensions. He acted the fool, charitably, to amuse others and woo them out of the boredom he accounted a sin, and to keep himself up to the level of intense enjoyment of the spectacle of existence, the serious mask slipping from the always absurd face of fact, the gap between profession and actuality in which was expressed the human condition, its idiot ambiguity.

And so his insistence on being a frustrated wooer of all the lovelies of an embarrassingly lavish world was perhaps in part an expression of a genuine uncertainty and modesty, as it was also certainly in part a game that he was playing with himself in order to enhance the rather dull everyday facts. At the same time he found a certain satisfaction in trying to live up to his fabricated role as chief actor in an endless *conte drolatique*: not so much out of any impulse of venery as out of a wish to see how things went, how a gambler's tosses worked out, how often he could actually bluff life into taking him seriously at his jesting word. He didn't really give a damn, but he foamed at the mouth as he blamed the stringent economic conditions of England that made women conscious of the marriage ring as their blither loose-foot sisters of Australia never were. It was a rhetorical exercise, a sketch of vituperation in the Roman style, with the force behind the outpouring and elaborated phrases coming from his fear of failure, his fierce resolve to cut a figure in the mocked-at world.

One day as we were homing by bus, he winked at me and

gave a nod. I realized that he was on petting terms with the gravely aloof girl beside him, and left him to it. About an hour later he turned up at the flat, in a ferocious rage against English virgins. The girl had grown scared when he got out at her stop, and had threatened to call a policeman. One needed to know Brian well to realize that the affair had gone exactly according to schedule, and that the anti-climax was just what he wanted, since it released him from the need for further action and at the same time proved his point, giving him the desired text for a denunciation. The satisfaction lay in the words, in the clowning, in the social excitement that had been generated, with Brian gesticulating at its heart.

However not long after he picked up in the Plough the wife of a well-known painter, who liked listening to his tirades and who gave him a different set of variants in his exposition of the inferiority of the English female to the Australian. She was a little kittenish ball of a thing, who did not bother to wear pants, at least when visiting gentlemen, as I unavoidably noted one day when she sat waiting for Brian in our front room, yawning wide-and-brawny-kneed on the sofa under a photogravure of Watts' Hope blindfolded on a spinning world. Brian arrived an hour late, voluble in his spattering way with excuses, and gave an uproarious imitation of the editor whom he had been interviewing.

With his capacity to be extremely charming, he won Elza's affection and spent much of his time at our flat while I was at the office or the B.M. Once, however, we went down the street to his lodgings, where the dyspeptic landlady had one of those rare and outlandish things, a radio-set, to hear John Gough's *Wallaby Track* being broadcast. During this period Elza was more uninhibitedly blithe and easy-going than I had ever known her; and I felt that Brian's attentions, blustering, wheedling, and flatteringly docile, had much to do with this change of mood. The three of us generally went out together; and she even found a certain pleasure in having a couple of drinks at a pub with us. She grew excited and flushed when we discussed the plans in which now Brian had his place; and even gave me an unsolicited kiss after emerging from the big tin bath with sunflowers knocking against the glass windows

– a bath that made a thunderous noise when one stepped in or out of it.

She had temporarily left Robinetta with the neighbours at Takeley. The intention was to bring her to London as soon as we had found some large premises. These arrangements had been entirely Elza's. But we had not been long in London when a letter arrived to say that Miss Edith Craig, motoring in the Rodings, had called in at Takeley and carried her grand-niece off. I still do not know who had notified her about Robinetta. Perhaps it was the neighbours who were keeping the child for a weekly fee; perhaps we had some enemy in the area of whom I knew nothing and who had decided the child was being neglected. Elza was normally a capable enough housekeeper in her quiet way; but during my absence in Florence and for a short while after, before she regained her health, things had certainly been in a mess, presided over by the friendly but hag-looking old woman. (In any event, how had anyone known of Edith Craig?)

Elza did not seem at all perturbed. She went to see Edith Craig and told her that she had no objection to Robinetta being kept till we were suitably settled. No doubt she had been so used to temporary residences for herself, Robert, or the child, with friends or relations, that she did not attach any particular importance to Edith Craig's actions. The latter said nothing about being determined to hold on to Robinetta. I was not present at the discussion; but Elza returned in a good humour.

Brian told us that his wife Olga was arriving. With his fervent imagination he drew a picture of an incredibly dainty and petite creature, which he supported with the only photo of Olga he possessed; in it she showed up as a small white summer-blur. On the day of her ship's arrival he had an appointment with Lloyd George – one of his important appointments which he never quite explained and which never came to anything. So I agreed to meet the train and take Olga to our flat. For some hours she waited there as patiently as she could; then the door crashed open and Brian rushed impetuously in. He at once recoiled, stuttered, and advanced again at a more sober pace. I now knew him well enough to understand what had happened. He had so impressed himself with his dream pictures of Olga that no earthly actuality, however charming, could be identical with the fabulous sylph of his prolonged conjurations.

We decided to set up house together, Lindsays and Pentons, and Elza found a large house in Woodchurch Road, West Hampstead, with a fair-sized strip of back-garden. We moved in and I bought two presses, one of the old screw-type and one a more modern platen. I had decided to start printing as many of our books as possible myself. I had in hand a complete Catullus on which I had been working, with a long and hastily compiled introduction, and for which, as for the Theocritos, Ellis did woodcuts at a small fee. I bought some Cloister type for main jobs, and, at Oliver Simon's advice, Weiss Antiqua – another type which we were the first to use in Britain. (We had been the first to use Koch Kursiv, in *Delighted Earth*.)

I had written telling Phil and Ray that we now had a big house, and inviting them over. Phil decided to come. In early September he arrived. I cannot do better than cite his account. He says that I was late to meet him at Waterloo; probably I was, though I did not know at the time I had given him such an excruciating time of waiting. He describes his anguish as the friends of the voyage streamed past and he clutched the borrowed two-shilling piece that was all his wealth. 'I had received a cable in reply to mine merely demanding to know whether I was a myth, and telling me not to be a damned fool and ask for money, as he didn't have any. This statement I put down to the usual base subterfuge to avoid paying someone else's beer bill, and all the voyage over I had ranted boastfully of my genius of a brother and of the mighty Fanfrolico Press; but now I stood alone in that colossal roosting barn for trains, with no sign of a brother, millionaire or otherwise, to meet me on a London Sunday.' He says that he had only the office address, which was no use on a Sunday, and remembered reading of down-and-outs in St Martin's crypt, so decided to go there if need be. At last our uncle Jack Elkington, who was holidaying in England, turned up.

Then the other Jack, the villain, my brother, appeared. He bounded towards me over the platform, and instinctively I paled and stepped back. Behind him trotted Brian Penton, lean-faced under the dark upstanding mop of hair, grinning, with his wife, dark slim Olga, at his side: I recognized them immediately, of course, but I scarcely knew my brother. I could but gape and stare at him. He had left Australia in perfectly tailored garments, with oil on his hair and a stick in his hand, a man-about-town who blanched at a speck of dust on his waistcoat, and who carried his cigarettes in a gold case for fear they spoil with a little crushing; but, now! his trousers slumped to his ankles, like a tramp's; his shoes had never known polish, and were cracked; his coat looked as though he had slept in it for weeks, as indeed he probably had; while instead of a collar or tie, around his neck was knotted a huge red bandana such as cowboys are alleged to have worn.* From under the black wide-brimmed shapeless felt hat, wisps of hair shot in every direction, and all were of different lengths; but more than such details, what froze the smile on my lips and kept my hands as if paralysed with horror at my side, was Jack's face. Rasputin boasted no beard such as his: I have never seen one quite like it before, and hope never to see one like it again.

This was no carefully clipped adornment such as Jack Elkington had once sported, like Conrad's, or any sailorman's. It was but a beard, a beard that had grown with a beard's will, haphazardly, in sportive riot, over cheeks, upperlip, and chin: thick and woolly here, wispy there, tangled, matted: a confusion of darkish hair that would have made an early Christian saint bilious with envy. Why did he keep it?

I could but groan and mutter – why?

'Couldn't afford razor-blades,' he explained, gripping my arms, and grinning through the jungle.

'A drink,' I croaked, 'let's have a drink.'

In a body we thundered down some steps into a street, and in the public bar of a nearby little house we crowded. There I saw my stoker

---

*In his satiric exaggeration Phil here goes too far. I have never in my whole life oiled my hair or owned a gold case; my ill-starred silver cane I have mentioned early in this book. True, I had left Sydney with a new suit, a good one paid for by Norman; that is all. (In Ellis's portrait I am wearing the artist's worn velvet coat, not my own shabby tweeds; and the white cravat was devised by him to show up the beard.)

pal sitting with a group, and I shuddered in the company of Jack. The stoker whispered: Could I give him the price of a drink? and I slipped the priest's two bob into his hand, eager to be rid of him with my crushing sense of shame. To appreciate my feelings you must remember that I am an Australian and was then, as yet, unused to sartorial and, in particular, barbered unconventionality. Badly dressed though I always was, and always am, and undoubtedly always will be, there is nothing unusual in my garments, apart from grease spots, cigarette burns, beer and ink stains, and lack of creases.

I have, however, the normal Australian phobia of wishing to be one of a mob ... I suffer from this inferiority phobia to this day, although naturally not in the extreme condition of my first arrival, for London's tolerance has taught me many a lesson; but it was months before I could walk the street beside my brother without wanting to run for my life when anybody looked at us, as everybody inevitably did at sight of such a Bolshy beard. My worship for him naturally remained, and I was therefore unable to tell him my horror as I would have done with Ray or any other friend. I was shocked, embarrassed, and tormented by his company in public.

'What are London beers?' I asked – a vital question.

Penton, who had never cared for drinking, suggested Burton. It was the real English drink, he explained, the working man's tipple, something I'd never tasted before. He was right. I never had tasted it before and swore then never to taste it again. So we ordered bitter; and I didn't like that greatly either, although it was a slight improvement; then we essayed brown ale, like burnt sugar; and lastly, a light ale, which I considered too thin and gassy.

Then truly did the prospect of England darken before me ...

In fact, what Phil did say as soon as he tasted the beer, was, 'Christ, take me straight back to Australia!'

In *I'd Live* he tells of his excited journey through London to our house, which he scanned wrathfully:

If he were so broke as he said, how could he afford this mansion? I demanded the truth indignantly, but Jack's reply was quite unanswerable. He couldn't afford it, he told me, with that bland smile of his from somewhere in his beard, his light blue eyes seeming as innocent as any babe's, while he pulled on some ragged strings of hair as if he plucked Pan's music from them.

Whatever might have been my surprise at the exterior of the mansion, it turned to amazement when an obsequious rather-handsome young man opened the door, bowing faintly, and offered to take our hats and coats, even calling me *Sir*! I could but gape at Jack who calmly, as if it were the most ordinary thing in the world, whispered: 'Our butler!' while we were ushered through a door to the right.

This led us into a long room that was, in fact, two rooms, with dividing doors, now open. Great windows opened on to Woodchurch Road, and french-windows at the back revealed a garden which looked, with its thigh-high weeds, that if it weren't haunted by satyrs, it should have been. The furnishings were simple to poverty: a table, a few chairs, an armchair, book-cases, and various paintings – mostly by Lionel Ellis – unframed on the walls, with a few of Norman's etchings.

'This is Elza,' said Jack, and I turned to greet a pale Pre-Raphaelitish girl, with very fair hair parted in the centre, and drawn tightly back from the forehead; round china-blue eyes; and a pale rosebud mouth; her complexion being of such transparency that it was as if a soft candle glowed inside her skull, diffusing the veins with golden ichor rather than blood. She was dressed in Pre-Raphaelitish fashion, to enhance her Burne Jones features, wearing a high-breasted simple white gown, reaching to her ankles, the stockingless feet being encased in sandals.

I forget what the house's rent was; but it was not so much when halved between Brian and myself. And when one considered that it was also a workshop, with the printing machines in the basement, it was quite cheap. The man-servant, whom we jokingly called a butler, was a brief experiment. Elza, who had grown tired of cooking for two families, found him somehow in Kilburn; he was an unpleasant homosexual, intensely genteel, who loathed us as much as we disliked him; and he soon went. He did his best to act in a butlerish way, serving our meals with extreme decorum, and Brian, expecially if there were any guests, tried to disconcert him by saying the most obscene or blasphemous things in his best upper-class accents. I will say for the butler that he never gave away the disgust he felt, though behind the scenes he complained bitterly to Elza. I was glad to see him go, not merely because I disliked him, but because the presence of any servant in the house has always given me a sense of humiliation.

Phil was installed in the topmost room and we settled down to live a happy united life. Brian had slid into P.R.S.'s managerial position. He worked hard and did his best; but he came into the firm after the first burst of energy had gone, and he lacked P.R.S.'s enkindling flairs. I left the office almost entirely to him and mainly stayed at home, writing or printing. Phil did any odd jobs and lent a hand in the basement, damping the handmade paper and so on.

I had a large number of projects on hand: the translations of Ausonius which Bawden illustrated; a version of the *Mimes* of Herondas for which Brian wrote an introduction; a selection of the letters of the first Earl of Chesterfield, which I had come on in my Rochester researches. Finding that the scheme of printing our own books was going successfully, I managed to get a capable printer, W. J. Hatton, whom I paid union rates for full employment. Among the books we printed were *Guenevere*, poems by William Morris with an introduction by Bottomley and some unpublished drawings by Rossetti; *Festival Preludes* by Bottomley; *Fleas in Amber*, an anthology of poems on vermin, for which I used the paper cut off one of the larger jobs – hence the odd shape of the book. I was also doing a lot of writing for myself. *Hereward*, in which I tried to define my divided condition between Betty and Elza, was finished in June; I asked Gough to devise some simple drum-rhythms to go between the scenes (which were linked by spoken lyrics), but he composed complex musical backgrounds, which were printed with the text. I also wrote a full-length play on Wycherley's marriage; and shorter plays on Rembrandt and Paracelsus, which were, I think, among my best things – as well as an experimental play based on Tuareg traditional songs. At the same time I had a shot at prose in a surrealist novel, which began with an episode based on a tale that Owens told of his first stay in Paris. The hero arrives at his hotel, then goes out wandering in the streets of the Parisian night, expecting some romantic adventure; nothing happens; he goes back disconsolate to the hotel, rings the bell by accident, a servant-girl comes in, and he suddenly recognizes the light of invitation in her eyes. The novel proper opened as he went to sleep in the girl's arms, entering into the dream world of his desires.

I had written to Alan Odle asking if he would illustrate the Herondas. He at once called on us, and both Phil and I were struck by his likeness to Norman. With his long yellowish hair, his dead-white face and large bright eyes, his long nails and slender hands, he was a sort of Beardsleyish caricature of Norman, yet a caricature that had a haunting aspect of the original: we felt that we had met our father in his youth, in an off-moment when he was trying for a joke to be aesthetical. We also found Odle most likeable, and he quickly produced his splendid baroque designs. I felt that he was extremely shy and modest, somehow lost and very grateful at our calling him out of a dungeon or Gothic cave in which he had gone to sleep.

In *Hereward* I carried on with the method of *Love*, adding a rapid kaleidescopic effect of short scenes organized on a cinematic system, with snatches of song in darkness between. Thus, a scene that ends with Alftruda (Betty) and Osulf embracing is followed by another which opens with Hereward embracing her; he has hastened in and Osulf has dodged off in the between-dark. And this second scene breaks through the dark of another sudden and contrasted song into a scene of argument between Hereward and Torfrida (Elza). Thus a nightmare effect of the divided self was built up, reaching a sustained climax in the battle for Ely, where battle effects, babbling voices, counter songs are mingled, and Hereward is shown in a paralysed state, with a repeated action and distracted meditations in the dark. The cinematic devices recur throughout, mainly in the sharp juxtaposition of linked but opposed scenes and in conflicting relationships. My aim was to depict a man struggling to carry on a great emprise while torn in different directions by unresolved contradictions. (Bottomley, praising the work, added that my Hereward was far from the hero of history.)

I felt the Fanfrolico days were drawing to an end, and discussed with Garman the possibility of our starting an experimental theatre which specialized in verse-drama.* Bottomley

*Garman had written a book of verse, *The Jaded Hero*; he had spent some

sent his blessing and I felt sure we could draw Yeats in. Garman and I went to shows at small theatres. I best recall a Toller play at the Gate under snorting Charing Cross station, a play about the frustrated German revolution after the war, with film-passages on a screen at the side. We did not doubt that the moment we decided to act we would find our theatre and begin work.

---

time in Moscow as an English teacher and I asked him many questions about the Soviet Union, but at that time he was not very political-minded. When I printed in the *L.A.* something about a better poet than T. S. Eliot (meaning Edgell) saying that the great need was a symbol for Hell, Garman surprised me by remarking that the comment had been his, not Edgell's. (I had sent some parts of *Between Two Kisses* – a section trying to put the *Liebestod* into words – to *Calendar* and had it promptly rejected. It must have been in relation to this that D.G. once said, 'People should call in with their contributions; only then can an editor quickly get a sense of someone with something new'.) He later had a chequered career: husband of the millionairess Peggy Guggenheim and then a functionary of the C.P. (after the amalgamation of Wishart's and Martin Lawrence's), retiring with stomach trouble to pig-accountancy in Dorset.

16 · BREAKDOWN

OUR united family did not last long. As soon as Olga arrived, Elza began to lose her liking for Brian. Perhaps he ceased to pay her such flattering attentions. Anyway her brief period of easy expansiveness came to an end. And for no reason at all she grew jealous of Olga and me. Once Olga came into my workroom half way up the stairs to chat for a quarter of an hour, and Elza was in a furious state. There were many episodes of chafed tempers, which Brian's spluttering efforts at humour and chaffing could not dispel. Before long Elza made things impossible for the Pentons, who moved out into a Bloomsbury room, in Brunswick Square.

Still, we had now and then some junketings. Once Alec Brown, whose poems we had printed in *Aphrodite*, turned up in a huge ramshackle car full of strange delicacies, goat cheese from Sicily and the like, to celebrate the acceptance of his first novel: a slightly diabolonian character in looks, with his fair pointed beard and his air of having been whisked away from archaeological excavations on the Danube on a journey to some world of lost elegances, full of subtleties that one couldn't decipher. Thus, some thirty years later, he recalls the moment:

My impression was one of surprise, after the more comfort-loving ways of Yugoslavia, to find you in a big, spacious dark, dank, indeed gloomy house. I was dismayed by the chilliness. I wondered if I really should have come then, and not in the morning. Elza appeared, looking like a poetess arriving from a Parthenon situated somewhere in Finland, and I felt unbelievably outer barbarian. I was over-awed to discover that you printed your own books and kept your printing press in a back room. It was rather as if an American President arrived and drew a cyclotron from his hip pocket. You had the aura of a magnate for me. In my simplicity I had never thought of just printing one's books oneself. And we sat down at an enormously long refectory table, if I recall it, with candles. And then you suddenly quoted Greek to me, and though I had learned my Greek without the strange English pronunciation, to which you added the especial flavour of Australian vowels and elisions, and although I am practically illiterate in Greek, by magic in your declamation I knew it was Sappho. That is the most memorable moment in the whole meeting, the intensity of that Greekness, and Elza sitting there, sphinx-like . . .

I had also met my Brisbane friend Rosemary at the large house of the Segals, Australians who lived not far off. She was now married to a bearish bumbling White Russian, who wrote pastoral poems and had been kept for many years by the wife of one of our leading novelists. (The novelist was a homosexual and his marriage was one of frank convenience, a social cover.) The amiable White Russian, suddenly discharged, had to find someone else ready to shoulder the pleasant responsibility of looking after him in a rough and rude world; so he married Rosemary, who was delighted at such aristocratic connections. The White Russian wasn't so delighted at finding her less rich and less easily led than he had thought; but he shrugged and wrote some more pastorals, which were printed in small Russian pamphlets at Rosemary's expense.

One evening at the Segal house I was cornered by a puzzled old Russian lady who talked for hours about Shakespeare. 'Of course you admit that he's hopelessly dull, overrated, positively unreadable and vulgar. And on the stage he's impossible, so crude, so empty. To what do you attribute his reputation? Perhaps you have found music in his sonnets? So have I.' She signalled to the others. 'It is most interesting, most consoling. I find that Mr Lindsay agrees entirely with me. Only the sonnets of that monster Shakespeare are any good.'

Rosemary gave Elza some fashionable clothes, perhaps thinking she wore her long dresses because she possessed only a box of stage-properties. Elza put one skirt on and came to me in my room. 'Look how tight it is across the bottom,' she said. She had brought a mirror with her and twisted round to see herself. 'I feel horrible, I can't bear it.' She pulled the skirt off and tore it up.

About this time occurred an episode which convinced me that I had really changed in my attitudes. One lunch-hour I had a pint with P.R.S. in the Plough. When I left, I was followed out by a young woman, Topsy, whom I had often seen there and chatted with. She was surprisingly small, her charming doll-face with its big serious eyes surrounded by a great mop of curly hair. She asked me to have a drink in the side-bar. There she took my hand and said in her childish voice, 'Why don't you ever notice anything? You go about in a dream. I've been trying to make you look at me for months.'

'But I've often looked at you.'

'No, you haven't. Look at me.'

I looked at her and I certainly saw something different.

After some more word-fencing I said I must go. She pouted. 'Meet me in here just before the pub shuts after lunch tomorrow, will you?'

I said yes, and went off. Next day I passed the pub at the trysting-time. I even stood a few moments on the opposite side of the street. But I knew I had no intention of going in. I knew I had broken the spell of the Fanfrolico ethic (the poet must submit to the pull of life, never evade the new experiences offered him, etc.); and I felt remarkably happy, despite a few faint twinges of regret that I'd never kiss the dollish girl with her pleadingly wet eyes and her small pouted mouth. I walked on.

I lost touch with Heseltine after he went to Wales. A while back he had responded with scholarly seriousness, as if to some important questionnaire on Elizabethan madrigals, when I suggested he might aid Douglas who was compiling a book of obscene limericks for his American market. This book, in which Douglas printed the verses with not-so-funny commentaries, was one of his money-making dodges. I contributed a couple of poems, but Heseltine laboriously typed out a vast number, some by himself, others anonymous, on a toilet-roll, which he unwound on to a typewriter and then rewound like an ancient book-roll. The only printable one of his own composition I can recall is that with the famous phallus pun:

> *Young girls who frequent picture-palaces*
> *don't hold with this psychoanalysis,*
> *and though Doctor Freud*
> *is distinctly annoyed*
> *they still cling to their long-standing fallacies.*

Now out of the blue came a letter violently denouncing me for the preface to my versions of Sappho. Heseltine accused me of being a masochist, concerned with what women felt in bed instead of being interested in my own satisfactions. I was surprised, but decided he must have written in one of his irritable hangovers, when he was liable to look round for an enemy to bombard with abuse. However, another matter of dissension came up through the anthology on drunks that he did for the Mandrake, *Merry-go-round*, under the signature of Rab Noolas (Saloon Bar seen on the window from the inside): 'a gallery of gorgeous drunkards through the ages. Collected for the use, interest, illumination and delectation of serious topers' with decorations by Collins. It was a rather lightweight book, P.R.S. mentioned, and though I had no connection with the Mandrake I offered to fill it out, which I did with some more seventeenth-century poems and a few ballads of Bloomsbury by myself. Heseltine of course should have been consulted, even though he was not putting his name to the book. I suppose P.R.S. expected me to get in touch with him, and I expected P.R.S. Heseltine angrily struck out all the additions from the proofs. I saw him once or twice, but he was prim-lipped and aloof, very much on his dignity. I did not take his angers seriously, feeling that in due time we'd make things up. I didn't realize how the clock was running down.

P.R.S., given a free hand by Goldston after the Lawrence success, was seeking for an active principle on which to build his press. For a while he found it in D.H.L.'s *Pansies* and Burns's *Merry Muses*. But D.H.L. had his own publisher and was soon to die. P.R.S. turned to Joyce, but again there was not much left to build on. He started an excellent small series to which Owens, Edgell, and himself contributed. His effort to draw Liam in was less successful, as Liam did not find it easy to write to order and turned out a potboiler. I wrote four short stories,

Girl, for him, which however never got into print; one of the tales was that of Betty and the commercial traveller.

For the Fanfrolico Press, Allardyce Nichol edited the works of Tourneur, which we did with decorations by Carter. And I commissioned versions of *Thus Spake Zarathustra* from Penton, the *Contes Drolatiques* from Phil, and Machiavelli's *Comedies* from Garman. The lease at Bloomsbury Square had come to an end, and as the owners wanted to raise the rent we did not renew. I approached the wholesalers Simpkin-Marshall, sold them £1000 worth of books, and arranged for them to take over all our distribution and despatch. For a while we had small and dusty offices near the old one, then we retreated wholly to Woodchurch Road. Phil was my sole helper during this period, apart from the machinist.*

Elza was growing more unstable. She had now made it impossible for any of my friends to come to the house, and soon she was to quarrel with Phil. He came home drunk one night. She made some sharp comment and he flared up. He was very rude to her, unable to control the dislike which he had been accumulating and which the hostile comments of the various anti-Elza parties had strengthened. She ordered him out of the house. I vainly and feebly tried to restrain the pair of them; and when he stumbled up to his attic, she told me that I must get rid of him at once. I was in the utmost misery. I could not defend Phil when he had been so rude, and yet I could not pack him off. Elza insisted that she would leave the house herself if I did not tell Phil to go. At last I forced myself up the stairs to where Phil was lying still dressed on his bed. I told him that he would have to go, gave him what small money I had on me, and sent him out into the chilly night.

*In *I'd live*, Phil tells the tale of his lost MS novel, much more kindly than he told it in conversation. Brian and myself placed with Fabers N.L.'s novel *Redheap* (about his hometown near Ballarat). Its excellent picture of the mining township in the nineties was spoiled by the intrusion of a character who talks Einstein and who wasn't in the version I read in Australia. I disliked the book for its abortion theme, sure that N.L. was there drawing on his own emotional resistances to the marriage which had been forced on him by my advent.

I watched him go without argument, and felt like one of the damned. In *I'd live* he tells the story of his wandering night, though he charitably disguises the reason for his sudden homelessness. After calling on the Pentons, he went to Victoria station, was ejected after a while from the waiting-room, drifted off to Kensington where Jeanne Ellis was staying (he was already in love with her), and ended, via Kilburn, outside the Segal house, thinking of Muriel, a gay young girl he'd met at our place. He slumbered on a bench, then tried to break into West Hampstead station, tearing his trousers, wandered off to a coffee-stall opposite Baker Street station, tried the tube, and came to rest at last in Blasco's room.

My surrender to Elza in Phil's ejection revealed what a change had been going on in me. The weakness I now showed towards her was the reverse side of the strengths shown in turning down the mop-headed girl and in trying to reorganize the Press on a less idiosyncratic basis. It portended dire things for me.

Elza herself was also undergoing some process of change which I could not fathom. She asked a young architect to tea, saying he had been a good friend of hers once. I recall his startled face when I arrived home. He lost no time in finding an excuse to depart. (Later I found he had been one of her clients in the pre-Young period.) She told me that she was with child. No doubt she really believed it, though in fact she was not pregnant. We had never taken any precautions, and I feel sure that her various operations had made her sterile. But the fear and the desire of pregnancy played an important part in her psychic life from now on.

One day, as I was coming home, I met the Owenses, who took me into a pub, and after some embarrassment told me that they had been worried by some of the anti-Elzas talking about the need to get rid of her by pushing her under a bus, or something like that. They did not specify which of her many enemies had been indulging in this loose talk, which I did not take very seriously, knowing how such schemes can be elaborated in the midnight of booze without having any reality in the hangover dawn. However, I made the mistake of telling Elza what had been said. I did so only because I wanted a good alibi for having come home later than usual with a smell of beer; but in her disturbed condition she was strongly affected and her feeling of being ringed by malignant foes was deepened.

Her poems were growing more assured in their style. On the one hand they expressed a direct gratitude to me:

> *Always my mind calls forth this day*
> *when naked in the wood I lay*
> *and you came by and suddenly stood*
> *above my body in the wood*
> *among the deathless flowers where*
> *the crocus budded from my hair.*
> *I spoke; you answered and awake*
> *stretched out your curving hands to take*
> *my beauty, and at last grown brave*
> *all I had sought to give I gave:*
> *older than earth that beauty lay*
> *among fears sleeping till this day.*

She was able to write unselfconsciously about her beauty because for her it was indistinguishable from the life of nature or from poetry itself.

> *O Beauty strike not but unbind this darkness*
> *knotted in my hair that smoulders*
> *to clouds of dust and clotted light*
> *behind my tired eyes.*

> *Music shall hear me now, if I but speak*
> *and at that echo you'll turn*
> *and see me standing there*
> *suddenly naked as a scent.*

But there was also a growing awareness of division in herself.

> *A woman resentful*
> *in her common pride,*
> *fear holds me down and turns*
> *my happiness to hate;*
> *crooning in her lustful rage*
> *pulls down my hair and rules*

my soul's uncrowned estate
while I crouch at her side,
my lot now the fool's.

Apollo, Apollo,
undo this snare again,
release me and let me
be happy in my pain . . .
And all true lovers take this warning!
be brave and love again.

She continually wrote of herself in the third person and was obsessed by the image of two birds of prey fighting.

She was still active in many ways. As the rent was now too high for us, she suggested dividing the house into two and letting the top half. She found a carpenter who did the necessary work without removing or damaging any part of the existing structure, and let the upper storey to a newly married Jewish couple. The husband was a furrier, and almost at once he began furious quarrels with his wife. The main point at issue, as far as we could learn from their shouted altercations, was his determination to make the wife accept his two brothers on terms that she didn't like; she insisted she had married him but not his brothers, and wasn't going to be made a mat for the three of them to trample. But, bitterly protesting, she had to give in.

One of the neighbours wrote in complaint to the house-agents, and a representative of the latter turned up one day, a wizened man in a bowler-hat, who did his best to be as sympathetic as possible to such weird clients as Elza and myself. Hatton was working the machine in the basement and I didn't like to go and tell him to stop; I expected the wizened man to ask at any moment to be shown the basement and to discover we were using the premises as a workshop. The thudding of the machine sounded to me hopelessly loud; I felt the house steadily shaking. But the man made no sign and went off, saying that he thought he could square the matter if we accepted an increase in the rent. So our profits from the furrier were almost all diverted to the house-owner.

P.R.S., looking for a hero as his firm's keystone, had come

on Aleister Crowley, or Crowley had crept up on him. About 1929, the latter had taken up with Maria Teresa Ferrari de Miramar of Nicaragua, who, though married once or twice before and the mother of a child, fell heavily for him and his magic. She suggested indeed that he should get astride a unicorn and depart in secret for Jericho. He was expelled from France despite her efforts to enlist the help of the Nicaraguan consul; at Tilbury they were both locked in their cabins by the British and returned to France; they then got a visa for Belgium. (Crowley was thought a secret agent for the Germans; he had many German supporters and some dubious connections.) He wanted to marry Maria but found it difficult to get the permission of her very aged father who was somewhere in the Nicaraguan wilds. Expelled from Belgium, he went to Germany and brought the marriage off before a British consul. After that he was allowed to land in England. There he smelt the Mandrake and made for it.

His biographer states:

The directors of the Mandrake Press were Crowley's friends. Brothers Uranus and Volo Intelligere had each contributed a thousand pounds towards this venture, five hundred of which Crowley, as a gesture of independence, diverted to another struggling firm of publishers, a transfusion which helped to ruin one and was insufficient to save the other. However, during its brief run the Mandrake Press managed to bring out two volumes of the *Confessions* (which covered Crowley's life to 1903); his novel upon a theme of magic, *Moonchild*; a booklet of three stories, *The Stratagem*, and an arid apologia of Crowley, *The Legend of Aleister Crowley*, by one P. R. Stephensen, a director of the Mandrake Press. (J. Symonds)

He adds that the Press published D.H.L.'s paintings and 'also showed the originals, but the police closed the exhibition' – hardly a correct statement. I have no means of checking the details about the directors and their financing; I certainly never heard any such story at the time. The account goes on:

The *Confessions* might have paid their way, or even made some money, if the bookshops could have been persuaded to take them. But such was Crowley's reputation that the salesmen employed by the Mandrake Press always, to their amazement, returned without any orders. Booksellers weren't having Crowley at any price; especially with his demoniac self-portrait on the cover and the phallus-like feature of the A for Aleister in the oversize signature beneath it.

P.R.S.'s own account runs succinctly:

The Mandrake Press did not 'lose money'. It wound up partly because Goldston could shrewdly anticipate that the effects of the 'Depression' in 1930 would be adverse to Limited Editions, and partly because our star author, Aleister Crowley, was so difficult to handle that Goldston and I sold our interests to three of Crowley's nominees, who carried it on for a while and then wound it up.

These nominees seem the directors to whom Symonds refers.

One amusing episode suited for P.R.S.'s dashing methods occurred in early 1930, when Crowley was billed to lecture at the Oxford University Society on Gilles de Rais. The Catholic chaplain of the University, Father Ronald Knox, wrote to the club's secretary and the lecture was called off. The Mandrake printed the text as a sixpenny pamphlet and undergraduates with sandwich boards sold it in the High.

To Symonds's and P.R.S.'s accounts of the Press's demise I may add Phil's. He was more in touch with P.R.S. and the Plough than I was at this time:

Inky had the misfortune to start just when the limited edition mania was dying, and his efforts to combine reprints with general publishing and fiction proved too great a strain for the Mandrake's low finances. Wilfred [Hanchant] had been called in, after Inky's retirement, to see if he could salvage anything or open with a new, more lucrative programme, but it was hopeless . . .

I had known of Crowley in Australia through Tinny Jerdan, who later committed suicide in London, as I tell in *The Roaring Twenties*. He had talked about Crowley with me on Mount Tambourine, and he lent me several of Crowley's works during my subsequent visit to Sydney. I thus glanced through the *Equinoxes* and endless yards of verse, including the obscene booklets. I felt Crowley a fraud at first sight, since no one with genuine insights could be such a second-rate imitator of Swinburne. (The link of the self-intoxicated quality of Swinburne's

poems with the Crowleyan self-deification is worth noting.) I
also had pointed out a Sydney disciple, Frank Benett, a Lancashire bricklayer, who dubbed himself Sir. Then in the fifties,
he frequented the Roma Café, reputed to perform mystical
dances in the nude at the rate of two to three guineas a time.
He established a branch of Crowley's Order and was at Cefalu
with Mary Butts.

In 1929 Maria, Crowley's wife, was drinking heavily. I met
the pair of them a few times, casually, in Goldston's shop. She
was a fairly well-blown woman, oozing a helpless sexuality
from every seam of her smartly cut suit, with shapely legs
crossed and uncrossed, and keeping all the while a sharp glittering gaze on her swarthy and unsavoury husband with his
bow-tie, his staring uneasy pop-eyes, his prim lax rosebud
mouth, his sallow skin and brown shaven egg-shaped head,
which at the time I mistook as naturally bald. There was a
mustiness about him that perhaps came from his scent of
mingled civet, musk, and ambergris, which was said to have
a compelling effect on women and to make horses neigh after
him in the street. Maria spoke in various languages, including
English, which I could not understand, and he listened attentively like a well-behaved poodle, giving an impression of
uxorious dependence. However I gathered that in private she
made many scenes, accusing him and his friends of attempting
to poison her. After about a year he left her.

Politically, Crowley was ready to offer his system to anyone
as 'the alternative to fascism and communism' – democracy
being 'the political idea of Christianity in its dying phase'. In
1924 he wrote to Frank Harris, 'To put it very crudely, Indus-
trial-Capitalism is heading for the cataract. The only alternative yet is Bolshevism, which won't do either. Now the Law of
Thelema offers a Third Way. These last years I have been
training various peoples to act as a Brain for the human race.'
He didn't mind who his allies were, as long as they paid divi-
dends. He asked Trotsky to put him in charge of a world-
crusade against Christianity, while writing to King George V
with proposals for a religious crusade led by himself. His one
unchanging panacea was the use of the sex act for reaching and
realizing God.

The only allies he ever actually found were in the Nazi underworld. He had long had German connections through the *Ordo Templi Orientis*, founded in 1902 by K. Kellner and taken over by T. Reuss, who was certainly in the German secret service. Reuss called on Crowley in 1912 and said, 'Since you know our hidden sex teachings, you had better come into the Order and be its head for Great Britain.' Crowley accepted. During the 1914 war, in America, he expressed astonishment that the British did not appreciate his subtle tactics of writing German propaganda in such exaggerated terms as to render it ridiculous! Goldring notes:

There were other *gurus* at work during the last (1914) war and no doubt even now active in this (second) one – whose teaching might be described as 'esoteric Nazism' flavoured with the sexual perversions of the Marquis de Sade. It is significant that mages of this type almost invariably pointed to the Germans as the future 'master race'.

Phil, I mentioned, had fallen in love with Jeanne Ellis. He thus describes her at this time:

I loved her at sight when she entered (the room at Woodchurch Road) in her shy, hesitant manner, poised tiptoe as if she half expected to be insulted and was prepared to run; and then heard her low voice, so quick that it stumbled, and she would hesitate, stuttering a little, mumbling. Her brownish curls, for (like Elza) she wore no hat, fell so far forward that they half obscured her face in an exasperating fashion; yet her blue eyes, I could see, peeped brightly at me from the shadows. Her gown was rather of the Bloomsbury fashion, narrow-hipped and wide-skirted, and of an old-gold colour. She wore no jewellery of any kind, save beads about her throat, naught but the simple gown and shoes, and appeared to me quite exquisite . . .

Her hair was of a light chestnut colour, and fell in curls to her strong, sloping shoulders, and it took me years of pleading and bullying to entice her to draw it back from the face, for I judged that the Grecian style of hairdressing would be most suitable to her. But she wished always to hide within her hair, letting it swing forward to conceal her cheeks and vizor her eyes . . .

His imagery is precisely correct. He catches Jeanne's guilty fears which by some subtle alchemy she transmuted into a peculiar charm, her dainty trepidations, her flaunted slink, her challenge masked as a rustling retreat, her use of modest evasions to suggest a body softly opening at the first thrust of penetration, like petals soundlessly falling apart at a bee's snuggling intrusion.

I did my best to deter him by unkindly retailing all the tales I knew of her fornications; but he was besotted. Clearly he meant to force their relations into the open, and clearly Ellis would blame me. I uneasily waited for the blow. About this time a couple of Serbs from the embassy visited Lionel's studio and we drank with them. One of them insisted that war was the ideal state of the human race. For some time I tried to draw him out, to find if he had some complicated philosophical defence of his position; but he merely grinned and kept saying, 'No, no, I just mean it's good. It's what I like.' Next day Lionel came to groan a little and lie on the cool linoleum of my floor to ease his stomach. It's the last memory I have of him.

Phil had been readmitted as press-worker, though Elza didn't want him to have his room again. I was helping him financially as much as I could, and asked Jeanne to make some little drawings for Chesterfield's *Letters*. I was now setting and printing Elza's second book of verse, *Older than Earth*. With most of the books I did the setting and Hatton the machining, though I recall toiling at the machine for long hours over the Catullus and the Herondas.

Phil had brought over some photos of Ray's paintings and I had the idea of doing a book in which the three of us collaborated. As two of the paintings dealt with the buccaneer Morgan and two others could be plausibly linked with him, I suggested Morgan as the theme. Phil wrote an essay, *Morgan in Jamaica*, and I a poem on Panama beginning, 'Thousands of parrots waited on his sleep'. (When Alec Brown read this poem, he startled me by crying out, 'I wrote that!' I thought for a moment I must have plagiarized him in a dream, then he explained, 'I mean it struck me so forcibly I felt that I ought to have.') We did the whole of this book together, and it seemed that the real reason we had come to England and carried on the Press was to beget the collaboration.

I now went out very seldom, and almost always with Elza.

We mainly went to the Kilburn cinemas, and lamented the advent of the Talkies; it seemed that the era of strong pattern and rhythmic sequence on the screen was over. (Through P.R.S. I had seen many of the early Russian films, including *Potemkin*.) We also saw the first film of a young Scandinavian, Greta Garbo, whom Elza much admired. We went to a party given by Bradley where I met Allen Lane. A very popular woman novelist was there, trying to look like a hollyhock or some simple but overgrown cottage-flower, and being coy about her books. 'One can't succeed at any level unless one is sincere,' I said. 'The populace can at least always spot insincerity.'

'Oh, I'm always sincere,' she said with a meek lisp, taking another cocktail, and turned back to the fair Gerhardi with his blue shirt and bluer eyes.

But in taking Elza to dine at the flat which the Atkinsons now inhabited in St John's Wood, I brought disaster on my head. Rupert, with his hair draped sideways over his head to hide the baldness, was his kind-hearted and slightly distracted self, praising the virtues of colon-irrigation and exhorting me to try it. (About this time he gave Phil the £5 enabling him to start off a ménage with Jeanne.) But twice during the excellent dinner and once over the coffee, Marie slyly introduced the name of Betty May and asked me questions about her, looking surprised when I answered curtly. I didn't dare to glance at Elza, but felt sure she was taking everything in. Rupert was quite unaware of any tension; he always studiously ignored what Marie did in her spare time, and this night he was absorbed in colon-irrigation.

I suppose I must have conveyed to Elza the sinking heart with which I listened to Marie's stressed questions. As soon as we reached home, she turned on me and demanded to know why Marie had kept on referring to this Betty. I tried to pass the matter off airily, but she was now convinced that I was hiding something. All that sleepless night we continued the argument, she demanding the truth and I denying that there was anything to tell. I suppose there was a guilty weakness in my speech, which drove her to persist. But she had for some time been developing a persecution-mania, which, as usual in such cases, had a certain basis in fact; for anyone obsessed with suspicious fears inevitably becomes surrounded with ill-wishers and enemies. She had been building up a feeling of my untrust-worthiness; for did I not fail to prevent all our acquaintances from turning into hostile witnesses and conspirators? She had made me the sole barrier between herself and the world; and so she felt that unless I were wholly hers, almost indistinguish-able from herself, I was liable to turn into the other thing, the threatening world. She was painfully sensitive to the least movement of emotion or action on my part that seemed to break our bond and link me with the known and unknown forces lurking darkly all round her. In a sense, then, it was not my relations with Betty May that now concerned her; it was the need to find if I belonged to her or to the others. And the matter of Betty May merely sparked off the inflammatory material that had been piling up over the last year.

I could not see it like that at the time. I could only feel that I was guilty of the thing she accused me of – though I felt at the same time bitterly oppressed by the unfairness of being charged with an infidelity after having at last overcome the forces that had made me unfaithful. Again and again I told myself that I had the right to deny the charge; for if I did not deny it, I would give the effect of replacing my present self with the self who had been fascinated by the fatal-woman in Betty. I would undo all the change I had brought about in myself through pang and struggle; I would wreck everything; I would merely hurt and weaken Elza herself.

These qualms were only too true. But in the face of another endless day and night of inquisition I could not sustain my res-olution. I ended by admitting that I had slept with Betty, though insisting that the whole thing was far in the past and had driven me through unhappiness into the very strengths of single-hearted devotion that Elza wanted. My explanations, pleas, assurances were brushed aside, were not listened to. Elza plunged into one of her black and numb silences, out of which she emerged to pull me down on to the couch in the big room that Phil described. But if I thought that that ended the matter, I was mistaken. At first Elza said that she was going to leave me. Instead of accepting the fact that our relation had reached an impasse, I pleaded with her for a chance to prove my change-of-heart. She insisted on my telling her every detail of my relations with Betty, and seemed both to absorb with an intense excitement, and to suffer at, any facts she could pluck out of me. Finally she said that she would stay, but that henceforth she would go everywhere with me, no matter where I went. I abjectly agreed. And at once knew that I wished her to go.

Yet the least suggestion on her part of going stirred me to a panic. The deepest emotion in me was a need to prove to her that I was now responsible; and this emotion was stronger than all my fears, irresolutions, desires to escape the whole wretched situation, to be alone and at peace with myself. Stronger even than the humiliations, the doubts I felt at the thought of being forever dogged by her, of knowing what all my friends would say: 'We were right, she has finally got him down and destroyed him – what a weakling, what a fool!' Stronger even than the desire to live. I wanted only to make reparation.

17 · LAST FANFROLICO DAYS

APART from Hatton at the machine, there was now no one helping me; Lionel Ellis was the only friend I had left – that is, the only friend not excluded by Elza's system. Yet as we both revived from the exhaustion of those scenes before Christmas, I felt a certain serenity: as if the worst had happened, as if I were at last cleansed of some perilous and poisonous stuff in my bosom. All my difficulties and shames seemed unimportant beside the gains. I felt sure that it was now only a matter of time and Elza would realize the changes in me, we would come through to the tranquilly assured bond which we both wanted. I was happy sitting in the garden on an old wooden seat, setting *Zarathustra* in Walbaum or a selection of Davenant's poems in Poliphilus.

For someone who like myself had accepted the Australian segregation of the sexes in their spheres of action and who scorned the henpecked male as the lowest specimen of his species, it was indeed a personal revolution to have broken with almost all my friends on behalf of a woman whom they disliked. I felt her to be half in the wrong; but when I tried to apportion blame or responsibility for what had happened, I was driven back on myself. All the arithmetics of guilt and innocence broke down, and I was left simply with the conviction that I could not do other than I was doing. As far as I was concerned, I was wholly responsible for the situation; to share our guilts led only to righteousness and resentment; I must work out my salvation by absolutely accepting Elza as she was, a creature of desperate anxieties. I had gone deep enough in her being to become for her the symbol of all fear and hope, and I must accept the fact or be damned for ever.

As we saw practically no one now, it did not matter that she wanted to go everywhere with me. As I was looking up various things at the B.M. and transcribing Chesterfield's letters, I got her a ticket for the Reading Room. She made notes for me and for some reason I cannot now recollect I asked her to read Otto Rank's book on the birth trauma. This was a sad mistake. The book much increased her psychic confusion, her sense of a primal wrong; it deepened her fear and convinced her that she had somehow been murdered. I did not at the time realize how far it had affected her, but I saw her anxieties intensified. Another book, which she read at home and which further upset her, was Hemingway's *Farewell to Arms*; the desolate conclusion and the death in childbed completed her recoil from life, her feeling of being trapped and surrounded by murderers. Sex became steadily identified with murder. Again it was to be some time before I understood what was going on in her mind.

In March D.H.L. died. I wrote a *Letter to his Spirit*, which I sent to Charley Lahrs, who said he'd print it; but it never appeared. I feel sure however that I was in too great a state of confusion to have said anything worthwhile. But at least I felt the need to make a summing-up statement, to round off the strange process that had been the dialogue of D.H.L. with all of us throughout the twenties. Already I dimly felt that a period had come to a full-stop. No doubt much of the emotion derived from my own personal, moral, artistic and economic crisis, but in fact that crisis was at every point bound up with the larger issue, the collapse of the twenties and all that they implied. It was simply my individual refraction of the larger issue.

Ellis blamed me for the theft of Jeanne by Phil; our friendship dissolved. If things had been normal, I should have sought him out and put my case, and we should probably have patched things up. But in my imprisoned state I accepted this last misfortune as in inevitable part of the pattern of isolation. I was finding it ever harder to run the Press. Our sales were not bad, and the £1000 from Simpkin-Marshall had got rid of our main debts. But the burden was too much in my lonely position. I was afraid of the Press's demise, because I had no alternative method of earning money. If things had been normal, I should have turned to others – P.R.S., Edgell and

Garman, or one or other of my various contacts in the publishing and periodical world. But in the circumstances I could not do that. I was enclosed by Elza's neurosis, which in some unexplained sense was my own – a complex of fears which precipitated all the feared things and made it impossible to find a way out.

However, a god-from-the-machine turned up: B., who had been a director of Simpkin-Marshall and with whom I had had dealings in that firm. He now had a publishing house of his own and asked me to come and see him. Elza and I went. He said that he was interested in having his own fine-press, but did not feel inclined to make an offer for taking over the Fanfrolico. I told him that I was thinking of calling a meeting of creditors, and he asked me to get in touch with him after that.

I called a firm of accountants in to take charge of our insolvency. Things were not in a particularly bad way. Phil records that the accountant said to him, 'This should be a banking, not a bankrupt firm.' But I was at the end of my tether. At last the creditors met and I was asked to attend. I sat on a bench outside the room, expecting to be called in. Till that moment I had not felt much about the proceedings; but there, outside the room with its faint buzz of discussion, I felt an unutterable shame and dismay, as if I had betrayed everyone. I was not called in. After a while the accountant came out and said that everyone was satisfied I had acted honourably, and had no wish to ask me any questions. I think it was above all the fact that I had used practically the whole £1000 to meet debts and had clearly not hoarded anything whatever, that thus gained the creditors' goodwill. I am not sure how much the firm ultimately paid; but from my last contact with the accountants I think it must have been more or less twenty shillings in the pound.

I handed over all the stock, including the incompleted sheets of *Zarathustra* and Davenant, keeping only our house furniture, the paintings by Ellis, and a few etchings by Norman. The agents accepted the relinquishment of the lease, though our tenants in the upper storey turned nasty, expecting to have their modest rent raised. We moved to a large room over a shop in Priory Road, in which our paltry things were packed, so that we could just crawl through tables and chairs to the divan. I went to see B. and he offered to finance me in a new press. The agreement was not set down on paper and was rather vague. We proposed to find a house in the country where we could install a press, which we would work for B. Meanwhile he was ready to pay me a few pounds a week against a book I wanted to write on John Donne. I had in hand about £5, and Elza had a few shillings.

Within a few days, with the aid of *Daltons*, we had found just what we wanted. Our first journey, to a site outside Chelmsford, was fruitless; then we came on a disused forge a few miles south of Dunmow, with cottage attached. By concreting the forge floor a good workroom could be created. The price was about £300. B. agreed to buy the place and to let us live in it free while our agreement operated.

We had only about three pounds a week and I could not pay the bill of the removalist who brought our things down. He held on to the paintings by Ellis – my portrait, a large nude in a sort of Venetian pastoral setting, and a sketch of Jeanne combing her hair. I wrote to Ellis asking him if possible to reclaim the pieces as I did not see how I was going to do it in any measurable future. There was no reply and I do not know if he got the letter.

18 · A BACKWARD GLANCE

WHAT had we achieved in the Fanfrolico Press? Nothing, if one is to judge by the total absence of any comment in the literary records. True, we played our part in the raising of book-production standards in general, which resulted from the expansion of fine-presses in the twenties; and we did some useful books, such as the edition of Tourneur, as well as stimulating interest in Beddoes.* It was in *The London Aphrodite* that we made our wider impact, and this was too unconventional a product to meet any recognition from the critics, then or later. In the U.S.A. where critics are less strangled by the public-school tie, there have been some attempts to see the magazine in a serious perspective. Thus F. J. Hoffman remarks:

. . . its exaltation of Life and its disregard of both past and future structure, has been one of the characteristics of the twentieth-century explosion. So, for example, the opening editorial of *The London Aphrodite*, edited by Jack Lindsay and P. R. Stephensen: 'We affirm Life, and for definition quote Nietzsche: Spirit is that life which cuts itself into life. We affirm Beauty, and by that term understand a sensual harmony, a homogeneous ecstasy, which, constructing intellectually, yet hates nothing so much as the dry cogs of the objectified and objectifying intellect.' (*Freudianism and the Literary Mind*, 1945)

And, pointing to *The Modern Consciousness*, he adds that 'the *Aphrodite* was perhaps the best modern exponent of Nietzsche's position'.

*When in 1959-60 a widely travelled exhibition of fine-press work as a tribute to William Morris was got together, our *Guenevere* was the only direct work of homage to Morris. In point of sales we were the most substantial Press by far after the Nonesuch.

Still, in our Dadaism and our Integrations alike, in our Neoplatonist individualism and our revolutionary glance at the proletariat, we were too violent, too intense, too out-of-step, behind the times and ahead of them, for any direct effects of our propaganda to be identifiable. We remained at root an Australian explosion in the English scene, which politely ignored the noise, held its nose, and went on with its own business.

But the question of direct influence in the immediately succeeding years does not help us much in assessing an expression of the twenties. Soon, with the Great Slump, there was an almost clean break in the intellectual scene. A different political and a different cultural situation arrived. Even D.H.L. went wholly out of fashion for many years; the only point raised about him during the thirties was whether or not one should call him an outright Fascist. Huxley became an outmoded petty-liberal with an atomized view of life. Rickword dropped out of poetry. Even where there were genuine anticipations of the new phase, the work of the twenties was ignored; for example, no one pointed out that P.R.S. had founded Marxist literary criticism in 1928-29. True, the achievement of the twenties, in all its diversity of positive and negative elements, necessarily underlay the struggles of the thirties; but for the most part the participants of the new phase were too interested in getting on with their jobs to bother about their debts to the previous decade.

We may drop then the question of obvious effects, and ask instead how typical we were of the period. Looking back, one sees that for all our idiosyncrasies, which provided a stumbling-block and a source of mockery for the profane, we had many points of close contact with the contemporary situation. Our aesthetic at many points was allied to Yeats's; our ethic was in some respects near to D.H.L.'s (as witness his letter to me about the rightness of my rages), though it contained some of the things he most denounced; our satiric angle often coincided with that of Douglas and Huxley, both of whom were friendly to us. Our critical dialectic had its roots in Romanticism, in Morris and in Nietzsche, but also looked to Marxism, the direct point of contact being established by P.R.S.

The main significance of the twenties lay in the blasting force of its critical attitudes. All conventional and traditional values were questioned and put in doubt. The emphasis shifted from the meandering intellectual criticism of Shaw and Wells, with a leap into vague utopias, and from the art-for-art's-sake dissidence, with its opposition of philistinism to a rather rootless or decadent art. What emerged instead was a conviction that the whole development of society and art was wrong, and that the burden of defence had shifted from the artist to the upholder of the existing world. The new criticism varied from the passionate quest of D.H.L. for the human essence in its uncorrupted state to the nihilistic cavillings of Douglas and Huxley; but, whether passionate or nihilistic, it regarded with scorn the entire smug set-up.

Our positions then, despite oddities, were highly typical of the period and contributed elements which were lacking in the other expressions. We can therefore claim our due place in the historical picture.

In one sense we were all phoney or confused revolutionaries; and P.R.S. initiated the awareness of this crucial point by applying words of Lenin to D.H.L. and Huxley:

Lenin's criticism applies, for example, to the raving 'transition' mob in Paris, who assume, amid a thousand other vagaries, that word-chopping and the use of lowercase for caps, is revolution. It applies also, splendidly home, to Wyndham Lewis, that fantastical 'enemy' of everything and nothing, who garbles and espouses in turn Communism, East-versus-West pictorial sociology, Shakespearean heterodoxy, and aesthetic Fascism – with photo of author and all his Press-cuttings.

Lenin's criticism applies also to a 'modern' of great literary genius, D. H. Lawrence, who in *Lady Chatterley's Lover* sets out a quasi-revolutionary thesis of attack upon the Gentry by means of sexual-social humiliation – first making the mistake of selecting the wrong opponents, for the unfortunate and dispersed English Gentry hardly matter at all now, having long been displaced from their feudal hegemony by capitalists à la Monde; and secondly, using a purely abstract weapon of attack upon the ruling class, viz. lumbar mysticism; and thirdly, not even relating his chosen characters and conflicts to actuality: making the gamekeeper an almost-gentleman with a foot in both class-camps, so that the Lady was not even properly humiliated 'from below', because she knew her lover could talk and behave like a Gentleman whenever he chose.

With various changes, the same general charges could have been made against ourselves. They could also have been made against Graves, who in *Goodbye to All That* had written: 'I had sworn on the very day of my demobilization never to be under anyone's orders for the rest of my life.' But to reject authority in the abstract is to come back to individualism in its most ego-centric form, back to the very thing that started off the chain-reaction leading into the authority one rejects. Graves traced the experiences that brought him to rejection, but omitted the revelatory crisis and the resolving consciousness. 'No more anecdotes, and, of course, no more falsities, religion, conversations, literature, arguments, dances, drinks, time, fun, unhappiness. I no longer repeat to myself: "He who shall endure to the end shall be saved." It is enough that I have endured.' That is stoic *apatheia*, but reduced to the point of low intensity in which not only the world of struggle, but the whole world of ideas is renounced; and Graves has remained remark-ably true to his oath, his creative work showing intellectual activity without the intrusion of a single idea (in any compre-hensive, dynamic, or organizing sense). A strange rigour. The revolutionary emotion is maintained in a vacuum; a conviction of integrity is preserved by a ceaseless hysterical *noli me tangere* masquerading as uncommitted judgment. (From a different angle the *noli* cry was deep in D.H.L.) Lenin had summed up these attitudes as specially characteristic of the 'the petty-bourgeois "gone mad" from the horrors of capitalism' with all 'the weakness of such revolutionism, its futility, its liability to transform itself into obedience, apathy, fantasy, and even into a "mad" infatuation with some bourgeois "craze" '.

I have already discussed the way in which Heseltine fled from his deep-going sense of a wholly corrupted world into a sort of deliberate schizophrene condition. Here we must look at his end, in which awareness of his betrayal of life caught up with him. The way in which this awareness struck him was closely parallel to the way in which I had broken down under

Elza's attack; he too felt his error, not in its wider social bearings, but in the attitudes to women which it had brought about.

He had been depressed at Collie's death by galloping consumption; and he found his sources of income drying up. The song market had been spoiled by radio, and he had largely used up the sort of music he wanted to transcribe. (For his last work of transcription, the brilliant version of Giles Earles's MS book, which was published after his death, I can claim some credit, since I had introduced him to the MS by asking him to copy out and edit the music for *Tom o'Bedlam*.) His many schemes, for a magazine and for opera, broke down; he asked Victor Carne to help him to a job in Columbia Gramophones; he wanted to write notes for classic recordings, and act as adviser, and offered as a start to conduct gratis his own *Capriol Suite*. The wage he asked was £5 a week; he was turned down. He applied to various official seats of musical learning; and again was turned down. He burst out in fantasy schemes such as letting caves in Kent and Sussex to flagellants. And his spirits hovered between the hope of a new start and the conviction of doom. From a farm in Hampshire he wrote:

I have a hopeful premonition of something extremely fortunate making its way towards me. In any case I shall live no more in London unless I have some definite work to keep me there . . . I shall sell practically everything I have except a few books, and then set out afresh, without impediments to tie me long in one place – and hope for the necessary god to descend from his machine.

He had returned to the mood of 1919-20, but without its social consciousness. He wanted a wholly new start, but was afraid of what the effort implied. He turned back to a girl he had loved some eleven years before, and turned back to Delius. In a letter of June 1930 to the girl W.B. we find him still yearning to get away from the London of evil and trying to realize what flaw had made him fail love:

On that miraculous day, now more than two months past, when I was with you in those lovely places, I was so oppressed by the beauty of it all – and you were the key to it and all the downs and rivers and birds were you – that I was quite inarticulate, and even a little afraid of you and all the loveliness around me . . . I know now – and you have known always, I believe – that in failing you I have deliberately betrayed my own soul and all the faculties of mind and spirit. I do not pretend to understand the source of the appalling perversity in my nature that has caused me now for years, with deliberate and callous cruelty, to torment and persecute that only precious part of myself, which is you, until I know not now whether the semblance of its death is death its very self and no semblance at all.

He says that he cannot understand why he betrayed, reviled, mocked, and ill-used her 'with a barbarity that must surely have been implanted in me by the fiends of Hell'. He keeps on examining himself and is tormented.

And though you who know my heart have known that I was so encompassing my own destruction, I am writing this because I want to make full confession to you myself, kneeling at your feet, not for forgiveness but that you may know that all my cruelties have come back to revenge themselves on me, and because my one remaining joy is in the awareness of the horrors of my past actions as revealed by the anguish I am suffering at this memory of them – and I like to hope that awareness is itself a sign that I am in some measure expiating them.

I cite this letter because it brings out so poignantly the inner conflict which Heseltine had been striving to hold down all those years, and because it shows him in an emotional fix extraordinarily like mine at the same moment. Both of us were forced by the logic of events to pull ourselves suddenly up and recognize that the dynamic on which we had been relying enclosed an unrealized or evaded cruelty. Heseltine, unable to bear the strain, put out the cat, and gassed himself. The door was broken in on the morning of December 17th; he had feared to face the Christmas which he loathed and for which he set so many carols. He had failed to link his remorse over personal cruelties with the sense of a murderous world which had obsessed him in the years leading up to 1920. I also was failing to make the same sort of correlation for myself; but by enduring to the end I was to make it, not telling myself it was enough to have endured.

There is an odd similarity in the way the various persons with a displaced revolutionary emotion whom I have discussed all used a woman in order to objectify their needs and define their positions. Heseltine used W.B. to turn back the whips upon himself; D.H.L. used Frieda to dramatize his inner conflicts; Graves used Laura to bring to a head his desire to say farewell to all that; and I in the same sense used Elza to ensure that I should accept no half measures, no egoisms disguised in highfalutin terms.

D.H.L. fought out his conflicts to the bitter end. Heseltine devised his schizophrenic mode of life to sever art and struggle; his deepest experience had been his revolt against the forces making for war and the city of corruption; but his art expressed nothing of this. The deepest experience of Graves was the discovery of the human hell revealed by war and the rejection of the authority that permitted and needed such a hell. But after his first recoil from the inhumanities of the war in France, his art expressed nothing of this. His novels do not raise even in abstracted forms the problems of his discovery and rejection. By a creed of *apatheia* he was able to seal down the crevasse, now and then opening small cracks in his poems and hastily closing them up again.*

Heseltine, living more dangerously, found the mask of

---

*Though the method flattens his novels and makes him a bizarre critic flying off at any tangential point, it has worked well for the kind of verse he wanted. I notice, as I write, a review of *More Poems*: 'He is thus a great rhetorician. The thoughts in his poems are always sprung on us in their purest possible shape and at their moment of maximum impact. It is a technical mastery which goes with a complete openness to experience, a resolve to find, not impose, form ... [He] does not write poetry so much as find poems, a succession of separate victories for spontaneity, propitiations of the White Goddess of changeable love and unpremeditated experience ... As an artist he never repeats himself and never develops.' (P. N. Furbank, *Listener*, 18 May 1961). I agree with the proviso that the 'maximum impact' is that of a momentary concentration and dispersion of personality, not that of the whole man in consistent struggle with life. (When I knew him he was still haunted by terror dreams; many of the poems of the twenties record nightmares of a strangling kind.)

Warlockism break up in his hands; but by then the split had gone too far. He could only dream of regeneration and die.

I think what I have said above touches the innermost conflicts of the twenties, its creative liberations and its limitations. A necessary part of the spiritual scene was the scepticism, the withering ironies, of Norman Douglas* and of Huxley; but whereas Douglas stuck out stubbornly for a hedonist egoism as providing a stable basis for the exposure of the irrationality and falsity of the social situation (atomized into its idiotic details), Huxley was aware of the insufficiencies of this position and tried to use the ironic method to state the inner conflicts developing underneath. In *Antic Hay* he found the finest balance between the witty exposure and the disconcerted yearning for some kind of integration; and it is significant that the material of this work owed so much to Heseltine-Warlock. After that his work weakened; for he was losing his ironic bases without effectively building up any lyrical integrations. (At root this is what P.R.S. analyses about him in the *Aphrodite* and what I wrote

---

*Though N.D. would have snorted angrily at the idea that he had a social conscience, such a conscience underlay much of his indignation. In Florence, the conversation having turned on excessive legal penalties, I mentioned a Sydney dentist who around 1900 had been hanged; it had been found that, when he gave women gas, he cut off a small bit of their pubic hair and gummed it in a book with their names added. There was no evidence that he did more than that. N.D. was strongly affected by the story, kept on repeating it, asked me to tell it to Mrs Compton-Mackenzie, and so on. (I did not meet him again till 1944 when I was stationed in London and Nancy Cunard asked me to lunch with him. I found him shrunken and cantankerous, but saw him a few times to listen to his rages against wartime conditions and Britain in general. A few years later he wrote me some words of liking for an essay on Fairies in *Life and Letters*, on a card of Nancy's from Capri.)

Even Nina who seemed always as impervious to a general idea as anyone can well be, had her brief revolt under the influence of Gaudier-Brzeska. 'Henry knew five languages and translated for me' at an anarchist meeting in Soho before the 1914 war. 'I did not know much about anarchy but I thought that any kind of revolt against anything was good. I decided that it was dreadful not to have been born in Whitechapel and that the proletariat were the only people who were capable of anything.'

to him of *Point Counter Point*.) Hence the way in which he turned to D.H.L., and then, unable to use his formulas without becoming a mere echo, to pacifist yogi-ism, in a revulsion from the sterile intellectualism he had landed in.

Huxley thus faded out along a side cul-de-sac. D.H.L., with all his limitations, held the centre of the picture, seeking in the last resort for what remained truly human in a dehumanized capitalist world, despite the cash nexus and all its deadening routines and mechanizations. And I think that although we made our attack on him, partly stupid and partly attempting to sift away the maddened and confusing element in his work, we were on his side and in many ways close to him. P.R.S. made one of the possible logical steps when he moved in the Mandrake to the championship of Lawrence; his misfortune was that Lawrence was near his death and could not provide much further ammunition in the fight.

It seems to me, then, that we did have a valid place in the decade and that if we are left out of the picture the intelligibility of that world is lessened.

One important writer has been omitted from the above generalizations: Edith Sitwell. Her early brilliant developments of what I called the colour image, the new concentrations on the basis of the Rimbaudian derangement of the senses, developed by 1928 into *Gold Coast Customs*, in which she brought out all the social relations inherent in the aesthetic struggle she was waging. This process of hers was an expression of what I was talking so much about, the deepening of the Image of Beauty; but I somehow missed *Gold Coast Customs* at the time. In this I merely reflected the *zeitgeist*; for that poem did not affect the movements of the thirties, to their great impoverishment. However the development from *Façade* to *Gold Coast Customs* (with its seminal image, its author has told me, in a blackened death-dance figure in a hunger march) was of the highest significance, and revealed precisely and deeply the creative pattern which underlay the twenties, though almost all the writers failed to find it in its fullness in their work. Edgell Rickword, who had initiated the poetic exploration of the city of alienation, stopped writing poetry after he arrived at Marxism. A great misfortune: for if he had persisted, he might well have kept intact the links with what was vital in the twenties, and thus have deepened the whole poetic movement of the thirties.*

*Of the other persons who come in the narrative, Moeran and Lambert drank heavily and thus destroyed themselves; Lambert was strong enough to survive into the post-war world but had dissipated his lively talent. Philip Owens, whose *Marlowe* never got past the proof-stage in our Press, wrote *Portrait of a Nobody* during the thirties and was killed in the war in a jeep on Mytilene, serving in Intelligence. Brian Penton returned to Australia and became editor of the Sydney *Daily Telegraph*, dying of cancer. P.R.S., after various literary exploits, founded a nationalist party, and spent the war years in a concentration camp. In a sense he was trying to live through D.H.L.'s *Kangaroo*, bring it true. Nina survived into the 1950s, still resolutely and toughly living as in the twenties. I last saw her about a year before her death, a sadly shabby sight, in a Soho wine-bar. I am told that 'hauntings' by Crowley played a main part in driving her to her death through a window.

AND AFTER

AND AFTER

19 · FORGE COTTAGE

We were happy settling in. The cottage had two rooms below and a small kitchen, two rooms above. There was a large open fireplace into part of which a range had been put. Next door was the family of a farm labourer, with whom we became friendly. A few more cottages, a pub, and a farm with outbuildings made up the hamlet of Onslow (or Hounslow) Green. Once B. came down to inspect. He approved of the place and I had a few beers with him at the pub: the only time I went in. He paid for the forge to have a concrete flooring, but went on delaying about the despatch of a press. I had told him that I would start work as soon as the press arrived. He was in fact drinking hard and was not, I think, doing well as a publisher; he had started in the midst of the slump and did not have any knowledge of books apart from a certain trade-gumption acquired in the wholesalers.

We came to know most of the people around. The old parson looked apologetically in and we had a chat about the Cappadocian Fathers and about Donne. There was also a retired civil servant who lived in a large house about a mile off and who tried to act the role of Lord of the Manor, scoffed at by the villagers. One of the neighbouring women told us that he used to get into the cottages by asking for a glass of water, then he'd make a grab at the woman of the place. She added that when he tried to put his hand up her skirt, she said, 'Lemme alone, you dirty old sod. I'm one man's whore and that's enough.' She was a handsome merry woman who might have come out of a medieval *fabliau*, broad in the beam, brown as a nut, honest as the day, and quite shameless. Elza liked her and her bawdy sayings. 'The parson's given up asking me to church,' she said. 'Last time I farted in the middle of his sermon. I didn't mean to be rude, you know, he's a dear old boy, but I got to dozing, and when I doze I don't know what I'm doing. Lucky it wasn't worse.' She gave her gusty rusty laugh.

There were tales of the last proper Lord of the Manor, a great cussing character, who once rode his horse into church and who had a score of bastards. In a tumbledown cottage a few miles to the west there lived a widowed man with his three daughters. They all slept together and one of the girls had a child which everyone said was her father's. The youngest of the three frowsy tattered girls used to hang about the back door of the pub on a Saturday night, offering herself to the men who came out to visit the Gents. Her price was sixpence. 'She makes up to five bob on a good night,' said our bawdy friend. 'Not to be sneezed at these hard times. I'd consider it myself, only that old Bob of mine is that particular, he'd say I was getting myself talked about.' She and Bob were a happy loving couple, without a care in the world, it seemed to us, except when the slugs got at their cabbages.

There was also an idiot girl who roamed about and stood staring at nothing. One day I found her staring in at the window while I sat typing. She didn't answer when I spoke; she had a cleft palate. But Elza gave her some biscuits and she went away, chewing one and putting the others in her torn blouse. 'She's handy for them that are too mean to pay sixpence,' said our bawdy friend. 'There's a lot of mean sods round here, you'd be surprised. Sometimes I think it's awful being a woman, only Bob wouldn't like it if I wasn't, so I shut my trap and put up with things.' With a broad wink and a great laugh that swung the loose breasts in her loose blouse.

There was also an old witch who drove over from the Rodings in a decrepit cart with a bony horse on its last legs. She went slowly past, with many creakings and clatterings, talking to herself and now and then shaking the reins. The kids watched her in subdued awe, from a safe distance. She sold herb medicines. 'Relieves you of your rheumatiz and gets young hussies out of trouble, sometimes anyway. I never tried her. I'm one of those that like trouble, I can't get enough of it.'

The old rustic life was still thriving in the hamlet; and Elza felt at home in it. We had quickly taken roots here as we hadn't at Alphamstone or Takeley, perhaps because I wasn't spending part of the time in London and because the hamlet had its own close-meshed communal life. Elza was stimulated to start a novel on Saturday night at a pub; but she could not sustain a long work in prose and after a while she took to dictating it to me. I revised the completed thing – one can hardly call it a novel; it was more an extended documentary account, with a very slight story – but nine-tenths of the result was Elza's. I wondered where she had gained her knowledge of what a country pub was like; for neither here nor at the other Essex places had we drunk in the local.*

About this time on a visit to London to give some information which the accountants dealing with the Press wanted, I called in with Elza at the exporters, W. Jackson, off Chancery Lane – I forget why! they must have written with some queries about their stock. Elza mentioned her book; they asked to see it; they liked and published it.

I was myself working at my book on Donne, which kept running away with me. From a biography it wandered into an extensive commentary on the poems; from a commentary on the literary aspects it meandered into a psycho-analytical study and then into a long prose-poem which attempted to show the stages by which the reckless witty *libertin* became the devoted lover of Anne More. The thing grew huge and unwieldy, and in my disturbed and bewildered state of mind I could not devise a clear scheme on which to cut and rewrite. I was trying to find where I was myself going, by the exploration and elaboration of Donne's stages; and without knowing my own destination I was creating a wilderness of analysis on the pretence of mapping out Donne's spiritual progress. When at last I sent the MS in desperation to B., he didn't know what to make of it.

But very soon afterwards he died. Whisky and anxiety had

---

*She had written a short tale for the *Aphrodite*, obviously a piece of direct autobiography, about a starving girl who wanders in the streets, at last is driven to make a pick up, yet, when the man leaves in the morning, cannot bring herself to ask him for money.

proved too much. My two or three pounds a week abruptly ended, and it was only a question of time before the house was sold up over our heads. I managed to place one article, in a weekly, *Everyman*, but had no other luck. I was determined not to appeal to those who had been my friends but whom I had allowed Elza to exclude, Edgell, Brian, P.R.S., or Phil. I felt that I had no right. Having accepted Elza's control of the circumstances of my life, I had to find my way forward within the terms of that control or perish. The matter was so simple that I do not recall debating it at all in my mind; I merely accepted it without question as the premise on which any action must proceed.

On top of these disasters Elza suddenly, without any discussion, decided that at all costs she must have Robinetta. This was the first time she had mentioned the girl since she called on Edith Craig. There had been nothing to stop her having the child with us at Woodchurch Road as far as I was concerned; there was a large house and garden. But with my many problems pressing in on me, I had not suggested it; I felt that any decision must come from Elza. I did not ask myself if it was fear of me that prevented her from proposing the child's return; besides, she had become so self-assertive after driving the Pentons out that there seemed no reason to doubt that if she had wanted the child she would have raised the matter.

Despite my difficulties I rather welcomed Elza's demand. I told myself that the child would produce an easing of the situation. She would stand between Elza and me; and Elza's affection for her would surely have the effect of breaking down her own intransigence, of ending her 'imprisonment' of me, and of letting me out 'on parole' in quest of the necessary money for the household. I wrote in Elza's name to Edith Craig.

No reply came. I was surprised, as I had understood that Robinetta was to be returned whenever Elza asked for her. Though we could ill afford it, we made a trip to London and called at Miss Craig's address; but were told that she was away. We realized that she had no intention of returning Robinetta, whether that had been her intention from the start or she had come to it in the process of looking after the child (who was attending a semi-dance school at Hampstead). We wrote to

Robert and he offered Elza his support; other persons whom Elza made an effort to involve did not reply.

Elza told me that I must get the child. I think she expected me to kidnap her, but I said that we would go to a solicitor at Braintree. We walked across, through Felstead, where I lingered a few moments to look at the old buildings, and went into the first solicitor's office we saw. We could not have made a better choice in all England; for the elderly man who listened to us was won over by Elza and threw himself heart and soul into our case. Except for some fees to Counsel we never paid anything; we never received any bill. The solicitor knew that we could not have met it. He advised us that our only recourse was a Chancery suit.

The suit went on a couple of years. Many of the countless affidavits and statements were drawn up by myself, and merely re-typed at the office. Elza had worked herself up into a state of deep angry tension, which she vented on me. She clearly now looked on me as a weakling, a useless person unable to reclaim her child from an unjust world, unable to make a living. I felt a certain bitter satisfaction in knowing that my futility derived in large part from the impotence she imposed on me; she wanted to have me her slave and at the same time a strong man. I knew how she resolved the opposition: if I loved her truly, I would be both entirely hers and strong. I agreed with that thesis, but felt that she was inhibiting me from being 'entirely hers' in any free and vital sense by trimming our relationship into rigid rules and expressing her insistence that I should be a complete lover by a flat distrust of me. The least attempt on my part to argue this point of view produced in her a blind rage and convinced her that I wanted to escape once more into irresponsibility.

I tried to understand why I had given in to her pressure and 'confessed'. There is always, I thought, an element of revenge in a confession: the classic Dostoevskian position. One confesses in a hope of purging one's guilt, of spreading the guilt out, of proving that in the last resort society itself, the family and all that conditions the family, are the guilty things, having made one what one is. One hopes to gain a new start. But the element of resentment, making the confession an accusation as well as a plea, at once cripples one. One pre-supposes that the listener (the wronged lover, the police inspector, the whole damned world) is going to feel exactly the same mixture of emotions as oneself, will reach out to embrace one and bring about an identity of aspiration: the same rejection of the past, the same intense desire for a new life, a new heaven and a new earth. But this embracing union of confessor and listener is about the last thing likely to come about. The listener wants a different set of pledges, while the confessor feels the act of confessing itself to be the proof of his deep need for a regenerated self.

Re-reading *Hereward*, I saw how I had there forecast just what I was going to do. I felt all the more confused, as if throughout I had schemed for the exposure of myself, as a strange test of us both, a test I still could not understand. At the play's climax Torfrida discovers Hereward's entanglement with Alftruda, and he protests:

HEREWARD: *I feared to break because I feared to bring*
this pain upon you that I've brought at last –
but it's your fault. Why was your heart so hard?
I would have come then and confessed to you.

TORFRIDA: *No man confesses.*

HEREWARD: *But I would, I would.*
It has been beating fists in every pulse,
thumping upon my life like terrible messengers –
ah, can you understand what it is like
to have your life a room with many doors
and terror knocking madly on every door?
That's what it's been. If but I could have told you –
why was your heart so hard?

TORFRIDA: *You never tried . . .*

They upbraid one another, with Alftruda mocking them. Torfrida goes and Hereward turns gladly to meet his death of betrayal.

Yet when the time came, I had not wanted to die, as my Bussy and Hereward had. The *liebestod* had lost its glamour; the romantic basis of my poetry had fallen away at the crucial point, and I was left with an unsolved problem. I was alive, and enduring. What I carried over from the previous phase was the belief that I must never impose a solution on my conflicts. Desire was good; all will was self-will and evil. For it worked by seeking to impose a solution, a goal, a system, on others, and so must work out as self-righteousness and dogmatism, as parasitism and power-lust. My only hope was that by desiring harmony and union I would break down self-will in Elza, in whom since Takeley it had burst ever more strongly out.

I had to keep working in the hope of writing something that would sell, though I could not plan anything on the basis of making it marketable. As I had no belief in my own prose, I took the drawings Norman had made for Abercrombie's *Phoenix* and which had never been used. I shut my eyes and shuffled them up, then I set myself to work out a story to correspond to the new sequence. I hoped that I would be able to sell the result on the strength of the illustrations. For a character sufficiently like the girl in *Phoenix*, and yet different, I chose Cressida, Phil's great love; he had written a short verse play in Australia, *Cressida's First Lover*, and I decided to steal his title, as he had done nothing with his play.

I was about half-way through when Elza suddenly deepened her attack. I had noticed that she was growing more hostile and difficult, suffering a revulsion from sex altogether and yet caught in a half dream that some simple earth-love, a peasant-force, might awaken her body and fulfil it as none of her lovers had done, as I had failed to do. Something like the unexpurgated version of D.H.L.'s tale *Sun* as a day-dream (which in fact it was anyhow on D.H.L.'s part: though he saw himself as the peasant and Elza saw herself as the woman-to-be-earthily-awakened). Now the revulsion aspect triumphed, and henceforth there were never any physical relations between us. But the rejection of sex was the least furious of the attitudes she now turned on me. I had failed to get her back her child, I was a failure in all aspects. I was a liar who had not succeeded in cleansing and freeing myself from all the hellish aftermath of the birth trauma. I must now proceed to become fully sane.

'You are hiding behind your beard,' she said. The remark was true enough, but she had forgotten that she made me grow it. She borrowed a razor from the farm labourer next door and I shaved. She tore up several of my books which had drawings by N.L. in them. She wanted to get rid of anything of the past. She gave my one warm coat – that which Gruner had given me – to the farm labourer.

With my shaven face I did indeed feel strangely naked. I agreed with her in general that I still had far to go before I had fully sloughed my old self; but I could not see what more I could do at the moment. The mere fact of being the person who had the responsibility of making money, so that we could survive, had a tightening up effect; it prevented me from entire surrender, from letting go and dying and becoming a new man. Her answer was that I had no business to take on myself the responsibility of money when I shelved the responsibility of becoming a whole man, a man freed from the curse of the past. Let money go to hell.

We had long arguments. I clung to the general scheme of my Australian notion of life: the man for action (in its pure form, creation), the woman for love and children, the home. The man begets the creative image, the woman the child. Elza's retort was that woman's capacity to bear children did not affect the essential fact that her personality was humanly no different than the man's; she too could be creative. There was no simple line of sex division; sexual characteristics were secondary.

I wanted to accept her viewpoint, but couldn't. Every idea I had of life and art broke down if I did. I had given up my thesis of the poet at the mercy of his instincts and impulses. Using John Donne as my admired exemplar, I now accepted the true progress as from the Libertine who loves the Centrique Part in any woman, in a kaleidoscopic world of variable Venus, to the Truelove of a single woman, who, as a living centre, illuminates the rest of the universe, including all other women. But I could not go further and say it was male vanity and sexual fear which differentiated between the sexes at all and allotted them different functions. I was now nearing the D.H.L. idea of sex as my final defence.

But all the while something in me was breaking up. My ideas grew more and more entangled and uncertain. I could neither revise my Donne book nor finish my *Cressida*. I no longer had any stable basis on which to evalue event or construct character. All personality seemed built on false premises, an unsafe structure flimsily set up on quicksands; consciousness as I had known it, a total false face, an illusion pasted over an illusion. Nothing was real but the need to crawl as far back as possible down the tunnel of memory, to the very mouth of the womb. If one could only somehow repeat the birth experience inside the focus of one's consciousness of failure, of warped patterns, then one could perhaps correct what had gone wrong, get a really fresh start from the very first moment of the blast of light, of joy-pain, of hope-fear, of life-death. Every other way allowed the primal flaw to reassert itself in unrealized forms, however earnest the wish for a new start might be.

I decided to fast in the belief that privation, by permitting no alleviations of the anxiety, the backward-quest, was the only sure guide to the depths, to the light-in-darkness. I retired to bed upstairs, taking with me some bread and lemon-water, and fasted. Exactly how long I stayed there, I am not sure; for after the first few days I lost count of time; but it must have been at least a fortnight, perhaps three weeks or more. Now and then Elza brought me some water in which lemon slices had been dropped; otherwise I had nothing. After the first few days I did not feel any hunger. But in my dreamy lost state I found it hard to concentrate. Just as I would seem to be nearing some significant trauma or twisted wound in my remote past, my mind slid away and I drifted from one vague dissolving image to another. When I regained control of my thought processes, I felt hopeless. The traumatic spot (assuming that it existed and I did manage to come near it) was impregnable. Without concentration I could not break through the intense resistances; with it I would not drop slowly down to the hidden levels where the wound festered.

After I had been about a week abed, Elza came hastily up one morning and said, 'Alec Brown is here.' I dressed myself as quickly as possible: that is, pulled on shirt, trousers and shoes, and went down. I felt rather shaky and light-headed, but did my best to disguise my condition. Alec was driving through to his home area in Norfolk, Diss, and was full of cheerful talk about his work. All I can remember is saying that I meant to write a book about local characters and ways of life, calling it

Roundabouts Dunmow; for later, seeing that I did not use the title, he published a book *Chadwick Roundabouts*. I could not avoid eating a little while he was with us; but as soon as he had gone, I stripped and retired to bed again, resuming my fast.

Now, however, some images did persist and seem to be really drawn up from my submerged self. I saw myself walking in a small public garden just after Ray was born; he was being wheeled down the path in his pram by my mother, a lacy Victorian figure, and I fell down some stone steps on to my face. Further back, when I was about one, a curtain caught fire above my cot and blazed whirling red and black into the window . . . Gradually I seemed to be nearing the birth moment. At last, after hours of wrestling with obscurely violent sensations, my body caught in rhythmic pangs, I leaped from bed and ran to a mirror. Frantically I searched my face and found thin white scar-lines, almost indecipherable but brought out by the seething of the blood around them. I was convinced that I had found where instruments had torn my throat and lower face in dragging me from the womb, and that I had had a very difficult birth. (I did not get out of bed with my idea of looking for the lines; I was simply driven to the mirror; and only when I saw the lines did the idea of birth-scars come to my mind.)

Now, I have no conviction as to whether I had indeed forced myself, in my fasting condition, back to the earliest level of memory in the completed organism, or whether I had desperately fabricated the images in order to prove to myself and Elza that I was regenerated. (If the latter case were true, I must have noticed the scars unconsciously and now used them as definite evidence of my return. I later wrote a little of these experiences of mine to Jack Elkington, whom someone, my mother I think, had mentioned as being present at my birth. But instead of answering any of my questions, he riposted with one of his own: Had I been taking drugs? I presume that he had in mind the fact that some drugs can produce a series of birth images such as we find in Coleridge's *Kubla Khan*.)

I called Elza and tried to persuade her that I had now come to the end of my quest. She turned a stony face on me. I went back to my fast. Now I no longer made any effort to direct my thoughts and a strange series of images rose and drifted before me, changing from the microscopically exact to the incoherently vast: great deserts and cosmic wastes. (No doubt a prolonged fast, under conditions of extreme anxiety, can act in much the same way as drugs. My theory later was that it released the accumulated toxins in organs like the heart and the liver, which had an intoxicating effect in the literal sense of that term. The toxins were brought out and cleared away; the visions were of the vanishing evils of the body.) I saw enormous skies of cataclysm, Turnerian in colour at the outset, and slowly hardening into a lurid coppery glow. A skurry of countless forms, cosmic tadpoles and starry viruses, a mad descent of the damned. The small spikes and blobs expanded hugely, then contracted to points again and fell to a level somewhere below my sight, where I could yet see them in a painfully oblique angle. My broken body flapped like slow wings over the infinitesimally tiny forms in their ant-trail of busy fury across the abyss. Great coppery suns set in ragged crevasses. Apocalyptic imagery: sudden storm and flight of flashing angelic figures in battle with dark cloud-veering shapes. Then nothing but geometric forms breaking and revolving round a lost centre, perpetually on the edge of attaining a perfect balance, which I feared. Once the symmetry interlocks, all things will end. Then back to the cosmic spaces, myself crushed between mating earth and sky.

Some of the images may have been drawn from art, others constructed out of mythology; but the experience was none the less disturbing and engrossing. In my weakened condition there were long periods of dull lassitude. I floated with outstretched wings over the void and was not interested; then came moments of extreme urgency when life and death (of myself, of all things) depended on the outcome. My son, in whom I am well pleased. And dark mocking laughter. Day and night as one, a slow alternation of shaken patterns, hovering on the point of chaos or of interlocked immobility. All the while Elza said nothing, though she came up at moments to look at me with an inscrutable challenge and contempt. I longed for one word of encouragement.

Finally, one afternoon, in a sudden long wave of coppery light, I saw the over-life-size figure of an Egyptian goddess with lion-head, Tefnut or Mehi-t, at the other end of the room. At the same time the form seemed Betty May lion-headed, standing in majestic unconcerned power, a strange animal power, not malign, yet terrible in its predatory innocence. I saw the form in a preternatural sharp light which revealed every detail in a flat microscopically near precision. I saw every hair of the lion-face, every pore of the large coarse milky breasts. At the moment of vision I had no fear, no belief or disbelief; I merely saw. All my being was absorbed in the act of seeing. Then I leaped out of bed. The image vanished. I was afraid. I ran for the window and stared at the roadway of common traffic with tremendous love and relief. No one was in sight. Then a dog passed across at the end near the farm. I loved the dog. I loved the world and wanted to escape from the pointless hell of my own mind with its vicious circle of remorse. If I had reached the stage of projecting my images as apparently real things I had better stop before I went mad. I went slowly downstairs, found some milk and drank it.

I told Elza that I was cleansed of my illusions; I had realized my relation to my father and my mother; it had been the failure to achieve this realization that had driven me along a compulsive path of romantic self-dedication, with a dream of *liebestod*. All the while I had been running away from my responsibility to my mother; I had feared to face my failure to take charge of her in the helpless state into which she had fallen when I was about fourteen; I had put myself at the service of the father who had thrown her into her lost misery; by accepting his ethereal art message I had felt redeemed from the earth-fate of my mother. Woman, what have I to do with you? I am doing my father's business. I had been relieved of my sense of guilt by a deepening of guilt, by making the guilty act seem the affirmation of a higher need, an overriding justice. What I had thought my creativeness was a false intoxication proceeding from my passion, my mysterious crucifixion under the father's will. But at the very heart of my acceptance of that will there had been a slowly growing revolt, an effort to understand the truth. I had turned to her, Elza, because I recognized in her my lost mother; I had wanted to redeem her from her trampled desolation. But I had been unable to grasp this impulse in its fullness except by the dramatization of my inner struggle through the conflicting claims of Elza and Betty – Janet now being obliterated as the image of the father-submission I rejected. It was therefore wrong to penalize me for my 'betrayal', which had been my only way forward to a complete devotion. Without it I could never have shocked myself into facing the truth of my relation to my parents. Now I was free from the repetition-compulsion uttered in my art theories, my romantic concept of the relation of art and life.

As an expression of my belated defence of my mother, I wrote an angry letter to Norman. I think it must have been Phil who told me that N.L. contemplated reducing my mother's not-large allowance (£5 a week was all she ever had to bring up us three boys and keep herself) on the grounds that her sons now made their own living. I am now not at all sure how definite the rumours of reduction were; but it suited me in my present mood to accept them. I wrote to N.L. accusing him of various meannesses towards my mother and demanding that he should not reduce the allowance. I assume that he got the letter and tossed it aside. He did not reply.

Though I was making the mistake of seeing my whole life as a mere projection of unrealized relations to my parents and of thus omitting the society in which the family operated, I had learned important truths about myself, without which I should never have made any decisive steps forward. And I owed these truths wholly to the relentless pressure that Elza had put on me. Previously, in discussing Freud, I had said: There seems a great deal of truth in his work – in his dynamic concepts of the unity of the psyche and in his subtle web of associations, in his understanding of the nature and action of symbols; but for the life of me I can't see how the Oedipus complex applies to myself; I have no feeling one way or another about my mother – though I can see how the complex has a wide application.

Now I felt whatever was the case with other people I certainly was a perfect example of the complex. I had been left by the disappearing (dying) father with my mother as the head of the family; and a peculiarly strong tension had been brought about as she lay increasingly helpless (at my mercy) from my puberty onwards. I was the family head (father) with my two young brothers and my mother looking to me; and I had been driven into ever-deepened revulsion from the position by my mother's collapse, which I did not know how to deal with. Inevitably then I was psychically in the classic role of Oedipus.

I expected Elza to turn to me now with happiness and say that the basis for a stably harmonious relation had been reached. But she merely listened with an aloof critical interest, as though I had had the first glimmerings of sanity but was not at all yet to be trusted. In an effort to find external verifications of my change of heart I burned all my MSS I could lay hands on: the many plays and poems written in both Australia and England, which had not yet been published, and surrealist novel, the translations of Essenin, and so on. I also burnt all the letters I had been keeping, of which the most important were those of N.L., Norman Douglas, and Gordon Bottomley. But no holocaust had the least effect in moving Elza. And I began to doubt my own sincerity. Was I acting like this because I really wanted to cut all past connections? or was I only trying to placate Elza? Her disbelief in me had the effect of creating afresh a division inside myself. I did not yet suspect how deep were her fears, how hopeless was the task I had set myself.

Once she said, 'Your eyes are sane while you're working.' I should have understood how all her energies were taken up in watching me. All her fears and revulsions had become concentrated in me; and I was therefore the last person in the world who could help her to throw them out and to become stable. I was in the position of a psychoanalyst who has seduced, cheated, and betrayed his patient, and who then cannot understand why the processes of transference fail to work. The more he tries to detach the patient from himself and return her in a balanced state to the world, the more he awakens her distrust. And in my case the situation was made yet more involved by the fact that I was simultaneously attempting the decisive analysis of myself and that the world to which the patient had to return was my own bed and bosom.

I had some vague understanding of the impasse already, and as things went on I saw it all clearly enough. But always it seemed too soon or too late to insist on a break. The uttered or unuttered threat of suicide always stayed my hand. Besides, it was not so easy to affect my own transference. The more difficult things became, the more I felt that I was facing a test, an ordeal, which I must accept if my humanity were not to perish. For a few years the mirage of a final reconciliation as a reward for suffering and submission also operated; then I ceased to believe in it. I simply endured.

She liked to be in control, even while resenting her position. My submission fed the tyrannical side of her fear, and it was illusion for me to believe that only flaws in my submission prevented her from turning afresh to me with love. Not that now I loved her in any normal sense of the term. One cannot love what one fears. Since fear had now come ineradicably between us, our love had become a form of hate, an uneasy alliance of enemies, so that my mirage of an ultimate reunion could only mean a reversal of the roles, myself supplanting her in control. She felt this well enough and was determined to keep the whip-hand. She was determined never again to be hoodwinked by 'love', by trust in anyone else's goodwill. I was the last person in the world she could ever trust, because of the complicated process that had gathered in me all the oppressors and betrayers of her defiled life. She hated me now with a steady calm hatred, which was tempered to a kind of tranquil benevolence as long as she felt sure that I obeyed her in all things and thus reflected her will without the least contradiction. So she too was tormented by her mirage. She wanted me to become an automaton of her needs, which she interpreted as my becoming my pure self; only if all self-will dropped away from me would she be able to give up her sleepless task of watching, which kept her hard and unbending, and took away all possibility of relaxation, let alone pleasure, from her life.

For the moment however there was a truce of exhaustion. I tried to complete *Cressida*, and finally managed to do so, keeping up as well as I could a manner in which I no longer could put my heart. Elza read the MS and insisted that Cressida and the lad she has carried along with her should be married at the end; I thought this out of key but did as she said. Then I sent the MS to the agents Curtis Brown. About the same time

I thought of the Limited Editions Club of New York as probably one of the few fine-book producers able to weather the economic storm. I wrote and proposed a version of the *Golden Ass*. They promptly commissioned the work for £100. However, £50 of this was used up before I got it, for at our solicitor's advice I agreed to put that sum into a trust-fund for Robinetta; they advanced the money as a loan.

Suddenly Elza announced that she was going to see her mother. She had previously always spoken of her mother as long dead, the distracted Mme de Locre of the aristocratic Paris Garden; but now, without any explanation, she told me that her mother was married to a market-gardener in Combe Martin and that she herself was an illegitimate child. Her father had been an elderly doctor who holidayed yearly with his family in north Devon; he fell in love with the young girl who worked for them, and got her with child; he arranged to go off with her to New York, but his wife proved too much for him; he gave in and allowed his child, Elza, to be looked after by an uncle of hers in Bristol. After a while Elza's mother married the market-gardener, and now had several children by him.

I had heard so many stories from Elza that I didn't believe this one; but it turned out to be completely true. I sent my few N.L. etchings to the Leicester Galleries and my books to Foyles, and got a very poor price. We also offered our few sticks of furniture to a Dunmow dealer. We now had enough cash in hand to buy our tickets for north Devon and live there a few weeks. Elza, concerned at the effect I'd have on her family, insisted on buying me two ready-made suits from the local Co-op. One, which we took on the spot, fitted me to a certain extent; the other, sent after us, proved about five sizes too large, but we made no effort to send it back and have it changed.*

---

*I recently revisited Onslow Green to take a photo of the house, and found it gone. At first I thought I must have mistaken the place, then I saw the concrete flooring I had had put in the smithy. At the pub close by I learned that shortly after we left an old man fell down the stairs with an oil-lamp and the house and smithy were burned down.

20 · ELZA GOES HOME

THIS is the part of my life when I am vaguest as to chronology; I was living so completely inside myself. However, my fasting experience must have occurred in mid-winter, helped on its way by the news of Heseltine's suicide; and it was some time in early spring that we arrived in Combe Martin, that long sprawling valley-town, with market-gardens on the slopes and the tall tapering shapes of ruined mine-towers on the skyline. Elza had taken a thin corridor of a bungalow, about half-way along the village and half-way up the northern slope. We went to see her mother, who proved a cheerful stocky country woman with a broad Devon accent. The only thing at all akin to Elza were her eyes, of a pale bright blue. But one could see, on a second glance, that she must have been a pretty thing at the age of seventeen before her waistline thickened and her face was burned by the suns and the ovens of a hard working life. Her husband was a bluff self-contained man, somewhat older, who received Elza with a friendly nonchalance, despite the fact that her arrival must have stirred up all the village gossips with the tales of his wife's young days. The children, boys and girls in their late teens, were clearly curious. One of the girls, bringing some vegetables and finding me at the washing up, reported that we were 'chicken': that is, tenderly devoted to one another.

It was necessary for Elza to make an impressive return, but we had none of the paraphernalia for it. I must have looked gauntly distracted, obviously no rich husband; and Elza's distinguished eccentricities of dress were not the sort of thing to evoke a village's respect. From this period she began to wear ordinary clothes. Her mother was certainly very relieved to see her. She had heard nothing since Elza left Ilfracombe, did not

711

even know of her marriage; she had given her up for lost, imagining a fate which in many aspects was all too exactly what had happened, but hardly guessing that her girl could have climbed so far out of the ruck and the muck as in some ways she had. Yet the relief was chequered by confused fears; she didn't enjoy her past coming up again after so many years of respectability; she sensed something was wrong and that our visit had an unstated motive.

Elza found her tongue loosed by the familiar setting of so much of her childhood. At about six she had left Bristol and had lived with her grandfather and grandmother here. Then she had run away to a job in a hotel at Ilfracombe, where the manager seduced her. Not that he was the first. She took me to meet a woman who as a girl had been her closest friend; they used to go out with this latter's two brothers and make love in a scrambled way among the bushes and nooks of the valley, changing round and laughing at one another. The friend, now a married woman with a couple of children, received us with a prim mouth and scared eyes.

There were endless tales of the troubles she had got into. She must have been a wild child, rebelling against the least show of authority and resentful at being relegated to her grandparents while her mother, now married, was near at hand. She had a conviction that the Bristol uncle, a commercial traveller, had embezzled the funds that the doctor had settled on her, and then tossed her back to the village. From a few remarks of her mother I think there was probably much truth in this belief, though she may have exaggerated the sums of which she was cheated. She also had a very circumstantial account of the various ways her uncle abused her in a small carpentry workshop he had at the rear of his suburban house. At the time I credited all she told me; but now I am not sure. She had suffered so much outrage and she had brooded so long on her uncle's theft of her 'birthright' that she may well have built up a fantasy of complete depravity on his part.*

*Among other things I now learned that she was a real connection with De Hérédia; before meeting Robert, Elza had had an affair with a youth of that name, whom she described as the poet's son. Presumably he was some

Various outlying relatives, hearing of her return, called in to see us, friendly and suspicious, and invited us to tea amid their best china ornaments. I found the whole thing wearying and felt in a false position, but did my best to help Elza keep her end up. In my spare time I was working at the *Golden Ass*, using a rickety writing desk, and feeling an ever-greater fellowship with Lucius transformed into a beast of burden and seeking the rose of regeneration. We were near the end of our cash. When I went to post the MS to the Limited Editions Club, I didn't have enough to pay the postage. I took the parcel back, removed most of the packing material and any unnecessary sheets, tied up what remained in a tubular form, and just managed to buy the stamps. As soon as I handed the parcel over, I felt scared that it would come to pieces before it reached New York. However, it arrived safely, and in a few weeks the cheque turned up.

Before that I had had some more luck. The Bodley Head accepted *Cressida*, with the proviso that the marriage was an unconvincing finale. I rewrote the passage and received a cheque for £25. To my surprise the firm said that they did not want the drawings with the tale. To keep going with our daily expenses Elza had meanwhile had a heart-to-heart talk with her mother and borrowed a few pounds, which we repaid as soon as the first cheque arrived. At the same time she told her mother about the Chancery suit. I had the feeling that the various revelations both worried and relieved her mother, who now felt that she understood better the strange daughter come back in a strange guise. Our solicitors had advised us that it would help us if we had an affidavit from Elza's mother supporting our case. We went with her to a firm they had named at Ilfracombe, and complied with the formalities.

A mistake was made in the document which our opponents tried to make much of, though I don't think the judge took it

---

descendant of the family, how directly from the poet I do not know. But he certainly existed; Elza had much to say of him; he seemed to have moved her a great deal.

seriously. Elza's mother was described as widow. Edith Craig's solicitors sent a detective down to Combe Martin to check up and found that the mother did exist but was not a widow. I hadn't noticed the error in the flurry of the moment and couldn't see that it mattered so much; but our solicitors said a widow had a much more free legal personality than a wife. (This was not the only mistake we made; but the other was an error of judgment, possible through the almost free hand I had in the affidavits. In a moment of wrath I put into a plea against Miss Craig some matters of libellous hearsay, purveyed to me by Elza, and was properly rebuked by the judge-in-chambers, who also, however, rebuked our opponents for trying to describe my writings as immoral.)

Shortly after the acceptance of *Cressida*, but before the cheque came in, I received a card from Allen Lane to say that he would be motoring in Devon and would like to call on us. (He was still in the family firm, the last of the name.) Though I would have liked to see him, I felt it would be impossible and wrote putting him off. For the next ten years no guest put his foot in our doors (except once a student at Truro, and once Randall Swingler at Dartmouth). I did not know that my uneasy card of late spring 1931 was putting off not only Allen Lane, but the world.

We now felt that we must retreat somehow from Combe Martin, but didn't know how to make a graceful exit. Elza found out that several miles to the east, at Blackmore Gate, a fine house was to let at 30s. a week. The person who had main control of the leasing was a rich woman living on our village's outskirts; and we called on her. She clearly did not quite know how to treat us. In the hopes of getting the house I laid what stress I could on my appearance in *Who's Who*, but on the other hand the woman clearly knew about Elza's parentage. She tried to ward us off, but without much decision. I managed to go over her head to the Barnstaple solicitors in charge of the estate, and they drew up a lease.

But the lease had still not arrived on the Saturday when we had arranged to leave Combe Martin. I felt desperate. We had to go somewhere; Elza's relations knew that we were negotiating the lease of the imposing house; a decrepit taxi was calling for us. I decided to assume that the lease was held up by some accident and to enter the house by hook or by crook. When we arrived, we piled up our things on the door-step and said goodbye to the car-driver, who would report to the village that we had duly taken possession. Then I prowled round the house and found a side-window open. So we entered without breaking anything. I then rang up the solicitors and told them that we were in. Some hours later a bewildered clerk came by train from Barnstaple with the lease. I had succeeded in forcing the hand of the uncertain owners. I presume that the solicitors had rung up the lady of Combe Martin, who hesitated about calling in the police to have us evicted.

Well, there we were, with our solitude established, in a sort of magnificent manor-house built of local grey stone, with about twenty rooms and large grounds. In the gentlemanly way of pre-war leases (which was to save me from ruin many times in the coming years) the first payment was due at the end of three months. Three months: time to write a couple of masterpieces and perhaps make some money. In a large cellar under the huge kitchen there was the complete apparatus for generating electricity; meanwhile we had some candles. But the days were lengthening and we could rise at dawn. We each chose one of the rooms upstairs with a splendid view, and put a suitcase and a small portmanteau in for furniture. That was all we had for the moment. We slept on the floor.

That night, after darkness came, I was disturbed by a loud scrabbling and banging at the back door, and went with some trepidation to see who was there. When I opened, I had a fleeting glimpse of a large white object that shot up, knocked me over, trampled on me, and rushed into the house. My candle had gone out, but there was another in the passage. I rushed to get it and found my assailant had been a sheep. With some difficulty, its hooves clatter-clattering on the wooden floors, I managed to push it out. It baa-ed disconsolately for some time, scrabbled, and went off. Some days later I found that the house had previously been tenanted by a caretaker with a couple of children who made a pet of a small lamb; the lamb grew into a sheep, but the children wept and clung to it; they saved it as their own till their departure about a week before. On the night of our arrival the sheep had broken loose and come in search of its playmates.

In a cupboard next day I found a gadget for impressing the address of the house on note-paper. I selected my best bits of paper and impressed the address; then I wrote to some shops in Barnstaple, the names of which I gained from a copy of the local newspaper. I ordered enough blinds to cover the windows of the ground floor; also some of the more durable groceries. At the last moment I also ordered a quantity of dried fish, with a few fresh ones, from a large fishery store. (I developed a feud with the latter shop, for they delivered the fish to a blacksmith at the cross-roads below in the valley: the place where they had left goods for the last inhabitants of the house. They didn't inform me, and the fish were unclaimed so long that they went bad. I refused to pay and was threatened with prosecution for debt.)

Luckily the caretaker had not taken away a fair amount of vegetables he had been growing; and in the barns and sheds at the back I found packing-cases and lengths of wood out of which I constructed tables and wardrobes. I started on a pair of beds; but as I had no tools except a defective hammer found in the pantry, I gave up and used my impressed note-paper to order the cheapest pair of camp stretchers I could get. Now we were fully equipped.

What was I to write? I couldn't follow *Cressida* up with a similar kind of work; and my ideas about people and life were still in too chaotic a condition for me to attempt an ordinary novel. I decided to try a fable about Satyrs and Centaurs – about the war that wiped out those odd creatures, so that only a memory of them remained in Greek art and poetry. Thus I felt I could continue my anatomizing of what was wrong with mankind and why they were heading for disaster. Once I had begun, I wrote with considerable speed and hopefully sent the work to The Bodley Head, from whom it soon came back. Depressed, I sent it to the agents, who failed to place it.

I thought the work had gone to join the limbo of so much of my writing; but after Phil's death in 1958 I found a copy of it in his big box, among other MSS of mine and a large number of his summonses and debt-writs. To my surprise the work was much more amusing than I had remembered; its weakness lay in the fact that there was no central idea to explain the stupidities, irrationalities, and highly involved confusions that led to the exterminating war. A ridiculous chain-series of events was shown accumulating disorders and antagonisms; but the only general idea to be inferred was that the inner disorganization of men prevented them from dealing in time with trivial alarms and conflicts, which gathered steadily their destructive momentum. The culmination came when the physicist of the Satyrs projected on to the Centaurland a terrific force which too late he realized would set up a chain-reaction and recoil on its begetters.

Once again I expressed my conviction that modern science was set on a road of disintegration which would threaten the earth's very existence. The physicist stays on at his mechanism, trying to find the flaw in his system in the few minutes of life left to him. ('I may find the necessary formula before I am exploded.' 'What use is that?' wailed Paniscos. 'What use is anything?' replied Assaon tartly. 'It will be a most important discovery.')

But what most surprised me in re-reading the MS was that the novel held in abstracted form the method I was later to apply in my historical fiction. It showed obsession with points of social explosion, with the causes of mass movements, the relation of individual aims to the larger whole which is seen only in refracted or distorted ways; and it strove to find a technique for gathering a multiple set of divergent lines into a single pattern. My fasting vigil under Freud's aegis had brought me half-way to the clear earth. It had rid me of other worldly fantasies and lodged me nakedly in the reality of the family; what remained was for me to place the family solidly in the reality of social process. But that was no easy task. Meanwhile I could see only individual acts and emotions in infinite interaction, with the aggregate of separate impacts making up a complex mass of turmoiling strains and stresses; I could not distinguish any organic unity or purposes in that mass. The birth trauma alone unified.

At the same time as I worked on *Satyrs* I began an attempt to generalize my experiences on a theoretical level, *Birth and*

Will. My aim was to show the way in which the birth trauma produced various repetition-compulsions, based on an unconscious attitude to the parents – an attitude which turned the parents into myths or god figures, images of authority or licence, fear or desire. As a result, an accumulative set of tensions and strains were created in the individual, who drove himself along the lines determined by his unconscious fantasy of the parents. Will was thus a destructive force, an effort to compel oneself along the fantasy lines, to impose a pattern of living on oneself; it always created more problems than it solved; it tied one up in knots of worsening frustration and bodily rigidity; it distorted the sexual flow into power-lust; it turned the self into a thing, a means to an end, and thus produced property-lust – all the possessed things being reduplications of the dead thing-self. The alternative was to relax, to stop fighting and driving oneself forward, to fall back into oneself and slowly break the tight grip of fear. Then one could begin to realize the truth of oneself, one's place in the family, one's place on the earth. By finding one's own true centre one entered into the fullness of life, realized oneself as a living part of all things. By straightening out the traumatic knots, twists, and cankers in one's being, one enabled the life-flow to pervade all aspects and levels of oneself. One released one's sex from its clotting in certain zones and points of irritation, and made it an harmonious part of the life-process in one's body-spirit, merging oneself with the universal process.

These ideas were worked out in long and precise detail; especially I used the evidence of language, in which the unconscious hope and fear are often fused. (At this stage I saw all social institutions and forms of expression as projections of the struggle in the individual psyche.) The general method was Freudian; but I did not know any psychoanalytic work with the same points of departure or arrival. I did not assume that the work of analysis had as its aim the smoothing out of inner conflicts so that the purged individual might fit into our given society. On the contrary, I assumed that our society was all wrong, the result of a mass projection of all the evils I grouped under the heading of will – power-lust, property-lust and so on. I wanted the individual to resist our society, to reject it, but had no scheme for changing it, beyond the assumption that if enough persons resisted and rejected along the lines I advocated, a different sort of social system would result, one that reflected the pure life-flow in the individual.*

I had a letter from Sherard Vines, asking for a contribution to a collection of satiric poems, *Whips and Scorpions*, and wrote *Philocyon*, aimed against my past self. I copied out my Blake book, added some variants, and sold it for a couple of pounds to Foyles' MSS department. I had only a shaky packing-case table and a typewriter in its last stages of collapse, continually jamming. I kept on racking my brains for fresh translation outlets; but the Limited Editions Club turned down my suggestion of *Daphnis and Chloe*, saying that they meant to do George Moore's version. Later in the year their fine edition of my *Golden Ass*, bound in soft ass-skin, turned up.

I loved the house we'd taken and dreamed of spending the rest of my days there. We went for a few walks over to Exmoor, but mostly stayed within our own bounds. Even there I sometimes encountered wild cats behind the sheds. The house itself, though built in the last century, seemed in its silvery-brown stone to have been hewn out of the earth, not something imposed on the landscape and rejected by it. The farmer below, with whom we became friendly, gave us a hare he had snared; but neither of us, despite our food straits, could bear to clean it, so that in the end I buried it. Once I used up a lot of our meagre supplies in making, very successfully, an elabor-

---

*Apart from the books by Freud then available in English, I had read fairly widely in psychoanalysis: the books of Jones (the essay on Salt much influenced me, and both Phil and I had recognized N.L. in his essay on the god fantasy), Stekel, Rank, Ferenczi, etc. (Ferenczi's 'shock-tactics' had impressed me.) I had studied a large number of case reports and thus had a good idea of the practical side, especially impressed by finding that the process of psychoanalytic self-knowledge was identical in structure with the poetic process of Greek and Shakespearean tragedy. Works like Freud's on dreams and the psychopathology of everyday life deepened what one had already surmised and thought out about the associative principle at work in the creative process. While admiring some of Jung's work on symbols, I disliked what I felt his vague and messy mysticism.

ate cake, just to prove that I too could be handy in the kitchen. Elza, with her sudden phobias that could be most inconvenient in the midst of other difficulties, decided that she could not bear the creeper covering one side of the house, and I called in a local builder to remove it and wash the walls with some preservative. He must have reported the matter to the Combe Martin lady, for a few days after the job was finished she turned up. I couldn't ask her in to have some tea, as there was no furniture – nothing on the ground floor at all, apart from the neat blinds, but a packing case in the middle of the vast kitchen. So I had to talk as fast as I could, wandering round the outside of the house and discussing the improvement we had made by removing the creeper, and jumping on to any other theme that came into my mind, to distract her. Finally after about an hour, during which I kept an anxious eye on the blinds, afraid that some had not been well drawn, I said, 'I'm sorry to keep you so long. Sorry there isn't time to ask you in for tea,' and shook hands. Being well mannered, she mumbled something about not wanting to bother us and went off, probably deciding we were mad and best left to our own devices.

Though with no market in mind, I began on *Daphnis*, and I got an idea for another novel. A group of people weekending in a remote country house (exactly like ours) dress up in the costumes of the 1640s; without realizing the transition, they find themselves transported back into the midst of the Cromwellian Civil War, the house is besieged, and various conflicts develop among them.

21 · WANDERINGS

The end of the first quarter was nearing and I had no means of meeting the bill of £20/10/-. Left to myself, I would have stayed on, hoping somehow to raise the money. But Elza decided that we must return to London. The hearing of the suit was soon to come on, and we should have to pay a visit anyhow. With our depleted finances, the only sensible choice was to evacuate. I wrote a letter to the Barnstaple solicitors and posted it as we left. I asked them to cancel the lease, wait for what was owing, and arrange to sell the blinds, sending what they fetched to the firm that had sold them, and letting me know the deficit. I was melancholy as we took the local train, but Elza was always cheerful during a move.

In London we found a flat in Portobello Road, a top-storey that was being given up by two old maids. The latter had decided that city air did not agree with their large number of pets, and they were moving on to the north outskirts of London. We had to listen to long accounts of the ailments to which canaries, cats, dogs (if pekes may be dignified with that name), and angora goats were liable. Not that they had goats in the flat, but they meant to acquire them in their new place. By these means we gained their confidence and their flat, escaping after four days from our Paddington room.

The episode of the uneaten hare and the general bias of my book on birth and will had inclined us against meat-eating. The more I thought about it, the more I felt that the roots of religion and the whole evil power-complex I was trying to understand were to be found entwined with meat-eating and all it involved – not the only roots, but an important set of them. The magical ideas of the hunting groups, and even more the religious ideas of the settled groups who raised animals for

slaughter, seemed to me to have created a series of irrational
fears and lusts which has later been rationalized in men's consciousness, but which still operated in their aboriginal form
from deep down. Only by discarding a diet based on rotting
corpses could men become sane. The fantasy of needing a
blood diet, a corpse diet, was inseparable from the distorted
relation to the parents I had been trying to clarify in myself
and which one way or another existed in everyone. The corpse
eater was still in fantasy feeding on the parents.

We discussed these ideas and decided to eat no more meat,
no more animal products of any kind (such as milk, cheese,
eggs) and to discard mineral salt. Apart from a few extreme
applications of our position, when I tried to eat such nauseous
things as raw potatoes, we found that we felt very much better
in health. Until I was called up into the Army in 1941 I kept
strictly to a vegetarian diet, with enormous benefit to my
health, getting rid even of the colds that used to bother me a
lot and had convinced me of a weak chest. I never had the least
illness during the decade to come, despite the many hardships
and anxieties, and despite the periods of lack of exercise.

Robert Craig turned up in reply to a letter from Elza, and
on learning our views took us to a vegetarian restaurant. I now
read some health-reform periodicals, and during the next few
years contributed articles and poems to them. The Chancery
suit did not come up as we expected. Some preliminary rounds
were completed, and the game of affidavits resumed. I was trying to finish the new novel, *Masquers*, and wrote a long short
story, *Come Home at Last*, set in the ancient Greek world, which
Elza read and tore up. (Later I wrote it down as close to the
first version as I could recall it, and it appeared in a book of
short stories with that title. The wife and the girl whose deaths
she brings about stood for the opposed aspects of Elza, her
cruelty and her tenderness.) I also re-wrote for her a play on
which she had got stuck – a typical romantic incest fantasy,
in which a father almost seduces his unrecognized daughter.*

---

*I was trying to write an introduction to *Daphnis*, citing examples of the
Rejected Babe Suckled by Beasts. As I was walking home from Notting Hill
I was thinking of Cyros, stopped at a tray of second-hand books and picked

Then we moved again. I cannot remember why. Elza's restlessness must have been the main cause; for, throughout the following years, I always wanted to burrow in, wherever we chanced to be, if only to avoid more moving costs – but also because I urgently wanted to grow roots. Within a week at any new place I had ransacked the public library for histories, records, and so on, and had begun to feel a local patriotism. Now, using our trusty *Daltons* we decided to settle in some seaside huts below Maldon. At the moment Elza had fantasies of our finding an island somewhere and of herself turning into a great matriarchal figure with hundreds of grandchildren and great-grandchildren.

Autumn was advanced. The Essex coast was bleak, an endless stretch of misty mudflats broken only by mournful seagulls. The damaged decaying huts, with shreds of summer gaiety, were all empty. Elza hated it at the first glance and sulked. I wanted to get at least our week's worth of money. But she wouldn't stay. We took a bus eastward, and by making inquiries put up at a farmstead where part of the main building was to let. We stayed there some weeks. My typewriter ceased to work, and I copied out the last parts of *Masquers* by hand as neatly as I could, afflicted by the stench of pigs and fowl-droppings. I felt the novel was weak. The idea was good, but I could not develop personal conflicts among my masqueraders which really had any deep connection with the historical scene into which they were dropped. As in *Satyrs* there was an effective mechanism, but no organic idea to draw the parts together. I looked out on the yard and said to myself: There is the earth, describe it in all its manifold details; bring it to life in its underlying unity. But I seemed to have no talent at all. I compiled a list of the things I saw; I could not reconstruct

---

up a copy of Herodotus that opened at the tale of Cyros. I bought the book for a penny (my limit for books), and felt an omen in the event as I translated the passage. But no one wanted the *Daphnis*. Elza had been convinced that Seymour Hicks would take her play; she had known him in her Craig-days. We sent the play (as later the one I rewrote for her in Cornwall), with no luck.

the scene or define what I felt when I looked at it. Either a dead enumeration of oddments or a retreat into a personal cavern of despair. I gave up and brooded through the long slow changes of the dusk. Then suddenly I found phrases coming from my pen: 'The knots and snarls of light in the tree are drawn too tight, they crack and explode in momentary spikes of silver. Nothing has happened. Time exists . . .' I felt Time as my enemy, tearing the world to shreds before I could grasp its pattern, taking me, too, to pieces, like a child with a clock, and unable to put half the cogwheels back. Time that went backwards as well as forwards, but was not reversible. I re-read what I had written. Words, words, words. Nothing to the point. But I did not know what the point was.

I had another problem to worry me. Just before we left the shore-hut a letter from my literary agents had arrived, addressed to me, which held inside a letter to Norman. From the letter it was clear that Norman was now in England; and I inclined to believe, no doubt incorrectly, that the misdirection to me had been deliberate – an oblique way on Norman's part of letting me know that he was in London, and of providing me with his address, without risking the snub that might come from any straightforward note or message. I was convinced that he had indeed come to England to see me; that he had been upset by my attacking letter and had finally decided to come over and see what had happened to me. In all these conclusions I doubtless over-estimated greatly my importance in his mind. From Rose's notes I learn that he had been much embittered by a renewal of abuse in Australia and that as they walked through the Sydney streets on their way to the liner they read the *Smith's Weekly* posters: Will Norman Lindsay Be Arrested? The Faber edition of *Redheap* had been banned and an *Art in Australia* edition dedicated to his work had been seized by the police. They felt the need to get away from Australia for a while, and visited the U.S.A. as well as England. In London, as Will Dyson was ill, the *Daily Herald* offered Norman his place as a guest cartoonist at a high fee. 'But Norman was only interested in getting on with his scheme for publishing books,' says Rose. I should guess however that he shrank from doing cartoons for any periodical with the least left tinge; he thus threw aside a ready-made opportunity for a strong impact on English opinion. He and Rose stayed at a hotel in Russell Square, complaining that the central-heating pipes gave no heat (while Elza and I shivered in Essex with no fires at all). He used to walk to the Pentons' flat in Corman Street for its piled-up grate: Brian at the time working on his novel *Landtakers*. When the Pentons moved to a larger place, Norman and Rose took over the Corman Street flat for six weeks, then left for Australia again. Rose mentions visits from Phil and Jeanne, the latter in her tight-bodiced velvet frocks and flowing skirts.

My father does not seem to have made any inquiries about me at all. The only persons who had my changing addresses were the agents; but since he shared them, he could easily have written me a note. Despite my angers, I still felt the strong pull of his personality. Deep in myself, I longed to go and see him. But I knew that if I did, I should succumb to his charm, I should begin to whittle down and modify my new convictions, I should end by returning, even if in a less intense form, to my discipleship. And deeper than the longing for reconciliation there was the need to hold myself apart and nurture the new life which was still a young and fragile thing. Here, as in all matters, for the next few years, Elza was my objectified conscience, sternly watching me for any backsliding. That was why, in the last resort, despite the many inconveniences and hardships it entailed, despite what may seem from the outside an intolerable narrowing of existence, I accepted her domination. The over-rigid elements in her attitudes may have been unfortunate; but I felt them as the price paid for keeping on a straight and perilous path from which it was all too easy to stray – especially for someone of my character, who, ready to set up absolutes in solitude, was given to caving in and compromising when faced with an opponent in the flesh. In part the reason for such compromises lay in my inability to avoid seeing a certain element of truth in the adversary's position and being driven to imagine myself under his skin in order to understand why he had arrived at it. I was ready to fail myself, but I could not bear to fail Elza.

We took buses and reached Colchester. I visited the Castle with its Roman remains and long meditated there. We bought

Daltons and sat in a flyblown café. After Devon we felt the pull of the West. Why not go further on, further into the wilds? I longed for a landscape where I did not feel the shaping hand of man. The comfortable vistas all round London had ended by horrifying me as revealing only a toy world, a land ploughed and trampled into easy curves. I wanted the sterile stone and the waste that men had not dunged into prosperity. And looking out through the café window I watched the girls, the young men, hurrying or idling through a world they never questioned, a world that was now a madness to me. And I was sorry for them, and envied them, like a dead man looking through a crack in his gravestone. How happy if they only knew. But if they knew their happiness, they would know also its insufficiencies, they would reject it and seek wholeness, they would be lost, haunted with an irremediable ache and yet strangely proud. I have been chosen for this impossible task, the quest of the life-source; I chose myself for it. I am living in a folk-tale, I am Gilgamesh as well as Hamlet, and the end is the same for all of us. Only I have this secret pride. Perhaps it is nothing but a sense of wonder at the infinite riches of the least moment of living. I have discarded all the normal props and protections in order that I may have nothing whatever but life; that I may live in the perpetual wonder. But why then this distracting fear, which breaks the wonder?

'We shall take two cottages,' Elza is saying. 'There are two advertised at Portreath on the North Cornish coast.'

I nod. I too would like to live on my own. But all I can think of is the double rent. Such details never bother Elza; she decides what she wants, what she needs, what is right; and then she simply leaves me to find the means.

We took the next train to London and went to Paddington. From there we wrote for the cottages in Elza's name. By return post our tenancy was accepted. With our luggage and a bagful of apples we took the train; and with every westward mile my heart was lighter. I liked even the ugly town of Redruth and my heart leaped at the sight of Carn Brea before I knew anything of its history. The bus rattled with us down the green valley to Portreath, where the quay was still used for coal deliveries though the old tackle for hauling the coal up the hillside was broken. The houses stood in tiers on the valley-sides; our address was on the eastern slope. Once again we met one of the worried old maids who let houses distrustfully to us. 'I thought it was two ladies,' she moaned, wondering what to do with the tea she had brewed ready for us. Her lips puckered and quivered. I talked so fast that she gave up trying to make out what our relationship was, offered us tea, and surrendered the keys. With difficulty I held myself back from saying that if we had come to Portreath to live in sin in her houses, we should not have needed two of them.

It was now early 1932. A second £25 for *Cressida* had been keeping us going. Soon I was to get £50 for an American edition. For over a year no other money came in. And even then it was very little. I cannot now make out how we managed to exist at all, let alone move about, from now on till late in 1933. True, apart from rents, our expenses were extremely small. I did all my own washing and mending, as well as cooking (as indeed I did till 1941). I lived almost wholly on oats, cabbages, spinach and potatoes, which for the most part I bought from local farmers – if one can use the word farmers for men penuriously growing a few vegetables on small patches of dry and stony soil. I liked these men, and talked with them, as with the fishermen who had lost their boats, or with the miners encountered in some hollow of the hills – sharp, embittered, calm men. I liked the rough barren moorlands with their ruined mine-towers; even the crenellated small cottages and the miserable gardens of fuchsias. I spent a whole morning with men I struck washing and crushing with ancient apparatus in a lonely glen. 'What do they care for us?' they asked. 'Can't they make more money out of sweating the Malayans?' I felt an entire unity with these men, though I did not know how to express it, to them or to myself. The reference to Malaya reminded me of my sage remarks to P.R.S. in Paris; but what had been a bit of random economic information had here become human reality, knotted in the hands of these miners. And it seemed that I had had to come a long way round to understand my own words.

A few doors above Elza was a fisherman's family. The man was small and wiry, his wife large and snub-nosed, and they had an indeterminate number of children. They joked at one another rather in the vein of our bawdy friend at Onslow Green: she about the lovers she took while he was at sea, and he about his wives in every port. His mother lived on the opposite side of the valley, keeping a stern eye on the daughter-in-law whom she detested for her loose tongue and for her refusal to listen to advice about the rearing of children. The two women rejoiced the village by shouting abuse at one another across the valley; and the wife forced her husband to take out an insurance policy on his mother's life. Then, when she could think of nothing else to annoy, she flourished the paper and commented on the good time they were going to have after the old lady's death. The latter set her teeth. 'I won't die, to spite you. I'll make you pay out a mint of money and then I'll laugh in your face.'

I liked the suspicious Cornish, living in their stony caves of separateness, with a hunger for comradeship which seemed to find expression only in their Methodism. I liked their speech with its dying hint of a Celtic lilt. One day I heard a woman say to a friend, 'Yes, my dear, I haven't washed my feet for a year, and they're lily-white.' I got all the books I could from Redruth library about the locality and about Cornish mining and fishing, climbed Carn Brea, and dreamed of the ancient tinners. There had been food riots in the twenties in Redruth; the Cornish were capable of sudden violence, but found a continued union of resistance too hard to sustain. The co-operative fishing groups had just gone down before the steam-trawlers of commercialized fishing; always someone betrayed the group. And yet there was a strange smouldering desire for righteousness and unity. (I later put what I felt of Portreath and the region in the novel *End of Cornwall*, which Cape published, under the name of Richard Preston. It perhaps showed some knowledge of what was going on that I mentioned then a growth of solidarity among the miners in the very area where shortly afterwards the first trade-union organization emerged.)

But for the time I was having no luck with my writing. I tried a short novel, set in Portreath, in which I used an Australian episode. In Sydney, once visiting a well-known poet friend, I was told by his wife, when he was out of the room, that she had taken revenge on him by pouring boiling water on the roots of his favourite flower bush; during the evening he kept on lamenting the sad looks of this bush and wondering what pest was afflicting it. I transplanted this incident to Portreath, making the flower lover a retired Cornish seaman. The short novel was rejected when the agents sent it round, though later I included it as half of *End of Cornwall*.

For the rest I worked at *Birth and Will*, and collected a large amount of notes illustrative of its thesis, mainly using language and folklore for my material. I re-wrote a play of Elza's and worked up her early life into a novel under her name, taking down her tale and then expanding it. Neither of these works had any success; the Elza narrative was too strictly tied to the facts (as she remembered them) and the play was an odd mixture of the plays which Elza had acted in or been connected with, third-rate musical comedy and third-rate drawing-room comedy. I wrote a poem on the deep sea-blue eyes of the girl serving in the grocery-shop; the *Western Mail* printed it, but paid nothing; I gave up hoping for any cash-return from verse. However, I got some health-food goods in barter-return for poems in nature-cure monthlies.

At this moment I could easily have given up writing, as there seemed no way to connect my pre-fasting techniques with my post-fasting attitudes. Human personality had broken down into the vast network of complexes born from the birth trauma and reducible to a limited range of repetition-compulsions. What the world took for personality was only the fabricated mask of difference set over the shared flux of compulsions; as soon as one had seen behind it, one could not feel excited about defining or elaborating it. (D.H.L. had felt something like this when he early rejected 'character-drawing' as against the quest for the nuclear core.) I felt the need for anonymity, for completing my rejection of will by losing myself in the faceless mass, in any form of productive work where I was simply exploited and had no share whatever in the profits, in the advantages of the situation. For this reason I felt a wish to become a navvy, a farm-labourer, a craftsman; I should have preferred to die than to serve as any kind of office clerk or to take any kind of fragmented factory work, which seemed to me the antithesis of everything human: the degradation of labour by its reflection of the disintegrative nature of the cash nexus. I did not seek out a job, partly because I was automatically grinding away at the literary tasks before me, partly because there would have been a strenuous struggle with Elza, which I did not feel capable of carrying through to the bitter end. At moments, however, she talked about schemes of hers for a dress-making shop or the like, in which I tried to encourage her without giving away my eagerness; once she had shown any power to stand on her own feet, I should have taken a job on a farm, written poetry again for myself, and published nothing. Beyond that, there was the dream of earning enough to buy a small island where I could build, grow things, and live entirely without the use of money, severing the last ties with iniquity.

That I might have some claim on parish or national powers in the event of complete indigence was something that never came to my mind; and if it had, I should have thrown it out.

The Chancery action now at last came on. We went up to London and stayed in a Paddington room. At the hearing the judge was polite about me and my relations with Elza, despite the efforts of the other side to present the Fanfrolico Press as something disreputable. He, however, inevitably came to the conclusion that the child was best left in the control of Miss Craig for her education, though he gave Elza full freedom of access to her. I forget the exact wording, but his decision amounted to allowing Elza to see Robinetta as often as was reasonable and to have her for part of any holidays. Elza was enraged, but at first she seemed ready to make the most of the chances offered her. We changed our rooms to a better neighbourhood, Bayswater, and she fetched Robinetta for the day. She decided that we must stay in London so that she could be near the child; she meant to keep continually in touch and offset Edith Craig's influence. I suggested that I should go back alone to Portreath and fetch our luggage. Travelling by night train, I hastily crammed our things into various cases, lugged them down to the bus-stop, and caught a London train that got me back some time the following night.

But when I arrived in exhaustion, I found that Elza had abruptly changed her mind. She could not bear to share the child and compete with Edith Craig. She had decided to return to Portreath. Luckily in my rush I had spoken to no one; I had meant to write from London. So, without unpacking, we left London the next day and took up afresh our residences in Portreath, with no other effects than a waste of money we could ill spare, and the creation of some astonishment among Portreatheans who had seen the going and coming of the luggage. Though the loss of her child played a profound and pervasive part in Elza's psychic life, she never again referred to it in any way.

Our landlady now wanted one of her houses and asked me to change over into a small house in the grounds of the hotel nearer the sea. I did so. Farmers used the bit of roadway in front of the house for selling horses, and I much enjoyed the arguments, the sales jargon, the humorous comments. The shore was shingly, without sand, and rapidly shelving. Without Elza knowing it, I used to get up early and swim. I was afraid of the harsh undertow where the shingle banged against my legs and knocked me over, the choppy waves, in which I once bumped against a solid body, rose spluttering in dismay, and found myself staring into the questioning eyes of a seal. And once, expecting to find nobody about – for I never saw any of the Cornish bathing and visitors were rare, I had thrown off my clothes and walked round a rock to find a girl standing naked, stretching herself with her hands above her head; another girl was bent with her back turned, bare but for her stockings. I retreated, pulled on my blue trunks, and plunged into the sea. Later in the day I passed the two girls on the quay. The one who had been standing with her arms above her head smiled at me, but I gave no sign and went on. To ignore the smile was not easy. It wasn't that I wanted to make love to the girl. What I longed for was companionship without veils. Nakedness was a symbol of the ending of fear, of lies; the tenderness of undemanding touch; the lotus-peace of union with the elemental flow. I felt more fully one with the girl than with anyone I had ever known. But to speak with her would have dissolved the conviction of oneness. And yet in passing her I seemed to renounce all human warmth and contact.*

It was easier to ignore the smiles of the hotel manageress, her amber eyes and cat smile. She asked me now and then to help her with her arithmetic and suggested a drink of gin, which I refused. Every morning I called on Elza for a short while, then returned to my work. Occasionally we went for a long walk together, up the coast to St Agnes and beyond, or down, across the cliff tops and the dunes, to St Ives. What she did with her time I was careful not to ask. There was an assumption that both of us would emerge from the trammels of the past at the same moment, with the same powers of self-expression. But in fact she had given up any attempts at writing since the days of Forge Cottage, where she wrote her last poem when we returned one misty morning from an encounter with the redcoats and the hounds of a hunt among the ghostly trees.

The manageress now asked asked me to change into a round tower with a single large chamber above a store-room, at a few shillings less a week. Which I gladly did. Soon afterwards I received a letter from some Sydney solicitors acting for Janet, who asked for money to meet the expenses of a divorce. Instead of welcoming this letter, writing frankly about my financial situation, and promising to foot the bill as soon as I could, I sent a panicked reply that I could not pay a ha'penny. Perhaps because of this letter, perhaps because of the growing economic strain, Elza turned up in my tower one day and announced that she was staying with me, that her nerves made it impossible to go on alone. In a furious temper, she accused me of having messed everything up. I saw no reason to defend myself. But we could not live together long in my tower-room, however chastely, in a village that had known us as mere, if peculiar, acquaintances.

If only a divorce could then have been carried through, things might have worked out differently. I am thinking of the greater security Elza would have felt, but even more of the

---

*Something of the emotion of this moment went later into *Shadow and Flame*: myself drowned and Elza finding the moment of tender touch as a release from fear.

change I should have felt in our relation. Married, she would have had the law on her side, to enforce her rights; unmarried, she was dependent on my honour, and that was a court without appeal.

22 · MORE WANDERINGS

So we read *Daltons*, found a bungalow at Feock, at the top of
Falmouth Harbour, and removed there by devious buses. Elza
at once disliked the dilapidated place, though the situation was
excellent. We walked all over the area and bathed on the beach
below. Then we tried Truro, where Elza decided to settle. The
only possible house was at the end of a terrace, tenanted by
an accountant who wanted to move to a newly built suburban
residence he was buying through a society. He was a snobby
pretentious type we abhorred; and after some discussion he
referred us to the owner, a canny old Cornish dealer with a villainous twinkling eye, who, I think, guessed our unreliability
but dangled a lease before us. In the end the accountant moved
out and we moved in without any proper agreement, though
the person to blame was the amused pig-eyed owner, who still
had the accountant in his clutches. We were now extremely
hard up, and on our negotiating visits we walked all the way
to Truro and back to save bus fares. The time was late August
or early September, for I recall how we ate the ripe blackberries
from the hedges as we wandered endlessly on. It needs a very
large amount of blackberries to give even the temporary
illusion of a full stomach.

Just before we moved, Robert came down to see us; he was
arranging to divorce Elza. She was moved at the sight of him,
reluctant to accept the divorce, and clearly contemplating a
return to him at the last moment. And strangely I felt jealous.
I wanted her to stay: as though, despite the burden she was,
I had no trust in my continuing to strive for the new way of
life unless she were there driving me along.

With blackberries, cankered apples plucked across a fence,
and sixpenn'orth of turnips, we survived and reached Truro.

We had no furniture at all; but a bit of luck saved us. *John O'London* accepted three articles of mine on the ancient novel, and paid on the spot. We ordered a table, chairs, and beds on hire-purchase. About this time I got a letter from P.R.S. saying that he was on his way to Australia, wishing me all the best, and hoping he could be of service to me. I used a penny on a stamp to tell him to go to hell. It was highly ungrateful of me to respond so rudely, but I could not let pass any chance to throw a stone at my past.*

As soon as the *J.O'L.* cheque was cashed, we went to a health-food store and bought several shillings worth of things, unheard-of delicacies for us. But we had eaten so little for so long that we felt sick as soon as we started on the plenteous meal. However, I enjoyed having the town library nearby and began reading anything there on Roman history, my mind harking back to Catullus and his world. I got the idea of writing a biography of M. Caelius Rufus, Catullus's supplanter with Clodia. Not a great deal was known of him apart from the speech on his behalf, against Clodia, by Cicero; his handful of letters to Cicero and the latter's replies; and the fragment of a speech he gave – together, one assumes, with the abusive poems by Catullus to his rival Rufus. But I thought that I could eke the book out by extensively sketching the background.

*I give without comment his own statement about his development in Australia, made in August 1961: 'It began with my book, *The Foundations of Culture in Australia*, 1936. I was then associate editor with W. J. Miles (an old Tory Australian Nationalist, founder of the Rationalist Association in Sydney – and father of "Bea" Miles) and conducted a monthly paper, *The Publicist*, in Sydney for 5¾ years from July 1936 until March 1942, writing at least 5000 words a month for it, covering a very wide field of literary and political criticism. Our stand would nowadays be declared as Australian neutralism – no participation in England's obviously coming second war against Germany. This the Communists and Jews interpreted as pro-Nazism and anti-Semitism. Under their pressure, after Japan entered the war, I was interned without trial for 3½ years by order of H. V. Evatt, and was in an Australian concentration camp from March 1942 until September 1945. Of this incident I am inordinately proud, even though, as Nietzsche remarked, "Martyrdom *proves* nothing" '.

Somehow or other an Oxford undergraduate, who knew and admired the work of the Fanfrolico Press, got in touch with me. I have forgotten how he did it; perhaps the librarian told him I was in Truro. Anyway he called and we let him in, gave him a brief meal, and became friendly. On his return to Oxford he borrowed many books from his college library on the period of Caesar and sent them to me. Among them was E. S. Beasley's *Catalina, Clodius and Tiberius* (1878), a book which had a decisive effect on my thinking. It somewhat idealized Catalina and Clodius, but it brought out strongly the nature of the popular discontent in their period and the way that Cicero and the other ancient writers had blackguarded it. Slight as the work was, it was just what I needed to fertilize my mind at this moment, to release me into a radically critical attitude to the ancient sources I knew so well. For the first time (apart from vague adolescent intuitions) I felt, however crudely, the role of the people in history; my idealist preconceptions, sapped from one angle by my Freudian ordeals, now began breaking down in all directions. History was no longer moved by the Idea, but the Idea was born from History, from the masses, from the production and renewal of life in and by the masses. My long criticism of religion had prepared the way to this position: and now that I had reached the position I saw the nature of religion from a new angle. I grasped in sudden, sweeping intuitions how the abstractions had arisen from the fertility rituals in groups rent by inner divisions; I felt the desperate fears and hopes as forces rending my own flesh. Memories of my readings in Jane Harrison returned, consolidating my new convictions and opening up fresh vistas.

I did not however at a blow rid myself of the limitations of my Freudian period. A wild confused fight went on between my belief that all social forms were projections of psychic conflicts and compromises, and my new positions that the spirit could only be understood historically and that history itself arose in the last resort from the struggle to know and merge with the earth (in work, in sex, in art). I blundered along, rereading Catullus, Lucretius, Cicero, Propertius and the rest. At the same time I started on a novel, *Flatdwellers*, which tried to use a block of flats as a social group – refraction of the larger

whole. But I was bewildered in my ideas as to what part personality played in a world of psychic projections and mass cre-
ations of history. There was no coherence in my group of
flat-dwellers, and I tried to find a guiding idea in the dim struggles of the main heroine to develop and stand on her own feet
– Elza in her early years.

Elza was tired of Truro and the usual rent problems were
looming up. The accountant, asked to wait, turned nasty and
got a court order against me. Two bailiffs tried to break into
the house, but we baffled them, bolted all doors and windows,
and announced from the upper storey that we had no intention
of surrendering. After their threats and cajoleries had failed,
they swore that they'd besiege us. But they were negligent, and
it was easy for one or other of us to dodge out now and then.
Still, the periodical banging on the front door became irritat-
ing. Elza found a recently built bungalow at Portloe, not far
to the east, which we took, and we arranged to move on a Sunday when we knew our bailiffs would be at home enjoying a
well-earned rest.

We moved successfully. But about a week later the bailiffs
tracked us down and this time we didn't have time to bar them
out. 'Everything we have is personal belongings, tools of trade,
or things on hire-purchase with only the deposit so far paid,'
I told them. They said they believed me, but must report that
they'd seen over the house. So, all good friends now, we showed
them over and they made jocular remarks about our poverty.
'You see you couldn't escape us,' they said with pride, 'but
there's nothing here we can seize. We'll do the best we can for
you. We always do that for those that treat us decent.' They
shook hands and departed. No more was heard from Truro.

I decided against trying to revise *Birth and Will*, but couldn't
bear to burn it. I dug a deep hole and buried it in the hard
earth. Elza felt ill in a listless sort of way, but refused to let
me fetch a doctor. The house was situated on the upper ground,
with the road winding down to the small fishing village. Once
more I would have been ready to settle, but Elza wanted to
move. I had no money at all and wrote to Will Dyson asking
if he could help me; I mentioned that I was doing so because
I recalled the letter of his my mother had always carried in her

bag. He at once sent me a friendly note and a cheque for £15.

From some local paper we found rooms to let at Porthleven in a ropemill and took them by post. We got someone to carry us and our belongings across in a lorry. Our premises consisted of one room on the ground floor beside the firm's office, and two above. Elza took the room below as it had an oil-stove, and I took those above, where I had a small oil-burner of my own for the oats or vegetables which I cooked.

Once more I tried to drive roots in, talking to the old fishermen on the grey granite quay and walking along Looe Sands or towards St Michaels Mount. Also, I liked living in the middle of a workshop. From my windows I watched the rope twined or stretched. I finished *Flatdwellers*, which had become a large kaleidoscopic work, with much use of interior dialogue that owed more to surrealism than to Joyce; but there was still no central idea. I had regained high spirits in writing and used extended lyrical metaphors, trying to define Jenny (young Elza) so as to give myself faith in her purposes of self-renewal.

I sent the MS to the agents. Phil had written to me, care of the Bodley Head, and I replied that I was extremely hard up. I told him of the Caelius book. He wrote back: Why not drop straight history and try a novel on the period? I pondered over his words and suddenly felt the need to write a story about Catalina. I began *Rome for Sale*.

Oddly, about this time I developed the only strongly felt antagonism to socialism I ever had. As N.L.'s disciple I had paid lip-service to his anti-popular positions, but had not really felt them in my bones. Now, however, in my intense regard for individual responsibility, for my own special responsibility towards Elza, I felt fiercely hostile to any system which would make things easier for me, which would take Elza off my hands and in any way mitigate the rigours of my self-dedication. I wrote poems on the absolute rejection of property, of all possessive emotions, as the only way into a true humanity: *There is a State and Act called S. Francis*. For a while I turned my ascetic demand against socialism, feeling it to offer plenty without first purging the individual of his lusts for property and power. I did not yet see socialism as the form of society in which at last the struggle I wanted became generally possible.

I also completed a series of poems dramatizing my divided state of being in terms of a character James Allague. 'Drunken Christ, crucified Bacchus, we live and grow despite our shames.' But I made no attempt to place any verses, except a satirical *Cradle Song* and a lyric which I sent to Roger Roughton's *Contemporary Verse*, where they were printed. (An issue of this magazine had been sent me by my undergraduate friend: the only such periodical I saw during these years.)

I now received a note from Colin Still, a publishers' reader of much power at the time. Still said that he had read *Flat-dwellers* and was impressed, but felt there was no public for experimental novels. He encouraged me to keep writing and suggested it might be possible to cut the more unusual parts of the novel and trim it to a more conventional shape. I asked for the return of the MS, but soon found that to remove its extravagances was to kill it stone-dead. So I wrote to Still with an account of *Rome for Sale*, which I had not yet carried far. He expressed much interest.

I was then held up from the novel by a lucky chance. Noticing an advertisement for a school-series which included a book on the Greeks. I wrote to the editor Gerald Bullett, proposing one on the Romans. He asked for a specimen chapter, liked it, and commissioned the book. I thus earned £30. But meanwhile Elza's outbursts were growing worse. At any moment she was liable to come upstairs and start abusing me. After one of her outbursts I wrote in the blank pages at the back of my edition of Catullus by L. Mueller:

Let me recall this always, written after a scene with Elza. There is no question of self-pity or of fantasies that a life together is possible. Any such weakening in my part reacts most miserably upon her. She wants freedom underneath, the same as myself, but her form of father-fascination makes her tethered to me while I am tethered by a single point of weakness. The whole thing is not a question of sex or of anything beyond the fact that the psychoanalytic relationship must be broken, and it can only be broken by the most ruthless standing on my own feet. As soon as there is money to stabilize her position I must go. First, however, to break things we must get separate houses under different names. The merest expression of fear or uncertainty on my part breaks down her efforts to escape me. Things must ultimately turn out the same for both of us, but that does not mean we should not part. The responsibility of the psyche is that we should share revenues – nothing else. Let me put this down in case I forget it, the utter horror of contact with her, the poor tormented way in which everything I do or say is turned by her into hatred and murder. May I go mad myself if anything ever blinds me to this.

Well might I add that last sentence; for the least softening on her part, the least appeal to my pity, and all my resolutions crumbled away. However, at last I was goaded to say to her that it would surely be best for us to part since she had such a low opinion of me. She agreed. I left all the money I had, apart from the fare to London, with a note saying that I would send her more in the near future and see that she did not starve. Then I knocked at her door and announced my departure. She merely stared at me with hate.

I had Phil's address in London and went straight there. But there had been no time to warn him of my coming, and I had to wait outside for about three hours. I had only a few pennies left and didn't know what to do. Then he and Jeanne turned up, welcomed me joyously, and took me in. As soon as we were inside their small flat, I broke down and wept for some hours, in a mixture of relief, remorse, and inability to believe that I had come through into a life with my fellows again. Philip did his best to strengthen me, and Jeanne fluttered round me with her bird-hands and her small mellifluous voice. They were still hard up and had little furniture. The only article they could offer me to sleep in was a sort of big cradle, bought for their baby Cressida Anne, who had been sent to the country. My legs stuck out at the end, but it was more comfortable than the floor. In the morning, as we were breakfasting on toast and porridge, a wire arrived for me. I had left Phil's address in a note to Elza, so there could be no question who had sent the wire. I fumbled at the envelope, afraid that Elza might have done something violent to herself. But it was only a demand that I should return. Phil told me not to be a bloody fool, but I replied that I had no choice. With sinking heart I took the train back. (Phil and Jeanne had been married since April.) Phil gave me the fare.

To my surprise Elza did not show any particular emotion at my return. I realized that she had dared me to go because she was convinced I couldn't do it; she always tended to assume that I was in the same impasse as she was. That was the only way she could keep her sense of superiority. My return apparently had the effect of enabling her to reassert her conviction that after all I couldn't really go and stand on my own feet.

Soon we were back at the old tensions. I worked hard at *Rome for Sale*. I wanted to express the tragic role of Catalina, caught into accepting leadership of a doomed movement, and to show the change of all his hopes into their opposites as the expression of the contradictions in the movement itself. I still felt that the tragic pattern was the deepest revelation of the human condition, that consciousness was developed by a process which ensured that it arrived too late to affect things, that the flaw in life was discovered at the point where consciousness had decisively broken through, and that the peculiar struggle in tragedy was this tension between the doomed action and the liberated consciousness – one line going down, the other line going up at the same time, and the two meeting with full concentration and contradiction at the climax. Against Catalina I set Cicero the professional compromiser and falsifier, the rising middle-class character wanting to be accepted by the land-owners, and Caesar, the supple schemer who bided his time, waiting for the moment when a maximum amount of change would be possible, but making the possible always his limit. To bring out the lost tribal unity to which the angry hopes of the dispossessed looked back and from which the more complex aims of renewal in Catalina and Caesar drew sustenance, I sketched in a background of the recurrent rituals in which the life of the earth and men's fertility needs were expressed. The action thus had to cover a single year, a single twirl of the earth-cycle: to bring out, as strongly as my powers allowed, the way in which men's relations to nature pervaded all their economic and cultural activities. Further, as I struggled with the form, I realized that I must attempt to define the situation from a number of levels – personal, economic, legal, religious, and so on – all of which had to be grasped in the last resort in a single focus. And that for my colour key

I must draw on my total impression of the art, literature, and religion of the period. Thus the particular intonation of an age, its unique coloration and resonance, might be reproduced. And through all the individual movements and impacts there must run an organic connection with the deepest conflicts of the age – the conflicts between all that was most human and integrative, and all that was most inhuman, corrupted and divisive. Though I was by no means fully clear, I already had the intuition that the human aspects were linked with the unions of men for productive, creative and joyous purposes, and the inhuman with everything that divided up the human process, money, privilege, social and economic differentiation of any kind, the systems of power and parasitism begetting class-societies. I felt more and more that the creative key lay in the free and harmonious relations to nature, which were strengthened and deepened by the uncorrupted unions, and destroyed or perverted by the divisive forms.

Slowly and doggedly I was coming to see history as the pattern of this struggle. With moments of painful confusion and loss of the trail, and with moments of enormous delight, as I felt I had picked the trail up again. The year-pattern I saw in terms of Attic tragedy. In drawing away from the limiting aspects of psychoanalysis, I was re-discovering the cultural anthropology I had read, the work of Jane Harrison, Cook, Cornforth, Gilbert Murray, and others.

At the same time the feverish quest for an irreducible element in experience, in history, which I could accept and bless as good, as truly human, was given its force by my personal situation, my almost total isolation from normal everyday life and its consoling contacts. The imprisoning pressure of Elza's neurosis (reflected in my own anxieties and instabilities) helped to hold me back from accepting anything save that which satisfied the whole man. In a sense, while I thought I was sacrificing myself to help her, I was doing in fact the exact opposite – using her to knit my own resistances and drive myself along the lines which my deepest self wanted to follow.

Slowly and steadily, for the first time since the undermining of our Fanfrolico synthesis, I felt a growing zest, a simple sustained happiness, a sense of continual discovery which stayed with me even in my sleep – or so I was convinced. For I awoke fresh and filled with a sense of urgent tasks. (Ever since my Freudian fast I had had no dreams. I told myself that my unconscious was too afraid to provide me with symbols to analyse for its undoing, or that I had cleansed myself of the need to throw up the masked ghosts of fear and desire. I had absorbed my mythopoeic or symbolizing powers, such as they were, into my working faculties.) I had, as I had never had before, a pervasive and secure sense of union with sea, sky, earth – and despite, or because of, my isolation, a sense of equal union with people. I felt that my relation to nature was becoming serene and pure, and that therefore my feeling for people was being purified. The pity I had felt and still felt for Elza had become a pity for all living, a sense of my unity with all the torn and suffering lives. For all were crucified: that was the truth of Christianity. I felt anew an intense sympathy for, and antagonism against, that creed. In some of its aspects it seemed to me to have reached the deepest truths yet stated about the human condition; in others it turned away from its profundities and did everything possible to distort them, to hand mankind over to the murderers.

My departure for London had upset Elza more than had appeared. She grew restless and less harsh. Finally she said that she wanted to go to London. I would have preferred to wait till I had finished *Rome*; but I at once agreed. I sent the MS, as far as it was completed, to Still. We left our few bits of furniture to be sold, and as soon as I had any cash in hand I paid off the debt on it. The ropemaker, I am sure, was glad to see the end of us. A kindly man, he could not but have been aware of the discords between Elza and myself, and the separate way we lived. But he was too mild and easy-going to throw us out.*

---

*Edith Young in *Lisa* strangely makes Michael and Liza (myself and Elza) go near Porthleven at the point of tragic breakdown. Also, I was interested later to find that Christopher Caudwell went to Porthleven not long after our stay, to think out his new world-outlook of Marxism.

23 · LONDON AND A NEW START

We found a top flat in a house in the Paddington area, and I set to work on *Rome for Sale*. I visited Phil, who now had a large ground-floor flat only partly furnished; his fortunes had started going uphill. I also went a couple of times to see Still and discussed among other things his thesis that *The Tempest* incorporated the structure of the mystery rite as carried out at Eleusis. I felt he was correct enough – but not because of any esoteric lore on Shakespeare's part. In *The Tempest*, the first great work in which we may say that the creative process is made the object of the poetic consciousness, we inevitably find the tragic structure glossed and illuminated in a new way, though in the work itself tragedy dissolves in dream and symbol. Still told me to take my time; he was going to instruct Nicholson and Watson that they must do *Rome*, and he could get me an advance if necessary. Elza refused to call on Jeanne and as a result Jeanne shrank from calling on her.

I completed the novel. Still asked me to prune it a bit if I could, but not to worry if I couldn't. I cut out two episodes. Nicholson, whom I met, was an intelligent publisher, and I felt that I had at last got somewhere and found a basis of existence as well as a form of work that interested me and allowed me to make a maximum use of my past preoccupations while revaluing method and material in terms of my new attitudes. Elza was much affected by my success in having a work thus accepted. She assumed that she too would very soon find her way forward along similar lines. I discussed things with her, and she said that she wanted to study the eighteenth century; she even decided that it would be best to live on her own. She had made a brief effort to contemplate a resumption of normal relations between us; but the idea terrified her and brought her to the decision of a break.

I agreed with her. We once more consulted *Daltons*. I had a look at a place advertised in the apple area of Kent, but found it too small. Then I decided to take a cottage advertised in a lonely part near Speen in Buckinghamshire, while Elza thought she would like to go somewhere along the south coast in Dorset or Devon. She found a place near Lyme Regis.

I bought her several books on the social history of the eighteenth century; and we parted with something like goodwill. She was firm and calm; it was rather I who tended to feel and show some regret. After seeing her off at Victoria, I went to Paddington and took a ticket for High Wycombe. By bus I reached Speen and then walked out to the cottage, which was on the top of a hill. There was another house not far off, and a farm screened by some trees. Otherwise the site was lonely and deep in greenery. Away to the back were large woods. The country woman who owned the cottage I found was living in some rooms built by the well at the side, but I hardly ever saw her. To my delight the old timbered cottage itself, sparsely furnished, with a huge fireplace, was thickly stocked with books, mainly dealing with the history of religion and with anthropology. From my landlady I learned that they belonged to the previous tenant, who had committed suicide; his relations had not yet collected the books. The man had written for the Rationalist Press under a pen-name; a melancholy recluse, he had ended by being crushed under the weight of an irrational world.

I stayed in this cottage for some three or four months, over the worst of the cold weather of 1933-34. I had no thought of the dead man except gratitude for his library, which was just what I wanted after *Rome for Sale*. I read through the whole of Frazer's works, those of Hartland and many other anthropologists whose work I had known only slightly, as well as a large number of works in various languages on Biblical criticism and the origins of Christianity. Nicholson had agreed to do two anthologies of translated poetry and prose: *I am a Roman* and *Medieval Latin Poems*. First I concentrated on the latter, and often went up to the British Museum to copy out medieval

texts. I also wrote to Stephen Gaselee, with whom I had corresponded earlier about Petronius, and was invited several times
to his house near Gloucester Road. Here I ate a conventional
meal and drank some wine – my only lapses before 1941. He
had a young, handsome and silent wife; and to my shame I
once spilled a whole glass of wine on the table linen. But we
soon retired to his book-lined study. Though his lines of interest
were very different from mine, he was always ready to spend
any amount of time to help me in difficulties or to advise me
what editions or commentaries to read. After I left Speen, I
kept in touch with him by letters; and generally I got a reply
dealing with any knotty point in medieval Latin by return
post. Once, however, he was gravelled and consulted A. E.
Housman, sending me on that scholar's authoritative answer.

I enjoyed the journeys into London. Often I walked all the
way from Speen to High Wycombe, and once I was jostled by
the portly Chesterton on his way back to Beaconsfield. I did
not call on Ramsay Macdonald's daughter, whom I had met
at Oxford and who had taken the Speen pub which I passed
on my way out to my lonely hill. Arriving home in the dark,
I lighted an oil-lamp, put a match to the pile of wood I had
prepared in the brick fireplace before leaving in the morning,
warmed up some of my perennial vegetable stew and opened
a tin of soya beans, and settled down to read Frazer or the
verses of Hugo of Orléans and the Archpoet. When I did not
go to London, I walked in the woods or went westward to where
the hills fell away into open vistas. I felt intensely happy, but
always over my happiness there hovered a slight cold shadow
of fear that Elza would not keep to our bargain.

I wrote to her a few words every day, and sent her money
weekly, cutting my own expenses to the bone so that I could
give her twice as much as myself – though the agreement had
been equal shares. I spoke to no one. At moments in London
I was tempted to ferret out Phil or Edgell. But I never did. I
had a feeling that I best warded off the danger of a new attack
from Elza, a collapse on her part, by living with an ever more
sharp discipline. My ideas were rapidly expanding, on the basis
cleared by *Rome for Sale*, and I enjoyed working on medieval
Latin.

Elza asked for more money. I drew further on the publishers and sent what she asked. Then came the expected and dreaded telegram, to say that she was ill. At once I went, arriving about 10 p.m. In the morning I got her on to the train and brought her back to my cottage. She was not suffering from any specific illness; she was merely worn out and miserable. For about six weeks I nursed her, doing all the cooking and housework. She gradually regained her spirits and found a house in Brixham in South Devon. Again I gave her all the money I had in hand, and promised a weekly sum; but I had the feeling that this time I should be called to her even sooner.

I was right. Within a couple of weeks she wrote saying that she would go mad; I must come to her. I went, leaving my cottage with deep regret. Furniture had been sent from one of the large hire-purchase firms, selected by Elza from a catalogue. I now ordered exactly the same ugly things for myself. Already she was on bad terms with our neighbours; and a day or so after the second lot of furniture arrived, the police called, saying that these people had complained of someone stealing their firewood; obviously they had hinted that we were the culprits. I told the police to look in the house if they wanted; and rather apologetically they glanced vaguely around and went off. The house was new and jerrybuilt, on the high ground east of the harbour, overlooking the sea. I liked the fishing-port and did my best to settle down.

Rome for Sale was now published and went quickly into a second edition; it also appeared in the U.S.A. Still had added an introduction, which I did not see till I got the book. In it he made a rough comparison of the Catalinarian revolt with Fascism. I was a bit staggered at this, but did not protest – though I was sufficiently uneasy to ask Harper's to omit the preface from the American edition. Mussolini's régime I had disliked and despised, but had not taken it very seriously except as one among many symptoms of social decay; I had used the term 'Fascist skull-and-crossbones' in the *Aphrodite*. Of Hitler and Nazism I as yet knew practically nothing, since I read no newspapers, partly through poverty and partly through obsession with my own problems. All I knew of the Nazis came from a translation of their basic points in a *John-O'London* picked up at Porthleven: a programme that read as a demagogically radical creed. I had no means of telling how truly or untruly it reflected the party policy; and indeed had only glanced at it, assuming the Nazis to be some ephemeral gang of noisy cranks. Though I now began a desultory scanning of newspapers, it was not till the end of 1935 I realized anything of the significance of the international events going on. For one thing, I had a profound Australian distrust of anything whatever in newsprint.

I was working on *I am a Roman*, prose and verse extracts translated from Latin to exemplify the Roman way of life; and had sketched out the idea for a second novel, *Caesar is Dead*. I had realized now that the only way for me to compose was from the mass effect to the particular, from the large-scale rhythm to the individual involvement; I had to begin with a feeling of vast forces at work, clashing, fusing, breaking apart, and by holding fast to the epical pattern, to make out, inside the stormy whole, the faces of people at the key points of death and renewal. Then gradually the individuals grew in size, taking into themselves the original tumult of clashing masses and big involving rhythms, so that they became significant of the main lines of force. Here I decided that I must open with a long many-angled account of the day of Caesar's murder, without Caesar himself being directly shown, and then, after the explosive moment seemed to blast the multiple individual purposes into unrelated shreds, to express the mounting tide of popular and legionary wrath, which deified Caesar and swung Antony into power as the Avenging Mars. In *Rome for Sale* the religious rituals had been deliberately kept apart from the narrative of events, to bring out the gap between the past group united in the fertility cult and the present conflicting classes. But now I needed to show the fresh liberation of the religious emotions slumbering in the masses, who had been caught up in a revolutionary situation – though a situation which halted far short of actualizing freedom and equality. I needed to show how the masses deeply affected the direction of events and yet in the end appeared only to have intensified oppression and state power. The form of the book thus emerged as a sharp broken pattern of rapidly changing events, with the mass pressure reflected by the development of a growing coherence of narrative movement. The uprush from below steadily shatters all the ambitious plots, cabals, and temporary compromises of the politicians. Antony, the leader least driven by personal schemes (except in so far as he seeks to evade the push of his wife and to enjoy himself), is the one who becomes the vehicle of the mass emotion. The book was to end in his effort to find a point of arrest in conjunction with the young man, Octavius, who comes up in rivalry with him as the actual heir. I felt the need to convey the way in which the baffled aspirations of the populace, which led to Caesar's deification and disrupted the balances of the schemers, were in essence begetting both the Empire and the Christian protest against the state.

The books I had read in the Speen suicide's library thus turned out to be the best possible aid to my tackling the second volume of the trilogy I had decided to write.

I had arranged for the publishers to pay me £5 a week against royalties; and as I was able to keep this system going till I was called up into the Army I henceforth had a stable basis for my existence, even if the sum at times was hardly adequate.

. I was working hard. The noise of my typewriter must have grated on Elza's nerves as a proof that I had mysteriously managed to come through into earning a livelihood while she was further off than ever from such a thing. She had long given up any pretence of studying the eighteenth century; and from now on, as far as I know, she never read another book of any kind. She was becoming violent and could not bear even to see me. At the back of my *Catullus*, under what I had written at Porthleven, I find I scrawled about this time: '. . . all truces are lies. That is why they afflict us both with dependence, an effort to bring out the truth. She wants the same as me – to escape. Look out for self-pity – which is *the lie*.' And then in pencil: 'If I am such a stinking lunatic as to forget all this, may I be boiled in oil. Remember how she smashed my window merely because I opened the door at the same time as she was going into the hall.' My extreme weakness in the face of the slightest appeal from her was the reason for the vehemence of the last sentence, as with the similar exhortation at the end of the Porthleven entry. But no matter how strongly I called on myself to remember in all its anguish and horror the moment of contact with her suffering resentments, I could not sustain the oath of cold objectivity. The next moment I saw only her misery, her vicious circle of frustrations, for which in their final stages of precipitation I had been responsible.

Often at this time she came into my bedroom and switched on the light, holding the hot and glaring bulb close against my face, my eyes, and stared at me. Painful as the sensation was, I felt only pity for her maddened effort to recognize the unknown murderer. Once she came into my work-room and flung my typewriter on the floor, so that I had to send it away to be mended. Once, as I opened my door, she threw a carving-knife and missed my eye by an inch or so. Knives at this time fascinated her and I knew she wanted to attack me with one. I did not however at any moment feel fear; only disgust and pity. Perhaps she knew this. During these months when I often thought she might come in and attack me in my bed, I never slept more soundly. An extreme fatalism mingled with my spiritual weariness. If it works out like that, I thought, it's too bad; but felt no impulse to protect myself. I do not know if this calm of mine saved me or made her worse.

Strangely, she now had no physical resemblance to the delicate Pre-Raphaelitish dreamer I had first met. Ever since her return home she had been growing more like her mother, and now she had turned into a plumpish, heavily built person, her face rounding out and losing the translucent pallor which had struck everyone in her earlier days. Her complexion had coarsened and had a rough redness about it. She often reverted roughly to the tones and idiom of North Devon, which had been quite absent from her speech. No doubt a mixture of psychological and glandular disturbances worked to produce these effects.

My efforts to psychoanalyse her had all recoiled on me. She had gained only a deepening of certain fears and obsessions, had turned the tables and forced me to psychoanalyse myself. So while I had been liberated, she had been more closely bound down. Our isolation had the effect of cutting her off blankly in a dead space, paralysing her whole emotional being. On me it had the effect of intensifying my social consciousness and making me feel with a terrible poignancy the need of union with my fellows in a worthy cause. The quest for this cause had become one with my search for a creative method, for themes in which I could embody all that I had experienced of deep-going change and renewal. I had turned from the groping journey down the dark tunnel of my own buried past, into the effort to enter into the conflicts and aspirations of history; but into the latter I brought the agonized dynamic of my need to cleanse myself, to find bedrock.

About this time Graves published his first Claudius book, which the *Bookman* sent me to review. It happened that I had just read Tacitus through in the Latin, and Graves's novel struck me as almost a straight paraphrase, with a minimal amount of invention and without any central idea or any effort to build the social picture. But, feeling that perhaps I was jealous of its success, I leaned over backwards to praise it, though pointing out a few errors such as the misdating of Catullus's death (through an antiquated mis-reading of the squib on Vatinius). Apparently these quite minor cavillings annoyed Graves; for when the *Bookman* sent him my *Caesar is Dead* he made no comment on the work as a whole in his review, but contented himself with trying to find factual errors. I disagreed with all his points and dropped him a note, saying why and mentioning some real mistakes I had myself spotted after publication, e.g. the mention of stirrups. Graves had said my passage purporting to be from an elegy by Gallus was too coloured, and in that he was correct, though I could formally defend each phrase: which I did by looking up examples under the key words in the dictionary. Replying, Graves remarked that he had a dictionary as well as I: which was smart on his part but did not dispose of the examples. However, his contention in general was right, and I re-wrote the passage. (Later, during the war, I heard that Graves had gone to Brixham: no doubt a pure accident, but giving me an odd feeling of his following in my track.)

One day Elza opened my door suddenly and threw a note in. The note demanded a move, but the wording was vague and I assumed that she wanted once more to be on her own. Gladly I found a house in Lincombe Drive, Torquay – a rambling complicated three-storey structure of wood, built on the slope overlooking the eastern coastline, almost directly above Kent's Cavern. I arranged for the furniture to be taken there and sent on my typewriter to Phil in London. Then at the last moment I found that Elza expected me to go with her. For a brief moment I felt inclined to walk out; but as usual I accepted her wish without question.

For a short while she was happier, as she always was in a new place. She settled in on the ground floor, then decided to move upstairs. The house was easily divisible: both the ground floor and the upper section had their own entries, kitchens, baths. I reclaimed my typewriter by railway from Phil and set to work on the third novel about the Caesarian revolution. I had now realized that the connecting character in the trilogy was Mark Antony and the last volume must deal with the breakdown of Cleopatra's schemes. Her vision of a theocratic empire on the system of Ptolemaic Egypt in many ways anticipated what was to happen in the fourth century A.D., with herself as Isis suckling the Divine Babe (Caesar's Son) providing the iconography of the Virgin Mary; but history would have been incomparably poorer if the leap had been made at once to the conclusion, without the slow working out of the inner struggle between the remnants of republican *libertas* and the new centralizing power. I tried to express the full contradictions of the situation, taking Antony in his final phases of collapse; to catch the difference of the historical level from that of *Caesar is Dead* I used a straightforward narrative dealing with two persons, a boy and a girl, who were in themselves unimportant and through whose problems we saw the last convulsions of the slowed-down revolution and the enhancement of personality which was to appear both in the extensions of Roman law and in the protests of Christianity. In the last pages, where the lad in his flight with the girl up the Nile had to deal single-handed with the pangs of childbirth, I hoped to convey the feeling of the new epoch that was being born.

In choosing the Caesarian revolution as my theme I had in a sense been exploring the poems of Catullus, which had always meant a great deal to me: finding myself through the discovery of all their social and political implications, or rather

of the dialectical relation between their intense personal definition and the larger aspects. While from one angle I had
begun by trying to grasp the historical events as projections or
facets of the poet's passionate personality, in the process of
realization I was forced to invert this effort and to explore the
roots of personality in the social process. A set of tensions was
thus set up between outer and inner reality, through which I
sought to define the full structure of movement. While in one
way the story was an allegory of my own struggles, in another
and more important way it was a vehicle through which those
struggles were enlarged and I transformed my isolation, my
sterile reductions of experience to the early pangs and
traumata of growth, into a sympathy with human life in its
entangled richness of good and evil, its distorting compulsions
and its liberating leaps into new dimensions, new wholes.

There is much more I should like to say of my struggle with
the trilogy and the ideas I sought to embody. But I have said
enough to show the general lines of approach. Perhaps I may,
however, once more stress what I felt about the enclosing
relationship to nature as providing both the moral and artistic
clue. The dialectics of social struggle remained barren unless
realized within this larger whole; and by the touchstone of the
pervasive relation of individual men and of society to natural
process one gained a true understanding of what was at stake
in all the conflicts, in the conscious and the unconscious aims.
One saw what alienation was, and what human unity and freedom were. In all my work I have continued the effort to apply
this moral criterion, which is also an artistic method.

24 · BREAKTHROUGH

MY main interest at the moment, apart from my continuing pre-occupation with the meaning and pattern of history, was biology. I had read Darwin's *Origin of Species* and was powerfully affected. The effect came, not from the book's conclusions which I already accepted in a general way, but from the tremendous force and weight of the exposition, the method. The slow remorseless way in which all interpretations but the materialist are excluded, the masterly insistence on the simple and the concrete, had a decisive influence on my thinking. I then read all Darwin's other books, and followed up with many contemporary ones on biological themes. I was also reading D.H.L. for the first time with a strong sympathy. I still rejected much of his ideas and tendencies, but I had found out the quick of the man, all that he meant when he declared that our civilization 'has almost destroyed the natural flow of common sympathy between men and men, and men and women. And it is this that I want to restore into life.' I realized the deepmost nature of his criticism of our cash nexus society, and what he had meant when he told me to stick to my hates, since they were the best and truest part of me; and I felt bitterly sorry that I had neglected my chances of meeting him when he was alive. I was also re-reading Dostoevsky, Tolstoy, Dickens, and reading Proust for the first time – previously I had been put off by the kind of person who admired him. Also, after Darwin, I read Spinoza, and came through him to Bruno. (I wrote a long poem on Spinoza, which was printed in the *Irish Quarterly*.)

I had also begun writing a considerable amount for the *Freethinker*, with a few contributions to the *Literary Guide*. I should like to mention an article in the latter, dealing with an attack on Darwin by Belloc, since it brought out clearly the philosophic position I had now reached, synthesizing Freud, Jane Harrison, ancient Stoicism, Spinoza, Darwin.

Defending the latter from the charge of mechanism, I argued that one gained from his work the conviction that there was no teleological universe, no 'purpose-behind'. There was only the vital totality of forces at any given moment, from which the future organically evolved. My argument implied that the living moment, the existential present, included freedom as well as determination, it was spontaneous as well as fated by the previous moment. Though I did not go any further, I should have claimed that the totality could not be seized by analytic thought – though such thought played a necessary part in one's comprehension of it. Intuition and analysis merged in the whole man; and by one's existential wholeness one could know, even if one could not ever finally encompass by analysis, the living moment.

I was now at a half-way point between my Fanfrolico positions and those of Marxism. In *Dionysos* I had rejected all abstractions in the name of the ceaseless experience of existence.

Do we strive to make life approximate to an abstract idea? That is to hate all that breaks the abstract law, to hate all that is vitally alive and moves by the laws of its unique and dynamic identity. That is to hate life.

For life eternally outruns all statements that can be made of life, its complexities for ever go one step further than the ground covered by the widest of generalities. We must continually formulate our experience in image and thought; but once we conceive that the thought exists in itself and not as part of a continuous and deepening process, it becomes completely false. Once we try to substitute re-experience of the thought for the developing experience of the energies loosed by the thought, we are growing abstract.

I had now lost the bias to the irrational present in that passage; I accepted history and evolution as fully real, as the wider processes in terms of which any individual existence alone could develop; I saw that any biological, social or individual purpose must be inherent in the material situation and could not represent a transcendent or abstract intrusion of mind or spirit;

I believed that the processes of knowledge, in so far as they proceeded from the whole man, were knowledge of a real and
material world. But I had not yet properly separated out the
social from the biological, and as a result I still was confused
as to the dialectical relation of the individual and society. My
concept of a totality of given forces at any moment, with an
inner dynamic of organic purpose, still had an element of *mystique* about it. This came, not from stressing the element of the
unknown and unknowable, but from the lack of any guiding
principles for the analytic attack. I was aware emotionally of
the importance of love and work for individual and social
development; I felt their link with the brotherhood of struggle.
But I was still far from any clear idea as to the precise effect
of productive forces and relations in determining the general
structure of history. Still, though Darwin had temporarily
made me think of society in biological terms, he also prepared
me for a materialist explanation of its movement and changes;
and as a novelist I had already begun investigating and concretely defining relations which I could not yet formulate as
a thinker.

I kept on writing poems, wholly for myself, in which the
unslackening pang of loss was fused with my deepened sense
of unity with nature. In some the pang spoke harshly:

> *I have nothing left and nothing remains to be done.*
> *In me is enacted the ancient sacrifice*
> *and it means nothing. Nothing. That is my hope.*
> *Put it aside now, put it aside at last,*
> *let nakedness be gaunt with the thistle, and dumb.*
> *Say nothing. Lean and turn with the thinning shadow.*
> *Put it aside and wait till the Agony's past*
> *here on the winter's slope . . .*

But for the most part a sense of intolerable sweetness had the
last word, which I tried to put into a poem on Van Gogh, my
hero of this phase.

I was indeed intensely happy, with a daily sense of vast discovery and a crystalline conviction of harmony with nature.
I lay naked in the sun outside my bedroom window where there
was a sort of cavern guarded by flowers and bushes; and to

listen through the night to the faint clear sounds of Mozart or Wagner from a house higher up the hill, gave me a purer sense of what music was, than any concerts or records I had ever heard. My gratitude was infinite. There were a few moments of friendliness with Elza, when we visited Kent's Cavern or watched the butterflies with long curved beaks which they inserted, hovering delicately, into the flowers on our terraces. But soon she grew hostile and retreated into herself. She was continually harassed by smells. First she insisted on having all her floors lined with cork-lino, then she said the smell drove her out of her senses, and so on. I had so much that I needed to read and think about, to write, that I did not want to disturb her and provoke her rages. For weeks I did not go out. Such groceries or vegetables as we needed could be delivered – a note being left out for the man from the delivery-van. I kept myself fit by sunbathing and exercises; I had never felt better. But my happiness did not lie only in perfect health and satisfying work; it derived in the last resort from the secure feeling I had of a total renunciation, above all my sense of owning nothing and wanting nothing. During these years I was a better person than I had ever been before or have ever been since, because of my complete elimination of any property sense from my being; and for this reason I was also deeply and stably happy.

Mary Butts, who had published a novel on Alexander the Great, *The Macedonian*, wrote to me. She was working on another about Cleopatra, and sent me the MS when she completed it. I ran through it for factual errors and found about fifty. She thanked me and said she'd incorporate my corrections, but a while later she wrote to say that she was feeling very depressed and ill, having fallen down a cliff. She had lost my list of errors and asked if I could remember what I had written. I compiled a fresh list as best I could, and sent it to her. I did not hear from her again. (She died in March 1937, a few weeks before her Gabriel.)

After my trilogy I felt winded for a short while. Then I wrote *Despoiling Venus*: the story of Caelius Rufus, done in the first person. I had wanted to compose something which would define his strong, lost, embittered personality. This novel was a pendant to the trilogy, making the direct link with Catullus and Clodia. Next I decided to go further back in time and used the Egyptian record of an envoy who went to Lebanon after timber near the end of the second millennium B.C. Egypt at that time was on the downgrade, and Wenamen's difficulties and mishaps amusingly brought out this situation. I followed the record closely, though introducing a Greek, a tough rough character, to represent the up-and-coming culture, which seems very crude next to the highly sophisticated though tired culture of Egypt. Through Phil I had got in touch with an Australian working at Saggara under Emery. I sent him the MS, which both he and Emery read. Neither of them could find any mistakes or slips in fact or in tone, though Emery queried one botanical detail. I had soaked myself in ancient Egyptian art, literature, and religion before I began the work.

I also wrote a boy's book, a tale set at the time of Spartacus, *Runaway*, for the O.U.P., and a long short-story, *Storm at Sea*, for the Golden Cockerel Press, which was illustrated with woodcuts by John Farleigh. Further, I found that the daily papers had started competing with short stories. I wrote large numbers of these, all of which were printed. The best I collected in a book *Come Home at Last*. One longer story about the heroic end of Cleomenes in Alexandria was published in the *London Mercury* (now not Squire's). I was working about fourteen hours a day. Having no interruptions, I was able to stick to any job day after day without a break, using pen or typewriter ten to twelve hours at a time. My simple meals took little time to prepare.

A letter arrived from Jeanne, saying that Phil had accused her of being unfaithful, and asking me to convince him of her innocence. I was moved by the letter, and besides I was ready to champion any woman in the name of the united family. So I wrote to Phil in her defence. He replied, with testy correctness, that I was butting into a matter about which I knew nothing, that Jeanne had been playing hell with him, and that he was going off to the West Indies. He had obtained a librarian's job at Government House, Jamaica, through the offices, I think, of Compton Mackenzie. The work was easy and the Indies were congenial, but he could not bear the way the

Whites treated the West Indians, with whom he hobnobbed on friendly terms.

The English, I gathered, sat on the stage or somewhere near it during shows, while the locals were kept to the pit, where Phil sat among them. He soon found himself choked out of his job and decided to return to England. For some time he had been doing much work, or, to be more precise, earning a lot of money by wasting time, in connection with films. He had been artistic director for Korda's film on Henry VIII, on the strength of the novel, *Here Comes the King*, which had been very successful; and after that he became friendly with Wallace Beery and the Fairbanks. At the time I had written to him sarcastically suggesting that he choose definitely between films and books; and indeed my advice was good. But he could not resist the easy money and the excitement of pottering about in the film world, going on trips to Spain or somewhere else to get local colour for never-made films. And this just at the time when he should have been concentrating on his novels if he were to develop them with full effect.

Once again Elza suddenly decided that she must move. We found a house at the back of Preston further west along the bay. This was a fine house with a large garden and many fruit trees. Elza was always friendly during moves, perhaps because then she had something to interest her. I was aware that her total lack of any form of activity stood heavily in the way of her recovery, and in our friendly periods I did my best to develop the least show of attention on her part into some more enduring line of thought or action. I had to be careful, as the slightest effect of pushing her aroused instant antagonism. But though she momently took up this or that subject, she was incapable of any sustained action on her own. I never knew how she spent her time in her long withdrawn phases.

I had myself now reached a point where I needed to deepen and extend my understandings of history and individual existence. I had found that I could enter effectively into the latter only if I was at the same time exploring in some new way the relations of individual and social movement, historical change. The timeless element only came alive when I was deeply involved in the colours and patterns of a particular time. In the hopes of extending my method I wrote a slight contemporary novel *Shadow and Flame*. The main character was a gentler sort of Elza, the person she had seemed at our first meetings. She has married a young bookish chap who knows nothing of her past, and they are holidaying at Portreath; as strain develops, he is drowned in the shingly undertow and she is thrown back on her old ways. But now she manages to escape the spiritual undertow which has always brought her down; she finds, with an artist's aid, what I may call her Lawrencian body; she achieves calm, relaxation from the rigours of fear, acceptance of herself in the tenderness of undemanding touch – unpossessive contact with another. The tale was thus once more an allegory of Elza standing on her own feet, with myself eliminated and with the solution using something of D.H.L.'s terms reinterpreted in terms of my own experience.

The book was promptly accepted by Chapman and Hall, the reader being L. A. G. Strong. (He did not know at the time I had written it, as it was signed Richard Preston, under which name it appeared.) I got an amusing letter from a reader, who described herself as highly musical and married to an unappreciative husband; she added that she would like to spend a weekend with a witty young writer, giving herself 'without reserve'. I replied that Richard was neither so witty nor so young, but out of curiosity asked for a photo. She answered at length, but without the photo; and though I did not write again, she went on pouring out her soul, even sending small presents. What had convinced her that I was the witty young writer she needed was a passage where the heroine walks along the cliff top from St Ives with her bladder near bursting, too shy to withdraw behind one of the scanty bushes.

However my uncertainties as to what next to do were settled by Warburg, then in Routledge's, asking me to write a biography of Mark Antony. I was thus plunged afresh into the Caesarian world. And shortly afterwards I found what I needed for a fresh stimulus. I saw an advertisement for works by Marx, Engels, Lenin, and decided I ought to look at them. My knowledge so far had been almost all derived from P.R.S.'s writings in the *Aphrodite*, his copy of Marx's *18th Brumaire* which I had read and which had in fact merged with Beasley's book in providing much of the political outlook in *Rome for Sale*, together with a few scattered remarks in conversation. I had a woefully inadequate idea of Marx's positions: which had not prevented me in the past from laying down the law about them. Now, however, I obtained and read the main works of Marx and Engels in English, with *State and Revolution* and some other writings of Lenin. From almost the first moment I felt that at long last I had come home; I had found the missing links in my dialectical system. I had brought that system from its idealist basis in Plato-Blake-Nietzsche down to earth and had at moments intuited something of the nature of productive activity; but only now did I see that activity in the fullness of its nature. The conflict of liberty and brotherhood which I had tried to discuss in *Last Days with Cleopatra* was now seen as securely resolved by the return of the means of production to the producers.

My ripeness for Marxism was shown by the fact that in a few weeks I had read and absorbed all the main works by Marx and Engels, with a sprinkling of Lenin's theses. Needless to say, I had not understood them as fully as I thought I had, nor were the answers to all the problems so unanswerably present as I thought they were. All the same, I had really reached bedrock; and though in the twenty-five years since January 1936 I have found the problem of developing Marxism adequately to be incomparably more difficult than I had imagined, I have never wavered in my conviction that Marxism does lay the basis for a world of unity (of equality, brotherhood, justice) and for a unitary consciousness in which the old contradictions and limitations of thought and feeling are overcome. What I have had to learn, often very painfully, is the depth of those contradictions and limitations, and the complexity of the struggle that has to be waged in order to overcome them – a struggle which is simultaneously social, political, intellectual (scientific and artistic), and which is going to take a long time.

I thus inevitably oversimplified things in my delighted discovery of Marxism. Where I have differed perhaps from the many other intellectuals of the period, who in their own ways then came to Marxism, has been that when I bumped in due time up against the brick walls, I blamed myself for the over-simplifications, not Marxism. From the outset I took seriously the proposition that the dialectical method must expand and deepen to admit every new truth, every new exploration of reality; I did not believe that the way forward lay in trimming the truths and editing the explorations so that they did not jar against the already built system. In consequence my progress as a Marxist has led to many conflicts with my comrades, in some of which, though not all, I have been wrong.

But that experience lay ahead. For the moment I was enjoying all the excitement of the secrets of heaven and earth laid bare. I subscribed to the *Daily Worker* and plunged into immediate politics as zealously as I had once avoided them. It was with much satisfaction I realized that Edgell, Garman, Alec Brown and others had reached the same conclusions as myself, though by less devious byroads; and that in *Left Review* there was a rallying-point of the movement. With a shock I grasped something of what the rise of Fascism in the thirties had meant: the breaking-out, through the thin crust, of the evil forces I had often talked about in the twenties as sure to reassert themselves. I got hold of any books I could about the Soviet Union, and in particular searched eagerly for translations of Soviet novels or plays. I soon had read a couple of score or more, most impressed by Sholokhov, Gladkov (*Cement*), and Leonov (*Skutaresky*, done by Alec Brown). With enormous love and gratitude I looked towards the new world into which my aloneness had suddenly turned: the Soviet Union and the Communist Parties.

I wanted to join the C.P. at once, but was deterred by the unsolved problem of Elza. There was no branch close by, but I could have found one at Exeter or somewhere nearer. I had learned that the only thing with any strong effect on Elza was an accomplished fact. If I had joined up and then told her, she might have accepted my action and have made some effort to go out into the world again. Probably things would not have worked out that way; but they might have. I should have tried. My failure to act at this moment haunts me as the one real error of those years.

But in positing the issue so simply I know that I do not do

justice to the complexity of each changing moment at the time. After more than five years' daily crushing of my own self-will, I did not find it easy to assert myself, even when now I had discovered an authority in the world which I could respect. When I had diverted my immature revolutionary emotions in 1919 into the championship of Norman's ideas of art, I had found life infinitely exciting; in effect I had accepted him as authority. My unstable and conflicting emotions of admiration and anger towards him and his work were supplanted by a single-hearted allegiance, and there was a powerful identity between the actual father and the father-image of authority, built up in my spirit out of complex family and social elements. The authority I now accepted was set flatly against all the existent forms of authority that I knew in the social scene. In my Fanfrolico years in London I began to break up the N.L. image and ended by losing any faith in it; I turned instead to Elza as the martyred mother (in whom I slowly recognized an identity with all the suffering and downtrodden elements of life). Elza then, in her suffering self and in her remorseless need to keep insisting on moral purification, became my sole image of authority. However, as I dramatized my experience and situation in my work, I gradually got an objective basis, which had ended by splitting the authority-image in Elza. Now I saw her pitiful self on one side and the claims of the suffering and downtrodden on the other side. The Soviet Union and the C.P.s of the world became the new form of authority to which I could yield a pure allegiance, for they were pledged to the ending of the class-system and all the sufferings and contradictions that that system implied – all that Marx had gathered under the term which I still did not know, alienation.

This was the moment then when I should have been able to break from Elza in the sense of standing up against her, obeying my need to express the new allegiance openly and *then* seeing what I could do to help her.

All that sounds simple. But in fact I was caught in a set of contradictions that were not at all easy to resolve. My new position, which brought to a head the striving of many years, involved as its essence the need to achieve a unity of theory and practice. As long as Elza could contain the authority-

image I had expressed that unity by my submission to her; now
I could express it only by joining the C.P. Deep in myself I felt
sure that I would drive her to suicide if I did. How could I
express my solidarity with the oppressed and exploited of the
world by stepping over Elza's dead body to give them a cheer?
The more I felt sure that I would kill her or drive her out of
what remained of her wits by the step it was necessary for me
to take, the less I could take that step. I felt more cornered than
ever. The whole mechanism of fear and self-pity which had put
me at the mercy of Elza took control once more.

Clearly throughout my post-1930 relations with Elza I was
revealing the masochism of which Heseltine had scornfully
accused me. Without that masochistic strain I could not have
carried out the steady sacrifice of my self-will; I must have
gained a certain satisfaction from being Elza's victim. And yet
I do not feel that the whole thing can be reduced to such simple
terms. There was indeed the weak side to which they apply;
but the need for moral self-renewal which expressed itself
through my weakness seems to me the dynamic of the process,
the ultimate touchstone. I renounced my freedom in order to
gain a place in the universe; and though for long it seemed that
I had lost any basis for reachieving human solidarity, in fact
the drive throughout was the need to reachieve it. Step by step
I moved towards a fuller sense of what constituted humanity;
and that progress was the proof, the only possible proof that
my submissions were not as irrationally masochistic as they
might well appear. I had come through to the point which has
been well defined thus:

. . . submission is not the only way of avoiding aloneness and anxiety.
The other way, the only one which is productive and does not end
in an insoluble conflict, is that of *spontaneous relationship to man and
nature*, a relationship that connects the individual with the world
without eliminating his individuality. This kind of relationship – the
foremost expressions of which are love and productive work – are
rooted in the integration and strength of the total personality and
are therefore subject to the very limits that exist for the growth of
the self. (E. Fromm, *The Fear of Freedom*)

In the sense that this passage gives to the words, I had used submission to break through into a spontaneous relationship to man and nature, realizing that the key expressions of this relationship were love and productive work; and I had struggled to define this attitude in my writing. Through Marx I saw that history was more than a cyclic conflict between freedom and brotherhood, individual self-expression and social unity, and that the logical step after the creation of an industrial proletariat was the socialist ownership of the means of production and distribution. But this new idea was not merely the addition of a corner-stone to an edifice in process of construction, it involved a radical re-organization of my whole dialectic. I had been tending in this direction ever since I wrote *The Modern Consciousness* in 1928; but the moment of arrival was none the less shattering.

After my fast at Forge Cottage I had had a long period when I struggled against the reduction of society, history, people, to a set of psychological projections and traumatic compulsions. Now I had to struggle against the reduction to economic forces and relationships. Once again personality seemed unreal, a rationalization imposed on an unrealized complex of compulsions. I decided to write a novel on the last days of Bruno, his return to Venice which led to his being handed over to the inquisition. He had known the danger he was putting himself into; in a sense he had sought destruction. But more deeply, he had tired of his rootless wandering life, his intellectual activity without a basis in any apparent group or people; he wanted to find again his place in the Catholic body, with a desperate hope that by the sheer force of truth he could convert that body or at least find in it a minimal basis for the propagation of his ideas – so that out of the resulting conflict a union of his lonely truths and of Catholic solidarity might result. (In historical fact, some 250 years were to be needed before the line of thought Bruno-Spinoza-Kant-Hegel-Marx could find its Catholic body with which to unite, and then his body turned out to be the international proletariat. Bruno was trying to short-circuit history by turning to the one world-body of his epoch; he was also perhaps showing a nostalgia for his own childhood and an intuitional revolt against the new individualism which he was helping to found and which was to play

its part in making capitalism possible.) There could only be
a tragic end to his quest; and in his possessed distracted days
in Venice I strove to show the hopeless contradictions that
drove him on. In his agony before the inquisition I was drawing
on my own memory of the demoralizing dilemma of facing
with rational arguments a force which is simply asking a total
submission – a submission which one may want to give but
which one cannot fabricate. As I had put it in one of my Elza-
poems:

> The walls of the world have fallen, yet I'm enclosed.
> No man, imprisoned in a foul jail,
> may know this suffering; for while he rots,
> he writhes with renewed worms of rancour and plots
> to escape, and when his efforts fail
> he still can blame and hate
> the men who thrust him there.
> For me all such evasions come too late.
> I cannot even claim the right
> to be sad because I am lonely.
> I am ravaged by the ceaseless Face of light.
>
> I cannot blame, because I know
> that I am alone in the world, mated only
> with the untouched Accuser. Nothing avails
> to repay where what is demanded is not part
> of self or the world, not coins or the heart's idols,
> but the whole of a life. This is the clutch
> in ancient days called Christ, the insatiable voice
> of pain insisting upon absolute choice.
> In vain I cry: You ask too much, too much.
> It is not mine to give.

But I was also thinking of the victims of Fascism being tortured as I wrote. And though I did not know it, I was exploring
also the pangs of a communist brought up cruelly against the
dogmatisms developed in his own creed as part of such aberrations as occurred under the later Stalin. I was dealing with the
conflict of freedom and unity which carries on into socialism,
however much it is being steadily resolved by the forward
movement of the socialist society towards communism.

I am speaking here of the completed work; but nothing I have written caused me greater pangs and confusions. I had to write and re-write, I had to fight every inch of the way – as if I were reliving all my past years with Elza as well as sharing a cell with some anti-fascist fighter in Hitler's Germany; I had to rediscover in Bruno the complex origins of my Marxism and regain through my reconstruction of his personality, his thought, his desperation, a belief afresh in the individual as well as in the forces of history.

When the book appeared, nothing of what I had attempted was visible to my fellow anti-fascist intellectuals. This was the first shock, giving me a slight inkling that I had a somewhat romantic and over-simplified idea of what our anti-fascist unity was, and of the way in which Marxism acted as a liberating force.

I inevitably carried an existentialist stress into Marxism, but I did not, and do not, see that this was necessarily wrong. Existentialism in its modern form is a one-sided dialectic which seeks to correct certain abstractions and distortions in the Hegelian system. It goes too far in its swing and achieves an aberration far greater than anything in Hegel; yet its protest remains of significance as an attempt to vindicate concrete experience and the whole man. In so far as Marxism has carried over abstractions from Hegel, the existential protest has a certain validity, which however diminishes with each step of Marxism towards a fuller concrete grasp of life in all its aspects. That is, existentialism in its protest has an absolute value against Hegelianism, but not against Marxism. It keeps its value only insofar as Marxism holds mechanist, idealist, and over-rationalized elements – as Marxism will continue to do in some degree until the realization of world communism and the total withering-away of the state.

Here is a crucial point in my outlook, and I feel that I must clarify it further in order to bring out as richly as possible the inner struggle of my advance into Marxism, a struggle which, at a different level, is still with me now. Kierkegaard put ethics in the forefront as the key to the release of the whole man; Nietzsche stressed an aesthetic view of the world for the same reason. Both were reacting against the views of the rationalist eighteenth and nineteenth centuries which in effect identified Being and Thinking. I think, therefore I am. This abstract elevation of thought and reason is linked with the expansion of mechanist science, and reveals a key aspect of the alienating process, which above all drives a wedge between reason and emotion, logic and imagination. Kierkegaard saw that the purely intellectual or rational (scientific) mode of life was insufficient, and he used all his sharp irony against the idea that an intellectual system could set things to rights by merely offering the rejected elements a place in its rational ordering. Nietzsche in the same vein attacked the notion of scientific objectivity, not in the name of relativism, but in that of the whole man; scientific values must not be cut away from the values and purposes of the whole man; he saw the science of his day as hopelessly compromised with the deadening forces of dehumanization.

I believed, and still believe, that such contentions were correct, however much I dissent from the ways they were worked out. Kierkegaard split his 'existentialist simultaneity' with an abstract concept of choice between belief and unbelief, between finite and infinite, and so on. Nietzsche lost his concept of the whole man in a medley of biological and subjective fantasies, and never faced what he meant by Eternal Recurrence (a blind repetition or the acceptance of necessity which becomes freedom). Jaspers was thus able to formalize the split at the heart of the existentialist notion of wholeness, a split which inverted the struggle against alienation into an acceptance of alienation as the precondition of choice. He divided Being into three forms: being-there (the world of scientific 'objectivity'), being-oneself (the transcending of being-there), and being-in-itself (the world of transcendence itself). The weaknesses and errors of the unsystematic dialectics of Kierkegaard and Nietzsche are thus systematized, upheld, and brought within the general framework of philosophy. The vital intuitions of those thinkers are carefully undermined. Though in Jaspers's system the thinker is said to participate in all three realms of being and thus to approach the unity to which his reason aspires, in fact the interrelations are metaphysical and we are back at rationalist domination, against which existentialism made its protest. A gap has been driven between being-there (the given self, the given world) and being-oneself (the dynamic self of living experience, with all its potentialities and complex changes); the task of achieving a true dialectical unity has been evaded once more in the name of abstract choice. (The dilemma made manifest in Jaspers is in fact present in Kierkegaard and Nietzsche; but because they do not system-atize, it is disguised under a brilliant handling of momentary aspects of experience, with their contradictions and their impulses towards resolution brought out.)

Something of the Jaspers system had still clung to me in my defence of Darwin, though I was already rejecting the gap between being-there and being-oneself. At the same time I was also beginning to comprehend that scientific method and fact were not given, unalterable things. Now that comprehension became explicit and drew me forever away from the existen-tialist gap of passivity. I saw that it was necessary to distinguish between scientific methods and views as developed in a world of alienation and those that would develop in a classless society moving towards communism. The deadly gap between science and feeling, reason and imagination, which was the clearest mark of the alienating process, would have to be closed if the whole man was to be more than a ghostly figment used as a merely logical link between the two spheres; and this implied a struggle to develop both science-reason and imagination-feeling along new lines so that they could fuse in a higher syn-thesis. Existentialism, I saw, used its genuine insights into alienation to obscure the real solutions, to return to the meta-physical sleight-of-hand it had set out by rejecting. The prob-lem was to end the gap between being-there and being-oneself, not to rivet it by a scheme of transcendences which were in fact only a sanctification of the divisions of alienation. The gap must be closed by a steadily deepening unity of thought and act, theory and practice – whereby both thought and act them-selves would be changed.

Where I differed from most of my fellow Marxists, though it took me some time to grasp the meaning of this difference, was that I refused to assume that the taking over of the given mechanism of Marxist dialectics automatically solved the problem of alienation and closed the gap. I saw it, indeed, as the first and necessary step towards the solution. But the insufficiencies of the existing scientific outlook and method remained even when science was set socialist tasks instead of capitalist ones. The social aims were bettered, but the actual modes of thought and being were still tethered to the insufficiencies and distortions of a discipline developed under the full blast of alienation.

At the same time, I realized, one could not hope to step overnight into a science from which all the old mechanisms and idealisms had been purged; those limitations went deep into the premises on which all scientific thinking had been built up, under the Greeks or in the epoch starting with the sixteenth century. In carrying on from those given bases, a fierce struggle was needed to work out new fundamental methods and ideas expressing the dialectical unity of process. Similarly, old methods of art could not express the new man developing under socialism.

There seemed, and seems, then, to me a deep conflict between the socialist struggle for the new man and the methods which a socialist society is compelled to take over in order to develop its science and its art. This conflict seems to me to have been recognized so far only in its superficial aspects. But I had faith, and still have, that the conflict will grow powerfully in due time, and that from it will emerge the single line of thought-feeling which will unify science and art in undreamed of ways and finally dispose of the heresy that being and thinking are the same, without succumbing to existentialist dilemmas or irrationalities.

I should like to follow out these problems further in their general bearing; but here I must restrict my remarks to the struggle rending me in 1936. I felt the existentialist stress on the unceasing urgencies of choice to be essential, but I wanted to discard the abstract mechanism that made the moment of choice a repetition-compulsion going round in a vicious circle where one chose nothing, one merely vindicated the right or liberty to keep on choosing. That abstract mechanism is what vitiates existentialism from Kierkegaard to Sartre (though the latter, as artist, continually breaks through it). Kierkegaard's system was the perfect consecration of the alienating process; for the person practising it went on as if nothing had happened and impacted on nothing outside himself; he had merely tied himself up in a knot of absolute anxiety. To choose abstractly is to choose nothing; it is to deify the *angst* of alienation as the only concrete aspect of experience. If, however, one straightens out the dogmatic kink in existentialism, one is left with a moral urgency and a sense of the immediate reality of living, which Marxism needs for the unfolding of its ethic and for a protection against all hardening of the arteries, all mechanist application of terms, methods, definitions, categories.

Through psychoanalysis, anthropology, and biology, I had broken down the divisions in my thinking between being-there, being-oneself, and being-in-itself; but I lacked terms adequate to grasp the inner conflict of the unitary process I was intuiting. I still could not satisfactorily explain the nature of real choice, which involved not only oneself but also others, not only the existential moment but also history. I needed Marxism to move from existence to history without losing the concrete texture of the moment. My struggle since then, often leading me into confusions and mistakes, has been to hold true to the existential moment, in which the unexpurgated colour and richness of experience is alone preserved, without blurring the significance of the long-distance choice, the complete self-dedication to the work of achieving human unity through association with others in the field of history.

Thus Marxism released me from the spell of my relations with Elza; nothing else could have done so. For, though I might attempt, in works like *Birth and Will* or in the novels, to analyse my own motivation and to understand what moved Elza, I was not strictly concerned to assess my relations to her. Those relations came under the existentialist heading of a Nietzschean *amor fati*. I had made an absolute act of choice and was bound to it. In the last resort I was not interested in understanding it so that I could overcome it; I wanted to grasp it in order to give it more power, make it more fully an aspect of myself. True, each step I had made forwards had undermined our relations; but despite my temporary revolts or plans of escape I could not have broken the spell of the relationship without snapping the existentialist *huis clos* of which it was the expression. I had to make the full philosophical exploration and find the flaw in the existentialist position, find the dialectic which emerged from the full comprehension of the flaw, before I could feel free.

Also, there was a powerful life-and-death pressure driving me on. To those who feel no need to unify their life and to make a consistent relation of theory and practice, the above arguments must seem nonsensical. Why be bound by such a desperate need to find a coincidence of theory and practice? why tie oneself to an intensely difficult mode of life merely because of a philosophical point? I can only answer that I have never been able to live, have never seen any reason to live, except in a unity of idea and action. And so I carried over into my post-1930 relations with Elza my Nietzschean concept of tragedy, my acceptance of *amor fati*. In *Bussy* and *Hereward* the hero (poet) when brought to the end of the tether of his existentialist contradictions can only affirm himself by a triumphant and mocking death. When, in 1930, my bluff was called, I had to decide how far my Bussy-Hereward role held. Heseltine committed suicide. Such an end was not possible for me; but the time-space I had entered was a death. That was why I could not make an easy re-adaptation to the world, go to Phil, Edgell and the others, and find some way of jogging along as they did. I accepted Elza as a form of death, of total isolation. I felt that only by such an acceptance could I live out my death and find some way back to life that was not a cowardly retreat from all my premises. I had to live out that death of isolation and existentially find my rebirth. That is, I had to make each step forward as a fiercely contested victory over the existentialist contradictions; I had to invoke those contradictions at their strongest and most effective, and only then find if I could overcome them. And I could believe that I had overcome them only to the extent that they were concretely resolved in immediate experience, in love, in work, and in my relation to nature. My love was the discovery of otherness as a dialectical part of myself; my work was the creation of images in which this dialectical conflict was resolved; my relation to nature was the joy in love and in work, which supplanted the tragic ecstasy and slowly evolved a new sensuous harmony in my momentary living. The problem was to achieve love, work and joy in a time space that was their ceaseless negation, the death-isolation incarnated in Elza. All the while, the existentialist conflict was deepening into the Marxist conflict, converting otherness into my own life and thus making a dynamic unity of being-there, being-myself, and being-in-itself.

At the crucial point, reached round the New Year of 1936, the new balance triumphantly asserted itself as a definitely organized system, and I found it was Marxism: not simply the particular system labelled Marxism at that moment, but Marxism the vital stream of thought-feeling which in that system had reached the highest world level then possible. Marxism as a vital stream broadening into the future and implying an ever greater unity of consciousness, unity of man and nature, unity of man and man. Not that I did not welcome and accept the system as it had evolved up to that moment. To do otherwise would have been to sever potentiality from existence, otherness from self – the primary existentialist errors. I had found the open gate into a united movement, which, however many errors, corruptions, distortions it might incidentally produce, held the only fully valid clue to past, present, and future alike, and the one compact that could not in its essence be corrupted. I was free, with all the new problems that freedom raised – the relations to other people as well as the effects on myself that the moment of choice now brought about.

But in this digression I have omitted the events which went on as I wrote *Adam of a New World* and which had such a profound effect on the anti-fascist groupings: the conflict in Spain that led to the Civil War. In a newspaper of 17 February I read that shock troops in Spain had disobeyed their officers and joined the mob. I wrote a rough poem, *Warning of the End*, which I sent to *The Eye*, a sort of trade journal issued by Lawrence and Wishart. It has at least the interest of being a prophecy of the civil war to come in July and the first of the vast number of poems to be written on the Spanish theme; for me it meant the first direct expression of a new stirring loyalty.

About the same time, reading the review of a book by Allen Hutt in the *T.L.S.*, which remarked that what he said was all very well, but he didn't know the English, I wrote a longish declamatory poem, *Who are the English?* I sent it to *Left Review*, where it was published and received with such acclamation that it was reprinted in large numbers as a pamphlet. Also, a group at the recently formed Unity Theatre, who wanted to develop a form of dance-mime together with spoken verse, took it up and produced a stage version of it which was very successful and provided the basis of an English form of mass-declamation with mime and movement. When the Spanish Civil War broke out, Edgell wrote and asked me to do a similar sort of poem on the theme of the war, and I produced *On Guard for Spain*, which was also developed into a mass declamation.

On Guard was even more successful than *Who are the English?* and in the following years was continually done all over England by Unity Theatre or groups connected with the Left Book Club. It was performed in Trafalgar Square and at countless rallies; the typical meeting in support of the Spanish Republic consisted of speeches by Victor Gollancz, Harry Pollitt, and the Duchess of Atholl, with a performance of *On Guard*. Harry once felt impelled to write to me after such a meeting that he had never in all his life seen an audience so powerfully affected as by the declamation.

The Civil War had itself affected me as no other event in my whole life. Coming just at the moment when I had discovered my new allegiance, it represented the new life with the immediate threat and attack it aroused from all the forces of evil, of power and property. Till the final defeat of the Republicans in 1939 my own aspirations were indistinguishable from what I felt of the Spanish people. There were, of course, oversimplifications in all this, but at the same time a profound element of truth. There was a peculiarly tragic quality in the struggle, with the Spanish people doomed from the outset through the help given by Mussolini and Hitler and the betrayal by the 'democracies', and with the anarchist spontaneities and confusions of the people themselves. I suffered extremely from a bad conscience at not being in the International Brigade, and yet at the same time felt an intensely urgent need to get on with my writings, to attempt to absorb into my own painfully evolved dialectics, and to express, the full meaning of proletarian unity. Perhaps I did not force the issue with Elza because my deepest need lay in my writing, and I felt underneath that if I joined the C.P. I would be hurried along by participation in the many activities of the day, thrown off my balance just as I was anxiously trying to find it in the new complexity of ideas and impulses that had gripped me. To join the C.P. was for me tantamount to going into the International Brigade – though in fact after the deaths of Fox, Cornford, Caudwell, every barrier was put in the way of intellectuals sacrificing themselves.

Also, for a while Elza listened to my political ideas and was moved by them; I had hopes that I had at last found a way of awakening her from her deathly withdrawals. It seemed that with a little patience I should be able to carry her with me, and that I must not frighten her too much by stressing the activities stemming from the ideas. However, she began to feel that contact with people would be the logical consequence, and at once closed herself against what I said.

Despite the sado-masochistic character of our relationship, I had escaped by facing the real nature of my isolation; she could not escape, could not work, because she had long given herself up to a retreat from reality in which she had staked her all on me as a 'magical helper'. She had lost all her spontaneity and waited for a miraculous moment that would restore it, restore her power to work (above all to write poetry) and her power to love; and that moment she had identified with the moment when I regained 'sanity'. But in this system of hers I could never regain sanity, for the test did not lie in anything I became, anything I said or did; it lay solely in the miraculous return of her spontaneity, her effective connection with the life-process. And as the miracle did not and could not happen without the effort it was beyond her to make, she could never consider that I had become 'sane'. So she was returned to her need to dominate me and the situation; but whereas I had freed myself from dependency through my work, she had grown evermore dependent on me, though this dependency took the form of her sense of domination. She needed me ever more as the one person with whom she could feel safe, the sole person she had as a symbol of the world and also as a victim.

In fact I had now long lost my original sense of guilt towards her; I merely felt that by an involved set of circumstances I had become responsible for her; I pitied her and could not face the suicide or breakdown which I felt sure would result from my leaving her. It may be argued that this pity and this fear of what she would do if left alone were a delusion; and indeed a strong masochistic tincture pervaded the emotions. But after all there was the practical problem which no amount of chiding myself for self-pity and masochism could whisk away. I kept on hoping that one of my books would make a lot of money; I should then be able to take steps to see that she was well looked after when I went. But though after *Rome for Sale* I always had at least £5 a week, I could not advance beyond that level. Such extra sums as I made were swallowed up by our moves and similar expenses. The result was that I had to keep on working all the while if we were to subsist; and the unrelenting economic pressure had a great deal to do with my accepting the situation, because I feared any long break that would disorder my earning system. In the first years, when anxiety was strong, I had longed for illness, for a breakdown on my own part, which would solve the situation by putting me in hospital and forcing Elza to stand on her own feet. But, partly through my sparse vegetarian diet, my health could not have been better and I never came even remotely within reach of the coveted breakdown. Elza, on the other hand, was several times vaguely ill, though she always refused to see a doctor.

She, on her part, would have liked to stop me working. She recognized to a certain extent that I was escaping from our interlocked situation through my work. After Portobello Road, she never read a line I wrote. She knew that if she did she could not stop herself dictating and tearing up; and she had enough sense to know that if she did that, she would destroy my earning power and bring about a state of collapse in which she could not maintain her control. So, to maintain that control, she had to permit the process which made it impracticable. Her one resource was to dream of the miraculous day when she, too, would become 'creative', able to earn her living. But this dream was liable to fall away, leaving her with melancholic depressions or a sadic outburst in which she wanted to smash my typewriter. I realized that ever since she left Combe Martin, she had been seeking the magical helper who would restore her birthright and release her energies, her spontaneity and her expansiveness; and that her history had throughout been a series of disappointments and disillusions. Robert, who had introduced her into the refined world of his mother, the world of Ellen Terry and of Nicholson, had seemed for a while to offer her a key into a magical realm: but the inner release did not come. I had done more than anyone else to convince her that the release was possible, by my headstrong fantasies of our Fanfrolico purpose and our great aims, and by enabling her to begin writing poems. Therefore my letting her down had come with a decisive blow of derangement; and the fact that she discovered my 'betrayal' at the time when the Press was breaking down and I was going through a very painful and prolonged process of inner change was crucial for bringing out her sado-masochistic components in the form of an effort to take complete charge of me. The economic decline and insolvency of the Press lay at the core of our spiritual fall; for she was thus led to a belief that I was a fraud, not at all the strong and fated character she had taken me to be, whose guidance had to some extent released her. The more I lost faith in what I had been and honestly sought to rid myself of my flaws and illusions, the more I convinced her that I was a weakling. Her respect for the demonic force of my Fanfrolico days (begotten in me by N.L.'s ideas and my feeling of a dedicated purpose in serving them) completely died away; and it was this ending of her respect for my 'power' which led her to feel the need of filling the vacuum with her own domination. To the extent that she had previously respected my demonic possession as the mark of her fated magical helper, she now feared and despised me. Her angers over Betty May had not been the key thing at all; they had expressed her final conviction that I was a weakling and that she had discovered a means of dominating me. (I do not mean she thought consciously along those lines; I mean that that was how the situation worked on her.) In the same way, it was the economic collapse and the crisis of ideas which it precipitated that was the dynamic of my fall, not the guilty

conscience over Betty in which I concentrated my dissatisfaction with my past self.

The plain proof of this analysis is to be found in the fact that
the collision leading to the breakdown of our relations in
1930-31 occurred then, and not earlier, when I was still meeting
Betty, or just after I had ended things with her. Elza was certainly feeling uneasy at that earlier period, as was shown by
her sudden advent one morning to confront me and find out
what was going on; yet she did not tackle me then, nor did I
feel burdened by the sense of disaster and doom that made me
'confess'. Elza was still controlled by her respect for my strong
sense of inner purpose. Long before she had heard the name
Betty May she responded to the weakening purpose in myself
to start petty tyrannies such as throwing out the Pentons. At
the same time she made the vague effort to return to the persons she had known in her days of selling herself – a further
expression of the fact that she was beginning to feel she could
not rely on me. But she found that she could not make a return
to her old way of life, and that sharpened her sense of dependence on someone whom she no longer felt carried along by
a magical aim.* She was impelled to begin direct attacks on
me to find out just how weak I was, just how unlike her pristine
image of me I had become. Her taking up of the Betty hints
thrown out by Marie was the expression of this need to get
inside me; and the cheat she felt was the discovery of the man
of straw behind the Apollonian disguise. Therein lay my
betrayal of her; the Betty theme was the mere emblem of the
deeper letting down; her misery lay in feeling tied to someone
who was now shown to be an imposter. She could not move
forwards a poet or return to the one role, prostitution, where
she could use her helplessness to get her own back on an out-

---

*In the first days at Forge Cottage, brooding over Donne's symbols of the
Two Indies (gold and spice) and on Freud's idea of anal-eroticism, I said
to Elza, 'Perhaps a man ought to give a woman money every time he lies
with her.' The next moment I thought the idea a bad one (reducing all sex
to the Baudelairean position of guilt); but Elza enthusiastically took it up
and kept talking of it. Clearly it met her feeling of castration in the act that
proved her woman.

raging world. She felt the need to take whips and scorpions to my unreliable self; and thus it was, as I have said, that my vulnerable condition – ever more vulnerable the more I tried to change myself – provoked her distrust and hostility instead of making her feel that at last there was the basis of a stable and happy union between us.

Though I did not yet analyse things quite as bluntly as I have just done, I had steadily arrived at this position; and my discovery of Marxism, which was the natural completion of the process going on in me ever since 1928, brought me to the point of finally discarding the mechanism of guilt. But it did not, as I have said, solve the practical problem of what I was to do with Elza. I could not, now as before, accept a way out which was an expression of my self-will and disregard the consequences for her, however good a rationalization I could put up in its defence. My pity and my responsibility remained, however much their focus had changed.

25 · CONCLUSIONS

In essence the conflict with Elza had been fought out and I had found the resolution of the contradictions which had been lurking in my thought and action since 1928, or more precisely since 1919. But to round off the story, I will rapidly describe what happened between 1936-37 and 1941, when I was called up. As usual, Elza's disconcerted mood found expression in a change of residence. We went to Dartmouth and stayed awhile in the upper storey of a long, thin house, packed with useless furniture. Then we found a small bungalow on the western side of the river, looking towards the sea, with a brewery deep below. Almost at once she wanted to move again. Fish had been driven into the estuary, shoals of them piling up in the shallows, and the fishermen were complaining that the dealers had dropped their prices so low it was best to sell the easy catches to the farmers for dunging the fields. The scream of excited gulls filled the river valley. Elza spent day on day away, looking for a house. I recall the posters saying that Madrid was on the eve of capture, and I grieved. For the first time since Forge Cottage I went into a pub and had a few half pints. The local cinema manager, acting the goat, was babbling about the gallons of pee that the kids left on his seats and floor on Saturday afternoons; I talked to a miserable-looking joiner and found that the P.A. officer had been telling him that he must sell his tools. I rowed up the river past the serried lines of chained ships rusting away.

Elza found a house at the end of the bay west of Paignton. We moved there. The beach was only about twenty yards distance and I bathed for a few moments all the year round. Still wrote to say that Nicholson had died, and he was arranging for me to go to Methuens. I wanted now to turn to English history, to use the novel to revive revolutionary traditions; and to finish off my Nicholson contract I wrote *Sue Verney* as a preparation for a large novel on the Cromwellian Revolution. *Sue*, based on the Verney Papers, dealt with the breakdown of the last stages of the manorial system; at the end Sue, married to a small landowner, finds that her hopes are based in the Cromwell whom she had once detested. Methuens asked me to do a biography of Bunyan: a proposition I was glad to accept, as it fitted in with my Cromwellian studies and enabled me to pay a tribute to a man whom I greatly admired as a character and as one of the founders of the novel. A reconsideration of *The Pilgrim's Progress* chimed in with my ponderings on the nature and form of a consciously revolutionary art which attempts a fresh start, a comprehensive vision of human activity and of the role of the individual breaking away in the struggle for a new life. Methuens also published, as *Anatomy of Spirit*, some essays I had written as part of a large book, *Homage to Bruno*, which I abandoned through the difficulty of reading and evaluing his Latin poems and his relation to Renascence mathematics. In *Anatomy* I tried to deal with the question of what elements of Freud remained useful for a Marxist.

I still had a considerable fan mail; and two girls, without seeing me, fell in love. One I managed to divert into becoming a party member; the other was not so easily interested in politics and kept on writing that she wanted to meet me. Luckily Elza had had one of her interfering bursts and had been abusive because she found I was in correspondence with Edgell, so I had all letters addressed to the bank in Paignton. The girl thus did not know where I lived; but she came down to stay in the neighbourhood and wrote urgently asking me to see her. I was in the habit of walking in to Paignton three mornings a week to buy food, and I arranged to have coffee with my pursuer, saying that I could only see her once and for an hour. We met and I did my best to make her feel the meaning of the Spanish struggle. She had banged into something the day before and injured her brow on one side: a handsome girl with a remarkably clear, frank look. Anyway, after our one brief meeting, she wrote less emotionally; I kept up my political arguments, and about three months later she stopped writing.

In 1940 she sent me a short note with some wedding cake.

Edgell asked me to review novels for *Left Review*; also to compile an anthology, *Handbook of Freedom*, which he himself cut and added to; it was later re-issued as *Spokesmen for Liberty*. The poetry section of the Left Book Club asked me to be chairman and I co-edited their monthly; I further suggested and edited verse broadsheets. I completed my novel *1649*, in which I sought to apply all I had learned through my Caesarian novels to the English Revolution, taking afresh the cycle of a year, attempting a multiple series of levels and angles and interspersing passages from contemporary writings. (One reason for this latter detail was to provide a touchstone which would show if the rest of the book had the tone and colour of the period. My method here as always was to avoid anachronisms, to be as factually correct as possible in all things large or small, but not to try for a pastiche of the period's style. Nothing must jar as out of period, but otherwise one should write in a modern style. The effect should be simultaneously: how like ourselves, how unlike.)

The reception of the Bruno novel and *1649* made me realize that nothing of what I was trying to do had got over to my fellow intellectuals, who saw only the political bearings. My Roman novels had been in general very well received, though without any insight into their intentions. Now, however, I came up against hostilities. I do not mean on the part of right-wing critics; for in these years almost the whole of the literary world had swung into support of the Spanish people and the anti-Hitler cause. But the element of whole-hearted acceptance which made the declamations so successful with audiences made me suspect with the intellectuals: and Spender attacked *On Guard for Spain* in *Fact*, taking some lines spoken by a dead man as a call on the part of the living for death. Calder-Marshall reviewed the Bruno book in *Left Review* without a flicker of penetration into what I had struggled to express. And so, oddly, from this moment when I had come through to an enduring sense of union with the revolutionary forces everywhere, I found myself odd man out, a continuing outsider, whose work was rejected by the conservative or liberal as crudely committed to the proletarian cause, and was not much welcomed on the Left, which complained steadily over the years about all sorts of unorthodox elements, over-complex and subtle, over-psychological, mystical, over-lyrical, lewd, over-naturalistic or psychopathological, over-concerned with sex, etcetera.* It was perhaps characteristic that at the moment Spender attacked me in *Fact*, John Allen, producer at Unity, wrote to me that he had been at the *Daily Worker* office to find why the report and photos of a performance of *On Guard* in Trafalgar Square had omitted my name, and had been told there was a rule I was not be to mentioned. But I went on doing my best to struggle ahead into the unknown by the light of my own experience, my deepest convictions, and Marx's critique of class-society. I have not been deaf to criticism; perhaps I have listened too much to it. I have often learned something from the letters or discussion of readers, and recently I have had letters from young people in the Soviet Union which reveal a clear understanding of my aims; this I find the most encouraging thing that has ever happened to me.

From *1649* on I worked direct on the typewriter, and till I was called up I made only a single draft of my historical novels. After long and thorough preparation I typed each work straight out and merely made local corrections before sending the MS off. I still, however, could not handle the contemporary scene. I roughed out a novel on the anti-conscription fight of 1917 in Australia; a semi-autobiographical novel of the twenties set in Sydney, which I sank by putting too much into it; and part of a novel on Elza and Mrs Craig. Then I wrote *End of Cornwall*, which Cape published as by Richard Preston.

*If I were asked to put in a phrase what my work since 1933 is about, I should answer: the alienating process (in Marx's sense) and the struggle against it. But even in the essay by my friend Alick West in his *Sunlight on the Mountain*, while he stresses the central significance of the relation to nature in my work, he says nothing whatever of what this entails in method and how it involves the many-sided struggle against alienation, how the latter is artistically presented, what the total effect is, and so on. Instead, he queries some isolated passages without relating them to the central problem, in terms of which alone can the position and negative qualities be determined.

All the while I kept sketching out plays, some straightforward, some lyrical and fantastic, but my isolation from the theatre held me back from finding what I was after. I continued with many articles and stories, e.g. in *New Writing* and in anthologies edited by J. Rowland and E. Martin. Rowland worked for the *Literary Guide* and we corresponded a lot; Martin, enthusiastic for my philosophy, was working on a life of me and Phil. I also wrote articles for *New Masses* and a small book on Blake for the Critics Group, New York, which never came out on account of the war and is lost. Harry Moore and Isidore Schneider, whose writings I had liked in *Transition*, were my main correspondents; I think Moore at that time meant to follow up his work on Steinbeck by dealing with me. Further, taking up a request from John Sommerfield to protest against a narrow-minded Russian review of his *Mayday*, I was drawn into considerable article writing and verse translation for *International Literature*. I made the first English versions of the Ukrainian poet, Shevchenko, and Partridge published some of the Provençal troubador poems I translated. I was also continually composing declamations for small and large occasions. Strike committees or trades councils from all over England wrote in with requests; and I produced long poems for a Chinese event at the Phoenix Theatre and for the L.B.C. Theatre Guild in support of Soviet policy. The latter declamation, *Defend the Soviet Union*, was printed and performed fairly extensively. A boys' story about the Eureka Stockade was published by Lawrence and Wishart.*

Finally I accepted an invitation to speak at the L.B.C. summer camp of 1938. When the time came, I simply told Elza what I was going to do, and said I'd be back in two days. She was so overwhelmed that she said nothing. In London I dropped in at 16 King Street – why, I cannot recall – and encountered Harry Pollitt in the street. Recognizing him from

---

*My seclusion seems to have made me rather a mysterious figure at this time. Various efforts were made to visit me, which I baffled. In 1939 one of the many young poets with whom I corresponded, Maurice Carpenter, set out to walk down from London to find my lair, but was caught in Bristol by the war, married a working-class girl, and went into an aircraft factory.

his photos, I introduced myself. At the moment a shower came up. I wore only a slight summer suit, and he pulled off his raincoat and handed it to me, 'Here, lad, your need is greater than mine.' At the camp I gave a very bad lecture, but had the pleasure of meeting Norman Alford, whose friend Marley Denwood had written to me a couple of years back about my *Freethinker* articles. (The Denwoods were a remarkable Cumbrian family. The father, a village tailor, had been a follower of Ernest Jones in his last days and spent much time in Carlisle Gaol for poaching – a traditional defiance to which his poverty drove him. While in jail he wrote poems attacking the water bailiffs and the landlords, which were printed as broadsheets and sold for the benefit of the family. Marley's brother, Jonathan, was the last important folk poet in Britain, and Marley and John were keen collectors of Cumbrian lore.) Alford at this time was absorbed in poetry. He told me how he went round the pubs of Cumberland, reciting poems by Burns and myself: a compliment, which, however undeserved, I found pleasant. He was a tall eager fellow, so full of energy and ideas that he had to stride about as soon as he began talking. We paced up and down in the moon shadows while he talked and talked. Once the subject of John Strachey came up, and, in reply to some derogatory remark, I protested about his Marxist staunchness: Alford replied, 'You just wait. As soon as things grow more entangled and set new problems, he'll turn to the Labour Party.'

But I was pleased to drive back next morning to London with Strachey. Gollancz had recently accepted my summary of a book I wanted to write, *A Short History of Culture*. I tried to discuss it, but Strachey didn't seem interested. On my arrival back home, Elza made no complaints and I felt that after all nothing had been needed beyond decisive action on my part. However in a few days she was restless and wanted to move. We found a bungalow with large grounds on the eastern side of the Teign. The first night after we had moved she lay out in the dews and contracted severe rheumatism. For three or four months she was unable to leave bed. I did all the housework, cooking, washing. After a few weeks in the big room at one end of the long front corridor, she said that the wall-panelling was driving her mad with its smell; so I took it all down, leaving the roughly finished brickwork underneath. Myself, I loved the place, with its broad gardens sweeping down towards the river, and would have liked to stay on for good. I rowed up the river and thought of Keats and talked with the old ferryman who had a tame seagull perched on his shoulder.

Here at Teignmouth I finished *A Short History*, which was sent back as about three times too long. I hacked it about, which was one of the reasons for the unsatisfactory form in which it appeared. But in any event I had bitten off more than I could chew, and over-simplified a number of anthropological and cultural issues. I next worked on the second novel of what I meant to be an English trilogy: *Lost Birthright*, set in the 1760s during the Wilkite agitations. I attempted a form that corresponded to the period's tensions and outlook, working at extreme pressure. In the middle I was diverted by an urgent request from Randall Swingler, who had taken over the editing of *Left Review* and was about to start a series of Key Books for mass circulation at the price of 2d. He wanted to start off with a selection of Haldane's scientific articles and a long essay by myself on the revolutionary side of the English tradition, which I composed and called *England my England*. Randall wrote that he would be passing through Teignmouth on his way back from a farm holiday in the West and would like to see me. I met him at the station and we walked back to the house across the toll-bridge; after a too-short chat he had to rush to catch another train. The tract sold some 80 000 and had a strong effect in the factories.

We were still in the house when the Munich crisis arrived. There was a small party group in the town, led by a man with a fried-fish shop. I used to call in and discuss things with him, as also with the workers at the railway-station; and I should have joined up if Elza had not been bed-ridden. I was sure that though she had certainly been suffering at first from rheumatism, she was kept in bed by the simple fear of getting up again. But suddenly she decided that she could not bear the house. I was faced with the problem of restoring the panelling in her large room – a job that would have taken me weeks on my own.

I found an unemployed carpenter at the Labour Exchange, and the two of us repanelled the room in four days. Elza couldn't bear to stay in the house another moment; she was sure it had developed all sorts of hostile smells. So we moved to some rooms down nearer the river and the bridge. I felt that we were in for a wandering period; and as I had been put behind my schedule by Elza's illness, I drank coffee and worked for about a week without more than a few hours of snatched sleep. I thus completed *Lost Birthright* and sent it in to Methuens.

No sooner had I done so than Elza wanted to move into a house on the other side of the river. We were there only a few days and she wanted to move again. We had a look at houses along the coast, at Dawlish and Exmouth, and ended by taking some temporary rooms at Exeter. There we looked round and almost leased a lonely place inland to the west, which was owned by a titled descendant of the Shelley family (who had water-colours of appalling taste in her house). Elza, however, decided to revisit her home area of North Devon. We went to Barnstaple and then Ilfracombe, where we found a small furnished bungalow and visited various houses to let in the neighbourhood. I recall one place in Ilfracombe of truly palatial dimensions – huge ballrooms and the like – which we could have had for 30s. a week if we had undertaken repairs. (The reader may wonder at the ease with which we changed our residence; but at this time there was no difficulty in finding houses or rooms almost anywhere, and thirty shillings a week provided one with quite fine houses.) At Ilfracombe I was able only to write stories and articles. One article, which I did for *Life and Letters* on Savage, a book of whose poems I had picked up for sixpence in a small bookshop, started me off on an enquiry into our eighteenth-century poetry (and thence into that of the seventeenth and nineteenth century) which has now extended into many million words, though I have published only a few chapters of the various sections as essays.

Elza suddenly decided that she wanted to go back to Torquay. We found a barnlike house a little inland; and while we were there, on 7 March, the Spanish War ended. With a feeling as of world end, I read the report in an evening paper bought near the sea-front. The Negrin government had fallen. Stricken on a seat, I watched the unconcerned passers and tried to find words that would express my sense of horror and disaster. When, next day, I heard some girls laughing in the lane by our rambling house, I felt an anguish that seemed deeper than any pang I had ever known on my own behalf.

> . . . And yet the laughter was lovely and unstained
> as poplar-fountains flutterleafed with blue.
> It was their scream I heard upon the day
> when fear comes true.
> They do not know the barrier's down which kept
> the blackbird-whistle safe, the cherry-snow.
> They do not know what foulness roots the earth,
> but soon they'll know.

In six months our war was to come. That afternoon I read, again on the sea-front, 'Communist troops refused to accept the coup against Negrin and were bombed in Madrid by forces that included Anarchists.'

> . . . Out of the newsprint blows this wind of honour,
> pause reading amid the traffic-blast, seal down
> red as the heart the oath that we must swear
> if we are still to live on such an earth,
> and so it ends and ending so begins.

We moved to a bungalow in a new estate being built on high ground to the west of Torquay. I did not like this locality and was pleased enough when Elza wanted to move again. (Here I corrected the proofs of *A Short History* hastily, missing many errors.) We went to Bournemouth and stayed awhile in the dim dank lower storey of a house in one of the central chines. Here I reduced to normal novel-size and method the strange vast MS of Dorothy Johnson about Giuliano Medici for Dakers. He and Ludovici were the persons in Methuens with whom I had been dealing; and during my visit to London in 1938 I had met Ludovici and discussed my work with him. About this time Dakers left Methuens and Ludovici went with him. Still wrote and told me to transfer to the new firm they were setting up, as they were particularly keen on my work and would give it special attention. I did so, but still owed Methuens two novels: the first of which I now wrote, *Bright Light*, on the life of Catullus, a companion piece to *Despoiling Venus*. Elza found a house in the northern part of Bournemouth, unpleasantly sur-burban. One day, out walking, we stopped in a small café for lemonade and heard the depressed voice of Chamberlain announcing that Britain was at war with Germany.

Ever since the days of Munich, the inevitability of war had been obvious; and that was another reason why I felt I had to do my best to help Elza. We now moved out to a small bunga-low on the sandbanks close to the ferry across the mouth of Poole Harbour. Soon the rigours of the 1939-40 winter closed in and the Harbour froze. In walking up to the shops I passed through some woodland and scattered for the birds all the scraps of food I had. The grocer was an Italian, terrified that Mussolini would come into the war and that he himself would be interned, losing all the work he had put into the shop. I was working at a large book, *Mirror of Antiquity*, in which I tried to overcome the weaknesses of *A Short History* and in particular to grapple with the phases betwen the totemic tribe and class-society, which I felt to be a crucial and little-explored matter for anthropology. (Dakers, however, held this work on account of the war and it was never published.) I also completed my contract with Methuens by writing the third novel of my Eng-lish trilogy, *Men of Forty-eight*. In those bitter days of the phoney war, with the feeling that at any moment hell would be let loose, I strove to let myself go and to pack my deepest emotions about alienation and the class-world into the novel.

We had a look round Swanage, then moved over to Upwey, half-way between Weymouth and Dorchester. For thirty shill-ings a week we got a fine solidly built Victorian house with a big garden. To save money, I used to walk into Dorchester for the public library, and sometimes visited Maiden Castle on the way. I wrote *Hannibal Takes a Hand* for Dakers, dealing with the situation at Carthage when the defeated Hannibal turns on his class, the nobles, and attempts to build a city democracy on the remnants of the old clan-elements; the nobles call in the enemy Rome against their own disarmed city. Writing in the period of the *drôle de guerre*, I was symbolizing the betrayal of

the anti-fascist cause by the French government and prophesy-
ing the fall to Hitler; but at the same time I tried to develop
from several angles the theme of ancient religion turned back
in on itself, as the social situation grows more complex and the
original bases break down. Then I did *Stormy Violence*, using for
the first section a long short story I had written for an anthology
edited by E. Martin, about one of the branded bondmen or
slaves of Elizabethan times. To this story, in which human desperation was carried to its limits, I added a second half about
the bondman after he had escaped to London and been pressed
into service as a sailor; the ship is captured by Moors and practically single-handed he regains it – driven solely by his love
of one of his fellow sailors and of the ship itself; he has regained
his humanity through comradeship and work, regained his
sense of a place in nature. Dakers wrote that the book was
rather short; so, without even the MS of the two parts before
me to check, in four days I wrote a middle part describing the
man's experiences among the poor in London, when his hand
is still against all others and it seems likely he will succumb
to crime. This work, which sold well, I wrote in less than three
weeks.

My contract with Dakers was now ended, and I wrote to Gollancz, who commissioned two novels: *Light in Italy*, centred on
a painter in Italy about 1816, and *The Barriers are Down*, dealing
with a world in collapse and renewal (the Western part of the
Roman Empire round A.D. 450). In these years I was reading
a great deal of archaeology and anthropology, making full
notes from scores of books. I found that by writing very fast,
in a small script, I could get down in one day practically all
the argument and the illustrative facts, with references, of a
book of about 250 pages. I tried to persuade Lawrence and
Wishart to publish a collection of my mass declamations,
including *Defend the Soviet Union*, as an expression of my
unchanged political position; but perhaps they disliked the
preface in which I declared that the war would become genuinely anti-fascist as it developed. This attitude I had expressed
in many letters to the newspapers. Though I held the phoney
war with its efforts to mobilize political opinion against the

Soviet Union rather than against Hitler, to express an imperialist stand, I never doubted that the dynamic contradictions of the situation would develop the war along anti-fascist lines; and I stated this in print. Which meant that as usual I was odd man out. I also tried to concentrate in a simple form my ideas on *The Pattern of History*. This, too, was rejected as unorthodox. I made a fresh start on my theses about English poetry, in *Decay and Renewal* attempting to show how the poets from Thomson on, while generally acclaiming the Newtonian universe, in fact were reacting against it; and that this reaction was a key aspect of the Romantic movement, which begins with Thomson – the moments of elemental change such as dawn, moon-rise, storm-flare, and dusk (especially the latter) being taken as symbols of a total transformation of life; the same struggle, I showed, was going on in the fields of science, psychology, history, art, as well as literature. I sent this to the Cambridge University Press, which rejected it – though eight years later, in Cracow, Waddington told me that he fought to get the Syndics to publish it. I continued amassing material for a large-scale extension of my theses; tried to tackle what seemed to me the fundamental problems of cultural anthropology (above all, the sequence of motives, the interrelation of ritual, society, and myth in an historical series – all that was ignored in the scholastic method of Frazer's compilation). I particularly sought to grapple with the origin, meaning and development of the Bear's Son motive, starting from an analysis of *Beowulf* – much stirred by the Chadwicks' *Growth of Literature*, which had brought out the enormous significance of the mantic or shamanist individual in the phases between the totemic tribe and the settled literate society. And so on.

I had the feeling that I must somehow conquer all the problems of culture before I was called up. Almost nightly the German planes came over, sometimes seeking to bomb Portland, sometimes using the landmark of Weymouth-Portland to give them their bearings as they struck inland. All round us were powerful anti-aircraft guns, which made the house tremble and shook down the strongly built brick barn at the back. I had my curtains well drawn and my light shaded, but did not stop work even when the bombs and the shrapnel were falling around us. And when I went to bed, I slept at once, waking only with the light of day.

I was called up for my medical inspection at Dorchester the day after Hitler launched his attack on the Soviet Union. Elza was not much perturbed, as she assumed that I would be rejected. I said nothing. Some weeks later came my call-up papers, telling me to go to Trowbridge. At Dorchester, in reply to questions, I had said, 'Put me in the infantry.' But I found that I was directed to Signals, presumably because I had a university degree and Signals were counted the brains of the Army. In my squad were a number of postmen, considered likely to prove good signallers because post offices had once used Morse a lot. But I do not want to tell the story of my life in the Army. What matters here is simply that a force against which arguments and screams had no effect had intervened to snatch me from Elza. I was pleased that the parting had come, even in such an ignominious way; yet I felt utterly miserable that Elza was being thrown back on her poor resources in such a difficult situation and that I had not been able to find some rational method of settling things. One of the chaps in my intake told me later that he had never seen anyone so stricken as I looked that first day in the barrack-room. But my misery was wholly about Elza and the way she would be feeling at that moment. At Trowbridge I soon joined the Party, though as soldier I could not hold a card or attend branch meetings.

I was ashamed that I should so crudely express in my life that element in men which made them accept and even long for war, as the only release from the intolerable but unrealized tensions of their daily existence. My failure to find a way out from my Elza-conflicts by my own exertions showed me as all too clearly representative of the very worst aspects of the *angst* of alienation, which made war possible; I had been in the divided state of realizing this weakness in myself while fighting against the drift to war. But now at least that division was over. I had failed to carry Elza with me; the struggle against war had failed; I was in the Army. But the war, for all its confusions and complex trends, was in its strongest aspect an anti-fascist war; and so, beyond all the remnants of unresolved conflicts, I could assent to my position and be happy in it.

It must have taken Elza some time to realize I had really become a soldier and was thriving on it. She would have assumed I must break down under a strain that would have broken her; I think the fact of my being at home in the Army baffled, perplexed, and wore her down. The impersonal nature of the force separating us did, however, make her accept the situation without violence or complaint. She became much more emotionally settled than she had been at any time since 1930, but also shrunken, deflated, as if she had at last awoke from a painful dream to find herself changed from a beautiful girl to an ageing chubby country woman who lacked charm, culture, or any reason for existence. She bought a wireless and tried to follow what was happening. She even attempted to write verse again, but could not manage it: only a few fragments, about the planes continually overhead like silver bees enigmatically burning. The doctor who lived next door to us at Upwey had promised to keep an eye on her; I had had a long talk with him before leaving. After a while, at his advice, she voluntarily went into a mental home close to Dorchester. I got special leave to see her there. She was not happy, but had no strong dislike of the place, no clear objections, no alternative to propose. Before long, however, she left and went to Brighton. There she wrote me long confused letters of detailed incoherent complaints about the people around her. (From the time I left her I wrote daily to her as encouragingly as I could.) She wilted away and died of cancer.

Thus sadly and undramatically our relation ended. What I felt and still feel was the intolerable waste of fine human material. It was so pathetically pointless that she should have fought her way up from the misery and degradation of her childhood and youth into the world of Ellen Terry, into the creation of the strange dream-charm that Edith Young has recorded in *Lisa*, into the limited but deeply original poetry of our days in Museum Street – only to decline into the desperate manic-depressions of the last decade. Endlessly I proved to myself that there was something warped and crippled in her from early days and that if she hadn't gone to pieces one way she'd have done it some other way; endlessly I found myself convinced that in 1926-28 she had made a deep-going effort to draw herself out of the slough, and while helping her out with one hand, I had pushed her back with the other. An equally good case could be made out for my exoneration and for my condemnation. But remorse was useless. Beyond both exoneration and condemnation was the image of the beautiful girl with her dream-charm, her childlike pathos.

The poem of hers in the *Aphrodite* defined the lyrical dream which had persisted through her early defeats:

> *She walks with the drunken wind for lover, this girl –*
> *this mad girl who can't tell the thighs of shadows*
> *from those of Dick and Tom and drunken Harry*
> *as she goes walking with the wind along the meadows.*
>
> *This girl is a spirit who is not yet born,*
> *but wed to sun and air and to the drunken wind.*
> *She cares not how she treads, so young are her thoughts,*
> *and nobody knows how young is her unborn mind.*
>
> *She lays her languid body out under the trees;*
> *and lying with the drunken wind, round her lover's eyes*
> *she curls her slender body, round and round,*
> *like a young tree curling its branches round the skies.*
>
> *The wind runs up out of the grass and over her.*
> *She listens to the wind running up out of the grass,*
> *and sighs to hear the shepherd's pipe, and sighs,*
> *shutting her eyes, and waits for him to pass.*

And there is a passage in *Lisa*, which subtly suggests the peculiarly magical strength of her presence in those years: the power she had to make of her body an immediately convincing thing of spiritual depth and integrity:

I noticed then the thin border of lawn – or was it lace? – that topped Liza's bodice and lay next to her skin: it showed more of her nature to me than much of what she said and probably all she did; by it I knew her delicacy, and I also knew that the fineness of her complexion showed her sensitivity. What did it matter, I said to myself, how many men she has lived with, what experiments she has made in her search after some kind of fulfilment, some satisfying beauty between man and woman? She herself is so sensitive that the most subtle of life's impacts are registered by her, are woven into this fabric of herself, and because of this she becomes subtle herself, her mind fine, made so by the acute registration of the most delicate shades of feeling.

The image of her fine dreaming self haunted and haunts me; and I have written this book, not to exorcise the ghost, but to give it a home. How could I pay her a fitting tribute except by attempting to tell the whole truth as far as I understood it in my long wrestling with her, my long brooding over her? To obscure her failings and the darker sides of her life would be to belittle the desperate struggle that she ceaselessly waged, and to make a doll-thing out of her poor bruised humanity and her achievement, for a while, of a rare beauty. Even the years of her derangement had something of stark moral nobility, in her hopeless search for nothing less than complete freedom and harmony. She herself wanted the truth, and nothing but it. Let me end with one of her last poems written in 1930:

> *How like to Satan is this hand of mine.*
> *How cunning these fingers, twisting these words*
> *to shapes I never guessed at, dragged from me,*
> *and jeers at my remaining fears, so pitiless.*
> *I see my hand stretched forth to take the pen*
> *to wring from me remorselessly all secrets*
> *that I had longed to keep from common ears.*
> *Yet I cannot stay my hand, nor would I.*
> *I have my pride and laugh at it –*
> *the devil may take me.*

EPILOGUE

Here is a brief, highly compressed account of my development after the events recorded in the trilogy. At the end there I disappeared into the Army. My branch of Signals was the Special Operators Training Battalion, dealing with high Morse speeds and with interception of enemy messages, and thus closely linked with Intelligence. I liked the weeks of basic training but felt lost when I had to tackle Morse messages tapping wildly away in the air, in my brain. So I was brought up for an interview with the colonel, who looked at my records and said bleakly, 'Send him off to Catterick': that is, let him carry on with the ordinary run of Signals. But I could bear Morse no longer. I went to my company commander, a decent old chap who had risen from the ranks, and broke my vow of anonymity. 'I'll only be a disaster for the Army as any sort of signalman. I'm an author, you'll find my name in *Who's Who.*' He smiled and said he'd arrange another interview. This time the colonel looked up amiably and said, 'What can I do for you, Lindsay?' I explained, and he turned to the adjutant: 'Put him in the battalion orderly room.'

'But there are no vacancies there.'

'Put him in.'

So I became a clerk in a fairly stable position. I learned later that the colonel had two passions: trout-fishing and Cleopatra. He had read, or looked at, my novel, *Last Days with Cleopatra.*

At Trowbridge barracks, settling in to Army life, I wrote two novels: *We shall Return*, on the Dunkirk campaign, and *Beyond Terror*, on the fighting in Crete. In these I drew on the experiences of friends in the battalion, who had taken part in the events. To write a novel in the Army, even when in barracks, is not an easy matter. After about a year and a half the battalion moved to Douglas, Isle of Man. There I began a novel, *Hullo Stranger*, dealing with women in war industry; I based it on the accounts of the young wife of a signalman also in the orderly room, who had come over to join him and who had been the first woman in Handley Page. I also published two books of verse: *Into Action* (on the Dieppe attack) and *Second Front*. A.T.S. were now supplanting most of the men in the battalion, showing that the Second Front was near. But I again escaped posting to a signals unit. One day, passing through London on leave, I met Mary Wren (heroine of Frank Hardy's novel, *Power without Glory*). She said a script-writer was wanted in the War Office for a new Army theatre project. I protested that I'd written everything but such scripts. She insisted on ringing up Captain MacOwan, and I went along to see him. I found he had known my uncle, Will Dyson. We had a pleasant chat and I thought that was all; but he applied for my transfer. Some weeks later I was ordered to report to the War Office.

So I became script-writer for a new unit, the A.B.C.A. Army theatre. But the Army Council had neglected to include such a necessary person on the strength. I remained on paper a signalman seconded to the Education War Office as actor. I thus became the only private in the War Office, actually doing a captain's job. Stephen Murray was in general charge of the unit, while also acting. He, MacOwan, and I were the group making up and working out the plays, though others such as Ted Willis were drawn in at times. (Later Bridget Boland, skilled at film-scripts, came in as a captain.) The scripts were built up collectively, rather in the way of film-scripts, and I had the final job of putting the bits together in a completed play. We thus created an experimental theatre with an original type of documentary play, expository and evocative, using any suitable device of realism, symbolism, expressionism, argument, poetry, and audience involvement. The best plays, I think, were *Lend Lease* and *Where do we go from here?* I also did on my own for Martin Brown and his Pilgrim Players, *The Whole Armour of God*, with emphasis on the poetry; it dealt with Christian resistance to Hitler in Europe and was performed in churches all over England. I finished *Hullo Stranger* and wrote a book on the cultural activities liberated widely among our people in their response to an anti-fascist war. Also a booklet, *Perspective for Poetry*, on what seemed the new possibilities of poetic development in such a situation. Calling on the offices of *Tribune*, I came to know Orwell, who printed various pieces I wrote.

In 1945 I was demobbed. I had married Ann Davies of Unity Theatre, who had a marvellous voice for poetry and who was a first-rate organizer as well as actress. Among my close friends was Dylan Thomas, and I had re-met my old friend, Edgell Rickword. Our activities were now for some years centred on the hopes of developing further what we called, with jesting seriousness, the Cultural Upsurge, the release of cultural energies and interests by the war, which we felt could be encouraged, expanded, powerfully linked together as a necessary part of the large-scale social advance signalled by the 1945 elections. I was now chief director of Fore Publications with its monthly *Our Time*, in which we sought to record and stimulate the Cultural Upsurge, and to which we added *Theatre Today*, edited by Montagu Slater. The latter led in time, with the aid of J. B. Priestley, to the Theatre Conference, which did much to lay down the guiding lines for national and regional drama. C.E.M.A. had become the Arts Council, and we did our best to support the secretary, Mary Glasgow, in the policy of taking art to the people and aiding local activities. She was defeated and W. E. Williams took the Council over with the motto of Few but Roses.

I was lecturing in London and elsewhere on Documentary Drama and the Cultural Upsurge. We started the Script Centre, with Ann as secretary, to provide plays, pageant scripts and so on for the Labour movement. We did work for various co-ops. I wrote several film-scripts for trade unions, though we failed in the project for a magazine on documentaries which I discussed with some leading directors like Basil Wright. Ann was active in the British Drama League, helping to form new guilds which drew local groups together, and in the Arts Committee of the National Council of Social Services. At one time she went round as the voice of a puppet theatre, then organized a company of actors for the London Co-op. and produced the play, *Men of Rochdale*, which she took on tour. She also got together a Unity group for my declamation, *Voice of Greece*. I joined in with Montagu Slater and Bernard Miles in Theatre 46, at the Scala. Montagu had been commissioned by the Engineers to write a centenary play, and we hoped to build a theatre based on trade-union support. I wrote *Face of Coal*, on mining and the struggle for nationalization, drawing in B. L. Coombes to ensure authenticity. An attempt to found a dance theatre with Ernst Bergk, for which I wrote a ballet scenario, *John Barleycorn*, failed to raise enough money. (One of our ideas was to link ballet with tribal and ancient ritual and to use poetry in various ways.) I was also trying to develop drama at the Anglo-French Centre (close to the house we had taken opposite Lords), with the aid of David Tutaeff. To help the widespread growth of community centres, which had come about in the war, I did the script for an M.O.I. film, visiting groups round Glasgow and Edinburgh to hear their debates and discussions. The script was accepted, but the project was later quashed from above.

There were many other activities in these full years. I wrote essays for *Life and Letters*, and edited it briefly while Robert Herring was in the West Indies. I did selections of Herrick and Morris for the Grey Walls Press, and was editing Donne's letters for it when it broke down; I wrote an essay for a book on Leslie Hurry's art, plus a poem (hoping to start something like the link of artist and poet found in France). I was drawn in by Krishna Menon to start the Meridian Press: an odd experience, since in his fanatical devotions he had come to believe that sheer force of will made up for lack of money or organization. Our first book sold without any sales effort, for it was Nehru's *Discovery of India*, published just at the time when India gained its independence. (The one positive aspect of this venture was that it gave my friend C. A. Adams, met in Trowbridge, his first chance in publishing; he later played an important part in suggesting and publishing books of mine. At this time I gave him my version of *Daphnis and Chloe*.)

Our struggle to carry on and extend the Cultural Upsurge was defeated. This defeat was linked with the failure of the Labour government to meet the challenge of vested interests

and to build the new sort of society that would have expressed
the emotions of the people who voted it in in 1945: emotions
which in a powerful though undogmatic way hoped for a new
start, a no-return to the situation resulting in the depression
of the 1930s, a democracy developed out of the elements of
genuine anti-fascist unity built up in the war years. By 1947-48,
paper was getting more plentiful; commercial interests were
getting the means in the publishing and entertainment worlds
to 'give the people what they wanted,' and so on. I almost
brought off a linkage of Fore Publications with a sympathetic
firm that would have given us a new lease of life, but was
defeated by some political sectarians on the board.

The story of these years, briefly told, thus seems one of failure, and from one angle that was what it was. But the long and
complex struggle had its steady exhilaration as well as its
momentary triumphs, its broad historical perspective as well
as its limited objectives. I had turned to the contemporary
novel, to help me to get inside the situation in its human fullness. *Time to Live* dealt with a victory street party. *The Subtle
Knot* told of a group with shared war experiences who get
together to produce *Everyman* in a half-wrecked Soho church,
with the result of emerging conflicts and deepening unions. I
also wrote historical novels. *Fires in Smithfield* dealt with the
Protestant underground under Bloody Mary, which sowed the
seeds of resistance leading in time to the revolution of the
1640s. In Poland they told me it read as a story of their own
underground struggles against the Nazis. *The Great Oak* told of
Kett's revolt of 1549. It was only published later in a cut version, but in 1948 my *Men of Forty-eight* (written 1939-40) came
out at last. *Song of a Falling World* was direct history, dealing
with the sources of cultural renewal in the provinces as the
Roman imperial state broke down.

All this while I was working hard to develop my Marxism.
In November 1945 a Communist Party conference discussed
a lengthy document of mine on the nature of culture. Everyone
condemned it but the young E. P. Thompson. (It defined culture as a form of production as against the notion that it was
part of a superstructure with determining economic base.) In
other discussions I attacked the Zhdanov theses. In 1949

appeared my *Marxism and Contemporary Science*, which sought to work out a unitary dialectic overcoming what I saw as mechanist or idealist elements in the accepted system of dialectical materialism. Again my ideas were roundly condemned (except in one long review in Poland). I tried to learn from the criticisms, but could not see that my main positions were undermined. J. D. Bernal, among others, tried to argue me out of my views. About this time I had met L. L. Whyte through my friend Mulk Raj Anand, and felt that there was much force in his thesis of development occurring through a reassertion of symmetry in an unsymmetrical situation. For a while we had a sort of anti-Newtonian society meeting for discussions at our house in St John's Wood: Whyte, R. Silver, physicist, Blair Scott, rheologist, and a few others.

In these years the Cold War had been steadily worsening, linked with the factors breaking down our Cultural Upsurge. The U.S. was seeking to assert its dominance as the sole owner of the atom bomb. Lewis Mumford said to me in 1947 that the situation was dire: only the war-weariness of the peoples prevented the U.S. from launching a war against Russia. As part of the struggle to preserve and deepen the antifascist positions, I had sought to learn about the resistance struggles in Europe and to get into contact with the French writers who had used poetry against the Nazis. Partly with the aid of Nancy Cunard I met many of them and became friendly with Aragon, Eluard, Tzara, Vercors, Guillevic and others. They had used poetry as a political weapon without weakening it and were now struggling to rebuild a stable popular culture on the basis of the resistance systems, with local and national organization. The U.S. in its Cold War was attacking them even more directly than it was sapping the advances made in Britain. In these years I was also struggling to help the large number of Greek writers thrown into concentration camps through the British betrayal of their resistance movement. I raised the matter in the P.E.N. Committee, of which I was a member round 1947, and worked through the Committee for Democracy in Greece. Communications from many writers were smuggled out, and letters of mine were smuggled in.

An important step forwards was taken when the Poles arranged for a Peace Conference of intellectuals at Wroclaw in 1948. I did what I could to help the Poles in London in preparations, proud at being the first person they invited. Ann and I went to the conference, which was attended by Picasso (whom I met in Warsaw) and most of my French friends; there was a large English delegation. I found the event most stimulating and was able to meet Russian writers like Leonid Leonov, whom I greatly admired. At Warsaw I spent much time with Lukacs and Ernst Fischer, and went on to Cracow (from where I visited Auschwitz) and then Zakopane in the mountains. In spring 1949 came the huge peace gathering in Paris, where I met Howard Fast, Mike Gold, and others, and spent some more time with Lukacs as well as with Fadeyev and K. Simonon.

Out of Wroclaw came the Authors World Peace Appeal, with A. E. Coppard and Louis Golding at first playing a leading part. A large number of writers were drawn in, including Dylan Thomas and Naomi Mitchison. Edith Sitwell, now a close friend of mine, signed the appeal. I worked on the committee. Then came the broader peace movements. But the Cold War worsened. Ann and I, with Tony Adams and his wife, took a house at Penshurst, Kent, where I wrote most of my *Life of Dickens*, which I may claim to be the first modern book on him. Ann and I moved into a forester's cottage in Ashour Woods on the Medway. Here I wrote *The Passionate Pastoral*, set in the 1790s, with the Woods as its background. In 1949, partly through the enthusiastic reception of my *Men of Forty-eight* in Russia, I was invited to the Pushkin Celebrations, and I spent six weeks in the U.S.S.R. Among the writers with us were Pablo Neruda, Nexo of Denmark, Laxness of Iceland, Theun de Vries of Holland. The whole thing was immensely exciting. The Russians had just got over the worst of their reconstruction of the war devastations; there was a genuine enthusiasm for Pushkin as exemplar of their national culture. Our experiences seemed to verify my highest hopes for a socialist society. Starting from Moscow, we went to Leningrad and Pushkin City, then on to Pskov and the poet's homeland, Mikhailovskoye; and on the way I grew friendly with several Russian writers, especially the poet, Tikhonov. With Neruda and others we visited Stalingrad. Then we had the choice of going to whatever part of the Soviet Union that most interested us. We chose Kiev, as I was working on Byzantine history, and with us went a Korean writer with a sardonic sense of humour, Lee Gee Eng. On our return home (by boat via Helsinki and Stockholm) I wrote an account of the visit, *A World Ahead* as well as *Three Letters to N. Tikhonov* (in verse).

I had no idea of the Stalinist repressions behind the scenes. In Moscow I was invited by the writer Gergel to visit his native Hungary, and I discussed English history with the Hungarian Ambassador, who had a keen interest in the subject. About the same time the writer Paloczi-Horvath, whom I met briefly before his return to Hungary, was being interrogated by the secret police there about that traitor, Jack Lindsay, who would be liquidated in due time by the heroic British working class.

I had already started the quarterly *Arena*, with John Davenport's help. This hoped to bring together the best work of resistance writers. The first issue had contributions by Tzara, Edith Sitwell, MacDiarmid, Pasternak, Cassou, Eluard, Tikhonov, Camus, Malcolm Lowry, Illes (Hungarian). The editorial note spoke of the task of distinguishing 'the valuably formative from the false and merely fashionable' (a feeble conformity seeking to exploit what was for a moment a genuine adventure). It was fiercely attacked in the *Daily Worker* and nothing else of the contents here or in later issues was mentioned. The establishment, including the booksellers, turned an equally blind eye. Disregarded too were the twelve issues of Key Poets (a shilling each), which included a booklet of new poems by Edith and George Barker's *Confessions* (hailed when it appeared later under a different imprint). The last two issues of *Arena* consisted of speeches at big conferences we held on the American threat to British culture and on the national tradition.

I was working on *Byzantium into Europe*, a large-scale account of Byzantine history and culture, which sought to break down the artificial barrier set up by historians between east and west in the dark ages and the medieval period. Though now such an approach would be welcomed, in the Cold War of the 1950s it was violently repudiated, and in a full page review the *Times Literary Supplement* called for the exclusion of all Marxists from university posts. I was also working on Meredith, to follow up my Dickens biography, and had conceived a series of novels, *The British Way*, which would deal with the experiences of our people in the post-war years, combining the close study of individuals with a clear historical structure. The method would fuse all that I had learned from my historical novels and from my efforts to come close to the lives, defeats, and aspirations of the people who had gone through the anti-fascist war and were now being subjected to the pressures of the Cold War.

I began with *Betrayed Spring*, dealing with a group of demobbed soldiers and with the situation in the mines, the textile areas (Bradford), London, and the Tyne. I wanted to get to grips with what was really happening to people, away from the trivialities of most novel writing – and this at the time when the Cold War was scaring writers away from the larger truths of our world, not by overt penalties but by the general atmosphere created, with effects still dominant as I write here (1981). *Betrayed Spring* was translated into Russian, in at least a million copies, and into the various East European languages; it even appeared in Chinese. I followed it by *Rising Tide* (the dockers' strike) and *Moment of Choice* (mainly set in Yorkshire and dealing with the peace movement). The *Times Literary Supplement* refused to review these novels, then attacked them in a leading article. I should not have managed to get any of these works, or the Byzantine history, into print if it had not been for Nicholson of the Bodley Head; his politics were not at all of the left, but he was a genuine liberal who refused to be dictated to by Cold War pressures. A book of translations of French resistance poetry I failed to get published; one publisher had the frankness to say, 'Nobody will print it. Don't you know these people were a lot of brigands?'

Meanwhile I had made visits to Czechoslovakia (1950), Poland (1951), Rumania (1952 and 1953), in which I went extensively about and had many discussions on culture. In Warsaw, Brecht and Helene Weigel were also staying at the Hotel Bristol, and I breakfasted with them as well as joining them on other occasions. (I met Brecht again in Amsterdam in 1954.) In Rumania I went at length into the question of the treatment of the many minorities, and wrote a book on the subject, *Rumanian Summer*. Ann had developed cancer in 1951 and we moved to Castle Hedingham, North Essex, to be near the

Swinglers. She died in early 1954. Edith Sitwell wrote to me, 'I loved Ann very much. I think she was nearer being a saint than almost anyone I have ever known, saintly without censoriousness, good without weakness, sweet without weakness.' And, 'I think I never saw any face with such a light of goodness on it, and of peace.' In 1954 in my unhappiness I did much travelling: Italy and Sicily, Holland, Cornwall, the Soviet Union. I was asked to Moscow to give a lecture in the Fielding Celebrations, then, as the Second Congress of Writers was near, I was invited to stay on for it. Postponements meant that I stayed over three months, during which I visited Georgia, where I grew friendly with the poet Leonidze, Abhkasia and the Black Sea. I saw much of the writers V. Azhayev, Lukonin, Marshak, Simonov, Tikhonov. With Oksana Krugerskaia, who went round with me, I worked on Russian poetry, and published (1956 and 1959) two collections of translations. I saw a large number of plays and ballets, old and new, and was much impressed. *Romeo and Juliet*, with Ulanova dancing, I saw three times. Despite noting various shortcomings, especially in the question of Marxism, I maintained my general enthusiasm. The discussions at the Congress were serious, thorough, with the promise of important advances. 'What holds us back but an inner censor?' demanded the poet Yashin.

Back in England, I continued work on my novel series, and, encouraged by Jim Reynolds of Mullers, began afresh on history: *Civil War in England, The Writing on the Wall* (Pompeii interpreted through its graffiti), *The Romans were Here, Arthur of England, 1764* (the year treated for its daily events). In *After the Thirties* I tried to draw attention to the real achievements of the 1930s, the weaknesses, the way that the positive elements could be carried forward. Then came the Kruschev revelations of 1956. For a while I was shattered. I had never imagined such derelictions possible in a socialist society, and found it difficult for some time to see in a single focus the regressive and the valuable aspects. However, it seemed likely that under Kruschev the evil heritage would be eliminated, even if slowly. I went to the Third Writers' Congress in 1959, with Ewan MacColl. It was a small event next to the Second, but again held many promising elements. The problem of understanding the Soviet Union became a test of one's ability to grasp historical process in its multiple aspects of good and evil, of release and distortion.

The great setback came in 1968 with the invasion of Czechoslovakia. Not that it brought about anything like a reversion to Stalinism. Rather we see a conservative bureaucratic system that is afraid of any changes and seeks in every way to maintain the *status quo*. Not that there is a lack of positive elements, of vitalities in cultural life, which would vastly increase with the required advent of active participation by the people in all spheres. Certainly one thing that holds back popular pressure is the international situation. While there is danger of attack from the U.S. and its allies, the Soviet folk are not likely to agitate for decisive changes, afraid that their enemies would take advantage of any disorder.

I had written *Local Habitation*, which carried on with the broad base and interlinked sections of *The British Way* series. While keeping the historical approach, I now felt driven to concentrate on a particular aspect of development rather to attempt a large perspective of interrelated moments or scenes. I began with *The Revolt of the Sons*, dealing with a country family where the father keeps the sons in subjection (in his timber firm) by a mixture of discipline and inheritance promises. I had now become interested in field archaeology and found many Roman sites in my North Essex area as well as medieval kilns. I told the story in *Discovery of Britain*. I had married Meta Waterdrinker, a Dutch potter, and we had a son, Philip, in 1959, a daughter, Helen in 1961.

I was now living a less active life and concentrated on studies and writing: more of *The British Way*, accounts of life in Graeco-Roman Egypt as revealed by the papyri, and cultural anthropology. In the novels I wrote *All on the Never-never*, in which I sought to catch the essence of the new consumer society with its credit systems, using as symbol the housewife who sells herself to meet the payments. I thus equated the consumer society with prostitution, arguing that capitalism was entering a new phase which needed a vast extension of internal sales and which would issue in time in general inflation of a new kind. (I could not find any fellow Marxists who agreed with this analysis.) *The Way the Ball Bounces* dealt with the Korean War. A clerk who has been conscripted is trying to push clean out of mind his painful war experiences but is forced by circumstances (which include an affair with a West Indian girl) to face the reality of his world. The book sought to define a society where everyone knew the likelihood of total destruction by nuclear forces, but did anything rather than face the facts. *Masks and Faces*, using the moment of a father's deathbed, sought to define the same sort of revelatory moment in an upperclass family. *Time to Live* depicted the growing petty-bourgeois tendencies of the working class against memories of a very different world in Oldham in the old textile days, with the question of evaded choice coming up through the Cuban crisis. I wrote next an historical novel on Nero's Rome, called *Thunder Underground*. Here the theme is the unavailing effort to revive traditions of freedom in a world where an overall tyranny is invading every sphere. In *Meetings with Poets* I described my relations with Dylan Thomas, Edith Sitwell, Aragon, Tzara and Eluard.

In 1968 Bernard Miles at the Mermaid Theatre put on my versions of four Euripides plays, making a Trojan War cycle, as well as a version of Lessing's *Nathan the Wise*. In the seventies, Roy Fuller and I arranged a large number of Sunday performances at the theatre, and held discussions and lectures with readings of poetry.

Through suggestions from Tony Adams, working at first for firms like Studio Vista, then in his own firms, I was drawn afresh into cultural anthropology, doing a completely new version of *A Short History of Culture* and then exploring culture and myth in early Greek society: *The Clashing Rocks* and *Helen of Troy*. I did for him a translation of Giordano Bruno's *Cause, Principle and Unity*. He also started me off on a series of books on art. First, *The Death of the Hero*, a study of the art of the French Revolution, then lives of Turner, Cézanne, Courbet, Hogarth, William Morris, Blake. Here I sought a method which would draw together, clarify and dialectically unite the personal, social, and aesthetic elements in artistic expression. I wrote three long books on life, enjoyment, culture, religion, in Graeco-Roman Egypt, then moved into the study of ancient science with books on the origins of alchemy and astrology, and in *Blastpower and Ballistics* dealing with concepts of force and energy in the ancient world, and developing a general critique of science and of nuclear fission in particular. I wrote as well a *Life of Cleopatra*, a book on the Troubadours and their world (with many translations carrying over the original complex verse forms, *The Normans* (which deals at length with the Normans in their homeland, in France and England, in Southern Italy and Sicily), *The Monster City* (Defoe's London), *Decay and Renewal*, essays mainly on modern writers, with several on Australian novelists. This year is to see a *Life of Gainsborough*, carrying further my art biographies, and *The Crisis in Marxism*, which analyses various modern trends (in the work of Lukacs, Bloch, Adorno, Marcuse, Althusser, Colletti, Della Volpe, Gramsci) and then sets out my own formulations. This book completes the attempt to create an open Marxism, freeing itself from all dogmatisms, which I began in 1945. A large *Collected Poems* is appearing in the U.S.

I may claim then that I have worked in an unusually wide number of fields. The main reason is that my enduring interest at all phases has been in the nature of development, in the ways in which change and forward movement occur with a leap into new levels: conflict and contradiction driven to the decisive point, then bringing about either breakdown or the liberation into a qualitatively new dimension. The concern with such things, the effort to test out generalizations in field after field, in situation after situation, and to grasp yet more finely and fully how fundamental change occurs is what I call Marxism; and it has been the restless movement of my Marxism, the need to grapple with new problems of conflict and of the resolution of conflict, that has driven me on in what has been I trust a quest not without its rewarding moments, its realizations as well as its continual probing and enquiry. The same method, the same impulse, is at work, I should claim, in my novels and my historical works, my analyses of art and science, my anthropological attempts to grasp the forms in which humanity has kept on realizing itself and its relation to nature.

JACK LINDSAY
Castle Hedingham
February 1981

HANDLIST OF PUBLICATIONS

Works by Jack Lindsay

1. *Fauns and Ladies*, poems, 1923
2. *The Pleasante Conceited Narrative of Panurge's Fantastically Brocaded Codpiece*, poem, 1924
3. *Spanish Main and Tavern*, poem, 1924
4. Aristophanes's *Lysistrata*, translation, 1925; 1926 (pirated in U.S.A.)
5. Petronius's *Satyricon and Poems*, translation, 1927 (pirated in U.S.A.)
6. *Propertius in Love*, translations, 1927
7. *Marino Faliero*, verse play, 1927
8. *Helen Comes of Age*, three verse plays, 1927
9. *William Blake*, 1927
10. *Dionysos: Nietsche contra Nietzsche*, 1928
11. *Homage to Sappho*, translations and adaptations, 1928
12. *Theocritos*, translation, 1929
13. *Women in Parliament*, translation of Aristophanes's *Ecclesiazusai*, 1929
14. *William Blake*, reprint with an extra chapter, 1929
15. *Catullus*, translations, 1929
16. *Mimes of Herondas*, translations, 1929
17. *The Passionate Neatherd*, lyrics, 1929
18. *Hereward*, verse play, 1929
19. *Homer's Hymn to Aphrodite*, translation, 1930
20. *Patchwork Quilt*, translations from Ausonius, 1930
21. *A Retrospect of the Fanfrolico Press*, 1931
22. *Golden Ass*, Apuleius, translation, 1931; revised edition with essay, 1960
23. *Cressida's First Lover*, a fantasy novel set in ancient Greece, 1931
24. *Time — please!*, contemporary novel by Elza de Locre and Jack Lindsay published under the name of Ailsa Lindsay, 1932
25. *Rome for Sale*, novel on the period of Catilina, 1934

26. *Caesar is Dead*, historical novel, 1934

27. *I am a Roman*, translations, 1934

28. *Medieval Latin Poets*, translations, 1934

29. *Last Days with Cleopatra*, historical novel, 1935

30. *Despoiling Venus*, historical novel on Clodia and Caelius Rufus, 1935

31. *Storm at Sea*, long short story set in the early Roman Empire (Golden Cockerel Press), 1935

32. *Runaway*, novel for boys, period of Spartacus, 1935

33. *The Romans*, 1935

34. *Wanderings of Wenamen*, novel set near the end of the second millenium B.C., 1936

35. *Come Home at Last*, short stories of the Graeco–Roman world, 1936

36. *Adam of a New World*, novel on Giordano Bruno, 1936

37. *Who are the English?* verse declamation, 1936

38. *Shadow and Flame*, contemporary novel published under the name of Richard Preston, 1936

39. *Mark Antony*, biography, 1936

40. *Rebels of the Goldfields*, boys' novel on the Eureka Stockade, 1936

41. *Sue Verney*, novel set in the Cromwellian period, 1937

42. *End of Cornwall*, contemporary novel published under the name of Richard Preston, 1937

43. *John Bunyan*, biography, 1937

44. *Anatomy of Spirit*, 1937

45. *On Guard for Spain*, verse declamation, 1937

46. *Five Thousand Years of Poetry*, prose and verse declamation, 1938

47. *1649*, the novel of a year, 1938

48. *To Arms*, boys' book set in ancient Gaul, 1938

49. *England my England*, long pamphlet on the English tradition, 1939

50. *Short History of Culture*, 1939

51. *Brief Light*, historical novel on Catullus, 1939

52. *We Need Russia*, verse declamation, 1939

53. *Lost Birthright*, novel set in the 1760s, 1939

54. *Giuliano the Magnificent*, version of a novel by D. Johnson, 1940

55. *Light in Italy*, novel set in 1816, 1941

56. *Hannibal Takes a Hand*, novel set in ancient Carthage, 1941

57. *The Stormy Violence*, novel set in early Elizabethan period, 1941

58. *The Dons Sight Devon*, boys' book (Elizabethan period), 1941

59. *Into Action*, long poem on Dieppe, 1942

60. *We Shall Return*, novel on the Dunkirk campaign, 1942

61. *Beyond Terror*, novel on the Cretan campaign, 1943

62. *Second Front*, army poems, 1944

63. *Perspective of Poetry*, critical survey, 1944

64. *The Barriers are Down*, novel on the collapse of the Roman Empire in the West, *c.* 450 (written 1941), 1945

65. *Jolly Swagman: The Australians at Home*, Army Bureau of Current Affairs pamphlet, 1945

66. *Hello Stranger*, novel on women in war industry, 1945

67. *British Achievement in Art and Music* (in series on developments during the war), 1945

68. *Time to Live*, contemporary novel, 1946

69. *The Subtle Knot*, contemporary novel, 1947

70. *Men of Forty-eight*, historical novel (written 1939), 1948

71. Longus's *Daphnis and Chloe*, translation, 1948

72. *Catullus*, completely new translation and essay, 1948

73. *Song of a Falling World*, account of Latin poetry 4th–8th centuries, with translations, 1948

74. *Clue of Darkness*, poem (Theseus theme), 1949

75. *Marxism and Contemporary Science*, 1949

76. *Fires in Smithfield*, novel set in reign of Mary, 1950

77. *A World Ahead* (account of travels in Russia and the Pushkin celebrations), 1950

78. *Charles Dickens*, biography, 1950

79. *Peace is Our Aim*, poems, 1950

80. *The Passionate Pastoral*, 18th-century novel, 1951

81. *Three Letters to Nikolai Tikhonov*, poems, 1951

82. *Song of Peace* by V. Nezval, translation from Czech (with S. Jolly), 1951

83. *Byzantium into Europe*, history, 1952

84. *A Month in Rumania*, 1952

85. *Betrayed Spring*, contemporary novel, 1953

86. *Rising Tide*, contemporary novel, 1953

87. *Rumanian Summer*, travels in Rumania (with chapters by M. Cornforth), 1953

88. *Civil War in England*, the Cromwellian Revolution, 1954

89. *Moment of Choice*, contemporary novel, 1955

90. *George Meredith*, biography, 1956

91. *After the Thirties*, critical survey, 1956
92. *The Romans were Here*, history of Roman period in Britain, 1956
93. *Russian Poetry 1917–55*, translations, 1956
94. *Three Elegies*, poems, 1957
95. *A Local Habitation*, contemporary novel, 1957
96. *Poems of Adam Mickiewicz*, translations from Polish, 1957
97. *The Great Oak*, novel on the peasants' revolt of 1949, 1957
98. *Arthur and his Times*, history, Britain in the 5th century A.D., 1958
99. *Discovery of Britain*, field archaeology, 1958
100. *Life Rarely Tells*, autobiography, 1958
101. *Askelpiades in Love*, translations, 1957
102. *1764*, a day-by-day account of the year, 1959
103. *Revolt of the Sons*, contemporary novel, 1960
104. *Petronius*, new translation, with essay, 1960
105. *The Writing on the Wall*, history, account of Pompeii, 1960
106. *The Roaring Twenties*, autobiography, 1960
107. *Modern Russian Poetry*, translations, 1960
108. *The Death of the Hero*, French painting from David to Delacroix, 1960
109. *William Morris, Writer* (lecture, W. M. Society), 1961
110. *All on the Never-never*, contemporary novel, 1961
111. *Ribaldry of Rome*, translations of Roman writers, 1961
112. *Ribaldry of Greece*, translations of Greek writers, 1961
113. *The Way the Ball Bounces*, contemporary novel, 1962
114. *Our Celtic Heritage*, history, 1962
115. *A Short History of Culture*, a completely new work, 1962
116. *Cause, Principle and Unity*, by G. Bruno, translation with essay, 1962
117. *Fanfrolico and After*, autobiography, 1962
118. *Masks and Faces*, contemporary novel, 1963
119. *Daily Life in Roman Egypt*, history, 1963
120. *Nine Days' Hero: Wat Tyler*, biography, 1964
121. *Choice of Times*, contemporary novel, 1964
122. *Thunder Underground*, novel on Nero's Rome, 1965
123. *The Clashing Rocks*, study of Greek culture and the origins of drama, 1965
124. *Our Anglo–Saxon Heritage*, history, 1965
125. *Leisure and Pleasure in Roman Egypt*, history, 1965
126. *J. M. W. Turner*, biography, 1966

127. *The Age of Akhenaten*, by Eléonare Bille–de Mot, translation, 1966
128. *Our Roman Heritage*, history, 1967
129. *Meeting with Poets*, memories of Dylan Thomas, Edith Sitwell and others, 1968
130. *Greece I keep my Vigil for you*, by Teskros Anthias, translation, 1968
131. *The Ancient World: manners and morals*, 1968
132. *Men and Gods on the Roman Nile*, history, 1968
133. *Cézanne*, biography, 1969
134. *The Origins of Alchemy in Graeco–Roman Egypt*, history, 1970
135. *The Origins of Astrology*, history, 1971
136. *Cleopatra*, biography, 1971
137. *Gustave Courbet*, biography, 1973
138. *Helen of Troy*, biography, 1974
139. *Blast Power and Ballistics: Concept of Force and Energy in the Ancient World*, 1974
140. *Faces and Places*, poems, 1974
141. *Death of a Spartan King*, short stories, 1974
142. *The Normans and their World*, history, 1974
143. *William Morris*, biography, 1975
144. *Decay and Renewal*, criticism, 1976
145. *The Troubadours and their World*, history, 1976
146. *Hogarth*, biography, 1977
147. *The Monster City: Defoe's London, 1688–1730*, history, 1978
148. *William Blake*, biography, 1978
149. *Gainsborough*, biography, 1981
150. *Crisis in Marxism*, criticism, 1981

Works edited
151. *Vocal and Instrumental Recital of the Works of Adolphe Beutler*, concert programme, 1923
152. *Poetry in Australia* (with K. Slessor), 1923
153. *Metamorphosis of Aiax* by Sir John Harrington (with P. Warlock), 1927
154. *Loving Mad Tom*, Bedlamite poems of the 17th century, 1927
155. Eliot's *Parlement of Pratlers*, 1928
156. Herrick, *Delighted Earth* (as Peter Meadows), 1928
157. *Inspiration*, anthology of statements on the creative process, 1928
158. *Letters of Philip Stanhope*, second Earl of Chesterfield, 1930

159. *Handbook of Freedom*, anthology (with E. Rickword), 1939: re-issued as *Spokesmen for Liberty*, 1941
160. *New Lyrical Ballads* (with M. Carpenter and H. Arundel), 1945
161. *Anvil*, miscellany, 1947
162. *Herrick*, selection with essay (Crown Poets), 1948
163. *William Morris*, selection with essay (Crown Poets), 1948
164. *Paintings and Drawings of Leslie Hurry*, 1950
165. Z. Stancu's *Barefoot* (Rumanian novel), 1950
166. William Blake: 200 years, commemorative leaflet, 1957
167. *The Sunset Ship*, poems by J. M. W. Turner, 1966
168. Joseph Priestley, autobiography, 1970

Magazines edited
Vision (with K. Slessor and F. Johnson), 1923–24
The London Aphrodite (with P. R. Stephensen), 1928–29
Poetry and the People (co-editor), 1938–40
Arena (with J. Davenport and R. Swingler), 1948–49

Series edited
New Development Series (The Bodley Head), 1947–48
Key Poets (with R. Swingler), 1950
Background Books, 1962

Articles and journalism
For a list of the major articles see John Arnold, 'Jack Lindsay: towards a bibliography', *Overland*, 1981, pp. 53-5. A selection of his criticism was published as *Decay and Renewal*, Sydney, Wild and Woolley, 1976.

JOHN ARNOLD
Melbourne, 1981

INDEX OF NAMES

Throughout this index J. L. indicates Jack Lindsay.